Lecture Notes in Computer Science 5408

Commenced Publication in 1973
Founding and Former Series Editors
Gerhard Goos, Juris Hartmanis, and

Vijay Garg   Roger Wattenhofer
Kishore Kothapalli (Eds.)

Distributed Computing and Networking

10th International Conference, ICDCN 2009
Hyderabad, India, January 3-6, 2009
Proceedings

 Springer

Volume Editors

Vijay Garg
IBM India Research Laboratory
New Delhi 110070, India
E-mail: vkgarg@gmail.com

Roger Wattenhofer
ETH Zurich
8092 Zurich, Switzerland
E-mail: wattenhofer@tik.ee.ethz.ch

Kishore Kothapalli
International Institute of Information Technology
Hyderabad 500032, India
E-mail: kkishore@iiit.ac.in

Library of Congress Control Number: 2008942101

CR Subject Classification (1998): C.2, D.1.3, D.2.12, D.4, F.2, F.1, H.4

LNCS Sublibrary: SL 1 – Theoretical Computer Science and General Issues

ISSN   0302-9743
ISBN-10   3-540-92294-6 Springer Berlin Heidelberg New York
ISBN-13   978-3-540-92294-0 Springer Berlin Heidelberg New York

springer.com

© Springer-Verlag Berlin Heidelberg 2009
Printed in Germany

Typesetting: Camera-ready by author, data conversion by Scientific Publishing Services, Chennai, India
Printed on acid-free paper   SPIN: 12590384   06/3180   5 4 3 2 1 0

Message from the General Chairs

As General Chairs it is our pleasure to welcome you to the proceedings of the International Conference on Distributed Computing and Networking (ICDCN 2009). This year marked the 10th ICDCN. This conference, which started as a workshop (IWDC) in 2000, has grown steadily in its scope, reach, and stature. It now attracts quality submissions and top speakers annually in the areas of distributed computing and networking from all over the world, thereby strengthening the connection between Indian research, which has been on the rise, with the rest of the world. The choice of Hyderabad for this year's location declares ICDCN's intent to be open to any location in India.

There are many people who worked tirelessly behind the scenes over the last year to make this a first-class event. We were honored to work with a truly superb team who made our job considerably easier. We had an excellent program this year, with 20 papers, 32 short presentations, 4 tutorials, a panel discussion, 3 keynote speakers, and the A.K. Choudhury Memorial Lecture.

Critical to the success of any technical program is the quality, dedication, and leadership of the Technical Program Chairs. We were very fortunate to have Vijay Garg and Roger Wattenhofer at the helm of the committee. Vijay and Roger are a pleasure to work with and we thank them and their Technical Program Committee for putting together a great program of quality papers. We would also like to thank the Keynote Chair, Sajal Das, for organizing an excellent invited program. Krithi Ramamritham (IIT, Mumbai) was the A.K. Choudhury Memorial Speaker and Maurice Herlihy (Brown University), P.R. Kumar (University of Illinois, Urbana-Champaign), and Andrew T. Campbell (Dartmouth College) gave the keynote addresses.

We would like to thank Kishore Kothapalli as Publication Chair for dealing with the many details of putting the proceedings together and our Publicity Chairs Romit Roy Choudhury and Niloy Ganguly for doing a good job of getting the word out about the event this year. We had a set of excellent tutorials this year on a broad set of important topics in theory and systems. Topics included: middleware by Jiannong Cao, Hong Kong Polytechnic University; digital media distribution by Sanjoy Paul, Infosys Technologies Limited; game theory by Yvonne-Anne Pignolet, ETH, Zurich; and finally, Internet outages by Krishna Kant, NSF & Intel Research. We would like to thank Sushil K. Prasad and Sriram Pemmaraju for putting this outstanding tutorial program together.

We are very grateful to Bruhadeshwar Bezawada and Kishore Kothapalli for their initiative to host the conference at IIIT-H which, incidentally, is also celebrating its 10th anniversary this year.

On this 10th anniversary, we want to especially thank Sajal Das and Sukumar Ghosh whose vision, commitment, and hard work have been largely responsible for the successful growth of ICDCN. From our note it's clear that many people volunteer their time and energy and work in a dedicated fashion to pull everything together each year, including our very supportive Steering Committee members led by Sukumar Ghosh. However, the success of ICDCN is mainly due to the hard work of all those people who submit papers and/or attend the conference. We thank you all.

January 2009   Prasad Jayanti
                                                 Andrew T. Campbell

Message from the Technical Program Chairs

Welcome to the proceedings of the 10th International Conference on Distributed Computing and Networking (ICDCN) 2009. As ICDCN celebrates its 10th anniversary, it has become an important forum for disseminating the latest research results in distributed computing and networking.

We received 179 submissions from all over the world, including Algeria, Australia, Canada, China, Egypt, France, Germany, Hong Kong, Iran, Italy, Japan, Malaysia, The Netherlands, Poland, Singapore, South Korea, Taiwan, and the USA, besides India, the host country. The submissions were read and evaluated by the Program Committee, which consisted of 25 members for the Distributed Computing Track and 28 members for the Networking Track, with the additional help of external reviewers. The Program Committee selected 20 regular papers and 32 short papers for inclusion in the proceedings and presentation at the conference. We were fortunate to have several distinguished scientists as keynote speakers. Andrew Campbell (Dartmouth College, USA), Maurice Herlihy (Brown University, USA), and P.R. Kumar (University of of Illinois, Urbana-Champaign) delivered the keynote address. Krithi Ramamritham from IIT Bombay, India, delivered the A.K. Choudhury Memorial talk.

The main conference program was preceded by a day of tutorial presentations. We had four tutorials, presented by Jiannong Cao (Hong Kong Polytechnic University, Hong Kong) on "Middleware for Pervasive Computing," Krishna Kant (Intel Research, USA) on "Surviving Large-Scale Internet Outages," Sanjoy Paul (Infosys, India) on "Digital Media Distribution: Trends, Challenges and Opportunities," and Yvonne-Anne Pignolet (ETH, Zurich) on "Game Theory for Distributed Computing and Networking."

We thank all authors for their interest in ICDCN 2009, and the Program Committee members and external reviewers for their careful reviews despite a tight schedule. We thank the creators of the EasyChair system which handled the submissions, reviews, discussions, and notifications for the conference.

January 2009

Vijay K. Garg
Roger Wattenhofer

Organization

ICDCN 2009 was organized by International Institute of Information Technology, Hyderabad, India.

General Chairs

Andrew Campbell   Dartmouth College, USA
Prasad Jayanti   Dartmouth College, USA

Program Chairs

Roger Wattenhofer   ETH Zurich, Switzerland, Networking Track
Vijay Garg   IBM India Research Lab, Distributed
                          Computing Track

Keynote Chair

Sajal Das   University of Texas at Arlington, USA

Tutorial Chairs

Sushil K. Prasad   Georgia State University, USA
Sriram Pemmaraju   University of Iowa, USA

Panel Chair

Rajeev Sangal   IIIT Hyderabad, India

Publicity Chairs

Romit Roy Choudhury Duke University, USA
Niloy Ganguly   IIT Kharagpur, India

Organizing Committee Chairs

Gen. R.K. Bagga   IIIT Hyderabad, India
V. Ch. Venkaiah   IIIT Hyderabad, India

Publication Chair

Kishore Kothapalli   IIIT Hyderabad, India

Registration Chair

Bezawada Bruhadeshwar IIIT Hyderabad, India

Finance Chair

K.S. Rajan   IIIT Hyderabad, India

Steering Committee Chair

Sukumar Ghosh   University of Iowa, Iowa City, USA

Steering Committee Members

Gautam Barua   IIT Guwahati, India
Pradip K. Das   Jadavpur University, Kolkata, India
Sajal Das   University of Texas at Arlington, USA
Anurag Kumar   Indian Institute of Science, Bangalore, India
David Peleg   Weizmann Institute of Science, Israel
Michel Raynal   IRISA, France
Indranil Sengupta   IIT Kharagpur, India
Bhabani Sinha   Indian Statistical Institute, Kolkata, India

Organizing Committee

Kishore Kothapalli   IIIT Hyderabad, India
Bruhadeshwar Bezawada   IIIT Hyderabad, India
Kannan Srinathan   IIIT Hyderabad, India

Program Committee

Marcos Aguilera   Microsoft Research Lab, Silicon Valley, USA
Bezawada Bruhadeshwar   IIIT Hyderabad, India
Mainak Chatterjee   University of Central Florida, USA
Samir R. Das   SUNY Stony Brook, USA
Pierre Fraigniaud   University of Paris, France
Vijay K. Garg   IBM India Research Lab, India
Sukumar Ghosh   University of Iowa, USA
Mohamed Gouda   University of Texas at Austin, USA
Rachid Guerraoui   EPFL, Switzerland
Arobinda Gupta   IIT Kharagpur, India
Isabelle Guerin Lassous ENS Lyon, France
Krishna Gummadi   MPI, Germany
Indranil Gupta   University of Illinois at Urbana-Champaign,
                             USA

Magnus Halldorsson	Reykjavik University, Iceland
Maurice Herlihy	Brown University, USA
Prasad Jayanti	Dartmouth College, USA
Shivkumar Kalyanaraman	RPI, USA
Holger Karl	University of Paderborn, Germany
Roger Karrer	Deutsche Telekom Labs, Germany
Kishore Kothapalli	IIIT Hyderabad, India
Prashant Krishnamurthy	University of Pittsburgh, USA
Ajay Kshemkalyani	University of Illinois at Chicago, USA
P.R. Kumar	University of Illinois at Urbana-Champaign, USA
Santosh Kumar	University of Memphis, USA
Shay Kutten	Technion, Israel
Xiang-Yang Li	Illinois Institute of Technology, USA
Victor Luchangco	Sun Microsystems, USA
Madhav Marathe	Virginia Polytechnic Institute, USA
Neeraj Mittal	University of Texas at Dallas, USA
Gopal Pandurangan	Purdue University, USA
Sriram Pemmaraju	University of Iowa, USA
Atul Prakash	University of Michigan, Ann Arbor, USA
Bozidar Radunovic	Microsoft Research, USA
Sergio Rajsbaum	UNAM, Mexico
C. Pandu Rangan	IIT Madras, India
Shrisha Rao	IIIT Bangalore, India
Michel Raynal	University of Rennes, France
Grigore Rosu	University of Illinois at Urbana-Champaign, USA
Yogish Sabharwal	IBM India Research lab, India
Paolo Santi	Instituto di Informatica e Telematica, Pisa, Italy
Alper Sen	Freescale Semiconductor Inc., USA
Koushik Sen	University of California, Berkeley, USA
R.K. Shyamsundar	IBM India Research Lab, India
Mukesh Singhal	University of Kentucky at Lexington, USA
Kannan Srinathan	IIIT Hyderabad, India
Lakshmi Subramanian	New York University, USA
Subhash Suri	University of California, Santa Barbara, USA
Srikanta Tirthapura	Iowa State University, USA
K. Vidyasankar	Memorial University of New Foundland, Canada
Anil Vullikanti	Virginia Polytechnic Institute, USA
Roger Wattenhofer	ETH Zurich, Switzerland
Klaus Wehrle	RWTH Aachen, Germany

Additional Referees

Aseem Gupta	Aylin Aksu	Balakrishnan Prabhakaran
Bibudh Lahiri	Bojian Xu	Christos Stergiou
Claude Chaudet	Debabrata Das	Dongyun Jin
Elias Weingaertner	Elyes Ben Hamida	Faith Ellen
Frank Olaf Sem-Jacobsen	Galigekere Dattatreya	Georg Kunz
Gheorghe Stefanescu	Hai Vu	H. B. Acharya
Hongtao Huang	Hugues Fauconnier	Imran Pirwani
Ismet Aktas	Jacob Burnim	Jayanthi Rao
Jianqing Zhang	Jo Agila Bitsch Link	Juan de Lara
Korporn Panyim	Mark Hills	Muhammad Hamad Alizai
Mukundan Venkataraman	Olaf Landsiedel	Pallavi Joshi
Pankaj Kohli	Partha Dutta	Petr Kuznetsov
Raimondas	Rajesh Karmani	Ralf Klasing Sasnauskas
Remi Vannier	Ricardo Jimenez	Roman Vitenberg
Sai Sathyanarayan	Saptarshi Debroy	Saurav Pandit
Sharmila Devi Selvi	Shiguang Wang	Sivaramakrishnan Subramanian
Soumya Ghosh	Stefan Goetz	Subbarayan Venkatesan
Subramanian Neelakantan	Swades De	Taehoon Kim
Tahiry Razafindralambo	Tarun Bansal	Tobias Heer
Traian Serbanuta	Uday Chakraborty	Umesh Deshpande
Vasu Singh	Venkatesan Chakaravarthy	Vibhor Bhatt
V. C. Vinayak	Vincent Villain	Vinit Ogale
Vishal Singh	Xiaobing Wu	Xiaohua Xu
Xufei Mao	Yanwei Wu	Y. Narahari

Table of Contents

Peer-to-Peer Computing

Reliability and Security

Distributed Computing

Network Algorithms

Fault Tolerance and Models

Sensor Networks 2

Fault-Tolerance and Replication

Wireless Networks

Sensor Networks 3

Grid and Cluster Computing

Tracking Dynamics Using Sensor Networks: Some Recurring Themes

Krithi Ramamritham

Dept of Computer Science & Engineering
Indian Institute of Technology Bombay

Abstract. Much of the data consumed today is dynamic, typically gathered from distributed sources including sensors, and used in real-time monitoring and decision making applications. Large scale sensor networks are being deployed for applications such as detecting leakage of hazardous material, tracking forest fires or environmental monitoring. Many of these "natural" phenomena require estimation of their future states, based on the observed dynamics. Strategically deployed sensors can operate unattended (minimizing risk to human life) and provide the ability to continuously monitor the phenomena and help respond to the changes in a timely manner. In this paper, we show that in-network aggregation, in-network prediction, and asynchronous information dissemination form sound building blocks for addressing the challenges in developing low overhead solutions to monitor changes without requiring prior knowledge about the (dynamics of) the phenomena being monitored.

1 Introduction

More and more of the information we consume is dynamic and comes from sensors. Networks made up of sensor nodes are being increasingly deployed for observing continuously changing data. Numerous interconnected sensors are being used to build

- smart buildings that make efficient use of energy,
- smart vehicles that improve efficiency, assist drivers and help in navigation,
- robots to monitor water bodies, for better pollution control, and
- systems to track weather patterns.

These *cyber-physical systems* blend sensing, actuation, computation, networking, and physical processes. In these systems, there is a need to process enormous amounts of changing, time-sensitive data and to continuously update query results (energy) efficiently, adaptably, i.e., continuously evolve to changing conditions, and resiliently – to message/sensor losses.

Continuous queries are appropriate for such monitoring applications since a user is updated as and when source data changes. But this continuous updating is a challenging requirement because sensing devices are often battery powered, making energy efficiency in processing sensor data and updating users

V. Garg, R. Wattenhofer, and K. Kothapalli (Eds.): ICDCN 2009, LNCS 5408, pp. 1–7, 2009.

a primary design consideration; since energy expended for communication is significantly higher than that for local computations, data dissemination and query-processing techniques should minimize the amount of communication so as to increase the lifetime of the network.

This paper outlines some simple techniques to address these challenges in the context of aggregate query processing. We show that in-network aggregation, in-network prediction, and asynchronous information dissemination form sound building blocks for addressing the challenges in developing low overhead solutions to track changes without requiring prior knowledge about the (dynamics of) the phenomena.

2   Data Dissemination in Sensor Networks

A canonical sensor network application involves sensors wirelessly interacting through multi-hop protocols with their neighbours. Queries are posed typically at a base station and hence results are also expected to be produced at the base station. A very simple model for processing sensor data is to push all data to the base station and compute at base station. This simple technique floods the data through the network. It strains sensor nodes near the base, draining their batteries and disconnecting network. An alternative is to pull only the relevant data to the base station and compute at the base station. Here the query needs to be flooded. But, it begs the question: "which of the (new) sensor data is relevant to a given query?".

Only new data that is required to meet user specified accuracy or coherency requirements, e.g., 2 degree temperature, 10m distance, etc. need be deemed to be relevant. This exploitation of user specified coherency requirements reduces the number of updates in sensor networks.

This implies that we require a query to request the value of an aggregate with an associated coherency, c. This denotes the accuracy of the results delivered to the query node relative to that at the sources, and thus, constitutes the user-specified requirement. For example, a query injected for building monitoring is: "Report the average temperature of the southern wall of the building whenever it changes by more than 2 degrees". Thus, any change in the average temperature value that is within two degrees of what the query node knows need not be reported and the current value known to the query node is considered accurate enough. The resulting reduction in the number of update messages improves both fidelity of query results (by reducing the probability of message losses due to collisions) and lifetime (by reducing communication-related energy needs).

Essentially, we relax strong coherency by adopting the notion of Δ_v - coherency: The difference in the data values at the source and the base bounded is by Δ_v at all times. For example, if we are only interested in temperature changes larger than 2 degrees, $\Delta_v = 2$.

3 Routing Relevant Data to Base

Typically, an overlay network is constructed to route messages from a set of source nodes to the base station. Many ways to realize the overlay tree have been proposed in the literature. Even those which incur nontrivial overheads can be justified since the overlay tree construction costs can be amortized over the monitoring period, that is the period over which the continuous query will execute. Tree construction, i.e., choosing the node to which a node with an update sends the update can depend on how many hops away it is from the source, the length of expected time that the node can serve, etc.

Also, to ensure that single node failures do not lead to failure of the network as a whole, there is a need to adjust the overlay tree after such failures. In [3] we propose a tree construction algorithm that has the following features:

1. It does **take into account the coherency requirements associated with the query, the remaining energy at the sensors, and the communication and the message processing delays**, thereby contributing to higher lifetime and fidelity of query results.
2. It is able to exploit the presence of common sources across multiple queries. This leads to further increase in fidelity and lifetime.
3. It incorporates optimizations to efficiently handle complex aggregate queries with **group by** clauses.
4. Upon the death of a node, the dissemination tree can be locally adjusted allowing query results to be provided. This increases lifetime.

4 Asynchronous In-Network Aggregation and Prediction

For many types of aggregate queries, the number of message transmissions can be reduced significantly by computing partial aggregates wherever possible while the messages are being routed towards the query node. Overlay network allows in-network partial aggregation. For example, consider computing the max of a set of sensed values. When each node in the overlay tree hears from its children, it can compute the max of the received values and send it to its parent. This technique called in-network aggregation has been exploited to increase the lifetime of the sensor network. The nodes at which this is done are called aggregator nodes. Existing approaches to answering coherency based aggregate queries perform in-network aggregation by synchronizing transmissions of nodes level-by-level on an aggregation tree [5]. Any message that is received by an aggregator node is delayed for a certain amount of time before it can be propagated up the tree. This leads to a definite loss in fidelity. Moreover, these approaches do not address the issues of energy efficiency and timeliness of query results in their tree construction mechanisms. In [3] we present an asynchronous prediction-based approach for answering aggregate queries. In it, each node in the tree computes a partial aggregate of the values sensed by the source nodes which belong to the subtree rooted at that node. The computed value of the partial aggregate is pushed by a node to its parent node in the aggregation tree. It incorporates several novel ingredients:

It makes use of asynchronous in-network aggregation wherein an aggregator node computes a partial aggregate *asynchronously*, i.e., whenever an update that may affect the current partial aggregate is received from one of its serving nodes in the aggregation tree. Thus, every received message that is required to be sent to the query node should be pushed up the tree as soon as possible, i.e., **change in values sensed at the sources must be propagated to the query node as soon as possible**. In contrast, existing approaches compute aggregates *synchronously*, often delaying propagation of the effect of received partial aggregates.

Suppose node B receives a partial aggregate from node E. In order to compute a new partial aggregate, B needs the current value of the partial aggregate computed by node F. Since this value is unknown to B, what value should B use for the current value at node F? When an aggregator node receives a partial aggregate from a serving node and computes a new partial aggregate, what values should it assume for all other serving nodes? In our approach, **the aggregator node predicts the missing values from the previously received values using a computationally efficient prediction mechanism**. This *prediction-based* approach is in contrast to existing *last-value-based* approaches that use the last received values for this purpose.

If each partial aggregate computed as above were to be disseminated towards the source, would it not lead to significant energy consumption? This is where the idea of *in-network prediction* proves to be useful again. When an aggregator node computes a partial aggregate asynchronously, it also calculates the value of the partial aggregate as would be predicted by the receiving node. **If the difference between the previous value and the new value is within a specified fraction of the coherency associated with the partial aggregate (derived from user specified coherency on the aggregate), it does not send the computed value**, thus saving energy in transmissions.

The latter idea of *Prediction based In-network Filtering* implies that a child node F need not send a new partial aggregate to B if (a) if it is not *too different* from the previously sent value, or (b) B's new prediction will not be *too different* from prediction based on previous values received by B from F.

Let us make the notion of *too different* somewhat more concrete. Let us denote by c, the user specified coherency on the aggregate query and by c', the coherency associated with the partial aggregate. c and c' are related as:

$$c' = c \times \beta$$

where β is a real number in the interval $[0, 1]$. To understand β, consider an aggregation tree. In an aggregation tree, the number of messages exchanged between nodes increases as we traverse from the leaf nodes in the tree towards the root. Due to higher number of messages near the source nodes, the possibility of messages being lost due to collisions is higher. We use coherency c to suppress the number of messages exchanged between nodes. β effectively controls the number of messages suppressed and ensured that the query node receives results at the desired accuracy.

In order to ensure accurate prediction of partial aggregates, we use the notion of *NoActivityThreshold* to guard against loss of messages (and thus loss of model parameters and partial aggregate values) due to collisions. *NoActivityThreshold* at a node for its dependent node is defined as the amount of time for which a node waits before pushing the value of its partial aggregate to the dependent, i.e. if a node has not pushed the value of the partial aggregate to its dependent for a duration greater than *NoActivityThreshold*, the node pushes the value of the partial aggregate.

We would like to point out that our asynchronous approach is in direct contrast with the epoch-based synchronization schemes, for example, TAG [4] and TiNA [5]. In that approach each epoch is divided into time slots and all serving nodes at a given level in the tree are allowed to transmit within a particular time slot. The dependents of these nodes listen during this time slot. At the end of this time slot, each dependent computes a partial aggregate of the data received from its serving nodes. During the next time slot, the dependents transmit the partial aggregates to their dependents. In synchronous computation methods, the duration of the time slot for which the message is withheld at each aggregator node decides the amount of delay for each value that is generated at a source to reach the query node. This delay can lead to loss in fidelity, unacceptable for scenarios that require online decision making. Using an asynchronous approach minimizes this delay, thus providing the potential to deliver higher fidelity. In terms of lifetime, with the asynchronous approach it may seem that computation of an aggregate on receiving a message from any serving node, and a subsequent push to the dependent, if required, may lead to unnecessary transmissions and thus a decrease in lifetime. Our approach of using in-network filtering and in-network prediction for energy efficient aggregation ensures that this is not the case.

In [3], we show that for simple aggregates, for improved query lifetime and correctness, overlay tree construction algorithm should be (remaining) energy-aware, and that we should exploit in-network processing ability. The latter translates to exploiting coherency requirement, using asynchronous prediction based aggregation, and using prediction based In-network filtering. Experimental results demonstrate that (a) the resulting scheme has only one fifteenth of the fidelity loss along with a 40% improvement in lifetime compared to a synchronous last-value-based aggregate computation method; (b) simple approaches to predicting partial aggregates work well for real-world phenomena.

5 Aggregations While Tracking Dynamic Natural Phenomena

As was mentioned in the introduction, time critical data sensed in-situ or remotely – from many mobile/stationary nodes have to be continuously aggregated to track phenomena in the physical world, e.g., movement of oil slicks, gas plumes, etc. Here we briefly show that asynchronous in-network filtering, prediction & aggregation are themes that are useful even in more complex aggregation scenarios.

Consider tracking a dynamic boundary. A dynamic boundary has mainly two types of variations: spatial and temporal. So, the effective tracking of dynamic boundaries requires handling both of these variations. In [2] we describe an algorithm for dynamic boundary tracking which combines a spatial estimation technique and a temporal estimation technique to effectively track a dynamic boundary using static range sensors that measure the distance to the boundary from their current location. The first step is to estimate the boundary at a location x using a spatial estimation technique. It uses spatial correlations among (error-prone sensor) observations at a given time by sensors within a small neighbourhood of x. Aggregator nodes in the overlay network perform aggregation operations on sensor observations to estimate a number of boundary points. Partial information of the boundary from aggregator nodes is then sent to the base station where the final estimate of the boundary at x is computed. In order to exploit in-network aggregation possibility, the aggregation is done using kernel smoothing that is amenable to being "broken-up" into subcomputations that can be done within the network, by the aggregator nodes. A similar approach is used to perform in-network subcomputations needed to determine the confidence interval associated with the boundary estimated at x. A confidence band is estimated from multiple boundary points around the entire boundary using an interpolation scheme executed by the base station.

The second component of the overall approach is a temporal estimation technique which ensures that the estimates are updated whenever due to changes in the boundary the confidence band does not cover the boundary with a desired accuracy. We use a Kalman Filter based technique to predict future boundary locations based on its model of the boundary dynamics. Once the boundary has moved by more than a certain threshold, the spatial estimation technique is invoked to get an accurate estimate of the boundary. As a result, boundary estimates are updated based on only the local dynamics of the boundary and partial estimates track changes in sections of the boundary. Both of these lead to reduction in communication overhead for accurate boundary estimation. Effectiveness with respect to tracking efficiency and correctness have been demonstrated on real contours [2].

Our current work involves applying the building blocks discussed in this paper for handling aggregations of sensor observations when using mobile in-situ sensors [1].

6   Conclusions

Given a sensor network and aggregate queries over the values sensed by subsets of nodes in the network, how do we ensure that *high quality results* are served for the *maximum possible time*? The issues underlying this question relate to the *fidelity* of query results and *lifetime* of the network. To maximize both, we propose a novel technique called *asynchronous in-network prediction* incorporating two computationally efficient methods for in-network prediction of partial aggregate values. These values are propagated via a tree whose construction is cognizant of (a) the coherency requirements associated with the queries, (b) the remaining energy at the sensors, and (c) the communication and message processing delays. Finally, we exploit *in-network filtering* and *in-network aggregation* to reduce the energy consumption of the nodes in the network. Experimental results over real world data used to track dynamic physical phenomena support our claim that for aggregate queries with associated coherency requirements, a prediction based asynchronous scheme provides higher quality results for a longer amount of time than a synchronous scheme.

References

1. Srinivasan, S., Ramamritham, K., Kulkarni, P.: ACE in the Hole: Adaptive Contour Estimation Using Collaborating Mobile Sensors. In: IPSN: ACM/IEEE International Conference on Information Processing in Sensor Networks (IPSN 2008) (April 2008)
2. Duttagupta, S., Ramamritham, K., Kulkarni, P., Moudgalya, K.: Tracking Dynamic Boundary Fronts using Range Sensors. In: Verdone, R. (ed.) EWSN 2008. LNCS, vol. 4913, pp. 125–140. Springer, Heidelberg (2008)
3. Edara, P., Limaye, A., Ramamritham, K.: Asynchronous In-network Prediction: Efficient Aggregation in Sensor Networks. ACM Transactions on Sensor Networks (November 2008)
4. Madden, S., Franklin, M.J., Hellerstein, J.M., Hong, W.: TAG: a Tiny AGgre- gation service for ad-hoc sensor networks. SIGOPS Oper. Syst. Rev. 36 (2002)
5. Sharaf, M.A., Beaver, J., Labrinidis, A., Chrysanthis, P.K.: TiNA: A Scheme for Temporal Coherency-Aware in-Network Aggregation. In: Third International ACM Workshop on Data Engineering for Wireless and Mobile Access (MobiDE) (2003)

Distributed Computing and the Multicore Revolution

Maurice Herlihy

Computer Science Department
Brown University Providence, RI 02912, USA

Abstract. Computer architecture is undergoing a sea-change: very soon, nearly all computers will be "multicore" architectures in which multiple processors reside on a single chip. It is widely recognized that the switch to multicore presents a daunting challenge in areas that range all the way from architecture to software engineering, to raw system performance.

V. Garg, R. Wattenhofer, and K. Kothapalli (Eds.): ICDCN 2009, LNCS 5408, p. 8, 2009.

The Rise of People-Centric Sensing

Andrew Campbell

Computer Science Department
Dartmouth College
Hanover, NH 03755, USA

Abstract. Technological advances in sensing, computation, storage, and communications will turn the near-ubiquitous mobile phone into a global mobile sensing device. People-centric sensing will help drive this trend by enabling a different way to sense, learn, visualize, and share information about ourselves, friends, communities, the way we live, and the world we live in. It juxtaposes the traditional view of mesh wireless sensor networks with one in which people, carrying mobile devices, enable opportunistic sensing coverage. In the MetroSense Project's vision of people-centric sensing, users are the key architectural system component, enabling a host of new application areas such as personal, public, and social sensing.

V. Garg, R. Wattenhofer, and K. Kothapalli (Eds.): ICDCN 2009, LNCS 5408, p. 9, 2009.
© Springer-Verlag Berlin Heidelberg 2009

Temporal Considerations in Wireless Networks and Cyberphysical Systems

P.R. Kumar

Department of Electrical and Computer Engineering
University of Illinois, Urbana-Champaign, IL 61081, USA

Abstract. As we move towards cyberphysical systems, temporal considerations in information delivery will play an ever larger role. Timeliness of delivery of packets will be just as important as throughput or reliability. Accurate and consistent time-stamping of information will be necessary for information fusion. Temporal coordination of action over a network will be important for the safety and efficiency of the underlying physical systems. We will address these issues vis-a-vis wireless networks, sensor networks and cyberphysical systems.

V. Garg, R. Wattenhofer, and K. Kothapalli (Eds.): ICDCN 2009, LNCS 5408, p. 10, 2009.
© Springer-Verlag Berlin Heidelberg 2009

Finding Facilities Fast

Saurav Pandit and Sriram V. Pemmaraju

University of Iowa, Iowa City IA 52242-1419, USA
{spandit,sriram}@cs.uiowa.edu

Abstract. Clustering can play a critical role in increasing the performance and lifetime of wireless networks. The *facility location* problem is a general abstraction of the clustering problem and this paper presents the first constant-factor approximation algorithm for the facility location problem on unit disk graphs (UDGs), a commonly used model for wireless networks. In this version of the problem, connection costs are not *metric*, i.e., they do not satisfy the triangle inequality, because connecting to a non-neighbor costs ∞. In non-metric settings the best approximation algorithms guarantee an $O(\log n)$-factor approximation, but we are able to use structural properties of UDGs to obtain a constant-factor approximation. Our approach combines ideas from the primal-dual algorithm for facility location due to Jain and Vazirani (*JACM*, 2001) with recent results on the *weighted minimum dominating set* problem for UDGs (Huang et al., *J. Comb. Opt.*, 2008). We then show that the facility location problem on UDGs is inherently *local* and one can solve local subproblems independently and combine the solutions in a simple way to obtain a good solution to the overall problem. This leads to a distributed version of our algorithm in the $\mathcal{LOCAL}$ model that runs in *constant* rounds and still yields a constant-factor approximation. Even if the UDG is specified without geometry, we are able to combine recent results on *maximal independent sets* and *clique partitioning* of UDGs, to obtain an $O(\log n)$-approximation that runs in $O(\log^* n)$ rounds.

1 Introduction

The widespread use of wireless multi-hop networks such as ad hoc and sensor networks pose numerous algorithmic challenges. One of these algorithmic challenges is posed by the need for efficient *clustering* algorithms. Clustering can play a critical role in increasing the performance and lifetime of wireless networks and has been proposed as a way to improve MAC layer protocols (e.g., [1,2]), higher level routing protocols (e.g., [3,4,5]), and energy saving protocols (e.g., [6,7]). Clustering problems can be modeled as combinatorial or geometric optimization problems of various kinds; the *minimum dominating set (MDS)* problem, the *k-median* problem, etc. are some popular abstractions of the clustering problem. Since wireless networks reside in physical space and since transmission ranges of nodes can be modeled as geometric objects (e.g., disks, spheres, fat objects, etc.), wireless networks can be modeled as geometric graphs, especially as intersection graphs of geometric objects. This has motivated researchers to consider a

V. Garg, R. Wattenhofer, and K. Kothapalli (Eds.): ICDCN 2009, LNCS 5408, pp. 11–24, 2009.

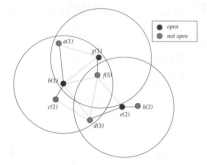

Fig. 1. A UDG with eight vertices. Opening costs are integers shown next to the vertex names and connection costs of edges are assumed to be Euclidean lengths. Vertices b, g, and e have been opened as facilities. The solid lines indicate the assignments of vertices (clients) to open facilites and the dotted lines indicate edges in the UDG that are not being used for any facility-client connection. Only the disks around the three open facilities are shown in the figure. The cost of this solution is 4 units (for opening facilities) plus $|fg| + |ab| + |cb| + |de| + |he|$.

variety of clustering problems for geometric graphs [8,9,10,11,12] and attempt to develop efficient distributed algorithms for these. Most of these clustering problems are NP-hard even for fairly simple geometric graphs and this has motivated attempts to design fast distributed *approximation* algorithms. In this paper, we present the first constant-factor approximation algorithm for the *facility location* problem on *unit disk graphs (UDGs)*. For points u and v in Euclidean space we use $|uv|$ to denote the Euclidean distance in L_2 norm between u and v. A graph $G = (V, E)$ is a *unit disk graph (UDG)* if there is an embedding of the vertices of G in $\mathbb{R}^2$ (the 2-dimensional Euclidean space) such that $\{u, v\} \in E$ iff $|uv| \leq 1$. The *facility location problem on UDGs* (in short, UDG-FacLoc) takes as input a UDG $G = (V, E)$, opening costs $f : V \to \mathbb{R}^+$ associated with vertices, and *connection costs* $c : E \to \mathbb{R}^+$ associated with the edges. The problem is to find a subset $I \subseteq V$ of vertices to open (as "facilities") and a function $\phi : V \to I$ that assigns every vertex ("client") to an open facility *in its neighborhood* in such a way that the total cost of opening the facilities and connecting clients to open facilities is minimized. In other words, the problem seeks to minimize the objective function $\sum_{i \in I} f(i) + \sum_{j \in V} c(j, \phi(j))$. See Fig. 1 for an illustration. The opening cost $f(i)$ reflects the available battery power at node i; less the battery power, greater the cost $f(i)$. The connection cost $c(j, \phi(j))$ represents the power needed for j to communicate with $\phi(j)$. Hence it is safe to assume that the connection costs of edges are determined by their Euclidean lengths via a fairly general function. More precisely, let $g : [0, 1] \to \mathbb{R}^+$ be a monotonically increasing function with *bounded growth*, i.e., for some constant $B \geq 1$, $g(x) \leq B \cdot g(x/3)$ for all $x \in [0, 1]$. We assume that each edge $\{i, j\} \in E$ get assigned a connection cost $c(i, j) = g(|ij|)$. Note that the restriction that g has bounded growth still permits cost functions that are quite general from the point of view of wireless networks. For example, if $g(x) = \beta \cdot x^\gamma$ for constants β and γ

(as might be the case if connection costs represent power usage), then $B = 3^\gamma$. It should be noted that every vertex in G is a "client" and every vertex has the potential to be a "facility." Furthermore, a vertex ("client") can only be connected to (i.e., "serviced" by) another vertex ("facility") in its neighborhood and thus the set of open facilities forms a dominating set.

Note that UDG-FacLoc is inherently *non-metric*, i.e., connection costs of edges do not satisfy the triangle inequality. This is because a vertex cannot be connected to a non-neighbor, implying that the connection cost of a vertex to a non-neighbor is ∞. There are no known constant-factor approximation algorithms for the non-metric version of facility location, even for UDGs. In one sense, this is not surprising because UDG-FacLoc is a generalization of the *weighted minimum dominating set (WMDS)* problem on UDGs. This can be seen by noting that an instance of WMDS, namely $G = (V, E)$, $w : V \to \mathbb{R}^+$, can be interpreted as a UDG-FacLoc instance in which the connection costs (of edges) are set to 0 and each opening cost $f(i)$ is set to the vertex weight $w(i)$. Unlike the WMDS problem that ignores the cost of connecting to *dominators*, the facility location problem explicitly models *connection costs*. As a result, solutions to WMDS may lead to clustering that is quite poor. There have been no constant-factor approximation algorithms for WMDS on UDGs until recently, with the result of Ambühl et al. [11] being the first constant-factor approximation for WMDS on UDGs. Subsequently, Huang et al. [13] have improved the approximation ratio significantly. Our technique combines the well known *primal-dual* algorithm of Jain and Vazirani [14] with these recent constant-factor approximation algorithms for WMDS on UDGs, to obtain a constant-factor approximation for UDG-FacLoc. Applicability of our technique to more general models of wireless networks, for example, *unit ball graphs* in higher dimensional spaces or *doubling metric spaces*, *disk graphs*, *growth-bounded graphs* etc. is only limited by the availability of good approximation algorithms for the WMDS problem on these graph classes. Using our technique, a constant-factor approximation algorithm for WMDS on any of these graph classes would immediately imply a constant-factor approximation for facility location on that graph class.

UDGs are simple and popular models of wireless networks and the facility location problem on UDGs is a general abstraction of the clustering problem on wireless networks. To be more specific consider one common application of dominating sets in wireless networks, which is to save energy by sending all dominatees into a low power *sleep mode* and having the network be serviced exclusively by the dominators. While it makes sense to keep the size or weight of the dominating set small so that most nodes are in the sleep mode, ignoring the connection costs could yield a dominating set in which each dominator has to spend a lot of energy in order to reach its dominatees. By using an objective function that takes opening costs as well as connection costs into account, UDG-FacLoc yields a set of cluster heads that can service the network with smaller overall cost and for a longer duration. For more background see the recent survey by Frank [15] on the facility location problem as it arises in the context of wireless and sensor networks.

1.1 Related Work

Facility location is an old and well studied problem in operations research ([16,17,18,19,20]), that arises in contexts such as locating hospitals in a city or locating distribution centers in a region. A *standard* instance of the facility location problem takes as input a complete bipartite graph $G = (F, C, E)$, where F is the set of facilities and C is the set of cities, opening costs $f : F \to \mathbb{R}^+$, and connection costs $c : E \to \mathbb{R}^+$. The goal, as mentioned before, is to find a set of facilities $I \subseteq F$ to open and a function $\phi : C \to I$ that assigns every city to an open facility so as to minimize $\sum_{i \in I} f(i) + \sum_{j \in C} c(j, \phi(j))$. In this context, the connection costs are said to satisfy the *triangle inequality* if for any $i, i' \in F$ and $j, j' \in C$, $c(i, j) \leq c(i, j') + c(i', j') + c(i', j)$. In the *metric facility location* problem the connection costs satisfy the triangle inequality; when they don't we have the more general *non-metric facility location* problem. UDG-FacLoc can be seen as an instance of the non-metric facility location problem by setting $F = V$, $C = V$, setting connection costs between a facility and a city that correspond to non-adjacent vertices to ∞, setting $c(i, i) = 0$ for all $i \in V$, and inheriting the remaining connection costs and opening costs in the natural way. $O(\log n)$-approximation algorithms for the non-metric facility location problem are well known [21,22]. Starting with an algorithm due to Shmoys, Tardos and Aardal [23] the metric facility location problem has had a series of constant-factor approximation algorithms, each improving on the approximation factor of the previous. In this paper we make use of an elegant primal-dual schema algorithm due to Jain and Vazirani [14] that provides a 3-approximation to the metric facility location problem. Since UDG-FacLoc is not a metric version of the facility location problem, we cannot use the Jain-Vazirani algorithm directly. We use the Jain-Vazirani algorithm to get a "low cost," but infeasible solution to UDG-FacLoc and then "repair" this solution via the use of a "low weight" dominating set and show that the resulting solution is within a constant-factor of OPT.

Several researchers have attempted to devise distributed algorithms for the facility location problem; these attempts differ in the restrictions placed on the facility location problem and in the network and distributed computing models. For example, Moscibroda and Wattenhofer [24] present a distributed algorithm for the standard non-metric facility location problem. The network on which their algorithm runs is the complete bipartite graph on F, the set of facilities and C, the set of cities. Since this network has diameter 2, one way to solve the problem would be for a node to gather information about the entire network in constant number of communication rounds and just run a known sequential algorithm locally. Thus this problem is uninteresting in the $\mathcal{LOCAL}$ model [25] of distributed computation. The problem becomes more interesting in the $\mathcal{CONGEST}$ model, where a reasonable bound, such as $O(\log n)$ bits, is imposed on each message size. The message size of $O(\log n)$ bits allows each message to contain at most a constant number of node identifiers and constants that are polynomial in n. In such a model, exchanging a lot of information costs a lot of rounds and Moscibroda and Wattenhofer [24] present an approximation algorithm for non-metric facility location that, for every k, achieves an $O(\sqrt{k}(m\rho)^{1/\sqrt{k}}\log(m+n))$-approximation in $O(k)$ communication rounds. Here m is the number of facilities, n is the number of clients, and ρ is a coefficient that depends on the numbers (i.e., opening costs and connection costs) that are part of the input. The main thrust of this result is that even with a constant number of communication rounds, a non-trivial approximation factor can be achieved. However, it should be noted that no matter how large k is (e.g., $k = \text{polylog}(n)$), the approximation factor of this algorithm is $\Omega(\log(m+n))$.

Frank and Römer [26] consider facility location on multi-hop networks (like we do), but assume that given edge weights, the connection cost $c(i,j)$ for any pair of vertices i and j is simply the shortest path distance between i and j. This turns their problem into a *metric* problem and thus they can use known sequential algorithms; in particular, they use the 1.61-approximation due to Jain et al. [27]. Frank and Römer [26] show how to implement the sequential algorithm of Jain et al. [27] in a distributed setting without any degradation in the approximation factor, but they do not provide any non trivial running time guarantees. These authors [26] do mention the version of the problem in which connection costs between non-neighboring vertices is ∞, but they just observe that since this is a non-metric problem, constant-factor approximation algorithms are not known.

Gehweiler et al. [28] present a constant-approximation, constant-round distributed algorithm using only $O(\log n)$-bits per message, for the *uniform* facility location problem. In this problem, all opening costs are identical and the underlying network is a clique. The authors make critical use of the fact that all facility opening costs are identical in order to obtain the constant-approximation. The uniform opening costs assumption is restrictive for certain settings. For example, if we want opening costs to reflect the amount of battery power that nodes have available – more the available power at a node, cheaper it is to open that node, then this assumption requires the battery power at all nodes to remain identical through the life of the network. This may be untenable because nodes will tend to expend different amounts of power as they perform different activities. The interesting aspect of the Gehweiler et al. [28] algorithm is that all message sizes are bounded above by $O(\log n)$.

1.2   Main Results

We assume that we are given a UDG along with its geometric representation. Let $g : [0,1] \to \mathbb{R}^+$ be a monotonically increasing function with *bounded growth*, i.e., there exists a constant B such that $g(x) \leq B \cdot g(x/3)$ for all $x \in [0,1]$. Each edge $\{i,j\} \in E$ gets assigned a connection cost $c(i,j) = g(|ij|)$, representing the dependence of the connection cost on the Euclidean distance between the involved vertices. For any $\varepsilon > 0$, we present a $(6+B+\varepsilon)$-approximation algorithm for UDG-FacLoc. To put this result in context, observe that if connection costs are exactly Euclidean distances, i.e., $g(x) = x$, then $B = 3$ and we have a $(9 + \varepsilon)$-approximation. If the connection costs are meant to represent energy usage, then a function such as $g(x) = \beta \cdot x^\gamma$ for constants β and $2 \leq \gamma \leq 4$ may be reasonable. In this case, $B = 3^\gamma$ and we get a $(3^\gamma + 6 + \varepsilon)$-approximation, still a constant-factor approximation. We then present a distributed implementation of our algorithm that runs in just $O(1)$ rounds and yields an $O(B)$-approximation.

In the $\mathcal{LOCAL}$ model, every node $v \in V$ can send an arbitrarily large message to ever neighbor u in each round of communication. This model abstracts away all the restricting factors (e.g. congestion and asynchronicity) and focus on the impact of *locality* on distributed computation. To obtain this result we show that UDG-FacLoc can be solved "locally" with only a constant-factor degradation in the quality of the solution. One aspect of our result, namely the constant approximation factor, depends crucially on the availability of a geometric representation of the input UDG. If we are given only a combinatorial representation of the input n-vertex UDG, then our algorithm runs in $O(\log^* n)$ rounds yielding an $O(\log n)$-approximation. This result depends on two recent results: (i) an $O(\log^* n)$-round algorithm for computing a *maximal independent set (MIS)* in growth-bounded graphs [29] and (ii) an algorithm that partitions a UDG, given without geometry, into relatively small number of cliques [30]. Overall, our results indicate that UDG-FacLoc is as "local" a problem as MIS is, provided one is willing to tolerate a constant-factor approximation. Our techniques extend in a straightforward manner to the *connected* UDG-FacLoc problem, where it is required that the facilities induce a connected subgraph; we obtain an $O(1)$-round, $O(B)$-approximation for this problem also.

2   Sequential Algorithm

Now we present a high level *three step* description of our algorithm for finding a constant-factor approximation for UDG-FacLoc. Let $G = (V, E)$ be the given UDG with an opening cost $f(i)$ for each vertex $i \in V$ and connection cost $c(i, j)$ for each edge $\{i, j\} \in E$. We assume that there is a monotonically increasing function $g : [0, 1] \rightarrow \mathbb{R}^+$ satisfying $g(x) \le B \cdot g(x/3)$ for all $x \in [0, 1]$ for some $B \ge 1$, such that $c(i, j) = g(|ij|)$.

Step 1. Convert the given instance of UDG-FacLoc into a standard non-metric instance of facility location. This transformation is as described in the previous section. Run the primal-dual algorithm of Jain and Vazirani [14] on this instance to obtain a solution S. The solution S may contain connections that are infeasible for UDG-FacLoc; these connections have connection cost ∞ and they connect pairs of non-adjacent vertices in G.

Step 2. Assign to each vertex i of G a weight equal to $f(i)$. Compute a dominating set of G with small weight. For this we can use the $(6 + \varepsilon)$-approximation algorithm due to Huang et al. [13]. Let D^* denote the resulting solution.

Step 3. For each vertex $i \in V$ that is connected to a facility by an edge of cost ∞, reconnect i to an arbitrarily chosen neighbor $d \in D^*$. Think of the vertices $d \in D^*$ as facilities and declare them all open. Let the new solution to UDG-FacLoc be called S^*.

We will prove the following theorem in the next subsection.

Theorem 1. *Let OPT denote the cost of an optimal solution to a given instance of* UDG-FacLoc. *Then* $cost(S^*) \leq (6 + B + \varepsilon) \cdot OPT$.

2.1 Analysis

To analyze our algorithm we need some details of the Jain-Vazirani primal-dual algorithm used in Step 1. For a more complete description see [14]. The starting point of this algorithm is the following Integer Program (IP) representation of facility location. Here y_i indicates whether facility i is open and x_{ij} indicates if city j is connected to facility i. The first set of constraints ensure that every city is connected to a facility and the second set of constraints guarantee that each city is connected to an open facility.

$$
\begin{aligned}
\text{minimize} \quad & \sum_{i \in F, j \in C} c(i,j) \cdot x_{ij} + \sum_{i \in F} f(i) \cdot y_i \\
\text{subject to} \quad & \sum_{i \in F} x_{ij} \geq 1, & j \in C \\
& y_i - x_{ij} \geq 0, & i \in F, j \in C \\
& x_{ij} \in \{0,1\}, & i \in F, j \in C \\
& y_i \in \{0,1\}, & i \in F
\end{aligned}
$$

As is standard, we work with the LP-relaxation of the above IP obtained by replacing the integrality constraints by $x_{ij} \geq 0$ for all $i \in F$ and $j \in C$ and $y_i \geq 0$ for all $i \in F$. The dual of this LP-relaxation is the following:

$$
\begin{aligned}
\text{maximize} \quad & \sum_{j \in C} \alpha_j \\
\text{subject to} \quad & \alpha_j - \beta_{ij} \leq c(i,j), & i \in F, j \in C \\
& \sum_{j \in C} \beta_{ij} \leq f(i), & i \in F \\
& \alpha_j \geq 0, & j \in C \\
& \beta_{ij} \geq 0, & i \in F, j \in C
\end{aligned}
$$

The dual variable α_j can be interpreted as the amount that city j is willing to pay in order to connect to a facility. Of this amount, $c(i,j)$ goes towards paying for connecting to facility i, whereas the "extra," namely β_{ij}, is seen as the contribution of city j towards opening facility i. Initially all the α_j and β_{ij} values are 0. The Jain-Vazirani algorithm initially raises all of the α_j values in synch. When α_j reaches $c(i,j)$ for some edge $\{i,j\}$, then the connection cost $c(i,j)$ has been paid for by j and any subsequent increase in α_j is accompanied by a corresponding increase in β_{ij} so that the first dual constraint is not violated. The quantity β_{ij} is j's contribution towards opening facility i and when there is enough contribution, i.e., $\sum_j \beta_{ij} = f(i)$, then the facility i is declared *temporarily open*. Furthermore, all unconnected cities j that make positive contribution towards $f(i)$, i.e., $\beta_{ij} > 0$, are declared *connected* to i. Also, any unconnected city j that has completely paid its connection cost $c(i,j)$, but has not yet started paying towards β_{ij}, i.e., $\beta_{ij} = 0$, is also declared *connected* to j. The opening of a facility i corresponds to setting $y_i = 1$ and declaring a city j connected to i corresponds to setting $x_{ij} = 1$. Once a facility i is open and cities connected to it, then the dual variables of these cities are no longer raised; otherwise the dual constraint $\sum_{j \in C} \beta_{ij} \le f(i)$ would be violated. The algorithm proceeds in this way until every city has been connected to some open facility. This is the end of Phase 1 of the algorithm.

It is easy to check that at the end of Phase 1, $\{\alpha_j, \beta_{ij}\}$ define a feasible dual solution and $\{y_i, x_{ij}\}$ define a feasible *integral* solution. If the cost of the primal solution is not too large compared to the cost of the dual solution, then by the Weak Duality Theorem, we would have a solution to facility location that is not too far from a lower bound on OPT. However, the gap between the costs of the dual and the primal solutions can be quite high because a single city may be contributing towards the connection costs and opening costs of many facilities. To fix this problem, Phase 2 of the algorithm is run. Let F_t be the set of temporarily open facilities. Define a graph H on this set of vertices with edges $\{i, i'\}$ whenever there is a city j such that $\beta_{ij} > 0$ and $\beta_{i'j} > 0$; in other words, city j is contributing a positive amount towards the opening of both facilities i and i'. Compute a *maximal independent set (MIS)* I of H and declare all facilites in I open (permanently) and close down all facilities in $F_t \setminus I$, i.e., set $y_i = 0$ for all $i \in F_t \setminus I$. Due to the shutting down of some facilities, some cities may be connected to closed facilities implying that the primal solution may be infeasible, due to violation of the $y_i - x_{ij} \ge 0$ constraints. Call a city j a *Class I city* if it is connected to an open facility. Denote the set of Class I cities by C_1. We will call cities outside of C_1, *Class II cities*. At this point in the algorithm the primal and the dual solution satisfy the following properties.

Lemma 1 *[Jain-Vazirani [14]]. The dual solution $\{\alpha_j, \beta_{ij}\}$ is feasible. The primal solution $\{y_i, x_{ij}\}$ is integral, but may not be feasible. Furthermore,*

$$\sum_{j \in C_1} \alpha_j = \sum_{j \in C_1} c(j, \phi(j)) + \sum_{i \in I} f(i).$$

The above Lemma is essentially saying that the Class I cities completely pay for connections to and the opening of facilities in I. The goal now is to fix the infeasibility of the primal solution, i.e., find connections for cities outside C_1, without increasing the cost of the primal solution too much relative to the cost of the dual. Let j be a city that is connected to a closed facility. If there is an open city i to which j has already paid connection cost, i.e., $\alpha_j \ge c(i, j)$, then simply connect j to one such city. Since $\alpha_j \ge c(i, j)$, the connection cost is paid for by α_j and furthermore the opening cost of i has been paid for by other cities. This leaves a set C' of cities such that for each $j \in C'$, $\alpha_j < c(i, j)$ for all open cities i. This may happen, for example, if none of j's neighbors in G have been opened as facilities and therefore for every open facility i, $c(i, j) = \infty$. Note that at the end of Phase 1, there was a temporarily open facility, say i, to which j was connected and in Phase 2, i was shut down. This implies that (i) $\alpha_j \ge c(i, j)$ and

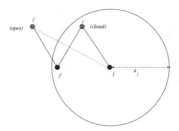

Fig. 2. Client j is connected to temporarily open facility i at the end of Phase 1. Client j' contributes positively to the opening cost of both i and i'. Facility i' is closed at the beginning of Phase 2 and facility i becomes a candidate for connecting j to.

(ii) there exists a city j' that is paying a positive amount towards the opening of two facilities i and i' and this "double payment" is responsible for i being shut down. See Fig. 2 for an illustration. In such a case, the Jain-Vazirani algorithm simply connects j to i'. In the *metric* facility location case, Jain and Vazirani are able to show that the connection cost $c(j, i')$ is not too big relative to $c(i, j)$ (they show, $c(j, i') \leq 3 \cdot c(i, j)$). In our case, i' may be outside the neighborhood of j and therefore $c(j, i') = \infty$ and therefore connecting j to i' is too costly. This possible mistake is fixed in the subsequent two steps of our algorithm, via the use of a WMDS solution. We now include the last two steps of our algorithm in the analysis to show that we are able to find a facility that is not too costly for i to connect to. More precisely, if j' is in the neighborhood of i, then $c(i, j') < \infty$ and we are able to show that connecting i to j' is a good idea. On the other hand, if j' is not a neighbor of i, then we show that connecting i to some neighbor in the WMDS solution D^* will not increase the cost of the solution too much. We make use of the following inequalities that Jain and Vazirani prove. The first inequality was mentioned earlier in this paragraph, but the remaining two inequalities take a little bit of work to prove and we refer the reader to the Jain-Vazirani paper [14].

Lemma 2 [Jain-Vazirani [14]]. $\alpha_j \geq c(i, j)$, $\alpha_j \geq c(i, j')$ and $\alpha_j \geq c(i', j')$.

Lemma 3. *Let B satisfy $g(x) \leq B \cdot g(x/3)$ for all $x \in [0, 1]$. If j' is a neighbor of i, then i is connected to j' in Step 1 and $c(i, j') \leq B \cdot \alpha_j$. If j' is not a neighbor of i, then i is connected to some neighbor $j^* \in D^*$ in Step 3 and $c(i, j^*) \leq B \cdot \alpha_j$.*

Proof. Since Euclidean distances satisfy triangle inequality, we have

$$|ij| + |i'j| + |i'j'| \geq |ij'|.$$

Let y denote the largest of the three terms on the left hand side above. Then $y \geq |ij'|/3$. Suppose that j' is a neighbor of i. Then $|ij'| \leq 1$ and $c(i, j') = g(|ij'|) < \infty$. Then,

$$c(i, j') = g(|ij'|) \leq B \cdot g\left(\frac{|ij'|}{3}\right) \qquad \text{(due to bounded growth of } g\text{)}$$

$$\leq B \cdot g(y) \qquad \text{(due to monotonicity of } g)$$
$$\leq B \cdot \alpha_j \qquad \text{(due to Lemma 2).}$$

Now suppose that j' is not a neighbor of i. Then $|ij'| > 1$ and for any neighbor j^* of i, $|ij'| > |ij^*|$. Since $y \geq |i'j|/3$, it follows that $y > |ij^*|/3$. Then, by the same reasoning as above, we get

$$c(i, j^*) = g(|ij^*|) \leq B \cdot g\left(\frac{|ij^*|}{3}\right)$$
$$\leq B \cdot g(y)$$
$$\leq B \cdot \alpha_j. \qquad \square$$

Lemma 4. *Let S^* be the solution produced by our algorithm. Then, $cost(S^*) \leq (6 + B + \varepsilon) \cdot OPT$, where OPT is the cost of an optimal solution to* UDG-FacLoc.

Proof. The cost of the entire solution can be expressed as

$$\left(\sum_{i \in I} f(i) + \sum_{j \in C_1} c(\phi(j), j)\right) + \left(\sum_{i \in D^*} f(i) + \sum_{j \in C_2} c(\phi(j), j)\right).$$

By Lemma 1, the first term in the above sum equals $\sum_{j \in C_1} \alpha_j$. Let OPT_{DOM} denote the weight of an optimal dominating set when each vertex i of G is assigned weight $f(i)$. Then,

$$\sum_{i \in D^*} f(i) \leq (6 + \varepsilon) \cdot OPT_{DOM} \leq (6 + \varepsilon) \cdot OPT \qquad (1)$$

because we use the $(6 + \varepsilon)$-approximation algorithms of Huang et al. [13] to compute a dominating set of small weight. Also, by Lemma 3,

$$\sum_{j \in C_2} c(\phi(j), j) \leq B \cdot \sum_{j \in C_2} \alpha_j. \qquad (2)$$

Together the above inequalities yield

$$cost(S^*) = \left(\sum_{i \in I} f(i) + \sum_{j \in C_1} c(\phi(j), j)\right) + \left(\sum_{i \in D^*} f(i) + \sum_{j \in C_2} c(\phi(j), j)\right)$$
$$\leq \sum_{j \in C_1} \alpha_j + (6 + \varepsilon) \cdot OPT + B \cdot \sum_{j \in C_2} \alpha_j$$
$$\leq B \cdot \sum_{j \in C} \alpha_j + (6 + \varepsilon) \cdot OPT \qquad \text{(since } B \geq 1)$$
$$\leq (B + 6 + \varepsilon) \cdot OPT \qquad \text{(by Weak Duality Theorem).} \qquad \square$$

By making simple modifications to an example due to Jain and Vazirani ([14]), we can show that the above analysis is tight in the sense that there exists a UDG along with an assignment of opening and connection costs for which our algorithm produces a solution with cost at least $B \cdot OPT$, independent of the quality of the WMDS used.

3   Distributed Algorithm

In this section, we present an $O(1)$-round distributed implementation of the above algorithm in the $\mathcal{LOCAL}$ model [25]. In this model there is no upper bound placed on the message size and due to this, a node can collect all possible information (i.e., node IDs, topology, interactions) about its k-neighborhood in k communication rounds. We show in this section that UDG-FacLoc is inherently a "local" problem provided we are willing to tolerate a constant-factor approximation in the cost of the solution. This property of UDG-FacLoc allows us to solve a version of the problem independently on *small squares* and combine the solutions in a simple way to get the overall solution. We partition the plane into squares by placing on the plane an infinite grid of $1/\sqrt{2} \times 1/\sqrt{2}$ squares. This is a standard and simple way of partitioning a UDG with geometric representation into cliques. The square S_{ij} for $i, j \in \mathbb{Z}$, contains all the points (x, y) with $\frac{i}{\sqrt{2}} \leq x < \frac{i+1}{\sqrt{2}}$ and $\frac{j}{\sqrt{2}} \leq y < \frac{j+1}{\sqrt{2}}$. Let $G = (V, E)$ be the given UDG. For a square S_{ij} that has at least one node in V, let $V_{ij} \subseteq V$ be the set of vertices whose centers lie in S_{ij}. Let $N(V_{ij})$ denote the set of all vertices in $V \setminus V_{ij}$ that are adjacent to some vertex in V_{ij}. Now consider the subproblem, denoted UDG-FacLoc$_{ij}$, in which we are allowed to open facilities from the set $V_{ij} \cup N(V_{ij})$ with the aim of connecting all the nodes in V_{ij} as clients to these facilities. The objective function of the problem remains the same: minimize the cost of opening facilities plus the connection costs.

Let $\{F_{ij}, \phi_{ij}\}$ denote a solution to UDG-FacLoc$_{ij}$, where $F_{ij} \subset V_{ij} \cup N(V_{ij})$ is the set of open facilities and $\phi_{ij} : V_{ij} \to F_{ij}$ is the assignment of clients to open facilities. Let $\cup_{ij}\{F_{ij}, \phi_{ij}\}$ denote a solution to UDG-FacLoc in which the set of open facilities is $\cup_{ij} F_{ij}$ and the assignment $\phi : V \to \cup_{ij} F_{ij}$ is defined by $\phi(v) = \phi_{ij}(v)$ if $v \in V_{ij}$. Thus $\cup_{ij}\{F_{ij}, \phi_{ij}\}$ defines a simple way of combining solutions of UDG-FacLoc$_{ij}$ to obtain a solution of UDG-FacLoc. The following Lemma shows that if the small square solutions $\cup_{ij}\{F_{ij}, \phi_{ij}\}$ are good then combining them in this simple way yields a solution to UDG-FacLoc that is also quite good. This Lemma is a generalization of a result due to Ambühl et al. [11] that was proved in the context of the WMDS problem for UDGs. The proof of this Lemma is omitted due to space constraints, but it appears in [31].

Lemma 5. *For each $i, j \in \mathbb{Z}$, let OPT_{ij} denote the cost of an optimal solution to UDG-FacLoc$_{ij}$ and let $\{F_{ij}, \phi_{ij}\}$ be a solution to UDG-FacLoc$_{ij}$ such that for some c, $cost(\{F_{ij}, \phi_{ij}\}) \leq c \cdot OPT_{ij}$. Then $cost(\cup_{ij}\{F_{ij}, \phi_{ij}\}) \leq 16c \cdot OPT$. Here OPT is the cost of an optimal solution to UDG-FacLoc.*

The above Lemma implies the following simple distributed algorithm.

Step 1. Each node v gathers information (i.e., coordinates of nodes, opening costs of nodes, and connection costs of edges) about the subgraph induced by its 2-neighborhood.

Step 2. Each node v in S_{ij} then identifies V_{ij} and $N(V_{ij})$. Recall that $V_{ij} \subseteq V$ is the set of nodes that belong to square S_{ij} and $N(V_{ij}) \subseteq V \setminus V_{ij}$ is the set of nodes outside of V_{ij} that have at least one neighbor in V_{ij}.

Step 3. Each node v locally computes the solution of UDG-FacLoc$_{ij}$, thereby determining whether it should be opened as a facility and if not which neighboring facility it should connect to.

Based on the above description, it is easily verified that the algorithm takes 2 rounds of communication. Note that the instance of UDG-FacLoc$_{ij}$ solved in Step 3 is slightly different from UDG-FacLoc, in that only certain vertices (namely, the vertices in V_{ij}) need to connect to open facilities, whereas every vertex (both in V_{ij} and in $N(V_{ij})$) is a potential client. This difference is minor and the $(6 + B + \varepsilon)$-approximation algorithm described in the previous section, can be essentially used without any changes, to solve UDG-FacLoc$_{ij}$. Lemma 5 then implies that the distributed algorithm above would yield a $16 \cdot (6 + B + \varepsilon)$-approximation algorithm. We can do better by making use of an intermediate result due to Ambühl et al. [11] that presents a 2-approximation algorithm for the WMDS problem on each square S_{ij}. Using arguments from the previous section, we can use this to obtain a $(B + 2)$-approximation for UDG-FacLoc$_{ij}$ and a $16 \cdot (B + 2)$-approximation for UDG-FacLoc.

4   Conclusion and Future Work

One open question implied by this work is whether we can obtain a constant-factor approximation algorithm for facility location on more general classes of wireless network models. We believe that a first step towards solving this problem would be to obtain a constant-factor approximation algorithm for UDG-FacLoc when the input UDG is given without any geometry. The only obstacle to obtaining such an approximation, using our techniques, is the lack of a constant-factor approximation to WMDS on UDGs given without geometry. Without geometry, the best algorithm we could design is one that, in $O(\log^* n)$ rounds, outputs an $O(\log n)$-approximation to the UDG-FacLoc problem. That algorithm is omitted due to space constraints, but it appears in [31].

The distributed algorithm we present runs in $O(1)$ rounds in the $\mathcal{LOCAL}$ model, which assumes that message sizes are unbounded. We would like to extend our distributed algorithm to the $\mathcal{CONGEST}$ model where only messages of size $O(\log n)$ are allowed.

References

1. Heinzelman, W.R., Chandrakasan, A., Balakrishnan, H.: Energy-efficient communication protocol for wireless microsensor networks. In: HICSS 2000: Proceedings of the 33rd Hawaii International Conference on System Sciences, vol. 8, p. 8020 (2000)
2. Wu, T., Biswas, S.: Minimizing inter-cluster interference by self-reorganizing mac allocation in sensor networks. Wireless Networks 13(5), 691–703 (2007)
3. Wan, P.J., Alzoubi, K.M., Frieder, O.: Distributed construction of connected dominating set in wireless ad hoc networks. Mob. Netw. Appl. 9(2), 141–149 (2004)

4. Wang, Y., Li, X.Y.: Localized construction of bounded degree and planar spanner for wireless ad hoc networks. In: DIALM-POMC 2003: Proceedings of the 2003 joint workshop on Foundations of mobile computing, pp. 59–68 (2003)

5. Wang, Y., Wang, W., Li, X.Y.: Distributed low-cost backbone formation for wireless ad hoc networks. In: MobiHoc., pp. 2–13 (2005)

6. Deb, B., Nath, B.: On the node-scheduling approach to topology control in ad hoc networks. In: MobiHoc 2005: Proceedings of the 6th ACM international symposium on Mobile ad hoc networking and computing, pp. 14–26 (2005)

7. Kang, J., Zhang, Y., Nath, B.: Analysis of resource increase and decrease algorithm in wireless sensor networks. In: ISCC 2006: Proceedings of the 11th IEEE Symposium on Computers and Communications, pp. 585–590 (2006)

8. Talwar, K.: Bypassing the embedding: algorithms for low dimensional metrics. In: STOC 2004: Proceedings of the thirty-sixth annual ACM symposium on Theory of computing, pp. 281–290 (2004)

9. Bilò, V., Caragiannis, I., Kaklamanis, C., Kanellopoulos, P.: Geometric clustering to minimize the sum of cluster sizes. In: Brodal, G.S., Leonardi, S. (eds.) ESA 2005. LNCS, vol. 3669, pp. 460–471. Springer, Heidelberg (2005)

10. Cheng, X., Huang, X., Li, D., Wu, W., Du, D.Z.: A polynomial-time approximation scheme for the minimum-connected dominating set in ad hoc wireless networks. Networks 42(4), 202–208 (2003)

11. Ambühl, C., Erlebach, T., Mihalák, M., Nunkesser, M.: Constant-factor approximation for minimum-weight (connected) dominating sets in unit disk graphs. In: APPROX-RANDOM, pp. 3–14 (2006)

12. Erlebach, T., van Leeuwen, E.J.: Domination in geometric intersection graphs. In: Laber, E.S., Bornstein, C., Nogueira, L.T., Faria, L. (eds.) LATIN 2008. LNCS, vol. 4957, pp. 747–758. Springer, Heidelberg (2008)

13. Huang, Y., Gao, X., Zhang, Z., Wu, W.: A better constant-factor approximation for weighted dominating set in unit disk graph. Journal of Combinatorial Optimization (2008)

14. Jain, K., Vazirani, V.V.: Approximation algorithms for metric facility location and k-median problems using the primal-dual schema and lagrangian relaxation. J. ACM 48(2), 274–296 (2001)

15. Frank, C.: Algorithms for Sensor and Ad Hoc Networks. Springer, Heidelberg (2007)

16. Kuehn, A.A., Hamburger, M.J.: A heuristic program for locating warehouses. Management Science 9(4), 643–666 (1963)

17. Stollsteimer, J.F.: A working model for plant numbers and locations. Management Science 45(3), 631–645 (1963)

18. Balinski, M.L.: On finding integer solutions to linear programs. In: Proceedings of IBM Scientific Computing Symposium on Combinatorial Problems, pp. 225–248 (1966)

19. Kaufman, L., Eede, M.V., Hansen, P.: A plant and warehouse location problem. Operational Research Quarterly 28(3), 547–554 (1977)

20. Cornuejols, G., Nemhouser, G., Wolsey, L.: Discrete Location Theory. Wiley, Chichester (1990)

21. Hochbaum, D.S.: Heuristics for the fixed cost median problem. Mathematical Programming 22(1), 148–162 (1982)

22. Lin, J.H., Vitter, J.S.: e-approximations with minimum packing constraint violation (extended abstract). In: STOC 1992: Proceedings of the twenty-fourth annual ACM symposium on Theory of computing, pp. 771–782 (1992)

23. Shmoys, D.B., Tardos, É., Aardal, K.: Approximation algorithms for facility location problems (extended abstract). In: STOC 1997: Proceedings of the twenty-ninth annual ACM symposium on Theory of computing, pp. 265–274 (1997)
24. Moscibroda, T., Wattenhofer, R.: Facility location: distributed approximation. In: PODC 2005: Proceedings of the twenty-fourth annual ACM symposium on Principles of distributed computing, pp. 108–117 (2005)
25. Peleg, D.: Distributed computing: a locality-sensitive approach. Society for Industrial and Applied Mathematics (2000)
26. Frank, C., Römer, K.: Distributed facility location algorithms for flexible configuration of wireless sensor networks. In: Aspnes, J., Scheideler, C., Arora, A., Madden, S. (eds.) DCOSS 2007. LNCS, vol. 4549, pp. 124–141. Springer, Heidelberg (2007)
27. Jain, K., Mahdian, M., Markakis, E., Saberi, A., Vazirani, V.V.: Greedy facility location algorithms analyzed using dual fitting with factor-revealing lp. J. ACM 50(6), 795–824 (2003)
28. Gehweiler, J., Lammersen, C., Sohler, C.: A distributed O(1)-approximation algorithm for the uniform facility location problem. In: SPAA 2006: Proceedings of the eighteenth annual ACM symposium on Parallelism in algorithms and architectures, pp. 237–243. ACM, New York (2006)
29. Schneider, J., Wattenhofer, R.: A Log-Star Distributed Maximal Independent Set Algorithm for growth-Bounded Graphs. In: 27th ACM Symposium on Principles of Distributed Computing (PODC), Toronto, Canada (2008)
30. Pemmaraju, S., Pirwani, I.: Good quality virtual realization of unit ball graphs. In: Arge, L., Hoffmann, M., Welzl, E. (eds.) ESA 2007. LNCS, vol. 4698, pp. 311–322. Springer, Heidelberg (2007)
31. Pandit, S., Pemmaraju, S.: Finding facilities fast. Full Paper (2009), http://cs.uiowa.edu/~spandit/research/icdcn2009.pdf

Large-Scale Networked Systems: From Anarchy to Geometric Self-structuring

Anne-Marie Kermarrec[1], Achour Mostefaoui[2], Michel Raynal[2], Gilles Tredan[2], and Aline C. Viana[3]

[1] INRIA Rennes-IRISA
[2] Université de Rennes 1-IRISA
[3] INRIA Saclay, France

Abstract. We define geometric self-structuring in a large-scale networked system as the ability of the participating nodes to collaboratively impose a geometric structure to the network. Self-structuring is hard to achieve when no global positioning information about the network is available. Yet this is an useful capability in networked autonomous systems such as sensor networks. In this paper, we present the design and the evaluation of a fully decentralized geometric self-structuring approach. This approach heavily relies on the ability of each node to estimate its position in the network. The contribution of the paper is twofold: (i) a simple and fully decentralized virtual coordinated system (VIN-COS) is proposed, relying only on local connectivity information and per-neighbor communication; (ii) a network geometric self-structuring approach (NetGeoS) is presented that enables a large set of nodes to configure themselves in arbitrary geometric structures. The evaluation shows that the approach is both efficient and accurate while achieving the geometric structuring.

1 Introduction

Context. *Self-structuring* refers to the ability of a networked system to let emerge a specific structure, from scratch, without requiring external information. Self-structuring is an important dimension of system autonomy (especially in terms of scalability issues [14]). In sensor networks for example, self-structuring represents an important requirement for common operations such as forwarding, load balancing, leader election, or energy consumption management (see again [14]). Examples include the partitioning of an area in several zones for monitoring purposes or the selection of sensors to ensure specific functions for energy saving.

Motivation. The complexity of a self-structuring mechanism strongly depends on the amount of knowledge that is initially provided to nodes in the network. If all nodes in the system have a complete knowledge of the system, structuring the network is trivial. Otherwise, if nodes are only aware of their own neighborhood, ensuring that a given structure emerges from individual decisions is challenging. Let the *external knowledge* be the information provided to a node by an external

V. Garg, R. Wattenhofer, and K. Kothapalli (Eds.): ICDCN 2009, LNCS 5408, pp. 25–36, 2009.

entity or device. This is to oppose to *intrinsic knowledge* that consists of the information that each entity gathers itself from its observation of the network. The more external knowledge is required, the less robust a system is (especially in environments where human intervention is difficult). Instead, approaches relying mostly on intrinsic knowledge definitively increases system autonomy at the price of a higher communication overhead. In short, the autonomy degree of a networked system is inversely proportional to the external knowledge required to structure the network. It is however, crucial to come up with a reasonable trade-off between autonomy and overhead.

This paper presents a robust structuring mechanism, leading to geometric organization that can be deployed from scratch in a networked system where the initial knowledge of each node is limited to its own identity and communication range. Nodes can then be assigned to different adaptive behaviors based on the established organization. In the context of this work, we focus on wireless sensor networks (WSNs). To the best of our knowledge, this is the first *geometric structuring autonomous system* deployed upon those conditions in the literature.

Network structuring becomes a very challenging goal, as soon as neither positioning referential, boundary delimitation, nor density distribution is provided. One solution for this is to allow the nodes to access a coordinate system from which they can obtain a coordinate assignment. Such a coordinate system represents the basic layer on top of which adaptive behaviors can be designed. This constitutes our second contribution.

Most of positioning approaches in the literature [1, 6, 8, 10, 12] rely on some specific assumptions and this shows striking evidence that even more autonomy is required. This has been coped by solutions that use *no position-aware referential points* and that result in *virtual coordinates* being assigned to nodes, instead of geographic coordinates [4,6,15]. Virtual coordinates better reflect the real network connectivity, and can consequently provide more robustness in the presence of obstacles. Despite having clearly defined outlines and presenting good approximation solutions, previous works on virtual coordinates are computationally- (and message) costly, or hardly practical in wireless sensor networks [4,6]. This situation is slowly changing though [16]. In addition, the solutions presented in [4,8,15], although not accounting for position-aware landmarks, require the nomination of well placed entities in the systems to work as anchors or bootstrap beacon nodes.

This paper proposes a versatile virtual coordinate system for WSNs. The main difference with related works is that the proposed approach does not rely on any anchors, position-aware landmarks, or signal measurement. Yet, nodes get assigned virtual coordinates in a fully decentralized way. Nodes derive local connectivity information, solely leveraging their per-neighbor communication.

Contribution. In summary, the contributions of the paper are the following ones.

- A simple and fully decentralized, *VIrtual Networked COordinate System* (VINCOS) that achieves a good coordinate assignment.
- A *Networked Geometric Structuring* approach (NetGeoS) for autonomous systems. Here, we show how NetGeoS builds upon VINCOS.

Outline. After introducing our system model in Section 2, we present the design rationale of our approach and give an overview of related works in Section 3. The virtual coordinate system (VINCOS) is described in Section 4. In Section 5, we show how VINCOS can be used to obtain specific geometric structuring. Performance results are presented in Section 6. We give an overview of related works and conclude this work in Section 7. More development can be found in [7].

2   System Model

Area monitoring is one of the most typical applications of WSNs. It consists in deploying a large number of sensors in a geographic area, for collecting data or monitoring events. It is not unusual that human intervention is hardly feasible in such settings. Sensors are then deployed in mass and must be able to form a network and to operate in a decentralized self-organized manner, maintaining connectivity and area monitoring for as long as possible. These are typical applications considered here.

Nodes. We consider a system composed of a (finite) set of N resource-limited wireless sensor devices scattered on a geographical area. Each node gets assigned a unique identifier i. This represents both the only difference between two nodes and the only information that nodes have about the configuration. Nodes are all "equal" with respect to their capabilities. No synchronization is required.

Communication. Each node i is able to directly communicate wirelessly with a subset of nodes that are reachable (we refer to this subset as the *neighbors* of the node i). No node is provided with geographical topology information (such as physical obstacles). We assume *bidirectional* communication and that the density of nodes is such that the resulting communication network is connected (*i.e.*, the network is not partitioned). The presented hereafter approaches relies solely on node connectivity.

Initial knowledge. Initially a node only knows its identity, the fact that no two nodes have the same identity, and a parameter d that will define the size (or dimension) of the virtual coordinate space. The design of the parameter d depends on the application requirements.

3   Design Rationale

This section discusses the fundamental principles that underlie each of our contributions.

3.1   VINCOS: Virtual Coordinate System

Position awareness is a key functionality to build and maintain autonomous networked systems. A coordinate system provides each node with a "position"

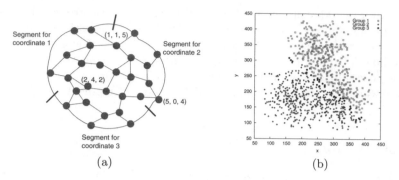

Fig. 1. (a) An example of virtual coordinates. (b) "Line partitioning" in a topology with three hot spots of different nodes densities.

that is both individual and globally consistent. As already observed, a node network awareness may come from two sources: an *intrinsic knowledge* resulting from the algorithm execution (*e.g.*, neighbors set, hop distance to a specific node, etc.), and *external knowledge* supplied by external devices (*e.g.*, satellite or radio signal device), or design hypothesis (such as "all sensors have a unique *id*", "the network is initially connected", etc.).

In VINCOS, each node is initially configured with the parameter d indicating the dimension of the coordinate system (number of coordinates). The virtual coordinates of a node i are consequently a tuple $(x_1, \ldots, x_d)$, where x_j is the projection of i on the jth axis of the d-dimensional virtual space.

The virtual d-dimensional space is defined as follows. The border of the geographical area covered by the nodes is partitioned into d "segments". These border segments can have the same size or different sizes (we assume in the paper that they have the same size). This depends only on the algorithm and may easily be changed. Let us consider any axis j, $1 \le j \le d$, of the coordinate system. The coordinate x_j is the length, in hops, of a shortest path from the node i to the border segment j (*i.e.*, to the closest node on that border segment). This is illustrated on Fig. 1(a) through a simple example. The coordinate system is 3-dimensional ($d = 3$). The virtual coordinates of three nodes are indicated. The coordinates $(2, 4, 2)$ mean that the corresponding node is at distance 2 of both borders 1 and 3, and at distance 4 of border 2.

The coordinate assignment of VINCOS depends on an accurate definition of the *border segments*, *i.e.*, the d "segments" dividing the border of the considered geographical area. To define the border segments, VINCOS relies on a *belt* construction mechanism. The resulting belt, defined as a set of *border-belt nodes* (nodes located on the perimeter of the area), is a connected structure that (*1*) enables communication among border-belt nodes along two different paths; (*2*) allows an order assignment to these nodes; (*3*) is one-hop wide; and (*4*) has proportional size wrt the network size[1]. This ensures that, given the broadcast

---

[1] A too small belt could generate inaccuracies in the coordinate system resulting in many non-neighbor nodes being assigned to the same coordinates.

communication pattern, any message forwarded along the belt (complete round) reaches every border-belt node.

Nevertheless, discovering a connected border at a low cost and in an accurate way is difficult. We quickly describe at the Section 4, how VINCOS computes such a belt, referred hereafter as *border-belt*.

3.2   NetGeoS: Geometric Structuring

In the literature, network coordinates are mainly used for routing. We argue that their interest goes far beyond. When appropriately manipulated, network coordinates represent a powerful tool for different kinds of network management. A main contribution of this paper lies in showing how to rely on such a coordinate system for a different purpose: geometric structuring.

NetGeoS defines organization laws that, once applied to the virtual coordinates of each node, let emerge a specific *geometric structuring* so that nodes get assigned different behaviors/functionalities depending on their position in the network. Geometric structuring can be (1) defined as a logical partitioning of the network and (2) used as a powerful tool for structuring wireless networks and assigning different functionalities to nodes for clustering, data aggregation, or energy consumption management. Although this can be easily done upon any polar coordinates, we show here how NetGeoS is deployed upon VINCOS.

As an example, consider sensors disseminated in a large geographical area and that are partitioned in three groups, the *North* group, the *South* group, and the *Equator* group. The Equator group is a simple "straight line" of nodes that separating the north and south groups. Let us consider the application scenario where the nodes in the North and South groups are in charge of collecting some information, subsequently sent (via a routing protocol) to the Equator group. Periodically, a plane flies over the Equator line and collects the relevant data stored in the Equator sensors [3]. To implement such an application, the sensor network should be partitioned in such three groups. It turns out that this can be easily achieved with a 2-dimensional virtual coordinate system. Let (x_1, x_2) be the VINCOS coordinates of node i. i belongs to the North group if $x_1 < x_2$, the South group if $x_1 > x_2$ and to the Equator group if $x_1 = x_2$ (see example in Fig. 1(b)).

4   VINCOS: From Anarchy to Virtual Coordinates

To build a meaningful coordinate system, the nodes need to acquire some consistent knowledge of the network. This approach provides nodes with a novel and fully decentralized way of acquiring that knowledge. The protocol is composed of four consecutive phases summarized in Table 1 and described in a nutshell in the following paragraph. A full description of the protocol is available in [7].

Bootstrap. The first phase consists in identifying a set of initiators (act as landmarks). In short, nodes chosen as initiators are more connected than any of

Table 1. Summary of the four phases of VINCOS

P.	Input	Output
1	*none*	*initiators*: nodes with more neighbors
2	*initiators*: flood their id	*all*: learn score (average distance to initiators) *perimeter bootstrap nodes*: nodes that are for sure on the border
3a.	*perimeter bootstrap nodes*: send probes *highest scoring nodes*: relay the probes	*segment definer node*: node that knows a connected border belt with the probes it received
3.b	*segment definer nodes*: split the belt	*border-belt nodes*: nodes that own the border-belt
4	*border-belt nodes*: flood their segment number	*all*: learn the smallest distance to each segment (*i.e.* coordinates)

their neighbors therefore representing a local density maximum. During the second phase, each initiator then floods the network. This allows each node to learn its *distance to each initiator*[2]. Nodes then compute a *score* that is the average of all distances to the initiators.

Border belt construction. This phase identifies a belt of nodes on the border. To this end, a set of nodes is in charge of sending *probes*. Probes are assumed to never travel backwards: let node i receive a probe from node j. i chooses the next probe destinator among i's neighbors that are not j's neighbors. In addition, among the eligible neighbors a node always chooses the node with the highest score. This ensures that the probe remains on the border. Eventually, the probe reaches the node that originated it. The probe path thus defines a suitable border belt: it is connected and thin (less than one hop wide). Note that at this point, more than one border could be detected. In this case, the following phases happen concurrently on each detected border. Nodes only adopt coordinates originated from the longer border.

Segment definition. The goal is here to devide the border in d segments. The belt allows border nodes to easily elect one of them as leader during Phase 3.a. The leader computes the total length of the border and sets the direction of the border. A node is able to uniquely decide to which of the segments it belongs based on its distance to the leader and the information about the direction (Phase 3.b).

Coordinate definition. Finally, each border node floods the rest of the system (Phase 4), allowing all nodes to get their distance to each border segment. This results in each node i being provided with a set of coordinates $(x_1, \ldots, x_d)$ in the d-dimensional space. Section 5 shows how these coordinates can be used to easily define geometric structuring.

5   From Virtual Coordinates to Geometric Structuring

Geometric structuring can be defined as a logical partitioning of the network into geographical zones for application-dependent purposes. The aim of NetGeoS is

---

[2] In the following, a distance always refers to the minimal distance between two nodes in terms of number of hops.

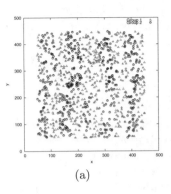
(a)

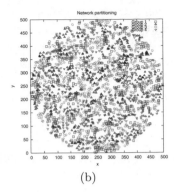
(b)

Fig. 2. Geometric partitioning examples

to provide in a fully decentralized way and based only on a local observation of the neighborhood, each node with a partition number. Partitions are then used to fulfill specific applications requirements or systems properties, for example. Formally, let $\mathcal{K}$ be the coordinate space (in our application, $\mathcal{K} \in \mathbb{N}^d$), and let p be the number of partitions. Let c_i and p_i be the coordinates and the partition number of node i, respectively. Then a geometric structuring function is a function f s.t. $f : \mathcal{K} \rightarrow \{0, \ldots, p\}$, where $f(c_i) \mapsto p_i$. Let us observe that such a definition allows any node to compute the partition number of any other node whose coordinates are known: *each node has a global foresight of the system layout.*

Let (x_1, x_2) be the VINCOS coordinates of node i. In Section 3.2, the following *line partitioning function* was used to produce the introductory example, where nodes were structured into *North, South,* and *Equator* groups ($f : \mathbb{N} * \mathbb{N} \rightarrow \{1, 2, 3\}$):

$$f(x_1, x_2) \mapsto \begin{cases} 1 \ when \ x_1 > x_2 \\ 2 \ when \ x_1 = x_2 \\ 3 \ when \ x_1 < x_2, \end{cases}$$

where node i belongs to the North group if $x_1 < x_2$, to the South group if $x_1 > x_2$ and to the Equator group if $x_1 = x_2$ (see Fig. 1(b)).

Another useful geographic partitioning is the *target-like partitioning*. This is a straightforward structuring to achieve using $d = 1$. In this structure, each node gets as a partition number, its minimum hop distance to the border ($f : \mathbb{N} \rightarrow \mathbb{N}$): $f(x_1) \rightarrow x_1$. This can be a useful structure, for example, for tracking applications where all the inner rings could be set in sleep mode, the only active partition being the border. Whenever a node from a partition p senses something, it wakes up the partition $p + 1$, so that the network is gradually woken up.

Using the line partitioning, one can also create parallel vertical lines at each j_v hop in the network. In this structure, each node i belongs to the vertical line resulted from ($f : \mathbb{N}^4 \rightarrow \{0, 1\}$): $f(x_1, x_2, x_3, x_4) \mapsto max(x_1, x_3) \mod j_v$ (see Fig. 2(a)). In this way, parallel vertical or horizontal lines can be used to select well distributed nodes in the network to be responsible for performing data aggregation. In addition, a lattice partitioning as shown in Fig. 2(b) can be used to distribute nodes between awake and sleep states for energy consumption management.

6   Performance Evaluation

This section describes the experiments we have conducted to assess both the performance and the accuracy of the proposed approach. The experiments have been done using a discrete event simulator implemented in Java. Note that, as we are mostly interested in the algorithmic evaluation, our simulator deliberately does not model all the details of a realistic MAC protocol. Instead, we considered a simplified MAC layer where neither messages losses, nor collisions and duplications are considered. We argue they will not affect the correctness of the proposed algorithms. This is mainly due to the fact that the well performance of the presented mechanisms are independent of the order of messages' arrival, even if it may cause a longer convergence time. A realistic MAC protocol would have the major effect of introducing arbitrary delays on messages due to messages re-transmission, which will be studied in a future work.

Experimental setup. We implemented the system model described in Section 2. Our simulations involve scenarios where the number of nodes varies from 250 to 2600. The nodes are distributed over a 2-dimensional plane, in an area of 500×500 square units. A node range is simulated as a circle area. Radio ranges from 30 to 50 distance units have been used in the simulations. Nodes broadcast Hello messages within their radio range, containing information required in each phase of VINCOS.

We conducted experiments under various node distributions in the network (*i.e.*, uniform, normal, multi-centered normal distribution) and various border shapes, like topologies with concave shapes (*e.g.* rectangle- and cross-shaped topologies) or that contains a large void in the center (*e.g.* donuts-shaped[3] topologies). Each point of an experimental curve results from 20 independent experiments.

Metrics. Fig. 3(a) presents the average results of 20 experiments as the network size increases from 250 to 2600 nodes, for a 40-unit radio range. Network size and radio range are the two main parameters of the simulations since they impact the average number of neighbors, the system size, and the density (which globally impact initiators detection). Another key parameter is the system shape: the regularity of the border is important to ensure a correct border detection.

Communication Costs. The $O()$ communication cost imposed by each phase during the execution of the VINCOS algorithm has been evaluated in [7] for a square grid shaped network of N nodes. With y and z being respectively the number of initiators and the perimeter bootstrap nodes, and d being the size of the coordinate system, the total cost of VINCOS is : $O((2+y+d)*N+4*z\sqrt{N})$.

---

[3] *I.e.*, circle-shaped topologies in presence of voids.

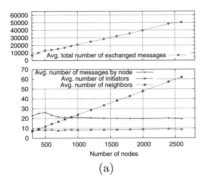 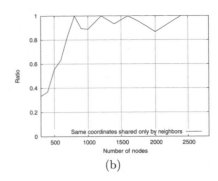

(a)   (b)

Fig. 3. (a) Cost analysis as a function of the network size, for $d = 4$. (b) Ratio of neighbors with the same coordinates.

Figure 3(a) confirms the theoretical results by showing that the message communication cost per node for the VINCOS construction is low and independent of the size of the network. It can be observed that for increasing network size and neighbors density, the number of initiators is constant and remains low. In addition, even if the total number of messages exchanged in the network grows nearly linearly with the number of nodes, the average number of messages per node is kept low and presents a slight decrease with the increase of the network size. This can be explained by the fact that inner nodes have a constant number of messages to exchange and that only border-belt nodes exchange additional messages[4]. The proportion of border-belt nodes, however, decreases with the size of the system, which by consequence, decreases the average cost.

Time of convergence. Similarly to communication cost, the theoretical time cost was discussed through the VINCOS extended description available in [7]. The total expected convergence time is $2 + (2\sqrt{2} + 4)\sqrt{N}$ interactions.

Accuracy. Even though we do not focus on the routing capabilities over VINCOS, it is well known in the literature [15] that accurate coordinate systems lead to correct greedy routing. This is highly dependent on the number of nodes which get identical coordinates as well as their respective physical positions. In order to assess the accuracy of VINCOS, and consequently its routing capabilities, we measured the number of nodes in the system sharing the same coordinates. Among those, we considered the following metric at the granularity of an experiment: *"any two nodes having the same coordinate are neighbors"*. Systems that meet this metric are perfectly suitable for greedy routing: a message reaching the destination's coordinates also reaches the final destination. Fig. 3(b) shows the ratio of experiments that respect the considered metric, for different number of nodes and 50-unit radio range. The figure shows that for some node densities, the considered metric is nearly always respected. For example, consider the point of the curve $x = 1500$ nodes, it

---

[4] This does not happen in [6], since perimeter nodes flood all the network to discover each other.

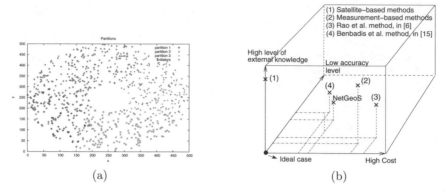

Fig. 4. (a) VINCOS's segment definition for a topology with a large void in the center. (b) VINCOS w.r.t. cost, accuracy, and external knowledge.

means that in 96% of the experiments, all nodes sharing the same coordinates are neighbors. For networks with a small number of nodes (less then 800 in the figure), the low ratio is explained by the low density in the system.

Different shapes and node distribution. As previously discussed, the shape of the system is a parameter that can impact the coordinate system correctness. In this section, we explore this issue by showing the resulting segment definition of VINCOS under two specific topologies. Fig. 4(a) depicts the result for a donut-shaped topology with $d = 4$ in a 2000-node network. We observe that even in the presence of voids (*i.e.*, regions inside the network that do not contain any nodes), VINCOS performs well and correctly defines the required $d = 4$ partitions. The presence of the void leads to the detection of multiple border-belts: the biggest one is used for the virtual coordinate definition.

Fig. 2(a) shows a geometric structuring for a rectangle-shaped topology of 2000 nodes and 40-unit radio range. The obtained geometric structuring shows that VINCOS performs well in a topology with sharp angles too (this will be addressed in future). Similarly, Fig. 1(b) shows the partitioning of a 900-node network and 30-unit radio range, where nodes were scattered following a normal distribution. The topology presents three hot spots of different densities. By applying a "line" predicate, the figure shows the correct partitioning of the network in *North*, *South*, and *Equator* groups.

7   Related Work on Positioning Systems and Conclusion

Fig. 4(b) compares the features of related works in the literature compared to the VINCOS coordinate assignment approach. It shows their differences with respect to cost (message complexity), coordinate assignment accuracy (in terms of number of nodes sharing the same coordinate), and initial knowledge. The closest to the origin, the better is the compromise between these three criteria.

The importance of a coordinate system for autonomous systems is demonstrated by the vast literature on the topic [1,2,4,5,6,8,10,11,12,13,15]. Regarding absolute positioning systems, the literature is dominated by the satellite-based methods, like GPS and Galileo. Equipping all entities with a satellite receiver constitutes the best way to provide them with a very high level of external knowledge, resulting in a very accurate coordinate assignment (point (1) in Fig 4(b)). Unfortunately, this approach suffers from important drawbacks when applied to sensor networks: it is expensive, energy-inefficient, and cannot work when the sensors are deployed in a zone that is out of satellites receiver scopes.

This problem can be solved by equipping only a few entities (i.e., position-aware landmarks) with a satellite receiver, and let the other entities infer their position from connectivity information, or signal strength measurements [1,4,9, 10,11,12,13]. While allowing systems to be designed with fewer external knowledge (*i.e.*, only few entities know their position), such hybrid approaches are costly and are not accurate from a coordinate assignment point of view[5] (point (2) in Fig. 4(b)). Differently, solutions that are based only on connectivity [1,9,10] are algorithmically simpler. Nevertheless, they have a high communication cost, being their coordinate assignment accuracy strongly dependent of the landmarks density and good positioning [8, 15] (point (4) in Fig. 4(b)). A more attractive approach is then, when no position-aware referential is used. Recent researches propose solutions that result in *virtual coordinates* being assigned to nodes, instead of geographic ones [4, 6] (point (3) in Fig. 4(b)).

The coordinate assignment procedure of VINCOS is similar to the approaches described in [6, 8] with respect to initial knowledge assumptions. In these approaches, perimeter nodes or landmarks are considered to be known, situated on the border of the network topology, or are determined based on the distance to a well centered node. In particular, compared to [6], VINCOS exploits border knowledge in a much different way. Moreover, our segment definition's result gives the perfect landmarks positioning for the coordinated assignment mechanism described in [8]. In addition, the upper layer *NetGeoS* relies also on simple design principles. Its versatility dimension makes it relevant for defining a geometric partitioning on top of which upper layer scalable services can be implemented. Simulation results attest of the accuracy of both VINCOS and NetGeoS. Future work includes considering more realistic MAC layer models and non-convex irregular-shaped topologies.

References

1. Bischoff, R., Wattenhoffer, R.: Analyzing Connectivity-Based, Multi-hop Positioning System. In: Proc. of IEEE Percom, pp. 165–176 (March 2004)
2. He, T., Huang, C., Blum, B., Stankovic, J., Abdelzaher, T.: Range-free Localization Schemes in Large Scale Sensor Networks. ACM Mobicom, 81–95 (2003)
3. Ben Hamida, E., Chelius, G.: Analytical Evaluation of Virtual Infrastructures for Data Dissemination in Wireless Sensor Networks with Mobile Sink. In: SANET 2007 (September 2007)

---

[5] For example, the signal measurement-based solutions [12] are less efficient in indoor or underground environments besides being algorithmically costless.

4. Moscibroda, T., O'Dell, R., Wattenhoffer, M.R.: Virtual Coordinates for Ad Hoc and Sensor Networks. In: ACM Workshop DIAL-POMC, pp. 8–16 (2004)
5. Nagpal, R., Shrobe, H., Bachrach, J.: Organizing a global coordinate system from local information on an ad hoc sensor network. In: Zhao, F., Guibas, L.J. (eds.) IPSN 2003. LNCS, vol. 2634, pp. 333–348. Springer, Heidelberg (2003)
6. Rao, A., Ratnasamy, S., Papadimitriou, C., Shenker, S., Stoica, I.: Geographic Routing without Location Information. In: Mobicom, pp. 96–108. ACM Press, New York (2003)
7. Kermarrec, A.-M., Mostéfaoui, A., Raynal, M., Trédan, G., Viana, A.C.: Large-scale networked systems: from anarchy to geometric self-structuring. Tech Report #1876, 19 pages, IRISA, Université de Rennes (December 2007)
8. Benbadis, F., Obraczka, K., Cortès, J., Brandwajn, A.: Exploring landmark placement strategies for self-organization in wireless sensor networks. Eurasip Journal on Advances in Signal Processing (to appear, 2008)
9. Benbadis, F., Friedman, T., Amorim, M.D., Fdida, S.: GPS-free-free positioning system for sensor networks. In: Proc. of WOCN, pp. 541–545 (April 2005)
10. Caruso, A., Chessa, S., De, S., Urpi, A.: GPS free coordinate assignment and routing in wireless sensor netwoks. Infocom, 150–160 (2005)
11. Shang, Y., Ruml, W., Zhang, Y., Fromherz, M.: Localization from mere connectivity. In: Proc. of ACM Mobihoc, pp. 201–212 (June 2003)
12. Gustafsson, F., Gunnarsson, F.: Positioning using time-difference of arrival measurements. In: Proc. of ICASSP, vol. 6, pp. VI-553–556 (April 2003)
13. Doherty, L., Pister, K.S.J., El, G.L.: Convex position estimation in wireless sensor networks. In: Proc. of IEEE Infocom, pp. 1655–1663 (April 2001)
14. Dohler, M., Watteyne, T., Barthel, D., Valois, F., Lu, J.-L.: Kumar's, Zipf's and Other Laws: How to Structure an Optimum Large-Scale Wireless (Sensor) Network? In: 13th European Wireless Conference (April 2007)
15. Benbadis, F., Puig, J.-J., Amorim, M.D., Chaudet, C., Friedman, T., Simplot-Ryl, D.: JUMP: Enhancing hop-count positioning in sensor network using multiple coordinates. Ad Hoc and Sensor Wireless Networks Journal (to appear, 2008)
16. Pemmaraju, S.V., Pirwani, I.A.: Good quality virtual realization of unit ball graphs. In: Arge, L., Hoffmann, M., Welzl, E. (eds.) ESA 2007. LNCS, vol. 4698, pp. 311–322. Springer, Heidelberg (2007)

Cheapest Paths in Multi-interface Networks*

Ferruccio Barsi, Alfredo Navarra, and Cristina M. Pinotti

Department of Computer Science and Mathematics, University of Perugia,
Via Vanvitelli 1, 06123 Perugia, Italy
{barsi,pinotti}@unipg.it, navarra@dipmat.unipg.it

Abstract. Multi-interface networks are characterized by the property
that each node in the network might choose among several communication interfaces in order to establish desired connections. A connection
between two neighboring nodes is established if they both activate a
common interface. Each interface is associated with an activation cost.
In this context we investigate on the so called *Cheapest Path* problem,
i.e., given a node s of the network, for each other node j, we look for
the cheapest set of interfaces that must be activated among the nodes
in order to establish a path between s and j. Polynomial algorithms are
provided.

1 Introduction

Nowadays wireless devices hold multiple radio interfaces. This allows to switch
from one communication network to another. The selection of the "best" radio
interface for a specific connection might depend on various factors. Namely, availability of specific interfaces in the devices, the required communication bandwidth, the cost (in terms of energy consumption) of maintaining an active interface
and so forth. Challenging optimization problems arise in this context.

In [2,4,3] the *Coverage* problem is investigated under several assumptions. The
requirement was to activate all the connections expressed by the input graph
G while minimizing the overall cost. In [5], connectivity issues are addressed.
This paper is then a natural continuation in investigating the context of multi-
interface networks. We study the *Cheapest Path* problem which corresponds to
the well-known shortest path tree determination for standard graphs. Given a
graph $G = (V, E)$ and a source node $s \in V$, we are interested in determining
all the paths of minimum costs from s to any other node. The cost of a path is
given by the cost of the cheapest set of interfaces necessary to cover the edges of
the path. We consider the most general unbounded case, i.e., when the number
k of available interfaces among the whole network is not known a priori but
depends on the input instance. We provide a general algorithm which works in
$O(k|V||E|)$ time. When $k \in O(E)$, a faster algorithm for CP makes use of the
standard Dijkstra's algorithm and requires $O(k^2|V|+k|E|+k|V|\log(k|V|))$ time.
For the unit cost interface case, i.e. when every interface is associated with the
same cost, an algorithm which works in $O(k|E|)$ is given [1].

* The research was partially funded by the European project COST Action 293,
"Graphs and Algorithms in Communication Networks" (GRAAL).

V. Garg, R. Wattenhofer, and K. Kothapalli (Eds.): ICDCN 2009, LNCS 5408, pp. 37–42, 2009.
© Springer-Verlag Berlin Heidelberg 2009

2   Definitions and Notation

Unless otherwise stated, the network graph $G = (V, E)$ with $|V| = n$ and $|E| = m$ is always assumed to be simple undirected and connected. The set of neighbors of a node $v \in V$ is denoted by $N(v)$, the set of all the available interfaces in v by $I(v)$. Let k be the cardinality of all the available and distinct interfaces in the network, that is, $k = \left| \bigcup_{v \in V} I(v) \right|$. For each node $v \in V$, an appropriate interface assignment function W guarantees that each network connection (i.e., each edge of G) is *covered* by at least one interface.

Definition 1. *A function* $W: V \to 2^{\{1,\dots,k\}}$, *with* $k = \left| \bigcup_{v \in V} I(v) \right|$, *is said to* cover *graph* $G = (V, E)$ *if for each* $(u, v) \in E$ *the set* $W(u) \cap W(v) \neq \emptyset$.

Moreover, for each node $v \in V$, let $W_A(v)$ be the set of switched on (activated) interfaces. Clearly, $W_A(v) \subseteq W(v) \subseteq I(v)$.

The cost of activating an interface for a node is assumed to be identical for all nodes and given by cost function $c: \{1, \dots, k\} \to \mathbb{R}_+$. The cost of interface i is denoted as c_i. Moreover, in the *unit cost interface* case, all the interfaces have the same cost $c > 0$.

A path P in G from a given source node s to a target node v is denoted by a sequence of couples: for each node $v_j \in P$, besides node v_j itself, the interface i_j used to reach v_j is given. Namely, $i_j \in W_A(v_j)$. For example, the sequence $P = \langle (s \equiv v_0, 0), (v_1, i_1), \dots, (v \equiv v_t, i_t) \rangle$, denotes a path P from s to v that moves on the nodes $s, v_1, \dots, v_{t-1}, v$ and that reaches node v_j via interface i_j, for $1 \leq j \leq t$. Interface 0 is used to denote "no interface" because the source is not reached by any other node in P. In general, the cost for activating the path P is $d_P(v) = \sum_{j=1}^{t} cost\left((v_{j-1}, i_{j-1}), (v_j, i_j)\right)$ where

$$cost\left((v_{j-1}, i_{j-1}), (v_j, i_j)\right) = \begin{cases} 2c_{i_j} & \text{if} \quad i_{j-1} \neq i_j \\ c_{i_j} & \text{otherwise} \end{cases}$$

Clearly, $c((s, 0), (v_1, i_1)) = 2c_{i_1}$.

Let $\delta(v)$ be the minimum cost to activate a path from the source node s to node v, that is, $\delta(v) = \min\{d_P(v) : P$ is any path from s to $v\}$. In addition, let a *cheapest path* CP_v from the source s to v be any path P from s to v such that $d_P(v) = \delta(v)$. An i-path P from s to v is a path from s to v that reaches v via interface i. Let $d_P(v, i)$ denote the cost of the i-path P, whereas $\delta(v, i)$ denotes the minimum cost among all the i-paths from s to v. Besides, let a *cheapest i-path* $CP_{v,i}$ from the source node s to node v be any i-path P such that $d_P(v, i) = \delta(v, i)$. Clearly, $\delta(v) = \min\{\delta(v, i) : i \in W(v)\}$.

3   Cheapest Paths

In this section we study the usually called Shortest Path problem but in the context of multi-interface networks. The *Cheapest Path* (*CP* for short) problem can be formulated as follows.

Input:	A graph $G = (V, E)$, an allocation of available interfaces $W: V \to 2^{\{1,\dots,k\}}$ covering graph G, an interface cost function $c: \{1, \dots, k\} \to \mathbb{R}_+$ and a source node $s \in V$.
Solution:	For each node $v \in V \setminus \{s\}$, a path P from s to v must be specified by a sequence of couples of the form (v_j, i_j), with $v_0 = s$, $i_0 = 0$, $v_t = v$ and $v_j \in V$, $i_j \in W(v_j)$ for $1 \le j \le t$ with the meaning that node v_j is reached by means of interface i_j.
Goal:	For each node $v \in V$, find $\delta(v)$ along with a cheapest path CP_v.

Recalling that a *simple* path is a path not passing through the same node more than once, as the activation costs associated to the interfaces are non negative, it holds (see [1] for proofs):

Lemma 1. *Given a graph G, the cheapest path between any two nodes of G can be found among the simple paths.*

Corollary 1. *Given a graph G, the cheapest path between any two nodes of G is composed of at most $n - 1$ hops, where $n = |V|$.*

Proposition 1. *A subpath of a cheapest path is not necessarily a cheapest path itself.*

While the sub-optimality property does not hold in general, it holds when we consider a subpath of a cheapest path characterized not only by its final node, but also by the interface used in its last hop.

Lemma 2. *Given a graph $G = (V, E)$ and a source node $s \in V$, let CP_v be a cheapest path from s to v that passes through node u and reaches u via interface i. Then, the i-subpath of CP_v from s to u is a cheapest i-path.*

As a consequence, the cost of a cheapest path from s to v can be easily determined when the endpoints of the final edge of such a path and the interface used to reach v are given. In fact:

Lemma 3. *Given a graph $G = (V, E)$ and a source node $s \in V$, the cost $\delta(v, i)$ of the cheapest i-path $CP_{v,i}$ from s to v which has node u as the parent of v satisfies: $\delta(v, i) = \min\{\delta(u, i) + c_i, \delta(u) + 2c_i\}$.*

The CP problem, for a given graph $G = (V, E)$ and a given source $s \in V$, is solved by Procedure `Parents_Setup`. In order to make use of Procedure `Parents_Setup`, we initialize variables $d(v)$, $d(v, i)$ to $+\infty$ for each $v \in V$ and $i \in I(v)$ (see Procedure `Initialize` in [1]). Such variables estimate $\delta(v)$ and $\delta(v, i)$, respectively. At any step, the Procedure `Parents_Setup` computes, for the cheapest i-path from s to v visited so far, its cost $d(v, i)$ and the parent node $\pi(v, i)$ of v on such a path. The values $d(v, i)$ and $d(v)$ are updated according to Lemma 3. At the end of the procedure, since all the possible simple paths in G have been visited, it yields $d(v, i) = \delta(v, i)$ and $d(v) = \delta(v)$, for each node $v \in V$, $v \ne s$ and for each interface $i \in W(v)$.

```
Procedure Parents_Setup(graph: G; set of nodes: U; int: count)
    TMP := ∅;
    for each u ∈ U
        TMP := TMP ⋃ N(u);
        for each v ∈ N(u)
            for each i ∈ W(u) ⋂ W(v)
                if (d(v,i) > d(u,i) + cᵢ)
                    d(v,i) := d(u,i) + cᵢ;
                    π(v,i) := u;
                if (d(v,i) > d(u) + 2cᵢ)
                    d(v,i) := d(u) + 2cᵢ;
                    π(v,i) := u;
                if (d(v) > d(v,i))
                    d(v) := d(v,i);
    if − − count > 0
        Parents_Setup(G,TMP,count);
```

As regard to the time complexity of Procedure `Parents_Setup`, it is worth noting that the double *for* leads to $m = O(|E|)$ executions of the third *for*. In fact, such double *for* explores at most all the possible connections among nodes when $U \equiv V$. Since Procedure `Parents_Setup` is called $n - 1$ times, and the third *for* iterates for at most k rounds, the time complexity of the algorithm is $O(k|V||E|)$.

Clearly, as `Parents_Setup` is called $n - 1$ times, by Lemma 1, all the simple paths have been generated and for each $v \in V$ and $1 \le i \le k$, $d(v,i) = \delta(v,i)$ and $d(v) = \delta(v)$.

Once all the parents have been sorted out, for each node v, we can make use of Procedure `Cheapest_Path` with input parameters $(G,s,v,0)$ in order to obtain the cheapest path CP_v as the sequence of couples (node, interface). Such a procedure takes $O(kn)$ time.

```
Procedure Cheapest_Path(graph: G; node: s, t; interface: j)
    if (s ≠ t)
        i := 0;
        while (d(t) ≠ d(t,i))    i + +;
        if (j! = 0 and d(t,j) + cⱼ < d(t,i) + 2cⱼ)    i := j;
        Cheapest_Path(G,s,π(t,i),i);
        return (t,i);
    else
        return (s,0);
```

Another way of solving CP on a graph $G = (V, E)$ makes use of the standard Dijkstra's algorithm for the determination of a shortest path tree spanning the directed weighted graph $\vec{G} = (V', E')$ obtained from G as follows. Each node $x \in V$ is replaced by $|I(x)|$ nodes connected by the directed edges (x_i, x_j), $i, j \in I(x)$ of costs c_j, respectively. Moreover, each edge $\{x, y\} \in E$ is replaced by $|I(x) \bigcap I(y)|$ edges, of costs c_i, $i \in I(x) \bigcap I(y)$, respectively. A further node s' representing the source of the shortest path tree is added, and it is connected by the directed edges (s', s_i), $i \in I(s)$ to the nodes which replace the original source node s. The costs of each edge (s', s_i) is equal to the c_i. It can be shown that the Dijkstra's algorithm applied on $\vec{G}$ also solves CP with time complexity $O(|E'| + |V'| \log |V'|) = O(k^2|V| + k|E| + k|V| \log(k|V|))$ which is better than or equal to $O(k|V||E|)$ for $k \in O(|E|)$.

4   Unit Cost Interface Case

In this section, the CP problem for multi-interface networks with unit cost interfaces is studied. In this case, each interface has the same cost c, and without loss of generality $c = 1$. A path edge costs then 1 or 2 depending on whether it uses or not the same interface as the previous edge on the path. Hence, according to Corollary 1, any cheapest path from s to v satisfies $\delta(v) \leq 2(|V| - 1)$. Moreover, due to the unit cost interfaces restrictions, one has:

Lemma 4. *Given a graph G and a pair of nodes s and v, in the unit cost interface case, there is at least a cheapest path CP_v from s to v whose subpaths are, at their turn, cheapest paths as well.*

Let $W_\alpha(v)$ be the set of all the interfaces that allow to reach a node v from the source s with optimal cost $\delta(v)$. Note that $W_A(v) \subseteq W_\alpha(v) \subseteq W(v) \subseteq I(v)$. Besides, to build a cheapest path CP_v, for each node v and each interface $i \in W_\alpha(v)$, a parent node $\pi(v, i)$ of v on a cheapest path that reaches v via interface i has to be maintained. The cheapest path from s to v, along with its cost $\delta(v)$, can be easily determined when the parent node u of v and the interfaces used to reach u are known. In fact:

Lemma 5. *Given a graph $G = (V, E)$ and a source node $s \in V$, the cost $\delta(v)$ of the cheapest path CP_v from s to v which has node u as the parent of v is:*

$$\delta(v) = \begin{cases} \delta(u) + 1 & \text{if } W_\alpha(u) \cap W(v) \neq \emptyset \\ \delta(u) + 2 & \text{otherwise} \end{cases}$$

Moreover, the set of interfaces that allow to reach v from u with cost $\delta(v)$ is:

$$W_\alpha(u, v) = \begin{cases} W_\alpha(u) \cap W(v) & \text{if } W_\alpha(u) \cap W(v) \neq \emptyset \\ W(u) \cap W(v) & \text{otherwise} \end{cases}$$

Procedure Unit_Cost_Setup greedily builds a set S of nodes for which the cost of the cheapest path has been found. For each node $u \in S$, the procedure maintains the cost $\delta(u)$ of CP_u, the set of all the interfaces $W_\alpha(u)$ that allow to reach u with cost $\delta(u)$ and, for each $i \in W_\alpha(u)$ a parent node $\pi(u, i)$ of u on some CP_u that reaches u via interface i.

   To start, Procedure Unit_Cost_Initialize (see [1]) sets $S = \{s\}$, $\delta(s) = 0$, $W_\alpha(s) = \emptyset$ and $\pi(s, 0) = -1$ (conventionally, -1 means that no node is parent of s). Moreover, for each vertex $u \in V \setminus S$, the procedure sets the estimated cost $d(v)$ for CP_v to $2|V|$, $W_\alpha(v) = \emptyset$ and $\pi(v, 0) = -1$.

   Procedure Unit_Cost_Setup examines the nodes in the neighborhood of the last node inserted into S. For each node $v \in N(u)$ and $v \in V \setminus S$, according to Lemma 5, the procedure computes the cost of the path obtained by extending the cheapest path CP_u up to v and also finds the interfaces to traverse (u, v). If the new path has cost smaller than or equal to the current estimated cost to reach v, all the information, $d(v)$, $\delta(v)$, $W_\alpha(v)$, and $\pi(v, i)$ for each $i \in W_\alpha(u, v)$, are updated accordingly. Procedure Unit_Cost_Setup is called $|V| - 1$ times until $V \setminus S$ becomes $\emptyset$. Its time complexity is $O(km)$, see [1] for the detailed proof.

```
Procedure Unit_Cost_Setup(graph: G; set: S, node: u, int: count)
    for each v ∈ N(u) and v ∉ S
        if (W_α(u) ∩ W(v) ≠ ∅)
            cost := 1;
            W_α(u, v) := W_α(u) ∩ W(v);
        else
            cost := 2;
            W_α(u, v) := W(u) ∩ W(v);
        if (d(u) + cost < d(v))
            d(v) := d(u) + cost;
            for i ∈ W_α(v)
                π(v, i) := -1;
            W_α(v) := W_α(u, v);
            for i ∈ W_α(u, v)
                π(v, i) := u;
        if (d(u) + cost = d(v))
            W_α(v) := W_α(v) ⋃ W_α(u, v);
            for i ∈ W_α(u, v)
                π(v, i) := u;
    u := v such that v ∈ V\S and d(u) = min d(v);
    δ(u) := d(u); S := S ⋃ {u};
    if (- - count > 0)
        Unit_Cost_Setup(G, S, u, count);
```

Finally, for each node v, we can make use of Procedure `Unit_Cost_Cheapest_Path` (similar to Procedure `Cheapest_Path`, see [1]) with input parameters $(G,s,v,0)$ in order to obtain the cheapest path CP_v as the sequence of couples (node, interface). Such a procedure takes $O(n)$ time.

5 Conclusion

We have considered a basic problem in the context of multi-interface networks. Namely, the well-known shortest path tree determination has become the *Cheapest Path* problem. We have shown how the complexity of the original problem has increased, and we have provided suitable algorithms. Many other interesting problems remain unexplored in the context of multi-interface networks.

References

1. Barsi, F., Navarra, A., Pinotti, C.M.: Cheapest paths in multi-interface networks. Technical Report 2008/08, Department of Mathematics and Computer Science, University of Perugia (June 2008),
   http://www1.isti.cnr.it/~pinotti/PUBBLICAZIONI/TRCP.pdf
2. Klasing, R., Kosowski, A., Navarra, A.: Cost minimisation in wireless networks with bounded and unbounded number of interfaces. Networks (to appear)
3. Klasing, R., Kosowski, A., Navarra, A.: Cost minimisation in multi-interface networks. In: Chahed, T., Tuffin, B. (eds.) NET-COOP 2007. LNCS, vol. 4465, pp. 276–285. Springer, Heidelberg (2007)
4. Kosowski, A., Navarra, A.: Cost minimisation in unbounded multi-interface networks. In: Wyrzykowski, R., Dongarra, J., Karczewski, K., Wasniewski, J. (eds.) PPAM 2007. LNCS, vol. 4967, pp. 1039–1047. Springer, Heidelberg (2008)
5. Kosowski, A., Navarra, A., Pinotti, C.M.: Connectivity in Multi-Interface Networks. In: Proceedings of the 4th Symposium on Trustworthy Global Computing (TGC). LNCS. Springer, Heidelberg (to appear, 2008)

Concept-Based Routing in Ad-Hoc Networks[*]

Radosław Olgierd Schoeneich, Jarosław Domaszewicz, and Michał Koziuk

Institute of Telecommunications, Warsaw University of Technology
Warsaw, Poland
{rschoeneich,domaszew,mkoziuk}@tele.pw.edu.pl

Abstract. In concept-addressable messaging, network nodes are both described and addressed by concepts derived from an ontology domain model. The paper presents a routing protocol for the concept-addressable messaging in mobile ad-hoc networks. The domain model is a taxonomy, and the address is any concept from the taxonomy. The protocol uses restricted flooding (narrowcasting) to deliver concept-addressed messages. To that end, nodes' conceptual descriptions are proactively spread with Hello messages. If there is not enough room in the Hello message, selected descriptions are moved to a higher abstraction level and merged. The protocol is a single layer solution (not an overlay). Preliminary ns2-based performance results are provided.

Keywords: Ad-hoc networks, concept-based addressing, taxonomy, narrowcast.

1 Introduction

In [1], [2] we proposed a method for addressing network nodes, called Concept-Based Addressing. Messaging with concept-based addressing is based on a predefined domain model. In general, the domain model is an ontology. In this paper we assume that the domain model is a collection of concepts (classes) organized in a taxonomy tree, as in Fig.1.

A node is assumed to belong to (or represent) a single entity from the domain, e.g., a person, object, or place. For example, the node may be carried by a fireman or be attached to a piece of equipment. Owing to this association, the node is described as being an instance of a class from the bottom of the taxonomy tree. The node's class membership may either be permanent (then it is the node's profile), or it may change at runtime (then it is the node's context). In this paper we focus on the case where the class membership does not change at runtime.

In this paper, a concept-based address is a single class from the domain model, and the addressees are all the instances of the class. Contrary to the node's profile, a concept-based address need not be a leaf class. When delivering concept-addressed messages, the sub-class/super-class relationship is taken into account. For example, a message sent to `EmergencyWorker` should be delivered to both `Fireman` and `Paramedic`.

---

[*] This work was supported by the 6FP MIDAS IST Project, contract no. 027055.

V. Garg, R. Wattenhofer, and K. Kothapalli (Eds.): ICDCN 2009, LNCS 5408, pp. 43–48, 2009.
© Springer-Verlag Berlin Heidelberg 2009

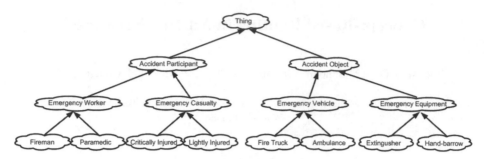

Fig. 1. A taxonomy-based domain model for emergency situations

In this paper we present a routing protocol that supports concept-based addressing. The main idea behind the protocol, hereafter referred to as Concept-Based Routing (CBR), is to minimize the number of transmissions by means of narrowcast forwarding (i.e., using only some neighbors as forwarders). The CBR protocol does not use any traditional node addresses (e.g., IP or MAC).

The CBR protocol consists of concept maintenance and concept-based message forwarding. The task of the concept maintenance is to proactively spread nodes' profiles around the network and to form concept-based routing tables. This is done by means of periodically broadcasted Hello messages. If there is too much profile information to be put in a Hello message, taxonomy-based concept compression takes place. A concept routing table contains, for each concept, a list of neighbors to which a message addressed with that concept should be forwarded. The concept routing table is used in the concept-based message forwarding.

This paper is organized as follows. Related work is given in Section 2. In Sections 3 and 4, concept maintenance and concept-based message forwarding are presented. Simulation results are provided in Section 5. The paper is concluded in Section 6.

2   Related Work

There is conceptual closeness between concept-based addressing and publish- subscribe systems. The nodes' profile or context could be looked at as "subscriptions," while concept-addressed messages as "events." Taking into account our taxonomy-based domain model, topic-based publish-subscribe systems (e.g., [3]), and especially hierarchical ones [4], are most relevant. Content-based networking (e.g., [5]) is another important family of publish-subscribe. Messaging with concept-based addressing could be implemented by means of a publish-subscribe system and vice-versa. The important difference is that most publish-subscribe systems are built as an overlay on top of the IP routing layer. We use one integrated layer, without possibly redundant mechanisms necessary to maintain two separate layers.

We identified several solutions similar to ours, both in terms of the messaging service functionality (addressing nodes by their profiles or context) and in terms of the single layer approach. One of them is FlavourCast [6], a context-based messaging system, where context is propagated through the network in order to construct a "topographical map," with minima representing clusters of nodes with similar profiles.

The map is then used by a message delivery algorithm. The key difference in our work is the domain model: we use a taxonomy, while in [6] a "flat" set of attributes is used.

The content-based query support system presented in [7] is the closest one to our work that we could identify. There, a taxonomy-based domain model is used, and narrowcasting is used for message forwarding. However, while in [7] the profile is spread with obligatory "fading" (going to a more general concept) for each concept at each hop, in our system two concepts are "compressed" into a more general one only if there is no room in a Hello message. This results in slower loss of information.

3   Concept Maintenance: Spreading and Compression

In order to enable narrowcast forwarding of concept-addressed messages, CBR uses periodic Hello messages to distribute profile information among nodes. Ideally, each Hello message contains all profile information available to the sending node, both about the sending node itself and about other nodes. The Hello message consists of triples. Each triple contains: (a) a concept describing the profile of a node (Concept), (b) a hop-count distance to the node (Hop Count), and (c) the identifier of that node (ID Source of concept). The Hello message has to fit in the single physical frame. The period for the Hello messages is fixed.

In a large network it may happen that not all profile information available to a node can fit in a single Hello message. Whenever a new triple has to be inserted into a full Hello message buffer, a pair of triples already in the buffer is replaced by a single triple that tries to capture the information present in the two triples being replaced. The replacement makes room for the new triple. We call this concept compression.

The concept compression algorithm picks for replacement those two concepts that have the highest number of common super-classes. For example, consider the full Hello message buffer at the top of Fig. 2 (assuming that up to three triples can fit in the Hello message). When yet another triple is to be inserted, concept compression has to take place. The possible pairs of concepts, to be considered for replacement, are (Fireman, Paramedic), (Fireman, Lightly Injured), and (Paramedic, Lightly Injured). Out of the three, (Fireman, Paramedic) has the highest number of common super-classes (see the domain model shown in Fig. 1), and the corresponding two triples are replaced with a single one.

The concept in the replacement triple is the most specific super-class of the both concepts being replaced. In our example, the most specific super-class of (Fireman, Paramedic) is Emergency Worker. The ID Source of concept and the hop count in the replacement triple come from that of the two triples being replaced which has the least hop count.

As a result of the concept compression, the Hello message buffer looks as at the bottom of Fig. 2. After compression, a single triple no longer represents a single node; instead, it represents a number of nodes – instances of the triple's concept. The ID Source of concept and the hop count are those of the closest among the instances.

The described compression method is lossy in that the replacing concept is less specific than the two concepts being replaced. Also, the ID Source of concept and the hop count are preserved only for the closest node. The benefit of compression is that the overhead due to the concept spreading depends on the (fixed) period of sending the Hello messages and not on the amount of profile information present in the network. Moreover, even though some profile information is lost, the resulting replacement triple still carries information useful for routing (as explained below).

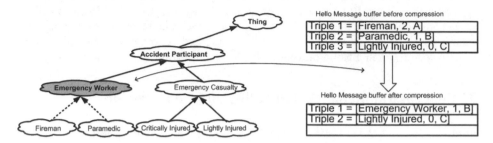

Fig. 2. Hello message buffer before and after compression

The heuristic to maximize the number of common super-classes serves the purpose of keeping the profile information as specific as possible. The maximization of the number of super-classes allows triples to be the subject of a number of compression steps, without concepts "degenerating" into Thing, which does not carry any information useful for routing.

All Hello message triples, except one, are generated from entries of a concept routing table. One triple (called the local triple) contains the node's own profile description. The order in which triples are inserted into the buffer is important, as triples inserted earlier can be subject to compression more times than those inserted later. In our solution, the local triple is always inserted last. This order ensures that the description of the node sending the Hello message is never compressed.

4   Concept-Based Message Forwarding

Concept-based message forwarding is used to deliver concept-addressed messages to their addressees. At each hop, the protocol uses the concept routing table to select some neighbors (not all) as forwarding nodes (narrowcasting); the message is then sent, by unicast, only to those nodes. Whenever the message reaches a node, a determination is made if the node belongs to the address class (to possibly pass the message to the application layer).

The forwarding is illustrated in Fig 3. As can be seen, there are two nodes described with the profile Fireman. As a result of concept maintenance, knowledge of these nodes spreads throughout the network and ends up in concept routing tables. Arrows originating at a node represent the contents of the node's routing table for the concept Fireman; they point towards forwarding nodes for that concept. Importantly, not all the neighbors are forwarding nodes.

Now assume that a node sends a message addressed to Fireman (as marked in Fig. 3). The forwarding history for that particular message is depicted with thick arrows, each representing one unicast transmission. The advantage of narrowcasting is that, contrary to flooding, the message does not reach all the nodes in the network. In Fig. 3, the message reaches only six nodes out of twelve (the sender node is not counted).

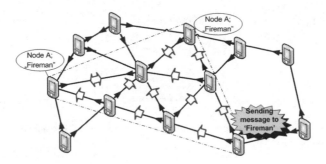

Fig. 3. The narrowcast message forwarding for Fireman

We now explain the selection of forwarders in more detail. A message addressed to a given class should be delivered to all nodes described either by that class or any of its sub-classes. For each sub-class of the concept-based address, the concept routing table is searched for matching entries, and respective forwarders are retrieved. We refer to those forwarders as "sub-class forwarders."

As described above, the profile of nodes is compressed during the distribution of Hello messages. This means that a specific concept can be replaced by a concept which is higher in the hierarchy. Thus a message should be forwarded towards all nodes described in a concept routing table by any of the super-classes of the address class. The super-classes of the address class give rise to "super-class forwarders" in the same way as for sub-classes and sub-class forwarders. The difference is that while the latter are guaranteed to be closer to an actual addressee, the former are not. To limit the overall number of forwarders (and, in turn, the number of flooded nodes), the super-class forwarders are used only if there are no sub-class forwarders.

5 Simulation Results

The simulations were made using the ns2 simulation environment, with the CMU-Monarch wireless extension. We assume a static network (without node mobility), with a random placement of nodes. A selected concept, Fireman, was randomly assigned to a certain number of nodes and used as the address. The main goal of the simulation was to check the performance of narrowcast concept-based message forwarding. Both CBR and Flooding (as the simplest solution) were simulated.

In Fig. 4, the number of nodes flooded per one addressee discovered is provided, as a function of the number of network nodes. There is a significant gap between CBR and Flooding, but it tends to decrease as the number of addressees increases. The gap is likely to be more substantial, even with many addressees, if the addressees are organized in clusters (for Fig. 4, the node distribution is uniform, with no correlation).

In the presented cases, the CBR concept-based message forwarding is significantly more effective than Flooding in terms of flooded nodes. However, we stress that the effectiveness of forwarding is achieved at the expense of overhead incurred due to Hello messages. Full results will be presented in a future paper.

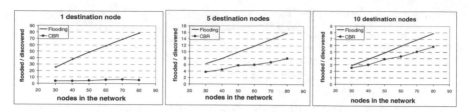

Fig. 4. Number of nodes flooded per one addressee discovered (CBR and Flooding), for 1, 5, 10 addressee nodes

6   Conclusion and Future Work

In this paper we present the idea of Concept-Based Routing – an approach to handling concept-based addresses in MANET networks. We present preliminary results of ns2 simulations. The concept-based message forwarding is more effective than flooding, but the overhead due to Hello messages has to be taken into account to make a complete comparison.

References

1. Domaszewicz, J., Koziuk, M., Schoeneich, R.O.: Context-Addressable Messaging with ontology-driven addresses. In: 7th Intl. Conference on Ontologies, Databases, and Applications of Semantics (ODBASE 2008), Monterrey, Mexico (2008)
2. Koziuk, M., Domaszewicz, J., Schoeneich, R.O.: Mobile Context-Addressable Messaging with DL-Lite Domain Model. In: 3rd European Conference on Smart Sensing and Context (EuroSSC 2008), Zurich, Switzerland (2008)
3. Chockler, G., Melamed, R., Tock, Y., Vitenberg, R.: SpiderCast: A Scalable Interest-Aware Overlay for Topic-Based Pub/Sub Communication. In: 2007 Inaugural International Conference on Distributed Event-based Systems (DEBS 2007), Toronto, Canada, pp. 14–25 (2007)
4. Eugster, P., Felber, P., Guerraoui, R., Kermarrec, A.: The many faces of publish/subscribe. ACM Comput. Surv. 35, 114–131 (2003)
5. Carzaniga, A., Rosenblum, D.S., Wolf, A.L.: A Routing Scheme for Content-Based Networking. In: IEEE INFOCOM 2004, Hong Kong (2004)
6. Cutting, D., Corbett, D., Quigley, A.: FlavourCast: Context-based Messaging for Ad Hoc Networks. Univ. of Sydney technical report no. 570 (2005) ISBN 1864877235
7. Bhaumik, P., Scalem, M., Roy, S., Bandyopadhyay, S.: Content-based Query Support in Ad-Hoc Wireless Networks using Information-Fading and Narrow-Casting for Efficient Resource Handling in Disaster Management. In: 14th IST Mobile & Wireless Communications Summit, Dresden (2005)

Heuristics for Minimizing Interference in Sensor Networks

Amit K. Sharma[1], Nikunj Thakral[1], Siba K. Udgata[2], and Arun K. Pujari[1]

[1] The LNM Institute of Information Technology
Jaipur-303 012, (Rajasthan) India
[2] Department of Computer and Information Sciences, University of Hyderabad,
Hyderabad (A.P.) India

Abstract. Reducing interference is one of the main challenges in sensor networks and also in ad hoc networks. The amount of interference experienced by a node v corresponds to the number of nodes whose transmission range covers v. We study the problem of minimizing maximum interference for a given set of nodes in a sensor network. This requires finding a connected topology which minimizes the maximum interference for set of nodes. It is proved to be NP-hard by Buchin[5]. In this paper, we propose an algorithm named "Minimizing Interference in Sensor Network (MI-S)", to minimize the maximum interference for a set of nodes in polynomial time maintaining the connectivity of the graph. We also present a variation of this algorithm based on local search technique. We check the results by applying the standard approximation algorithms and study different cases in which they are applicable. Finally we analyze some typical instances as well as average case instances to verify the proposed algorithm.

Keywords: Sensor network, topology control, interference, Heuristic.

1 Introduction

One of the primary issues in sensor network is interference. A node u interferes with the node v if the transmission radius of u is greater the distance between nodes u and v. High interference increases the probability of packet collision and therefore packet retransmission, which significantly affect the efficiency and energy consumption. Thus, it is desirable to keep the interference level low at every node. In this paper, we study to find a connected network on the given set of nodes in Euclidean plane that minimizes the maximum interference in the network. Locher et al. [6] posed five challenge problems and the Problem 2, is a problem related to topology control.

Problem: Given n nodes in a plane, connect the nodes by a spanning tree. For each node v we construct a disk centering at v with the radius equal to the distance to v's farthest neighbor in the spanning tree. The interference of a node v is then defined as the number of disks that include node v. find a spanning tree that minimizes the maximum interference

Early work focus on topology control algorithms emphasizing locality while exhibiting more and more desirable properties [8,9,10]. All these approaches deal interference minimization implicitly by reducing the node degree.

It is considered that by keeping the transmission radius small, we then not only reduce the power consumption and density but also the interference. But Burkhart et al.

V. Garg, R. Wattenhofer, and K. Kothapalli (Eds.): ICDCN 2009, LNCS 5408, pp. 49–54, 2009.

[1] shows that this is not always correct. Various mechanisms that have been developed to conserve energy in sensor networks show neither low degree nor less transmission radius can explicitly guarantee low interference. Out of several possible models, the model by Burkhart et al. [1] measures the number of nodes affected by the communication of single communication link and gives optimal results using Minimum Spanning Tree (MST) for their model. They also show experimentally that graph spanners do help in reducing interference for a given network. Rickenbach et al. [2] suggests that it is improper to study sender centric model, as interference is always detected by receiver. They propose an algorithm for a special case when all the nodes are positioned linearly, which is also called Highway model. This algorithm constructs a network with an $O(\sqrt{\Delta})$ interference. Halldorsson et al. [4] show that it is possible to construct a network with $O(\sqrt{\Delta})$ interference for any node set extending the theory of Rickenbach et al. [2] to a planner case. Buchin in [5] proves the posed problem to be NP-hard. Moscibroda et al. in [3], give a nearly tight logarithmic approximation bound algorithm for bounding the average interference at a node.

2 Proposed Algorithm

The sensor network is modeled as a graph G(V,E) consisting of a set of nodes V and a set of edges $E \subseteq V^2$. Nodes represent hosts and edges represent communication links. The maximum power is not equal for all nodes. Gg(V, Eg) is the resulting topology where Eg are the communication links obtained by the proposed algorithm Minimizing interference in communication networks (MI-S) that minimize interference. Let μ be the condition which states that edges should not form cycles in T* where T* is the state of Gg at any instant. Let E* be a set of edges for all the vertices satisfying μ in T*. Only that edge $e \subseteq E^*$ appear in Eg which is either the smallest of the edges that do not affect the maximum interference of T* (here maximum interference of T* is being calculated corresponding to edges added at each stage to Eg) or the smallest amongst the remaining edges. We add n-1 (where |V|=n) such edges to Eg such that E* and T* are redefined after adding each edge.

Algorithm 1. Minimizing Interference in Sensor networks (MI-S)

INPUT node set V
    1. Eg =Φ
    2. Gg=(V,Eg)
    3. count =0
    4. while (count <n-1) where n=|V|
    5. E* = set of all edges satisfying μ ,in sorted order of their length
    6. for(each $e \subseteq E^*$)
    7. if (e does not affects maximum interference of Gg)
    8. Eg = Eg ∪ {e}
    9. break for
    10. end if
    11. end for
    12. if (all $e \subseteq E^*$ affects maximum interference of Gg)

13. Eg = Eg ∪ {smallest e ⊆ E*}
14. end if
15. count++
16. end while
17. T= G(V,Eg)
OUTPUT T

2.1 Example

We illustrate working of the MI-S algorithm (Fig-1) in stages where each stage corresponds to addition of an edge to Gg.

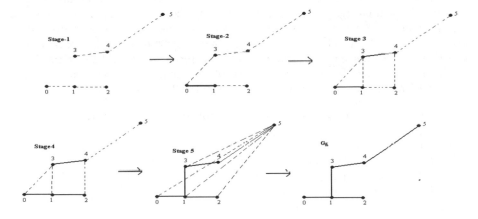

Fig. 1. At each stage dashed edges shows E* and bold lines shows edges added to Gg

Stage-1. At this stage first edge adds to Gg.E* thus obtained for this stage is ((0,1), (1,0), (2,1), (3,4), (4,3), (5,4)).As all edges increases the interference of current Gg hence edge (0,1) adds to Gg as it is smallest in E*.

Stage-2. E* thus obtained for this stage is ((0,3), (1,2), (2,1), (3,4), (4,3), (5,4)). As edge (3,4) does not increases the maximum interference hence this gets added to Gg.

Stage-3. E* for this stage is ((0,3), (1,2), (2,1), (3,1), (4,2), (5,4)). As all edges in E* increases the interference of current Gg, edge (1,2) adds to Gg as it is smallest in E*.

Stage-4. E* for this stage is ((0,3), (1,3), (2,4), (3,1), (4,2), (5,4)). As all edges in E* increases the interference of current Gg, edge (1,3) adds to Gg as it is smallest in E*.

Stage-5. After this stage, we will obtain spanning tree on given node set. E* thus obtained for this stage is ((0,5), (1,5), (2,5), (3,5), (4,5), (5,4)). As all edges in E* increases the interference of current Gg, edge (4,5) adds to Gg as it is smallest in E*.

Theorem 2.1. MI-S runs in polynomial time and gives a connected graph.

Proof. If n points are given, K_n (Complete graph) will be connected and either of the conditions in lines 7 or 12 of Algorithm-1 will be true as there will always be a smallest edge among the remaining edges and all the statements are executable in polynomial time. Since there are n-1 iterations, n-1 edges will be added to Gg without forming any cycle so Gg will always be a connected graph.

2.2 Time Complexity Analysis

Iteration at line-4 of algorithm-1 executes n-1 times. For each iteration, checking of condition μ and calculating E* correspond to checking all edges on node set V. As edges are $O(n^2)$ bound, obtaining E* is also $O(n^2)$ bound. Hence MI-S is $O(n^3)$ bound.

3 Local Search Technique

In this section, we consider application of local search technique for the given problem posed by Locher et.al. [6]. Local search technique starts with an arbitrary solution and applies small changes to it in order to improve the solution [7]. This is repeated until no more improvement is possible. Consider spanning tree obtained from MI-S (Algorithm-1) as T on node set. If we add any new edge e' to T, it shall form cycle in T. Removing the edge e (e≠e') from the cycle thus formed will yield a new tree T'. If T' has maximum interference less than that of T or number of nodes having maximum interference is less in T' then T' is considered as T-improvement.

Algorithm 2. Local Search – Improvement MI-S(LS-IM)

---

1. INPUT node set V
2. Let T be spanning tree obtained from MI-S on node set V
3. While there exists a T-improvement on T
4. Let T := T-improvement.
5. end while
6. OUTPUT T

This algorithm runs in polynomial time as at each stage we are decreasing maximum interference for T which is bounded by n and each improvement is achieved by adding a new edge to T and removing an existing edge from T. Each newly added edge and removal of existing edge is bounded by the complexity n^2 and n respectively.

4 Experiments, Results and Analysis

In this section we consider performance of MI-S on worst, best and average cases. We consider exponential node chain as worst case because maximum interference of optimal solution is bound by Ω ($\sqrt{n}$) [2]. Orthogonal grid as best case as we prove later in this section that maximum interference of optimal solution is O (1) bound.

4.1 Exponential Node Chain

Exponential node chain is a one dimensional setup of nodes where distance between two consecutive nodes grows exponentially from left to right. For the exponential node chain Wattenhoffer et.al [2] gives an algorithm which gives optimal results. The maximum interference for their topology on exponential node chain is given as

$$I = \left\lfloor \frac{\sqrt{8n - 15} + 1}{2} \right\rfloor \quad n>1 \tag{1}$$

Where |V|=n. It is clear from eqn.1 that Interference in exponential node chain is $\Omega(\sqrt{n})$bound. The topology resulting from application of MI-S on exponential node chain seems to be quite close to optimal solution given by Rickenbach et.al [2] as shown in fig.2.The maximum interference using MI-S on V comes out to be

Fig. 2. Resulting topology from MI-S on exponential node chain

$$I = \left\lceil \frac{\sqrt{8n - 23} - 1}{2} \right\rceil + 1 \quad n>4 \tag{2}$$

It is clear from eqn.2 that MI-S result in exponential node chain is also $\Omega(\sqrt{n})$ bound. Comparison of eqn.1 and eqn.2 shows that for n ≥ 10, MI-S's result exceeds results shown by Rickenbach et.al [2] by a factor of 1. Hence, MI-S's result in case of exponential node chain is not optimal but differs from optimal by a factor of one only.

4.2 Orthogonal Grid

Orthogonal grid is two dimensional setup of points in which consecutive nodes are unit distance apart. Maximum interference of optimal solution to the given problem for orthogonal grid is O(1) bound as proved in Theorem 4.1.

Theorem 4.1. Given a orthogonal grid graph G(V,E) where no vertex has degree grater than k (2 ≤ k ≤ 4), then maximum interference of the solution spanning tree on vertex set of G is equal to k.

Proof. Let *v* is the vertex having maximum degree in G(V,E) which is always unit distance away from it's neighbors. In any spanning tree drawn on vertex set V, each neighbor of *v* will be connected with a transmission radius of 1 unit to maintain connectivity and all neighbors of v shall interfere v. Thus we can not have a spanning tree on vertex set of G(V,E) which has maximum interference lower than k.

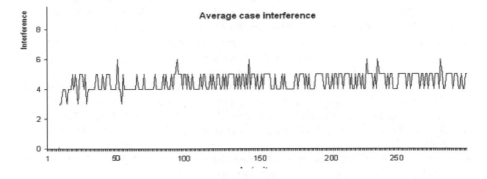

Fig. 3. Maximum interference on y-axis and node density on x-axis

The spanning tree obtained from MI-S and LS-IM have interference equal to k which is the optimal solution with minimum possible maximum interference.

4.3 Average Case Interference

In addition to the above restricted scenarios, we consider some general cases. We apply MI-S on arbitrarily distant nodes in two dimensions generated by the Random class of 'util' package of java for the generation of nodes in a specified Euclidean plane. This class is based upon method depicted by Knuth [11]. The results are shown in figure-3.

5 Conclusions

In this paper, we propose two algorithms namely MI-S and LS-IM for the minimization of maximum interference in a sensor network. We analyzed the performance of these algorithms for best and worst cases. We also analyzed MI-S on average cases. In all cases, we found their performance to be good. We performed many experiments to find the experimental bounds for the problem where the interference upper bound is the interference exhibited by the MST of the graph.

References

1. Burkhart, M., von Rickenbach, P., Wattenhofer, R., Zollinger, A.: Does Topology Control Reduce Interference. In: Proc. of 5th ACM International Symposium on Mobile Ad Hoc Networking and Computing, MOBIHOC 2004, pp. 9–19 (2004)
2. von Rickenbach, P., Schmid, S., Wattenhofer, R., Zollinger, A.: A robust interference model for wireless ad-hoc networks. In: Proceedings of the 19th IEEE International Parallel and Distributed Processing Symposium (IPDPS 2005), p. 239 (2005)
3. Moscibroda, T., Wattenhofer, R.: Minimizing interference in Ad Hoc and sensor networks. In: Proc. 3rd ACM Joint Workshop on Foundations of Mobile Computing (DIALM-POMC), Cologne, Germany, pp. 24–33 (September 2005)
4. HalldÓorsson, M.M., Tokuyama, T.: Minimizing interference of a wireless ad-hoc network in a plane. In: Nikoletseas, S.E., Rolim, J.D.P. (eds.) ALGOSENSORS 2006. LNCS, vol. 4240, pp. 71–82. Springer, Heidelberg (2006)
5. Buchin, K.: Minimizing the maximum interference is hard, arXiv: 0802 2134v1 [cs.NI] (February 15, 2008)
6. Locher, T., von Rickenbach, P., Wattenhofer, R.: Sensor networks continue to puzzle: Selected open problems. In: Rao, S., Chatterjee, M., Jayanti, P., Murthy, C.S.R., Saha, S.K. (eds.) ICDCN 2008. LNCS, vol. 4904, pp. 25–38. Springer, Heidelberg (2008)
7. Ravi, R.: Local Search: Max-leaf Spanning Tree, Min Degree Spanning Tree. Lecture notes, http://www.cs.cmu.edu/afs/cs/academic/class/15854-f05/www/scribe/lec05.pdf
8. Wattenhofer, R., Li, L., Bahl, P., Wang, Y.M.: Distributed Topology Control for Power Efficient Operation in Multi-hop Wireless Ad Hoc Networks. In: Proc. of the 20th Annual Joint Conf. of the IEEE Computer and Communications Societies (INFOCOM) (2001)
9. Santi, P.: Topology Control in Wireless Ad Hoc and Sensor Networks. Wiley, Chichester (2005)
10. Li, X.Y., Song, W.Z., Wan, W.: A Unified Energy Efficient Topology for Unicast and Broadcast. In: Proc. of the 11th MOBICOM (2005)
11. Knuth, D.: The Art of Computer Programming, vol.2, Section 3.2.1

Non-blocking Array-Based Algorithms
for Stacks and Queues

Niloufar Shafiei

Department of Computer Science and Engineering, York University
niloo@cse.yorku.ca

Abstract. We present new non-blocking array-based shared stack and queue implementations. We sketch proofs of correctness and amortized time analyses for the algorithms. To the best of our knowledge, our stack algorithm is the first practical array-based one and it is the first time that bounded counter values are employed to implement a shared stack and queue. We verify the correctness of our algorithms by the Spin model checker and compare our algorithms to other algorithms experimentally.

Keywords: Shared memory, Non-blocking, Asynchronous, Stacks, Queues.

1   Introduction

Concurrent stacks and queues are fundamental data structures in distributed systems and are widely used in parallel applications. *Non-blocking* algorithms guarantee some process completes its operation in a finite number of steps regardless of other processes' failures or delays. It is impossible to implement non-blocking stacks and queues using only read/write registers [7]. We present new non-blocking array-based stack and queue algorithms using *Compare&Swap* (C&S) objects. A C&S operation writes a new value into a variable if the current value of the variable is equal to some value. Our new non-blocking array-based stack algorithm uses unbounded counters. We describe how to make the counters bounded and use the same technique to design a new non-blocking array-based queue algorithm using bounded counters. Our algorithms are *linearizable*: Each operation takes effect instantaneously between its invocation and response.

Most distributed data structure implementations can be classified as either *link-based* if they use dynamically allocated nodes and pointers or *array-based* if they primarily use arrays. (If a data structure uses both and must therefore deal with memory reclamation problems, we consider it link-based.) Most existing distributed algorithms for stacks and queues are link-based and therefore require memory management. Herlihy et al. [9] showed that several dynamic memory management methods perform poorly with non-blocking synchronization. Shann, Huang and Chen [18] suggested that link-based algorithms may not be as efficient as claimed, because the time required for memory reclamation is not fully considered. Benefits of array-based ones include the lack of memory management overhead, good locality of reference and their compactness.

V. Garg, R. Wattenhofer, and K. Kothapalli (Eds.): ICDCN 2009, LNCS 5408, pp. 55–66, 2009.

Table 1. Related Work on Stack and Queue Implementations

Stack	Array-based	Primitive Used	Progress Property
[21]	No	C&S	non-blocking
[8]	No	C&S	wait-free
[6]	No	C&S	non-blocking
[3]	No	C&S	almost non-blocking
[1]	infinite array	Swap, Test&Set, Fetch&Add	wait-free
[13]	Yes	DC&S	non-blocking
[19]	Yes	read/write	non-blocking (not linearizable)
[20]	Yes	read/write	lock-based
This paper	Yes	C&S	non-blocking

Queue	Array-based	Primitive Used	Progress Property
[8]	No	C&S	wait-free
[16]	No	C&S	non-blocking
[23]	No	C&S	non-blocking
[14]	No	C&S	non-blocking
[12]	No	C&S	non-blocking
[15]	No	C&S	non-blocking
[10]	infinite array	Swap, Fetch&Add	wait-free
[23]	Yes	DC&S	non-blocking
[4]	Yes	C&S	non-blocking
[22]	Yes	C&S	non-blocking (low probability of error)
This paper	Yes	C&S	non-blocking

The correctness of algorithms using C&S often depends on the fact that, if a process's C&S succeeds, the value has not been changed since the process last read it. However, if changes to the shared variable are performed after the read and then it is set to the same value that the process read, the C&S can incorrectly succeed. This is called the ABA problem. To deal with it we associate a counter value with each shared variable in our algorithms. In a C&S, both the shared variable and its counter are checked and updated atomically. In our array-based algorithms we store indexes instead of pointers, so there is enough room in a word to store the counter. One disadvantage of using arrays is their fixed size. If the size of the array is unknown, dynamically resizable arrays can be used [5].

Table 1 compares previous algorithms of stacks and queues. All except [19] are linearizable. Some are link-based [3,6,12,14,15,16,21,23]. Of the array-based ones, some are impractical because either they use some primitives that many systems do not support [13,21,23] or they require an infinite array even when the size of the stack or queue is bounded [1,10]. To the best of our knowledge, no practical non-blocking array-based stack algorithm has been proposed.

Tsigas and Zhang proposed an array-based queue algorithm [22], but they only decrease the probability of the ABA problem; their algorithm can return incorrect results in some unlikely executions. Shann, Huang and Chen introduced an array-based queue algorithm [18] using C&S, but it has some bugs which were corrected by Colvin and Groves [4]. The algorithm uses unbounded counter values and needs two successful C&S operations to complete the dequeue operation, whereas our new queue algorithm needs only one. Sect. 4 gives more comparisons between the queue algorithm of Colvin and Groves and ours.

In a non-blocking algorithm, an individual operation can take arbitrarily many steps as long as some other operation is making progress. So we give an *amortized analysis* of our algorithms. This evaluates the performance of the system as a whole. The *point contention* at time t, denoted $\dot{c}(t)$, is the number of processes running concurrently at t. The worst-case amortized costs of our algorithms are adaptive to the point contention, meaning their time complexity depends only on the maximum point contention in the execution.

2 Non-blocking Stack Algorithm

Here, we present a non-blocking algorithm for stack. (See Algorithm 1.) The $Stack$ array is employed to store the entries of the stack and the Top variable is used to store the index of the top element of $Stack$. Top and entries of $Stack$ are changed using C&S. To avoid the ABA problem, Top and each entry of $Stack$ has an unbounded counter. Changing Top using a C&S is the key step and every successful operation is linearized at that point. If a push fails after successfully performing a C&S on Top, we must ensure that the pushed value is not lost. So, the C&S also stores that value in Top. Then, the algorithm uses *helping*: some process updates $Stack$ using the information that was saved in Top. To avoid updating $Stack$ more than once, the C&S on Top also stores the increased counter of the top element of $Stack$. Then, before the next successful operation, some process writes $Top.value$ and $Top.counter$ in the appropriate location in $Stack$ to complete the previous operation. $Stack$ is empty when $Top.index$ is 0 and full when $Top.index$ is $size - 1$ ($size$ is the size of $Stack$). An operation that returns $Empty$ or $Full$ is linearized at its last read of Top. Initially, Top is $(0, Null, 0)$ and for all i, $Stack[i]$ is $(Null, 0)$. The implemented stack has a capacity of $size - 1$. ($Stack[0]$ always stores a dummy entry.)

Algorithm 1. Stack Algorithm

$push(v)$
1. **while (true)**
2. $(index, value, counter) \leftarrow Top$
3. $finish(index, value, counter)$
4.   **if** $index = size - 1$ **then return** $Full$
5. $aboveTop \leftarrow Stack[index + 1].counter$
6.   **if** **C&S**$(Top, (index, value, counter), (index + 1, v, aboveTop + 1))$ **then**
          return ack

$pop()$
1. **while (true)**
2. $(index, value, counter) \leftarrow Top$
3. $finish(index, value, counter)$
4.   **if** $index = 0$ **then return** $Empty$
5. $belowTop \leftarrow Stack[index - 1]$
6.   **if** **C&S**$(Top, (index, value, counter), (index - 1, belowTop.value,$
          $belowTop.counter + 1))$ **then return** $value$

$finish(index, value, counter)$
   F1. $stackTop \leftarrow Stack[index].value$
   F2. **C&S**$(Stack[index], (stackTop, counter - 1), (value, counter))$

For a detailed proof of correctness, refer to [17]. We sketch the main ideas here. Consider any execution, consisting of a finite or infinite sequence of atomic steps. We refer to a step and the time at which that step occurs interchangeably. For any push or pop, a complete iteration of the loop is called an *attempt*. An attempt is *successful* if it ends with a successful C&S at line 6. If S is a step, $op(S)$ is the operation that does S and $att(S)$ is the attempt that includes S. We first show no shared variable ever gets set to the same value twice, so the ABA problem is avoided. This is easy to show for $Stack[i]$: Only line $F2$ can change $Stack$ and when $F2$ changes an element of $Stack$, it increases its counter.

Lemma 1. *Top does not get set to the same value twice.*

Proof Sketch. If the claim is false, consider the first step S that sets Top to some value (i, v, c) that it has had before. It can be shown that $Stack[i].counter$ is changed to c between the two times Top is set to (i, v, c) and hence $att(S)$ reads a value $c' \geq c$ in $Stack[i].counter$. But then S must write $c' + 1 > c$ in $Top.counter$, a contradiction.   □

Let $T_1, T_2,...$ be the steps, in order, that change Top. Let $top_j = (i_j, v_j, c_j)$ be Top just after T_j. Let d be the number of operations that change Top. If d is finite, then $T_{d+1} = \infty$. For $1 \leq k \leq d$, let S_k be the first line $F2$ inside an attempt that starts after T_k. If $T_{k+1} \neq \infty$, by Lemma 1, $att(T_{k+1})$ starts after T_k and line $F2$ inside $att(T_{k+1})$ is executed between T_k and T_{k+1}. Thus, if T_{k+1} exists, S_k exists. Lemma 2 is the heart of the proof: it states that between any two consecutive linearization points of successful operations, some operation updates the top entry of $Stack$. In the case of a push, this writes the newly pushed value and updates the counter. For a pop, it just updates the counter.

Lemma 2. *Before T_1 the Stack array does not change. Between T_j and T_{j+1} where $j \geq 1$, only S_j, which writes (v_j, c_j) into $Stack[i_j]$, changes Stack.*

The proof is similar to Lemma 7, so we omit it. The main steps in the inductive proof are: (1) No attempt that starts before T_k changes $Stack$ between T_k and T_{k+1}. (2) Between T_k and S_k, no process changes $Stack$. (3) S_k writes (v_k, c_k) into $Stack[i_k]$. (4) Between S_k and T_{k+1}, no process changes $Stack$.

The *abstract stack* at time T is the stack that would be formed by doing all the operations linearized before T in the order they are linearized (starting from an empty stack and assuming pushes do not change the stack when it already has $size - 1$ elements). We describe exactly how the shared $Stack$ array is changed and show what happens in the data structure exactly matches the abstract stack. We use the notation $Stack[1...g].value$ ($g > 0$) for the sequence $Stack[1].value, Stack[2].value, ..., Stack[g].value$. If $g \leq 0$, $Stack[1...g].value$ is the empty sequence. Lemma 3 shows that the data structure always accurately represents the abstract stack's contents.

Lemma 3. *(1) Before T_1 the abstract stack is empty and $Top = (0, Null, 0)$. (2) Between T_k and S_k, the abstract stack contains $Stack[1...(Top.index - 1)].value$, $Top.value$. (If $Top.index = 0$ then the abstract stack is empty.) (3) Between S_k and T_{k+1}, the abstract stack contains $Stack[1...Top.index].value$.*

Proof. Part (1) follows from the fact that no push linearized before T_1 can return Full or change Rear, since $Top.index \neq size - 1$. We show every change to the abstract stack and to $Stack$ and Top preserves the lemma.

Assume the lemma is true up until T_k for some $k \geq 1$. First assume a push(v_k) is linearized at T_k. Just before T_k, the abstract stack contains $Stack[1..i_k - 1].value$. Since $i_k - 1 \neq size - 1$, the abstract stack has fewer than $size - 1$ elements just before T_k. Thus, for any k, the abstract stack contains $Stack[1...i_k - 1].value, Top.value = v_k$ just after T_k. Now, assume a pop is linearized at T_k. Just before T_k, the abstract stack contains $Stack[1..i_k + 1].value$. Since $i_k + 1 \neq 0$, the abstract stack is not empty just before T_k. Since, by Lemma 1, $att(T_k)$ starts after T_{k-1}, line 3 in $att(T_k)$ is not executed before S_{k-1}. Thus, no operation changes $Stack[i_k]$ between line 3 in $att(T_k)$ and T_k and $Top.value$ is equal to $Stack[i_k].value$ just before T_k. So just after T_k, the abstract stack contains $Stack[1...i_k - 1].value, Top.value$.

Assume the lemma is true up until S_k for some $k \geq 1$. The abstract stack does not change at S_k. By Lemma 2, $Top.value = v_k$, is written into $Stack[i_k].value$ at step S_k. Just before S_k, the abstract stack contains $Stack[1..i_k - 1].value, Top.value$. So just after S_k, the abstract stack contains $Stack[1..i_k].value$.

Assume an operation op is linearized at $T \neq S_k$ between T_k and T_{k+1} and the lemma is true just before T. Neither $Stack$ nor Top changes at T. If op is a push, then it returns $Full$ because it does not change Top. Thus, $i_k = size - 1$. So, the abstract stack contains $size - 1$ elements at T and op does not change the abstract stack at T. Similarly if op is a pop, then it returns $Empty$. □

Using Lemma 3, it can be shown that the result returned by each operation is consistent with the abstract stack at the moment the operation is linearized. Hence, the implementation is linearizable.

Now we describe the amortized time complexity. Consider any finite execution E. Let f be the number of operations that fail or return $Full$ or $Empty$. Each iteration of loop 1-6 takes constant time. The total number of iterations of loop 1-6 performed by all operations is the number of unsuccessful and successful C&S's on Top performed by all operations plus f. Each time an operation has an unsuccessful C&S on Top, we blame the first operation that changed Top during the C&S's unsuccessful attempt. Thus, the successful C&S on Top at T_i may cause up to $\dot{c}(T_i) - 1$ unsuccessful C&S's on Top. So, the total time complexity of all operations is at most $f + \sum \dot{c}(T_i)$. Let $\dot{c}(E)$ be the maximum point contention at any time during execution E. The amortized time per operation is $O(\dot{c}(E))$. This argument also proves the algorithm is non-blocking.

We can modify the algorithm to use bounded counters. Since the technique is similar to the one in Sect. 3, we omit it here. For more details, refer to [17].

3 Non-blocking Queue Using Bounded Counters

Here we present the queue algorithm using bounded counters. To make counters bounded and avoid the ABA problem, we use *collect objects* [2]. Each process can store some value into its component of a collect object and collect the values that have been stored. These operations are not atomic. However, a collect operation returns, for each component, either the last value stored there or some value whose store is concurrent with the collect. A simple implementation of a collect object uses an array: a process stores a value by writing it into its own array location and collects by reading the whole array. Processes employ a collect object to inform one another about counters currently in use. Processes store the old (and new) counter(s) of a shared variable into the collect object after reading a shared variable and delete them before exiting an operation. To generate a new counter, a process chooses a value different from the values in the collect object.

The overall approach is similar to the one used in Sect. 2. (See Algorithm 2.) The $Queue$ circular array is used. The $Rear$ variable stores the index, value and old and new counter of the rear element of $Queue$. The $Front$ variable stores the index of the front element of $Queue$ and a counter (which is not related to $Queue$). The operations must get a consistent view of $Rear$ and $Front$ to check whether $Queue$ is full or empty. $Queue$ is full when $Front$ is above $Rear$ in the circular array and there is just one empty entry between them. $Queue$ is empty when $Front$ is above $Rear$ in the circular array and there is no entry between them. Initially, to check for a full queue, the enqueue reads $Rear$, then $Front$ and then checks whether $Rear$ has been changed since last reading it. If $Rear$ has not been changed, it means when the enqueue was reading $Front$, $Rear$ was the same as it read before. The dequeue checks for an empty queue in a symmetric way. If an operation returns $Full$ or $Empty$, it is linearized at its last line 6. Otherwise, it is linearized at its successful C&S on $Rear$ or $Front$.

We use two collect objects, $CollectRear$ and $CollectFront$. At most $2n + 2$ different counter values are used (or even fewer if contention is low), so $O(\log n)$ bits are sufficient to store counters. E.g., if you have a 64-bit word and there are 128 processes and 32 bits are required for values which are stored in the queue, in $Rear$, 18 bits would be enough for old and new counters and 14 bits remain for the index. So, the queue size could be up to 16384. Initially, $CollectRear$ and $CollectFront$ are empty, $Rear$ is $(0, Null, -1, 0)$, $Front$ is $(1, 0)$ and for all i, $Queue[i]$ is $(Null, 0)$. The implemented queue has a capacity of $size - 1$.

Now we sketch the proof of correctness using the same pattern as in Sect. 2. For details, see [17]. For any operation, an $attempt$ is the interval of time from the last line 7 in an iteration of the outer loop until the execution of line 13 in the same iteration of the outer loop. Successful attempts, $op(S)$ and $att(S)$ are defined as in Sect. 2. Let $T_1, T_2,...$ be the steps, in order, that change $Rear$. Let $rear_j = (i_j^r, v_j^r, old_j^r, new_j^r)$ be $Rear$'s value just after T_j. Lemma 4 guarantees that the ABA problem on $Rear$ and $Front$ are avoided. Let d be the number of enqueues that change $Rear$. If d is finite, then $T_{d+1} = \infty$. For $1 \le k \le d$, let S_k be the first line $FE2$ inside an attempt that starts after T_k. If $T_{k+1} \ne \infty$, by Lemma 4, $att(T_{k+1})$ starts after T_k and line $FE2$ of $att(T_{k+1})$ is executed between T_k and T_{k+1}. So, if T_{k+1} exists, S_k exists between T_k and T_{k+1}.

Lemma 4. *Rear is not changed during a successful attempt of any enqueue and Front is not changed during a successful attempt of any dequeue.*

Algorithm 2. Queue Algorithm

enqueue(v)
1. **while (true)**
2.   **while (true)**
3. $(index^r, value^r, old^r, new^r) \leftarrow Rear$
4.   store new^r and old^r into $CollectRear$
5.   **if** $Rear = (index^r, value^r, old^r, new^r)$ **then**
6. $(index^f, counter^f) \leftarrow Front$
7.   **if** $Rear = (index^r, value^r, old^r, new^r)$ **then exit loop**
8.   finishEnqueue($index^r, value^r, old^r, new^r$)
9.   **if** $index^f = (index^r + 2) \bmod size$ **then** $result \leftarrow Full$ and **exit loop**
10. $aboveRear \leftarrow Queue[(index^r + 1) \bmod size].counter$
11. $myCollect \leftarrow$ collect $CollectRear$
12. $myCounter \leftarrow$ a value in $\{0...2n + 1\}$ but not in $myCollect$ or $aboveRear$
13.   **if** **C&S**($Rear, (index^r, value^r, old^r, new^r), ((index^r + 1) \bmod size, v,$
            $aboveRear, myCounter)$) **then** $result \leftarrow ack$ and **exit loop**
14. store $\emptyset$ into $CollectRear$ and **return** $result$

dequeue()
1. **while (true)**
2.   **while (true)**
3. $(index^f, counter^f) \leftarrow Front$
4.   store $counter^f$ into $CollectFront$
5.   **if** $Front = (index^f, counter^f)$ **then**
6. $(index^r, value^r, old^r, new^r) \leftarrow Rear$
6'.   **if** $(index^f = index^r)$ **then** store old^r into $CollectRear$
7.   **if** $Front = (index^f, counter^f)$ **then exit loop**
8.   **if** $(index^f = index^r)$ **then** finishEnqueue($index^r, value^r, old^r, new^r$)
9.   **if** $index^f = (index^r + 1) \bmod size$ **then** $result \leftarrow Empty$ and **exit loop**
10. $result \leftarrow Queue[index^f \bmod size].value$
11. $myCollect \leftarrow$ collect $CollectFront$
12. $myCounter \leftarrow$ a value in $\{0...n\}$ but not in $myCollect$
13.   **if** **C&S**($Front, (index^f, counter^f), ((index^f + 1) \bmod size, myCounter)$)
            then exit loop
14. store $\emptyset$ into $CollectFront$ and $CollectRear$ and **return** $result$

finishEnqueue($index^r, value^r, old^r, new^r$)
 FE1. $queueRear \leftarrow Queue[index^r].value$
 FE2. **C&S**($Queue[index^r], (queueRear, old^r), (value^r, new^r)$)

Proof Sketch. If not, consider the first time that $Rear$ is changed at T during $att(T_i)$. $Rear$ must change back at T' between T and T_i. Since $att(T')$ chose new^r_i, it must start collecting before $att(T_i)$. So, $Rear$ is changed during $att(T')$ before T, a contradiction. $\square$

Operations must obtain a consistent view of $Rear$ and $Front$ to check whether $Queue$ is full or empty. Lemma 5, which is proved in a similar way to Lemma 4, states that op's last iteration of the inner loop, denoted itr_{op}, does this.

Lemma 5. *In the last iteration of the inner loop of an enqueue (or dequeue), Rear (or Front, respectively) is not changed from line 5 to line 7.*

To update *Queue*, if the counter of the rear element of *Queue* is *old*, some operation changes it to *new* by a C&S. To avoid updating *Queue* more than once between two consecutive linearization points of enqueues, the values of *new* and *old* must be different. The counter value of *new* that is chosen at line 12 must be different from *old* which is *aboveRear.counter*. Lemma 7 is the heart of the proof: it states that between any two consecutive linearization points of successful enqueues some operation updates the rear entry of *Queue*.

Observation 6. *At any time, the new and old fields of Rear are different.*

Lemma 7. *Before T_1 the Queue array does not change. Between T_j and T_{j+1} where $j \geq 1$, only S_j, which writes (v_j^r, new_j^r) into $Queue[i_j^r]$, changes Queue.*

Proof. Base case: Any call to finishEnqueue before T_1 has parameters $(0, Null, -1, 0)$. Just before a successful C&S at $FE2$, $Queue[0].counter$ must be -1. But, $Queue[0].counter$ is initially 0, so *Queue* is not changed before T_1.

Induction Step: Assume the lemma is true up until T_k. We show only S_k changes *Queue* between T_k and T_{k+1}, writing (v_k^r, new_k^r) into $Queue[i_k^r]$.

Claim 1: No attempt that starts before T_k changes *Queue* between T_k and T_{k+1}.

Proof of Claim 1: Assume not. Let C_1 be the first step that violates Claim 1. The value of $(index^r, value^r, old^r, new^r)$ in $att(C_1)$ is $(i_x^r, v_x^r, old_x^r, new_x^r)$ for some $x < k$. First, assume $x = 0$. Then $att(C_1)$ starts before T_1 and its value of $(index^r, value^r, old^r, new^r)$ is $(0, Null, -1, 0)$. Since C_1 is a successful C&S, $Queue[0].counter$ must be $old^r = -1$, just before C_1, but counter values are always at least 0. So $x \geq 1$. By the induction hypothesis, step S_x writes (v_x^r, new_x^r) into $Queue[i_x^r]$ at step S_x between T_x and T_{x+1}. For the successful C&S at step C_1, $Queue[i_x^r].counter$ must be old_x^r just before C_1. By Observation 6, $old_x^r \neq new_x^r$. So, between S_x and C_1, an operation writes old_x^r into $Queue[i_x^r].counter$ at T between T_y and T_{y+1} for some $x < y \leq k$. (By the induction hypothesis, we must have $y \neq x$.)

If $y = k$, $att(T)$ starts after T_y since C_1 is the first time *Queue* is changed between T_k and T_{k+1} by an attempt that starts before T_k. If $y < k$, the only change to *Queue* between T_y and T_{y+1} is S_y by the induction hypothesis. So, $T = S_y$ and $att(T)$ starts after T_y by definition of S_y. Thus, in either case, the value of $(index^r, v^r, old^r, new^r)$ that $att(T)$ uses is $(i_y^r, v_y^r, old_y^r, new_y^r)$. Since $op(T)$ writes old_x^r into $Queue[i_x^r].counter$, $i_y^r = i_x^r$ and $new_y^r = old_x^r$. So, at T_y, $op(T_y)$ changes *Rear* to $(i_x^r, v_y^r, old_y^r, old_x^r)$. Since $Rear.index$ is i_x^r just after T_x and T_y, T_x and T_y cannot be two consecutive linearization points. So, $y > x+1$. If $op(C_1)$ is an enqueue, it stores old_x^r into $CollectRear$ before $att(C_1)$ starts. If $op(C_1)$ is a dequeue, it means $index^r = index^f$ during $itr_{op(C_1)}$, so it stores old_x^r into $CollectRear$ before $att(C_1)$ starts. Thus, $op(T_y)$ started to collect $CollectRear$ to choose the counter value old_x^r in $att(T_y)$, before $op(C_1)$ finishes storing old_x^r into $CollectRear$, which is before T_{x+1}. So, $att(T_y)$ starts before T_{x+1} and ends at T_y ($y > x + 1$), contradicting Lemma 4.

By Claim 1 and the definition of S_k, no attempt that starts either before T_k or after T_k changes $Queue$ between T_k and S_k.

Claim 2: S_k writes (v_k^r, new_k^r) into $Queue[i_k^r]$.

Proof of Claim 2: First we show $Queue[i_k^r].counter$ is old_k^r just before T_k. By Lemma 4, $Rear$ has not been changed during $att(T_k)$, so $att(T_k)$ starts after T_{k-1} and, by definition of S_{k-1}, execution of line $FE2$ inside $att(T_k)$ is not executed before S_{k-1}. So, $att(T_k)$ reads $Queue[i_k]$ at line 10 after S_{k-1}. So, the value of $Queue[i_k]$ that $op(T_k)$ reads in $att(T_k)$ is not changed between that read and T_k, by the induction hypothesis. Let (v', c') be the value of $Queue[i_k^r]$ that $op(T_k)$ reads in $att(T_k)$. Since $att(T_k)$ changed $Rear$ to $(i_k^r, v_k^r, old_k^r, new_k^r)$ at T_k, $c' = old_k^r$. No process changes $Queue$ between T_k and S_k. Therefore, just before S_k, $Queue[i_k^r]$ is still (v', old_k^r). Since $att(S_k)$ starts after T_k, the value of $(index^r, value^r, old^r, new^r)$ in $att(S_k)$ is $(i_k^r, v_k^r, old_k^r, new_k^r)$. So, the C&S at step S_k succeeds and changes $Queue[i_k^r]$ from (v', old_k^r) to (v_k^r, new_k^r).

By Claim 1, no attempt that starts before T_k changes $Queue$ between S_k and T_{k+1}. Consider any attempt that starts between T_k and T_{k+1}. Its value of $(index^r, value^r, old^r, new^r)$ is $(i_k^r, v_k^r, old_k^r, new_k^r)$. By Claim 2, $Queue[i_k^r].counter$ is new_k^r just after S_k. For a successful C&S at $FE2$ in such an attempt, $Queue[i_k^r].counter$ must be old_k^r just before $FE2$. By Observation 6, $old_k^r \neq new_k^r$. So, no such attempt can change $Queue$ between S_k and T_{k+1} for the first time.   □

Lemma 8 shows no enqueue can change $Rear$ when the queue is full and no dequeue can change $Front$ when the queue is empty. Lemma 9 states if $Front$ and $Rear$ point to the same cell in $Queue$, no dequeue happens before writing the last enqueued value into the cell. Assume d' is the number of successful dequeues and $T_1', T_2', ..., T_{d'}'$ are the steps, in order, that change $Front$.

Lemma 8. *For all $k \geq 1$, $Front.index \neq (Rear.index + 2)$ mod $size$ just before T_k and $Front.index \neq (Rear.index + 1)$ mod $size$ just before T_k'.*

Lemma 9. *For all $k \geq 1$, $Rear.index \neq Front.index$ just before the linearization point of any dequeue operation that changes $Front$ between T_k and S_k.*

The *abstract queue* at time T is the queue that would be formed by doing all the operations that are linearized before T in the same order as they are linearized (starting from an empty queue and assuming enqueues do not change the queue when it already has $size - 1$ elements). For simplicity, we use the notation $Queue[k...g]$ for $k \neq (g + 1)$ mod $size$ instead of $Queue[k], Queue[(k + 1)$ mod $size], ..., Queue[(k + i)$ mod $size]$ where i is the smallest nonnegative integer such that $(k + i)$ mod $size = g$. If $k = (g + 1)$ mod $size$, $Queue[k...g]$ is the empty sequence. For example, if $size = 10$, $Queue[9...1]$ is the sequence $Queue[9]$, $Queue[0], Queue[1]$. Lemma 10 states that the data structure contents accurately represent the abstract queue's contents at all times.

Lemma 10. *(1) Before T_1 the abstract queue is empty, $Rear$ is $(0, Null, -1, 0)$ and $Front$ is $(1, 0)$. (2) Between T_k and S_k, the abstract queue contains $Queue$*

$[Front.index...(Rear.index-1) \bmod size].value$, $Rear.value$. (If $Front.index = Rear.index + 1$, then the abstract queue is empty.) (3) Between S_k and T_{k+1}, the abstract queue contains $Queue[Front.index...Rear.index].value$.

The proof is similar to the proof of Lemma 3. It follows that each operation returns a value consistent with the abstract queue when the operation is linearized. Hence, the implementation is linearizable and uses bounded memory.

Now we analyze the amortized time complexity. Consider any finite execution E. Let f be the number of enqueues that return $Full$ or fail. The total number of iterations of the inner loop performed by all enqueues is at most the number of unsuccessful tests in line 5 and 7 and successful tests in line 7 performed by all enqueues plus f. If the test in line 7 returns true, then the enqueue returns full, fails or reaches line 13. So the number of successful tests in line 7 is at most f plus the number of C&S's on $Rear$. Let $\dot{c}_e(t)$ be the point contention of enqueues only at time t. Using a similar argument to Sect. 2, each successful execution of C&S on $Rear$ at T_i may cause up to $\dot{c}_e(T_i) - 1$ unsuccessful executions of line 5 and 7 and C&S's on $Rear$. Each iteration of the inner loop is dominated by the time of storing into the collect object, denoted $storeTime$. Thus, the total time for the inner loop of all enqueues is $O((f + \sum \dot{c}_e(T_i)) \cdot storeTime)$. Each iteration of lines 8-14 is dominated by the time of collecting the collect object, denoted $collectTime$. Thus, the amortized time per enqueue is $O((\sum \dot{c}_e(T_i)) \cdot (collectTime + storeTime)/(f + d))$.

Let f' be the number of dequeues that return $Empty$ or fail. Let $\dot{c}_d(t)$ be the point contention of only dequeues at t. By a symmetric argument, the amortized time per dequeue is $O((\sum \dot{c}_d(T_i')) \cdot (collectTime + storeTime)/(f' + d'))$.

Let $\dot{c}_e(E)$ be the maximum point contention of enqueues during E. There is a collect algorithm [2] whose time complexity is $O(\dot{c}(E)^2)$. Thus, the amortized time per enqueue is $O(\dot{c}_e(E)^3)$ and the amortized time per dequeue is $O(\dot{c}(E)^3)$. (If the queue always contains at least two elements, line 6' is never executed and the time complexity of dequeues become adaptive to the point contention of only the dequeues.) This argument also proves the algorithm is non-blocking.

4   Conclusion

We used the Spin model checker [11] using exhaustive search to verify the correctness of our algorithms. We defined abstract variables, e.g., an abstract stack for the stack algorithm. For each operation that returns empty (or full), we assert that the abstract stack or queue was empty (or full) at its linearization point. At the linearization point of a successful operation, we atomically change the abstract variables and assert that the contents of the shared data structures are the same as the state of the abstract stack or queue. To specify all operations terminate, we define end-state labels when an operation returns. All operations must reach an end-state label. We verified our algorithms for four operations and the array of size three. For a larger number, Spin gives out-of-memory errors.

We performed experimental comparisons of our stack algorithm (using unbounded counter values) to Treiber's stack algorithm [21] and our queue

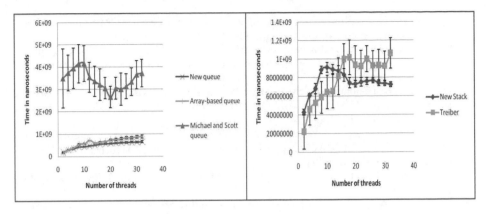

Fig. 1. Comparison of stack and queue algorithms

algorithm (using unbounded counter values) to the algorithm of Michael and Scott [14] and the array-based algorithm of Colvin and Groves [4]. Since there are no other implementations using bounded counter values, we did not compare our algorithms using bounded counter values. We implemented all algorithms in Java using the java.util.concurrent.atomic package. and ran them on a system with two quad core Intel Xeon processors, 2.66 GHz clock speed and 4 GB of memory. To make a fair comparison with link-based implementations, we chose the array size large enough that pushes or enqueues never returned *full*. The total number of the operations in any execution is 1441440 with varying numbers of threads. The charts in Fig. 1 show our comparison results. Each data point represents the mean of fifty runs. The bars on the charts show the standard deviations. One possible reason that algorithm of Treiber and Michael and Scott have bigger error bars is that the link-based memory management problems cause a wider range of execution times. Compared to Treiber's implementation, our stack implementation scales slightly better. Our queue implementation outperforms Michael and Scott's and is slightly better than Colvin and Groves's.

Our algorithms are simple, fast, efficient and practical. Our implementations might be made more scalable using an elimination backoff scheme [19] which allows pairs of opposing operations, such as stack pushes and pops, to meet and exchange values without accessing the shared data structure. This technique has been used for other implementation of stacks [6] and queues [14].

Acknowledgments. I would like to thank my supervisor, Eric Ruppert for his guidance, advice, encouragement and support.

References

1. Afek, Y., Gafni, E., Morrison, A.: Common2 extended to stacks and unbounded concurrency. In: PODC 2006: Proc. 25th ACM Symposium on Principles of Distributed Computing, pp. 218–227 (2006)
2. Attiya, H., Fouren, A.: Algorithms adapting to point contention. J. ACM 50(4), 444–468 (2003)

3. Boehm, H.-J.: An almost non-blocking stack. In: Proc. 23th ACM Symp. on Principles of Distributed Computing, pp. 40–49 (2004)
4. Colvin, R., Groves, L.: Formal verification of an array-based nonblocking queue. In: ICECCS 2005: Proc. 10th IEEE International Conference on Engineering of Complex Computer Systems, pp. 507–516 (2005)
5. Dechev, D., Pirkelbauer, P., Stroustrup, B.: Lock-free dynamically resizable arrays. In: Shvartsman, M.M.A.A. (ed.) OPODIS 2006. LNCS, vol. 4305, pp. 142–156. Springer, Heidelberg (2006)
6. Hendler, D., Shavit, N., Yerushalmi, L.: A scalable lock-free stack algorithm. In: SPAA 2004: Proc. 16th ACM Symposium on Parallelism in Algorithms and Architectures, pp. 206–215 (2004)
7. Herlihy, M.: Wait-free synchronization. ACM Trans. Program. Lang. Syst. 13(1), 124–149 (1991)
8. Herlihy, M.: A methodology for implementing highly concurrent data objects. ACM Trans. Program. Lang. Syst. 15(5), 745–770 (1993)
9. Herlihy, M., Luchangco, V., Martin, P., Moir, M.: Nonblocking memory management support for dynamic-sized data structures. ACM Trans. Comput. Syst. 23(2), 146–196 (2005)
10. Herlihy, M.P., Wing, J.M.: Linearizability: a correctness condition for concurrent objects. ACM Trans. Program. Lang. Syst. 12(3), 463–492 (1990)
11. Holzmann, G.J.: The model checker SPIN. IEEE Trans. Softw. Eng. 23(5), 279–295 (1997)
12. Ladan-Mozes, E., Shavit, N.: An optimistic approach to lock-free FIFO queues. In: Guerraoui, R. (ed.) DISC 2004. LNCS, vol. 3274, pp. 117–131. Springer, Heidelberg (2004)
13. Massalin, H., Pu, C.: A lock-free multiprocessor OS kernel. SIGOPS Oper. Syst. Rev. 26(2), 108 (1992)
14. Michael, M.M., Scott, M.L.: Simple, fast, and practical non-blocking and blocking concurrent queue algorithms. In: Proc. 15th ACM Symposium on Principles of Distributed Computing, pp. 267–275 (1996)
15. Moir, M., Nussbaum, D., Shalev, O., Shavit, N.: Using elimination to implement scalable and lock-free fifo queues. In: Proc. 17th ACM Symposium on Parallelism in Algorithms and Architectures, pp. 253–262 (2005)
16. Prakash, S., Lee, Y.H., Johnson, T.: A nonblocking algorithm for shared queues using compare-and-swap. IEEE Trans. Comput. 43(5), 548–559 (1994)
17. Shafiei, N.: Non-Blocking Array-based Algorithms for Stacks and Queues. Master's thesis, York University, Toronto, ON, Canada (December 2007)
18. Shann, C.-H., Huang, T.-L., Chen, C.: A practical nonblocking queue algorithm using compare-and-swap. In: ICPADS 2000: 7th International Conference on Parallel and Distributed Systems, p. 470 (2000)
19. Shavit, N., Touitou, D.: Elimination trees and the construction of pools and stacks. Theory of Computing Systems 30(6), 545–570 (1997)
20. Shavit, N., Zemach, A.: Combining funnels: A dynamic approach to software combining. J. Parallel Distrib. Comput. 60(11), 1355–1387 (2000)
21. Treiber, R.K.: Systems programming: Coping with parallelism. Technical Report RJ 5118, IBM Almaden Research Center (April 1986)
22. Tsigas, P., Zhang, Y.: A simple, fast and scalable non-blocking concurrent fifo queue for shared memory multiprocessor systems. In: Proc. 13th ACM Symp. on Parallel Algorithms and Architectures, pp. 134–143 (2001)
23. Valois, J.D.: Implementing lock-free queues. In: Proc. 17th International Conference on Parallel and Distributed Computing Systems, pp. 64–69 (1994)

Provable STM Properties: Leveraging Clock and Locks to Favor Commit and Early Abort

Damien Imbs and Michel Raynal

IRISA, Université de Rennes 1, 35042 Rennes, France

Abstract. The aim of a Software Transactional Memory (STM) is to discharge the programmers from the management of synchronization in multiprocess programs that access concurrent objects. To that end, a STM system provides the programmer with the concept of a *transaction*: each sequential process is decomposed into transactions, where a transaction encapsulates a piece of code accessing concurrent objects. A transaction contains no explicit synchronization statement and appears as if it has been executed atomically. Due to the underlying concurrency management, a transaction commits or aborts.

The major part of papers devoted to STM systems address mainly their efficiency. Differently, this paper focuses on an orthogonal issue, namely, the design and the statement of a safety property. The only safety property that is usually considered is a global property involving all the transactions (e.g., conflict-serializability or opacity) that expresses the correction of the whole execution. Roughly speaking, these consistency properties do not prevent a STM system from aborting all the transactions. The proposed safety property, called *obligation*, is on each transaction taken individually. It specifies minimal circumstances in which a STM system must commit a transaction T. The paper proposes and investigates such an obligation property. Then, it presents a STM algorithm that implements it. This algorithm, which is based on a logical clock and associates a lock with each shared object, is formally proved correct.

1 Introduction

Software transactional memory. The concept of *Software Transactional Memory* (STM) has been proposed in [12]. It originates from the observation that the programmers were missing something when their applications are made up of concurrent processes that access sets of shared data structures (base objects). Roughly speaking, the main tools proposed to solve their synchronization problems were the locks and the notion of object multi-versioning (and associated version numbers): a lock allows preventing conflicting accesses to an object, while multi-versioning allows providing a process (without delaying it) with the appropriate version of an object (i.e., a version consistent with the other objects last values it has already obtained). Basically, locks are used to guarantee consistency (at the inherent price of possibly entailing delays), while versioning (when used) is employed to improve efficiency (by allowing to circumvent locking). The main problem with locks is that they are difficult to manage: locks controlling large sets of data reduce drastically parallelism, while locks controlling fine grain data are difficult to master and error-prone. Moreover, versioning can be very memory demanding.

V. Garg, R. Wattenhofer, and K. Kothapalli (Eds.): ICDCN 2009, LNCS 5408, pp. 67–78, 2009.

The STM approach is a middleware approach that provides the programmers with the *transaction* concept. (As we will see, this concept is close but different from the notion of transactions encountered in databases [3].) More precisely, a process is designed as (or decomposed into) a sequence of transactions, each transaction being a piece of code that, while accessing any number of base objects, always appears as being executed atomically. The job of the programmer is only to define the units of computation that are the transactions. He does not have to worry about the fact that the base objects can be concurrently accessed by transactions. Except when he defines the beginning and the end of a transaction, the programmer is not concerned by synchronization. It is the job of the STM system to ensure that transactions execute as if they were atomic.

Of course, a solution in which a single transaction executes at a time trivially implements transaction atomicity but is irrelevant from an efficiency point of view. So, a STM system has to do "its best" to execute as many transactions per time unit as possible. Similarly to a scheduler, a STM system is an on-line algorithm that does not know the future. If the STM is not trivial (i.e., it allows several transactions that access the same objects in a conflicting manner to run concurrently), this intrinsic limitation can direct it to abort some transactions in order to ensure both transaction atomicity and object consistency. From a programming point of view, an aborted transaction has no effect (it is up to the process that issued an aborted transaction to re-issue it or not; usually, a transaction that is restarted is considered as a new transaction).

Related work: STM consistency. In the past years, several STM concepts have been proposed and several STM systems have been designed. They differ mainly in the consistency criterion (global safety property) they implement, and in the operational mechanisms their design is based on.

Two main consistency criteria have been considered so far, namely, serializability (as in databases), and opacity. Serializability requires that the committed transactions appear as if they have been executed sequentially. This total order is not required to respect their commit order, nor even their real-time order. The two important points here are that serializability (1) places no requirement on the transactions that abort, and (2) is weaker than linearizability [6] (basically, linearizability requires that the total order respects the real-time order).

Differently, opacity places requirements on all the transactions (whatever their commit/abort fate), and involves linearizability. Suggested informally in [2], and given a name and formalized in [5], opacity is the addition of two properties. First, it requires that any transaction, whether it commits or aborts, always sees a mutually consistent state of the objects it accesses. (This means that a transaction has to be aborted before obtaining values that are not mutually consistent, or writing a value not consistent with the values it has read.) This means that an aborted transaction could be replaced by a maximal prefix (without write operations and subsequent read operations on the same objects) that would commit. The second property lies in the fact that the committed transactions and the appropriate prefixes of the aborted transactions are linearizable: they can be totally ordered in a consistent way, respecting the real-time order.

Related work: Operational point of view. Locks, versioning and (logical or physical) clocks are the main operational tools from which STM are built. We present here only a few STM systems that have been recently proposed. We focus on them because they all ensure the opacity criterion ([2] and [11] have been proposed before opacity has been formalized).

TL2 [2] is a single version, clock-based STM system. The logical clock is used to associate a date with each object, ensuring that the values read by a transaction define a consistent snapshot (belong to a consistent global state). TL2 satisfies the opacity property, but can abort a transaction T despite the fact that T is not conflicting with alive transactions. TL2C [1] is an extension of TL2 where the logical clock is distributed.

LSA-RT [11] is a STM system based on a real-time clock that manages several versions of each object. It does not use locks and satisfies the opacity property. As they are based on increasing clocks, both TL2 and LSA-RT have unbounded variables.

Differently from TL2 and LSA-RT, the protocol described in [7] does not use clocks and has only bounded variables. It requires a single version per object (as TL2), never aborts a write-only transaction, and aborts a transaction only in presence of conflicts (as LSA-RT, but differently from TL2). A comparison (from a property point of view) of this STM system with TL2 and LSA-RT is presented in [7].

Content of the paper: Favoring commit and providing early abort. The design of nearly all the STM protocols proposed so far has mainly been driven by efficiency, measured as the number of transactions that commit per time unit, without taking into account the number of aborted transactions. But an aborted transaction can access the shared memory, consumes resources, and has to be restarted (usually as a new transaction). Very recently, a new efficiency measure has been proposed, that considers the ratio made up of the number of committed transactions divided by the total number of transactions [4]. On another side, nearly none of the protocols proposed so far has been formally proved correct. At best, they are only explained with a sketch of an informal proof.

The paper has several contributions. The first is a first step in proposing a provable commit property. While both an aborted transaction and a committed transaction terminate, an abort has to be considered as an unsuccessful termination while a commit is a successful termination. Considering this commit/abort dilemma, the paper introduces a transaction property that, when satisfied by a transaction T, requires that T commits. This property is designed incrementally. A property, called $P1(T)$, is first formulated that states whether the snapshot of object values read by the transaction T is consistent (i.e., could have been obtained by an atomic read of the shared memory). Then, this property is enriched to take into account the write operations issued by a transaction. This enriched property, called $P2(T)$, is such that $P2(T) \Rightarrow P1(T)$. It states whether both the snapshot of the values read by a transaction *and* its shared memory write operations could have been issued in a single atomic "macro-operation". These properties $P1(T)$ and $P2(T)$ are abstract in the sense that they are expressed in the model capturing the transaction executions. It is important to see that $P1(T)$ and $P2(T)$ are safety properties. They can be used to force a STM system to commit transactions at least in "good circumstances", and so they are called *obligation* properties[1]. An interesting side effect of $P2(T)$ is the fact it can be used to direct all the write-only transactions to commit.

---

[1] This is similar to the specification of the *Non-Blocking Atomic Commit* problem where a transaction must commit when there is no failure and all the transactions have voted "yes".

Then, the paper presents its second contribution: a simple algorithm that implements a STM system satisfying the previous obligation properties. From an operational point of view, this algorithm is based on a logical clock (the logical clock could be replaced by a real-time clock or distributed real-time clocks as proposed in [11]; for simplicity, we only consider here a scalar clock). It uses the following shared control variables: (1) a lock, a date and a read set are associated with each object, and (2) a date is associated with each transaction. Combined with the local control variables managed by each transaction, the shared control variables allow to express predicates that are correct implementations of the abstract properties $P1(T)$ and $P2(T)$ previously introduced. From an underlying design principle, a read of an object X from a transaction T announces only that X is read by T. Differently, when an update transaction T commits (and only at that time), T manages the read/write conflict it gives rise to, and announces possible future write/read conflicts. Moreover but not least, the algorithm is formally proved correct.

Finally, let us observe that the abort of a transaction is a stable property. It follows that, when the irrevocable decision to abort a transaction has been taken, there is no reason for that transaction to continue its execution: it has to be stopped as soon as possible. The proposed algorithm implements this observation in a simple way (at the additional price of possibly more shared memory accesses).

Roadmap. The paper is made up of 4 sections. Section 2 presents the computation model and the obligation properties $P1()$ and $P2()$. Then, Section 3 presents a specification of a STM system, that takes into account the proposed obligation property for each transaction taken individually, and the opacity property (formalized in [5]) as the global consistency property linking all the transactions. Then, Section 4 presents a corresponding STM algorithm. Albeit the formal proofs of the theorems and the algorithm are an important part of the paper and its design philosophy, due to page limitation it was not possible to include them in the paper. The reader will find them in [8].

The paper leaves open the problem of finding less constraining obligation properties (i.e., properties forcing more transactions to commit) and algorithms implementing them, the challenge being to find properties that do not require the implementation protocols to add "too many" control variables and not to be too synchronized (as these would not constitute acceptable solutions for a STM system).

2   Computation Model and Property Statement

2.1   Computation Model

Transaction. As indicated, a transaction is a piece of code defined by the programmer. When (s)he defines a transaction T, the programmer considers that T is executed atomically (he does not have to worry about the management of the base objects accessed by the transaction). A transaction returns either commit or abort. Differently from a committed transaction, an aborted transaction has no effect on the shared objects. A transaction can read or write any base object. Such a read or write access is atomic. A transaction that does not write base objects is a *read-only* transaction, otherwise it is an *update* transaction. A *write-only* transaction issues only write operations.

Events and history at the shared memory level. Each transaction generates events defined as follows.

- Begin and end events. The event denoted B_T is associated with the beginning of the transaction T, while the event E_T is associated with its termination. E_T can be of two types, namely A_T and C_T, where A_T is the event "abort of T", while C_T is the event "commit of T".
- Read events. The event denoted $r_T(X)v$ is associated with the atomic read of X (from the shared memory) issued by the transaction T. The value v denotes the value returned by the read. If the value v is irrelevant $r_T(X)v$ is abbreviated $r_T(X)$.
- Write events. The event denoted $w_T(X)v$ is associated with the atomic write of the value v in the shared object X (in the shared memory). If the value v is irrelevant $w_T(X)v$ is abbreviated $w_T(X)$. Without loss of generality we assume that no two writes on the same object X write the same value. We also assume that all the objects are initially written by a fictitious transaction.

Given an execution, let H be the set of all the (begin, end, read and write) events generated by the transactions. As the events correspond to atomic operations, they can be totally ordered. It follows that, at the shared memory level, an execution can be represented by the pair $\widehat{H} = (H, <_H)$ where $<_H$ denotes the total ordering on its events. $\widehat{H}$ is called a *shared memory history*. As $<_H$ is a total order, it is possible to associate a unique "date" with each event in H. (In the following an event is sometimes used to denote its date.)

Types of conflict. Two operations conflict if both access the same object and one of these operations is a write. Considering two transactions $T1$ and $T2$ that access the same object X, three types of conflict can occur. More specifically:

- Read/write conflict: $conflict(X, R_{T1}, W_{T2}) \stackrel{\text{def}}{=} \big(r_{T1}(X) <_H w_{T2}(X)\big)$.
- Write/read conflict: $conflict(X, W_{T1}, R_{T2}) \stackrel{\text{def}}{=} \big(w_{T1}(X) <_H r_{T2}(X)\big)$.
- Write/write conflict: $conflict(X, W_{T1}, W_{T2}) \stackrel{\text{def}}{=} \big(w_{T1}(X) <_H w_{T2}(X)\big)$.

History at the transaction level. Let TR be the set of transactions issued during an execution. Let $\rightarrow_{TR}$ be the order relation defined on the transactions of TR as follows: $T1 \rightarrow_{TR} T2$ if $E_{T1} <_H B_{T2}$ ($T1$ has terminated before $T2$ starts). If $T1 \not\rightarrow_{TR} T2 \wedge T2 \not\rightarrow_{TR} T1$, we say that $T1$ and $T2$ are concurrent (their executions overlap in time). At the transaction level, that execution is defined by the partial order $\widehat{TR} = (TR, \rightarrow_{TR})$, that is called a *transaction level history* or a *transaction run*.

2.2 Two Properties

This section investigates two properties that involve a transaction and the run in which it appears. These properties will be used in the specification of a STM system to force it to commit all the transactions that satisfy them. Given a run, let $\mathcal{C}$ denote the set of transactions that commit in that run.

A Property Ensuring Snapshot Consistency. Let a *snapshot* be a set of object values obtained by a transaction. A snapshot is *consistent* if there is a time t at which all the values it contains are the last values written in the shared memory before or at time t.

Let us consider the property $P1(T)$ defined as follows: $\forall T1, T2 \in C, \forall X1, X2 :$ $\big(conflict(X1, R_T, W_{T1}) \wedge conflict(X2, W_{T2}, R_T)\big) \Rightarrow \big(E_{T2} <_H B_{T1}\big)$.

Assuming a transaction reads an object at most once, the following theorem shows that, if $P1(T)$ is satisfied, the snapshot of values obtained by T is consistent.

Theorem 1. [8] $P1(T) \Rightarrow$ the snapshot obtained by T is consistent.

It follows from this theorem that a read-only transaction that satisfies the property $P1()$ can always be forced to commit [8].

A Property Ensuring Atomicity. A transaction T is *atomic* if (1) its reads (if any) define a consistent snapshot, and (2) its writes appear as if they have been executed immediately after the reads, meaning "with no write operations (from other transactions) between its reads and writes". The transaction appears as if it is executed at a given point of the time line, no two transactions being associated with the same point.

Let $P2(T)$ be the property: $\forall T1, T2 \in C, \forall X1, X2 : \big(conflict(X1, R_T, W_{T1}) \wedge$ $conflict(X2, W_{T2}, R_T)\big) \Rightarrow \big(E_{T2} <_H E_T <_H B_{T1}\big)$.

It is easy to see that $\forall T : P2(T) \Rightarrow P1(T)$. The following theorem shows that, if $P2(T)$ is satisfied, T is atomic.

Theorem 2. [8] $P2(T) \Rightarrow T$ is atomic.

It follows from this theorem that both the update transactions that satisfy the property $P2()$ and all the write-only transactions can always be forced to commit [8].

3   Problem Specification

Safety properties specify which runs are correct. This paper considers two safety properties for a STM system. The first is opacity [5]. The second is an obligation property stating when a transaction is forced to commit. This section first presents opacity (in a way different from [5]), and then defines a STM specification. As already indicated, C is the set of transactions that commit. Let A denote the set of transactions that abort.

3.1   Preliminary Definitions

A transaction history $\widehat{ST} = (ST, \rightarrow_{ST})$ is *sequential* if no two of its transactions are concurrent. Hence, in a sequential history, $T1 \not\rightarrow_{ST} T2 \Leftrightarrow T2 \rightarrow_{ST} T1$, thus $\rightarrow_{ST}$ is a total order. A sequential transaction history is *legal* if each of its read operations returns the value of the last write on the same object.

A sequential transaction history $\widehat{ST}$ is *equivalent* to a transaction history $\widehat{TR}$ if (1) $ST = TR$ (i.e., they are made of the same transactions (same values read and written) in $\widehat{ST}$ and in $\widehat{TR}$), and (2) the total order $\rightarrow_{ST}$ respects the partial order $\rightarrow_{TR}$ (i.e., $\rightarrow_{TR} \subseteq \rightarrow_{ST}$).

A transaction history $\widehat{AA}$ is *linearizable* if there exists a history $\widehat{SA}$ that is sequential, legal and equivalent to $\widehat{AA}$ [6].

3.2   The Opacity Property

Given a run $\widehat{TR} = (TR, \rightarrow_{TR})$, and $T \in \mathcal{A}$, let $T' = \rho(T)$ be the transaction built from T as follows (ρ stands for "reduced"). As T has been aborted, there is a read or a write on a base object that entailed that abortion. Let $prefix(T)$ be the prefix of T that includes all the read and write operations on the base objects accessed by T until (but excluding) the read or write that entailed the abort of T. $T' = \rho(T)$ is obtained from $prefix(T)$ by replacing its write operations on base objects and all the subsequent read operations on these objects, by corresponding write and read operations on a copy in local memory. The idea here is that only an appropriate prefix of an aborted transaction is considered: its write operations on base objects (and the subsequent read operations) are made fictitious in $T' = \rho(T)$.

Finally, let $\mathcal{A}' = \{T' \mid T' = \rho(T) \,\wedge\, T \in \mathcal{A}\}$, and $\widehat{\rho(TR)} = (\rho(TR), \rightarrow_{\rho(TR)})$ where $\rho(TR) = \mathcal{C} \cup \mathcal{A}'$ (i.e., $\rho(TR)$ contains all the transactions of $\widehat{TR}$ that commit, plus $\rho(T)$ for each transaction $T \in TR$ that aborts) and $\rightarrow_{\rho(TR)} = \rightarrow_{TR}$. Informally, opacity expresses the fact that a transaction never sees an inconsistent state of the base objects [2,5]: the transactions in $\mathcal{C} \cup \mathcal{A}'$ can be consistently and totally ordered according to their real-time order. With the previous notation, Opacity can be formally stated as follows: $\widehat{\rho(TR)}$ is linearizable.

3.3   A STM Specification

Similarly to serializability, opacity alone is too weak a safety property as it does not prevent trivial STM systems that would abort all transactions. (This observation was the main motivation in defining the properties $P1(T)$ and $P2(T)$.) Let $read\_only(T)$ be a predicate that is true iff T is a read-only transaction.

- Termination. Let T a transaction that terminates when executed in a concurrency-free context. Then, it terminates (commits or aborts) despite concurrency.
- Strong global consistency (Opacity). $\widehat{\rho(TR)}$ is linearizable.
- Obligation. $\forall\, T\colon (P1(T) \wedge read\_only(T)) \vee P2(T) \Rightarrow (T \subset \mathcal{C})$.

While the termination property is a liveness property (on a per transaction basis), global consistency and obligation are safety properties. The first is on the whole execution: it states that the execution is consistent. The second concerns each transaction taken individually: it states conditions where a transaction is obliged to commit. Those are characterized by the predicates $P1()$ and $P2()$ (consistency of the snapshot defined by the values read by a transaction, and atomicity of a transaction -its reads and writes appear as being executed without interfering operations from other transactions).

It is worth observing that a weaker specification of a STM system can be obtained by replacing the global consistency property by the following weaker property: $\widehat{\rho(TR)}$ is sequentially consistent [9,10] (both linearizability and sequential consistency require a "witness" equivalent legal sequential history $\widehat{ST}$, but only linearizability requires that $\widehat{ST}$ respects the real-time order defined by $\rightarrow_{TR}$, i.e., $\rightarrow_{TR} \subseteq \rightarrow_{ST}$).

4 A STM Protocol Based on Clock and Locks

This section presents an algorithm that implements an STM system. The next section proves that it satisfies the previous specification.

4.1 The STM System Interface

The STM system provides the transactions with three operations denoted $X.\text{read}_T()$, $X.\text{write}_T()$, and $\text{try\_to\_commit}_T()$, where T is a transaction, and X a base object.

- $X.\text{read}_T()$ is invoked by the transaction T to read the base object X. That operation returns a value of X or the control value $abort$. If $abort$ is returned, the invoking transaction is aborted.
- $X.\text{write}_T(v)$ is invoked by the transaction T to update X to the new value v. As we will see, that operation never forces a transaction to immediately abort (when we do not consider the early abort mechanism).
- If a transaction attains its last statement (as defined by the user) it executes the operation $\text{try\_to\_commit}_T()$. That operation decides the fate of T by returning $commit$ or $abort$. (Let us notice, a transaction T that invokes $\text{try\_to\_commit}_T()$ has not been aborted during an invocation of $X.\text{read}_T()$.)

4.2 The STM System Variables

To implement the previous STM operations, the STM system uses the following atomic control variables. The shared objects accessed by the transactions, and the shared control variables -i.e., the variables kept in shared memory- are denoted with uppercase letters.

- A logical clock denoted $CLOCK$. This clock, initialized to 0, can be read, and atomically increased with the $Fetch\&Increment()$ operation.
- A lock per base object X. Locks are assumed to be fair (assuming each lock is eventually released, every transaction that requires a lock eventually gets it).
- A set RS_X per base object X. This set, initialized to $\emptyset$, contains the ids of the transactions that have read X since the last update of X. A transaction adds its id to RS_X to indicate a possible read/write conflict.
- Each base object X is made up of two fields: $X.value$ denotes its current value, while $X.date$ denotes the logical date at which that value has been written.
- A control variable MAX_DATE_T, initialized to $+\infty$, is associated with each transaction T. It keeps the smallest date at which an object read by T has been overwritten. That variable allows the transaction T to safely evaluate the abstract property $P2(T)$. As we will see, we have $P2(T) \Rightarrow (MAX\_DATE_T = +\infty)$, and the STM system will direct T to commit when $MAX\_DATE_T = +\infty$ [8].

In addition to accessing the previous variables kept in the shared memory, a transaction T manages the following local variables. The local control variables are denoted with lowercase letters.

- lrs_T and lrw_T are sets where T keeps the ids of the objects it has read and written, respectively.
- $read\_only_T$ is a boolean, initialized to $true$, that is set to $false$, if T invokes a $X.\text{write}_T(v)$ operation.
- For each object X is accesses, T keeps a copy lcx in its local memory. Its two fields are denoted $lcx.value$ and $lcx.date$.
- min_date_T contains the greatest date of the objects T has read so far. Its initial value is 0. Combined with MAX_DATE_T, that variable allows a safe evaluation of the abstract property $P1(T)$. As we will see, we have $P1(T) \Rightarrow (min\_date_T \le MAX\_DATE_T)$, and the STM system will not abort a read-only transaction T if $min\_date_T \le MAX\_DATE_T$[8].

4.3   The Algorithms of the STM System

The three operations that constitute the STM system $X.\text{read}_T()$, $X.\text{write}_T(v)$, and $\text{try\_to\_commit}_T()$, are described in Figure 1. As in a lot of other protocols (e.g., STM or discrete event simulation), the underlying idea is to associate a time window, namely $[min\_date_T, MAX\_DATE_T]$, with each transaction T. This time window is managed as follows:

- When a read-only or update transaction T reads a new object (from the shared memory), it accordingly updates min_date_T, and aborts if its time window becomes empty. A time window becomes empty when the system is unable to guarantee that the values previously read by T and the value it has just obtained belong to a consistent snapshot.
- When an update transaction T is about to commit, it has two things to do. First, write into the shared memory the new values of the objects it has updated, and define their dates as the current clock value. These writes may render inconsistent the snapshot of a transaction T' that has already obtained values and will read a new object in the future. Hence, in order to prevent such an inconsistency from occurring (see the previous item), the transaction T sets $MAX\_DATE_{T'}$ to the current clock value if $((T' \in RS_X) \wedge (X \in lws_T))$ and $(MAX\_DATE_{T'} = +\infty)$.

The operation $X.\text{read}_T()$. When T invokes $X.\text{read}_T()$, it obtains the value of X currently kept in the local memory if there is one (lines 01 and 08). Otherwise, T first allocates space in its local memory for a copy of X (line 02), obtains the value of X from the shared memory and updates RS_X accordingly (line 03). The update of RS_X allows T to announce a read/write conflict that will occur with the transactions that will update X. This line is the only place where read/write conflicts are announced in the proposed STM algorithm.

Then, T updates its local control variables lrs_T (line 04) and min_date_T (line 05) in order to keep them consistent. Finally, T checks its time window (line 06) to know if its snapshot is consistent. If the time window is empty, the value it has just obtained from the memory can make its current snapshot inconsistent and consequently T aborts.

Remark. Looking into the details, when a transaction T reads X from the shared memory, two causes can make true the window predicate $(min\_date_T > MAX\_DATE_T)$:

```
operation X.read_T():
(01)  if (there is no local copy of X) then
(02)     allocate local space lcx for a copy;
(03)     lock X; lcx ← X; RS_X ← RS_X ∪ {T}; unlock X;
(04)     lrs_T ← lrs_T ∪ {X};
(05)     min_date_T ← max(min_date_T, lcx.date);
(06)     if (min_date_T > MAX_DATE_T) then return(abort) end if
(07)  end if;
(08)  return (lcx.value)
===================================================================
operation X.write_T(v):
(09)  read_only_T ← false;
(10)  if (there is no local copy of X) then allocate local space lcx for a copy end if;
(11)  lcx.value ← v;
(12)  lws_T ← lws_T ∪ {X}
===================================================================
operation try_to_commit_T():
(13)  if (read_only_T)
(14)     then return(commit)
(15)     else  lock all the objects in lrs_T ∪ lws_T;
(16)           if (MAX_DATE_T ≠ +∞) then release all the locks; return(abort) end if;
(17)           current_time ← CLOCK;
(18)           for each T' ∈ (∪_{X∈lws_T} RS_X)
                      do C&S(MAX_DATE_{T'}, +∞, current_time) end for;
(19)           commit_time ← Fetch&Increment(CLOCK);
(20)           for each X ∈ lws_T do X ← (lcx.value, commit_time); RS_X ← ∅ end for;
(21)           release all the locks;
(22)           return(commit)
(23)  end if
```

Fig. 1. A clock+locks-based STM system

min_date_T has just been increased, or MAX_DATE_T has been decreased to a finite value (or both). If the abort is due to an increase of min_date_T, T is aborted due to a write/read conflict on X. Differently, an abort caused by the fact that MAX_DATE_T has been set to a finite value, is due to a read/write conflict on $Y \neq X$.

The operation X.write$_T()$. The text of the algorithm implementing X.write$_T()$ is very simple. The transaction first sets a flag to record that it is not a read-only transaction (line 09). If there is no local copy of X, corresponding space is allocated in the local memory (line 10); let us remark that this does not entail a read of X from the shared memory. Finally, T updates the local copy of X (line 11), and records that it has locally written the copy of X (line 12). It is important to notice that an invocation of X.write$_T()$ is purely local: it involves no access to the shared memory, and cannot entail an immediate abort of the corresponding transaction.

The operation try_to_commit$_T()$. This operation works as follows. If the invoking transaction is a read-only transaction, it is committed (lines 13-14). So, a read-only transaction can abort only during the invocation of a X.read$_T()$ operation (line 06).

If the transaction T is an update transaction, try_to_commit$_T()$ first locks all the objects accessed by T (line 15). (In order to prevent deadlocks, it is assumed that these objects are locked according to a predefined total order, e.g., their identity order.) Then, T checks if $MAX\_DATE_T \neq +\infty$. If this is the case, there is a read/write conflict: T has read an object that since then has been overwritten. Consequently, there is no guarantee for the current snapshot of T (that is consistent) and the write operations of T to appear as being atomic. T consequently aborts (after having released all the locks it has previously acquired, line 16).

If the predicate $MAX\_DATE_T = +\infty$ is true, T will necessarily commit. But, before releasing the locks and committing (lines 21-22), T has to (1) write in the shared memory the new values of the objects with their new dates (lines 19-20), and (2) update the control variables to indicate possible (read/write with read in the past, or write/read with read in the future) conflicts due to the objects it has written. As indicated at the beginning of this section, (1) read/write conflicts are managed by setting $MAX\_DATE_{T'}$ to the current clock value for all the transactions T' such that $((T' \in RS_X) \land (X \in lws_T))$ (lines 17-18), and consequently RS_X is reset to $\emptyset$ (line 20), while (2) write/read conflicts on an object X are managed by setting the date of X to the commit time of T.

As two transactions $T1$ and $T2$ can simultaneously find $MAX\_DATE_{T'} = +\infty$ and try to change its value, the modification of $MAX\_DATE_{T'}$ is controlled by an atomic compare&swap operation (denoted $C\&S()$, line 18).

Remark 1. In order to save (expensive) $C\&S(MAX\_DATE_{T'}, +\infty, current\_time)$ at line 18, this invocation can be replaced by the following statement:

"**if** $(MAX\_DATE_{T'} = +\infty)$ **then** $C\&S(MAX\_DATE_{T'}, +\infty, commit\_time)$ **end if**".

Remark 2. It is worth noticing that the proposed algorithm does not address write/write conflicts. As we will see, the write-only transactions are never aborted.

4.4   Reducing the Aborts and Favoring Early Aborts

Reducing the aborts. The predicate used at line 06 can be satisfied for $MAX\_DATE_T = d$ (and then T is aborted), while it would be false for $MAX\_DATE_T = d+1$ (or a greater value). This means that, when it is updated to a finite value, MAX_DATE_T has to be set to a value as great as possible. On another side, $CLOCK$ can be increased by an arbitrary number of transactions between two successive accesses to $CLOCK$ by the transaction T (at line 17 and line 19).

If the aim is to abort as few transactions as possible (without adding other control variable, a best effort strategy can be obtained by exploiting the previous observations. More precisely, replacing the lines 17 and 18 by the following statement

"**for each** $T' \in \left(\cup_{X \in lws_T} RS_X \right)$ **do** $C\&S(MAX\_DATE_{T'}, +\infty, CLOCK)$ **end for**"

can reduce the number of aborts. It is important to notice that a price has to be paid for this improvement: each $C\&S()$ invocation now requires an additional access to the shared memory to obtain the last value of $CLOCK$.

Favoring early abort. As indicated in the introduction, as soon as the fate of a transaction is to abort, it has to be aborted as soon as possible. In the proposed algorithm, the fate of a transaction T is to abort as soon as the predicate

$$(min\_date_T > MAX\_DATE_T) \vee (\neg read\_only_T \wedge (MAX\_DATE_T \neq +\infty))$$

becomes true. Consequently, in order to expedite aborts, it is possible to:

- Add the following statement before line 01: "**if** $(min\_date_T > MAX\_DATE_T) \vee (\neg read\_only_T \wedge (MAX\_DATE_T \neq +\infty))$ **then** return $(abort)$ **end if**",
- Replace the statement of line 06 by the statement used in the previous item,
- Add the statement "**if** $(MAX\_DATE_T \neq +\infty)$ **then** return $(abort)$ **end if**" before line 09,
- And add the previous statement at line 15, just before locking the locks.

This is obtained at the additional price of increasing the number of shared memory accesses to the atomic variables MAX_DATE_T. (It is worth noticing that these predicates could easily be used by an underlying contention manager).

References

1. Avni, H., Shavit, N.: Maintaining Consistent Transactional States without a Global Clock. In: Shvartsman, A.A., Felber, P. (eds.) SIROCCO 2008. LNCS, vol. 5058, pp. 121–140. Springer, Heidelberg (2008)
2. Dice, D., Shalev, O., Shavit, N.: Transactional Locking II. In: Dolev, S. (ed.) DISC 2006. LNCS, vol. 4167, pp. 194–208. Springer, Heidelberg (2006)
3. Felber, P., Fetzer, C., Guerraoui, R., Harris, T.: Transactions are coming Back, but Are They The Same? ACM Sigact News, Distributed Computing Column 39(1), 48–58 (2008)
4. Gramoli, V., Harmanci, D., Felber, P.: Towards a Theory of Input Acceptance for Transactional Memories. LPD-REPORT-2008-009, Distributed Programming Lab, EPFL (2008)
5. Guerraoui, R., Kapałka, M.: On the Correctness of Transactional Memory. In: Proc. 13th ACM SIGPLAN Symposium on Principles and Practice of Parallel Programming (PPoPP 2008), pp. 175–184. ACM Press, New York (2008)
6. Herlihy, M.P., Wing, J.M.: Linearizability: a Correctness Condition for Concurrent Objects. ACM Transactions on Programming Languages and Systems 12(3), 463–492 (1990)
7. Imbs, D., Raynal, M.: A Lock-based STM Protocol that Satisfies Opacity and Progressiveness. In: Baker, T.P., Bui, A., Tixeuil, S. (eds.) OPODIS 2008. LNCS, vol. 5401, pp. 226–245. Springer, Heidelberg (2008)
8. Imbs, D., Raynal, M.: Provable STM Properties: Leveraging Clock and Locks to Favor Commit and Early Abort. Tech Report, #1894, IRISA, Univ. de Rennes 1, France (May 2008)
9. Lamport, L.: How to Make a Multiprocessor Computer that Correctly Executes Multiprocess Programs. IEEE Transactions on Computers C28(9), 690–691 (1979)
10. Raynal, M.: Sequential Consistency as Lazy Linearizability. BA. In: Proc. 14th ACM Symposium on Parallel Algorithms and Architectures (SPAA 2002), Winnipeg, pp. 151–152 (2002)
11. Riegel, T., Fetzer, C., Felber, P.: Time-based Transactional Memory with Scalable Time Bases. In: Proc. 19th annual ACM Symposium on Parallel Algorithms and Architectures (SPAA 2007), pp. 221–228. ACM Press, New York (2007)
12. Shavit, N., Touitou, D.: Software Transactional Memory. Distributed Computing 10(2), 99–116 (1997)

Aspectising Concurrency for the RTSJ

Nathar Shah

Faculty of Inormation Technology, Multimedia University, Jalan Multimedia, 63100
Cyberjaya, Malaysia
nathar.packier@mmu.edu.my

Abstract. The Real-Time Specification for Java (RTSJ) supports concurrency mainly by using object-oriented mechanisms. Hence it entangles with functional components. This crosscutting nature does not promote coherence and traceability between real-time systems requirement specifications, designs, and implementations. Such qualities are only possible by separating it. We show how to separate concurrency, a non-functional concern, from thread-safe functional concerns using "aspectisation". The paper's contributions are in devising a systematic separation approach, and elaboration of challenges and requirements for "pluggable" concurrency.

Keywords: Concurrency, Aspect-Orientation, Object-Orientation.

1 Introduction

The Real-Time Specification for Java (RTSJ) [1] aims to elevate Java for real-time applications. The Java concurrency model, implemented using threads, does not have notions to capture real-time systems' specifics such as release period, deadline, handlers (for cost-overrun, and deadline miss), arrival time, and minimum interval arrival time. The RTSJ supports these constructs using powerful object-oriented mechanisms such as encapsulation, abstraction, and inheritance.

Development of real-time systems is complex and normally its functional components are crosscutting with non-functional implementations such as in the concurrency [2, 3]. The crosscutting has the following problems:-

1. The design and implementation are not coherent and traceable from the requirement specification when concurrency is introduced. This is because it entangles with functional implementation, hence, resulting in a less maintainable system.
2. The inflexibility in the real-time thread timing control either during the development, testing, or maintenance.

For an example, when functional classes implement concurrency in the RTSJ by extending RealtimeThread class, unintentionally, the semantic of the functional classes is also changed. Such side effect implies that the functional classes inherit both the behaviour and the properties of the non-functional class. Hence, there is incoherence between what is intended in the specification, what is designed, and the outcome behaviour of the implementation. Therefore, functional requirements and concurrency

V. Garg, R. Wattenhofer, and K. Kothapalli (Eds.): ICDCN 2009, LNCS 5408, pp. 79–84, 2009.

must be handled separately. Besides that, the entanglement also scatters the implementation of timing parameters such as the release parameters. It is a hindrance to the systems maintenance and fine-tuning.

These issues motivated us to explore aspect-orientation, a development paradigm evolved from the concept of separation of concerns [4], with an intention to make it possible to transform a non-concurrent object to a real-time concurrent object by means of concurrency concern weaving. The transformation demonstrates that the concurrency concern is separable from the functional concerns and hence can be depicted separately in the design for traceability yet maintaining the coherence with the implementation. Such an approach also modularises crosscutting concerns [5], which allows for an elegant encapsulation of code scattering and tangling.

This paper contributes in the following ways. It elaborates on the effects and implications of the current object-oriented paradigm in handling concurrency crosscutting concern. Section 2 discusses the challenges in aspectising concurrency. Section 3, will systematically aspectise concurrency, and implement concurrency in two paradigms: absolute object-orientation and aspect-orientation. Section 4 highlights requirements in aspectising concurrency, justify the soundness of new approach. The final section discusses other related work and future work.

2 Challenges in Aspectising the RTSJ Concurrency

There are two important issues of concurrency in the RTSJ. The first is the introduction of concurrency into objects, and the second is the interaction between concurrent objects, which among others is achieved by using synchronisation construct for mutual exclusion. There are two general approaches to introduce concurrency to the RTSJ objects. The first is by extending the super class *RealtimeThread* and overriding the *run()* method to express task. In the second approach, an object of a class implementing *Runnable* interface is passed as an argument to the *RealtimeThread*. [6, 3] investigated aspect orientation of interactions between concurrent objects; this paper will focus on aspect orienting concurrency introduction. The crosscutting constructs in the introduction of concurrency concern are the extension and implementation of *RealtimeThread* and *Runnable*. It is difficult to cleanly introduce concurrency to a non-concurrent object due to the levels of thread safety support in the non-concurrent environment. The five levels in Bloch's thread safety [7] are: immutable, thread-safe, conditionally thread-safe, thread-compatible, and thread-hostile.

Difficulty arises if thread-hostile classes are used in a non-concurrent environment, hence the transformation into concurrent objects should be prohibited. Conflicts would still arise at conditionally thread-safe and thread compatible levels and prior analysis would be needed to ascertain whether locking on the calling thread environment is required. Multiple locks on the same object by a thread results in the lock count on the object incremented by the Virtual Machine and decremented only when the lock associated with the object is released. This redundant locking is inefficient. Besides that, other real-time threads will not be able to obtain the lock associated with the object if not all the locks associated with the object are released by that real-time thread. In addition, transformation is also required between non thread specific constructs to thread specific constructs. For example, in a non-concurrent environment, an object may be required to be passed between two non-concurrent objects, where as in concurrent environment, the thread information might need to be passed between two concurrent environments.

3 Aspectising the RTSJ Concurrency

This paper specifically focuses on separating the concurrency in Bloch's thread-safe objects using aspectisation. We show this in the readers-writers problem, which is a standard concurrency control problem [8]. The transformation of non-concurrent implementation to concurrent implementation extending *RealtimeThread* can be done in 8 steps. Example implementation in the AspectJ[9], a Java based aspect-oriented language follows next.

Step 1: Inter-type declaration is used to effect static structural change to the non-concurrent class such that it now extends the *RealtimeThread* class.

Step 2: Inter-type declaration is used to introduce the run() method. Since a reference to the non-concurrent object is not known yet, only at step 4 the logic for the run() is specified. This is because the run() method may need to reference the non-concurrent object.

Step 3: Pointcut to the introduced run() method is specified. References to the non-concurrent objects can be elicited here.

Step 4: The logic for the RealtimeThread run() method is given by using the around advice and the pointcut from Step 3. The logic can also reference step 3 elicited objects. This effectively allows us to maintain the functional logic at the functional object and separated the non-functional concurrency to an aspect.

Step 5: Pointcut to the non-concurrent implementation is specified. This is the join point where the concurrency will be introduced.

Step 6: An around advice that setup and start the real-time thread at the join point identified by the step 5 pointcut is specified.

Step 7: Pointcut to the concurrent execution of the non-concurrent implementation is specified.

Step 8: Constraints specific to the concurrent environment (such as shared object's entry and exit protocols, and the pre and post conditions) are specified using before() and after() advice to the pointcut identified in step 7.

```
aspect ReaderConcExtend{
  declare parents: NonConcurrencyReader extends
  RealtimeThread; //Step 1
  PriorityParameters pp = new PriorityParameters(5);
  public void NonConcurrencyReader.run(){
  }//Step 2
  pointcut concurrency(NonConcurrencyReader ncr):
  target(ncr) && execution(void
  NonConcurrencyReader.run());//Step 3
```

```
pointcut directExecution(NonConcurrencyReader ncr):
target(ncr) && execution(void
NonConcurrencyReader.performReading()); //Step 5
pointcut concurrencyCall(NonConcurrencyReader ncr):
target(ncr) && cflow(execution(void
NonConcurrencyReader.run())) && execution(void
NonConcurrencyReader.performReading()); //Step 7
void around(NonConcurrencyReader
ncr):directExecution(ncr) &&
!cflow(adviceexecution()){
    ncr.setSchedulingParameters(pp);
    PeriodicParamaters per1 = new
    PeriodicParamaters(new RelativeTime(1000,0), new
    RelativeTime(100, 0), null, null, null, new
    DeadlineHandlerConc(ncr, "Reader"));
    ncr.setReleaseParameters(per1);
    ncr.start();
}//Step 6
before(NonConcurrencyReader ncr):  //Step 8 (1)
concurrencyCall(ncr){
  //preprocessing code for precondition checking
  //preprocessing code specifying reader's entry
  //protocol
}
after(NonConcurrencyReader ncr): // Step 8 (2)
concurrencyCall(ncr){
  //postprocessing code for postcondition checking
  //postprocessing code specifying reader's exit
  //protocol
}
void around(NonConcurrencyReader ncr):  //Step 4
concurrency(ncr){
  boolean go = true;
  while(go){
      ncr.performReading();
      go = RealtimeThread.waitForNextPeriod();
}}}
```

In the concurrency environment, real-time threads are susceptible to thread safety issues. Necessary guards and protections are needed depending on the attained level of Bloch's thread safety before a functional object is executed. Step 7 and 8 does exactly that by ensuring pre and post processing before and after concurrent execution of the functional object. For an example, in the before advice, it may perform precondition checks and try to obtain locks whereas in the after advice, it may perform postcondition checks and release locks.

The transformation aspect for the second approach is similar to the first approach. However, the following changes are necessary.

Step 1: The required class will have to implement *Runnable* interface using the inter-type declaration.

Step 6: RealtimeThread instance is created with the Runnable reference as part of the real-time thread setup in the around advice. Then it is started.

4   Review of the Approach

The requirements for aspect-oriented encapsulation of concurrency introduction are:-

- The software resources interfaced in a class to be weaved with concurrency aspect must conform to Bloch's "immutable" or "thread-safe" levels. Whilst interfacing resources of Bloch's hostile thread safety level should be avoided, care must be taken for objects of Bloch's conditionally thread-safe or thread compatible level.
- Real-time thread specific constructs such as the code to change a thread's priority should only be done by weaving. This will promote "information hiding".

It is naturally unlikely that non-concurrent functional components will be accessing thread-safe software resources in a sequential environment. Though it can, but it will result into unnecessary overheads of "synchronization". However, in a planned inclusion, it may be a help in concurrent environments. But it is not necessarily true for all scenarios. For an example, unlike its counterpart in a non-concurrent environment, the logic of functional component in the concurrent environment may need atomicity. Using software resources of thread-safe level alone will not guarantee atomicity [10]. Therefore, it is important to aspectise concurrency so that the synchronization for atomicity can be included in the aspect separately. Software resources with conditional thread-safe and thread compatible levels can still make safe concurrent execution with lock and unlock requests in the before and after advices. However, it will require more discipline to standardize the locking mechanism between thread accesses.

The ability of aspect-oriented implementation to execute concurrently just as how absolute object-oriented implementation does indeed signifies the soundness of the new approach. As the aspect only deals with concurrency introduction, the thread's behaviour is not a factor in determining the soundness of the implementation

5   Related Works and Future Work

The work that is closest to this paper is the one by [6]. The paper implemented both object and aspect oriented versions of concurrency synchronisation, and then compared them. In this paper, we aspectised concurrency introduction. Another related research was done in 1993 by Karaorman et al. [11]. They devise a technique to introduce concurrency to sequential object-oriented Eiffel language by using class libraries approach. Our work is a reverse of what they had done; we opted to separate concurrency from functional modules, whereas they integrated concurrency to functional modules.

Kienzle [12] presented the challenges in aspectising concurrent systems in particular transaction based systems. The issues were on the aspectisation of transaction semantic, transaction interface, and transaction mechanism. This paper's scope does not include transaction systems but rather general concurrency. We are able to show that aspectising concurrency concern from the concurrent functional components allows better object-oriented interpretation to the component. The functional component's design semantic is better analysed without the intermingling of non-functional concurrency.

Future work will include extending the ability to introduce concurrency to other objects having Bloch's "conditionally thread-safe" and "thread compatible" levels. A technique also needs to be developed to pass thread information during conversion of non-concurrent object to concurrent object. Assuming several of the "to-dos" stuffs are completed, we anticipate that concurrent-software development can be greatly simplified. Like how our current GUI application development is simplified with drag-and-drop features, future IDEs for concurrent-software will have "pluggable" concurrency to functional components. This will be the direction of our research.

References

1. Bollella, G., Gosling, J., Brosgol, B.M., Dibble, P., Furr, S., Hardin, D., Turnbull, M.: Real-Time Specification for Java. Addison Wesley, Reading (2000)
2. Raje, R.R., Zhong, M., Wang, T.: Case Study: A Distributed Concurrent System with AspectJ. ACM SIGAPP Applied Computing Review (2001)
3. Holmes, D., Noble, J., Potter, J.: Aspects of Synchronisation. In: Proc. of the Technology of Object-Oriented Languages and Systems (1997)
4. Hursch, W., Lopes, C.: Separation of Concerns, Technical Report, College of Computer Science, Northeastern University (1995)
5. Kiczales, G., Lamping, J., Mendhekar, A., Maeda, C., Lopes, C.V., Loingtier, J.-M., Irwin, J.: Aspect-Oriented Programming. In: Aksit, M., Matsuoka, S. (eds.) ECOOP 1997. LNCS, vol. 1241, pp. 220–242. Springer, Heidelberg (1997)
6. Tsang, S.L., Clarke, S., Baniassad, E.: An Evaluation of Aspect-Oriented Programming for Java-based Real-time Systems Development. In: Proc. of Seventh IEEE International Symposium (2004)
7. Bloch, J.: Effective Java: Programming Language Guide. Addison-Wesley, Reading (2001)
8. Wellings, A.J.: Concurrent and Real-Time Programming in Java. John Wiley & Sons, Chichester (2004)
9. The AspectJ Organisation: The AspectJ^{TM} Programming Guide, Xerox Corporation and Palo Alto Research Centre (2001)
10. Goetz, B., Peierls, T., Bloch, J., Bowbeer, J., Holmes, D., Lea, D.: Java Concurrency in Practice. Addison-Wesley, Reading (2006)
11. Karaorman, M., Bruno, J.: Introducing Concurrency to A Sequential Language. Communication of the ACM (1993)
12. Kienzle, J., Guerraoui, R.: AOP: Does it make sense? The case of concurrency and failures. In: Magnusson, B. (ed.) ECOOP 2002. LNCS, vol. 2374, pp. 37–61. Springer, Heidelberg (2002)

An Asymptotic Performance/Energy Analysis and Optimization of Multi-core Architectures

Jeong-Gun Lee[1], Eungu Jung[2], and Wook Shin[3]

[1] Dept. of Computer Engineering, Hallym University, South Korea
Jeonggun.Lee@hallym.ac.kr
[2] Attached Institute of ETRI, South Korea
[3] KDDI R&D Laboratories, Inc., Japan

Abstract. In this paper, we develop asymptotic analysis models for better understanding the performance and energy consumption characteristics of multi-core processor architectures using Amdahl's law in order to foresee their performance and energy impacts for given workload characteristics (e.g. available parallelism). Through the asymptotic analysis and optimization based on the models proposed in this paper, we can make system-level architectural design decisions on "the number of cores" and "core size" of a multi-core architecture with regarding performance and energy consumption at an initial phase of designs.

1 Introduction

It is getting harder to improve the performance of traditional monolithic cores as the number of transistors integrated on the monolithic cores increases due to the limit of instruction level parallelism. The approach of integrating more functional units to a single core and increasing clock frequencies has met the saturating limit of performance. This phenomenon is called *"diminishing return"* [1]. In order to cope with the severe diminishing return problem and better utilize the large number of available transistors provided by advanced CMOS technology, industries have started to produce multi-core processors providing high-performance, energy-efficient and reliable computation. More than one hundred cores are expected to be integrated into a single chip by 2015 [2].

In this paper, asymptotic analytical models for evaluating performance and energy-consumption of a multi-core architecture are derived *for exploring a high-level design space of a multi-core architecture*, and optimizations are performed based on the proposed analytic models. In particular, we issue design problems such as *"how many cores and how powerful cores do we need to get the best performance or minimum energy consumption of a multi-core system for a given workload ?"* and we try to answer the question by using the proposed analytical models.

The analytic model-based design space exploration is important to understand the fundamental relationship between the core configurations of multi-core designs and their performance and energy consumption characteristics. Through

V. Garg, R. Wattenhofer, and K. Kothapalli (Eds.): ICDCN 2009, LNCS 5408, pp. 85–90, 2009.

the asymptotic analysis based on the models proposed in this paper, we can make the architectural design decisions such as *"the number of cores"* and *"core size"*. Further, with the proposed models, we expect that we can probe the possible research direction of optimizing the performance and energy of multi-core architectures.

- **Related Work:** The Amdahl's law has been used to give the speedup estimates we can achieve from multi-core architectures in [1,4], but they did not perform further in-depth analysis on the issue. Very recently, Amdahl's law based performance and energy analyses have been published in [5,6]. In [5], simple architecture models for three different types of heterogeneous multi-core processors are constructed and corresponding performance equations are derived. Finally numerical performance simulations have been performed. In [6], different clock frequencies are assumed to be used for executing serial code and parallel code. Then, two optimal clock frequencies for running serial code and parallel code are derived in order to minimize energy consumption. Their main focus was the impact of dynamic clock frequency scaling on energy consumption of multi-core architecture.

2 Multi-core's Speedup

To evaluate the performance tradeoff of possible configurations of multi-core architectures including different core size and different number of cores under resource-constrained design, a speedup analysis model of the multi-core architectures is derived based on an Amdahl's law and it can be described in the following equation.

$$Sp = \frac{\frac{IC}{\text{perf}(n)}}{\frac{IC \cdot s}{\text{perf}(r)} + \frac{IC \cdot (1-s)}{\left(\frac{n}{r}\right) \cdot \text{perf}(r)}} \tag{1}$$

In this equation, s is the percentage of serial codes as we mentioned before and 'n' denotes the total number of available transistor resources. The number of transistors allocated per core is denoted by 'r'. The function perf(r) models the performance of a core utilizing r transistor resources. IC is the total number of instructions in applications. The number of cores is easily calculated by n/r (only integer number of cores is valid).

To evaluate Sp, we need a model for perf(r). The function, perf(r), can be measured in *instruction per second*, and thus the perf(r) can be expressed in the product of *instruction per cycle* (IPC) and clock frequency f (that is, perf(r) = $IPC \times f$). In [7], we derived the function as "perf(r) = $k \cdot G^{\beta}$" with two parameters k and β. If "perf(r) = $k \cdot r^{\beta}$" is applied to Eq. 1 then the speedup equation based on an Amdahl's law for a resource-constrained multi-core architecture can be rewritten in the followings.

$$Sp = \frac{\frac{IC}{k \cdot n^{\beta}}}{\frac{IC \cdot s}{k \cdot r^{\beta}} + \frac{IC \cdot (1-s)}{\left(\frac{n}{r}\right) \cdot k \cdot r^{\beta}}} = \frac{\frac{1}{n^{\beta}}}{\frac{s}{r^{\beta}} + \frac{(1-s)}{\left(\frac{n}{r}\right) \cdot r^{\beta}}} \tag{2}$$

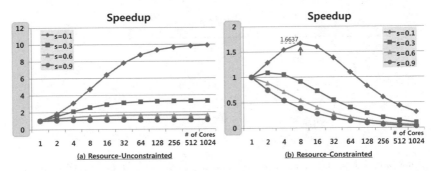

Fig. 1. Speedup as the number of cores increases when resources are constrained

In a resource unconstrained case as shown in Fig. 1(a), around 10 times speedup is achieved when 90% parallelism is extractable from applications [7]. On the other hand, in resource-constrained multi-core architectures (β is set to 0.5 for Fig. 1(b)), it is interesting to see that the speedup is quite smaller than that of the resource-unconstrained case. Maximum speedup is around 1.66 (66% improvement) at the system of employing **eight** cores when applications are exploiting 90% parallelism from their instruction codes. This is a very disappointing result when compared with the resource unconstrained case.

• **Optimal Core Partitioning for Performance:** For a given resource restriction, by finding r satisfying $\delta Sp/\delta r = 0$, we can get an optimum solution, r (optimum number of resources allocated to a core). From Eq. 2, by solving the equation $\delta Sp/\delta r = 0$, r_{opt} and Sp_{opt} can be derived as $r_{opt} = \frac{n \cdot s \cdot \beta}{(1-s)\cdot(1-\beta)}$ and $Sp_{opt} = \left(\frac{1-\beta}{s}\right)^{1-\beta} \cdot \left(\frac{\beta}{1-s}\right)^{\beta}$, respectively.

When r_{opt} is found, the optimum number of cores is simply calculated by $\frac{n}{r_{opt}}$ and described in $nc_{opt} = \frac{n}{r_{opt}} = \frac{(1-s)\cdot(1-\beta)}{s \cdot \beta}$.

3   Energy Models of Multi-core Architecture

• **Problem Formulation:** Fig. 2 shows the concept of normalized workload and execution time. ① shows the serial portion (s) and parallel portion ($p = 1 - s$) of total workload normalized to '1'. ② illustrates the normalized execution time when a multi-core architecture is designed using fixed (limited) amount of transistor resources. T_s and T_p are normalized execution times of serial code portion and parallel code portion, respectively.

If the number of cores increases, the number of transistors allocated to one core decreases due to the limit of resources. As a result, the performance of individual cores is degraded and the time to execute serial workload increases. On the other hand, the execution time of parallel code portion can be reduced thanks to parallel execution. This is described in the graph ② of Fig. 2.

Assuming that x is used to denote the speedup obtained by employing a multi-core architecture. Then, total execution time is '$1/x$', and the execution time to

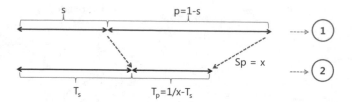

Fig. 2. Normalized workload and time

complete parallel portion, T_p, is expressed in '$1/x - T_s$'. If T_s is replaced by t, T_p can be redefined as $(1/x - t)$. In resource-constrained multi-core architectures, T_s increases as the number of cores increases since the transistor resource assigned to the individual cores is reduced.

In general, energy consumption can be described as the product of execution time and power consumption. Power consumption is expressed in a well-known equation, $C_{eff} \cdot V_{DD}^2 \cdot f$, where C_{eff} is an effective capacitance considering switching activity, V_{DD} is a supply voltage, and f is a clock frequency. It is well known that f is proportional to a supply voltage (V_{DD}) and thus, power consumption can be modeled asymptotically by f^α where α is a value around '3'. The α can be varying according to a process technology and parameters. In this paper, the frequency, f, is derived from the amount of transistor resources assigned to an individual core.

• **Frequency modelling for an energy model:** In a normalized system model, total workload (that is, total instruction count) and total execution time are normalized to 1. In this model, the maximum clock frequency also has a relative speed of 1 [6]. In our normalized model, f is expressed in s/t for serial code portion and $\frac{1-s}{(1/x-t) \cdot (n/r)}$ for parallel code portion with slight modification of the equations given in [6]. Note that, in [6], clock frequencies for serial and parallel code portions are different to the other, and it means *dynamic clock scaling* is utilized in the model.

Since we do not consider clock frequency scaling, clock frequencies for serial and parallel code portions are same to the other. Thus, we use the frequency f expressed in s/t for the both of serial code and parallel code portions. It is noteworthy that the clock frequencies are depending on the number of transistor resources allocated to a core (that is, core size) in our model. The clock frequency of a core utilizing r transistors, f_r, can be expressed in $s/t = s/\frac{s}{(r/n)^\beta} = (r/n)^\beta$ when t is normalized execution time expressed in $\frac{s}{(r/n)^\beta}$ $(= \frac{s}{perf(r)})$.

• **Energy Model with Resource Constraints:** By combining the basic energy equation presented in [6] and parameters f_s, f_p, T_s and T_p presented before, new energy model can be derived as $E(r) = T_s \cdot f_s^\alpha + (n/r) \cdot T_p \cdot f_p^\alpha + E_{Static}$.

The first term indicates dynamic energy consumption of a core running a serial code and the second term expresses dynamic energy consumption in n/r cores executing a parallel code. The last term is for modelling static energy by leakage current.

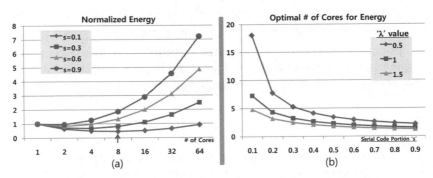

Fig. 3. (a) Energy consumption as the number of cores increases, (b) Optimum number of cores for minimum energy consumption

When T_s is set to a variable t, T_p and E_{Static} can be expressed in '$1/x - t$' and '$\lambda \cdot (1/x)$', respectively. The λ is used for denoting the proportional ratio between dynamic energy and static energy. The λ is a parameter depending on semiconductor technology. $1/x$ is total execution time, where x is speedup achieved by multiple cores. The f_s and f_p are set to f_r. Then, $E(r)$ can be rewritten in $E(r) = t \cdot f_s^\alpha + (n/r) \cdot (1/x - t) \cdot f_p^\alpha + \lambda \cdot (1/x)$.

The static energy, E_{Static}, is the leakage current consumed during $1/x$. By employing multi-core parallel processing, the total execution time is reduced by factor of speedup, x, and the corresponding static energy is reduced as well. Now, $E(r)$ can be rewritten in "$E(r) = t \cdot (r^\beta/n^\beta)^\alpha + (n/r) \cdot (1/x - t) \cdot (r^\beta/n^\beta)^\alpha + \lambda \cdot (1/x)$" when f_r is r^β/n^β.

Fig. 3(a) shows normalized energy consumption of a multi-core processor when λ is set to 1. With respect to energy consumption, the optimum number of cores are observed to be less than 10 cores when s is in the range between 0.1 and 0.9. When s is 0.9, the optimum number of cores is **eight** and the normalized energy consumption of the eight-core system is about 0.34 (34% of total energy consumption of single monolithic core processor). It is also noteworthy that the optimum number of cores with respect to performance and energy is relatively smaller than the expected.

● **Optimal Multi-Core Partitioning for Energy:** The equation "$\delta E(r)/\delta r$" includes a term, $r^{\alpha \cdot \beta}$, and thus it is not a polynomial equation. In consequence, we cannot directly derive r satisfying $\delta E(r)/\delta r = 0$. To solve this difficulty, we assign generally accepted values to α and β in order to make the equation in a polynomial form. When frequency is proportional to a supply voltage, α can be set to '3' and the variable β is set to '2/3' in order to make α/β to be a known integer value. Since the normal value of β lies in the range between 0.4 and 0.7, '2/3' is a reasonable value for the β in a general processor architecture [7]. The derived equation at $\alpha = 3, \beta = 2/3$ is as follows.

$$\left. \frac{\delta E(r)}{\delta r} \right|_{\alpha=3, \beta=2/3} = \frac{\frac{1}{3} \cdot r \cdot (1-s) \cdot \lambda + \frac{2}{3} \cdot n \cdot \left(2 \cdot \frac{r^2}{n^2} - s \cdot \lambda\right)}{n^{1/3} \cdot r^{5/3}} \tag{3}$$

Finally, by solving Eq. 3, the number of cores in a optimum energy-efficient multi-core processor is expressed by $nc_{opt} = \frac{8}{\left\{ \sqrt{\lambda} \cdot \sqrt{32 \cdot s + \lambda - 2 \cdot s \cdot \lambda + s^2 \cdot \lambda} - (1-s) \right\}}$.

The optimum number of cores in a multi-core processor is presented in Fig. 3(b) with some possible values of s and λ. The graph implies that the ratio between dynamic energy and static energy has significant impact on optimal core size.

4 Conclusion

For better understanding those performance and energy characteristics of the multi-core architectures regarding different core configurations, in this paper, we developed asymptotic analysis models for investigating optimum core partitioning of resource-constrained multi-core architectures. Although the models are simple, through the asymptotic analysis, we foresee their optimum core configurations and performance/energy benefits for given workload characteristics (e.g. available parallelism). We hope that the model guides the architectural decision and research direction of optimizing the performance and energy consumption of multi-core architectures.

Acknowledgement

This work was financially supported by IT Scholarship Program supervised by IITA & MIC, Republic of Korea.

References

1. Borkar, S.: Thousand Core Chips A Technology Perspective. In: ACM/IEEE Design Automation Conference (DAC), pp. 746–749 (June 2007)
2. Semiconductor Industry Association, International Technology Roadmap for Semiconductors (2007)
3. Amdahl, G.M.: Validity of single-processor approach to achieving large-scale computing capability. In: Proceedings of AFIPS Conference, pp. 483–485 (1967)
4. Asanovic, K., Bodik, R., Catanzaro, B., Gebis, J., Husbands, P., Keutzer, K., Patterson, D., Plishker, W., Shalf, J., Williams, S., Yelick, K.: The Landscape of Parallel Computing Research: A View from Berkeley, UCB Technical Paper (2006)
5. Hill, M.D., Marty, M.R.: Amdahl's Law in the Multicore Era, Univ. of Wisconsin Computer Sciences Technical Report CS-TR-2007-1593 (April 2007)
6. Cho, S., Melhem, R.: Corollaries to Amdahl's Law for Energy. IEEE Computer Architecture Letters (December 2007)
7. Lee, J.-G., Jung, E., Lee, D.-W.: Asymptotic Performance Analysis and Optimization of Resource-Constrained Multi-Core Architectures. In: Proceedings of the IEEE International Conference on Microelectronics (December 2008) (to appear)

A Cost-Optimal Algorithm for Guard Zone Problem

Ranjan Mehera[1] and Rajat K. Pal[2]

[1] Subex Limited, Adarsh Tech Park, Outer Ring Road, Devarabisannalli,
Bangalore 560 037, India
[2] Dept. of Computer Sc. & Engg., University of Calcutta, 92, A. P. C. Road,
Kolkata 700 009, India
ranjan.mehera@gmail.com, rajatkp@vsnl.net

Abstract. Given a simple polygon P, its guard zone G (of width r) is a closed region consisting of straight line segments and circular arcs (of radius r) bounding the polygon P such that there exists no pair of points p (on the boundary of P) and q (on the boundary of G) having their Euclidean distance $d(p,q)$ less than r. In this paper we have designed a time-optimal sequential algorithm to solve the guard zone problem, and developed a cost-optimal parallel counterpart of the same problem for solving it in distributed environment.

Keywords: Guard zone problem, Minkowski sum, Convolution, Analytical geometry, Coordinate geometry, Computational geometry, Resizing of VLSI circuits.

1 Introduction

Guard zone problem is well defined in literature as an application of computational geometry. Often this problem is also known as safety zone problem [6]. Given a simple polygon P, its *guard zone* G (of width r) is a closed region consisting of straight line segments and circular arcs (of radius r) bounding the polygon P such that there exists no pair of points p (on the boundary of P) and q (on the boundary of G) having their Euclidean distance $d(p,q)$ less than r.

In this paper we design a time-optimal sequential algorithm for finding the guard zone of an arbitrarily shaped simple polygon, as shown in Figure 1. A *simple polygon* is defined as the polygon in which no two boundary edges cross each other. In addition, in this paper we also develop a cost-optimal parallel algorithm for the guard zone problem for solving the problem in a distributed computing environment.

In this context, it is worth mentioning that, given two polygons P and Q in R^2, their *Minkowski sum* [8] is defined as $P \oplus Q = (p+q \mid p \in P, q \in Q)$, where $p+q$ denotes the vector sum of the vectors p and q, i.e., if $p = (p_x, p_y)$ and $q = (q_x, q_y)$, then we have $p+q = (p_x+q_x, p_y+q_y)$. The *guard zone* (of width r) of a convex polygon P is surely obtained by taking the Minkowski sum of the polygon P and a circle C of radius r. But for a simple nonconvex polygon (i.e., a simple polygon with some concave vertices), the *guard zone* is a super set of the region A obtained by taking the Minkowski sum of the polygon P and the circle C. Here the area indicated by the Minkowski sum may be composed of the guard zone of the polygon P with some holes inside it such that the boundaries of the holes also satisfy the guard zone property [6].

V. Garg, R. Wattenhofer, and K. Kothapalli (Eds.): ICDCN 2009, LNCS 5408, pp. 91–98, 2009.

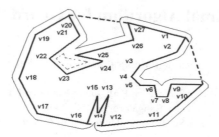

Fig. 1. Guard zone of a simple polygon

2 Literature Survey

If P is a simple polygon and G is its guard zone of width r, then the boundary of G is composed of straight-line segments and circular arcs of radius r, where each straight-line segment is parallel to an edge of the polygon at a distance r apart from that edge, and each circular arc of radius r is centered at a (convex) vertex of the polygon. The boundary of a guard zone describes a *simple* region in the sense that no two edges (straight line segment(s) and/or circular arc(s)) on its boundary intersect in (or pass through) their interior. This has been explained in Figure 1. The problem originates in the context of resizing of VLSI layout design [11].

The computational complexity of the Minkowski sum of two arbitrary simple polygons P and Q is $O(m^2n^2)$ [1], where m and n are the number of vertices of these two polygons, respectively. In particular, if one of the two polygons is convex, the complexity of the Minkowski sum reduces to $O(mn)$. In [3], a number of results are proposed on the Minkowski sum problem when one of the polygons is monotone.

An algorithm for finding the outer face of the Minkowski sum of two simple polygons is presented in [10]. It uses the concept of convolution, and the running time of the algorithm is $O((k+(m+n)\sqrt{l})\log^2(m+n))$, where m and n are the number of vertices of the two polygons, k and l represent the size of the convolution and the number of cycles in the convolution, respectively. In the worst case, k may be $O(mn)$. If one of the polygons is convex, the algorithm runs in $O(k\log^2(m+n))$ time.

In this context, a linear time algorithm is developed for finding the boundary of the minimum area guard zone of an arbitrarily shaped simple polygon in [6]. This algorithm uses the idea of Chazelle's linear time triangulation algorithm [2], and requires space complexity of $O(n)$ as well, where n is the number of vertices of the polygon. After having the triangulation step, this algorithm uses only dynamic linear and binary tree data structures.

3 Formulation of the Problem and the Algorithm

A simple polygon may contain both convex and concave vertices in it. We define these vertices as follows: A vertex v of a polygon P is defined as *convex (concave)*, if the angle between its associated edges inside the polygon, i.e., the internal angle at vertex v, is less than or equal to (greater than) $180°$. In Figure 2, angle θ_1 (between edges a and b) at vertex (x_2,y_2) is convex whereas angle θ_2 (between edges c and d) at vertex (x_4,y_4) is concave.

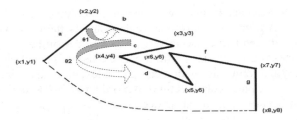

Fig. 2. Part of a polygon with vertices (x_1,y_1) through (x_8,y_8), and edges *a* through *g*; the dotted line indicates the inner portion of the polygon

Let us consider a simple polygon P with n vertices and n edges. A polygon P is given implies that the coordinates of the successive vertices of the polygon are given; where no two polygonal edges cross each other rather two consecutive polygonal edges intersect only at a polygonal vertex. We can assume that a portion of this polygon is as shown in Figure 2. To know whether an angle θ, inside the polygon, is either convex or concave at vertex v, we do a constant time computation of determining the value (of θ) at vertex v. Thus, all the n internal angles of P are identified as convex or concave in $O(n)$ time.

At this point, we can conclude that the guard zone is computed only with the help of n straight line segments and n circular arcs, if all the n internal angles of the polygon are convex. But for a given simple polygon, we may have concave internal angles as well, in P. Problems may arise in computing guard zone for those portions of polygon P with concave internal angles. In this context, we introduce the concept of notch as defined below.

A *notch* is a polygonal region outside polygon P that is formed with a chain of edges of P starting and terminating at two vertices of a false hull edge [6]. A *false hull edge* is a hull edge introduced in obtaining a convex hull, shown in Figure 1. Here we have three false hull edges drawn by dotted lines, between vertices v_1 and v_{10}, v_{12} and v_{16}, and v_{20} and v_{27}. A *convex hull* is a convex polygon (having no concave internal angle) of minimum area with all the points residing on the boundary or inside the polygon for a given set of arbitrary points on a plane.

Clearly, if P is a given simple polygon and CH(P) denotes the convex hull of polygon P, then the area CH(P)–P consists of a number of disjoint notches outside polygon P. According to this definition, a notch is formed outside the polygon in Figure 3, below the dotted line v_2v_8, as this edge is a false hull edge.

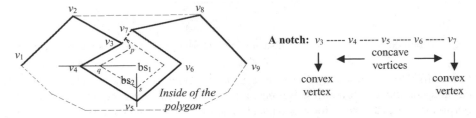

Fig. 3. A notch is formed between vertices v_3 and v_7, and a guard zone is obtained for this notch

For the sake of convenience in developing our algorithm *Guard_Zone*, we redefine notch as follows. A *notch* is a polygonal region outside the polygon that is starting and terminating between two consecutive convex vertices of the polygon that are not adjacent. That means a notch starts with a convex vertex, goes through one or more concave vertices, and terminates with a convex vertex, along the edges (and vertices) of the polygon (in one particular direction). According to this definition, in Figure 3, a notch is formed between polygonal vertices v_3 and v_7, as v_4, v_5, and v_6 are concave vertices whereas v_3 and v_7 are convex.

Now we develop a time-optimal (sequential) algorithm *Guard_Zone* for computing a guard zone G of a simple polygon P, and in developing the algorithm, we consider the edges of P one after another and do the following. Consider edge v_2v_3 in Figure 3. Here both the vertices v_2 and v_3 are convex. So a line segment parallel to v_2v_3 and of length same as v_2v_3, for G is computed at a distance r apart the polygonal edge with a circular arc of radius r centered at vertex v_2. Clearly, the line segment parallel to v_2v_3 is a tangent to the circular arc centered at v_2.

Then consider edge v_3v_4. Here v_3 is a convex vertex whereas v_4 is concave. So, the length of the line segment of G parallel to v_3v_4 is less than that of v_3v_4. Surely the line segment of G touches (as a tangent) the circular arc centered at v_3 at point p (in Figure 3), but on the other end (near v_4) the line segment of G is prolonged up to point q. Point q is the intersection point of the bisection bs_1 (of the angle at v_4), and the line segment of G passes through p and parallel to v_3v_4.

Now consider polygonal edge v_4v_5, where both the vertices v_4 and v_5 are concave. So it is not required to draw any circular arc here for this portion of G. The line segment of G is obtained by computing a line going through q up to s, where s is the intersection of the line segment of G parallel to v_4v_5 and the bisection bs_2 of the internal angle at vertex v_5. Note that the length of qs is less than that of v_4v_5.

It may so happen that the length of v_4v_5 is sufficiently small and the internal angles at v_4 and v_5 are large enough such that the distance between the intersection point f of bs_1 and bs_2 to v_4v_5 is less than the distance between the intersection point g of the two line segments of G parallel to v_3v_4 and v_5v_6 to v_4v_5 (see Figure 4). In this case, there is no line segment of G parallel to v_4v_5. In general, instead of a single edge like v_4v_5, several edges or even several notches of a simple polygon may be there for which no guard zone is distinguishingly computed.

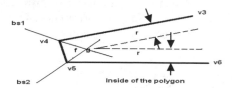

Fig. 4. A portion of the guard zone without any line segment parallel to the polygonal edge v_4v_5

Needless to mention that all these measures are achievable with the help of analytical and coordinate geometries. Besides, all these computations required to obtain a portion of the guard zone for a polygonal edge or for a polygonal vertex can be performed in constant time.

Computational Complexity of Algorithm *Guard_Zone*

It is easy to observe that the guard zone of an n-vertex convex polygon is a convex region with n straight line segments and n circular arcs only, and the time required for computing the guard zone of such a polygon is $O(n)$.

The situation is complicated, if concave vertices rather notches belong to a simple polygon. For the presence of a concave polygonal vertex, we bisect the angle and draw a line parallel to the edge under consideration. For a polygonal edge or an angle of the polygon, either convex or concave, all these computations take constant time. Therefore, for a polygon of n vertices (and n edges), the worst-case time required in computing a guard zone of a simple polygon is $O(n)$.

The remaining part of our algorithm is to exclude the portions of guard zone G that are at a distance less than r apart from some edge or vertex other than the edge or vertex for which the segments of G were computed earlier. This could also be realized in time $O(n)$.

This is also worthwhile to mention that the lower bound of computing a guard zone of a simple polygon of n vertices is $\Omega(n)$, as we have to consider each of the n vertices (and n edges) exactly once. Hence we establish the following theorem.

Theorem 1: *Algorithm Guard_Zone computes a guard zone of a simple polygon of n vertices in $\Theta(n)$ time. This algorithm is time-optimal, as the lower bound of the problem of computing a guard zone of a simple polygon of n vertices is $\Omega(n)$ and the worst-case computational complexity of algorithm Guard_Zone is $O(n)$.*

4 A Cost-Optimal Algorithm for Distributed Environment

In this section, we develop a constant time, cost-optimal algorithm *Parallel_Guard_Zone* for computing a guard zone of a simple polygon with n vertices in a distributed environment. This algorithm is based on the sequential algorithm developed in Section 3. Here, instead of using a single processor, we use $O(n)$ processors on a CRCW PRAM [7].

At the very beginning of our algorithm, we keep the n vertices, $v_1, v_2, \ldots, v_n$, as input of a given polygon P in n (shared) memory locations [4]. A processor P_i, $1 \le i \le n$, concurrently reads the coordinates of vertices v_{i-1}, v_i, v_{i+1}, and v_{i+2}, and computes the equations of edges (v_{i-1},v_i), (v_i,v_{i+1}), and (v_{i+1},v_{i+2}) along with their lengths. We may rename the edges as e_{i-1}, e_i, and e_{i+1}, respectively. Then processor P_i computes the internal angles flanking edge e_i, at vertices v_i and v_{i+1}. It is easy to understand that for $i = 1$, $i-1 = n$, and for $i = n$, $i+1 = 1$, etc. as we have indexed the vertices and kept into memory.

In our algorithm, primarily processor P_i is responsible for considering one of the four possibilities, as explained in Figure 5, and draws portions of G for vertex v_i and edge e_i, if they exist. If line segment(s) and/or circular arc(s) of G intersect, the processor excludes these portions of G drawn by itself that are at a distance less than r apart from a polygonal edge or vertex (outside the polygon).

Consider a polygonal edge e_i with its end vertices v_i and v_{i+1}, either convex or concave (see Figures 5(a)-5(d)). In developing the parallel algorithm, P_i draws a circular arc of radius r centered at such a vertex if it is convex, or bisects the internal angle at such a vertex if it is concave. Then P_i draws a line parallel to e_i at a distance r apart from e_i (outside the polygon), in a way analogous to its sequential counterpart, algorithm *Guard_Zone*, described in Section 3.

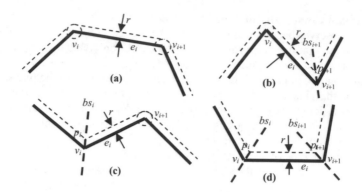

Fig. 5. Computation of guard zone for a polygonal vertex v_i and a polygonal edge $e_i = (v_i, v_{i+1})$. (a) Edge e_i with both its end vertices v_i and v_{i+1} convex. (b) Edge e_i with its end vertex v_i convex and v_{i+1} concave. (c) Edge e_i with its end vertex v_i concave and v_{i+1} convex. (d) Edge e_i with both its end vertices v_i and v_{i+1} concave.

Now it is easy to develop the parallel algorithm that computes a guard zone of a simple polygon in constant time, and that can be executed in a distributed computing environment. The remaining part of the algorithm is to exclude the portions of line segment(s) and/or circular arc(s) of G that are at a distance less than r apart from a polygonal edge or vertex (if such line segment(s) and/or circular arc(s) of G intersect, outside the polygon) as described earlier.

Computational Complexity of Algorithm *Parallel_Guard_Zone*
Now we analyze the time complexity of algorithm *Parallel_Guard_Zone*, for computing a guard zone G of a simple polygon P in parallel. In order to do that we consider a *Concurrent Read Concurrent Write* (*CRCW*) *Parallel Random Access Machine* (*PRAM*) in a *Single Instruction stream Multiple Data stream* (*SIMD*) parallel computing environment [5,9], where a control unit issues an instruction to be executed simultaneously by all processors on their respective data.

In our algorithm we primarily perform the following accession of memory and computation required. We keep all the coordinates of n vertices of polygon P in $O(n)$ shared memory locations of the PRAM. A *Concurrent Read* (*CR*) instruction is executed by $O(n)$ processors, where two or more processors can read from the same memory location at the same time. This instruction is executed constant times as the coordinate of a vertex is read by four processors. As for example, the coordinate of vertex v_{i+2} is accessed by processors P_i through P_{i+3}.

Thus when instruction CR is executed, $O(n)$ processors simultaneously read the contents of $O(n)$ memory locations such that processor P_i reads the coordinates of vertices v_{i-1}, v_i, v_{i+1}, and v_{i+2}. This could also be executed using an *Exclusive Read* (*ER*) instruction in constant time by $O(n)$ processors, where processors gain access to memory locations for the purpose of reading in a one-to-one fashion (as CR includes ER as a special case).

Then processor P_i computes the edges (v_{i-1},v_i), (v_i,v_{i+1}), and (v_{i+1},v_{i+2}) (i.e., e_{i-1}, e_i, and e_{i+1}, respectively), and computes the internal angles at vertices v_i and v_{i+1}. So, processor P_i finds one of the four possible situations, as explained in Figure 5. Accordingly, the processor draws circular arc(s), if the angle(s) is (are) convex and/or bisects the angle(s) if it is (they are) concave, as it has clearly been described above. In addition, the processor draws a line parallel to e_i at a distance r apart from the polygonal edge (outside the polygon), as a portion of G.

Hence, a guard zone for polygon P is computed in constant time, which may contain several redundant portions of (overlapping) line segments due to presence of notch(es) in P. To remove these undesired portions of G, we execute a *Concurrent Write* (*CW*) instruction in the form of *COMBINED SUM* CW by O(n) processors, where two or more processors can write into the same memory location at the same time. Moreover, when this instruction is executed, in our algorithm, O(n) processors simultaneously write into one memory location, whereas the memory location involved can be written into by all the processors.

It is now straightforward to verify that the running time of this algorithm is O(1). As O(n) processors are involved in computing a guard zone, the cost of algorithm *Parallel_Guard_Zone* is O(n), which is same as the worst-case computational complexity of the sequential version of this algorithm that is time-optimal (see Theorem 1). Hence we conclude the following theorem.

Theorem 2: *Algorithm Parallel_Guard_Zone computes a guard zone of a simple polygon of n vertices in constant time. This algorithm is cost-optimal, as the cost of the algorithm is O(n), which is same as the worst-case running time of the best known sequential algorithm for solving the problem of computing a guard zone of a simple polygon of n vertices.*

5 Conclusion

In this paper we have considered the problem of computing a guard zone of a simple polygon, and developed a time-optimal (sequential) algorithm for computing the same that uses the concepts of analytical and coordinate geometries. This problem finds several applications in practice. In VLSI layout design, the circuit components are not supposed to be placed much closer to each other in order to avoid electrical effects among them [11]. The guard zone problem finds another important application in the automatic monitoring of metal cutting tools. In this paper we also have developed a cost-optimal (parallel) algorithm for solving the guard zone problem using the same set of geometric concepts for its implementation in a distributed computing environment. Our work can also be extended for computing a guard zone of a three dimensional solid object.

References

1. de Berg, M., van Kreveld, M., Overmars, M., Schwarzkopf, O.: Computational Geometry: Algorithms and Applications. Springer, Berlin (1997)
2. Chazelle, B.: Triangulating a Simple Polygon in Linear Time. Discrete Computational Geometry 6, 485–524 (1991)
3. Hernandez-Barrera, A.: Computing the Minkowski Sum of Monotone Polygons. IEICE Trans. on Information Systems E80-D(2), 218–222 (1996)

4. Hwang, K.: Advanced Computer Architecture: Parallelism, Scalability, Programmability. McGraw Hill, New York (1993)
5. Hwang, K., Briggs, F.A.: Computer Architecture and Parallel Processing. McGraw-Hill, New York (1984)
6. Nandy, S.C., Bhattacharya, B.B., Hernandez-Barrera, A.: Safety Zone Problem. Journal of Algorithms 37, 538–569 (2000)
7. Patterson, D.A., Hennesy, J.L.: Computer Architecture: A Quantitative Approach, 2nd edn. Morgan Kaufman, San Francisco (1996)
8. Pottmann, H., Wallner, J.: Computational Line Geometry. Springer, Berlin (1997)
9. Quinn, M.J.: Parallel Computing: Theory and Practice, 2nd edn. McGraw-Hill, New York (1994)
10. Ramkumar, G.D.: An Algorithm to Compute the Minkowski Sum Outer Face of Two Simple Polygons. In: Proc. of the 12th Annual ACM Symposium on Computational Geometry, pp. 234–241. Association for Computing Machinery, New York (1996)
11. Sherwani, N.A.: Algorithms for VLSI Physical Design Automation. Kluwer Academic, Boston (1993)

Underlay Aware Resiliency in P2P Overlays

S.D. Madhu Kumar[1], Umesh Bellur[1], and V.K. Govindan[2]

[1] Department of Computer Science and Engineering,
Indian Institute of Technology Bombay
Powai, Mumbai - 400076, India
[2] Department of Computer Science and Engineering,
National Institute of Technology Calicut
Calicut-673601, Kerala, India
{madhu,umesh}@cse.iitb.ac.in,
vkg@nitc.ac.in
http://www.cse.iitb.ac.in/~madhu,
http://www.cse.iitb.ac.in/~umesh

Abstract. Modern distributed applications that run on P2P overlays need the overlay to be resilient to failures in the underlying communications network. An example application is that of event dissemination where the P2P overlay (the event broker network) delivers events published by a client to subscribers based on subscription filters. Achieving high availability requires that the overlay be aware of, and utilize the path redundancies in the underlying physical network. In addition, the overlay should be self organizing, as broker nodes may dynamically join or leave the network and centralized control is not an option in large scale networks. In this paper, we present **Trimarg**, an efficient distributed algorithm for achieving a self organizing overlay with an availability degree of three. Our algorithm is based on a graph theoretic foundation for highly available overlay networks and is designed to handle the concurrency issues of a large scale distributed system. The resulting unstructured P2P overlay ensures **3-degree of availability** in the presence of node and link failures in the underlying physical network. We have proved the correctness of the algorithm and analyzed its complexity to show that the time complexity is $O(diameter * degree)^2$ of the network and the message complexity is $O(diameter * degree)$. Our algorithm is the first of its kind to deal with concurrency issues and self organizing capabilities of the resultant overlay.

Keywords: P2P overlays, Event Broker Networks, Availability, Distributed Algorithm.

1 Introduction

Data Dissemination using push models of events is a typical example of an application that uses P2P overlays. Event brokers [1] (used for routing events from publishers to subscribers) form an overlay that is a logical graph over the physical network (referred to as the underlay) that consists of broker nodes as well as other (non-broker) nodes. Such overlay networks free the application designer from having to understand the intricacies and variations of the underlying physical network. Routing is done at the level

V. Garg, R. Wattenhofer, and K. Kothapalli (Eds.): ICDCN 2009, LNCS 5408, pp. 99–113, 2009.

of the overlay without references to the physical path (overlays cannot dictate IP layer routing).

In recent years, the focus on overlay QoS has revealed the need for the overlay to have greater control over the physical network on which it depends, to deliver its QoS requirements like event delivery latencies. This has led to the notion of underlay aware overlay networks [2]. Such networks include a partial knowledge of the physical nodes and links corresponding to the paths between overlay nodes, and/or mechanisms for extracting knowledge from the underlying network layers to provide more deterministic routing services. Much research has been done on using underlay information for improving latency and reducing bandwidth requirements [2]. However availability of the overlay network, which is a necessary condition for guaranteed event delivery, bears closer scrutiny. Availability is defined not only with respect to redundancies in the overlay paths between any two overlay nodes but also with respect to node-disjointness of the underlay paths that represent the overlay paths under consideration. The challenge in building such an underlay-aware, available overlay stems from three major factors.

1. The asynchronous distributed nature and the dynamism of the network.
2. The size of the underlay makes it more feasible for the nodes to efficiently gather and store information about a portion of underlying network rather than the whole underlay.
3. The underlay cannot be changed or reconfigured in any manner by the overlay network, the broker software or applications, to provide QoS requirements. Moreover, the changes in the underlay due to external factors have to be observed by the overlay and the overlay has to adapt to these changes to provide the required QoS.

The above reasons call for an asynchronous distributed algorithm for overlay formation and maintenance. The routines to be executed by each node should be independently executed while maintaining the required conditions of availability and correctness under possible concurrent executions. Underlay aware overlays have to be designed to provide the services with a smallest possible set of details of the physical network and its benefits need to be analyzed taking into account the overheads associated with the acquisition and storage of this knowledge. Despite this, self organizing underlay aware overlay networks, which use knowledge of the underlay to provide guaranteed levels of availability can be efficiently built and maintained dynamically, as we demonstrate in this paper. The algorithms presented in this paper are general and relevant for all P2P overlays. However since one of the most popular applications of P2P overlays is EBN (Event Broker Networks) used for data dissemination, we take EBN as a case for illustrating our algorithms. We henceforth use the phrases *overlay node, event broker node* and *broker node* interchangeably in this paper.

In this paper, we present *Trimarg*, an asynchronous distributed algorithm for the construction and maintenance of an overlay network which guarantees the existence of three *node disjoint* underlay paths for every overlay link, on a distributed asynchronous network of computers. The algorithm has three main functions to handle a node *JOINING*, a node *LEAVING* and *MAINTENANCE* of the overlay for ensuring the availability requirement. The broker nodes execute the routines outlined by the algorithm at the time of joining the network to ensure that the network's availability conditions would not be violated as a result of their *join*. When a broker node leaves the overlay, it executes the algorithm to ensure that the network's availability requirement is preserved even after the node leaves. Also every broker node executes the maintenance algorithm which dynamically maintains the availability conditions in the network. Broker nodes can independently execute these routines, using information that is locally available. The time complexity of the algorithm is $O((diameter * degree)^2)$ and the message complexity is $O(diameter * degree)$. The other major contribution of this paper is a method to overcome the inherent complexity of the problem of building available overlays on given underlay networks. We also briefly outline the formalization of underlay aware overlays, and review the graph theoretical basis for the construction of a general high availability overlay network.

Our literature survey reveals the fact that all the above concepts, essential for P2P networks with availability guarantees, are as yet unexplored by other research efforts.

We start with a description of the related work on overlay networks mainly used for EBNs in Section 2. In Section 3 we give the theoretical background necessary for the Trimarg algorithm. In Section 4, Trimarg, the main contribution of this paper, the distributed, three degree of availability algorithm is presented. Its analysis and proof of correctness under concurrent executions in the distributed system, are discussed in Section 5.

2 Related Work

Assuring QoS for applications on peer to peer overlays is a vast research area and a good amount of research work has been reported in this area. But, due to the space constraints, here we mention only those efforts that address issues like availability, underlay awareness and fault tolerance. RON (Resilient Overlay Network)[3] allow applications to detect and recover path outages and degraded performance quickly, and integrate routing and path selection with applications more tightly. Each RON node monitors the quality of the underlying network by itself and uses this information to route packets according to application specified routing metrics. Bayeux[4] is a P2P overlay for streaming multimedia applications with arbitrarily large receiver groups. It provides fault tolerance in routers and network links using the application level routing protocol called Tapestry[5].

Peer to Peer networks of event brokers are extensively used in event based middleware. Hermes[1], Rebecca[6], Gryphon[7], Siena[8] are a few of them. These EBNs use standard topologies for the event broker overlays. But these efforts do not consider resiliency as a central issue. The type of overlays used and the support for fault tolerance in these major research prototypes are summarized in [9]. Gero et al.[10] presents the concepts of self stabilizing publish/subscribe systems with self stabilizing content based routing algorithms.

[11] outlines an algorithm that automatically discovers the failed section of an overlay and repairs the failed overlay with the help of an assumed distributed backup service. However, it is not underlay aware. Chiping Tang[2] et al. have studied the potential costs and benefits of exploiting underlay information to facilitate overlay construction and adaptation. They have reported efficient algorithms for path monitoring and construction of high quality overlay networks using underlay information. The CAIDA (Cooperative Association for Internet Data Analysis)[12] provides many tools like Traceroute, Xtraceroute etc.

which are useful for obtaining underlay path composition and monitoring the underlay paths. Network tomography[13] is another approach which can be used to obtain underlay topology information from end nodes.These tools and approaches make the underlay topology information collection feasible. In [14], an asynchronous distributed algorithm for the construction of overlays for event broker networks with two node disjoint paths between every pair of overlay nodes is described. It is based on the expansion lemma of Whitney's theorem[15], which implies that any node joining a biconnected network with two edges to two different nodes, results in a biconnected network. The technique does not directly scale to higher degrees of availability (number of node disjoint paths), as the underlying network cannot be expected to be triconnected, or in general k-connected, where $k > 2$. In this paper, graph theoretic concepts are first developed to form the basis for the algorithm for higher degrees of availability. Even though resilience to failures in P2P networks has been a topic of research for many years, a formal graph theoretic approach to the construction of P2P overlays with high availability guarantees, by correlating the overlay network to the underlay, has not been pursued in any previous work. However, the existing works like RON[3] and the referred tools developed by the research community supplement the feasibility of our methodology.

3   Theoretical Background

In this section we briefly outline the theoretical concepts necessary for the Trimarg algorithm. This section contains just the essence of the theoretical concepts developed-a more detailed and complete reference is [16].

Formalization of underlay aware overlay: The underlay [16] is represented by the underlay graph $G_u =< V_u, E_u >$ where V_u is a set of nodes each corresponding to a physical node in the computer network and E_u is a set of edges corresponding to each physical link existing between a pair of computers in the network.

$E_u =\{(p, q)|p, q \in V_u$, and there exists a communication link in the computer network between nodes corresponding to p and q$\}$.

Some computers in the underlay are selected as broker nodes. A link in the overlay network (between two broker nodes) is conceptual and implies the existence of at least one physical path in the computer network between the two nodes. An overlay network is represented by the overlay graph $G_o =< V_o, E_o >$, where V_o is the set of overlay nodes, and

$E_o = \{(p, q)|p, q \in V_o$, and there exists an overlay link in the overlay network between nodes p and q$\}$.

Each overlay node has a unique underlay node associated with it. The function $VERTEXMAP : V_o \rightarrow V_u$ maps every overlay node to a unique underlay node. We define $PATHS_u$ as the set of all simple paths in G_u. For any simple path, $path \in PATHS_u$, we define $INT\_NODES(path)$ to be the set of nodes in $path$ which are not the end points of $path$. We also define $END\_NODES(path)$ to be the set of end points of path. Corresponding to an edge in the overlay, there is a simple path in the underlying network. An overlay graph, the underlay graph and $VERTEXMAP$ also define a set $(EDGEMAPS)$ of functions (MAP). A MAP is defined as a function which has E_o as its domain and $PATHS_u$ as its range and maps every edge in the overlay graph to a simple path in the underlay graph. If MAP is a member of $EDGEMAPS$, then for any overlay link $l = (b, c)$, $MAP(l) = p$ where $p \in PATHS_u \wedge END\_NODES(p) = \{VERTEXMAP(b), VERTEXMAP(c)\}$.

We define *degree of availability* [14] as the number of node disjoint paths guaranteed between every pair of overlay nodes.

*A **latent availability overlay network of degree k.** [16] is a general overlay network which has the property that there are at least k distinct vertex disjoint paths in the underlay network between every pair of nodes in the underlay network corresponding to the nodes in the overlay.*

It has been proved that the problem of determining whether a given underlay can support a latent availability overlay of a given degree with a given number of overlay nodes, is NP complete[16]. However, under a set of practically relevant constraints the latent availability problem becomes polynomial time solvable. These constraints state that the set of mapping of overlay nodes to underlay nodes is fixed, the overlay nodes join and leave the overlay dynamically and independently, and that a full knowledge of the underlay is difficult to extract and maintain.

Underlay Awareness: The overlay nodes gather and store information about the underlying path for the overlay links originating from them including information about the underlay nodes in the path and the underlay node overlap in the overlay links from the node.

This information is required only for some nodes.

All the nodes in the underlying graph are classified as follows - overlay nodes, expander nodes, connector nodes and trivial nodes[14].

Overlay nodes are the nodes selected to be brokers. Their degree should be at least k, where k is the degree of availability required. **Expander nodes** are nodes (non brokers) with degree more than 2. They have the potential to exist in more than one physical path. **Connector nodes** (degree=2) and **pendant nodes** (degree=1) can be ignored for overlay construction as they cannot cause overlay path overlaps [14]in the underlay. The links associated with every node in the physical network are ordered and specified by their link numbers for the node.

The overlay node stores a sequence of three tuples for each of its overlay links. The three elements of the tuple are (node_id, link1, link2), where node_id identifies the nodes in the sequence, and link1 and link2 are the link numbers of the links of the node. The end nodes in this sequence correspond to broker nodes and the intermediate nodes are expander nodes.

All this underlay information is used by the broker nodes for overlay construction.

We define a ***reduced underlay graph*** G_{ru} of an underlay graph (G_u) as a multigraph $G_{ru} = < V_{ru}, E_{ru} >$ in which the nodes of degree 1 (pendant) are not included and the connector nodes are simply "joined across" by their adjacent nodes and removed from the picture. It has been proved[16] that an overlay graph G_o forms a latent availability overlay of degree k on an underlay graph G_u if and only if G_o forms a latent availability overlay of degree k on the reduced underlay graph G_{ru}.

We hereby refer to the reduced underlay as the underlay graph in the remaining sections of this paper. The underlay information stored with the broker nodes corresponds to the reduced underlay.

Graph theoretic basis for the algorithms. Whitney's theorem - expansion lemma [15] states that if a node x is added to a k connected graph with k edges to k distinct nodes, then the resulting graph is also k-connected. This lemma forms the basis for the algorithms we develop for available overlay formation. But this theorem is not directly applicable as the availability constraints are different from connectivity in a graph. The approach used in [14](where k=2) cannot be directly applied here as the underlay network cannot practically be k connected for $k > 2$ because that would imply that every node should have a degree at least as large as k, which is not true for an underlay graph for a practical large scale network. However it can be proved that if a new prospective overlay node can find k pairwise node disjoint paths, each to different overlay nodes of an overlay network with an availability degree of k, where $k \geq 2$, then the new overlay network obtained by adding the new overlay node to the existing network also satisfies latent availability of degree k [17]. With k=3, the above result forms the basis of the Trimarg algorithm. A new underlay node is allowed to become a broker node provided it is able to find 3 pairwise node disjoint paths to the existing broker network. The condition is that there should be an existing latent availability overlay of degree k to start with, and it should have at least k nodes, so that the new nodes can find node disjoint paths to k different brokers. The graph with fewest nodes satisfying this non trivially is a $k + 1$-clique, i.e a collection of four nodes with overlay edge between each pair of nodes, such that each edge is internally node disjoint to other edges. This is a manifest availability overlay [16]. Determination of such a k-degree overlay having $k + 1$ nodes is an NP complete problem [16]. For k=3 we can have a polynomial time solution which is $O|V_u|^4$ as each group of four nodes can be tested polynomially for six edges to be node disjoint, and there are $^nC_4$ such combinations to be tested.

The phase of finding this $k + 1$ node, k degree overlay is done statically, as the initialization phase. In our algorithm, we call it *the stellar broker network*. Moreover, these nodes are taken to be fault tolerant and permanent, they practically never cease to be broker nodes. These nodes are statically made known to a prospective broker node as a part of the installation software. The prospective broker node then tries to form k node disjoint paths to these stellar nodes. However, it is not essential that it ultimately forms overlay links to these very nodes, as we see in the algorithm in the next section.

4   The Trimarg Algorithm

4.1   Design

The overlay network is initialized with four special broker nodes called the *stellar* nodes. The stellar nodes network form a wheel [15] network of four nodes (a 4-clique). The edges in the wheel network are physically disjoint. The stellar broker network is illustrated in Figure 1. Figure 2 shows a general underlying physical network of the stellar broker network.

The initial (stellar) broker has *manifest* (and also *latent*) availability of degree three, as can be observed by listing out the paths between broker pairs in Figure 2. The paths contain expander nodes as well as connector nodes. The identities of the expander nodes in the adjacent links are stored at the broker nodes. A node that wishes to join the overlay network of broker nodes does so by connecting itself to existing broker nodes.

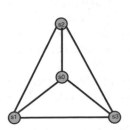
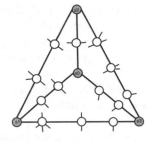
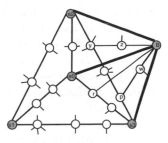

Fig. 1. The Stellar Broker Network

Fig. 2. The Stellar Broker network structure

Fig. 3. Broker joining

The overlay links so formed need not necessarily be node disjoint with existing links. *However, the broker network should ensure that the new broker has three pairwise underlay node disjoint paths to every broker node in the existing network.* The steps in the distributed algorithm work as follows. The new node to join is statically aware of the ids of the stellar broker nodes. It sends a *Join_Stellar_Broker* message to stellar broker nodes through all its links. It receives messages in return from stellar brokers or other intercepting brokers. It finds three node disjoint paths from the messages it receives and establishes broker links through them. The algorithm is formally stated in Subsection 4.2.

4.2 Algorithm

The routines described here are:

1. *Make_Broker(B):* This is executed when a node B wants to join the broker network.
2. *Leave_Broker(B):* This is executed by a broker B to leave a broker network.
3. *Execute_Broker(B):* This is a routine executed throughout by a broker which is a part of the network.

The set of messages exchanged by the broker nodes is:

1. **Join_Stellar_Broker(B).** This is sent by a node B wishing to join the broker network.
2. **New_Contact(R, B, path, list).** This is a message sent by a broker R which intercepts the *Join_Stellar_Broker()* message, or by the stellar broker (in case the *Join_Stellar_Broker()* was not intercepted by any other broker) to the broker B which wishes to join. It contains the knowledge of the path by which the message reached R from B, and also a list of other brokers and expander nodes, that B should try to contact, to get three node disjoint paths to the broker network.
3. **Establish_Broker_Link(B, A, path).** This is a message sent by a broker B to broker A to establish an overlay link between them with the underlay information in *path*.
4. **Confirm_Broker_Link (A, B, path).** This is a message sent by a broker A which receives the *Establish_Broker_Link* message from B, meant for A itself or some other broker X to which B had sent the *Establish_Broker_Link* message, if A was an expander node on the path from B to X, and subsequently became a broker. Then the broker link is established between A and B, instead of X and B.

5. **Check_Path (A, B, nodelist).** This is sent by a node A to a node B to check whether the path by which the *Check_Path* message reaches node B has more/less expander nodes than listed in *nodelist* (nodes in path). This is a periodic refresher message sent between overlay nodes, for the purpose of dynamically monitoring changes in the physical network.

6. **Leave_Stellar_Broker(B, nodelist).** This is sent by a node B to inform all the overlay neighbours that B has ceased to be a broker. The list *nodelist* contains the list of neighbours of B.

7. **Bye (A, B).** This message is sent by a neighbouring broker A or stellar node to allow B to stop its routing activities in the overlay.

$Make\_Broker(B)$ executed by an aspiring broker B enables it to find three node disjoint paths to three different nodes in the existing broker network, and it starts the process of establishing the links.

Algorithm 1. $Make\_Broker(B)$

---

1. **if** (degree(B)<1) **then** exit /* *does not qualify*/
2. send $Join\_Stellar\_Broker(B)$ from all the links of B to the stellar brokers
3. **while** (**not** timeout)
4.   **if** receive($New\_Contact(A, B, path, list)$)
5.   **then** store (path, list) in pathset
6. **if** pathset is empty
7.   **then** exit /*brokers unreachable*/
8.   **else** select three node disjoint paths from pathset
9.   **if** found
10.   **then** Send($Establish\_Broker\_Link(B, A, path)$)
11.   **else if** (suggested_path present in the *pathset*)
12.   **then** send ($Join\_Stellar\_Broker(B)$) through suggested_path in list of one $New\_Contact$ message
13.   delete suggested_path from *pathset*
14.   **goto** step 3
15.   **else** exit /* fails to find node disjoint paths*/
16. **while** (**not** timeout)
17.   receive($Confirm\_Broker\_Link(A, B, pathlist)$)
18. start $Execute\_Broker(B)$
19. start routing activity

Different cases in the algorithm are illustrated. As shown in Figure 3, B's *Join_Stellar_Broker()* sent via its three links may contact the brokers S0, S2 and S3 on node disjoint paths through expander nodes (r), (z, y) and (w, p) respectively. Nodes S0, S2 and S3 respond with paths and suggested brokers. Node B, on getting these messages, finds the three disjoint paths and decides to establish these links.

Now let us consider a second case, arising when there are more broker nodes in the broker network. Figure 4 illustrates the case in which the *Join_Stellar_Broker* message from an aspiring broker node N, to S2 is intercepted by a broker B on the path and subsequently the overlay link is established between the new node N and the intercepting

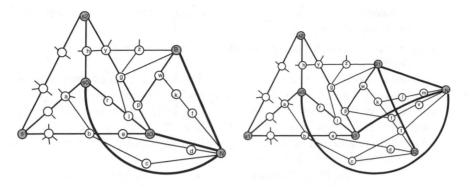

Fig. 4. Broker joining non stellar broker   **Fig. 5.** Overlay overlapping paths

broker B. The three disjoint paths found are (f, k, w) to B, (c, b, a) to S0 and (d, e) to S3 respectively. The new overlay links are shown with thick lines in Figure 4.

The third case illustrated is the establishment of three node disjoint paths, to three different brokers, but the paths having nodes in a common overlay link. Consider Figure 5. The aspiring broker node N finds three node disjoint paths, (m, j, k, w) to B1, (v, f, p) to S3 and (t, c, b, a) to S0, and is allowed to join the broker network B with three overlay links to B1, S3 and S0 respectively. The nodes are a part of the overlay link B1-B2, which maps to the physical path (w, k, f, t). But there is no smaller *separating cut*[15], hence the new broker node will have three node disjoint paths to the broker network.

A broker that wishes to stop being a broker executes a *Leave_ Broker(B)*. It still remains a part of the physical network. This message is also intercepted and replied to by the neighbouring broker which has B as its overlay neighbour with a *Bye* message. If this node had already ceased to be a broker the *Leave_Broker* message travels up all the way to the stellar node which replies with a *Bye* message.

Algorithm 2. *Leave_Broker(B)*

/* this is executed by a broker B to leave a broker network.*/
1. leaving = **true**
2. safe = **false**
3. over= **false**
4. **while** (**not** safe) wait;
5. stop(*Execute_Broker(B)*)
6. send(*Leave_Stellar_Broker($B, brokerlist$)*) through all the links of B.
7. **while** (**not** timeout or not over)
8.   **for** each node in neighbourlist
9.   **if** not receive($Bye(A, B)$) message then wait
10.   over=**true**
11. Stop routing in overlay.

We can visualize the process of a new broker node trying to join the broker network as an ancient ship trying to reach land by following a star. The ship stops when it finds land. The new broker node tries to reach the stellar brokers in the sea of IP addresses in the physical network, and in the process stops its search when it finds another broker already a part of the network.

Maintenance of the Overlay. Every overlay node executes the *Execute_Broker()* for overlay maintenance.

The routine for broker addition is also executed by a node already existing in the broker network as an underlay node, on turning into a broker. When the *Join_Stellar_Broker* message is received by the brokers on the links from the joining broker node, they respond with *New_Contact* and new broker links get established. If in the time interval between sending *New_Contact* and receiving an *Establish_Broker*, a new broker joins on the path, then the *Confirm_Broker* is sent by the new broker node, and the overlay link is only to that node. When the broker gets a *Leave_Broker* message meant for itself, it replies with a *Bye* message and establishes overlay links to the neighbour of the neighbours, which is present in the list sent by the leaving broker. Otherwise, it ignores the message and lets it proceed further up the path to the stellar node. In the overlay network every node checks its links information periodically to confirm the underlay knowledge. If new expander nodes are added in the path (say, by adding a new link to a physical node), then that knowledge is updated in the overlay node, so that further node sharing information among links can be correctly assessed. The *Check_Path(A, B, brokerlist)* message does this. The receiving node compares *nodelist* with the path by which the message actually comes and updates it. While checking the overlay information the old broker links may be modified by the old broker nodes, and new links to the new broker are added.

Algorithm 3. $Execute\_Broker(B)$

---

1. **while** (true) /* execute until terminated*/
2. **if** receive($Join\_Stellar\_Broker(A)$ **and** leaving==**false**)
3.   **then** intercept message
4.   send $New\_Contact(B, A, path, list)$
5.   enqueue $(B, A, path, list)$
6. **if** receive($Establish\_Broker\_Link(A, B, path)$)
7.   **then** send $(Confirm\_Broker(A, B, path))$
8.   dequeue(A, B, path,list)
9.   add overlay path (A,B,path)
10.   **if** (queue is empty) safe=**true**
11. **if** receive($Leave\_Stellar\_Broker(A, brokerlist)$
12.   **then** add new overlay links to the nodes in brokerlist
13.   send Bye message(A)
14. **for** all brokers x in neighbourlist of B
15.   send($Check\_Path(B, x, nodelist1)$)
16.   **if** receive($Check\_Path(x, B, nodelist2)$ **and** $nodelist2 \neq nodelist1$)
17.   **then** update path()

---

5 Evaluation

5.1 Complexity Analysis

Time Complexity: As the algorithm is based on probing upto the stellar node in the worst case, the maximum diameter of the network would determine the upper bound on the time for sending and receiving messages. Comparing node disjointedness in the obtained paths is O(number of paths^2*path length^2). As the number of paths is determined by the degree, and path length is bounded by the diameter, node disjointedness can be found in $O(degree * diameter)^2$.

Message complexity: The maximum number of messages are sent for the *Make_Broker()* routine, as the *Join_Stellar_Broker* message has to be sent by the joining broker to stellar brokers through all its links. The number of hops of this message is bounded by maximum diameter and the number of links is bounded by the maximum degree. Hence, the message complexity is $O(degree * diameter)$.

5.2   Proof of Correctness

We start by giving an inductive proof for the correctness for the algorithm.

Lemma: *An overlay graph B' obtained by the sequential or interleaved executions of the **Make_ Broker()** and **Leave_Broker()** procedures by different physical nodes and concurrent executions of the **Make_Broker()** and **Leave_Broker()** procedures by different physical nodes in a given physical network G, containing an availability latent overlay B of degree three, is an availability latent overlay of availability degree three, i.e., any broker node in B' has three node disjoint paths to every other broker node in B'.*

Base: The initial network formed by stellar brokers has three node disjoint paths to each other by construction as shown in Figure 2.

Inductive step: If the network of brokers and expander nodes, B, has three node disjoint paths between every broker pair, then a network of broker nodes and expander nodes, B', obtained by the execution of *Make_Broker()* by a single node, or concurrent execution of *Make_Broker()* by two different nodes, or *Leave_Broker()* executed by a non stellar node, or concurrent *Leave_Broker()* executions by non stellar nodes, or the concurrent execution of *Make_Broker()* and *Leave_Broker()* by non stellar nodes, also has three node disjoint paths between every pair of broker nodes which form a part of B'.

Proof: We prove the inductive step by considering the execution of the routines.

Case 1: Execution of a $Make\_Broker()$ by a node b.

  (i) If b has degree less than three or it is not connected or too far off (time-out) from B, then no change is made to B, hence B'=B.
  (ii) If b gets at least three replies that include node disjoint paths to three different broker nodes in B, x,y and z, then it joins with those links. Suppose the paths it gets are $(b, p_{11}, p_{12}, ... , p_{1n}, x),(b, p_{21}, p_{22}, ..., p_{2m}, y)$ and $(b, p_{31}, p_{32}, ..., p_{3k}, z)$. In each of these sequences there is a first node which is already a part of the existing overlay. Removing any one node, before this first expander node each from any two of these paths, will not disconnect b as there is a third node-disjoint path from b to B. As B already has three node disjoint paths between each of its broker nodes, the removal of any two of these nodes does not disconnect B either. The removal of any two nodes including those subsequent to these first nodes also

does not disconnect b from the network as B is known to have no separating pairs, and there exists a third path from b to B which does not include these two nodes. The three expander nodes at which b joins B, form a separating cut for B'. If b itself was an expander node in B, then it is allowed to join only if it has three disjoint paths, thus ensuring it has no separation cut of size less than three.

(iii) If it does not get two disjoint replies, it uses the information given by one of the replying brokers, which contains information about other expander nodes and broker nodes to contact. Hence if the node is able to link to that expander node, and this path is node disjoint to two other paths already obtained, then also B' satisfies the availability criteria.

(iv) If it is not possible, the node b does not join, so B'=B.

Case 2: Concurrent execution of Make_Broker().
Suppose nodes b_1 and b_2 execute *Make_Broker()*.

(i) If one or both of b_1, b_2 have lesser degree or get timeout then the proof enumerated in Case 1 holds.

(ii) If nodes b_1 and b_2 get three node disjoint paths each and these are to different broker/expander nodes in B, then they can simultaneously join B, and the proof for case 1 holds.

(iii) If two nodes b_1 and b_2 select paths that are mutually disjoint but overlap with each other's paths - this could happen in different ways as we enumerate:

1. Both join to same expander nodes/node, but with disjoint paths. Both still get node disjoint paths to each other and to the rest of the network, as they have separating cuts of size at least three. This is illustrated in Figure 6.
2. Both join same nodes, but with overlapping paths. This is illustrated in Figure 7.

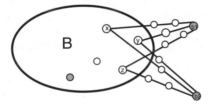   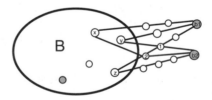

Fig. 6. Concurrent joins with disjoint paths   **Fig. 7.** Concurrent joins with overlapping paths

3. One of the nodes lies in the path selected by the other as illustrated in Figure 8.
4. Both nodes lie in paths selected by each other. This is illustrated in Figure 9.

Case 3: Leave_Broker() execution.
Leave_Broker() calls, whether executed simultaneously or individually, do not affect the underlying network connectivity, as it is just a change in status of the node(s) from broker to expander.

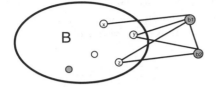 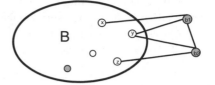

Fig. 8. Concurrent joins with single broker in-   **Fig. 9.** Concurrent joins with two broker inclu-
clusive path   sive paths

Case 4: Leave_Broker() and Make_Broker() execute concurrently.

(i) If the brokers contacted by *Make_Broker()* are different from the node executing
Leave_Broker() then they would each execute correctly individually as proved in
cases 1 and 3.

(ii) If the broker executing *Leave_Broker()* is one of the nodes that is contacted by
the node executing *Make_Broker()*, then if the contact is made after it starts executing *Leave_Broker()* then the *Join_Stellar_message* is simply forwarded, as it
would have executed *leaving* = **true**. If *Leave_Broker* is executed by a broker that
has already sent *New_Contact*, it is not allowed to proceed (by *wait*) until it has
confirmed the path. Also, it does not send new $New\_Contact$ messages.

Once the leaving broker confirms the path, the other broker would put this as a neighbour and vice-versa, so while continuing with *Leave_Broker( )*, the leaving broker will
wait for a *Bye* message from the new broker node, confirming that it has created other
overlay links. Hence the algorithm ensures that B' satisfies the required availability
criterion in the presence of concurrent *Leave_Broker()* and *Make_Broker()* executions.

Experimental Evaluation. The *Trimarg* algorithm has been tested on a simulated environment using an event based network simulation framework. This simulation framework has been developed by extending the Distributed System SIMulator (DSSIM)
used in Hermes [1]. The underlying physical network for the simulation is generated
using the Boston University Representative Internet Topology gEnerator(BRITE)[18].
The performance results show that our algorithm is scalable, and the time and message
overheads are reasonable [19].

6   Conclusions

The major contribution of this paper is an asynchronous distributed algorithm for a
self organizing underlay aware overlay network that ensures 3-degree of availability,
resilient to failures in the underlying physical network. A graph theoretic proof of correctness of the algorithm in the distributed, concurrent environment and complexity
analysis are included. As the primary focus is on the algorithm, and due to space constraints, a detailed discussion on the simulations are excluded in this paper. As *Trimarg*
overlays guarantee resilience to underlay failures, reliable routing algorithms which can
tap the power of the Trimarg overlay to guarantee event delivery, become feasible. We

foresee this as an interesting research area. Dynamic overlay node selection, underlay aware load balancing at the overlay links, dynamic routing path selection, dynamic creation of overlay nodes for offloading of overloaded brokers are a few of the interesting possibilities opened up by the *Trimarg* technique.

References

1. Pietzuch, P.R.: Hermes: A Scalable Event-Based Middleware. PhD thesis, Computer Laboratory, Queens College, University of Cambridge (February 2004)
2. Tang, C.: Underlay-Aware Overlay Networks. PhD thesis, Michigan State University (June 2005)
3. Anderson, D., Balakrishnan, H., Kaashoek, F., Morris, R.: The Case for Resilient Overlay Networks. In: Proceedings of Eighth Workshop on Hot Topics in Operating Systems(HotOS 2001), pp. 152–157. IEEE Computer Society, Los Alamitos (2001)
4. Zhuang, S.Q., Zhao, B.Y., Joseph, A.D., Katz, R.H., Kubiatowicz, J.D.: Bayeux: An Architecture for Scalable and Fault Tolerant Wide-area Data Dissemination. In: Proceedings of the Eleventh International Workshop on Network and OS support for Digital Audio and Video (NOSSDAV 2001) (2001)
5. Zhao, B.Y., Kubiatowicz, J.D., Joseph, A.D.: Tapestry: An Infrastructure for Fault Tolerant Wide-area Location and Routing. Technical Report, University of California-Berkeley, Berkeley, CA (2001)
6. Fiege, L., Muehl, G., Buchmann, A.: An Architectural Framework for Electronic Commerce Applications. In: Proceedings of Informatik 2001: Annual Conference of the German Computer Society (2001)
7. IBM T J Watson Research Center. Gryphon: Publish/ Subscribe over Public Network (2001), http://researchweb.watson.ibm.com/gryphon/Gryphon
8. Carzaniga, A.: Architectures for an Event Notification Service Scalable to Wide-Area Networks. PhD thesis, Politecnico di Milano, Milano, Italy (December 1998)
9. Mahambre, S.P., Madhu Kumar, S.D., Bellur, U.: A Taxonomy of QoS-Aware, Adaptive Event-Dissemination Middleware. IEEE Internet Computing 11(4), 35–44 (2007)
10. Muehl, G., Jaeger, M.A., Herrmann, K., Weis, T., Fiege, L., Ulbrich, A.: Self-stabilizing publish/subscribe systems: Algorithms and evaluation. In: Cunha, J.C., Medeiros, P.D. (eds.) Euro-Par 2005. LNCS, vol. 3648, pp. 664–674. Springer, Heidelberg (2005)
11. Porter, B., Taiani, F., Coulson, G.: Generalized Repair for Overlay Networks. In: Proceedings of the Twentyfifth IEEE Symposium on Reliable Distributed Systems (SRDS 2006), Leeds, UK (October 2006)
12. Performance Measurement Tools Taxonomy, http://www.caida.org/tools/taxonomy/performance.xml
13. Coates, M., Hero, A., Nowak, R., Yu, B.: Internet Tomography. IEEE Signal Processing Magazine (May 2002)
14. Madhu Kumar, S.D., Bellur, U.: A distributed algorithm for underlay aware and available overlay formation in event broker networks for publish/subscribe systems. In: Proceedings of the First International Workshop on Distributed Event Processing Systems and Applications (DEPSA 2007) Colocated with ICDCS 2007, Toronto, Canada (June 2007)
15. West, D.B.: Introduction to Graph Theory. Prentice Hall of India (1999)
16. Madhu Kumar, S.D., Bellur, U.: Availability Models for Underlay Aware Overlay Networks. In: Proceedings of the second International Conference on Distributed Event-Based Systems (DEBS 2008), Rome,Italy, pp. 169–180. ACM Digital Library, New York (2008)

17. Madhu Kumar, S.D., Bellur, U.: Graph Theoretic Concepts for Highly Available Underlay Aware P2P Networks. Technical Report IITB/CSE/2008/October/18, Department of Computer Science and Engineering, Indian Institute of Technology Bombay, IIT Bombay, India (October 2008)
18. Medina, A., Lakhina, A., Matta, I., Byers, J.: Brite: An Approach to Universal Topology Generation. In: Proceedings of the International Workshop on Modeling, Analysis and Simulation of Computer and Telecommunication Systems- MASCOTS 2001, Cincinnati, Ohio (August 200)
19. Madhu Kumar, S.D., Bellur, U.: Trimarg: A Distributed Algorithm for the Formation of Highly Available Underlay Aware Overlay Networks of Event Brokers. Technical Report IITB/KReSIT/2007/May/49, Kanwal Rekhi School of Information Technology, IIT Bombay (May 2006)

HPC5: An Efficient Topology Generation Mechanism for Gnutella Networks

Santosh Kumar Shaw, Joydeep Chandra, and Niloy Ganguly

Indian Institute of Technology, Kharagpur, India

Abstract. In this paper, we propose a completely distributed topology generation mechanism named HPC5 for Gnutella network. A Gnutella topology will be efficient and scalable if it generates less number of redundant queries and hence consists of lesser short length cycles. However, eliminating cycles totally, reduces the coverage of the peers in the network. Thus in the tradeoff between the cycle length and network coverage we have found that a minimum cycle length of 5 provides the minumum query redundancy with maximum network coverage. Thus our protocol directs each peer to select neighbors in such a way that any cyclic path present in the overlay network will have a minimum length of 5. We show that our approach can be deployed into the existing Gnutella network without disturbing any of its parameters. Simulation results signify that HPC5 is very effective for Gnutella's dynamic query search over limited flooding.

1 Introduction

Peer-to-peer (P2P) network is an overlay network, useful for many purposes like file-sharing, distributed computation, etc. Depending upon the topology formation, P2P networks are broadly classified as structured and unstructured. An unstructured P2P network is formed when the overlay links are established arbitrarily. Decentralized (fully distributed control), unstructured P2P networks (Gnutella, FastTrack etc) are the most popular file-sharing overlay networks. The absence of a structure and central control makes such systems much more robust and highly self-healing compared to structured systems [8,12]. But the main problem of these kinds of networks is scalability due to generation of large number of redundant messages during query search. Consequently as these networks are becoming more popular the quality of service is degrading rapidly [5,9].

To make the network scalable, *Gnutella* [1,2,3] is continuously upgrading it's features and introducing new concepts. All these improvements can be categorized into two broad areas: improvements of search techniques and modification of the topological structure of the overlay network to enhance search efficiency. In enhanced search techniques, several improvements like *Time-To-Live* (TTL), *Dynamic query*, *Query-caching* and *Query Routing Protocol* (QRP) have been introduced. One of the most significant topological modifications in unstructured network was done by inducing the concept of *super-peer* (ultra-peer) with a two-tier network topology.

The basic search mechanism adhered by Gnutella is *limited flooding* [1,2,3]. In flooding, a peer that searches for a file, issues a query and sends it to all of its neighbor peers. The peer that receives the query forwards it to all its neighbors except the neighbor from

V. Garg, R. Wattenhofer, and K. Kothapalli (Eds.): ICDCN 2009, LNCS 5408, pp. 114–126, 2009.

which it is received. By this way, a query is propagated up to a predefined number of hops (*TTL*) from the source peer. The TTL followed by Gnutella is generally 1 or 2 for popular search. However, the query with $TTL(3)$ (numeric value inside parenthesis represents the number of hops to search with) is initiated for rare searches.

The main goal of this paper is to improve the scalability of the Gnutella network by reducing redundant messages. One of the ways to achieve this is to modify the overlay network, so that small size loops get eliminated from the overlay topology. The rationale behind the proposition is explained through Fig. 1. In this figure, both networks have the same number of connections. With a $TTL(2)$ flooding, the network in Fig. 1(a) discovers 4 peers at the expense of 7 messages, whereas the network in Fig. 1(b) discovers 6 peers without any redundant messages. This happens due to the absence of any 3-length cycle in the network of Fig. 1(b). On generalizing, we can say that for a $TTL(r)$ flooding, networks devoid of cycles of length less than $(2r + 1)$ do not generate any redundant messages. In this paper, we propose a handshake protocol that generates a cycle-5 network topology (a network which does not have any cycles up to length $(r - 1)$ is referred as cycle-r network). However, some redundant messages are produced for rare searches ($TTL(3)$). Since this (rare search) is performed rarely, in this case we are more interested in having higher coverage than eliminating generation of redundant messages. The strength of our proposed mechanism is its simplicity and the ease of deployment over existing Gnutella networks along with its power to generate topologies having high efficiency in terms of message complexity and network coverage.

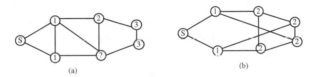

(a)   (b)

Fig. 1. Effect of topology structure on limited flood based search. The number inside the circle represents the TTL value required to reach that node from start node S.

Many algorithms exist in the literature that modify the topology in unstructured P2P networks to solve the excessive traffic problem. The structural mismatch between the overlay and underlying network topology is alleviated by using location aware topology matching algorithms [6,7]. A class of overlay topology based on distance between a node and its neighbors in the physical network structure is presented in [10]. Papadakis *et* al. presented an algorithm to monitor the ratio of duplicated message through each network connection. Consequently a node does not forward any query through that connection whose ratio exceeds certain threshold [11]. Zhu *et* al. very recently presented a distributed algorithm in [15] to improve the scalability of Gnutella like networks by reducing redundant messages. They have pointed the same concept of elimination of 3 and 4-length cycles. However this is demand driven and involves a lot of control overhead. Also it is not clear how the algorithm will perform in the face of heavy traffic and inconsistency. The algorithm also does not take care in preserving the Gnutella parameters (like degree distribution, average peer distance, diameter, etc), hence robustness of the evolved network is not maintained. In our work we take into considerations all the above aspects and propose a holistic and simple approach to topology formation. The algorithm initiates as soon as a peer enters in the network rather than having it demand driven. Thus the algorithm works during the bootstrap phase when the network is forming so that less overhead in involved afterwards.

A list of main notations that will be used throughout the paper is summarized in table 1 for ready reference.

Table 1. Notations

$TTL(r)$	Query search with $TTL = r$	d_{uu}	Avg. no. of ultra-neighbors of an ultra-peer
cycle-r	A cycle of minimum length r	d_{ul}	Avg. no. of leaf-neighbors of an ultra-peer
cycle-r network	A network which does not have any cycle up to length $(r-1)$	d_{lu}	Avg. no. of ultra-neighbors of a leaf-peer
cycle-3 network	Gnutella network	H_k	Hit ratio to select k^{th} ultra-neighbor
N	Total number of peers in the network	$\langle H \rangle$	Average hit ratio of a peer
U	Total number of ultra-peers in the network	$\langle H_{ev} \rangle$	Average evolved hit ratio of a peer
L	Total number of leaf-peers in the network	r^{th} neighbor	A peer at a distance of r hops. All immediate neighbors are 1st neighbors, all neighbors of 1st neighbors are 2nd neighbors and so on.

2   Basic System Model of Gnutella 0.6

In order to carry on experiments, a basic version of *Gnutella 0.6* [1,2,3] has been implemented. The basic Gnutella consists of a large collection of nodes that are assigned unique identifiers and which communicate through message exchanges.

Topology: Gnutella 0.6 is a two-tier overlay network, consisting of two types of nodes: *ultra-peer* and *leaf-peer* (the term peer represents both ultra and leaf peer). An ultra-peer is connected with a limited number of other ultra-peers and leaf-peers. A leaf-peer is connected with some ultra-peers. However, there is no direct connection between any two leaf-peers in the overlay network. Yet another type of peer is called legacy-peers, which are present in ultra-peer level and do not accept any leaves. In our model we are not considering legacy-peers.

Basic Search Technique: The network follows limited flood based query search. A query of an ultra-peer is forwarded to its leaf-peers with $TTL(0)$ and to all its ultra-neighbors with one less TTL only when $(TTL > 0)$. A leaf-peer does not forward query received from an ultra-peer. On the other hand ultra-peers perform query searching on behalf of their leaf peers. The query of a leaf-peer is initially sent to its connected ultra-peers. All the connected ultra-peers simultaneously forward the query to their neighbor ultra-peers up to a limited number of hops. Since multiple ultra-peers are initiating flooding, a leaf-peer's query will produce more redundant messages if the distance between any two ultra-neighbors is not enough. Gnutella 0.6 incorporates *dynamic querying* over limited flooding as query search technique. In dynamic querying, an ultra-peer incrementally forwards a query in 3 steps $(TTL(1), TTL(2), TTL(3)$ respectively) through each connection while measuring the responsiveness to that query.

The ultra-peer can stop forwarding query at any step if it gets sufficient number of query hits. Consequently dynamic querying uses $TTL(3)$ only for rare searches. Modern Gnutella protocol uses QRP technique over dynamic querying in which a leaf-peer creates a hash table of all the files it is sharing and sends that table to all the immediate ultra-neighbors. As a result, when a query reaches an ultra-peer it is forwarded to only those connected leaf-peers which would have query hits [1,2].

Basic Handshake Protocol: Many softwares (clients) are used to access the Gnutella network (like *Limewire, Bearshare, Gtk-gnutella*). The most popular client software, Limewire's handshake protocol is used in our simulation as a base handshake protocol. Through handshaking, a peer establishes connection with any other ultra-peer. To start handshake protocol a peer first collects the address of an online ultra-peer from a pool of online ultra-peers. A peer can collect the list of online peers from *hardcoded* address/es and/or from *GwebCache* systems [4] and/or through *pong-caching* and/or from its own hard-disk which has obtain list of online ultra-peers in the previous run [5]. The handshake protocol is used to make new connections. A handshake consists of 3 groups of headers [1,2]. The steps of handshaking is elaborated next:

1. The program (peer) that initiates the connection sends the first group of headers, which tells the remote program about its features and the status to imply the type of neighbor (leaf or ultra) it wants to be.
2. The program that receives the connection responds with a second group of headers which essentially conveys the message whether it agrees to the initiator's proposal or not.
3. Finally, the initiator sends a third group of header to confirm and establish the connection.

This basic protocol is modified in this paper to overcome the problem of message overhead.

Simulated Gnutella: To generate existing Gnutella network, we have simulated a strip down version of Gnutella 0.6 protocols which follows parameters of Limewire [1]. Our simulated Gnutella network exhibits all features (like degree distribution, diameter, average path length between two peers, proportion of ultra-peers, etc.) exhibited by Gnutella network. These features are obtained from the snapshots collected by crawlers [3,13,14].

3 HPC5: Handshake Protocol for Cycle-5 Networks

Fig. 2 illustrates the proposed HPC5 graphically. In Fig. 2, peer-1 requests other online ultra-peers to be its neighbor, given that, peer-2 is already a neighbor of peer-1. In Fig. 2(a) and 2(b), the possibility of the formation of triangle and quadrilateral arises if a 1st or 2nd neighbor of peer-2 is selected. However, this possibility is discarded in Fig. 2(c) and a cycle of length 5 is formed.

Each peer maintains a list of its 1st and 2nd neighbors, which contains only ultra-peers (because a peer only sends request to an ultra-peer to make neighbor). The 2nd ultra-neighbors of a leaf-peer represents the collection of 1st ultra-neighbors of the

Fig. 2. Selection of neighbor by peer-1 after making peer-2 as a neighbor

connected ultra-peers. To keep updated knowledge, each ultra-peer exchanges its list of 1st neighbors periodically with its neighbor ultra-peers and sends the list of 1st neighbors to its leaf-peers. To do this with minimal overhead, piggyback technique can be used in which an ultra-peer can append its neighbor list to the messages passing through it.

The three steps of modified handshake protocol (HPC5) is described below.

1. The initiator peer first sends a request to a remote ultra-peer which is not in its 1st or 2nd neighbor set. The request header contains the type of the initiator peer. The presence of remote peer in 2nd neighbor set implies the possibility of 3-length cycle. In Fig. 2, peer-1 cannot send request to peer 2 or 3, on the other hand peer 4 & 5 are eligible remote ultra-peers.
2. The recipient replies back with its list of 1st neighbors and the neighbor-hood acceptance/rejection message. If the remote peer discards the connection in this step, the initiator closes the connection and keeps the record of neighbors of the remote peer for future handshaking process. On acceptance of the invitation by the remote-peer, the initiator peer performs the following tasks.
3. The initiator peer checks at least one common peer between its 2nd neighbor set (say, A) and the 1st neighbor set of the remote peer (say, B). A common ultra-peer between sets A and B indicates the possibility of 4-length cycle.

    If no common peer is present between sets A and B then the initiator sends *accept connection* to remote peer.

    Otherwise the initiator sends *reject connection* to remote peer.

HPC5 prevents the possibility of forming a cycle of length 3 or 4 and generates a cycle-5 network.

4   Hurdles in Implementing the Scheme

Before embedding HPC5 in Gnutella network, we need to consider certain issues to assess the viability of HPC5 : whether this scheme is compatible with the current populations of Gnutella network, the average number of trials required to get an ultra-neighbor, and whether there is any possibility of inconsistency. Each of the issues are discussed one by one.

Compatibility with the Current Population of Gnutella
From ultra-peer point of view, the total number of ultra-leaf connections is $U \cdot d_{ul}$ and from leaf-peer point of view it is $L \cdot d_{lu}$. By equating both and considering $U + L = N$, we get

$$N = U \cdot \frac{(d_{ul} + d_{lu})}{d_{lu}} \tag{1}$$

Fig. 3 represents a part of an ultra-peer layer where P has immediate neighbors at level Q. Suppose, P is already connected with $(d_{uu} - 1)$ number of ultra-peers at Q level and wants to get d_{uu}^{th} ultra-neighbor. According to HPC5, P should not connect to any ultra-peer from R or S level as its next neighbor. However, T can be a neighbor of P. Thus, we can say that if P wants to make a new ultra-neighbor then P has to exclude at most $(d_{uu} - 1)$, $(d_{uu} - 1)^2$ and $(d_{uu} - 1)^3$ number of ultra-peers from Q, R and S level respectively. So, total $[(d_{uu} - 1) + (d_{uu} - 1)^2 + (d_{uu} - 1)^3] \approx d_{uu}^3$ number of peers cannot be considered as next neighbor(s) of P. Therefore the number of ultra-peers in the network needs to be at least

$$U \approx d_{uu}^3 \tag{2}$$

From equations 1 and 2 we get

$$N \approx \frac{(d_{ul} + d_{lu}) \cdot d_{uu}^3}{d_{lu}} \tag{3}$$

Presently Gnutella network is having the population of almost 2000k of peers at any time [1]. From equation 3 it can be seen that for the present values of $d_{uu} = 26, d_{ul} = 22$ & $d_{lu} = 4$ found in present day Gnutella networks, 120-130k peers are sufficient to implement HPC5 protocol. However, to form cycle-6 networks (HPC6) the number of peers

$$N \approx \frac{(d_{ul} + d_{lu}) \cdot d_{uu}^4}{d_{lu}}$$

required is more than 2000k. Hence the current population will not be able to support any such attempts.

Hit Ratio: Hit ratio is defined as the inverse of the number of trials required to get a valid ultra-peer neighbor. As our protocol puts some constraints on neighbor selection, a contacted agreeing remote ultra-peer may not be selected as neighbor. Mathematically, on an average if a peer (say, P) is looking for its kth ultra-neighbor and the m_k^{th} contacted ultra-peer satisfies the constraints and becomes k^{th} ultra-neighbor of P, then the hit ratio for k^{th} neighbor will be $H_k = \frac{1}{m_k}$. We first make a static analysis of hit ratio, then fine tune it considering that the network is evolving.

At the time of kth ultra-neighbor selection in HPC5, a peer (say, P) does not consider its 1st $((k - 1)$ ultra-peers) and 2nd $((k - 1)(d_{uu} - 1)$ ultra-peers) ultra-neighbors

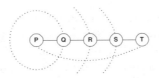

Fig. 3. A part of an Ultra-peer layer, where a node represents all nodes that are present in that level. Like, Q represents all 1st neighbors of P.

as a potential neighbor and this exclusion is locally done by checking the 1st & 2nd neighbors lists of P. The number of ultra-peers excluded (U') is then $[(k - 1) + (k - 1)(d_{uu} - 1)]$. According to step-3 of HPC5, P cannot make neighbor from any ultra-peer of level S (3rd ultra-neighbors of P) of Fig. 3 as its neighbor which are $U'' = [(k - 1)(d_{uu} - 1)^2]$ in number. So, total $[U' + U'']$ number of ultra-peers are excluded. We assume that the probability of getting any ultra-peer is uniform. So hit ratio can be given as $H_k = \frac{U - (U' + U'')}{U - U'}$. Assuming $U' \ll U$, $U' \ll U''$ and $U'' \approx d_{uu}^2 \cdot (k - 1)$, therefore H_k becomes

$$H_k \approx \frac{U - d_{uu}^2 \cdot (k - 1)}{U} \tag{4}$$

The upper bound of k and consequently average ultra-degree differs in leaf-peer and ultra-peer. To generalize further calculations, let m be the average ultra-degree of a peer. So, average hit ratio, denoted as $\langle H \rangle = \frac{1}{m} \cdot \sum_{k=1}^{m} H_k$ is,

$$= 1 - \frac{d_{uu}^2 \cdot (m - 1)}{2 \cdot U}. \tag{5}$$

The equation 5 shows the average hit ratio of peer joining the network when the population of ultra-peers in the network is U. It also reflects that $(1 - \langle H \rangle)$ is inversely proportional to the number of ultra-peers (U) in the complete network. Now as each node joins, the network grows. As a result the average hit ratio changes with the network growth. Therefore evolved hit ratio is the average value of all average hit ratios which are calculated at each growing stages of the network. Let U_0 and U_n be the number of ultra-peers in the initial and final networks. So, evolved hit ratio is

$$\langle H_{ev} \rangle = \frac{1}{U_n - U_0} \cdot \sum_{U_i = U_0}^{U_n} \langle H \rangle$$

$$= 1 - \frac{d_{uu}^2 \cdot (m - 1)}{2 \cdot (U_n - U_0)} \cdot \sum_{U_i = U_0}^{U_n} \frac{1}{U_i} \tag{6}$$

$$\approx 1 - \frac{d_{uu}^2 \cdot (m - 1)}{2 \cdot (U_n - U_0)} \cdot \log (U_n / U_0) \tag{7}$$

From equations 5 and 7 we get,

$$\langle H_{ev} \rangle \leq \langle H \rangle$$

As d and the maximum value of m are bounded, the value of $\langle H_{ev} \rangle$ increases with U. Again we have tested this phenomenon through our simulation and plotted the evolved hit-ratio against the network size of 200k-1000k in Fig 4 and observed the similarity between them. The similarity is not pronounced in the beginning as the approximations made to develop equations 4 and 7 play major role in smaller networks.

Consistency Problem: Periodically exchanging the list of neighbors facilitates the peers to get up-to-date information about their neighbors. In between two successive

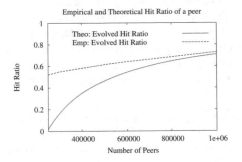

Fig. 4. Hit ratio of a peer against the number of peers in the network

updates, a peer may possibly have erroneous knowledge about it's neighbors. As a result, this inconsistency of the network leads to the presence of 3-length or 4-length cycles. Parallel update is possible when many peers enter simultaneously or there is a huge failure/attack in the network whereby many nodes have lost their neighbors and would now like to gain some.

1. *Parallel update:* In parallel update, due to inconsistency, smaller length cycles are formed as multiple peers from the same cycle handshake in parallel with a third common ultra-peer to become each other's neighbor. The parallel update situation is illustrated through an example (Fig 5(a)) where peer-1 and peer-5 execute the following actions according to steps of HPC5 and form cycle-3.
   (a) Both peer-1 and peer-5 find that peer-P is a valid remote peer to contact and both send request to P.
   (b) Peer-P gets their request more-or-less at the same time and sends back the neighbor-hood status to them.
   (c) As peer-1 and peer-5 do not know each other's activity or updated status, they make P as their new neighbor, therefore a cycle-3 is formed due to this inconsistency.
   Similarly smaller cycles may be created when multiple peers contact each other as a directed cycle (as in Fig. 5(b)) within the period of two successive updates.

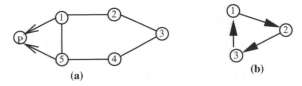

(a)

(b)

Fig. 5. A part of cycle-5 network, representing parallel update inconsistency

2. *Inconsistency arising in the face of failure/attack:*
   Here we discuss about the topological status of the network when x fraction (where $x \ll 1$) of nodes are left/removed from the network. We assume that the nodes have left uniformly from the different parts of the network. So each peer loses a fraction

of its neighbors and in effect the average degree of a peer in the network becomes less. To maintain the degree distribution of the network, each peer contacts other remote ultra-peers to fulfil neighbor deficiency. During this process, 3-length and 4-length cycles are created temporarily due to inconsistency between two successive updates. We calculate the effects of inconsistency due to peers removal from an ultra-peer point-of-view, so in this section the term peer will be used to represent an ultra-peer.

• *3-length cycle:* A 3-length cycle is created if two neighbor peers and third remote peer get involved in HPC5 as in Fig. 5. The initiation of handshake protocol in different combinations among three peers may create triangle. Here in calculation we are following the combination shown in Fig. 5(a) and peers are named as peer-1, peer-5 and P. After removal process $U_{rem} = (U - xU)$ number of ultra-peers remain in the network. According to HPC5, a peer cannot make any ultra-peers at level Q, R or S in Fig. 3 as its neighbor. We assume that the probability of getting any ultra-peer is uniform. So the probability of selecting an ultra-neighbor (here P) by peer-1 is

$$P_0 = \frac{U_{rem} - [d_{uu}(1-x)]^3}{U_{rem}}$$

The probability of choosing the same ultra-peer (P) as neighbor by any neighbor of peer-1 (here peer-5) is

$$P_1 \approx \frac{1}{U_{rem} - [d_{uu}(1-x)]^3}$$

So the probability of forming a 3-length cycle is

$$P_t = P_0 \cdot P_1 \approx \frac{1}{U_{rem}}$$

Therefore, the average number of 3-length cycles created around an ultra-peer is $[(d_{uu} + d_{ul})(1-x)/U_{rem}]$ and total number of 3-length cycles formed in the network is

$$L_3 = \bigcirc(\frac{(d_{uu} + d_{ul})(1-x)}{U_{rem}} \cdot U_{rem})$$
$$= \bigcirc((d_{uu} + d_{ul})(1-x)) = \bigcirc(d_{uu})$$

($\bigcirc(f)$ represents big-oh(f)).

• *4-length cycle:* A 4-length cycle is created if P and one of its 2nd ultra-neighbors or any two 1st neighbors (leaf or ultra) of P contact T and become neighbors. Similar to 3-length cycles calculation, the average number of 4-length cycles created around an ultra-peer is

$$\frac{[d_{uu}(1-x)]^2 + d_{uu}d_{ul}(1-x)^2}{U_{rem}}$$

and total number of 4-length cycles formed in the network is

$$L_4 = \bigcirc([d_{uu}(1-x)]^2 + d_{uu}d_{ul}(1-x)^2) = \bigcirc(d_{uu}^2)$$

So the total number of smaller length cycles created due to nodes removal is

$$L = L_3 + L_4 = \bigcirc(d_{uu}{}^2) \tag{8}$$

which is very less compared to network size.

In the same way we can prove that the effect of inconsistency from leaf-peer point-of-view is $\bigcirc(d_{uu} \cdot d_{lu})$.

Although, the presence of a small percentage of smaller length cycles in the network is tolerable, as they do not affect much on the performance but we have developed an algorithm for detecting and removing small length cycles arising due to inconsistency. However the details are avoided due to lack of space.

5   Evaluation by Simulation

To validate our approach, we have performed numerous experiments. We have taken different sizes (up to 1000k nodes) of networks and through these experiments, we have shown that HPC5 performs better than the existing protocols.

5.1   Search Performance

In our simulations, we have used message complexity and network coverage as performance metrics to analyze the search efficiency. *Message complexity* is defined as the average number of messages required to discover a peer in the overlay network. *Network coverage* implies the number of unique peers explored during query propagation in limited flooding. We have plotted the network coverage and message complexity (y-axis) with $TTL(2)$ and $TTL(3)$ flooding against the size of the network (x-axis) for leaf as well as ultra peers. To get the overall performance of the network, we have chosen the number of ultra-peers and leaf-peers for query flooding in the same $\frac{U}{L}$ ratio. The performance of the network is greatly influenced by the value of TTL used in search and thus we have discussed the performance metrics based on $TTL(2)$ and $TTL(3)$ separately. The search performance (specially message complexity) also depends on the implementation of QRP technique [1]. Thus we have discussed the search performance without and with QRP.

TTL(2) without QRP
It is clear from figures 7(a) and 7(b) that with $TTL(2)$, cycle-5 networks are better than cycle-3 networks in both message complexity and network coverage. In cycle-5 networks, the network coverage is approximately doubled and message complexity is almost 20% less than that of cycle-3 networks. With $TTL(2)$, a search query covers a significant portion (in our simulation it is more than 30%) of the cycle-5 network with lesser number of redundant messages. From the results we see that the message complexity is not close to 1 as expected. This is because the message complexity of the leaf-peer generated query is particularly high (Fig. 7(b)). In cycle-5 networks, a leaf-peer can be connected with two ultra-peers which are themselves 3rd or 4th neighbors of each-other and becomes a part of cycle-5 or cycle-6 (Fig. 6). From Fig. 6 we see, a leaf-peer search is initiated by its ultra-peers; both ultra-peers 1 & 4 (in Fig. 6(a))

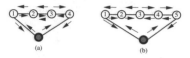

Fig. 6. Effect of leaf-peer layer with TTL(2) search. The arrows inside and outside of polygons indicate the directions of search by a leaf-peer and an ultra-peer respectively.

{1 & 5 (in Fig. 6(b))} start a $TTL(2)$ flooding. Consequently redundant messages are produced at ultra-peers 2 & 3 {3}. However, hardly any redundancy is generated in ultra-peer initiated query ((Fig. 7(b)).

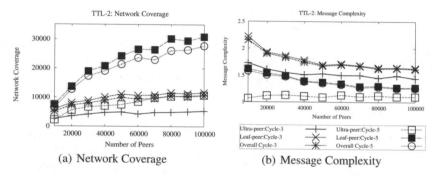

(a) Network Coverage   (b) Message Complexity

Fig. 7. Network Coverage and message complexity with TTL 2 for cycle-3 and cycle-5 networks

As a result, cycle-5 networks generate a large number of redundant messages which gets reflected in Fig. 7(b).

TTL(3) without QRP

Fig. 8(a) shows that in our simulation the entire cycle-5 networks are covered with $TTL(3)$ search which is almost double of the coverage attained in cycle-3 networks. If any pair of ultra-neighbors of a particular leaf-peer are not more than 6 hops apart from each other (in case of TTL(2) it was 4 hops), then query generates redundant messages. In cycle-5 networks the probability of forming cycle-5 and cycle-6 is very high. As a result, the message complexity of cycle-5 networks becomes higher than cycle-3 networks (Fig. 8(b)). As mentioned earlier, Gnutella (Limewire etc.) uses $TTL(3)$ in dynamic querying only for rare searches [1,2]. Therefore larger network coverage in this case, which increases the query hit probability, is more essential than slight increase of message complexity.

TTL(2) and TTL(3) with QRP

With QRP technique, searching is performed only at the ultra-peer layer, since ultra-peers contain the indices of their children [1,2]. So, the measurement of message complexity at the ultra-peer layer is more appropriate to compare results with Gnutella networks. The ultra-peer layer message complexity is shown in the Fig. 9. Simulation reflects that the message complexity in $TTL(2)$ of cycle-3 networks is almost 2-2.5

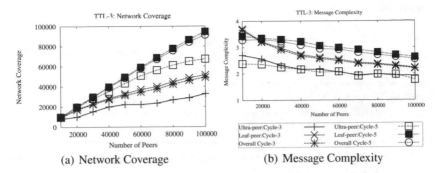

(a) Network Coverage   (b) Message Complexity

Fig. 8. Network Coverage and message complexity with TTL 3 for cycle-3 and cycle-5 networks

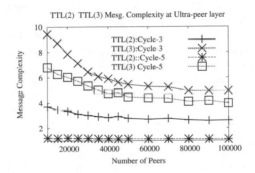

Fig. 9. Message Complexity with TTL(2) and TTL(3) at the Ultra-peer layer

times than that of cycle-5 networks. Even in $TTL(3)$ search cycle-3 networks generate 25% more messages than that of cycle-5 networks. So HPC5 protocol will be more effective in the Gnutella network in the presence of QRP protocol.

6   Conclusion and Future Work

In this paper, we have presented a handshake protocol which is compatible with Gnutella like unstructured two-tier overlay topology. We have shown that the protocol is far more efficient than existing protocols. A relation among TTL, minimum cycle length in the topology and network performance has been observed and proposed. A major fraction of internet bandwidth is occupied by Gnutella-like unstructured popular networks. P2P implementation of the 2nd generation web applications requires a huge internet bandwidth which initiates the optimum utilization of bandwidth. In this regard our protocol can be instrumental in improving the scalability of P2P networks.

In our future work we want to increase query hits through index table replication for cycle-5 networks. We are also planning to work on some design issues related to hit ratio, performance and bandwidth of the cycle-5 networks.

References

1. Gnutella and limewire, www.limewire.org
2. Gnutella protocol specification 0.6, http://rfc-gnutella.sourceforge.net
3. Gnutella, www.gnutellaforums.com
4. Gwebcache system, www.gnucleus.com
5. Karbhari, P., Ammar, M.H., Dhamdhere, A., Raj, H., Riley, G.F., Zegura, E.W.: Bootstrapping in gnutella: A measurement study. In: Barakat, C., Pratt, I. (eds.) PAM 2004. LNCS, vol. 3015, pp. 22–32. Springer, Heidelberg (2004)
6. Liu, Liu, Xiao, Ni, Zhang: Location-aware topology matching in P2P systems. In: INFOCOM: The Conference on Computer Communications, joint conference of the IEEE Computer and Communications Societies (2004)
7. Liu, Xiao, Liu, Ni, Zhang: Location awareness in unstructured peer-to-peer systems. IEEET-PDS: IEEE Transactions on Parallel and Distributed Systems 16 (2005)
8. Lua, K., Crowcroft, J., Pias, M., Sharma, R., Lim, S.: A survey and comparison of peer-to-peer overlay network schemes. Communications Surveys & Tutorials, 72–93 (2005)
9. Lv, Q., Cao, P., Cohen, E., Li, K., Shenker, S.: Search and replication in unstructured peer-to-peer networks. In: Proceedings of the 2002 International Conference on Supercomputing (16th ICS 2002), pp. 84–95. ACM, New York (2002)
10. Merugu, S., Srinivasan, S., Zegura, E.W.: Adding structure to unstructured peer-to-peer networks: The role of overlay topology. In: Stiller, B., Carle, G., Karsten, M., Reichl, P. (eds.) NGC 2003 and ICQT 2003. LNCS, vol. 2816, pp. 83–94. Springer, Heidelberg (2003)
11. Papadakis, C., Fragopoulou, P., Athanasopoulos, E., Dikaiakos, M.D., Labrinidis, A., Markatos, E.: A feedback-based approach to reduce duplicate messages in unstructured peer-to-peer networks. In: Integrated Research in GRID Computing (February 2007)
12. Saroiu, S., Gummadi, P.K., Gribble, S.D.: A measurement study of peer-to-peer file sharing systems. Technical report, July 23 (2002)
13. Stutzbach, D., Rejaie, R.: Capturing accurate snapshots of the gnutella network. IEEE INFOCOM, 2825–2830 (2005)
14. Stutzbach, D., Rejaie, R., Sen, S.: Characterizing unstructured overlay topologies in modern p2p file-sharing systems. In: Internet Measurment Conference, pp. 49–62. USENIX Association (2005)
15. Zhenzhou, Z., Panos, K., Spiridon, B.: Dcmp: A distributed cycle minimization protocol for peer-to-peer networks. IEEE Transactions on Parallel and Distributed Systems 19, 363–377 (2008)

Representation of Complex Concepts for Semantic Routed Network

Amitava Biswas, Suneil Mohan, Jagannath Panigrahy, Aalap Tripathy,
and Rabi Mahapatra

Department of Computer Science, Texas A&M University,
College Station, Texas, USA 77843
{amitabi,suneil,jagannath,aalap,rabi}@cs.tamu.edu

Abstract. Semantic Routed Network (SRN) can provide a scalable distributed solution for searching data in a large grid. In SRN, messages are routed in a overlay network based on the meaning of the message key. If the message key describes the desired data, then SRN nodes can be addressed and accessed by the description of their data content. The key challenges of materializing a SRN are: (1) designing a data structure which will represent complex descriptions of data objects; (2) computing similarity of descriptors; and (3) constructing a small world network topology that minimize the routing response time and maximize routing success, which depends on solving the first two problems. We present a design of a descriptor data structure and a technique to compare their similarity to address the first two problems.

Keywords: Semantic similarity, semantic routing, P2P systems.

1 Introduction

Search and retrieval of data from a large grid still remains a challenge because centralized search engines can only cover a very small portion (~0.25%) of the available information wealth [1]. Semantic Routed Network (SRN) which allows intention based searching can be a scalable solution to this problem.

SRN is an overlay network that can be implemented on top of the existing IP network. In SRN a message is routed to the final destination based on the meaning of the address key. Here two routing mechanisms, semantic routing and IP routing, operates together. Uniform Resource Identifier (URI, RFC 3986) is used as the unique handle to identify a resource (SRN node). To send a message to a particular resource, the message is loaded with a semantic key (denoted by "K", Fig. 1) which has a meaning similar to the description of the targeted resource (denoted by "D", Fig. 1), and then the message is injected into the overlay network of interconnected semantic routers (internet hosts). A semantic router maintains URI addresses of resources whose descriptions are similar to its own, in its semantic routing table.

Once a message is received, the semantic router identifies the URI name of the next semantic router or resource node whose description ("D") which is most similar to the message key "K" from the table (semantic lookup). Then the router carries out

V. Garg, R. Wattenhofer, and K. Kothapalli (Eds.): ICDCN 2009, LNCS 5408, pp. 127–138, 2009.

a DNS look up for this URI to ascertain the corresponding IP address to forward the message. In a SRN, once the message is delivered to the intended destination, the destination can respond back to the message source. Users need not know the exact description (matching keywords) of service/data or its schema. They can simply send a "call back" request with an appropriate semantic key which reasonably describes the desired service/data and get the handle to the resource they seek. In this manner semantic routing in SRN can enable distributed and scalable searching in a grid.

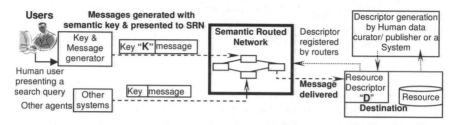

Fig. 1. Semantic Routed Network as a distributed information retrieval system

The challenges to realize a SRN include: (1) designing a suitable data structure to represent the semantic descriptors or keys; (2) developing an algorithm to compare any two arbitrary descriptors/keys; and (3) innovating suitable techniques to organize the overlay network which gives optimum search performance. The first two problems have to be solved in a way so that semantic routers will tolerate variability of keys as long as they contain same meaning. For example, using the SRN, users should be able to identify a bioinformatics data object (resource node) related to "neurotransmitter" by using any of these keywords: "dopamine", "serotonin" or "glycine". In biology the concept "neurotransmitter" encompasses (subsumes) "dopamine", therefore the semantically related keys should be interchangeable. This allows intention based semantic searching. Such semantic search capability can supplement the existing bioinformatics federation platforms like [2] and [3].

In addition the semantic descriptors should be able to represent complex concepts which are often needed to convey complex descriptions. Human beings comprehend and visualize complex concepts in terms of elementary and supporting concepts and their hierarchical compositions. Therefore the descriptor data structure should enable hierarchical concept composition. As a solution to the third problem, in [4] we showed how topology generation and semantic lookup algorithms can organize resource and router nodes in a small world network. However these algorithms depend on semantic descriptors and their comparison.

This paper presents the required techniques and algorithms that are needed to materialize high throughput semantic router hardware. First we present the algebraic theory and techniques to represent hierarchically composed concepts as a tensor which is amenable to efficient semantic similarity computation. Next we delineate a data structure for the semantic descriptors/keys and an algorithm to generate them. Then we describe an algorithm to compute the semantic similarity of two given descriptors (tensors). These techniques tolerate complex concepts (descriptions) while enabling query relaxation [5] and key interchangeability, while this is achieved without the routers having to maintain a knowledgebase (ontology) unlike in [5].

2 Preliminaries and Related Works

Semantic similarity comparison approaches. The vector space algebraic models represent description of an object as a vector where each dimension corresponds to an index term found in the vocabulary. A term can be a single keyword, or a phrase which indicates an entity or an idea. If a term occurs in the description, then a non-zero value (term weight) for the corresponding basis vector is considered. There are several alternatives ways to compute these values (e.g., TF-IDF [6]). The level of semantic similarity between two descriptor vectors, V_1 and V_2, is given by the cosine of the angle between them (Eqn.1). A similarity value of zero means that two vectors are dissimilar (orthogonal) and a higher value indicates more similarity.

$$\cos \ \theta \ = \frac{V_1 \bullet V_2}{\|V_1\| \cdot \|V_2\|} = \left\langle \frac{V_1}{\|V_1\|}, \frac{V_2}{\|V_2\|} \right\rangle \tag{1}$$

Lexical [7], ontological [8] and semantic network [9], formal concept analysis [4], [10] based approaches have been also proposed to compare semantic similarity between terms or descriptions/documents.

Limitations of existing approaches. Some of them (e.g, [4], [10]) do not support use of synonyms and hypernyms. All the above approaches are computationally expensive and can not represent complex descriptions which are based on complex meanings (concepts). This results in failure to discern between descriptions that have common keywords/terms but have very different meanings. In scientific applications, such keywords that are common between two vectors, may be statistically under represented in the corpus which causes a TF-IDF scheme to assign greater weights to these terms. This increases the similarity score when it should be minimal or zero.

3 Semantic Descriptor and Similarity Comparison

The network organization technique proposed in [4], groups destinations based on similarity of their descriptors (analogous to forming sub-nets) and enables routing table compression by replacing multiple key-destination map entries (routing table rows) with a single entry (row). Whereas route resolution essentially involves choosing a single (or few) forwarding destinations, based on which destination descriptor "D_i" is most similar to the message key descriptor "K" [4]. The techniques to represent and compare meanings using semantic descriptors are presented below.

3.1 Concept Composition and Tree Representation

We propose to represent a complex concept as a tree of hierarchically composed concepts with basic concepts as leaves (Fig. 2). Basic concepts are the ones which are represented by standard terms in domain lexicon or ontology like MeSH [2], Gene Ontology [11], Disease Ontology [12], etc. The other advantage of using this tree is that it can be represented as a tensor which is amenable for computationally inexpensive similarity computation. This is best explained by the example in Fig. 2 where we have considered a publication [13] as a resource. This kind of publication contains significant amounts of data. Quite often authors upload the related data set in bioinformatics databases. In that case we can consider the abstract of the publication as the textual description of the uploaded data in addition to the publication.

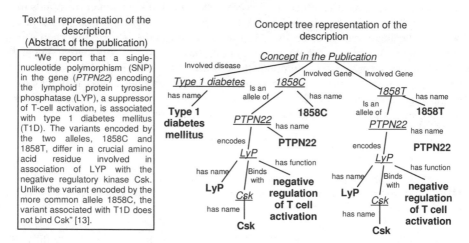

Textual representation of the
description
(Abstract of the publication)

"We report that a single-nucleotide polymorphism (SNP) in the gene (*PTPN22*) encoding the lymphoid protein tyrosine phosphatase (LYP), a suppressor of T-cell activation, is associated with type 1 diabetes mellitus (T1D). The variants encoded by the two alleles, 1858C and 1858T, differ in a crucial amino acid residue involved in association of LYP with the negative regulatory kinase Csk. Unlike the variant encoded by the more common allele 1858C, the variant associated with T1D does not bind Csk" [13].

Concept tree representation of the
description

Fig. 2. Representation of the content description

In Fig.2, the composed concepts are underlined and the basic concepts (terms) are in bold. The topmost concept, which is the publication's description, is composed of three child concepts: (1) the 1858T allele; (2) the 1858C allele; and (3) the resulting disease. A concept can be defined by multiple ways: by its label (name), by its function or by its relationships with other elementary concepts. For similarity matching, any one child concept may be sufficient in some cases, but additional supporting concepts as children can get a higher confidence. For example the concept LyP is known either: by its name "LyP" or by its "binds with" relationship with Csk or by the conjunction of all or some of these concepts. Thus this combination is actually a mix of disjunction (Boolean OR) and conjunction (AND) of the elementary concepts. This is modeled by designing a suitable algebraic binder (function) which is subsequently explained. The specific rules of constructing this tree will depend on the domain models and these can be codified as grammars of several domain specific Concept Description Language (CDL) dialects (e.g. CDL grammar for biochemistry of gene-disease interaction).

3.2 Mathematical Basis behind Tensor Representation of Concept Tree

An idea or concept is expressed as a tensor [14] in a Hilbert (vector) space, where the set of basis vectors includes the set of basic basis vectors "e_i", each of which corresponds to a unique basic concept (e.g. "Csk", "LyP", "negative regulation of T cell activation") in the domain lexicon, in addition to their polyadic combinations represented in the form "$e_ie_je_k.....$" which represent conjunction of concepts (e.g. "LyP" & "CsK" & "negative regulation of T cell activation" &...). This is needed because elementary concepts can combine with each other to form complex concepts which are entirely different from the elementary ones. The normalized inner (dot) product of the tensors, represented by $\langle \bullet, \bullet \rangle$, signifies the semantic similarity between the two concepts represented by these tensors. The basis vectors and their polyads are orthogonal hence $\langle e_i, e_j \rangle = \langle e_i e_j e_k \dots e_i \rangle = \langle e_i e_j \dots e_i e_k \dots \rangle = \dots = 0$.

To facilitate representation of concept composition we define two algebraic binders (functions): (1) $[\bullet, \bullet \dots]$; and (2) $\{\bullet, \bullet \dots\}$, that bind two or more tensors together. For example, by using $[\bullet, \bullet \dots]$, three tensors A, B and C, can be bound together to represent a composition [A,B,C]. These binders are used to generate the tensor which represents the composed concept tree in terms of its leaves. Both of these binders are commutative w.r.t their arguments. This ensures that all possible isomorphic trees (Fig. 3a) that convey the same meaning are expressed by a single tensor.

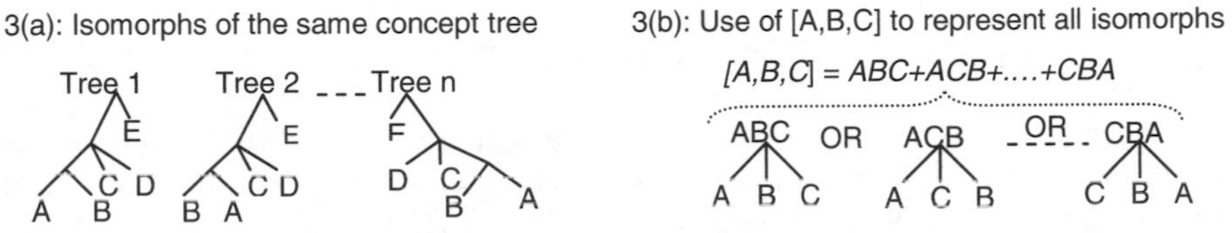

3(a): Isomorphs of the same concept tree   3(b): Use of [A,B,C] to represent all isomorphs

Fig. 3. Rational behind the descriptor data structure design

Definition of $[\bullet, \bullet \dots]$ **binder.** For case of one, two and three arguments we define:

$[A] \equiv A$, $[A, B] \equiv AB + BA$, $[A, B, C] \equiv ABC + ACB + BAC + CAB + BCA + CBA$, where AB denotes a dyadic tensor product, ABC denotes a triadic tensor and a polyadic tensor [14] is denoted by a juxtaposition (e.g., ABCD...). In general, $AB \neq BA$. This definition can be expanded for a general case of "n" arguments, where the sum of product form have all permutations of arguments: A,B,C, etc. Fig. 3b illustrates the usefulness of this binder.

Proof for the commutative property. Proof for two argument case is given which can be extended for "n" arguments. [A,B] = AB +BA = BA + AB = [B,A].

Definition of $\{\bullet, \bullet \dots\}$ **binder.** For one, two and three arguments we define:

$$\{A\} \equiv \frac{\sqrt{h_A} * [A]}{\sqrt{h_A^2}} = A \quad ; \quad \{A, B\} \equiv \frac{\sqrt{h_{AB}/2} * [A, B] + \sqrt{h_A} * [A] + \sqrt{h_B} * [B]}{\left\| \sqrt{h_{AB}/2} * [A, B] + \sqrt{h_A} * [A] + \sqrt{h_B} * [B] \right\|}$$

$$\{A, B, C\} \equiv \frac{(\sqrt{h_{ABC}/6} * [A, B, C] + \sqrt{h_{AB}/2} * [A, B] + \sqrt{h_{BC}/2} * [B, C] + \sqrt{h_{AC}/2} * [A, C] + \sqrt{h_A} * [A] + \sqrt{h_B} * [B] + \sqrt{h_C} * [C])}{\left\| (\sqrt{h_{ABC}/6} * [A, B, C] + \sqrt{h_{AB}/2} * [A, B] + \sqrt{h_{BC}/2} * [B, C] + \sqrt{h_{AC}/2} * [A, C] + \sqrt{h_A} * [A] + \sqrt{h_B} * [B] + \sqrt{h_C} * [C]) \right\|}$$

This binder encompasses all possible combinations and permutations of arguments. The resultant tensor is also normalized and used as an elementary tensor to be incorporated for next higher level of composition. Each instance of this binder has a corresponding set of co-occurring coefficients "H", having real valued scalar elements (e.g. H = set { h_{ABC}, h_{AB}, h_{BC}, h_{AC}, h_A, h_B, h_C }), each of which indicates the importance of the corresponding polyad to represent the meaning of the composed concept. For example, when only $h_{ABC} = 1$ and all other scalars $h_{AB} = h_{BC} \dots = h_C = 0$, then the composed concept is the one which is given by a strict conjunction of A,B and C. Whereas the set $h_A = h_B = h_C = 1$ and $h_{ABC} = h_{AB} = h_{BC} = h_{AC} = 0$ represents disjunction composition. A mix of all these extremes is possible by suitable choice of values for the co-occurring coefficients. Rules that guide assignment of these values can be codified under the CDL grammar. These parameters are normalized by $(n!)^{1/2}$, where "n" is the number of arguments in $[\bullet, \bullet \cdots]$.

Proof for the commutative property. When a function "F" is a linear composition (linear functional) of two other functions "F_1" and "F_2", such that $F = \lambda_1 * F_1 + \lambda_2 * F_2$ where λ_1 and λ_2 are real numbers, and if both function F_1 and F_2 is commutative, then their linear functional F is also commutative. The proof of this property is shown for two arguments, but it can be extended for "n" arguments. If $F_1(A,B) = F_1(B,A)$ and $F_2(A,B) = F_2(B,A)$, therefore $F(A,B) = \lambda_1 * F_1(A,B) + \lambda_2 * F_2(A,B) = \lambda_1 * F_1(B,A) + \lambda_2 * F_2(B,A) = F(B,A)$. As binder $\{\bullet, \bullet, \ldots\}$ is a linear functional of commutative $[\bullet, \bullet \cdots]$ binders, it is also commutative.

3.3 Tensor Representation of Concept Tree

A concept tree can be represented by a tensor which is expressed as a sum of scalar weighted polyads of the basic basis vectors that represent the leaves. In the example in Fig. 4a, all intermediate composed concepts for a tree are represented by the expressions present at corresponding node positions in the concept tree. These expressions are represented in terms of the binders defined earlier. On expanding these expressions we get the tensor in the form which is suitable for inner product computation. Each composition in this tree has its own co-occurrence set, for example the set "H" for binder {A,B} is denoted by ^{AB}H. For two compositions in example tree, the two co-occurrence sets: ^{AB}H, $^{(AB)C}H$, are also shown by arrows in Fig. 4a.

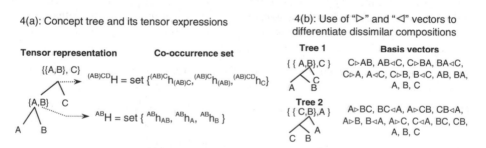

Fig. 4. Tensor expression for a concept tree

The expression {{A,B}, C} which represents "Tree 1" in Fig. 4b is expanded bottom up as an example. Basic basis vectors are denoted by lower case alphabets with arrow on top and scalars are without arrows. Delimiter vectors "▷" and "◁" are introduced between tensors which are at different tree levels. The delimiter vectors point toward the tensor which belongs to a lower tree level. For example, instead of "CAB" and "ABC" we write "C▷AB" and "AB◁C". The use of delimiter vectors ensure that trees having same leaves but different composition do not have similarity beyond which is contributed by the individual leaves (Fig. 4b). The scalar coefficients of the basis vectors are products of normalized co-occurring coefficients.

$$A = \vec{a}, B = \vec{b}, C = \vec{c}, \text{ and } \{A, B\} = \frac{^{AB}h_{AB}/\sqrt{2}*[A,B]+^{AB}h_A*[A]+^{AB}h_B*[B]}{\left\|^{AB}h_{AB}/\sqrt{2}*[A,B]+^{AB}h_A*[A]+^{AB}h_B*[B]\right\|} = \frac{^{AB}h_{AB}/\sqrt{2}\,(\vec{ab}+\vec{ba})+^{AB}h_A\,\vec{a}+^{AB}h_B\,\vec{b}}{\sqrt{(^{AB}h_{AB})^2+(^{AB}h_A)^2+(^{AB}h_B)^2}}$$

$$\{\{A,B\},C\} = \frac{^{(AB)C}h_{(AB)C}/\sqrt{2}*\{A,B\}\lhd C + {}^{(AB)C}h_{(AB)C}/\sqrt{2}*C\rhd\{A,B\}+^{(AB)C}h_{AB}*\{A,B\}+^{(AB)C}h_C*C}{\sqrt{(^{(AB)C}h_{(AB)C})^2+(^{(AB)C}h_{AB})^2+(^{(AB)C}h_C)^2}}$$

$$= \frac{1}{\sqrt{(^{AB}h_{AB})^2+(^{AB}h_A)^2+(^{AB}h_B)^2}}*\frac{1}{\sqrt{(^{(AB)C}h_{(AB)C})^2+(^{(AB)C}h_{AB})^2+(^{(AB)C}h_C)^2}}*(\frac{^{(AB)C}h_{(AB)C}}{\sqrt{2}}\frac{^{AB}h_{AB}}{\sqrt{2}}*(\overrightarrow{ab\lhd c}+\overrightarrow{ba\lhd c}+\overrightarrow{c\rhd ab}+\overrightarrow{c\rhd ba})+$$

$$\frac{^{(AB)C}h_{(AB)C}}{\sqrt{2}}*^{AB}h_A*(\overrightarrow{a\lhd c}+\overrightarrow{c\rhd a})+\frac{^{(AB)C}h_{(AB)C}}{\sqrt{2}}*^{AB}h_B*(\overrightarrow{b\lhd c}+\overrightarrow{c\rhd b})+^{(AB)C}h_{AB}*\frac{^{AB}h_{AB}}{\sqrt{2}}*(\vec{ab}+\vec{ba})+^{(AB)C}h_{AB}*^{AB}h_A*\vec{a}+^{(AB)C}h_{AB}*^{AB}h_B*\vec{b}+^{(AB)C}h_C*\vec{c})$$

3.4 Computation of Inner Product of Tensors and Bloom Filter Basics

The inner (dot) product $\langle E, F \rangle$ of two concept tensors E and F is the sum of product of the scalar coefficients of all basis vectors that are common in E and F. To quickly pair up the scalar coefficients for multiplications (as in Fig 5a) we use bloom filters.

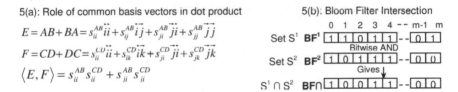

5(a): Role of common basis vectors in dot product

$$E = AB + BA = s_{ii}^{AB}\,\vec{ii} + s_{ij}^{AB}\,\vec{ij} + s_{ji}^{AB}\,\vec{ji} + s_{jj}^{AB}\,\vec{jj}$$

$$F = CD + DC = s_{ii}^{CD}\,\vec{ii} + s_{ik}^{CD}\,\vec{ik} + s_{ji}^{CD}\,\vec{ji} + s_{jk}^{CD}\,\vec{jk}$$

$$\langle E, F \rangle = s_{ii}^{AB}\,s_{ii}^{CD} + s_{ji}^{AB}\,s_{ji}^{CD}$$

5(b): Bloom Filter Intersection

Set S^1 **BF**^{1} | 0 | 1 | 2 | 3 | 4 | -- | m-1 | m
Set S^2 **BF**^{2}
Bitwise AND
Gives
$S^1 \cap S^2$ **BFn**

Fig. 5. Dot product and bloom filter basics

Bloom filter (BF) is a compact representation of a set [15]. The test of whether an arbitrary element is in the BF can result in false positives (returns true even when the element is not present), but not false negatives (will never return false when the element is present). The probability of false positives, $p_{false+ve} \approx (1 - e^{-kn/m})^k$, can be minimized by choosing large "m", and optimum "k" ($\approx 0.7*m/n$), where "m" is the number of bits in the BF, "k" is the number of independent hash functions and "n" is number of elements in the BF (Fig. 5b).

For example, a basic BF with m = 225 Kilobits, k = 16 can keep 10^4 elements with a small $p_{false+ve} \approx 2*10^{-5}$, which will have a negligible effect on similarity comparison. When two similar sized BFs (same "m", "k") represent two sets then the BF obtained by bitwise AND operation of these two parent BFs (BF_1, BF_2 in Fig. 5b) represents a set which is an intersection of the two sets. We use this property to filter out the common basis vectors from two tensors. When tensors' basis vectors are inserted in two BFs, then the intersection BF is a set of common basis vectors.

3.5 Technique to Generate Semantic Descriptor Data Structure

The tensor representation of the entire concept tree is encoded in a compact semantic descriptor data structure, which has two basic components: (1) a big "m" bit wide bloom filter BF using "k" hash functions; and (2) a coefficient look up table (Fig. 6a). Each element/row in the coefficient table has three columns: the 128 bit id for a basis vector (vector id); the scalar coefficient of the basis vector, as explained in sec 3.3;

and a set of "k" $\log_2 m$ bit integers which are indexes for the BF bits that should be set to 1 when the basis vector id is inserted in the BF. These data structure components together will be either: transmitted as query key, stored as semantic routing table row keys or used to compute semantic similarity. The steps to encode the concept tree tensor in this data structure are explained with the concept tree in Fig. 2:

- **Step 1:** The 128 bit vector identifiers for the basis vectors (polyads) are generated by hashing the concatenated textual representation of the polyad by MD5 algorithm. For example, one of the polyad in the tensor for the tree will be a combination of five basic terms/vectors: "LyP"; "Csk"; "negative regulation of T cell activation"; "◁"; and "PTPN22". We concatenate these three character strings together to get "LyPCsk negative regulation of T cell activation◁PTPN22" and then get its 128 bit MD5 digest. Henceforth we use the term vector ids and vectors interchangeably.
- **Step 2:** We insert the vector ids in the BF and note its BF bit cell indices.
- **Step 3:** For each basis vectors, we insert a row in the coefficient lookup table comprising of the vector id, the scalar coefficient of that vector; and the set of all the BF bit cell indices (Fig. 6a).

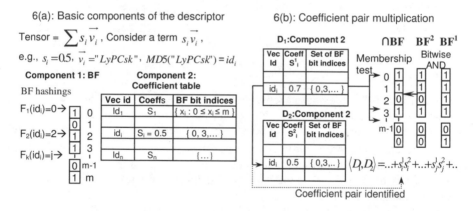

Fig. 6. Semantic descriptor generation and comparison

3.6 Technique for Fast Computation of Inner Product

The steps for computing of the inner product of two descriptors (D_1, D_2, Fig. 6b) are:

- **Step 1:** Two BFs of the data structures being compared are intersected (ANDed).
- **Step 2:** Once the set of common basis vectors has been filtered out in step 1, these are identified from the coefficient lookup table by verifying which vector ids are in the intersection BF by using the set of the BF bit indices.
- **Step 3:** If a vector is present in the intersection BF, then we use that common vector id as the key, and extract the coefficient value from the coefficient lookup table of the other data structure.

- **Step 4:** We multiply the pair of the coefficients for each identified common basis vectors and add all the products to get the similarity metric. With "n" basis vectors in the smallest descriptor (tensor) and "p" available parallel processor cells the complexity of this algorithm is O(n/p). Each of these operations in steps 1 to 4 can be executed in parallel at high speeds on simple hardware accelerators.

3.7 Extensions for Incorporating Synonym and Hypernyms

To incorporate synonyms and hypernyms for the elementary terms, the basic data structure described in sec. 3.5, is extended by a 3rd and 4th component: (3) a collection (set) of synonymous vector sets; and (4) a set of hypernym sequences.

Extensions for synonym. In the example of Fig. 2 the concept PTPN22, is denoted by multiple synonyms like "IPI00298016", "PTPN8: Tyrosine-protein phosphatase non-receptor type 22", in addition to "PTPN22", so there is a need to extend the concept tree tensor to incorporate all the known synonyms to enable correct comparison when two descriptors constructed using two different synonyms. The required technique is explained with an abstract example (Fig. 7a).

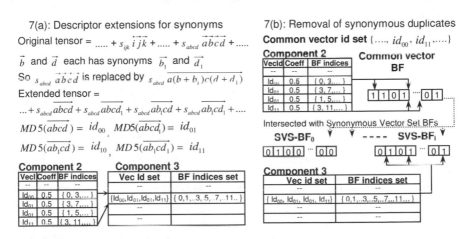

Fig. 7. Incorporation of synonyms in descriptor generation and comparison algorithms

Suppose the final tensor expression contains a term $s_{abcd}\,\overrightarrow{abcd}$, where the basis vector $\overrightarrow{abcd}$ is a polyad and the scalar coefficient is s_{abcd}. If the $\overrightarrow{b}$ and $\overrightarrow{d}$ each have one synonym: $\overrightarrow{b_1}$ and $\overrightarrow{d_1}$, then the term $s_{abcd}\,\overrightarrow{abcd}$ is replaced by sum of all combinations of the synonyms: $s_{abcd}\,\overrightarrow{abcd} + s_{abcd}\,\overrightarrow{abcd_1} + s_{abcd}\,\overrightarrow{ab_1cd} + s_{abcd}\,\overrightarrow{ab_1cd_1}$. We call $\overrightarrow{abcd_1}$, $\overrightarrow{ab_1cd}$, $\overrightarrow{ab_1cd_1}$, and $\overrightarrow{abcd}$ as synonymous vectors. This can be generalized to incorporate any number of synonyms for any number of basic concepts. The data structure generating algorithm is sec. 3.5 is extended as:

- **Step 4 & 5:** The 128 bit vector ids for all the synonymous vectors are generated and inserted in the BF as in step 1 and 2.

- **Step 6:** For each synonymous vectors, we insert a row in the coefficient lookup table comprising of the vector id, the scalar coefficient s_{abcd} ; and the set of all the BF bit cell indices (Fig. 7a).
- **Step 7:** The set of synonymous vectors ids are grouped together as a set and paired with the set of all their BF bit indices, and inserted as an element in the 3rd component, the "set of synonymous vector sets (SVS)" (Fig. 7a).

A step 2a is inserted between step 2 and 3 of the inner product algorithm in sec 3.6:

- **Step 2a:** The set of common vectors identified in step 2 is further filtered to remove the synonymous duplicates (e.g. $\overrightarrow{abcd_1}$, $\overrightarrow{ab_1cd}$, $\overrightarrow{ab_1cd_1}$) of a vector (e.g. $\overrightarrow{abcd}$), as follows. Using the BF bit indices from all the rows that contain the common vector ids a "common vector BF" is quickly constructed (Fig. 7b). Then we iterate (outermost loop in the nested iteration) over the "set of synonymous vector sets" and for each element, a synonymous vector BF is quickly constructed using BF indices and intersected with the common vector BF. If this intersected BF is not empty, we perform a nested iteration over this set of synonymous vector ids (in the middle loop) and over the set of common vector ids (in the innermost loop) to identify the ids that are in both sets. All subsequent common ids except the first one are dropped from common vector id set.

Extensions for hypernyms. To enable searching for a resource by a generic term (e.g. "Auto immune disease") instead of using the specific term for the concept (e.g. Type 1 diabetes), we have to incorporate all possible hypernyms for each term for similar reason as in case of synonyms. We consider a general model where the similarity value between a specific basic concept and its generic form is less than 1. The proposed hypernym incorporation technique is similar to that of synonyms. In the given example (Fig. 8a) we replace $\vec{c}$ in $s_{abcd} \overrightarrow{abcd}$ by a sum of scalar weighted hypernyms: $\vec{c}_1, \vec{c}_2, ... \vec{c}_n$, from the hypernym chain (Fig. 8b) where $\vec{c}$ corresponds to the term in the bottom most node. This chain is obtained from "is a" taxonomies or ontologies (e.g. Disease Ontology [12]). The hypernymous polyads have ranks and can be ordered to form a "hypernym sequences": $\overrightarrow{abcd} > \overrightarrow{abc_1d} > \overrightarrow{abc_2d} > ... > \overrightarrow{abc_nd}$. A set of all such ordered sequences form the 4th component, the "set of hypernym sequences". The data structure generating algorithm is extended by additional steps paired with the steps for the synonyms:

- **Step 4a (paired with step 4) & 5a (with step 5):** The 128 bit vector ids for all the hypernymous vectors are generated and inserted in the BF.
- **Step 6a:** Each of the vector ids of a set of hypernymous vectors are inserted in additional rows in the coefficient lookup table. The coefficient columns of these additional rows are filled with the coefficient s_{abcd} multiplied with the respective terms y_m for each hypernymous vector $\overrightarrow{abc_md}$, and with the set of BF bit indices.
- **Step 7a:** The set of hypernymous vectors ids are grouped together as a set and paired with the set of BF bit indices to generate "set of hypernym sequences".

We extend the inner product computation by a step 2b paired with step 2a:

Step 2b: The set of common vectors identified in step 2a is further filtered to remove the hypernymous vector duplicates. This is achieved in a manner similar to step 2a with only two differences. Here instead of "set of synonymous vector sets" the "set of hypernym sequences" is used. While performing the nested iteration, when a second common vector id is found between the set of common vector ids and the current hypernym sequence, the common vector id having the lowest rank in the sequence is dropped to get the final filtered common set of vectors.

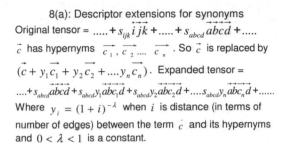

8(a): Descriptor extensions for synonyms

Original tensor $= \ldots + s_{ijk}\vec{i}\vec{j}\vec{k} + \ldots + s_{abcd}\overrightarrow{abcd} + \ldots$

$\vec{c}$ has hypernyms $\vec{c}_1, \vec{c}_2 \ldots \vec{c}_n$. So $\vec{c}$ is replaced by

$(\vec{c} + y_1\vec{c}_1 + y_2\vec{c}_2 + \ldots y_n\vec{c}_n)$. Expanded tensor $=$

$\ldots + s_{abcd}\overrightarrow{abcd} + s_{abcd}y_1\overrightarrow{abc_1 d} + s_{abcd}y_2\overrightarrow{abc_2 d} + \ldots s_{abcd}y_n\overrightarrow{abc_n d} + \ldots$

Where $y_i = (1+i)^{-\lambda}$ when i is distance (in terms of number of edges) between the term $\vec{c}$ and its hypernyms and $0 < \lambda < 1$ is a constant.

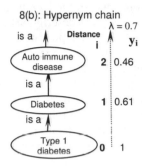

8(b): Hypernym chain

Fig. 8. Incorporation of synonyms in descriptor generation and comparison algorithms

4 Evaluation

We compared the performance of our tensor based semantic similarity computation scheme against the vector based approach. We obtained four publications (objects) from Pubmed [2] on gene-diabetes interaction studies, which are denoted by O_i in Table 1. The object pairs are ranked based on: (1) human interpretation; (2) semantic similarity values obtained by the tensor scheme; and (3) similarity values given by the vector based approach. MeSH index terms and their hypernyms were considered as the vectors in the vector model as in case of exploded search [2]. Semantic similarity ranking is our comparison criterion here, since it is the key primitive operation carried out during semantic lookup and semantic routing table optimization [4].

Table 1. Superior performance of tensor based approach for object similarity rankings

Object pairs	Semantic similarity rankings and (similarity values)		
	Human	Tensor approach	Vector approach
O_1, O_2	Rank 1	Rank 1 (0.864)	Rank 4 (0.442)
O_3, O_4	Rank 2	Rank 2 (0.689)	Rank 1 (0.653)
O_2, O_3	Rank 3	Rank 3 (0.557)	Rank 5 (0.395)
O_1, O_3	Rank 4	Rank 5 (0.443)	Rank 3 (0.521)
O_2, O_4	Rank 5	Rank 4 (0.525)	Rank 6 (0.376)
O_1, O_4	Rank 6	Rank 6 (0.317)	Rank 2 (0.608)
Kendall tau rank correlation	1	0.867	0.067

The non-parametric Kendall tau correlation of the rankings based on tensor and human interpretation is 0.867 which is much higher than that between vector approach and human interpretation (which is 0.067). This shows that the tensor based semantic descriptor model agrees more closely with humans in meaning comparison.

5 Future Work and Conclusion

In immediate future, we plan to design a technique to automatically generate concept trees from text descriptions and carry out larger scale evaluation of the proposed approach. We have presented the algebra, a data structure to represent complex concepts and a technique to generate the data structure. We have also illustrated an efficient computational technique to compute the semantic similarity of two given descriptors. To our knowledge this is the first work on representation and comparison of complex concepts that also allows query relaxation. These techniques will benefit materialization of semantic router hardware for the SRN, semantic search and retrieval of data from a grid of distributed databases, P2P networking and co-ordination among distributed internet search engines.

References

1. Bergman, M.: The Deep Web: Surfacing Hidden Value, White Paper (2001)
2. Pubmed, http://www.ncbi.nlm.nih.gov/pubmed/
3. SRS Server at EMBI-EBI, http://srs.ebi.ac.uk
4. Biswas, A., Mohan, S., Mahapatra, R.: Optimization of Semantic Routing Table. In: 17th International Conference on Computer Communications and Networks (2008)
5. Tempich, C., Staab, S., Wranik, A.: REMINDIN: Semantic Query Routing in Peer-to-Peer Networks Based on Social Metaphors. In: 13th Int. WWW Conf., pp. 640–649 (2004)
6. Salton, G., Buckley, C.: Term-weighting approaches in automatic text retrieval. Information Processing & Management 24(5), 513–523 (1988)
7. Yang, D., Powers, D.M.: Measuring semantic similarity in the taxonomy of WordNet. In: 28th Australasian Conference on Computer Science, vol. 38 (2005)
8. Hariri, B.H., Abolhassani, H., Khodaei, A.: A New Structural Similarity Measure for Ontology Alignment. In: Int. Conf. on Semantic Web & Web Services, pp. 36–42 (2006)
9. Lemaire, B., Denhière, G.: Incremental Construction of an Associative Network from a Corpus. In: 26th Annual Meeting of the Cognitive Science Society, pp. 825–830 (2004)
10. Rajapske, R., Denham, M.: Text retrieval with more realistic concept matching and reinforcement learning. Info. Processing and Management 42, 1260–1275 (2006)
11. Gene Ontology, http://www.geneontology.org/
12. Disease Ontology, http://diseaseontology.sourceforge.net/
13. Bottini, N., et al.: A functional variant of lymphoid tyrosine phosphatase is associated with type I diabetes. Nature Genetics 36, 337–338 (2004)
14. Irgens, F.: Tensors. Continuum Mechanics. Springer, Heidelberg (2008)
15. Broder, A., Mitzenmacher, M.: Network applications of Bloom filters: A survey. Internet Mathematics 1(4), 485–509 (2002)

Guaranteeing Eventual Coherency across Data Copies, in a Highly Available Peer-to-Peer Distributed File System

BijayaLaxmi Nanda, Anindya Banerjee, and Navin Kabra

Symantec Research Labs, Symantec Software India Private Ltd
RMZ ICON, Baner Road, Pune-411045, India
bijayalaxmi_nanda@symantec.com, anindya_banerjee@symantec.com
PuneTech.com
101 Twin Towers B, D. P. Road, Aundh, Pune-411007, India
navin@punetech.com

Abstract. Peer-to-peer systems use redundant data replicas to maintain high availability and improve on user response times. The consistency and coherency of these data replicas need to be maintained over time in face of various system changes like node joins, failures and network outages. In this paper we present a robust approach to guarantee eventual coherency of replicas in a multi-location large scale peer-to-peer distributed file system. We use a combination of data pull and push mechanisms, and a last coherent time stamp on each replica. These mechanisms ensure that no user read operation ever retrieves data that is older than a configurable upper bound in time.

Keywords: Peer-to-peer, wide-area file system, replication, data copies, coherency, consistency, push, pull, caching, high availability.

1 Introduction

Traditionally, peer-to-peer (P2P) based DFSs and file sharing systems have relied on file or data object replication to achieve better reliability in face of individual server failures. With replication, comes the problem of maintaining replica consistency and coherency. This problem has been of great interest in the research community, and many models have been proposed. In this paper, we briefly introduce our P2P protocol based DFS, named *StarFS*, and focus on how we have solved the problem of maintaining replica consistency and coherency in StarFS.

StarFS has been designed to run across wide area networks (WANs) to fit data hosting requirements of large enterprises. A typical enterprise will have multiple offices located in different countries and cities that are inter-connected through WAN. After performing a study of data access patterns for such types of enterprises, we observed that each file is normally updated from one location frequently, updated from other locations sparingly, and is read from different locations frequently. StarFS replica maintenance layer guarantees that no user will see stale data older than an interval set a-priori (*staleness threshold*). We do conflict prevention by maintaining enough number of replicas with latest data updated in a transactional manner. Cached replicas are synchronized asynchronously using a combination of push and pull mechanisms.

V. Garg, R. Wattenhofer, and K. Kothapalli (Eds.): ICDCN 2009, LNCS 5408, pp. 139–147, 2009.

2 StarFS Terminology

StarFS is designed to run on commodity servers using TCP/IP interconnections for
both control and data communications. Each such server is called a *Node*, which has
its own attached storage. The servers are aggregated hierarchically; a *Realm* is a collection of nodes within a LAN; a *Cloud* is a collection of realms connected by LAN
and/or WAN links.

Each file has a unique identifier associated with it, and has multiple copies on different nodes called *Replicas*. There are two types of replicas in the system described
in detail below.

P-replicas are *primary replicas*, which come into existence as part of the file 'create' operation and are persistent until a 'delete' operation is performed for the file.
Number of P-replicas per file is a known value configured at the set up time, and they
all reside within one realm called *P-replica realm* for the file. At least a quorum of
P-replicas is updated synchronously as part of file update using a distributed transaction. The transaction is always attempted on all P-replicas, and will not go ahead if at
least a quorum is not ready to perform the transaction.

R-replicas are *remote replicas* that are created in realms other than the P-replica
realm. They are automatically created and removed based on access pattern and space
availability. The R-replicas are updated asynchronously after updates to P-replicas.

Each replica has file specific metadata – creation/modification timestamps, access
permissions etc, and replica specific metadata – last coherent time stamp (described in
more detail later), and version number, maintained as part of on-disk metadata.

Data *coherency* implies the freshness of the data. A version number is associated
with every replica. If replicas that are up-to-date (have all updates to the file) are at
version v, any replica that is at version < v is called a *lagging* replica.

3 System Model

StarFS is built on top of a peer-to-peer infrastructure where every functional layer
communicates with its peers on other nodes to collaboratively provide a distributed
file service. Figure 1 shows the basic functional blocks of StarFS present on every

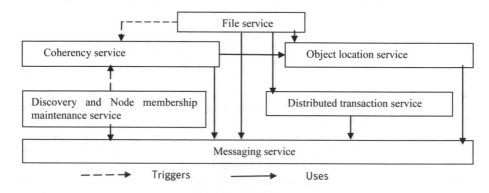

Fig. 1. StarFS functional block diagram on every node

node. *Messaging service* is responsible for sending and receiving message payloads from other service layers. *Discovery and node membership maintenance service* discovers new nodes joining the system, maintains node membership information and node status by doing heartbeat with immediate neighbors.

Object location service (OLS) maintains location records using file system metadata and a distributed hash table (DHT) on all nodes in a realm. Following points cover all aspects of locating a replica with respect to this paper (we don't go into details of how it is done as it is outside of the scope of this paper):

- The DHTs are realm specific and maintain location of replicas present in the same realm. Once the realm ID is known, any replica location can be obtained by querying the DHT.
- Parent directory entry of a file contains information about the realm in which the P-replicas are based, and this information is populated as part of the file 'create' operation.
- Root directory P-replica realm and file ID is known at every node to boot strap the file lookup process.
- A file's P-replica location information is maintained in the same realm DHT where the P-replicas are based. An R-replica is never created in the P-replica realm of a file.
- A file's R-replica location information is maintained in all corresponding realm DHTs where they have been created.
- When an R-replica is created, its realm ID is stored in every P-replica, as part of replica specific metadata. So, all R-replica realm IDs is available on all P-replicas. This location information is removed as part of the corresponding R-replica delete.
- When an R-replica is created, as part of populating its metadata, P-replica realm ID is stored into the replica specific metadata.

Distributed transaction service provides ACID properties to file updates. *File service* is the file maintenance layer that exposes file system interface to the end user, and internally uses all other services to provide DFS semantics. *Coherency service (CS)* is responsible for maintaining coherency among the P and R-replicas of each file.

4   Basic Concepts for CS Mechanisms

4.1   History Log

A list of recent updates to a file, called *history log*, is maintained on each P-replica node. It contains entries describing updates to that file along with a version number. For example, if the file operation was a regular file write operation, the corresponding history log entry would contain the changed metadata fields like time stamps, size, version number and the offset and region of the write operation. For update operations that involves only file system metadata update (ex: setattr, create, delete, rename etc), the history log entry will be sufficient to update a replica. If such self-contained entries are available starting with the version number on a lagging replica, the lagging replica can be brought up-to-date using the log entries only. Otherwise, a lagging replica needs complete data synchronization.

4.2 R-Replica Characteristics

R-replicas have additional information maintained for each region of its data. Each file is divided into a fixed number of regions, and a per-region status is maintained indicating whether the data for that region is valid. When most regions are invalid, the replica can be marked *invalid*. As new access operations are performed on the file from an R-replica realm, the *invalid* R replica populates its metadata and regions, on demand, with data fetched from P-replica. The R-replica then, marks itself valid.

An R-replica is deleted when there is space crunch on its hosting node and it is relatively less active compared to the R-replicas of other files on that node, or no accesses have happened for the file from this realm for a long time (which is configurable). An R-replica is also deleted when the file is deleted by a user operation on a best effort basis.

4.3 Last Coherent Time Stamp

A timestamp field is maintained on each replica for coherency purposes. This timestamp named *Last coherent timestamp (LCT)* is based on the local node system clock and is stored as part of the replica specific metadata. Note that a per-replica timestamp value is independent of that on other replicas. LCT is kept updated on a P-replica under following conditions: 1) as part of an update transaction, 2) after a successful coherent read and 3) after a successful synchronization with an up-to-date P-replica. LCT is kept updated on an R-replica under following conditions: 1) after a successful P-to-R synchronization and 2) on the return path of an access operation that was forwarded to a P-replica.

4.4 Typical File Update and Read Operations

Refer to Figure 2 for read request handling in the P-replica realm of a file (includes *coherent read* procedure), and to Figure 3 for read request handling in the R-replica realm of a file.

A typical file update operation in StarFS carried out by the *file service* would locate all the P-replicas of the file, perform a *distributed transaction* to update all of them, create history log entries on each P-replica node for replica synchronization purposes, inform the *CS* on one of the P-replica node(s) to initiate R-replica synchronization tasks and report the status of the operation to the user.

As the distributed transaction can go ahead with a quorum of P-replicas, a P-replica can be lagging if it did not take part in one or more recent distributed transactions. Similarly, an R-replica can be lagging when it did not receive latest changes from P-replicas.

5 Replica Update Mechanisms

5.1 P-to-R

As part of P-to-R, one of the P-replica nodes sends synchronization messages to all known R-replicas after an update operation completes successfully. This is a one way message and contains recent history log entries. This message to an R-replica might get lost if the P-replica node fails or the R-replica is inaccessible when the message is sent to it. To take care of cases where the P-replica node might fail before sending out the P-to-R synchronization message, we use a mechanism called *reliable P-to-R* where each node maintains a list of file IDs which were recently updated. If the designated P-replica node fails within a time window, one of the other P-replica nodes will send out the synchronization message to all R-replicas. For cases when the R-replica is inaccessible, it will remain lagging until during an access from its local realm, it is found that its LCT stale beyond threshold level.

5.2 P-to-P

As part of every transaction, answers are sought from all P-replicas along with their version numbers to make sure that at least a quorum of up-to-date P-replicas are available. If any P-replica replied with an older version number, then P-to-P synchronization operation is started from one of the up-to-date P-replicas asynchronously after the transaction completes.

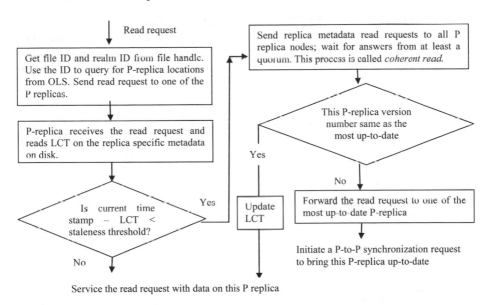

Fig. 2. Flow chart of read request in P-replica realm of a file

A P-to-P synchronization operation uses history log entries whenever possible, otherwise performs complete data synchronization. If this synchronization message is lost, then a lagging P-replica gets updated as part of the next access that finds the LCT older than the staleness threshold.

We also maintain a persistent list of file IDs on each node, for all P-replicas which could not participate in any of the transactions. A low priority agent on each node initiates P-to-P synchronization process for these file IDs. This ensures eventual synchronization for P-replicas outside of the most up-to-date quorum.

5.3 Some Considerations and Eventual Coherency

5.3.1 Stray R-Replicas

When a file is deleted, at least a quorum of its P-replicas is deleted as part of the operation and messages are sent to all registered R-replicas asking them to self-delete. If one or more such messages are lost, some R-replicas may still be present after the file is deleted. Read requests might get served from such R-replicas where accesses are coming through old file handles. When LCT becomes older than the threshold, the R-replica attempts to contact P-replicas and self-deletes itself after finding that the P-replicas are not present any more. Other R-replicas with no open handles are removed based on storage requirements on the local node as described in section 4.2.

Every time a read is forwarded from an R-replica to a P-replica, it is checked if the R-replica is registered. If not, the registration is attempted again. And if the P-replicas have been deleted in the mean time, the R-replica self-deletes itself in the access return path. This takes care of R-replicas those were not registered with P-replicas due to some transient error.

5.3.2 Sync Operations vs. Regular File Access Operations

A complete data synchronization operation for P-to-P may race with a user file access operation. If it is in process, and as it can potentially take several minutes to complete depending on the file size, the user operation will suffer. But, preempting the

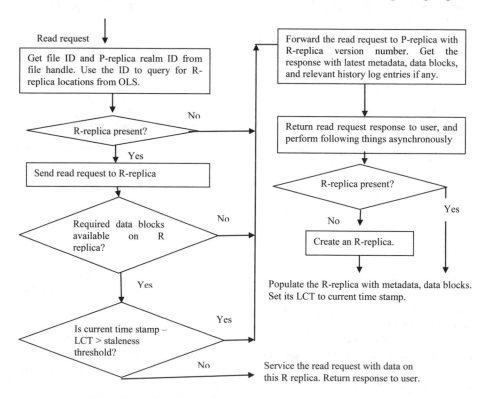

Fig. 3. Flowchart for read request in an R-replica realm of a file

synchronization operation might lead to starvation. To avoid this, we use checkpoint-based synchronization mechanisms where the operation is broken into smaller chunks that are serialized with user operations.

5.3.3 Eventual Coherency

Eventual coherency is assured in the form of not serving stale data beyond a certain period of time. Coherent read ensures that data stale beyond the threshold is never served to the user from any of the P-replicas (refer to Figure 2). Check for LCT on R-replica (Figure 3) ensures that data stale beyond threshold is not served from an R-replica. And when an R-replica contacts one of the P-replicas for up-to-date data, if that P-replica is too stale, it does a coherent read to make sure that the latest data is served for the read request. When coherent read is not possible due to a quorum of P-replicas being not accessible, read request is failed with transient error. This ensures that any user reading from anywhere will never see data older than that of the staleness threshold set for the system.

6 Observations

For StarFS, we started with the primary goal of ensuring that a user never retrieves inconsistent data from a file which we ensure through transactional update of files by preventing conflicts. As part of our testing for data coherency, we observed that with files up to a hundred million in the system, the *CS* could synchronize the R-replicas in other realms within a matter of seconds. As the number of active files in the system increases to thousands of millions, in each realm, the staleness of data in an R realm can amount to couple of minutes or more. Reducing the threshold for staleness will improve the experience, but number of messages goes up in such a case increasing the overall load in the system. Ideal threshold to put an upper limit for data staleness would depend on the workload and tolerance of the applications on StarFS. Setting a limit of 0 makes it a highly coherent system. Whereas setting it very high makes it quite unpleasant for many traditional file system users who are used to seeing most recent data always. So, it has to be carefully chosen to provide reasonable experience to the users in the domain for which data is hosted on StarFS.

7 Related Work

Update in distributed systems in the presence of replication is a widely researched field since many years. There are replication models proposed with weak consistency *[1]*, and with flexible coherency *[2]*. There are grid systems *[3]* that talk about adaptable replica consistency and coherency models. These systems are targeted towards read-only type of data hosting requirements, and compromise data consistency for heavier system loads. P2P systems like *Gnutella [4]* and *Freenet [5] take* the approach of not guaranteeing any upper limit for eventual coherency for replicas while *Farsite [6]* and *PAST [7]* assume a read-intensive access model. *Pangaea [8]* does not guarantee about staleness of the data, and does conflict resolution by compromising on data consistency. Initial design of *Oceanstore [9]* had a two-tiered update model similar to what we do in StarFS, but it also does not claim any coherency guarantees for the replica updates. However, as part of a later Oceanstore prototype- *Pond [10],* flexibility was provided to the user to choose data consistency models to support a variety of applications ranging from a database to a NFS like file service. Because of its generic design, it might have overhead for any particular class of applications. The abstraction layers and too many indirections will result in more message exchanges and higher overall system load. We have kept the regular update operation in StarFS simplistic to consume optimum number of messages, and do asynchronous update propagation to suit a particular access pattern well. While in *Pond [10]* there can be conflicts of updates requiring user intervention for resolution, we have taken conflict prevention approach to keep administrative intervention minimal. In *[11],* the authors talk about a replica update model that uses a hybrid approach of push and pull, but for a file that has not been accessed since long, when all its replicas are not coherent with each other, there is no care taken to validate that the user can see latest data on next access. In StarFS, we provide both these guarantees that there is an upper limit to how stale the data can be, and it is guaranteed even for files those have been inactive for a long time – by introducing coherent read concept on next access.

8 Conclusion

In this paper we described a set of protocols to ensure that a user never sees too old data even when multiple file copies are spread across multiple geographical locations. Our techniques should be efficiently applicable to any large scale peer-to-peer systems where strict data coherency is not a requirement.

Acknowledgements

This paper includes work of our StarFS team members: R SivaRamaKrishna, Dilip Ranade, Radha Shelat, Laxmikant Gunda and Mukund Agrawal.

References

1. Terry, D.B., Theimer, M.M., Petersen, K., Demers, A.J., Spreitzer, M.J., Hauser, C.: Managing Update Conflicts in Bayou, a Weakly Connected Replicated Storage System. In: Proceedings of the fifteenth ACM symposium on Operating systems principles (1995)
2. Sun, Y., Xu, Z.: Grid Replication Coherence Protocol. In: 18th International Parallel and Distributed Processing Symposium (IPDPS 2004) - Workshop 13, p. 232b (2004)
3. Chang, R.-S., Chang, J.-S.: Adaptable replica consistency for data grids. In: Proceedings of the Third International Conference on Information Technology: New Generations (2006)
4. Clip 2. The Gnutella protocol specification v0.4 (Document Revision 1.2) (2001), http://www.clip2.com/GnutellaProtocol04.pdf
5. Clarke, I., Sandberg, O., Wiley, B., Hong, T.W.: Freenet: A distributed anonymous information storage and retrieval system. In: Federrath, H. (ed.) Designing Privacy Enhancing Technologies. LNCS, vol. 2009, p. 46. Springer, Heidelberg (2001)

6. Adya, A., Bolosky, W.J., et al.: FARSITE: Federated, Available, and Reliable Storage for an incompletely trusted environment. In: Proceedings of OSDI 2002 (2002)

7. Druschel, P., Rowstron, A.: PAST: A large-scale, persistent peer-to-peer storage utility. In: Proceedings of the Eighth Workshop in hot topics in Operating Systems (2001)

8. Saito, Y., Karamanolis, C.: Pangaea: A symbiotic wide-area file system. In: ACM proceedings of the 10th workshop on ACM SIGOPS European workshop (2002)

9. Rhea, S., Wells, C., Eaton, P., Geels, D., Zhao, B., Weatherspoon, H., Kubiatowicz, J.: OceanStore: Maintenance-free global data storage. IEEE Internet computing 5(5) (2001)

10. Rhea, S., Eaton, P., Geels, D., Weatherspoon, H., Zhao, B., Kubiatowicz, J.: Pond: The OceanStore Prototype. In: Proceedings of the 2nd USENIX Conference on File and Storage Technologies (FAST 2003) (2003)

11. Datta, A., Hauswirth, M., Aberer, K.: Updates in highly unreliable, replicated peer-to-peer systems. In: ICDCS 2003 (2003)

On Minimal Connectivity Requirement for Secure Message Transmission in Asynchronous Networks

Ashish Choudhary[1,*], Arpita Patra[1,**], B.V. Ashwinkumar[1],
Kannan Srinathan[2], and C. Pandu Rangan[1,***]

[1] Dept of Computer Science and Engineering
IIT Madras, Chennai India 600036
{ashishc,arpita,ashwin}@cse.iitm.ernet.in, rangan@iitm.ernet.in
[2] Center for Security, Theory and Algorithmic Research
International Institute of Information Technology, Hyderabad India 500032
srinathan@iiit.ac.in

Abstract. In the PSMT problem, a sender **S** and a receiver **R** are part of a distributed network and connected through n node disjoint paths, also called as *wires* among which at most t are controlled by an all powerful Byzantine adversary $\mathcal{A}_t$. **S** has a message m, which **S** intends to send to **R**. The challenge is to design a protocol, such that at the end, **R** should correctly output m without any error (perfect reliability) and $\mathcal{A}_t$ should not get *any* information about m, what so ever, in information theoretic sense (perfect security). The problem of USMT is same as PSMT, except that **R** should output m with a small probability of error.Sayeed et al. [15] have given a PSMT protocol in an asynchronous network tolerating $\mathcal{A}_t$, where **S** and **R** are connected by $n = 2t + 1$ wires. However, we show that their protocol does not provide perfect security. We then prove that in an asynchronous network, if all the n wires are directed from **S** to **R**, then any PSMT protocol tolerating $\mathcal{A}_t$ is possible iff $n > 3t$. Surprisingly, we further prove that even if all the n wires are bi-directional, then any PSMT protocol in asynchronous network tolerating $\mathcal{A}_t$ is possible iff $n > 3t$. This is quite interesting because for synchronous networks, by the results of Dolev et al. [6], if all the wires are unidirectional (directed from **S** to **R**), then PSMT tolerating $\mathcal{A}_t$ is possible iff $n > 3t$, where as if all the wires are bi-directional then PSMT tolerating $\mathcal{A}_t$ is possible iff $n > 2t$. This shows that synchrony of the network *affects* the connectivity requirement for PSMT protocols. However, we show that $n > 2t$ wires are necessary and sufficient for the existence of any USMT protocol in asynchronous network tolerating $\mathcal{A}_t$, irrespective of whether the n wires are unidirectional from **S** to **R** or the n wires are bi-directional.

Keywords: Asynchronous Networks, Information Theoretic Security.

* Financial support from Infosys Technology India Acknowledged.
** Financial support from Microsoft Research India Acknowledged.
*** Work Supported by Project No. CSE/05-06/076/DITX/CPAN on Protocols for Secure Communication and Computation Sponsored by Department of Information Technology, Government of India.

V. Garg, R. Wattenhofer, and K. Kothapalli (Eds.): ICDCN 2009, LNCS 5408, pp. 148–162, 2009.

1   Introduction

In the problem of *perfectly reliable message transmission* (PRMT), a sender
S is connected to a receiver **R** in an unreliable network by n vertex disjoint
paths called wires. Moreover, they do not share any information beforehand. **S**
intends to send a message m chosen from a finite field $\mathbb{F}$ reliably to **R**, in a
guaranteed manner, in spite of the presence an *unbounded computing powerful*
Byzantine adversary $\mathcal{A}_t$ who controls at most t out of n wires. The problem of
perfectly secure message transmission (PSMT) has an additional constraint that
the adversary should get no information about m. Security against $\mathcal{A}_t$ is called
information theoretic security, which is also known as *perfect security*.

PRMT and PSMT are fundamental problems in the field of distributed computing. If **S** and **R** are directly connected by a secure link, as assumed in generic
secure multiparty computation protocols [3,8,14,19], then reliable and secure
communication between **S** and **R** is trivial. However, it is impractical to assume
the existence of a direct link between every two nodes in the network. In such
a situation PRMT and PSMT protocols help to simulate a *virtual* reliable and
secure link between **S** and **R**.

The problem of *unconditionally reliable message transmission* (URMT) [7] is
same as PRMT, except that **R** should correctly output m with probability at
least $(1 - \delta)$, where δ $(0 < \delta < \frac{1}{2})$ is the error parameter. Similarly, the problem
of *unconditionally secure message transmission* (USMT) [7] is same as URMT,
with an additional restriction that the adversary should not get any information
about m in information theoretic sense[1].

Existing Literature: PRMT and PSMT problem was first introduced and
studied by Dolev et al. [6]. Assuming the underlying network to be undirected
and synchronous, Dolev et. al have abstracted the underlying network and assumed that **S** and **R** are connected by n bi-directional vertex disjoint paths,
also called as *wires*, of which at most t could be under the control of $\mathcal{A}_t$[2]. In
such a model, any protocol is assumed to execute in phases, where a phase is a
send from **S** to **R** or vice-versa. So in a single phase protocol, only **S** is allowed
to communicate to **R**, while in a multi phase protocol, both **S** and **R** are allowed to communicate with each other along the n wires. Hence while in a single
phase protocol, the n wires can be viewed as unidirectional, directed from **S** to
R, in a multi phase protocol, they can be viewed as bi-directional. Dolev et al.
have given the necessary and sufficient condition on the connectivity (number of
wires n) for the existence of single and multi phase PSMT protocols, as shown
in Table given below. More recent efforts using the same adversarial model for
the problem of PSMT include [16,18,1,13,10].

---

[1] In [7], the authors have termed URMT and USMT as almost perfectly reliable and
almost perfectly secure message transmission respectively. However, to be consistent
with the terminologies of unconditionally secure multiparty computation [4,2], we
call them as URMT and USMT.

[2] The approach of abstracting the network as a collection of n wires is justified using
Menger's theorem [12] which states that a graph is $c - (\mathbf{S}, \mathbf{R})$-connected iff **S** and **R**
are connected by at least c vertex disjoint paths.

PSMT		USMT	
number of phases	number of wires (n)	number of phases	number of wires (n)
1	$n \geq 3t + 1$ [6]	1	$n \geq 2t + 1$ [5,9]
≥ 2	$n \geq 2t + 1$ [6]	≥ 2	$n \geq 2t + 1$ [7]

URMT and USMT problem was introduced by Franklin et al. [7] and later studied by [5,9] in synchronous network. The necessary and sufficient condition on the connectivity (number of wires n) for the existence of single and multi phase USMT, tolerating t-active Byzantine adversary is shown in the same Table.

Our Motivation and Contribution: The existing results for PSMT and USMT assumes the underlying network to be synchronous. Thus, if **S** (**R**) sends some information along a wire, then it is assumed that **R** (**S**) will get the information (possibly corrupted) along the wire after a fixed interval of time. However, a typical large network like Internet can be modeled more accurately by asynchronous networks than synchronous networks. In the literature, little attention has been paid to the study PSMT and USMT protocols in asynchronous network due to its complexity. This motivates us to study PSMT and USMT protocols in asynchronous networks. Our contributions in this paper are as follows:

1. In [15], Sayeed et al. have given a PSMT protocol tolerating $\mathcal{A}_t$ in the presence of $n = 2t + 1$ unidirectional wires from **S** to **R**, in an asynchronous network. However, we show that their protocol does not provide perfect security.
2. We show that: If there are n *unidirectional* wires from **S** to **R** in an asynchronous network under the influence of $\mathcal{A}_t$, then there exists a PSMT protocol iff $n > 3t$. Comparing this with first row of the Table shown above, we find that synchrony of the network does *not* effect the possibility of PSMT protocol, if all the n wires are unidirectional from **S** to **R**.
3. We show that: If there are n *bi-directional* wires between **S** and **R** in an asynchronous network under the influence of $\mathcal{A}_t$, then there exists a PSMT protocol iff $n > 3t$. This is surprising because from second row of the Table shown above, $n > 2t$ bi-directional wires are necessary and sufficient for the existence of PSMT protocol against $\mathcal{A}_t$ in synchronous network.
4. We show that USMT between **S** and **R** is possible in an asynchronous network, tolerating $\mathcal{A}_t$ iff $n > 2t$. Moreover, this is true, irrespective of whether the n wires are unidirectional or the n wires are bi-directional. Comparing this with the results in the Table, we find that irrespective of whether the n wires are unidirectional or bi-directional, synchrony of the network does *not* affect possibility of USMT.

In [17], the authors have studied PSMT and USMT problem in asynchronous networks tolerating a generalized non-threshold adversary, specified by an adversary structure. Informally, an adversary structure specifies the collection of potential corruptible sets of nodes where any one of the set of nodes will be activated/corrupted during the protocol execution. So, essentially the adversary can choose any one of the sets from the adversary structure and can corrupt the nodes in the set during protocol execution. It is easy to see that $\mathcal{A}_t$ is a special type of non-threshold adversary, where size of each set in the adversary structure is at most t. In [17], the authors have given the necessary and sufficient conditions for PSMT and USMT in asynchronous networks tolerating non-threshold adversary. However, though not explicitly stated in the paper, their characterization for PSMT is true under the assumption that **S** is honest, while their characterization for USMT is true under the assumption that **S** may be corrupted, where if **S** is corrupted, then he may not send anything to **R** along some path. However, in this paper, we derive all the necessary and sufficient condition, assuming **S** to be honest. The protocols given in [17] against general adversary are very complex. Though we can derive protocols for tolerating $\mathcal{A}_t$ from the protocols of [17] tolerating general adversary, the resultant protocols will be very complex and inefficient. Instead, since we work on threshold model, our protocols are very elegant and efficient.

Our results can be easily generalized for the case, when certain wires between **S** and **R** are unidirectional (directed either from **S** to **R** or vice-versa), while the remaining wires (if any) are bi-directional.

2   Model and Definitions

We consider an asynchronous network $\mathcal{N}$, where **S, R** are two special nodes in $\mathcal{N}$, modeled as probabilistic interactive Turing Machines, where randomization is achieved through internal random coins. The corruption in the network is modeled by a *centralized adversary* $\mathcal{A}_t$, who has *unbounded computing power* and can actively control at most t nodes in the network, excluding **S** and **R** in Byzantine fashion. $\mathcal{A}_t$ actively corrupting a node implies that it takes full control of the node and forces the node to (mis)behave in an arbitrary manner. The adversary is *adaptive* [4] and is allowed to *dynamically* corrupt nodes during protocol execution (and his choice may depend on the data seen so far), without exceeding the limit of t corrupted players. A node under the control of $\mathcal{A}_t$ will remain under its control throughout the protocol. Following the approach of Dolev et al. [6], we abstract the network and assume that **S** and **R** are connected by n vertex disjoint paths, called *wires*, of which at most t could be actively controlled by $\mathcal{A}_t$ in Byzantine fashion. Moreover, we consider two extreme cases: (a) when all the n wires are directed from **S** to **R**, thus do not allowing any interaction between **S** and **R**; (b) when all the n wires bi-directional, thus allowing interaction between **S** and **R**. A wire which is not under the control of $\mathcal{A}_t$ is called *honest*.

To model the asynchrony in the network, we assume that the adversary can schedule the message delivery along the wires; i.e., he can determine the time delay of all the messages along all the n wires. However, he cannot read or change those messages, except the ones which pass through the wires which are under its control. Moreover, the message sent through an honest wire will be eventually received by receiver. However, if a wire is under the control of $\mathcal{A}_t$, then $\mathcal{A}_t$ may not send the messages along that wire. Thus the receiver can not distinguish between honest wires which are slow (due to the malicious scheduling of messages by $\mathcal{A}_t$ on these wires) and corrupted wires which withhold/does not send information at all.

In our protocols, $\mathbf{S}$ and $\mathbf{R}$ do computation in a field $\mathbb{F}$, where $\mathbb{F}$ is a finite field of prime order. The only restriction on $\mathbb{F}$ is that $|\mathbb{F}| > n$. If some $x \in \mathbb{F}$ is sent through all the wires, then it is said to be broadcasted. If x is broadcasted over at least $2t + 1$ wires, then receiver will always correctly recover it. This is because out of the $2t + 1$ wires, at least $t + 1$ will be honest and will eventually deliver x. So receiver can wait to receive the same value over $t+1$ wires. We call the problem of PSMT and USMT in asynchronous networks as *asynchronous PSMT* (APSMT) and *asynchronous USMT* (AUSMT) respectively.

3 APSMT When All the Wires Are Unidirectional

In [15], the authors have given a single phase APSMT protocol tolerating $\mathcal{A}_t$, where $\mathbf{S}$ and $\mathbf{R}$ are connected by wires $w_i, 1 \leq i \leq n$, directed from $\mathbf{S}$ to $\mathbf{R}$, where $n = 2t + 1$. We briefly recall the protocol from [15] and show that the protocol does not achieve perfect secrecy; i.e., $\mathcal{A}_t$ can recover m. In the protocol, message m belongs to the set $Q = \{1, 2, \ldots, m_{max}\}$ of positive integers, such that $m_{max} > n$. Let $MAX = 2m_{max} + 1$. $\mathbf{S}$ sends m by doing the following:

1. $\mathbf{S}$ randomly selects n values $K_1, K_2, \ldots, K_n$ from the set Q and associates K_i with wire w_i. For each K_i, $\mathbf{S}$ forms a *key_carrying_polynomial* $p_i(x)$ of degree t, where $p_i(0) = K_i$ and other coefficients of $p_i(x)$ are randomly chosen from Q. $\mathbf{S}$ also forms a *secret_carrying_polynomial* $M(x)$ of degree n, where $M(0) = m$ and the coefficient of x^i is K_i.
2. Through w_i, $\mathbf{S}$ sends the values $p_j(i)$, where $1 \leq j \leq n$. $\mathbf{S}$ also broadcasts $M(1)$ and $M(MAX)$, where the values of $M(x)$ are in N, the infinite set of positive integers.

We now show how $\mathcal{A}_t$ can recover m from the values sent by $\mathbf{S}$. In the protocol, $\mathbf{S}$ broadcasts:

$$V_1 = M(1) = m + K_1 + K_2 + \ldots + K_i + \ldots + K_n \text{ and}$$
$$V_2 = M(MAX) = m + K_1 * MAX + \ldots + K_i * MAX^i + \ldots + K_n * MAX^n$$

Note that V_1 and V_2 do not belong to Q. They belong to N, the infinite set of positive integers; i.e., the protocol works with the exact values of V_1, V_2. However, $m \in Q$ and is always less than MAX. Since, V_1 and V_2 are broadcasted, $\mathcal{A}_t$ will also know V_1 and V_2. Also MAX is a publicly known parameter. If $\mathcal{A}_t$ computes (V_2 mod MAX), then he obtains m, because all other terms in V_2 are multiple of MAX, except m, which is less than MAX. Thus, protocol of [15] does not provide perfect secrecy. In fact, there does not exist any APSMT protocol tolerating $\mathcal{A}_t$ with $n = 2t + 1$ unidirectional wires from **S** to **R**. In the sequel, we present the true characterization of APSMT protocol tolerating $\mathcal{A}_t$, when all the n wires are unidirectional from **S** to **R**.

3.1   Characterization for APSMT

We now prove the necessary and sufficiency condition for the existence of any APSMT protocol tolerating $\mathcal{A}_t$, when the wires from **S** to **R** are unidirectional.

Theorem 1. *Suppose there exists n wires, directed from **S** to **R**, of which at most t could be under the control of $\mathcal{A}_t$. Then there exists an APSMT protocol only if $n > 3t$.*

PROOF: From [6], we know that $n > 3t$ wires are necessary for the existence of any synchronous PSMT protocol tolerating a t-active Byzantine adversary, when all the wires are unidirectional from **S** to **R**. Hence it is obviously necessary for the existence of APSMT protocol tolerating $\mathcal{A}_t$, if all the wires are unidirectional from **S** to **R**.   □

We now show that $n > 3t$ unidirectional wires from **S** to **R** are also sufficient for designing an APSMT protocol. Before that we briefly recall the properties of Reed-Solomon codes [11], which are used in our protocol.

Reed-Solomon (RS) Code [11]: Let $\mathbb{F}$ be a finite field and $\alpha_1, \alpha_2, \ldots \alpha_n$ be distinct elements of $\mathbb{F}$. Given $k < n \leq |\mathbb{F}|$, and an arbitrary block $\mathbf{B} = [m_1 \, m_2 \ldots m_k]$, the encoding function for the Reed-Solomon code is defined as $[p_{\mathbf{B}}(\alpha_1) \ldots p_{\mathbf{B}}(\alpha_n)]$ where $p_{\mathbf{B}}(x)$ is the polynomial $\sum_{i=0}^{k-1} m_{i+1} x^i$. Given an input RS codeword $W = \{(i_1, a_1), (i_2, a_2), \ldots, (i_l, a_l)\}$, which is RS encoded by a polynomial of degree k, there exists efficient error correcting procedure, like Berlekamp-Welch algorithm [11], that can correct up to r errors in W, provided that $|W| \geq k + 2r + 1$ [11]. We denote such an error correcting procedure as $RS - DEC(k, r, W)$, which takes as input an RS codeword W and tries to output a polynomial of degree k by correcting at most r errors in W. We are now ready to present our protocol.

Let **S** and **R** be connected by unidirectional wires $w_i, 1 \leq i \leq n$, directed from **S** to **R**, where $n = 3t + 1$. We design an APSMT protocol called $\Pi_{APSMT}^{Unidirectional}$, tolerating $\mathcal{A}_t$. The protocol is given below:

Computation and Communication by S: **S** selects a random polynomial $p(x)$ of degree t over $\mathbb{F}$, such that $p(0) = s$, where s is the secret message. Over wire $w_i, 1 \leq i \leq n$, **S** sends the tuple $(i, p(i))$ to **R**.

Message Recovery by R:

For $0 \leq r \leq t$, in iteration r, **R** does the following: /* **R** performs at most $t + 1$ iterations. */

1. Let $\mathcal{W}$ denotes the set of wires over which **R** has received the tuples and I_r denotes the tuples received over the wires in $\mathcal{W}$, when $\mathcal{W}$ contains $2t + 1 + r$ wires.

2. Wait until $|\mathcal{W}| \geq 2t + 1 + r$. **R** applies RS-DEC($t, r, I_r$) to get the polynomial $p'(.)$. If no polynomial is output, then **R** skips the next step and proceeds to next iteration.

3. If for at least $2t + 1$ elements $(i, a) \in I_r$, $p'(i) = a$, then **R** outputs $p'(0)$ as the secret message and terminates. Otherwise, **R** proceeds to the next iteration.

Theorem 2. *In* $\Pi_{APSMT}^{Unidirectional}$ $\mathcal{A}_t$ *gets no information about the message s.*

PROOF: It is easy to see that $\mathcal{A}_t$ gets at most t distinct points on $p(x)$, thus falling short of one point to completely interpolate $p(x)$. This implies that $p(0) = s$ is information theoretically secure. $\qquad \square$

Theorem 3. *In* $\Pi_{APSMT}^{Unidirectional}$, **R** *will always correctly output s.*

PROOF: Suppose $\mathcal{A}_t$ corrupts $\hat{r} \leq t$ wires during the transmission of values of $p(x)$. Now during $\hat{r}^{th}$ iteration, **R** receives $2t + 1 + \hat{r}$ points on $p(x)$, of which $\hat{r}$ are corrupted. So from the properties of Reed-Solomon codes [11] (as described above), polynomial $p'(.)$ which is output by RS-DEC during $\hat{r}^{th}$ iteration will pass through at least $2t + 1$ points in I_r. Since out of these $2t + 1$ points, at least $t + 1$ are honest and uniquely defines the original polynomial $p(.)$ ($t + 1$ points uniquely define a t degree polynomial), the output polynomial $p'(.)$ is same as $p(.)$. Thus $p(.)$ will be output in $\hat{r}^{th}$ iteration and all the iterations up to iteration $\hat{r}$ will be unsuccessful, as either they will not output any t degree polynomial or the output polynomial will not pass through $2t + 1$ points in I_r. $\qquad \square$

Theorem 4. *Let there exists n unidirectional wires from* **S** *to* **R**. *Then APSMT tolerating* $\mathcal{A}_t$ *is possible iff* $n > 3t$.

PROOF: The proof follows from Theorem 1 and protocol $\Pi_{APSMT}^{Unidirectional}$. $\qquad \square$

4   APSMT When All the Wires Are Bidirectional

In this section, we characterize APSMT tolerating $\mathcal{A}_t$, when all the n wires between **S** and **R** are bi-directional. Specifically, we show that APSMT tolerating $\mathcal{A}_t$ is possible iff there exists $n > 3t$ bidirectional wires between **S** and **R**. Thus, irrespective of whether the n wires between **S** and **R** are uni-directional or bidirectional, $n > 3t$ wires are necessary for the existence of any APSMT protocol tolerating $\mathcal{A}_t$. This is quite surprising because from [6], we know that if the n wires are bi-directional, then the presence of $n > 2t$ wires are necessary and sufficient for the existence of any synchronous PSMT protocol tolerating $\mathcal{A}_t$.

Theorem 5. *Let* **S** *and* **R** *be connected by* $n = 3t + 1$ *bi-directional wires, then there exists an APSMT protocol tolerating* $\mathcal{A}_t$.

PROOF: Any bi-directional wire between **S** and **R** can be treated as an unidirectional wire from **S** to **R**. Now we know that there exists an APSMT protocol $\Pi_{APSMT}^{Unidirectional}$ tolerating $\mathcal{A}_t$ if there exists $n = 3t + 1$ unidirectional wires from **S** to **R**. Hence the same protocol can also be executed if there exists $n = 3t + 1$ bi-directional wires from **S** to **R**. $\qquad \square$

We now show that if all the n wires between **S** and **R** are bi-directional, then APSMT tolerating $\mathcal{A}_t$ is possible only if $n > 3t$. The proof is by contradiction. We first show that there does not exist any APSMT protocol between a sender **S'** and receiver **R'**, with three bi-directional wires between **S'** and **R'**, of which one can be corrupted by the adversary (Theorem 6). Then by using a standard player partitioning argument, we show that if there exists an APSMT protocol tolerating $\mathcal{A}_t$ with $n = 3t$ bi-directional wires between **S** and **R**, then there exists an APSMT protocol between **S'** and **R'** who are connected by three bi-directional wires, of which at most one could be corrupted, which is a contradiction (Theorem 7).

Theorem 6. *Let there exists three bi-directional wires between a sender* **S'** *and a receiver* **R'**, *of which at most one wire could be under the control of the adversary. Then there does not exist any APSMT protocol between* **S'** *and* **R'**.

PROOF: The proof is by contradiction. Let **S'** and **R'** be connected by three bi-directional wires w_1, w_2, w_3, of which at most one wire can be under the control of adversary $\mathcal{A}_1$. Moreover, let there exists an APSMT protocol Π between **S'** and **R'** tolerating $\mathcal{A}_1$. Let E be an execution of Π. Then $time(E, \mathbf{R'}, w_i)$ denotes the arrival time of the different messages (with respect to local clock) received by **R** along wire $w_i, i \in \{1, 2, 3\}$, in execution E. Similarly, $time(E, \mathbf{S'}, w_i)$ should be interpreted. Let E^{time} be the total time taken (with respect to **R'**) by execution E; i.e., the time at which **R'** terminates by outputting the message in execution E. From the property of APSMT, each execution of Π will terminate. Moreover, in any execution of Π, the distribution of data sent along a wire will be same, irrespective of the secret message (which is sent by Π). Otherwise, the adversary can passively listen the wire and will get information about the secret message, thus violating the perfect secrecy property of Π. Now consider the following execution sequences of protocol Π:

1. E_1: The random coin tosses of **S'** and **R'** are r_1 and r_2 respectively. **S'** wants to send the secret m. The adversary strategy is to control wire w_3 and not allowing any data to pass over w_3 throughout E_1. Let α and β denote the messages that are exchanged between **S'** and **R'**, along w_1 and w_2 respectively and the protocol terminates at time E_1^{time}, outputting m.

2. E_2: The random coin tosses of **S'** and **R'** are r_1 and r_2 respectively. **S'** wants to send the secret message m. The adversary strategy is to passively control w_2 and delay any information along w_3 for time $E_1^{time} + E_3^{time} + 1$ (E_3 is defined below). In addition, the adversary schedules the messages along w_1 and w_2 in such a way that $time(E_2, \mathbf{S'}, w_i) = time(E_1, \mathbf{S'}, w_i)$, for $i \in \{1, 2\}$ and $time(E_2, \mathbf{R'}, w_i) = time(E_1, \mathbf{R'}, w_i)$, for $i \in \{1, 2\}$. Since the adversary has unbounded computing power, he can do so. Thus the view of **S'** and **R'** in E_1 and E_2 are same and hence the secret m is reconstructed. Also $E_1^{time} = E_2^{time}$ and α and β are exchanged between **S'** and **R'**, along w_1 and w_2 respectively.

Let $m^*(\neq m)$ be another secret message. Then from the perfect secrecy property of Π, there exists $r_3(\neq r_1)$ and $r_4(\neq r_2)$, such that the following holds: **S'** wants to send m^*, the random coin tosses of **S'** and **R'** are r_3 and r_4 respectively and the information exchanged between **S'** and **R'** along wire w_2 is β. Note that such an r_3, r_4 exists, otherwise it implies that data sent along wire w_2 is dependent on secret message, thus violating perfect secrecy property of Π. Now consider the following executions of Π:

3. E_3: The random coin tosses of **S'** and **R'** are r_3 and r_4 respectively. **S'** wants to send the secret message m^*. The adversary strategy is to control wire w_3 and not allowing any data to pass over w_3 throughout E_3. Let α^* and $\beta^*(=\beta)$ denote the messages that are exchanged between **S'** and **R'**, along w_1 and w_2 respectively and the protocol terminates at time E_3^{time}, outputting m^*.

4. E_4: The random coin tosses of **S'** and **R'** are r_3 and r_4 respectively. **S'** wants to send the secret message m^*. The adversary strategy is to passively control w_2 and delay any information along w_3 for time $E_1^{time}+E_3^{time}+1$. In addition, the adversary schedules the messages along w_1 and w_2 in such a way that $time(E_4, \mathbf{S'}, w_i) = time(E_3, \mathbf{S'}, w_i)$, for $i \in \{1, 2\}$ and $time(E_4, \mathbf{R'}, w_i) = time(E_3, \mathbf{R'}, w_i)$, for $i \in \{1, 2\}$. Since the adversary has unbounded computing power, he can do so. Thus the view of **S'** and **R'** in E_3 and E_4 are same and hence the secret m^* is reconstructed. Also $E_3^{time} = E_4^{time}$ and α^* and $\beta^*(=\beta)$ are exchanged between **S'** and **R'**, along w_1 and w_2 respectively.

5. E_5: The random coin tosses of **S'** and **R'** are r_1 and r_4 respectively. **S'** wants to send the secret message m. Let $\alpha', \beta'(=\beta)$ denote the messages that should have been exchanged between **S'** and **R'** along w_1 and w_2 in ideal situation, when w_1 and w_2 are honest (not under the control of adversary).

   Now the adversary strategy in E_5 is as follows: adversary delay any information along w_3 for time $E_1^{time} + E_3^{time} + 1$. In addition, the adversary controls w_1 in Byzantine fashion, such that instead of receiving messages from α', **R'** gets messages from α^*, while **S'** receives messages from α. Moreover, adversary schedules the messages along w_1 and w_2 in such a way that $time(E_5, \mathbf{S'}, w_i) = time(E_2, \mathbf{S'}, w_i)$, for $i \in \{1, 2\}$ and $time(E_5, \mathbf{R'}, w_i) = time(E_4, \mathbf{R'}, w_i)$, for $i \in \{1, 2\}$. Note that the adversary can do because he has unbounded computing power. Thus the view of **S'** is $\alpha \, \beta' = \alpha \, \beta$, while view of **R'** is $\alpha^* \, \beta' = \alpha^* \, \beta$.

Thus the view of **S'** in E_2 and E_5 are same, so **S'** will assume that m has been communicated securely. However, the view of **R'** in E_5 is same as in E_4 and hence **R'** will output m^*. But this violates the perfect reliability property of Π, which is a contradiction. Hence Π does not exist. $\qquad\square$

Theorem 7. *Let* **S** *and* **R** *be connected by n bi-directional wires, of which at most t can be under the control of $\mathcal{A}_t$. Then there exits an APSMT protocol tolerating $\mathcal{A}_t$ only if $n > 3t$.*

PROOF: The proof is by contradiction. Assume that there exist an APSMT protocol Π^{APSMT} between **S** and **R** tolerating $\mathcal{A}_t$, where **S** and **R** are connected by $n = 3t$ bi-directional wires. Now by using standard player partitioning strategy, we show how to transform protocol Π^{APSMT} into another APSMT protocol Π between a sender **S'** and a receiver **R'**, who are connected by three bi-directional wires, of which at most one could be corrupted by the adversary. Let the wires between **S** and **R** be numbered $1, 2, \ldots, 3t$. Similarly, let the wires between **S'** and **R'** be numbered as $1, 2, 3$. Now we define a mapping $M : \{1 \ldots n\} \longrightarrow \{1, 2, 3\}$ as follows: $M(x) = 1 : \forall x \in \{1 \ldots t\}, M(x) = 2 : \forall x \in \{t + 1 \ldots 2t\}$ and $M(x) = 3 : \forall x \in \{2t + 1 \ldots 3t\}$. We denote $M^{-1}(1) = \{1, 2, \ldots, t\}, M^{-1}(2) = \{t+1, t+2, \ldots, 2t\}$ and $M^{-1}(3) = \{2t+1, 2t+2, \ldots, 3t\}$. Now Π is obtained from Π^{APSMT} in the following way: if in protocol Π^{APSMT}, $k \in \mathbb{F}$ is sent from **S** to **R** on wire $w \in \{1, 2, \ldots, 3t\}$, then in protocol Π, k is sent from **S'** to **R'** on wire $M(w)$. We define the transmission from **R'** to **S'** in a similar fashion. Similarly, if the adversary controls wire $w \in \{1, 2, 3\}$ in protocol Π, then he controls the set $M^{-1}(w)$ in protocol Π^{APSMT}. It can be easily verified that the view of **S'** and **R'** in Π is same as the view of **S** and **R** respectively, in protocol Π^{APSMT}. So Π is an APSMT protocol between **S'** and **R'**, who are connected by three bi-directional wires, of which at most one can be corrupted. But from Theorem 6, Π does not exist. Hence Π^{APSMT} also does not exist. $\qquad \square$

Theorem 8. *Let* **S** *and* **R** *be connected by* n *bi-directional wires, of which at most* t *could be under the control of* $\mathcal{A}_t$. *Then there exists an APSMT protocol tolerating* $\mathcal{A}_t$ *iff* $n > 3t$.

PROOF: Follows from Theorem 7, Theorem 6 and Theorem 5. $\qquad \square$

5   AUSMT Tolerating $\mathcal{A}_t$

We now give characterization for AUSMT protocols tolerating $\mathcal{A}_t$, when all the wires are directed from **S** to **R**.

Theorem 9. *Let there exists* n *wires between* **S** *and* **R**, *directed from* **S** *to* **R**, *of which at most* t *could be under the control of* $\mathcal{A}_t$. *Then there exists an AUSMT protocol tolerating* $\mathcal{A}_t$, *only if* $n > 2t$.

PROOF: From [5,9], we know that $n > 2t$ wires are necessary for the existence of any synchronous USMT protocol tolerating an all powerful t-active Byzantine adversary, when all the wires are unidirectional from **S** to **R**. Hence it is obviously necessary for the existence of APSMT protocol tolerating $\mathcal{A}_t$, if all the wires are unidirectional from **S** to **R**. $\qquad \square$

We now show that $n = 2t + 1$ unidirectional wires from **S** to **R** are sufficient to design an AUSMT protocol tolerating $\mathcal{A}_t$. Let **S** and **R** be connected by $n = 2t + 1$ unidirectional wires, directed from **S** to **R**. Moreover, let $|\mathbb{F}| \geq \frac{n^3}{\delta}$, where $0 < \delta < \frac{1}{2}$. We now present an AUSMT protocol called $\Pi_{AUSMT}^{Unidirectional}$, which sends a message m containing $t + 1 = \Omega(n)$ elements from $\mathbb{F}$ by communicating $O(n^2)$ elements from $\mathbb{F}$, with an error probability of at most δ. Before describing the protocol, we describe the tools used in the protocol.

Extracting Randomness [18]: Suppose **S** and **R** by some means agree on a sequence of ℓ random numbers $x = [x_1 \; x_2 \; \ldots \; x_\ell] \in \mathbb{F}^\ell$ such that $\mathcal{A}_t$ knows $\ell - f$ components of x, but $\mathcal{A}_t$ has no information about the other f components.

However $\mathbf{S}$ and $\mathbf{R}$ do not know which values are known to $\mathcal{A}_t$. The goal of $\mathbf{S}$ and $\mathbf{R}$ is to agree on f elements $[y_1 \ y_2 \ \ldots \ y_f] \in \mathbb{F}^f$, such that $\mathcal{A}_t$ has no information about $[y_1 \ y_2 \ \ldots \ y_f]$. This is achieved algorithm **EXTRAND** [18]:

Algorithm EXTRAND$_{\ell, f}(x)$: Let V be an $\ell \times f$ Vandermonde matrix with members in $\mathbb{F}$. This matrix is published as a part of the algorithm specification. $\mathbf{S}$ and $\mathbf{R}$ both locally computes the product $[y_1 \ y_2 \ \ldots \ y_f] = [x_1 \ x_2 \ \ldots \ x_\ell]V$.

Lemma 1 ([18]). *The adversary has no information about $[y_1 \ y_2 \ \ldots \ y_f]$ computed in algorithm* **EXTRAND***.*

Asynchronous Unconditionally Secure Pad Establishment Technique:

We now propose a *novel* technique, which with probability at least $(1 - \delta)$, allows $\mathbf{S}$ and $\mathbf{R}$ to establish an information theoretically secure random one time pad $y \in \mathbb{F}^{t+1}$, by communicating $O(n^2)$ elements from $\mathbb{F}$. Let $\mathbf{S}$ and $\mathbf{R}$ be connected by unidirectional wires $\mathcal{W} = \{w_i : 1 \leq i \leq n\}$, directed from $\mathbf{S}$ to $\mathbf{R}$, where $n = 2t + 1$. $\mathbf{S}$ constructs a random non-zero matrix A of size $(t + 1) \times n$, where the $j^{th}, 1 \leq j \leq t + 1$ row of A contains the elements $M_{j,1} \ M_{j,2} \ \ldots \ M_{j,n}$, such that each $M_{j,i}$ is a non-zero element, selected uniformly from $\mathbb{F}$. For each $1 \leq i \leq n$, $\mathbf{S}$ constructs an unique t degree polynomial $q_i(x)$ passing through the points $(1, M_{1,i}), (2, M_{2,i}), \ldots, (t+1, M_{t+1,i})$. $\mathbf{S}$ then evaluates $q_i(x)$ at t additional points, namely at $x = t + 2, t + 3, \ldots n$ to obtain $c_{1,i}, c_{2,i}, \ldots, c_{t,i}$. Thus we can construct another matrix C of size $t \times n$ where i^{th} row in C is $(c_{i,1}, \ldots, c_{i,n})$. Finally, $\mathbf{S}$ obtains a square array D of size $n \times n$, where array D is the row concatenation of array A and C. Now note that column wise, elements of C are linear combination of the elements in A.

Claim.

1. Any $t + 1$ correct rows of D are enough to construct entire D.
2. If at most t elements of any column of D are corrupted, then it is detectable.

PROOF: The first property is easy to understand. For the second property, we recall that in D, the values along i^{th} column lie on a unique t degree polynomial $q_i(x)$. Now suppose at most t values along i^{th} column are changed in such a manner that they lie on some other t degree polynomial $q'_i(x)$, where $q_i(x) \neq q'_i(x)$. Since both $q_i(x)$ and $q'_i(x)$ are of degree t, they can intersect at additional t points. But still there is at least $n - 2t = 1$ points which lie on $q_i(x)$ (but not on $q'_i(x)$). Hence any attempt to interpolate a t degree polynomial passing through the elements of ith column (in which at most t values have been changed) will be a failure. $\square$

After constructing D, $\mathbf{S}$ does the following computation and communication:

---

1. $\mathbf{S}$ forms n polynomials $p_j(x), 1 \leq j \leq n$, each of degree n, where $p_j(x)$ is formed using the jth row of D as follows: the coefficient of $x^i, 0 \leq i \leq n - 1$ in $p_j(x)$ is the $(i + 1)^{th}$ element of the jth row of D.

2. $\mathbf{S}$ chooses n random, distinct, non-zero field elements, $\alpha_1, \alpha_2, \ldots, \alpha_n \in \mathbb{F} - \{1, 2, \ldots, n\}$. Over $w_j, 1 \leq j \leq n$, $\mathbf{S}$ sends the following to $\mathbf{R}$: the polynomial $p_j(x)$, the random value α_j and the n tuple $\{p_i(\alpha_j) : 1 \leq i \leq n\}$. Let $v_{ji} = p_i(\alpha_j)$.

3. Let E denotes the vector consisting of the coefficients of all n polynomials; i.e., concatenation of the rows of D. $\mathbf{S}$ computes $y = [y_1 \ y_2 \ \ldots \ y_{t+1}] = \text{EXTRAND}_{n \times n, t+1}(E)$.

Now out of the n wires, at least $t+1$ honest wires will correctly and eventually deliver the polynomials. If **R** is successfully able to identify these honest polynomials, then from the above claim, **R** will be able to reconstruct D and hence E. So **R** proceeds to reconstruct D by doing the computation shown below:

---

1. **R** waits for syntactically correct and complete set of values (i.e., an $n-1$ degree polynomial over $\mathbb{F}$, a random non-zero element from $\mathbb{F} - \{1, 2, \ldots, n\}$ and an n-tuple over $\mathbb{F}$) over $n - t = t + 1$ wires. Assume $\mathbb{W}$ represents the set of such $t + 1$ wires and **R** receives $p'_j(x)$, α'_j and the n tuple $\{v'_{ji} : 1 \leq i \leq n\}$ over $w_j \in \mathbb{W}$.

2. For each $w_j \in \mathbb{W}$, **R** computes $\text{support}_j = \{w_i : w_i \in \mathbb{W} \text{ and } p'_j(\alpha'_i) = v'_{ij}\}$ Thus support_j for $w_j \in \mathbb{F}$ represents the set of wires $w_i \in \mathbb{W}$, such that polynomial $p'_j(x)$ received over w_j, when evaluated at $x = \alpha'_i$, received over w_i, gives the value v'_{ij} which is also received over w_i. If $w_i \in \text{support}_j$, then we say that w_j is supported by w_i.

3. Repeat the following two steps until there exists $t + 1$ w_j's in $\mathbb{W}$ with $\text{support}_j \geq t+1$ /* **R** waits till it gets a set of $t + 1$ correct and consistent polynomials. */

   1. Let **R** receives syntactically correct and complete set of values (i.e., an $n-1$ degree polynomial over $\mathbb{F}$, a random non-zero element from $\mathbb{F} - \{1, 2, \ldots, n\}$ and an n-tuple over $\mathbb{F}$) over wire w_k, such that $w_k \notin \mathbb{W}$.

   2. For each $w_j \in \mathbb{W}$, **R** checks whether w_j is supported by w_k; i.e., **R** checks $p'_j(\alpha'_k) \overset{?}{=} v'_{kj}$. If yes then **R** updates support_j by including w_k in support_j. **R** then includes w_k in $\mathbb{W}$ and computes $\text{support}_k = \{w_i : w_i \in \mathbb{W} \text{ and } p'_k(\alpha'_i) = v'_{ik}\}$

4. Let $\overline{W}$ represents the sets of wires in $\mathbb{W}$, such that for each $w_j \in \overline{W}$, $\text{support}_j \geq t+1$. Except with probability at most δ, the polynomials delivered by the wires in $w_j \in \overline{W}$ are correct (see Lemma 2). Now by using these polynomials, **R** reconstructs D as follows: let $p'_j(x)$ be the polynomial delivered by wire $w_j \in \overline{W}$. **R** inserts the $i^{th}, 0 \leq i \leq n - 1$ coefficient of $p'_j(x)$ as $(i + 1)^{th}$ element in the jth row of D.

5. **R** will now have $t + 1$ rows inserted in D. Using them, **R** reconstructs all the n rows of D. From them, **R** constructs E and computes y by applying EXTRAND and terminate.

We now show that **R** will be able to recover y with very high probability.

Lemma 2. *Every corrupted wire w_j delivering incorrect $p'_j(x) \neq p_j(x)$ to **R**, will not be included in $\overline{W}$, except with probability at most δ.*

PROOF: In order that a wire $w_j \in \mathbb{W}$ delivering $p'_j(x) \neq p_j(x)$ to **R** is included in $\overline{W}$, $\text{support}_j \geq t+1$. In the worst case, there can be at most t corrupted wires in $\mathbb{W}$, such that w_j is supported by these t wires. However, in order to have $\text{support}_j \geq t + 1$, w_j should be supported by at least one honest $w_i \in \mathbb{W}$. Let π_{ij} be the probability that a corrupted $w_j \in \mathbb{W}$, which has delivered incorrect $p'_j(x) \neq p_j(x)$ is supported by an $w_i \in \mathbb{W}$. This means that $\mathcal{A}_t$ can ensure that $p_j(\alpha_i) = p'_j(\alpha_i)$ with a probability of π_{ij}. Since there are only $n - 1$ points at which these two polynomials intersect (the degree of p_j and p'_j is $n-1$) and α_i was selected uniformly in $\mathbb{F}$, we have $\pi_{ij} \leq \frac{n-1}{|\mathbb{F}|}$ for each i, j. Thus total probability that $\mathcal{A}_t$ can find $w_i, w_j \in \mathbb{W}$ such that corrupted w_j is not contradicted by an honest w_i is at most $\sum_{i,j} \pi_{ij} \leq \frac{n^2(n-1)}{|\mathbb{F}|} \approx \delta$, as $|\mathbb{F}| \geq \frac{n^3}{\delta}$. Thus except with probability at most δ, every $w_j \in \overline{W}$ delivers $p'_j(x) = p_j(x)$ to **R**. $\square$

Lemma 3. *Except with probability at most δ, **R** will be able to recover y.*

PROOF: From Lemma 2, except with probability at most δ, every $w_j \in \overline{W}$ delivers $p'_j(x) = p_j(x)$ to $\mathbf{R}$. Since there are $t + 1$ wires in $\overline{W}$, the proof follows from the earlier claim. □

Lemma 4. $\mathcal{A}_t$ will have no information at all about the pad y.

PROOF: Without loss of generality, let $\mathcal{A}_t$ controls first t wires. So $\mathcal{A}_t$ will know the polynomials $p_j(x), 1 \leq j \leq t$, from which it will know the first t rows of D. In addition, $\mathcal{A}_t$ will know t points on each of the n polynomials. Since $\mathcal{A}_t$ already knows the first t polynomials, the points on $p_j(x), 1 \leq j \leq t$ does not give new information to $\mathcal{A}_t$ and can be removed from his view. By the construction of D, the last t rows of D are linearly dependent on the first $t+1$ rows of D. Hence the t points on the last t polynomials, which are known to $\mathcal{A}_t$ can be expressed as a linear combination of the t points on the first $t+1$ polynomials which are known to $\mathcal{A}_t$. So the t points on last t polynomials can be removed from $\mathcal{A}_t$'s view. So overall, $\mathcal{A}_t$ will know the first t rows of D and t points on the polynomial $p_{t+1}(x)$. Hence $\mathcal{A}_t$ falls short of $n - t = t + 1$ points on $p_{t+1}(x)$ to know the complete array D and hence E. The proof now follows from the correctness and security of EXTRAND. □

Theorem 10. *Using Pad Establishment Technique, except with error probability of δ, $\mathbf{S}$ and $\mathbf{R}$ correctly establish a random pad y containing $t + 1$ elements from $\mathbb{F}$ by communicating $O(n^2)$ elements from $\mathbb{F}$. Moreover, y will be information theoretically secure from $\mathcal{A}_t$.*

PROOF: Over each wire, $\mathbf{S}$ communicates $O(n)$ elements from $\mathbb{F}$. The correctness and security follows from Lemma 2 and Lemma 4 respectively. □

Protocol $\Pi_{AUSMT}^{Unidirectional}$: The protocol $\Pi_{AUSMT}^{Unidirectional}$ is as follows:

$\mathbf{S}$ and $\mathbf{R}$ establishes a random one time pad y containing $t + 1$ elements from $\mathbb{F}$ by using **Pad Establishment Technique**. Parallely, $\mathbf{S}$ computes $c = m \oplus y$ and broadcasts c to $\mathbf{R}$. $\mathbf{R}$ correctly gets c, computes $m = c \oplus y$ and terminates.

Theorem 11. *If $|\mathbb{F}| \geq \frac{n^3}{\delta}$, then except with probability δ, in $\Pi_{AUSMT}^{Unidirectional}$, $\mathbf{R}$ correctly outputs m containing $t+1$ elements from $\mathbb{F}$. Moreover, m is information theoretically secure from $\mathcal{A}_t$. The total communication complexity of Π^{USMT} is $O(n^2)$ field elements.*

PROOF: The correctness and secrecy follows from the correctness and secrecy of pad establishment technique (see Theorem 10). It is easy to see that y is established by communicating $O(n^2)$ elements from $\mathbb{F}$. Parallely, $\mathbf{S}$ communicates c by sending $O(n^2)$ elements from $\mathbb{F}$. □

Theorem 12. *If there are $n = 2t + 1$ unidirectional wires from $\mathbf{S}$ to $\mathbf{R}$, then there exists an efficient AUSMT protocol tolerating $\mathcal{A}_t$.*

Theorem 13. *Let $\mathbf{S}$ and $\mathbf{R}$ be connected by n unidirectional wires, directed from $\mathbf{S}$ to $\mathbf{R}$. Then AUSMT tolerating $\mathcal{A}_t$ is possible iff $n > 3t$.*

PROOF: Follows from Theorem 9 and Theorem 12.   □

AUSMT when all the wires are bi-directional: The characterization for AUSMT tolerating $\mathcal{A}_t$, when all the n wires between **S** and **R** are bi-directional is given by following theorem.

Theorem 14. *Let **S** and **R** be connected by n bi-directional wires, of which at most t could be under the control of $\mathcal{A}_t$. Then there exists an AUSMT protocol tolerating $\mathcal{A}_t$ iff $n > 2t$.*

PROOF: Any bi-directional wire between **S** and **R** can be treated as an unidirectional wire from **S** to **R**. Now we know that there exists an AUSMT protocol $\Pi_{AUSMT}^{Unidirectional}$ tolerating $\mathcal{A}_t$ if there exists $n = 2t + 1$ unidirectional wires from **S** to **R**. Hence the same protocol can also be executed if there exists $n = 2t + 1$ bi-directional wires from **S** to **R**. This proves the sufficiency part.

From [7], we know that $n > 2t$ wires are necessary for the existence of any synchronous USMT protocol tolerating an all powerful t-active Byzantine adversary, when all the wires are bi-directional. Hence it is obviously necessary for the existence of APSMT protocol tolerating $\mathcal{A}_t$, if all the wires between **S** and **R** bi-directional.   □

References

1. Agarwal, S., Cramer, R., de Haan, R.: Asymptotically optimal two-round perfectly secure message transmission. In: Dwork, C. (ed.) CRYPTO 2006. LNCS, vol. 4117, pp. 394–408. Springer, Heidelberg (2006)
2. Beerliová-Trubíniová, Z., Hirt, M.: Efficient multi-party computation with dispute control. In: Halevi, S., Rabin, T. (eds.) TCC 2006. LNCS, vol. 3876, pp. 305 328. Springer, Heidelberg (2006)
3. Ben-Or, M., Goldwasser, S., Wigderson, A.: Completeness theorems for non-cryptographic fault-tolerant distributed computation. In: Proc. of 20th ACM STOC, pp. 1–10 (1988)
4. Cramer, R., Damgård, I., Dziembowski, S., Hirt, M., Rabin, T.: Efficient multi-party computations secure against an adaptive adversary. In: Stern, J. (ed.) EUROCRYPT 1999. LNCS, vol. 1592, pp. 324–340. Springer, Heidelberg (1999)
5. Desmedt, Y., Wang, Y.: Perfectly secure message transmission revisited. In: Knudsen, L.R. (ed.) EUROCRYPT 2002. LNCS, vol. 2332, pp. 502–517. Springer, Heidelberg (2002)
6. Dolev, D., Dwork, C., Waarts, O., Yung, M.: Perfectly secure message transmission. J. ACM 40(1), 17–47 (1993)
7. Franklin, M., Wright, R.: Secure communication in minimal connectivity models. Journal of Cryptology 13(1), 9–30 (2000)
8. Goldreich, O., Micali, S., Wigderson, A.: How to play any mental game. In: Proc. of 19th ACM STOC, pp. 218–229 (1987)
9. Kurosawa, K., Suzuki, K.: Almost secure (1-round, n-channel) message transmission scheme. Cryptology ePrint Archive, Report 2007/076 (2007)
10. Kurosawa, K., Suzuki, K.: Truly efficient 2-round perfectly secure message transmission scheme. In: Smart, N.P. (ed.) EUROCRYPT 2008. LNCS, vol. 4965, pp. 324–340. Springer, Heidelberg (2008)

11. MacWilliams, F.J., Sloane, N.J.A.: The Theory of Error Correcting Codes. North-Holland Publishing Company, Amsterdam (1978)
12. Menger, K.: Zur allgemeinen kurventheorie. Fundamenta Mathematicae 10, 96–115 (1927)
13. Patra, A., Choudhary, A., Srinathan, K., Pandu Rangan, C.: Constant phase bit optimal protocols for perfectly reliable and secure message transmission. In: Barua, R., Lange, T. (eds.) INDOCRYPT 2006. LNCS, vol. 4329, pp. 221–235. Springer, Heidelberg (2006)
14. Rabin, T., Ben-Or, M.: Verifiable secret sharing and multiparty protocols with honest majority. In: Proc. of 21st ACM STOC, pp. 73–85 (1989)
15. Sayeed, H., Abu-Amara, H.: Perfectly secure message transmission in asynchronous networks. In: Proc. of Seventh IEEE Symposium on Parallel and Distributed Processing (1995)
16. Sayeed, H., Abu-Amara, H.: Efficient perfectly secure message transmission in synchronous networks. Information and Computation 126(1), 53–61 (1996)
17. Srinathan, K., Ashwin Kumar, M.V.N., Pandu Rangan, C.: Asynchronous secure communication tolerating mixed adversaries. In: Zheng, Y. (ed.) ASIACRYPT 2002. LNCS, vol. 2501, pp. 224–242. Springer, Heidelberg (2002)
18. Srinathan, K., Narayanan, A., Pandu Rangan, C.: Optimal perfectly secure message transmission. In: Franklin, M. (ed.) CRYPTO 2004. LNCS, vol. 3152, pp. 545–561. Springer, Heidelberg (2004)
19. Yao, A.C.: Protocols for secure computations. In: Proc. of 23rd IEEE FOCS, pp. 160–164 (1982)

Response-Time Modeling of Controller Area Network (CAN)

Manoj Kumar[1,*], Ajit Kumar Verma[2], and A. Srividya[2]

[1] Control Instrumentation Division
BARC, Trombay, Mumbai-400085
kmanoj@barc.gov.in
[2] Reliability Engineering
IIT Bombay, Powai, Mumbai-400076
akv@ee.iitb.ac.in

Abstract. A probabilistic approach to determine response-time distribution for messages in Controller Area Network (CAN) is presented here. CAN is a field bus level communication network for exchanging short real-time messages. CAN is mostly used to carry periodic messages for control and automation systems.

Traditional response-time analysis of CAN messages only gives worst-case response-times. This introduces pessimism in analysis, resulting in over designing and under utilization of resources.

Response-time distribution is a probabilistic function. Response-time distribution provides a complete characterization of CAN message response-time. It can provide probability of meeting/missing any specified response-time limit. This probability is useful for system reliability and performance modeling.

In this paper response-time model of CAN messages is discussed. Technique to derive probabilistic parameters of response-time model, for periodic CAN messages with deterministic transmission times is given. The method has been applied to a standard data set, results are compared with that of worst-case analysis and reasons for deviations are discussed.

Keywords: CAN, DSPN, worst-case analysis, probabilistic, response-time analysis, real-time systems.

1 Introduction

Controller Area Network (CAN) is a well established field bus level networking system specially designed for real-time systems in mind [1]. CAN is extensively being used in real-time distributed applications such as automobiles, and medical applications. CAN came into existence in 1980s for interconnection of control components in automotive vehicles. Nowadays CAN has found its usage in diverse areas such as agriculture machinery, medical instruments, elevator controls, public transportation systems and industrial automation control components.

---

* Corresponding author.

V. Garg, R. Wattenhofer, and K. Kothapalli (Eds.): ICDCN 2009, LNCS 5408, pp. 163–174, 2009.
© Springer-Verlag Berlin Heidelberg 2009

During the last decade real-time researchers [2,3,4], all over the globe are working toward bringing CAN into safety critical applications. The inherent properties of CAN such as lossless collisions, priority of messages, limited message length, error detection and fault tolerance etc. makes it a possible to use it in applications where missing a deadline cannot be tolerated.

Meeting message deadline(s) is the primary requirement for real-time applications. Tindell et al. [3,4] have proposed a method for calculating an upper bound on message response times on CAN. Network parameters affecting response-time and condition(s) to ensure massage delivery before deadline is outlined in [5]. Effect of transmission errors due to EMI (Electromagnetic Interference) on message deadline is analyzed in [6,7]. Nolte et al. [8,9,10] have proposed probabilistic model for bit-stuffing, effect of bit-stuffing on response-time and message manipulation to minimize number of stuffed bits. All these methods although use probabilistic techniques to model interference and bit-stuffing, but use deterministic (worst-case) technique for response-time.

Response-time distribution gives a probabilistic complete picture of variation of response-time. Ref. [11] gives a method to numerically compute response-time distribution. This method is applicable for system with Poison (or combination of exponential) arrival and exponential service time distributions. Applications involving CAN bus are mostly time-triggered and have periodic arrivals and fixed transmission time.

In this paper, a stochastic model to numerically/analytically determine message response-time distribution is proposed. The model requires network parameters as probability and random variables (r.v.). A method to determine these probabilities and *pdf* (probability density function) of r.v. is given. With the help of an example, results are compared with worst-case and that of simulation.

In section 2, an introduction to CAN bus is given. Section 3 gives a brief background of worst-case response-time analysis of CAN from literature. A detailed stochastic model for response-time distribution along with parameter estimation is given in section 4. An example is taken in section 5, results of stochastic analysis are compared with worst-case and simulation. Finally conclusions are given in section 6.

2   CAN Bus

CAN is a broadcast bus- a single pair of wires- where a number of nodes are connected to the bus. It employs carrier sense multiple access with collision detection and arbitration based on message priority (CSMA/AMP) [1]. Data is transmitted as *message*, consisting of up to 8 bytes. Format of CAN message set is shown in Fig. 1. Every message is assigned a unique *identifier*. The identifier serves two purposes, filtering messages upon reception and assigning priority to the message.

The use of identifier as priority is the most important part of CAN regrading real-time performance. The identifier field of CAN message is used to control access to the bus after collision by taking advantage of certain electrical

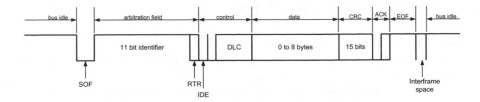

Fig. 1. CAN message format. It does not have source/destination address. 11-bit identifier is used for filtering at receiver as well as to arbitrate access to bus. It has 7 control bits- RTR (remote retransmission request), IDE (identifier extension), reserve bit for future extensions and 4 bits to give length of data field, DLC (data length code). Data field can be 0 to 8 bytes in length and CRC field contain 15-bit code that can be used to check frame integrity. Following CRC field is acknowledge (ACK) field comprising an ACK slot bit and an ACK delimiter bit.

characteristics. In case of multiple stations transmitting simultaneously, all stations will see 0 if any one of the node puts 0 bit (dominant), while all stations will see 1 if all transmitting node put 1 bit. So, during arbitration, by monitoring the bus a node detects if there is a competing higher priority message and stops transmission if this is the case. A node transmitting the last bit of the identifier without detecting a higher priority message must be transmitting the highest priority ready message, and hence can continue. Fig. 2 shows the arbitration mechanism and electrical diagram of CAN.

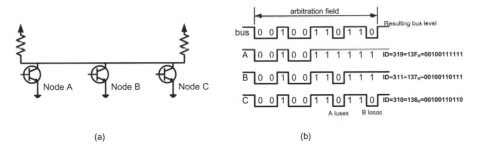

(a)   (b)

Fig. 2. (a) CAN's electrical interface (wired-OR) which enables priority based arbitration, (b) arbitration mechanism when 3 nodes are transmitting simultaneously

CAN uses principle of hard synchronization [12]. So, to allow receivers to synchronize and adjust internal timing, CAN insert a bit of opposite polarity when 5 consecutive bit of same polarity are transmitted on the bus. This process is called *bit-stuffing* and bits inserted by this process are called *stuff-bits*. The stuff-bits are removed at the receiver. Bit-stuffing affects the transmission time of message.

For more details on CAN, interested readers are requested to refer [1,12].

3   Worst-Case Response Time

Tindell et al. [3,4] present analysis to calculate the worst-case latencies of CAN messages. This analysis is based on the standard fixed priority response-time analysis.

The worst-case response-time of message is the longest time between the queueing of a message and the time message reaches at destination nodes. In case of CAN, it is defined to be composed of two delays, (i) queueing delay, q_i, (ii) transmission delay, C_i [4]. The queueing delay is the longest time that a message can be queued at a node and be delayed because of other higher- and lower-priority messages are being sent on the bus. The transmission delay is the actual time taken to send the message on the bus. Thus, worst-case response-time is defined as:

$$R_i = q_i + C_i \tag{1}$$

The queueing time, q_i is itself composed of two times, (i) longest time that any lower priority message can occupy the bus, B, (ii) the longest time that all higher priority messages can be queued and occupy the bus before the message i is finally transmitted.

$$q_i = B_i + \sum_{j \in hp(i)} \left\lceil \frac{q_i + J_j + \tau_{bit}}{T_j} \right\rceil C_j \tag{2}$$

Where J_i is the queueing jitter of the messages, i.e., the maximum variation in the queueing time relative to T_i, $hp(i)$ is the set of messages with priority higher than i, τ_{bit} (bit-time) caters for the difference in arbitration start times at the different nodes due to propagation delays and protocol tolerances. Equation (2) is recurrence relation for q_i. Considering effect of external interference and error, the worst-case response time [9] can be given as:

$$R_i = B_i + \sum_{j \in hp(i)} \left\lceil \frac{q_i + J_j + \tau_{bit}}{T_j} \right\rceil C_j + C_i + E\left(q_i + C_i\right) \tag{3}$$

4   Response-Time Distribution

The model presented here is based on following assumptions:

1. Queueing jitter is neglected.
2. Messages are not synchronized with each other.
3. Worst-case message transmission time is taken, i.e. with maximum number of stuff bits.(In the end, a method is discussed to accommodate bit-stuffing mechanism with the proposed model)
4. All parameters (*pdfs* and probabilities) are time invariant.

4.1   Response-Time Model

Response-time is the *time duration from the time instant a message is queued for transmission to completion of transmission.* Response-time model for a typical CAN message is shown in Fig. 3. This model is based on DSPN (Deterministic Stochastic Petri Net). The model is analyzed analytically. This DSPN model is chosen for better representation and explanation of analysis steps. As the DSPN model is only for explaining the model. A brief introduction to DSPN to understand the model is given below.

DSPN is Petri net based graphical tool to model stochastic phenomenon. It has two distinct class of nodes, *places* and *transitions*, where arcs are either from a place to transition or from a transition to place. In case of DSPN, node class, transitions have three variants-i) immediate, ii) exponential, and iii) general transitions. Immediate transitions are drawn as bars, exponential as dark rectangular box and general as gray rectangular box. Places can have tokens and transitions can fire. A transition is enabled for firing if all its input places have tokens, on firing it removes token from all input places and store one token in all output places. An enabled transition's time to fire could be immediate, exponential or general, based on type of transition immediate, exponential and general, respectively. Immediate transition has probability of firing as a parameter and used to model logical conditions. Exponential and general transitions are also known as timed transitions, and represent exponentially and generally distributed random variable. They are used to capture random time delays.

For more details on Petri nets and its variant, please refer to Murata [13].

To analyze the model of Fig. 3, values of all transitions, immediate (probabilities) and timed (*pdfs*) are required. The model gives response-time distribution of one message only. So parameter values need to be calculated for all the messages whose response-time distribution is required.

4.2   Parameter Estimation

Set of messages of the system are denoted by M. Parameter are estimated for a message m from set M. In parameters estimation sub-section, $i \in M$ means all messages except message m for which the parameter is being estimated.

Probability of finding bus free *bFree***:** Probability that a message finds the network free when it gets queued, is estimated based on the utilization of network. This utilization is by other messages of network.

$$P_{free}^m = 1 - \sum_{i \in M} \frac{C_i}{T_i} \qquad (4)$$

Probability of finding the bus free, by a message m is the complement of utilization. This is because in a closed system (with fixed number of messages/customers) with n messages, a message on arrival finds the system in equilibrium with $n-1$ messages [11].

Probability of no collision with high priority message *arbSuc***:** When network is free, a node with ready message can start transmission. Node will abort

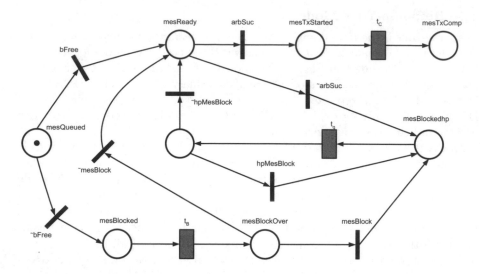

Fig. 3. Response-time model for CAN. A token in place *mesQueued* depicts that a message of interest is queued for transmission. Time taken by token to reach place *mesTxComp* is the response-time of message. Immediate transitions *bFree*, *hpmesBlock*, *arbSuc* are probabilities of bus being free, blocking due to higher priority message, and successful arbitration, respectively. Immediate transitions labeled with ˜ as prefix are complementary to transitions without this symbol. General transitions t_B, t_q, t_C represent time associated with blocking, queueing and transmission, respectively.

and back off transmission if it finds any higher priority message concurrently being transmitted. This can happen if a node start transmitting a higher priority message within the collision window τ_w.

$$P_{Suc}^m = \prod_{\substack{i \in M \\ i \in hp(m)}} P_C^i$$

where

$$P_C^i = \text{Prob}\,[\text{non occurrence of ith message in time } \tau_w]$$

$$= 1 - \left(\tfrac{1}{T_i} \times \tau_w\right)$$

(5)

Blocking time (t_B): A message in queue can be blocked by any message under transmission by any of the other nodes. This is because CAN messages in transmission cannot be preempted. *pdf* of this blocking time $p_b(t)$ is obtained by following steps:

1. Find the ratio r_i of all the messages. $r_i = \frac{1}{T_i \sum_j \frac{1}{T_j}}$, for $i, j \in M$

2. Construct a *pdf*, $p(t)$ of total blocking time by other messages

$$p(t) = \sum_{i \in M} r_i \cdot \delta\,(t - C_i)$$

(6)

3. Message can get ready at any time during the blocking time with equal probability. So, effective blocking time is given by following convolution

$$p_b^m(t) = \frac{1}{\max(C_i)} \int_0^t p(\tau)\left[U(t+\tau) - U(t+\max(C_i)+\tau)\right] d\tau \quad (7)$$

Blocking time by high priority message (t_q): When the ready node finds bus free and start transmission of ready message, then if within the collision time window, another node starts transmitting a higher priority message, node backs off. And the message need to wait till the time of completion of this transmission. *pdf* of blocking time by high priority message, p_{bhp} is obtained by following steps 1-3 of *Blocking time* with one variation, instead of all messages only high priority message of network are considered.

1. Find the ratio r_i^H of all the messages. $r_i^H = \frac{1}{T_i \sum_j \frac{1}{T_j}}$, for $i, j \in M$, $i \in hp(m)$

2. *pdf* of blocking after back off is given by

$$p_{bhp}^m(t) = \sum_{i \in hp(m)} r_i^H \cdot \delta(t - C_i) \quad (8)$$

where $\delta(\cdot)$ is Dirac delta function.

Probability of no new higher priority message arrival in t_B ($\tilde{~}mesBlock$): This is similar to *arbSuc* with the difference that instead of collision window time, mean of BlockTime is used.

$$P_{T_B}^m = \prod_{\substack{i \in M \\ i \in hp(m)}} P_{T_B}^i$$

where

$$P_{T_B}^i = \text{Prob [non occurrence of ith message in time } BlockingTime] \quad (9)$$

$$= 1 - \left(\frac{1}{T_i} \times E[t_B]\right)$$

Probability of no new higher priority message arrival in t_q ($\tilde{~}hpMes\text{-}$
Block): This is similar to previous.

$$P_{T_{Bhp}}^m = \prod_{\substack{i \in M \\ i \in hp(m)}} P_{T_{Bhp}}^i$$

where

$$P_{T_{Bhp}}^i = \text{Prob [non occurrence of ith message in time } BlockTimebyNew]$$

$$= 1 - \left(\frac{1}{T_i} \times E[t_{Bhp}]\right) \quad (10)$$

4.3   Total Queueing Time

Time to reach place *mesReady* from *mesBlockedhp* in i^{th} step is modeled as a single r.v. with *pdf* $B_{hp}^m(i, t)$.

$$B_{hp}^m(i, t) = \left[\left(1 - P_{T_{Bhp}}^m\right)^{i-1} P_{T_{Bhp}}^m\right] \eta^i(t)$$

where

$$\eta^i (t) = \eta^{i-1} (t) \otimes p_{bhp}^m (t)$$
$$\eta (t) = p_{bhp}^m (t)$$

$$B_{hp}^m (t) = \sum_i B_{hp^m} (i, t)$$

Symbol $\otimes$ is used to denote convolution.

In the same way, time to reach place $mesTxStarted$ in i^{th} attempt from $mesReady$ is modeled as a single r.v. with pdf $t_{rdy}(i, t)$.

$$t_{rdy}^m (i, t) = \left[(1 - Pfree)^{i-1} Pfree \right] (B_{hp}^m)^{i-1} (t)$$

where

$$(B_{hp}^m)^i (t) = (B_{hp}^m)^{i-1} (t) \otimes B_{hp}^m (t)$$
$$(B_{hp}^m)^0 (t) = \delta (t)$$

$$t_{rdy}^m (t) = \sum_i t_{rdy}^m (i, t)$$

From the instant message is queued, it can reach state $mesReady$ either directly or via state $mesBlocked$ and $mesBlockedhp$. State $mesBlocked$ has an associated time delay. So, using total probability theorem [14], total queueing time is given as:

$$q^m (t) = P_{free}^m t_{rdy} (t) + \left(1 - P_{free}^m\right) P_{T_B}^m \left[p_b^m (t) \otimes t_{rdy} (t) \right]$$
$$+ \left(1 - P_{free}^m\right) \left(1 - P_{T_B}^m\right) \left[p_b^m (t) \otimes p_{bhp}^m (t) \otimes t_{rdy} (t) \right]$$

4.4   Response-Time

Response-time of a message is sum of its queueing time and transmission time.

$$r^m (t) = q^m (t) \otimes C_m \delta (t) \tag{11}$$

Response-time distribution can be evaluated as

$$R^m (t) = \int_0^t r^m (\tau) \, d\tau \tag{12}$$

Let t_d^m is deadline for the message m. Then value of cumulative distribution at t_d^m gives the probability of meeting the deadline.

$$P (t \le t_d^m) = R^m (t_d^m) \tag{13}$$

Table 1. SAE CAN messages [4,10] used for analysis and comparison

Message ID	No. of bytes	Ti (ms)	Di (ms)
17	1	1000	5
16	2	5	5
15	1	5	5
14	2	5	5
13	1	5	5
12	2	5	5
11	6	10	10
10	1	10	10
9	2	10	10
8	2	10	10
7	1	100	100
6	4	100	100
5	1	100	100
4	1	100	100
3	3	1000	1000
2	1	1000	1000
1	1	1000	1000

4.5 Effect of Bit-Stuffing

Total number of stuffed bits in a message depends on bit pattern of message. A probabilistic treatment requires probability of each bit pattern to get distribution of bit-stuffing for each message as given in [8,10].

Once the distribution of number of stuff bits is available, distribution of transmission time can be obtained [10]

$$C_m(t) = C_m + (\varphi(n)) \tau_{bit} \tag{14}$$

where

C_m : time taken to transmit date without any stuff bits
$\varphi(n)$: prob. that stuff bits are n
τ_{bit} : time taken to transmit a bit on the bus

Response-time of a message considering bit-stuffing can be determined using above method, by replacing fixed C_i by distribution $C_i(t)$ in (6)(7)(8).

5 Example

To illustrate the method, benchmark message set of Society of Automotive Engineers (SAE) [10] is considered. The message set have messages exchanged between seven different subsystems in a prototype electric car. The list of messages along with other details are shown in Table 1. Message ID 17 is highest priority while message ID 1 is lowest priority.

Using the proposed method, parameters are calculated for each message considering worst-case transmission time. To compare the results with literature [10], CAN operating speed of 125Kbps (bit-time=7.745μs) is taken.

Using the proposed method all the parameters for all the message are estimated and response-time is calculated.

5.1   Results

The response-time distribution of 3 messages (message ID=1, 9 and 17) is shown in Fig. 4. For the purpose of comparison, worst-case response-time from literature and response-time from present analysis is presented in Table 2.

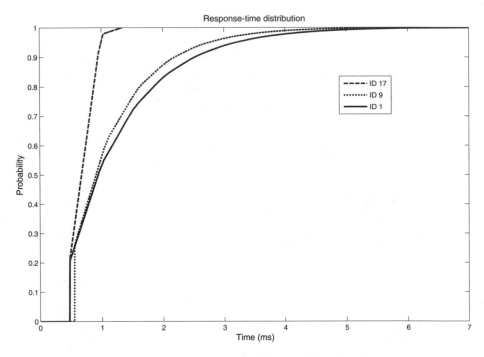

Fig. 4. Response-time distribution of 3 messages

5.2   Discussion

In Fig. 4 the offset at time axis is due to blocking when the message is queued. It is same for all messages irrespective of message priority, because CAN message transmissions are non-preemptive. Slope of response-time curves are different. Slopes are dependent upon the message priority, higher the message priority higher is the slope.

Response-times from worst-case analysis are giving upper bound on response-time, so probability at these times from response-time distribution is expected to be very high or even 1. Values in column 3 of Table 2 confirms this. Worst-case

Table 2. Comparison of response-time results of analysis with literature. Second and fourth column give worst-case response-time from literature. Third and fifth column gives probability of message delivery by corresponding time given in second and forth column, respectively. Last column gives response-time from present analysis assuming probability of message delivery to be 0.999.

Priority (ID)	R_i [10]	$P(R_i)$	R_i^{sim} [10]	$P(R_iSim)$	t_{min}
17	1.416	1.0000	0.680	0.5123	1.324
16	2.016	1.0000	1.240	0.9883	1.402
15	2.536	0.9997	1.720	0.9920	2.238
14	3.136	0.9997	2.280	0.9956	2.742
13	3.656	0.9995	2.760	0.9959	3.369
12	4.256	0.9995	3.320	0.9967	3.919
11	5.016	0.9991	4.184	0.9965	4.957
10	8.376	1.0000	4.664	0.9968	5.553
9	8.976	1.0000	5.224	0.9976	5.925
8	9.576	1.0000	8.424	0.9999	6.374
7	10.096	1.0000	8.904	0.9999	6.831
6	19.096	1.0000	9.616	0.9999	7.094
5	19.616	1.0000	10.096	1.0000	6.940
4	20.136	1.0000	18.952	1.0000	6.978
3	28.976	1.0000	18.952	1.0000	7.172
2	29.496	1.0000	19.432	1.0000	7.025
1	29.520	1.0000	19.912	1.0000	7.032

response-time from simulation is obtained from a limited simulation (2000000 ms [10]). Hence there is no consistence probability at these response-times.

Response-time of message with probability 0.999, is comparable for higher priority messages, while it is almost 25% of worst-case for lower priority. This is because worst-case analysis assumes all higher priority message will get queued deteministically, while response-time distribution gives probabilistic treatment to this.

6   Conclusions

CAN networks are used in application where message arrival are mostly periodic or mixture of periodic and sporadic. Response-time distribution is a probabilistic function. So, determination of response-time distribution of CAN messages require derivation of various probabilistic variable from periodic and deterministic parameters. A complete method to determine response-time distribution for a system with periodic message is presented. The analysis is applied on SAE CAN message set and results are compared and discussed. The model seems to be quite consistent, with CAN behavior, still thorough validation is needed.

Response-time distribution is quite useful for system design, reliability and performance evaluation. System design can be optimized for better network utilization and probability of missing deadline/specified time limit.

Acknowledgments. We thank Thomas Nolte for his valuable and timely suggestion at beginning of this work. We also thank Shri U. Mahapatra (BARC) and Prof. Varsha Apte (IIT Bombay) for useful discussions and guidance.

References

1. Farsi, M., Ratcliff, K., Barbosa, M.: An Overview of Controller Area Network. Computing & Control Engineering Journal, 113–120 (1999)
2. Wang, Z., Lu, H., Hedrick, G.E.: Message Delay Analysis for CAN Based Network. In: Proceedings of ACM/SIGAPP Symposium on Applied Computing Technological Challenges of the 1990's, pp. 89–94 (1992)
3. Tindell, K.W., Hansson, H., Wellings, A.J.: Analyzing Real-time Communications: Controller Area Network (CAN). In: Proceeding of Real-time Symposium, pp. 259–263 (2001)
4. Tindell, K.W., Burns, A., Wellings, A.J.: Calculating Controller Area Network (CAN) Message Response Times. Computing & Control Engineering Journal 3(2), 1163–1169 (1995)
5. Xiaodong, N., Yanjun, Z.: Determining Message Delivery Delay of Controller Area Networks. In: Proceedings of IEEE TENCON 2002, pp. 767–771 (1997)
6. Navet, N., Song, Y.-Q., Simonot, F.: Worst-case deadline failure probability in real-time applications distributed over controller area network. J. Systems and Architecture 46, 607–617 (2000)
7. Punnekkat, S., Hansson, H., Norstrom, C.: Response Time Analysis under Errors for CAN. In: Proceedings of RATS 2000-6th IEEE Real-time Technology and Applications Symposium, pp. 258–265 (2000)
8. Nolte, T., Hansson, H., Norstrom, C., Punnekkat, S.: Using bit-stuffing distributions in CAN analysis. In: IEEE/IEE Real-time Embedded Systems Workshop (RTES 2001) (2001)
9. Nolte, T., Hansson, H., Norstrom, C.: Minimizing CAN response-time jitter by message manipulation. In: Proceedings of the 8th Real-time and Embedded Technology and Application Symposium (RTAS 2002) (2002)
10. Nolte, T., Hansson, H., Norstrom, C.: Probabilistic Worst-Case Response-Time Analysis for the Controller Area Network. In: Proceedings of the 9th Real-time and Embedded Technology and Application Symposium (RTAS 2003) (2003)
11. Muppala, J.K., Mainkar, V., Trivedi, K.S., Kulkarni, V.G.: Numerical Computation of Response-Time Distributions using Stochastic Reward Nets. Annals of Operations Research 48, 155–184 (1994)
12. IEC: CAN Specification 2.0. Part A and B, CAN in Automation (CiA)
13. Murata, T.: Petri Nets: Properties, analysis and applications. Proceedings of the IEEE 77(4), 541–580 (1989)
14. Trivedi, K.S.: Probability & Statistics with Reliability, Queueing, and Computer Science Applications. Prentice-Hall, Englewood Cliffs (1982)

A Threat-Aware Anomaly-Based Intrusion-Detection Approach for Obtaining Network-Specific Useful Alarms

Subramanian Neelakantan[1] and Shrisha Rao[2]

[1] Centre for Development of Advanced Computing
No. 68, Electronics City, Bangalore 560 100, India
subbu@ncb.ernet.in
[2] International Institute of Information Technology - Bangalore
26/C Electronics City, Hosur Road
Bangalore 560 100, India
shrao@ieee.org

Abstract. We present a model and architecture that enhance anomaly based intrusion detection system(IDS) with threat-awareness capability. Anomaly based network IDS, profile network traffic to arrive base-line based on which it identifies anomalous events. However, due to dynamic changes in the threat level of a network, only a subset of these identified events are relevant to the network at any given instance. Hence, we introduce the notion of Threat-Awareness for anomaly based network IDS that periodically learns the changing threats in a network and enhance the capability of traditional anomaly based IDS to obtain network specific useful alarms. In this paper, we present a Threat-Aware Anomaly-Based IDS model for obtaining network-specific useful alarms. We also present our architecture and discuss its internal functions. Finally, we present our experiments based on various threat scenarios and the results obtained proves the efficiency of our model.

1 Introduction

This paper describes a threat-aware anomaly-based intrusion detection model that profile the dynamically changing threats in network and accordingly produce network specific useful alarms. The development of the threat-aware anomaly-based IDS is motivated by three factors: 1) current day IDS produce huge false alarms, 2) threat in any network is a dynamically changing entity and hence profiling of threat is a challenge and 3) utilizing the knowledge of the changing threats for Anomaly based IDS to produce network specific useful alarms in real-time. In this paper, we enhance the fundamental capability of anomaly-based IDS by providing the knowledge of threats that shall be very useful for IDS to detect intrusions more accurately.

Morin et al. [1] present a formal Gula [2] discusses the mechanisms for correlating IDS alerts with Vulnerability Information. Valeur et al. [3] present an event correlation framework to reduce the number of alarms generated by the intrusion detection, Axelsson [4] raises various questions related to alarm correlation. Kruegel and Robertson [5] present the ways of obtaining successful intrusion attempts by verifying the alerts, and

V. Garg, R. Wattenhofer, and K. Kothapalli (Eds.): ICDCN 2009, LNCS 5408, pp. 175–180, 2009.

Desai [6] tables the need for integrating vulnerability knowledge with IDS for reducing false alarms.

All the above related work, target the correlation of IDS alerts with vulnerability information to reduce the false alarms hence are off-line techniques. In this paper, we present a novel approach of threat-awareness at real-time to enhance the capability of anomaly based IDS. Our approach has two main advantages: one, our approach provides a real-time solution; and two, the outcome of the enhanced IDS generates network specific useful alarms.

The main contributions of this paper are, firstly in devising a threat-aware anomaly detection model for network IDS, secondly in developing a suitable architecture and thirdly in carrying out experiments and obtaining the results that proves the effectiveness of our approach.

The remainder of this paper is organized as follows. Section 2 discusses our Threat-Aware Anomaly-Based IDS model, Section 3 brings out the Threat-Aware Anomaly-based network IDS Architecture and its internal functions. In Section 4 presents the results of our experiments, Section 5 we provide conclusive summary.

2 Threat-Aware Anomaly-Based Intrusion Detection Model

Definition 1. *Global anomaly profiles G_P : Anomaly detection system uses Global Anomaly profiles that represents the combined behavioral changes of diverse entities such as hosts, user and services in a network. Let G_A be the total set of alarms generated using G_P.*

Definition 2. *Anomaly Blue Prints V_P: V_P is the deduced anomaly blue-prints derived from both the learnt the Vulnerability Profile and traffic profile. Since V_P is deduced based on the dynamically changing threats of any given network it can be utilised to produce local network specific useful alarms.*

Definition 3. *True Alarms TR_A: Is the set of alarms that are true, which may cause potential damage to the network. Hence,*

$$TR_A \subset G_A \tag{1}$$

In this paper, we introduce Verified Alarms. Once the anomaly detection module identifies deviations to normal behavior, these deviations G_A which are potential intrusions are verified against the learnt anomaly blue-prints.

Definition 4. *Verified Alarms V_A: Is the set of alarms that are produced after verifying against the deduced blue-prints. Hence, these sets of alarms are network specific and they can impact the network. Since we obtain V_A after applying V_P the Anomaly blue-prints over G_A,*

$$V_A \subset G_A \tag{2}$$

Analysis of our Model:

Let G_A be the set of total alarms generated by anomaly detection

Let TR_A be the true alarms at any given instance of time

Let V_A be the number of alarms generated after the verification

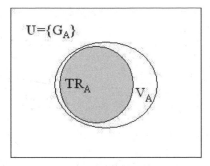

Fig. 1. Threat-Aware Anomaly-Based IDS Model

Since there could be false alarms in anomaly-based IDS, implies

$$TR_A \subset G_A \tag{3}$$

Since V_A is a filtered set of alarms generated from G_A using V_P, implies

$$V_A \subset G_A \tag{4}$$

and Based on the definition of true alarms that are critical intrusions that shall exploit the existing network vulnerabilities,

$$TR_A \subset V_A \tag{5}$$

Hence number false alarms are reduced using our model.

Best Case: Assuming that our model is able to learn all the traffic profiles and vulnerability profiles, the best case would be,

$$V_A = TR_A$$

Worst case: Worst case situation shall arise when for some reason the system is not able to generate the vulnerability profiles. During such a situation, total number of alarms generated shall be G_A which is still the total set of alarms that would have been generated even if our model is not used.

Challenge: Since we learn the threats periodically, there is a gap between instances of learning, which in real life may lead to some false alarms. Hence choosing the interval for periodic learning is a challenge and is specific to network.

3   Threat-Aware Anomaly-Based IDS Architecture

Refer Fig.2. that brings out the architecture of Threat-Aware Anomaly-Based IDS. It has modules to capture packets and profile the captured packets as any other anomaly detection IDS. In addition, modules such as vulnerability scanner, deduce anomaly blue-prints and anomaly verifier are specific to our architecture where by the traditional anomaly based IDS is empowered with threat-awareness capability.

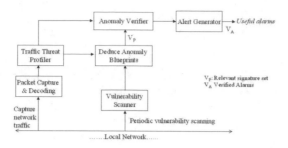

Fig. 2. Threat-Aware Anomaly-Based IDS Architecture

3.1 Packet Capture and Decoding

As any other IDS, Threat-Aware Anomaly-Detection IDS also, captures the entire network. Once the packets are captured, it is decoded to segregate various protocol information, headers and packet payloads, which are used for profiling and identifying anomalies.

3.2 Vulnerability Scanner

This component performs vulnerability scanning periodically. This component scans the entire network both horizontally and vertically to learn snap-shots of vulnerabilities and threats of hosts, applications and services. This produces a report at the end of every periodic learning and generates the threat information in XML format. This report can be parsed to deduce various threat profiles such as valid public hosts, valid internal services, valid public services, type and version of OS, and applications etc. A sample outcome of the parsed output is as given in the Table 1.

3.3 Threat Profilers

Using the Traffic Threat Profiler and Vulnerability scanner components, our system learns the dynamically changing threat profiles in network traffic, in host and in application.

(a) Traffic Threat Profiler This component is devised to learn various network threats based on packet counts, size of packets and interaction between hosts.
- Packet count based threat profiles: For profiling the packet count based traffic threats, entire traffic is taken as input by sniffing packets. Based on captured packet, packet count based threat matrix is built.
- Traffic size based threat profiles: Based on each captured packet, traffic size based threat matrix is built similar to that of the packet count based threat profiles.
- Internal and External Threat profiles: Both Internal and External threat profiles are learnt separately, based on the interactions between the internal hosts and ports with external hosts and ports and derives the normalcy pattern, and hence any deviation to this would be an abnormality in detection phase.

(b) Vulnerability threat profiler This performs vulnerability scanning periodically for the entire learning duration creates vulnerability threat profiles as shown in Table.1.

Table 1. Learnt Vulnerability Profile

Host IP	Valid Port	Kernel Info.	App. Info.	Threat Info.
172.16.1.2	80	Linux 2.4.2	Apache-2.0	warning notes
172.16.1.3	-	Win XP	-	Security Notes
172.16.1.4	25,63	Linux 2.6	Apache-2.2	Security hole
172.16.1.5	80	Win 2003	IIS 6	Security hole

3.4   Deduce Anomaly Blue-Prints

Above learnt threat profiles are utilized by this component to deduce various anomaly blue-prints to detect attacks during the detection phase. These blue-prints are maintained in the knowledgebase and periodically fed to the anomaly verifier to detect intrusions and attacks in the network.

(a) Internal Anomaly Blue-Prints
   - Interaction based anomaly blue-prints: To deduce the anomaly profiles for detecting attacks, this performs packet counts on client server interactions, based on which, traffic threat profile matrices are generated. These matrices are produced based on the intervals set. Then a 'or' operation is performed over all the matrices to get all possible interactions between hosts. Hence the result of this is a matrix, that has either 1's and 0's, where 1 represents the existence of interaction between hosts and 0 represent no interaction. This is then marked as the learnt base-line normalcy behavior and any deviation to this is a threat based anomaly.
   - Packet count and size of packet based anomaly blue-prints: To deduce the anomaly profiles to detect attacks based on packet counts and size, packet count and size based traffic threat profile matrices that are generated for the set duration. The chi-square averages are computed to produce the final matrix with learnt averages.
(b) External Anomaly Blue-Prints IP and Port based anomaly blue-prints: As discussed above, the Traffic Threat Profiler provides the list of internal IPs that are exposed outside for services, from which the anomaly blue-prints are deduced that any traffic aimed at other hosts and services are anomalous. Similarly, blue-prints based on profile of external ports that are accessible from inside are deduced.

Anomaly Verifier and Alarm Generator. Based on the deduced anomaly blue-prints, anomaly verifier performs validations of all the anomalous events using V_P to confirm the anomaly events and also marks the level of severity for all the generated events of severity of the events and respective alarms are generated.

4   Results

Test Environment: To validate our Threat-Aware Anomaly based IDS model, anomaly-based IDS modules, we prepared a test environment on a local area network with 5 hosts with various OS and applications being configured as per our scenarios explained.

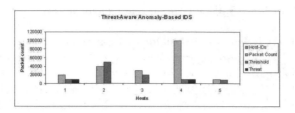

Fig. 3. Threat-Aware Anomaly-Based IDS Alarms

As presented in the graph shown in Fig.3, even though there are deviations to normal traffic for set of hosts, due to the vulnerability status of those hosts confirmation of the anomalous events are carried out. As seen in the graph, even though there are cases of anomalous events cross the expected normal threshold, only in certain cases these events gets mapped to vulnerable hosts and hence they are confirmed intrusions.

5   Conclusions

In this paper we presented a Threat-Aware Anomaly-Based IDS model along with a architecture that enhances the current Anomaly-Based IDS with this capability. Our experimental results shows the effectiveness of such an approach in obtaining network-specific useful alarms.

References

1. Morin, B., Me, L., Debar, H., Ducasse, M.: M2d2: A formal data model for ids alert correlation. In: Wespi, A., Vigna, G., Deri, L. (eds.) RAID 2002. LNCS, vol. 2516, pp. 115–137. Springer, Heidelberg (2002)
2. Gula, R.: Correlating ids alerts with vulnerability information. Tenable Network Security, Technical Report (2007)
3. Valeur, F., Vigna, G., Kruegel, C., Kemmerer, R.A.: A comprehensive approach to intrusion detection alert correlation. IEEE Transactions on Dependable and Secure Computing, 146–169 (2004)
4. Axelsson, S.: Research in intrusion-detection systems: A survey. Technical Report 98–17, Department of Computer Engineering, Chalmers University of Technology, Goteborg, Sweden (1998)
5. Kruegel, C., Robertson, W.: Alert verification: Determining the success of intrusion attempts. In: Proceedings of DIMVA 2004 (2004)
6. Desai, N.: IDS Correlation of VA data and IDS Alerts. Security Focus (2003)

Traffic Engineering Based Attack Detection in Active Networks

Jayashree Padmanabhan[1] and K.S. Easwarakumar[2]

[1] Department of Information Technology, Anna University, MIT, Chennai
[2] Department of Computer Science and Engineering, Anna University, CEG, Chennai
pjshree@annauniv.edu

Abstract. Distributed denial of service attacks are the serious candidates for traffic analysis next to traffic performance evaluation. As these threats deplete the network resources rapidly particularly link parameters, modeling these attacks provide a strong base for analyzing the attack characteristics. The solution domain uses active networks for implementation, as it supports active routers which can perform customized tasks on demand and ease of deploying. The paper presents a model based on packet attributes to characterize the attack traffic and a detection and response framework based on the model. The detection mechanism uses leaky buckets to rate limit the traffic based on the packet ranking using linear arithmetic. The simulation results depicting the attack traffic passed through the network as well as the legitimate traffic dropped at the active routers, under different attack scenarios, are found to be comparable to existing solutions with improved efficiency in detection rate and time.

Keywords: Denial of Service (DoS), traffic characteristics, leaky buckets, active network.

1 Introduction

Distributed Denial of Service (DDoS) attack is a coordinated attack launched through zombies on a victim network resource, with the purpose of preventing legitimate users from using that resource. With the advent of Internet based applications in dense volume, the availability of Internet services is of paramount importance and the damage that may be caused by DDoS attacks is more severe. Though a number of attack detection and defense mechanisms are available, achieving this goal is not an easy task due to the difficulty in distinguishing attack traffic from normal traffic.

Attack detection algorithms vary in granularity, network information needed and characteristics of the network that are used to detect the attacks [1]. An attack detection algorithm identifies specific characteristics of the network traffic used for rate limiting the traffic that may either queue or discard the packets based on the characteristics.

In this paper a proactive DDoS defense framework that rate limits traffic using leaky buckets and double checks a packet candidature for dropping using payload of packets as well.

V. Garg, R. Wattenhofer, and K. Kothapalli (Eds.): ICDCN 2009, LNCS 5408, pp. 181–186, 2009.
© Springer-Verlag Berlin Heidelberg 2009

2 Related Work

Modeling a DDoS attack has attracted lot of attention from researchers. [2] describes different DDoS models. A statistical model based on a multi-resolution non-Gaussian modeling is proposed in [3]. Path Identification model is proposed in [4]. A state transition model is used in [5]. [6] models a network as Markov chain model. In the model presented in [7], active networks uses a management station for detection.

A scheme to detect attacks by monitoring the increase of new IP addresses and a sequential change point detection algorithm have been proposed in [8]. [9] proposes a signal-processing approach based on frequency domain characteristics. [10] treats attacks as a congestion-control problem. A method to automatically fingerprint and identify repeated attack scenarios has been proposed in [11].

A collaborative overlay architecture called DefCOM has been defined in [12]. The DWARD [13] is a mechanism that is deployed in the source end networks. An architecture where a server under stress installs a router throttle at selected upstream routers to filter the packets has been introduced in [14]. PacketScore[15] is an online DDoS defense mechanism that performs score based selective packet-discarding.

The proposed work is based on the PacketScore approach amended with traffic engineering to collaboratively counter DDoS attacks in active networks.

3 System Model

Modeling the attack environment is a key challenge while designing a DDoS defense mechanism. The method proposed is based on the assumption that routers cannot be compromised. When the connectivity of the network(G) is high then launching an attack is easier and if the network is minimally connected, the node may crash even before the attack is detected. Therefore, a network should be optimally connected for the DDoS defense mechanisms to be deployed efficiently. This mechanism is also collaborative in that the routers share traffic information periodically to detect and mitigate the attack at the earliest.

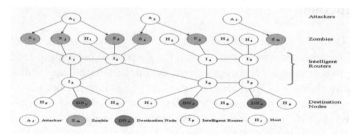

Fig. 1. System model

4 System Architecture

The defense framework defines a two level filtering at its core wherein it employs leaky buckets to bucket the flow and let out after making the first level filtering based on a threshold value computed using profiled packet attributes. The suspected flow is then passed to second level filter based on the payload of traffic to confirm attacks.

This work is based on the concepts of PacketScore[17] that makes use of conditional legitimate probability to compute a score for the packet and uses iceberg style profiles storing only the most frequently occurring attribute values along with their ratios. The computation time required for processing a packet is more which slows down the attack detection and providing an overload control mechanism for fast changing attacks is difficult in [17].

The candidate packet attributes considered for profiling are source network address, TTL value, TCP flags, port numbers and a leaky bucket is created for each of these attributes. Initially all leaky buckets have uniform preferences. However, over time, the preference value of each attribute varies dynamically based on the attack profile. This helps the system to adapt itself to fast-changing attack types.

In this work a current profile is also used to capture the characteristics of the traffic for each profiling period in addition to a nominal profile that contains the characteristics of legitimate packets accumulated over a period as well as the threshold score computed as a function of attribute values.

The current profile contains the packet score and the total number of legitimate packets received during that profiling period. At the end of the profiling period, a current profile score is computed and entered in the nominal profile for that profiling period. A dynamic threshold is computed from the values for successive current profile scores that are accumulated over time in the nominal profile.

The attack profile keeps track of the packet attributes as well as data signatures of attack packets. The attack packet attributes are used to dynamically compute the leaky bucket preference value for each attribute, while the data signatures of attack packets profiled in the attack profile are used during the second level of filtering.

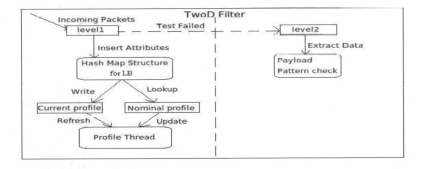

Fig. 2. System framework

5 Defense Mechanism

The defense mechanism is refined for effectiveness in detection overhead performance by attaching a weight to each attribute that is dynamically varied to detect fast changing attacks at the earliest. When a packet arrives, each attribute in the header is extracted and inserted into corresponding leaky bucket to check for overflow. A score for the packet is computed as a sum of the leaky bucket preferences for each bucket overflow. A packet is allowed to pass through, if the score is less then the threshold obtained from nominal profile. If the score exceeds the threshold then the packet payload is perused to determine the similarity with the data signatures of various attack packets already profiled in the attack profile.

At the end of a profiling period, a coordination capsule is created that contains information from both attack profile and current profile which is sent to the other routers in the network for collaborative attack defense so that each router in the optimal set updates its profile. It is assumed that the profiling period at each router is identical.

Initially, the nominal profile is empty and has to be trained before the packets can be filtered. A training period τ_t is chosen as $\tau_t = k*\tau_p$ where τ_p is the profiling period and k is any integer. During the training period, it is assumed that only legitimate packets arrive at the node. Based on the overflows during the training period, a current profile score is calculated after each τ_p that is part of τ_t. these scores are accumulated to compute the nominal profile $Th_{(n)}$.

After time τ_t, the nominal profile is used for packet filtering. The threshold $Th_{(n)}$ is updated dynamically every τ_p interval of time based on the current profile score value computed for that τ_p. The optimal set of routers is determined in the network G using an approximate vertex cover of G as vertex cover problem is an NP problem.

6 Simulation and Result Analysis

An active network is a network in which the nodes are programmed to perform custom operations on the messages that pass through the node. ANTS [16]is a Java based toolkit for constructing an active network and its applications. The proposed filtering scheme is deployed and tested in ANTS. The miniature network topology with 9 nodes is constructed using ANTS. Threads are used to simulate an attacker node which compromises the hosts and launches DDoS attacks.

The traffic flow, threshold and leaky bucket characteristics over a period of time are depicted for a single source and two sources as in Figure 3. Many simulation runs were performed using generic, nominal and SYN-flood attacks. The average false positive percentage is 2.65 for nominal traffic and 0 for others while the average false negative percentage is 2.51, 2.08, 3.65 for generic, nominal and SYN flood attacks.

Initially the Traffic filter was trained using legitimate packets for a training period. The testing data set used legitimate traffic for some time followed by bursty attack traffic. It can be seen from figure that all packets sent initially are legitimate and are allowed to pass. When the attack traffic begins, only some attack packets escape while the filter re-trains itself to the new traffic and all attack packets are dropped. It can also be seen that even during the attack period legitimate packets are not affected and are forwarded by the intelligent routers keeping false positives and false negatives to a minimum. The flooding attacks predictably give minimal false positive results as not many attack packets arrive before a bucket gets filled up. An attempt to reduce the profiling period may result in the rise of false positive results. It is found that the second level of filtering is responsible for minimizing this effect.

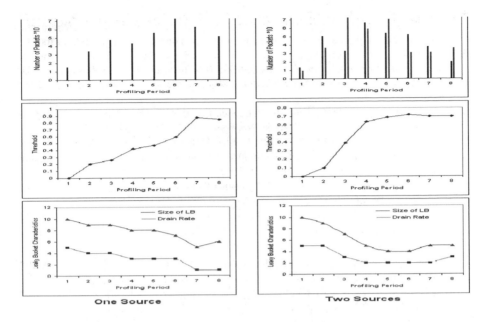

Fig. 3. Traffic Characteristics

7 Analysis and Conclusion

The paper proposes a novel traffic filtering framework using Leaky Buckets to counter DDoS attacks efficiently as well as effectively. A set of leaky buckets each with a preference value corresponding to the packet attribute's contribution for detection is used. For each packet causing bucket overflow, a score is computed and checked against a dynamic threshold obtained from the nominal profile. For packets exceeding the threshold next level of filtering based on payload comparison with the attack profile is done. As the weight associated with each packet attribute is dynamic, the scheme is able to adapt itself to varying traffic patterns. The scheme is deployed in ANTS. The two level packet filtering ensures that attack packets are detected with minimal false positives and false negatives and fast changing attack detection is made at ease, though comparative performance analysis with some existing schemes may appreciate the results well.

References

1. Chen, L.-C., Longstaff, T.A., Carley, K.M.: Characterization of Defense Mechanisms against Distributed Denial of Service Attacks. Computer and Security (2004)
2. Bouzida, Y., Cuppens, F., Gombault, S.: Detecting and Reacting against Distributed Denial of Service Attacks. In: IEEE ICC proceedings (2006)
3. Borgnat, P., Abry, P., Dewaele, G., Larrieu, N., Owezarski, P., Zhang, Y., Labit, Y., Aussibal, J., Gallon, L., Scherrer, A., Bernaille, L., Boudaoud, K.: Denial of service attack detection based on a non Gaussian and multiresolution traffic modeling. Research report Project METROSEC (2006)

4. Yaar, A., Perrig, A., Song Pi, D.S.: A Path Identification Mechanism to Defend against DDoS Attacks. In: Proceedings of the IEEE Symposium on Security and Privacy (2003)
5. Madan, B.B., Goseva-Popstojanova, K., Kalyanaraman, V., Trivedi, K.S.: A Method for Modeling and Quantifying the Security Attributes of Intrusion Tolerant Systems. In: Dependable systems and networks-performance and dependability symposium, pp. 167–186 (2002)
6. Wang, Y., Lin, C., Li, Q.-L., Fang, Y.: A queueing analysis for the denial of service (DoS) attacks in computer networks. Computer Networks 51(12), 3564–3573 (2007)
7. Nagesh, H.R., Chandra Sekaran, K., Kordcal, A.R.: Proactive model for Mitigating Internet Denial-of-Service Attacks. In: International Conference on Information Technology (2007)
8. Peng, T., Leckie, C., Ramamohanarao, K.: Detecting Distributed Denial of Service Attacks Using Source IP Address Monitoring. White paper (2002)
9. Chen, Y., Kwok, Y.-K., Hwan, K.: Filtering Shrew DDoS Attacks Using A New Frequency-Domain Approach. In: Proceedings of The First IEEE LCN Workshop on Network Security (2005)
10. Ioannidis, J., Bellovin, S.M.: Implementing Pushback: Router-Based Defense Against DDoS Attacks. In: Network and Distributed System Security Symposium (2002)
11. Hussain, A., Heidemann, J., Papadopoulos, C.: Identification of Repeated Denial of Service Attacks. In: Proceedings of the IEEE Infocom (2006)
12. Oikonomou, G., Reiher, P., Robinson, M.: A Framework for A Collaborative DDoS Defense. In: Proceedings of the 22nd Annual Computer Security Applications Conference, pp. 33–42 (2006)
13. Mirkovic, J., Reiher, P.: D-WARD: A Source-End Defense Against Flooding Denial-of-Service Attacks. IEEE transactions on Dependable and Secure Computing 2(3), 216–232 (2005)
14. Lam, H.-Y., Li, C.-P., Chanson, S.T., Yeung, D.-Y.: A Coordinated Detection and Response Scheme for Distributed Denial-of-Service Attacks. In: Proceedings of IEEE International Conference on Communications (2006)
15. Kim, Y., Lau, W.C., Chuah, M.C., Chao, H.J.: PacketScore: A Statistics-Based Packet Filtering Scheme against Distributed Denial-of-Service Attacks. In: Transactions on dependable and secure computing (2006)
16. Wetherall, D.J., Guttag, J.V., Tennenhouse, D.L.: ANTS: A Toolkit for Building and Dynamically Deploying Network Protocols. IEEE Open Architectures and Network Programming (3-4), 117–129 (1998)

Security against Sybil Attack in Wireless Sensor Network through Location Verification

Indranil Saha[1] and Debapriyay Mukhopadhyay[2]

[1] Computer Science Department
University of California, Los Angeles, CA 90095, USA
indranil@cs.ucla.edu
[2] Rebaca Technologies Pvt. Ltd.
Block EP & GP, Sector V, Salt Lake City, Kolkata 700091, India
debapriyaym@gmail.com

Abstract. A new functional for planar triangulation called Inner Core has been proposed in [4] for a location verification based defense against Sybil attack for sensor network, and also has been shown that the legitimacy of a new node inside the Inner Core of a triangle obtained by the triangulation of the set of sensor nodes can be established. In [4] it has been conjectured that Inner Core of a triangulation of a set of planar points achieves its maximum for Delaunay triangulation. In this paper, we present a formal proof of the conjecture. In order for the protocol proposed in [4] to work, what is required is an empty triangle formed out of three existing sensor nodes in whose Inner Core new node claims its presence. We present here an algorithm to find out such an empty triangle, so that it can be used for checking the legitimacy of the new node.

1 Introduction

Sensor networks are now being widely deployed in planned or ad hoc basis to monitor and protect different targeted infrastructures including life-critical applications such as wildlife monitoring, military target tracking, home security monitoring and scientific exploration in hazardous environments. The criticality of a large subset of applications triggers the need for providing adequate security support for them. Unlike in general data networks, the nodes of sensor networks may be physically captured by an adversary and thus can induce different modes of harmful attacks in addition to active and passive eavesdropping.

Douceur first introduced the notion of Sybil attack [2] in sensor networks, where a single entity illegitimately presents multiple identities. Physically captured nodes claiming superfluous misbehaving identities could control a substantial fraction of the system leading to malfunction of basic operational protocols including routing, resource allocation and misbehavior detection. Newsome et al. in [3] have pointed out that location verification can be a valid defense mechanism against Sybil attack. Following that line, a new functional for planar triangulation called Inner Core has been proposed in [4]. Also it has been shown that the legitimacy of a new node inside the Inner Core of a triangle can obtained by

V. Garg, R. Wattenhofer, and K. Kothapalli (Eds.): ICDCN 2009, LNCS 5408, pp. 187–192, 2009.

triangulation of the set of sensor nodes. But no algorithm has been provided to find out such a triangulation, where there is a triangle inside whose inner core the new node is present. It has also been conjectured in [4] that the functional Inner Core of a triangulation of a set of planar points achieves its maximum if and only if the triangulation is Delaunay triangulation [1].

   This paper presents an extension of the work presented in [4]. We present here a formal proof of the conjecture. We also have carried out simulation on several set of randomly scattered points and have found that Inner Cores of all the triangles obtained by Delaunay triangulation covers on an average 30-50% area of the convex hull of the planar points. Again, a new node's legitimacy cannot be checked if it is not inside the Inner Core of a triangle. So this reduces the applicability of the protocol proposed in [4] for defending Sybil attack. The protocol in [4] can work seamlessly if an empty triangle can be found out in whose inner core the query point lies. A triangle formed by three sensor nodes is called empty if it does not contain any other sensor nodes except the new one. Through simulation we have found that Inner Core of all the empty triangles covers on an average 75-95% area of the convex hull of the planar points and thereby increasing the applicability of the protocol.

2   Inner Core and Its Maximality for Delaunay Triangulation

The definition of Inner Core of a triangle as given in [4] is as follows.

Definition 1. *Inner Core of a triangle (Figure 1) T with A, B and C as vertices is defined as,*

$$IC(T) = Disk(V_A, l_A) \cap Disk(V_B, l_B) \cap Disk(V_C, l_C) \cap T,$$

where l_A = min {Length of the sides of the triangle T incident on V_A}, and $Disk(V_A, l_A)$ is the circular region with V_A as its center and l_A as its radius.

Definition 2. *Inner Core of triangulation Δ of a set $S \subset R^2$ of planar points is defined as the union of the Inner Cores of its constituent triangles, i.e.,*

$$IC(\Delta) = \bigcup_{T \in \Delta} IC(T).$$

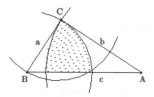

Fig. 1. Inner Core of Triangle T

For a set S of planar points, the set $\mathcal{F}$ of all triangulations becomes exponential in size with the number of planar points. So, a natural and obvious question is to find out the triangulation for which Inner Core gets maximized, i.e., to find out $\Delta \in \mathcal{F}$ for which the area of $ConvH(S) - IC(\Delta)$ is minimized, where $ConvH(S)$ denotes the convex hull of the set of planar points S.

Delaunay triangulation D of a set of points $S \subset R^2$ forming a regular triangular lattice coincides with the lattice itself and hence $ConvH(S) - IC(D) = \phi$ and thus maximizes Inner Core. From this observation it was conjectured in [4] that Inner Core is maximized for Delaunay triangulation among all the triangulations. Here we present a formal proof for the conjecture.

Let us first compute the area of the IC of the triangle $T = (\triangle ABC)$. Without loss of generality we assume that $\angle A \leq \angle B \leq \angle C$.

$IC(T) = \frac{1}{2}$ [The common area of intersection between two circles (one with radius $= a$ and another with radius $= b$), where the centers of the circles are distance c $(\geq a, b)$ apart]

$$= \int_{\frac{a^2-b^2+c^2}{2c}}^{a} \sqrt{a^2 - b^2} \; dx$$

$$- \frac{\pi a^2}{4} - \{(\frac{a^2-b^2+c^2}{4c})(\frac{\sqrt{(a+c+b)(a+c-b)(b+c-a)(b-c+a)}}{2c}) + \frac{a^2}{2} sin^{-1}(cos B)\}$$

$$\frac{IC(T)}{Area(T)} = \frac{\frac{\pi a^2}{4} - \{(\frac{a^2-b^2+c^2}{4c})(\frac{4\triangle}{2c}) + \frac{a^2}{2} sin^{-1}(cos B)\}}{\triangle}$$

$$\textbf{where,} \; Area(T) = \frac{1}{4}\sqrt{(a+b+c)(b+c-a)(a+c-b)(a+b-c)}$$

$$\frac{IC(T)}{Area(T)} = \frac{sin A}{sin(A+B)}[\frac{B}{sin B} - cos B]$$

It can be easily proved that for any B in $[0, \frac{\pi}{2}]$, $\frac{IC(T)}{Area(T)}$ increases monotonically with the increasing values of A (where $A \in [0, \frac{\pi}{3}]$). So we have now proved the following lemma:

Lemma 1. $\frac{IC(T)}{Area(T)}$ of a triangle increases monotonically with the increase in the minimum angle of a triangle.

In the process of obtaining the Delaunay triangulation we start with any triangulation and then successively replaces the illegal diagonals with the legal diagonals. In a quadrilateral, if we replace an illegal diagonal with a legal diagonal then that increases the minimum angle of the corresponding triangles, and hence following the lemma $\frac{IC(T)}{Area(T)}$ increases for the triangles. Hence we obtain the following result:

Theorem 1. *The functional $IC(\Delta)$ of a set of planar points S achieves its maximum if and only if Δ is the Delaunay triangulation of S.*

3   Modification of Location Verification Based Security Protocol [4]

In [4], it has been suggested to work with Delaunay triangulation if the triangulation in whose Inner Core the new node is located cannot be found out. In the Delaunay triangulation, the triangle inside which the new node is placed is found out, and it is checked whether the new node is present inside the Inner Core of the triangle. If it is inside the Inner Core of the triangle then the agent can check the legitimacy of the new node, otherwise legitimacy of the new node cannot be checked. We simulated random sensor network in a 400×400 plane to find out what percentage of area of the convex hull formed by the sensor nodes is covered by the Inner Cores of all the triangles obtained by Delaunay triangulation of the node points. The simulation result has been presented in Figure 2. It is evident from Figure 2 that Inner Core of Delaunay triangulation covers 30-50% of the area of the convex hull. It implies that in more than 50% cases the agent has to communicate with the setup server to check the legitimacy of the new node, which is not desired.

To make the protocol applicable for any randomly deployed sensor network, we modify the protocol proposed in [4] as follows. Previously, agent is required to start the protocol by finding a triangulation of the set of planar points S such that the new node is inside the Inner Core of a triangle. In absence of the knowledge of such a triangle, the agent works with Delaunay triangulation as it maximizes the area of the convex hull covered by inner core of the triangles.

The modified version of the protocol arises from the observation that we require an empty triangle for the central portion of the protocol to be workable. But, we start by finding Delaunay triangulation of the set of nodes, for it ensures maximum coverage of the convex hull of the set of nodes by Inner Core and also each triangle in it is empty. This is obviously a step towards limiting our search for an empty triangle in whose Inner Core the query point is located. The problem thus can be solved if the agent can find out an empty triangle formed

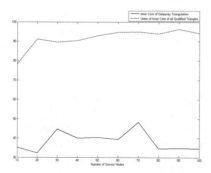

Fig. 2. Percentage area of Convex Hull covered by Inner Core of the Delaunay triangulation of the Convex Hull and union of Inner Core of all possible qualified triangles formed by any three sensor nodes for different number of nodes

out of the existing nodes, inside whose Inner Core the new node is placed.We call such a triangle a *qualified triangle*. Now instead of finding a triangulation, we directly seek for a qualified triangle. We simulated random sensor network in a 400×400 plane to find out what percentage of area of the convex hull formed by the sensor nodes is covered by the Inner Cores of all the possible triangles formed by any three sensor node points. Simulation result shows that Inner Core of all the qualified triangles covers on an average 75-95% area of the convex hull of the planar points and thereby increasing the applicability of the protocol(Figure 2).

4 Algorithm to Find Out a Qualified Triangle

We present here an algorithm to find out a qualified triangle and it is the task of the agent to run this algorithm. The algorithm takes a set of points S and another point p (the point corresponding to the new node), which is inside the convex hull of the set of points S. The algorithm returns a qualified triangle, if such triangle exists, otherwise it reports that no such triangle exists.

There may be at most nC^3 triangles formed by n nodes. The objective of this algorithm is to get rid of searching these $O(n^3)$ number of triangles. The agent starts the algorithm by triangulating the set of points representing N sensor nodes based on Delaunay's triangulation. Finding out Delaunay triangulation of a planar set of n points can be done in $O(nlogn)$ time [1]. Then the agent finds out the triangle inside which the new node is placed in $O(n)$ time [1]. This step of the algorithm essentially helps find out a triangle inside which the new node is placed in $O(nlogn)$ time. The objective of starting with Delaunay triangulation is to maximize the area of the Inner Core of the triangle with which the search process starts.

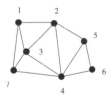

Fig. 3. An example of a network

After finding the triangle inside which the new node is placed, the agent checks if the triangle is a qualified one. If it is so the algorithm terminates reporting the triangle to the agent. Otherwise the search process to find out a qualified triangle continues in breadth first manner. Let us illustrate the algorithm through an example. The example has been shown in Figure 3. Suppose the new node is inside triangle (1, 2, 3). The agent finds out whether the new node lies in the Inner Core of this triangle. If the node does not lie in the Inner Core then consider the triangles formed with sides (1,2) (2,3) (3,1). For side (1, 2) the following triangles are obtained: (1,2,7), (1,2,6), (1,2,4) and (1, 2, 5). The agent verifies the appropriate triangles in the same procedure as done for triangle (1, 2, 3). The process is continued until all the triangles are covered before concluding that there is no qualified triangle. The algorithm stops at any time if agent finds a qualified triangle.

For every triangle the agent checks if the new node is inside the triangle and the triangle has not been already considered. To prevent repeated search two Boolean arrays are maintained. One of them keeps track of the triangles searched, and the other keeps track of the sides explored. Both of them are initialized to false for every element. When a triangle or a side is explored the corresponding entry in the array is set to true. The algorithm terminates when all the entries of the triangle array become true, or a qualified triangle is found.

5   Conclusion

In a sensor network, Inner Core based security against Sybil attack is possible if the new node is inside the Inner Core of an empty triangle formed by the existing sensor nodes. Given a set of points on a plane how to find out such a triangle efficiently was an open question. Though Delaunay triangulation maximizes the sum of the areas of the Inner Cores of the triangles, it cannot cover more than half of the area of the convex hull of the set of randomly generated planar points. Here we suggest to work with an empty triangle in whose Inner Core the query point lies, and that indeed enhances the applicability of the protocol.

References

1. Berg, M., Kreveld, M., Overmars, M., Schwarzkopf, O.: Computational Geometry-Algorithms and Applications. Springer, Heidelberg (1999)
2. Douceur, J.R.: The Sybil attack. In: Druschel, P., Kaashoek, M.F., Rowstron, A. (eds.) IPTPS 2002. LNCS, vol. 2429, p. 251. Springer, Heidelberg (2002)
3. Newsome, J., Shi, E., Song, D., Perrig, A.: The Sybil Attack in Sensor Networks: Analysis and Defenses. In: Proceedings of Third International Symposium on Information Processing in Sensor Networks (April 2004)
4. Mukhopadhyay, D., Saha, I.: Location Verification Based Defense against Sybil Attack In Sensor Networks. In: Chaudhuri, S., Das, S.R., Paul, H.S., Tirthapura, S. (eds.) ICDCN 2006. LNCS, vol. 4308, pp. 509–521. Springer, Heidelberg (2006)

Incentives to Tight the Runtime Estimates
of EASY Backfilling

Li Bo, Jun Chen, Man Yang, and Erfei Wang

School of Information Science and Engineering, Yunnan University,
Kunming, 650091, China
libo@ynu.edu.cn

Abstract. In standard backfill algorithms, a job will be terminated immediately it has been processed for its estimated runtime. This drives users not to provide tight estimates to make their jobs to be scheduled earlier but at the risk of being killed. This paper evaluated an enhanced mechanism to tolerate jobs to continue processing if they will not delay any other running or reserved jobs. By comparing the performance of this new mechanism with that of the standard easy backfill by simulation of real workloads, it is shown that both user- and system- centric performance metrics were improved. As more users underestimate the runtime of their jobs and make the estimates tighter, user-centric metrics always be improved, but the system-centric metric in some cases may degrade very slightly.

1 Introduction

Backfilling algorithms are widely used in parallel job scheduling to increase system utilization and user satisfaction over conventional non-backfilling scheduling algorithms. Different from traditional first-come-first-serve(FCFS) scheduling, backfilling requires the estimated running time of jobs to be known before making scheduling decisions. The estimation of a job is used by the scheduler to find out whether and when there are enough resources to execute the job without interfering running or reserved jobs. To prevent from possibly delaying other jobs, a job will be terminated or killed immediately by the scheduler once it can not finish itself within its estimated running time.

Because the scheduling behavior is heavily dependent on the estimation of jobs, many studies have been carried out to discover the characteristics of the estimations of jobs and their influences on the performances of the scheduler. A rational assumption is that users would be motivated to provide accurate estimates to have a better chance to make their jobs be backfilled. However, empirical studies of traces from sites using backfilling show that user estimates are generally inaccurate. A user tend to overestimate the running time of jobs to make sure that they would not be killed, rather than to provide a tight estimate to make the job to be scheduled earlier but at the risk of being killed. Ref. [Cirne and Berman '01] reported that in four different traces, 50% to 60% of jobs use less than 20% of their estimated time, and Ref. [Ward, Mahood and West '02] reported that jobs on a Cray T3E used on average only 29% of their estimates. Similar patterns are seen in many other workload analyses[Mu'alem and Feitelson '01].

V. Garg, R. Wattenhofer, and K. Kothapalli (Eds.): ICDCN 2009, LNCS 5408, pp. 193–199, 2009.
© Springer-Verlag Berlin Heidelberg 2009

In all those studies, all underestimated jobs will be killed, no matter they will delay other jobs or not. Ref. [Wong and Goscinski '08] suggested an enhanced EASY-backfilling algorithm in which a underestimated job would not be killed unless it would delay other job, and developed a batch scheduler for Linux cluster to evaluate the performances. Experimental results using static workloads of selected NAS parallel applications show that most of the jobs do not have to be aborted even though their job lengths are under estimated where the slowdown of jobs and the throughput of the system are only slightly degraded. However, the numbers of the jobs and the processing elements used in [Wong and Goscinski '08] are very small, and the actual runtime estimates of the jobs from users were replaced by the actual execution time. In this paper, we reevaluated the performance impact of extending underestimated jobs based on discrete event-based simulation and the newest cleaned version of the trace files of the Parallel Workload Archive[Feitelson]. Different from the results in [Wong and Goscinski '08] that the slowdown of jobs and the throughput of the system are only slightly degraded, our simulating results show that almost all performance metrics-including slowdown and throughput-were improved. As more users underestimate the runtime of their jobs and make the estimates tighter, user-centric metrics always be improved, but the system-centric metric in some cases may degrade very slightly.

This paper is organized as follows. Section 2 presents the implement of the enhance backfilling algorithm. Section 3 describes the profiles of the workload traces, the performance metrics and the simulator. Section 4 shows the experimental results. Finally section 5 presents the conclusion.

2   Underestimate Tolerance Mechanisms

In most of productive scheduler using backfilling algorithms or in research, a job will be killed immediately when it runs out of its runtime estimate. In this paper, a job will not be killed at the end of the estimated runtime unless it delays other jobs. This new mechanism can be implemented as follows:

(1) Within the estimated runtime of a job, check if it is finished completely. If yes, remove it from the running job queue. If not, go to (2).
(2) Check whether the job has been processing for the estimated runtime. If not, keep on processing; if yes, go to (3).
(3) Calculate the time period possible to extend the runtime of the job. If the time period exists, go on processing the job within the extended time period, go to (4). If not, kill the job and remove it from the running job queue.
(4) Check whether the job is finished within the extended time period. If yes, remove it from the running job queue. If not, go on processing until it is finished or reaches the end of the extended time period, remove it from the running job queue.

3   Experiment Descriptions

The experiments are based on an event-driven simulator of backfill scheduling. we have developed a simulator with enhanced backfill scheduling algorithms[Bo, Dongfeng and

Bin '06]. This simulator is based on SimJava[Howell and McNab '98]-a discrete event simulating package for Java and implemented all the aspects of backfilling algorithms. Workloads from real productive parallel systems were used to driven the simulator. After each simulation, a script written in Python was called to calculate the performance metrics.

All workloads in this work were derived from the newest cleaned version of the trace files of the Parallel Workload Archive. Each workload is represented by a single data file specifying the id, the arrival time, the number of processing elements, the estimated runtime and the recorded runtime of each job. Following three traces were used to drive the simulator, which are widely used for parallel scheduling simulations.

(1) KTH: the Swedish Royal Institute of Technology 100-node IBM SP2 from October 1996 to August 1997,
(2) CTC: the Cornell Theory Center 430-node IBM SP2 from July 1996 to May 1997,
(3) SDSC: the San Diego Supercomputer Center 128-node IBM SP2 from April 1998 to April 2000.

Both user- and system-centric metrics are used to evaluate the performances. The user-centric metrics are the number of successful jobs, average waiting time, average bounded slowdown; the system-centric metrics are utilization and the weighted throughput of success job. Let T_w and T_r denote a job's waiting time and runtime respectively. T_w is the period between the job's submittal and start time, and T_r is the period between the job's start and end time. These metrics are defined as follows:

(1) The number of successful job: the number of jobs not been killed. A job will be killed if its user estimate is shorter than the actual runtime needed. If an underestimated job is allowed to run longer than its user estimate, but during the extension, it delays other reserved jobs, it will be killed also. This metric reveals how many jobs, no matter underestimated or not, can be completely finished in the system.
(2) Average waiting time: the average amount of time that a submitted job has to wait for execution.
(3) Average slowdown: slowdown is the response time normalized by the running time, i.e. $(T_w + T_r)/T_r$. This measures how much slower the job ran due to scheduling conflicts with other competing jobs and it seems more reasonable than the average waiting time to capture users' expectations that a job's waiting time will be proportional to its runtime. In order to eliminate the influence of very short jobs on slowdown, a version known as " bounded slowdown"[Tsafrir, Etsion and Feitelson '07] were used in this study, in which a threshold of 10 seconds was set to T_r, and slowdown is redefined as $\max(1,(T_w + T_r)/\max(10, T_r))$.
(4) Weighted throughput of success job: the average of the products of the number of processing elements of successful jobs and its runtime per minute. Complementary to utilization, this metric is helpful to reveal how many resources are applied to successful jobs, rather than wasted by killed jobs.
(5) Utilization: the average percentage of the periods of all the processing elements being in busy.

4   Experimental Results

Easy backfill is practically used as the default configuration for most backfill schedulers. We will investigate the impact of killing and not killing underestimated jobs on easy backfill by measuring the performance metrics. Three workloads were scheduled by the simulator with EASY backfill and their metrics were calculated and collected in Table 2. The percentage for each metric is defined as $100*(V_1-V_0)/V_0$, where V_1 and V_0 represent the value of the metric in the enhanced backfill and that in the ordinary one respectively. A positive percentage means relative improvement and a negative one means relative degradation. Round-off errors of all numerical values were considered in this work.

The results of the enhanced backfill algorithms as shown in Table 1 can serve as a driving force to encourage users to provide a tight estimate of their jobs' runtime. In Table 1, the number of successful job, weighted throughout and utilization improved after extending underestimated jobs, whereas the average waiting time and the average bounded slowdown degraded. In the enhanced easy backfill scheduling, underestimated jobs are tolerated to extend their runtimes. However, the tolerance to minority underestimated jobs leads to longer waiting time of those majority normal jobs with correct or over estimates. Assume the users of those normal jobs are reluctant to suffer such losses. They want to share the benefits of underestimation by tightening their estimates: better chance to be scheduled to run earlier and low degree of risk of being killed during extended runtime. In the following, we will study the impact of more users with tighter estimates on easy backfill schedulers.

Table 1. Results for EASY backfill

workload	extend	success job		waiting time		slowdown		throughout		utilization	
KTH	No	28009		7400		83.9		4043		0.687	
	Yes	28447	1.56%	7415	-0.20%	83.7	0.24%	4096	1.31%	0.688	0.11%
CTC	No	70042		3959		11.6		12592		0.657	
	Yes	76683	9.48%	3858	2.55%	10.8	6.57%	14891	18.26%	0.660	0.40%
SDSC	No	49878		63766		175.4		4946		0.805	
	Yes	53628	7.52%	63261	0.79%	172.3	1.8%	5615	13.53%	0.806	0.13%

In aforesaid experiments, three traces were used to drive the simulator, without changing the number of users with underestimated jobs and the estimates of jobs. In order to examine the impact of more users with tighter estimates on easy backfill schedulers, new workload have to be generated synthetically. In our work this is a two step process and the three traces were used as a basis. In the first step, job records in the trace files were randomly chosen to shorten their estimated runtime. An input variable, *rate*, was used to define how many jobs should be chosen in total. The probability of a job being chosen is computed as random[0, *rate*]. In this way, as *rate* increases, more jobs are changed to be underestimated, i.e., more users will under estimate the runtime of their jobs.

In the second step, another input variable, factor, was used to calculate the tighter estimate for the job chosen in the previous step: new estimate=random[factor,1]* recorded estimate, where recorded estimate is the user estimate for the job recorded in the trace file. As *factor* decreases, the estimates for the selected jobs will be shorter.

With these two steps, all necessary properties of a new workload are copied and generated. For each {rate, factor} set, simulations were repeated for 10 times to calculate the statistics. Table 3,4, and 5 show the statistical results for KTH, CTC and SDSC with different {rate, factor} settings, where rate ranges from 0.1 to 0.3 and factor ranges from 0.9 to 0.7. As in Table 2, the percentage of each metric describes the relative improvement or degradation by comparing the values in the simulation with given {rate, factor} setting with that in the ordinary backfill.

Table 2. Results of KTH with different {rate, factor} settings

rate	factor	success job		waiting time		slowdown		w.throughout		utilization	
0.1	0.9	28374	1.3%	7286	1.5%	81.61	2.7%	4010	**-0.8%**	0.687	0.0%
	0.8	28351	1.2%	7276	1.7%	81.90	2.4%	3981	**-1.5%**	0.686	**-0.1%**
	0.7	28316	1.1%	7101	4.0%	80.37	4.2%	3960	**-2.1%**	0.685	**-0.3%**
0.2	0.9	28305	1.1%	7253	2.0%	80.18	4.4%	3918	**-3.1%**	0.687	**-0.1%**
	0.8	28250	0.9%	7113	3.9%	80.58	4.0%	3870	**-4.3%**	0.685	**-0.3%**
	0.7	28186	0.6%	6882	7.0%	78.07	7.0%	3846	**-4.9%**	0.682	**-0.7%**
0.3	0.9	28240	0.8%	7260	1.9%	82.18	2.1%	3861	**-4.5%**	0.686	**-0.1%**
	0.8	28143	0.5%	7043	4.8%	79.91	4.8%	3775	**-6.6%**	0.684	**-0.5%**
	0.7	28055	0.2%	6743	8.9%	78.23	6.8%	3697	**-8.6%**	0.679	**1.2%**

Table 3. Results of CTC with different {rate, factor} settings

rate	factor	success job		waiting time		slowdown		w.throughout		utilization	
0.1	0.9	76631	9.4%	3786	4.4%	11.21	2.9%	14802	17.6%	0.659	0.3%
	0.8	76574	9.3%	3760	5.0%	11.31	2.1%	14691	16.7%	0.658	0.2%
	0.7	76527	9.3%	3745	5.4%	11.05	4.3%	14657	16.4%	0.658	0.1%
0.2	0.9	76599	9.4%	3749	5.3%	11.02	4.6%	14724	16.9%	0.659	0.3%
	0.8	76474	9.2%	3617	8.6%	10.55	8.7%	14510	15.2%	0.657	0.0%
	0.7	76334	9.0%	3567	9.9%	10.72	7.2%	14409	14.4%	0.655	**-0.3%**
0.3	0.9	76541	9.3%	3615	8.7%	10.86	5.9%	14581	15.8%	0.658	0.1%
	0.8	76363	9.0%	3566	9.9%	10.87	5.9%	14388	14.3%	0.656	**-0.1%**
	0.7	76159	8.7%	3463	12.5%	10.98	5.0%	14147	12.3%	0.653	**-0.6%**

As shown in Table 2, 3 and 4, for simulations with given {rate, factor} setting of each workload, as rate increases or factor decreases, the level of underestimation increases, resulting in the improvement of user-centric metrics. As more users underestimate the runtime of their jobs, as what they wish, they do benefit from it with significant improvement in both of the average waiting time and the bounded

Table 4. Results of SDSC with different {rate, factor} settings

rate	factor	success job		waiting time		slowdown		w.throughout		utilization	
	0.9	53599	6.9%	61750	3.2%	167.59	4.5%	5615	13.5%	0.809	0.4%
0.1	0.8	53555	6.9%	59898	6.1%	165.58	5.6%	5577	12.8%	0.808	0.4%
	0.7	53518	6.8%	56668	11.1%	155.78	11.2%	5557	12.4%	0.808	0.4%
	0.9	53569	6.9%	59761	6.3%	163.29	6.9%	5597	13.2%	0.808	0.4%
0.2	0.8	53486	6.7%	53862	15.5%	148.97	15.1%	5535	11.9%	0.809	0.5%
	0.7	53393	6.6%	49573	22.3%	138.70	20.9%	5479	10.8%	0.809	0.5%
	0.9	53542	6.8%	57056	10.5%	157.30	10.3%	5584	12.9%	0.810	0.6%
0.3	0.8	53418	6.6%	51731	18.9%	144.80	17.5%	5481	10.8%	0.810	0.6%
	0.7	53288	6.4%	44238	30.6%	127.10	27.6%	5389	9.0%	0.808	0.4%

slowdown. However, system-centric metrics are not always improved in the same way, sometimes they degrade as the level of underestimation increases.

When we synthesize the results shown in Table 1 to Table 4, we can form a unified conclusion on the performance of the enhanced backfill algorithm. Compared with the standard easy backfill algorithm, simple extending of the runtime of underestimated jobs results in the improvement of the user-centric and system-centric performance metrics. The tolerance for underestimated jobs and potential benefits will drive the users to tight the runtime estimates for their jobs. As more users underestimate the runtime of their jobs and make the estimates tighter, user-centric metrics always be improved, but the system-centric metric in some cases may degrade very slightly.

5 Conclusions

Backfilling is widely used in parallel job scheduling to increase system utilization and user satisfaction over conventional non-backfilling scheduling algorithms. In standard backfill algorithms currently used by productive schedulers or in research, it is assumed that a job will be killed immediately it has been processed for the length of the estimated runtime. Consequently, users tend to over estimate the runtime of their jobs deliberately in order to avoid their jobs being aborted. This work investigated an enhanced backfilling algorithm in which an underestimated job would not be killed unless it delays other job, evaluated the performance impact of extending underestimated jobs from the viewpoints of both of the users and the system. Compared with the standard easy backfill, the benefits of extending the runtime of underestimated jobs are attractive and the degradations are very slight.

Acknowledgements

This work is partially supported by the Natural Science Foundation of China (No. 60663009), the Application Science and Technology Research Foundation of Yunnan Province (No. 2006F0011Q), the Research Foundation of the Education

Department of Yunnan Province (No. 6Y0013D) and the Research Foundation of Yunnan University (No. 2005Q106C).

References

1. Feitelson, D.: Parallel workloads archive,
   `http://www.cs.huji.ac.il/labs/parallel/workload`
2. Bo, L., Dongfeng, Z., Bin, S.: Simulating Platform for Grid Computing with Reservations. Journal of System Simulation 18(suppl.2), 373–376 (2006)
3. Cirne, W., Berman, F.: A comprehensive model of the supercomputer workload. In: Proc. 2001 IEEE International Workshop on Workload Characterization. IEEE, Los Alamitos (2001)
4. Howell, F., McNab, R.: SimJava: A Discrete Event Simulation Package For Java With Applications In Computer Systems Modelling. In: Proc. Proceedings of the First International Conference on Web-based Modelling and Simulation. The Society for Modeling and Simulation International, San Diego, CA (1998)
5. Mu'alem, A.W., Feitelson, D.G.: Utilization, predictability, workloads, and user runtime estimates in scheduling the IBM SP2 with backfilling. IEEE Transactions on Parallel and Distributed Systems 12(6), 529–543 (2001)
6. Tsafrir, D., Etsion, Y., Feitelson, D.G.: Backfilling using system-generated predictions rather than user runtime estimates. IEEE Transactions on Parallel and Distributed Systems 18(6), 789–803 (2007)
7. Ward, W.A., Mahood, C.L., West, J.E.: Scheduling jobs on parallel systems using a relaxed backfill strategy. In: Feitelson, D.G., Rudolph, L., Schwiegelshohn, U. (eds.) JSSPP 2002. LNCS, vol. 2537, pp. 88–102. Springer, Heidelberg (2002)
8. Wong, A.K.L., Goscinski, A.M.: The impact of under-estimated length of jobs on EASY-backfill scheduling. In: Proc. 2008 16th Euromicro Conference on Parallel, Distributed and Network-based Processing - PDP 2008, pp. 343–350. IEEE, Toulouse (2008)

An Index-Based Mobile Checkpointing and Recovery Algorithm

Awadhesh Kumar Singh, Rohit Bhat, and Anshul Kumar

Department of Computer Engineering, National Institute of Technology,
Kurukshetra, 136119, India
aksinreck@rediffmail.com, tihor2004@gmail.com,
anshul.nitk@gmail.com

Abstract. An index-based checkpointing and recovery protocol has been presented that uses time to indirectly coordinate the creation of consistent global
checkpoint for mobile computing systems. The protocol is computationally
more efficient because it takes fewer checkpoints than many other protocols and
does not need to compute dependency relationships. Also, the protocol is non-
blocking, adaptive, and uses very few control messages. Moreover, the number
of control messages is independent of the increase in the number of mobile
hosts and the size of control messages is also small.

Keywords: Mobile computing, Forced checkpoint, Time-coordinated.

1 Introduction

The index-based checkpointing protocol is a popular kind of CIC (Communication-
Induced Checkpointing) protocol, where a sequence number is assigned to each local
checkpoint. Any global checkpoint, consisting of local checkpoints with the same
sequence number, is guaranteed to be consistent. The index-based protocols are preferred because they piggyback smaller control information on the application
messages and force lesser checkpoints [1]. The present work aims at designing an
efficient index-based checkpointing protocol that uses time-coordination in order to
reduce the number of total checkpoints.

In the contemporary literature, most of the protocols handle only single message
reception in each checkpoint interval. However, our protocol successfully handles
multiple message reception in single checkpoint interval without taking more number
of forced checkpoints. It handles multiple process failure. The number of checkpoints
taken is application independent. The number of control messages, for the applications having low message sending rate would be very less and would be almost negligible for the fast message sending applications. In our protocol, the size of control
messages is also small as they contain only the most updated sequence number. Finally, the drift between processes is removed by a control message from mobile support station (MSS). Therefore, all the processes remain synchronized.

We assume that no message will be lost in the channel. A process saves its system
state as a checkpoint and assigns it a checkpoint sequence number. Any subsequent

V. Garg, R. Wattenhofer, and K. Kothapalli (Eds.): ICDCN 2009, LNCS 5408, pp. 200–205, 2009.

checkpoint is assigned higher checkpoint sequence number that increases monotoni-cally. Every mobile host (MH) and MSS contains a system clock. The system clocks of MSS's can be synchronized using internet synchronization services. Every application message m_j is piggybacked with two values viz. checkpoint sequence number N_j of the sender P_j and local timer of the MSS $Timer_M$, that is, time to next checkpoint. The MSS, closest to the receiver, is responsible for piggybacking its local timer $Timer_M$ in every application message m_j destined to the receiver.

2 The Checkpointing Algorithm

2.1 The Concept

We assume that each process takes an initial basic checkpoint and that, for the sake of simplicity, basic checkpoint is taken by a periodic algorithm [2]. Every process sends the snapshot of its initial state (termed as 0th checkpoint) to its local MSS when the application starts. A checkpoint period T, predefined by local MSS, is set on the tim-ers of all the MH's before starting the mobile computing application. For any process, whenever its local timer expires, it takes a local checkpoint with the updated sequence number and forwards the same to its MSS.

However, due to varying drift rates of local clocks, the timers at different sites are not perfectly synchronized. Hence, the checkpoints may not be consistent because of orphan message. In order to avoid this situation, every message sent between proc-esses is piggybacked with the sender's information that tells how many checkpoint intervals have passed at the sender process. Using this information, creation of orphan messages is avoided. At the expiry of MSS timer, the MSS identifies the MH's lag-ging behind and sends them a control message in order to resynchronize them with other MH's in the system.

Every message, originated from a process, reaches its destination via the MSS, where it is piggybacked 'time to next checkpoint' by the local MSS. When the mes-sage is received by the receiver node, it sets its local timer equal to the timer of local MSS. In this way, the timer synchronization is implemented.

After taking checkpoint, processes send their respective checkpoint information to their respective local MSS, where it is stored in a stable storage. A global checkpoint consists of all the Nth checkpoints of every process, where $N \geq 0$. If any process has not taken its Nth checkpoint (in case, it is idle and not performing any local computa-tion), its previous checkpoint would be included in the Nth global checkpoint. The construction of Nth global checkpoint is not complete unless every process sends either its Nth checkpoint or the information that N checkpoint intervals have passed.

2.2 The Working of the Algorithm

The algorithm uses the following local variables and messages:

```
N_i : Sequence number of latest checkpoint.
Timer_i : Timer of process P_i.
Timer_M : Timer of the MSS.
MAX: Maximum checkpoint sequence number received by MSS.
JoinList_M: List of mobile hosts that are currently connected to MSS_M.
```

Status$_i$: It indicates the current status of the MH's connected to any MSS at a particular time. If $status_i$ =ACTIVE then it implies that the corresponding MH is connected to MSS and is said to be active. However, if $status_i$ = DISCONNECT then it implies that the MH has disconnected from MSS voluntarily or due to some transient failure.
M$_i$: It is set to 1 if a MH receives a control message from MSS and it is set to zero after expiry of its local timer.
flag$_i$: It is set to 1 if a process takes a forced checkpoint after receiving a message from any other MH whose sequence number is greater than the current sequence number of the MH.
<IDLE, N$_i$> : It is sent by MH to MSS to inform that the MH was idle in the last time interval
m <m$_j$, N$_j$, TimerM>: Normal application messages.
M <N, TimerM>: Control message sent by MSS to those MH's which are lagging behind.
JoinM: Sent by a MH to the MSS when MH comes in the range of that MSS.
DM : Sent by MH to MSS to indicate disconnection.
LeaveM: Sent by MH to inform MSS that it is now joining some other MSS.

Process P_i takes a checkpoint when either its local timer $Timer_i$, has expired or when it receives a piggybacked message m_j from some other process P_j or when it receives control message M from its local MSS. If a process P_i receives a piggybacked message m_j but its local timer $Timer_i$ has yet not expired then it checks whether N_j of the sender P_j is greater than N_i of the receiver P_i. There are two possible cases:

Case 1. If it is true then P_i sets the flag variable ($flag_i$ =1) and takes a checkpoint, without recording the current reception event. Afterwards, P_i processes the received message m_j. As $flag_i$ is set to 1, P_i does not take checkpoint further, in the current checkpoint interval, after expiry of its local timer $Timer_i$.
Case 2. If it is false then process P_i directly processes the received message m_j without taking any checkpoint. However, process P_i takes a checkpoint, in the current checkpoint interval, after expiry of its local timer.

In order to synchronize the local timers of processes, whenever the MSS forwards an application message m_j to some process P_i in its local cell, MSS piggybacks its own 'time to next checkpoint', that is, $Timer_M$ in application message m_j and receiving process P_i synchronizes its timer accordingly.

In case, if a process P_i receives a control message M from MSS (in order to synchronize the mobile hosts) while its local timer $Timer_i$ has yet not expired then it checks whether $flag_i$ is set or not. The $flag_i$ value 1 indicates that checkpoint sequence number of MH$_i$ has already become equal to the most updated sequence number and it is in synchronization with other MH's. Hence, it need not take checkpoint. However, if $flag_i$ =0 then it takes a checkpoint, updates checkpoint sequence number to N and sets the variable M_i (i.e. M_i=1). Therefore, process P_i takes a checkpoint at the expiry of its local timer $Timer_i$ only if both $flag_i$ and M_i are not set i.e. $flag_i$ =0 and M_i=0.

2.3 The Pseudo Code

```
At each Process P_i (1<= i <= n)
if (Timer_i expires) then
{
    if (MH_i=idle)
    {
        N_i=N_i+1; do not take a checkpoint and send (IDLE, N_i) to MSS
    }
    if (flag_i == 1 or M_i= =1) then
    {
```

```
        flag_i=0 ; M_i=0 ; do not take a checkpoint
    }
    else
    {
        N_i= N_i+1; take checkpoint and send it and its sequence no. to MSS
    }
    resume normal computation
}
if (P_i receives a message m <m_j, N_j, Timer_M>) then
{
    Timer_i = Timer_M
    if (M_i = =0 and flag_i = =0) then
    {
        if (N_j > N_i ) then
        {
            flag_i=1
            N_i = N_j
            take checkpoint and send checkpoint and sequence number to MSS
        }
    }
    process message m_j
}
if (P_i receives a message M <N, Timer_M>) then
{
    Timer_i = Timer_M ; N_i = N
    if (flag_i ≠1) then
    {
        M_i = 1; take checkpoint and send it and its sequence no. to MSS
    }
    resume normal computation
}
if (MH_i Joins the cell of MSS_j) then send JoinM to MSS_j
if (MH_i wants to Disconnect) then send DM to MSS_p
if (MH_i leaves from MSS_p) then send LeaveM to MSS_p
At the MSS site:
if (MSS_p receives checkpoint C and sequence number N_i) then
{
    save checkpoint and N_i to stable storage;
    if (N_i>MAX) then {MAX=N_i;}
}
if (Timer_M expires) then
{
    N = MAX;
    for all processes P_i ε JoinList_M (1<= i <=n)
    if status_i = ACTIVE then
    {
        if ( N_i < N ) then
        {
            send C < N, Timer_M > to process P_i
        }
    }
}
if (MSS_j receives (IDLE, N_i) from MH_i)
{
    update sequence number of last checkpoint of MH_i to N_i
}
if (MSS_j receives a JoinM from MH_i)
{
    insert MH_i into JoinList_j; set status_i = ACTIVE
}
if (MSS_j receives a LeaveM from MH_i)
delete MH_i from Joinlist_j;
if (MSS_p receives a DM from MH_i or MH_i gets disconnected)
set status_i = DISCONNECT;
```

3   The Recovery Algorithm

Whenever a MH fails, it needs to recover back to its latest checkpoint that was before failure and, in turn, whole system should remain consistent. Hence, when an MH_i returns back from a failure it requests its latest checkpoint C from its local MSS_p, by sending *InitRollbackReq(i)* to MSS_p. If MH_i was in the *JoinList$_p$* of MSS_p, then MSS_p must have the latest checkpoint C_{Latest} of MH_i and it sends C_{Latest} to MH_i. Otherwise, it broadcasts a checkpoint request message *CReq(i)* to all MSS's. When an MSS_q receives *CReq(i)* message from MSS_p then it searches in its local storage whether it contains the checkpoint of MH_i. If an MSS_q finds the checkpoint of MH_i in its local storage then it sends the same to MSS_p that had requested for the checkpoint. When MSS_p receives, more than one checkpoints of MH_i, from various MSS's then it finds out the latest checkpoint among them and sends a *Rollback(C_{sn})* message to MH_i. It also sends a *RollbackReq(sn)* to all MH's via their respective MSS, where *sn* is the last checkpoint sequence number of the MH_i before failure. After receiving its checkpoint from MSS_p, MH_i restores itself to that checkpoint and resumes its normal computation. When other MSS's receive *RollbackReq(sn)* message from MSS_p then they send corresponding C_{sn} message to each MH that is in its *JoinList*. Each MH on receiving this message restores itself back to C_{sn} and resumes its normal computation.

4   The Performance Analysis

A time-coordinated checkpointing method that is closest to our work is Gupta *et al.*'s index-based protocol [3]. In their protocol, whenever a MH initiates a checkpoint, it broadcasts checkpoint request as a control message to each process in the system. Hence, the number of control messages in the system increase linearly with increase in the number of MH's. However, in our algorithm, no checkpoint initiation is required as each MH takes checkpoint independently when its timer expires.

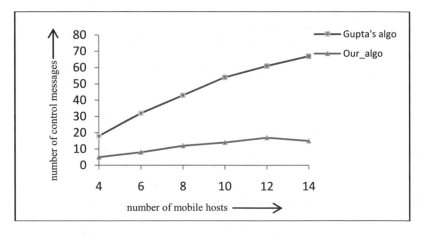

Fig. 1. The simulation result

However, a control message, having current timer information, is sent by an MSS only to its MH's that are not in synchronization with its other MH's. With the increase in the number of MH's, the number of application messages also increase. Hence, the number of control messages required would be less. As each application message also contains the timer information piggybacked into it, which helps in synchronizing the system. Consequently, when the system is synchronized, our algorithm does not send any control message. Therefore, with the increase in the number of application messages, there would be situations when the number of control messages in our algorithm would decrease even with the increase in the number of MH's. This fact is substantiated, also, by the downward slope in the simulation plot of our algorithm, presented in the following Fig. 1, when the number of MH's increases beyond 12.

5 Conclusion

The time-coordinated checkpointing protocols suit the applications where processes have high message sending rate [4]. However, for the applications where processes have low message sending rate, such protocols may perform poorly. Nevertheless, our protocol works well, in both situations, irrespective of the message sending rate.

References

1. Tsai, J.: An Efficient Index-Based Checkpointing Protocol with Constant-Size Control Information on Messages. IEEE Transactions on Dependable and Secure Computing 2(4), 278–296 (2005)
2. Baldoni, R., Quaglia, F., Fornara, P.: An Index-Based Checkpointing Algorithm for Autonomous Distributed Systems. In: SRDS 1997, pp. 27–34. IEEE Press, Los Alamitos (1997)
3. Gupta, B., et al.: A Low-Overhead Non-block Checkpointing Algorithm for Mobile Computing Environment. In: Chung, Y.-C., Moreira, J.E. (eds.) GPC 2006. LNCS, vol. 3947, pp. 597–608. Springer, Heidelberg (2006)
4. Chaoguang, M., Yunlong, Z., Wenbin, Y.: A Two-Phase Time-Based Consistent Checkpointing Strategy. In: ITNG 2006, pp. 518–523. IEEE Press, Los Alamitos (2006)

A Formal Framework and a Tool for the Specification and Analysis of G-Nets Models Based on Graph Transformation

Elhillali Kerkouche[1] and Allaoua Chaoui[2]

[1] Department of Computer Science, University of Oum El Bouaghi, Algeria
elhillalik@yahoo.fr
[2] Department of Computer Science, University of Constantine, Algeria
a_chaoui2001@yahoo.com

Abstract. This paper proposes a formal framework and a tool based on graph transformation to facilitate the design and analysis of complex software systems using G-Nets formalism. A G-Nets specification can be translated (manually) into an equivalent Predicate/Transition Nets specification (PrT-Nets). This transformation aims to use the formal analysis techniques developed for PrT-Nets to analyze G-Nets specifications. PROD is used to describe PrT-Nets models. So, we have proposed two automatic steps to perform the transformation of G-Nets models to their equivalent in PROD Language. The first one deals with the transformation of G-Nets models into Prt-Nets models. The second one transforms the resulted Prt-Nets models into PROD language. This work is a key step in a large project aiming at using graph transformation to formalize UML diagrams using G-Nets models.

Keywords: G-Nets, Predicate/Transition Nets, PROD, Meta-modelling, Graph Grammars, AToM[3], Models Transformation.

1 Introduction

G-Nets [5] are a kind of high level Petri Nets defined to support modular design and specification of distributed information systems. Once a G-Nets specification is done, it can be transformed [5] into a semantically equivalent Predicate/transition Nets (PrT-nets) model. This transformation aims to apply the formal analysis techniques of PrT-Nets on the obtained models. PROD analyzer [10 is one of the most used tools for PrT-Nets.

Building a modeling tool from scratch is a hard task. Meta-Modeling [4] approach is useful to deal with this problem since it allows (possibly in a graphical manner) the modeling of the formalisms themselves. Since a meta-model and a model are stored as graphs, further manipulations of the models can be described (modeled) graphically and formally as graph grammars [12]. The ideas presented above are implemented in ATOM[3]: A Tool for Multi-formalism and Meta-Modeling [2].

In this paper, we propose a formal framework and a tool based on graph transformation for the specification and analysis of complex software systems using G-Nets formalism. Our framework allows a developer to draw a G-Nets model and

V. Garg, R. Wattenhofer, and K. Kothapalli (Eds.): ICDCN 2009, LNCS 5408, pp. 206–211, 2009.

transform it into its equivalent PrT-nets model automatically. In order to perform the analysis using PROD analyzer, our framework allows a developer to translate automatically each resulted PrT-Nets model into PROD's net description language.

To this end, we have defined a Meta-Model for G-Nets formalism and another for PrT-Nets formalism. Then the Meta-Modeling tool AToM^3 is used to automatically generate a visual modeling tool for both formalisms. We have also proposed two graph grammars. The first one performs the transformation of the graphically specified G-Nets models to semantically equivalent PrT-Nets models. The second one translates the resulted PrT-Nets models into PROD's net description language.

This paper is organized as follows. Section 2 outlines some related works. We recall some basic notions of G-Nets formalisms in section 3. In section 4, we give an overview of the AToM3 tool. In section 5, we define a meta-model for G-Nets and another for PrTNets for generating visual tool for both formalisms. In section 6, we present our formal framework. In section 7, we illustrate our framework through an example. Finally, section 8 concludes the paper and gives some perspectives.

2   Related Works

In addition to AToM^3, there are other visual tools to describe formalisms using meta-modeling (DOME [6], Multigraph [13], MetaEdit+ [9] and KOGGE [7]). But these tools express formalism semantics by means of a textual language. In AToM^3, the user expresses such semantics by means of graph grammar. On the other hand, there are also similar tools to manipulate models by means of graph grammars, such as PROGRES [11], GRACE [8] and AGG [1]. However, none of these has a meta-modeling layer.

3   G-Nets Notation

A G-Nets specification is composed of a number of G-Nets. Each of them represents an independent module. A G-Net is composed of two parts: a special place called Generic Switch Place (GSP) and an Internal Structure (IS). The GSP provides the abstraction of the module, while the Internal Structure represents the detailed design of the G-Net [5]. The notation for G-Nets is shown in Fig.1.

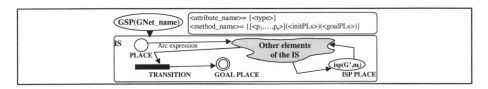

Fig. 1. Notations used to represent a G-Net

4   AToM^3: An Overview

AToM^3 [2] is A visual Tool for Multi-formalism Modeling and Meta-Modeling. The two main tasks of AToM^3 are meta-modeling and Model transformation. *Meta –modeling*

Fig. 2. Rule-based Modification of Graphs

refers to modelling formalisms concepts using UML Class Diagram formalism. Based on these descriptions, AToM[3] can automatically generate tools to manipulate (create and edit) models in the formalisms of interest [4]. For *Model transformation*, AToM[3] supports graph rewriting system, which uses Graph Grammar [3] to visually guide the procedure of model transformation. The main idea of graph transformation is the rule-based modification of graphs as shown in Fig. 2.

5   Meta-modeling of G-Nets and PrT-Nets

In this section, we will define two metamodels, the first one for G-Nets and the second one for PrT-Nets. The meta-formalism used in our work is the UML Class Diagram.

Following the description of G-Nets given in section 3, we have proposed to metamodel G-Nets with four Classes and five Associations as shown in the left side of Fig.3. Concerning PrT-Nets, we have proposed two classes (representing places and transitions) related with two associations (representing input arcs and out put arcs) as shown in the right side of Fig.3.

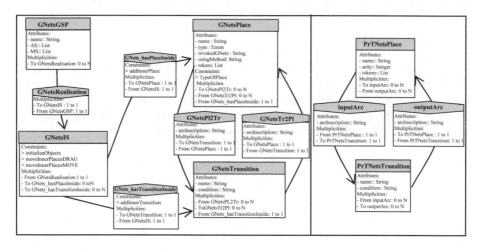

Fig. 3. G-Nets Meta-Model (left) and PrT-Nets Meta-Model (right)

Given our meta-models, we have used AToM[3] tool to generate a visual modelling environment for both formalisms. Since AToM[3] is a visual tool for multi-formalism modelling, we can show in a user interface of AToM[3] the two generated tools at the same time (see the generated tools in Fig.6).

In the next section we define two graph grammars for the obtained framework. The first one transforms the G-Nets specification into a PrT-Nets model. The last one generates PROD description (in PROD language) of the resulted PrT-Nets models.

6 Formal Framework for G-Nets

In this section, we improve the capabilities of the obtained framework by means of graph grammar. More precisely, we have defined two graph grammars. The first one translates a G-Nets specification into an equivalent PrT-Nets model. In order to perform the appropriate analysis of the resulted PrT-Nets models, the second graph grammar generates their PROD's net description (PROD language). Then the PROD analyzer can be used. The advantage of using a graph grammar is the formal and high-level representation of the transformation.

We have named the first graph grammar *G-Net2PrT-Nets*. During the execution of *G-Net2PrT-Nets*, the model is indeed a blend of G-Nets and PrT-Nets. But when the graph grammar execution finishes, the resulting model is entirely a PrT-Nets model.

In *G-Net2PrT-Nets* grammar, we have proposed twenty rules which will be applied in ascending order. Note that each rule has a priority. Due to the page limitations, we show only three rules in Fig. 4.

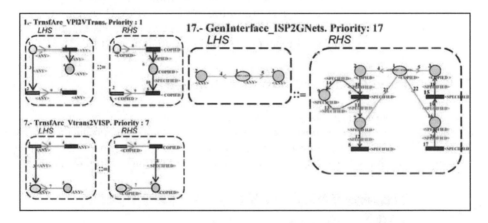

Fig. 4. Graph Grammar to Transform G-Nets specification into PrT-Nets

The main idea of the transformation in *G-Net2PrT-Nets* grammar is to transform the caller G-Net (which contain the ISP place) and the called G-Net into PrT-Net. Then create the interface in PrT-Nets model which mimics the invocation mechanism in G-Nets formalism and relate the two G-Nets. We note that before applying the rules of the grammar, the user is prompted to select a G-Net to be analyzed.

We have named the second graph grammar *PrT-Nets2PROD*. In *PrT-Nets2PROD* graph grammar, we have proposed *six* rules (see Fig. 5). We are concerned here by code generation, so none of these rules will change the input PrT-Nets model.

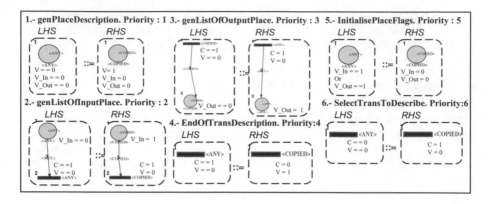

Fig. 5. Graph Grammar to generate PROD description from a PrT-Nets model

The idea behind the transformation can be described in three steps. The first one opens the file where the PROD description will be generated and decorates all transition and place elements in the model with temporary attributes. The second step is to generate PROD description for all places in PrT-Net model (*Rule1*). The last one is to produce the equivalent PROD code of all transitions in PrT-Net Model. To generate PROD code for a PrT-Net transition, *PrT-Nets2PROD* graph grammar selects a transition (*Rule 6*) and generates PROD code for its input places (apply *Rule 2* as many times as the number of input places) and for output places (*Rule3*).

7 Case Study: Producer/Consumer Problem

The producer/consumer problem consists of the synchronization between one or more producers and one or more consumers. For simplicity, we take one producer and one consumer. We have applied our tool on the G-Nets model of the produced/consumer example shown in Fig.6 and obtained the expected specification in PROD language.

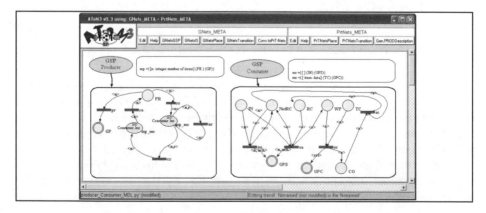

Fig. 6. Producer/Consumer problem created in our framework

8 Conclusion

In this paper, we have presented a formal framework based on the combined use of Meta-Modeling and Graph Grammars for the specification and verification of software information systems using G-Nets formalism. With Meta-modeling, we have defined the syntactic aspect of both G-Nets and PrT-Nets formalisms, then we have used the meta-modeling tool ATOM^3 to generate their visual modeling environment. By means of Graph Grammar, we have extended the capabilities of our framework to transform G-Nets specification into their equivalent PrT-Nets Models and to generate a PROD description of the resulted PrT-Nets Models for analysis purpose. In a future work, we plan to include the verification phase using PROD on a more complicated example and provide our tool by giving a feed back of the results (interpreting the results) of this verification in the initial G-Nets model. This work is an important step in a large project aiming at using graph transformation to formalize UML diagrams using G-Nets.

References

1. AGG Home page, http://tfs.cs.tu-berlin.de/agg/
2. AToM3 Home page, version 3.00, http://atom3.cs.mcgill.ca/
3. Bardohl, R., Ehrig, H., De Lara, J., Taentzer, G.: Integrating Meta Modelling with Graph Transformation for Efficient Visual Language Definition and Model Manipulation. In: Wermelinger, M., Margaria-Steffen, T. (eds.) FASE 2004. LNCS, vol. 2984, pp. 214–228. Springer, Heidelberg (2004)
4. De Lara, J., Vangheluwe, H.: Meta-Modelling and Graph Grammars for Multi-Paradigm Modelling in AToM3. Manuel Alfonseca, Software and Systems Modelling 3, 194–209 (2004); Special Section on Graph Transformations and Visual Modeling Techniques
5. Deng, Y., Chang, S.K., De Figueired, J.C.A., Psrkusich, A.: Integrating Software Engineering Methods and Petri Nets for the Specification and Prototyping of Complex Information Systems. In: Proceeding of The 14th International Conference on Application and Theory of Petri Nets, Chicago, June 21-25, pp. 206–223 (1993)
6. DOME Home page, Honeywell Technology Center. Honeywell, version 5.2.1 (1999), http://www.htc.honeywell.com/dome/
7. Ebert, J., Sttenbach, R., Uhe, I.: Meta-CASE in Practice: a Case for KOGGE. In: Olivé, À., Pastor, J.A. (eds.) CAiSE 1997. LNCS, vol. 1250, pp. 203–216. Springer, Heidelberg (1997), KOGGE Home page, http://www.uni-koblenz.de/_ist/kogge.en.html
8. GRACE Home page, http://www.informatik.uni-bremen.de/theorie/GRACEland/GRACEland.html
9. Kelly, S., Lyytinen, K., Rossi, M.: MetaEdit+: A fully configurable Multi-User and Multi-Tool CASE and CAME Environment. In: Constantopoulos, P., Vassiliou, Y., Mylopoulos, J. (eds.) CAiSE 1996. LNCS, vol. 1080. Springer, Heidelberg (1996), MetaEdit+ Home page, http://www.MetaCase.com
10. PROD Home page, version 3.4.01, http://www.tcs.hut.fi/Software/prod/
11. PROGRES Home page, http://www-i3.informatik.rwth-aachen.de/research/projects/progres/main
12. Rozenberg, G.: Handbook of Graph Grammars and Computing by Graph Transformation, vol. 1. World Scientific, Singapore (1999)
13. Sztipanovits, J., Karsai, G., Biegl, C., Bapty, T., Ledeczi, A., Misra, A.: MULTIGRAPH: An architecture for model-integrated computing. In: ICECCS 1995, Ft. Lauderdale, Lorida, pp. 361–368 (1995)

Fair Resource Allocation in Distributed Combinatorial Auctioning Systems

Lubna Rasheedi[1], Natasha Chatterjee[2], and Shrisha Rao[3]

[1] American Express India Private Limited
[2] ABB GIS Limited
[3] International Institute of Information Technology, Bangalore

Abstract. Combinatorial Auctions are auctions where bidders can place bids on combinations of items, called packages or bundles, rather than just on individual items. In this paper we extend this concept to distributed system, by proposing a Distributed Combinatorial Auctioning System consisting of auctioneers and bidders who communicate by message-passing. We also propose a fair division algorithm that is based on our DCAS concept and model. Our model consist of auctioneers that are distributed in the system each having local bidders. Auctioneers collect local bids for the bundles. One of the auctioneers acts obtains all the bids from other auctioneers, and performs the computations necessary for the combinatorial auction. We also briefly discuss how basic and extended fairness are implemented in resource allocation by our algorithm.

Keywords: Multi-agent systems, combinatorial auctions, fairness, distributed systems.

1 Introduction

In multi-agent systems (MAS) the autonomous agents act in a self-interested manner in their dealings with numerous other agents. This behavior is seen in MAS which mainly deal with issues like resource allocation [6]. The framework which exactly demonstrates this behavior is a combinatorial auctioning system (CAS). CAS is a kind of MAS whereby bidders can bid over, combination of items [4,3].

In this paper, we propose the concept of a Distributed Combinatorial Auctioning System (DCAS). A DCAS is a type of multi-agent system in a distributed environment composed of n auctioneers acting cooperative with each other, and p self-interested bidders who bid for sets of resources with the intention of procurement to satisfy their individual needs.

Possible applications of our work include different types of land and Internet auctions, both of which commonly use distributed systems. Our algorithm ensures fair resource allocation to bidders, and has the additional benefit of resolving the case of tied bids, by proportionately allocating the resource among bidders in distributed environment.

V. Garg, R. Wattenhofer, and K. Kothapalli (Eds.): ICDCN 2009, LNCS 5408, pp. 212–217, 2009.

2   Fairness in DCAS

CAS is a kind of MAS which comprises of an auctioneer and number of self interested bidders. Optimality and fairness are the key issues in a CAS. An algorithm was proposed by Saini and Rao [5] that uses a metric to measure fairness for each agent and determines the final payment made by the winners. Fairness has been classified by Saini and Rao [5] into two types, as Basic Fairness and Extended Fairness. Basic Fairness, in particular, is related to egalitarian social welfare [2] and envy-freeness [1], according to Saini and Rao.

2.1   Fairness in Distributed Combinatorial Auctioning Systems (DCAS)

In our proposed DCAS algorithm (Section 3), we assume that the auctioneers in the system are strongly connected with each other, and thus are able to successfully negotiate with each other. However, the local bidders are only connected to their respective auctioneers and not to other auctioneers or bidders in the system. The algorithm does not deal with resource management issues (e.g. maintenance of resources, physical transfer of resources to winning bidders, etc.). The resources in the system are divisible, and are not added to or removed from the system once the algorithm starts running. Message delivery is reliable, and the bidders and auctioneers are synchronous (possibly weakly synchronous), and also do not fail during the algorithm. As of now our algorithm does not discuss fault tolerance in DCAS. Last but not the least, all bids involved in the auction are sealed and are disclosed only to the auctioneers, not the bidders.

The auctioneers and each bidder under them have fair valuation for each of the individual resource(s).

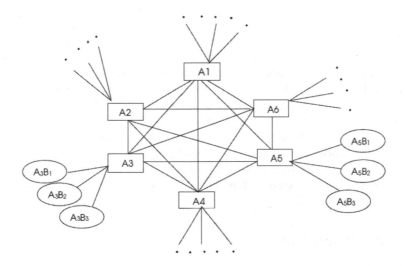

Fig. 1. DCAS Model

The auctioneer also maintains a table of the bid values from his local as well as from the other bidders of the system for each of the bundles.

In Figure 1, rectangular boxes represent auctioneers A_i, and ellipses represent bidders $A_i b_j$, which denotes the local bidder b_j of auctioneer A_i. A line shows a communication link.

2.2   Mathematical Formulation of Fairness in DCAS

Let our DCAS be represented as a 4-tuple $(\Phi, \mathcal{A}, \xi, \beta)$ which is defined as follows:

(i) A set Φ comprising m resources $r_0, r_1, \ldots, r_{m-1}$ for which the bids are raised.

(ii) A set $\mathcal{A}$ of auctioneers A_i who co-ordinate among themselves for the bidding to take place.

(iii) A set ξ comprising p bidders $A_j b_1, A_j b_2, \ldots, A_j b_p$ under each auctioneer A_j located geographically apart. These are the agents among whom the resources are to be allocated on basis of winning of bids. An agent cannot bid under more than one auctioneer.

(iv) A set β comprising set of resources against which the bidders bid. We term them as bundles.

According to the table structure defined by Saini and Rao for fair evaluation of resource (say, in dollars), we consider a case which comprises of four bidders $A_1 b_1, A_1 b_2, A_2 b_1, A_9 b_1$, auctioneer's fair evaluation value denoted as λ, and three resources r_0, r_1, r_2. Each bidder is privileged to bid upon any combination of these resources. The subsets of these resources are $\{(r_0)\}, \{(r_1)\}$, $\{(r_2)\}$, $\{(r_0, r_1)\}$, $\{(r_0, r_2)\}$, $\{(r_1, r_2)\}$, $\{(r_0, r_1, r_2)\}$. There is only one set of fair values for all auctioneers but under each auctioneer, each bidder has separate fair evaluation for a resource (say, in dollars). In DCAS we build the same *Fair Evaluation Table* when bidding details of a resource say R_i is requested by say auctioneer A_j.

According to the table structure defined by Saini and Rao for bids by different bidders , it contains bids raised by bidders under different auctioneers for the individual resource and different combination of resource. The bids raised by each of the bidder for different sets of resources may or may not be equal to his fair evaluation of the respective set of resources. A bidder can put zero bids for resources it does not wish to procure. In DCAS we build the same table as *Bid Value Table* when bidding details of a resource say R_i is requested by say auctioneer A_j. Bidding details of bidders under different auctioneers bidding for the resource R_i is collected under this table. This table is used to determine winner of auction and as well as for the deciding the payment amount to be made by winner.

3   DCAS Algorithm

Below we present our pseudocode for the n auctioneers and for p bidders in a DCAS.

```
while true do
    if round == k then
        while i < n do
            getValueT1();
            getValueT2($\beta_n$);
        end
    end
    if round == k+1 then
        while i<n do
            Send msg($A_j$);
            // message is sent to auctioneer $A_j$ where $n \neq j$;
            getBids($\beta_n$);
        end
    end
    if round == k+2 then
        compareBids();
    end
end
```

Algorithm 1. Pseudocode for Auctioneer

```
while true do
    if round == k then
        while j < n do
            while i < p do
                Send $fair\_msg(\| R_{A_j} \|_{A_j b_n})$;
                // fair value is sent to $A_j$ that populates Fair Evaluation
                Table
                Send $bid\_msg(\beta_n)$;
                // bid value sent to $A_j$ for Bid Value Table
            end
        end
    end
end
```

Algorithm 2. Pseudocode for Local Bidder

An auctioneer receives bids from local bidders in round k, gets bids from other auctioneers in round $k+1$, and does the allocation computation and notification in round $k+2$. This can happen concurrently as long as no new bids are received for any resource for which bids have already been received in a previous round.

In our pseudocode given above, $getValueT1()$ function returns the fair values decided by the local bidders which populates Fair Evaluation table. Similarly getValueT2(β_n) returns the bid values for the bundle (β_n) given by the local bidders to the auctioneer which populates Bid Value table. Next message msg(A_j) is sent to rest of auctioneers by an auctioneer asking for their respective local bids for all the bundles they have value for. This bid value is returned by the function $getBids(\beta_n)$. Finally $compareBids()$ returns the winner bidder decided by the auctioneer.

In the pseudocode for local bidders there are two messages sent by bidders $A_j b_n$ to auctioneer A_j. The first one is $fair\_msg(\parallel R_{A_j} \parallel_{A_j b_n})$ that returns the fair value given by bidders for individual resources populating the Fair Evaluation Table . The second message $bid\_msg(\beta_n)$ returns the bid value for bundles that is indicated in Bid Value table.

STEP 1: In round k, auctioneer A_j collects fair values for the individual resources denoted by set R_{A_j} where $R_{A_j} = \{r_0, r_1, r_2, \ldots, r_n\}$ from his local bidders and populates Fair Evaluation table with fair values of resources, denoted as$\parallel R_{A_j} \parallel_{A_j b_n}$, given by bidder $A_j b_n$. Also A_j collects local bids for the bundles and populates Bid Value table that is, $\{\beta_1 A_j b_1, \beta_2 A_j b_1, \ldots, \beta_i A_j b_1\}$ from his local bidder $A_j b1$

$\{\beta_1 A_j b_2, \beta_2 A_j b_2, \ldots, \beta_i A_j b_2\}$ from his local bidder $A_j b_2$

$\vdots$

$\{\beta_1 A_j b_n, \beta_2 A_j b_n, \ldots, \beta_1 i A_j b_n\}$ from his local bidder $A_j b_n$.

STEP 2: In next round $k + 1$, A_j sends message $msg(A_j)$ to fellow auctioneers asking for their local bids for all the bundles containing the resource(s) which auctioneer A_j is going to start auction for. They reply with a message containing the values of Fair Evaluation table and Bid Value table obtained from their local bidders returned by function $getBids(\beta_n)$. Let us consider that auctioneer A_0 sends message to auctioneer $A_1, A_2, ..., A_5$ requesting the values for Fair Evaluation table and Bid Value table. Each of the auctioneers receiving this message $msg(A_j)$ replies with all the values of both the tables that he has received from his local bidders.

STEP 3: In final round $k + 2$, after receiving responses from others, A_j does a comparative study of the bids and decides the winner following Saini and Rao [5] algorithm. Let us consider that after comparing bids from table 2 for a bundle β_i for all the bidder's values, auctioneer A_0 concludes that some bidder $A_3 b_5$ has won the auction for bundle β_i.

Remark 1. Resolving a tie: In case there is a tie amongst bidders for their bid value for any β then basic fairness is applied by calculating utility value for the respective bundle (this is explained in the full paper).

Remark 2. An auctioneer in one message asks for bid values from other auctioneers respectively. Thus if there are n auctioneers in the system, total number of messages sent would be $n - 1$.

4   Conclusion

Saini and Rao [5] presented a centralized algorithm for extended fairness where a single dedicated auctioneer receives bids, declares the winner and as well calculates the payment amount according to the circumstances in which the bidder won the auction.

Saini and Rao state that the fair value of the resources does not actually show the need of the resource for a bidder. But we have assumed that the fair values which they state for the resources depict their need for the resources. The bidders maximize the importance and their need for the resource to them by bidding higher or stating high fair values for that resource. Thus, the higher the fair value or the bidding value, the greater is the need for the resource set.

We have shown how our proposed algorithm incorporates fairness in DCAS, where all the agents receive their fair share if they behave rationally. We also discussed the application of basic and extended fairness in our work. Our proposed algorithm gives an appearance to the different bidders, both local and non-local, of the system to be non-distributed, as if controlled by a single auctioneer. The DCAS framework avoids the use of single dedicated auctioneer in favor of distributed auctioneers who cooperate among thenselves and perform fair allocation assuring basic and extended fairness. The algorithm achieves allocation efficiency in handling the tie situations by a new approach ensuring basic fairness where the resources are divided in proportion to the fair value of the bidder. A possible extension of our work would be to achieve generalized framework for multi agent systems that performs truly distributed auctions without any dedicated auctioneer.

References

1. Brams, S.J.: Fair Division. Oxford Handbook of Political Economy (2005)
2. Chevaleyre, Y., Endriss, U., Estivie, S., Maudet, N.: Multiagent resource allocation with k-additive utility functions. In: Proceedings of the First International Workshop on Computer Science and Decision Theory, vol. 14(3), pp. 83–100 (2004)
3. Narahari, Y., Dayama, P.: Combinatorial auctions for electronic business. Sadhna 30, 179–211 (2005)
4. Nisan, N.: Bidding and allocation in combinatorial auctions. In: Proceedings of the Second ACM Conference on Electronic Commerce, pp. 1–12 (2000)
5. Saini, M., Rao, S.: Fairness in combinatorial auctioning systems. In: Game Theoretic and Decision Theoretic Agents: Papers from the AAAI Spring Symposium, pp. 61–67 (March 2007), http://arxiv.org/abs/0809.2168
6. Sycara, K.: Multi-agent systems. AI Magazine 10(2), 79–93 (1998)

Compact Routing Schemes for Dynamic Trees in the Fixed Port Model

Amos Korman*

CNRS and Université Paris Diderot - Paris 7, France
amos.korman@gmail.com

Abstract. This paper considers the routing problem in dynamic trees under the *fixed-port* model, in which an adversary chooses the port numbers assigned to each node. We present two routing schemes for dynamic trees that maintain labels of asymptotically optimal size using extremely low average message complexity (per node). Specifically, we first present a dynamic routing scheme that supports additions of both leaves and internal nodes, maintains asymptotically optimal labels and incurs only $O(\log^2 n/\log^2 \log n)$ average message complexity. This routing scheme is then extended to supports also deletions of nodes of degree at most 2. The extended scheme incurs $O(\log^2 n)$ average message complexity and still maintains asymptotically optimal labels.

We would like to point out that the best known routing scheme for dynamic trees that maintains asymptotically optimal labels in the fixed port model has very high average message complexity, namely, $O(n^\epsilon)$. Moreover, that scheme supports additions and removals of leaf nodes only.

Keywords: Distributed algorithms, dynamic networks, routing schemes, trees.

1 Introduction

Background. The study of methods for designing *routing schemes* in *static* (fixed topology) settings is rather well developed. Typically, the main goal of such a scheme is to equip each node with a (hopefully short) label, such that efficient routing can be performed between any two nodes, based merely on the label of the destination node and the labels of intermediate nodes on the path. In particular, a classical *routing problem* for a family of graphs $\mathcal{F}$ consists of a method for assigning a *label* to each node in each graph $G \in \mathcal{F}$, such that given the label of any node v in some given graph $G \in \mathcal{F}$ and the label of any destination node $u \in G$, node v can find which of its incident port numbers (in G) leads to the next node on a shortest path connecting v and u. Most works on such routing schemes evaluate the scheme is by its *label size*, i.e., the maximal number of bits stored in a label (see e.g., [2,3,5,15,16]). Not surprisingly, the main objective was to construct *compact* schemes, which enjoy asymptotically optimal label size.

The quality of a routing scheme strongly depends on the model considered. In particular, it is known that the label size of a routing scheme for trees depends on who

---

* Supported in part by the ANR project ALADDIN, by the INRIA project GANG, and by COST Action 295 DYNAMO.

V. Garg, R. Wattenhofer, and K. Kothapalli (Eds.): ICDCN 2009, LNCS 5408, pp. 218–229, 2009.

has the power to assign the port numbers of the nodes. Specifically, two main models regarding port numbers are considered in the literature. For the *designer* port model, in which the designer of the routing scheme can freely select the port numbers assigned to each node (as long as they remain distinct), [5,16] independently constructed a routing scheme with label size $\Theta(\log n)$, for the family of n-node (static) trees. Under the *fixed port* model, in which the port numbers (encoded using $O(\log n)$ bits) are fixed by an adversary, [5] constructed a routing scheme on (static) n-node trees using labels of $O(\frac{\log^2 n}{\log \log n})$ bits. This bound was shown to be asymptotically optimal in [6]. Though it requires larger labels, the fixed port model (considered also in this paper) may be found more useful in certain applications, as it allows for more modular constructions; in this context, the adversary, choosing the port numbers, models constrains on port numbers which are given by other protocols running on the network and using the same ports.

In contrast to the static setting, the more complex *dynamic* setting, in which processors may join or leave the network or new connections may be established or removed, has received much less attention in the literature. In the dynamic scenario, in order to maintain the labels, the scheme needs to occasionally update labels following the topology changes, which may require the delivery of information from place to place. This raises the natural problem of maintaining short labels (hopefully asymptotically optimal) using low communication cost. Specifically, in addition to its label size, we evaluate a dynamic routing scheme by its *average message complexity*, i.e., the ratio of the number of messages sent during the execution to the number of nodes. This measure reflects the amount of work a typical node exerts for communication purposes.

The problem of maintaining a routing scheme in a dynamic tree was originally introduced by [4] (and implicitly in [1]). This problem was later studied in a series of papers [7,8,10,11], which proposed different tradeoffs between the label size and the message complexity. Still, the best known compact routing scheme on dynamic trees in the fixed port model[1] has very high average message complexity, namely, $O(n^\epsilon)$ [7]. Moreover, the types of topology changes supported by previous schemes on (fixed port) trees are limited to additions and removals of leaves only. On top of that, the correctness of previous such schemes is guaranteed only for *quiet* times, in which all updates concerning the previous topology changes, have already occurred.

Our contribution. In this paper we consider the fixed port model and present two compact routing schemes for dynamic trees that incur extremely low average message complexity.

The main contribution of the paper is the construction of an efficient compact routing scheme for growing trees, i.e., trees that undergo topology changes which are restricted to additions of both leaves and internal nodes. This routing scheme (given in Section 3) assigns and maintains asymptotically optimal $\Theta(\frac{\log^2 n}{\log \log n})$-bit labels, using $O(\frac{\log^2 n}{\log^2 \log n})$ average message complexity, where n denotes the current tree size.

---

[1] In the dynamic setting, the fixed port model assumes that, at any given time, the port numbers (assigned by the adversary) are encoded using $O(\log n)$ bits, where n is the maximal tree size until the given time. Moreover, once a port number is assigned, it remains fixed, and cannot be changed again (unless the port itself is removed).

Our scheme for growing trees can be extended to support also removals of degree 1 and 2 nodes using the method mentioned in [9]. For any given time, let n denote the maximal tree size until the given time. The extended scheme maintains $\Theta(\frac{\log^2 n}{\log \log n})$-bit labels using $O(\log^2 n)$ average message complexity (the average message complexity is taken with respect to all nodes existing in the tree, including deleted ones). Since the extended scheme is a straightforward application of the method in [9], its formal description is deferred to the appendix.

In contrast to the previous routing schemes on (fixed-port) dynamic trees, whose correctness is guaranteed only for quiet times, our schemes are correct at all times. Table 1 summarizes the complexities of our dynamic routing schemes in comparison to previously known results.

We would like to note that our dynamic schemes as well as the dynamic schemes in [7,8,9,10,11], assume the *controlled* dynamic model (see Section 2), in which the topology changes do not occur spontaneously, and instead can be delayed by the update protocol. Clearly, no routing scheme can be expected to be both compact and correct at all times, if nodes are being inserted to the tree in a very rapid succession. In particular, if an adversary can continuously insert internal nodes very fast, then it can prevent any message from reaching its destination. In the case where only leaves may join the tree, our schemes can be extended to support spontaneous insertions of leaves, however, in this case, the correctness is only guaranteed for quiet times (similarly to [7,10]).

Table 1. The table summarizes the performances of our dynamic routing schemes in comparison previous ones

Routing schemes	Paper [7]	Paper [10]	This paper (result 1)	This paper (result 2)
Label size	$\Theta(\frac{\log^2 n}{\log \log n})$	$O(\log^2 n)$	$\Theta(\frac{\log^2 n}{\log \log n})$	$\Theta(\frac{\log^2 n}{\log \log n})$
Average message complexity	$O(n^\epsilon)$	$O(\log^4 n)$	$O(\frac{\log^2 n}{\log^2 \log n})$	$O(\log^2 n)$
Types of topological changes	add leaf remove leaf	add leaf remove leaf	add any node	add any node remove a leaf or deg 2 node
Correctness guarantee	at quiet times	at quiet times	at all times	at all times

Related work. Routing schemes on static trees were investigated in various papers e.g., [14,17]. Compact routing labeling schemes on static trees were given in [5,6,16]. Specifically, for the *fixed* port model, [5] gave a routing scheme using labels of $O(\frac{\log^2 n}{\log \log n})$ bits. This bound was shown to be asymptotically optimal in [6].

The problem of maintaining a routing scheme in a dynamic tree under the fixed-port model was originally introduced by [1,4], and later studied in a series of papers [7,10,11], which proposed different tradeoffs between the label size and the message complexity. In [1], the authors implicitly describe a dynamic routing scheme on a dynamically growing tree (in which only leaves are allowed to join) using logarithmic average message complexity but huge labels, namely, the label size is $O(n \log n)$. In [4] the authors gave an improved dynamic routing scheme on dynamically growing trees using labels of size $O(\Delta \log^3 n)$ (where Δ is the maximum degree in the tree) and logarithmic average message complexity. Again, if only leaves can join the tree, [7,11] gave a dynamic routing scheme with logarithmic average message complexity and label size that is larger than the optimum by a factor of $O(\log n)$.

In the case where leaves can also be removed from the network, [10] gave a dynamic routing scheme with average message complexity $O(\log^4 n)$ and label size that is larger than the optimum by a factor $O(\log \log n)$. So far, the best known *compact* routing scheme on (fixed port) trees [7] uses $O(n^\epsilon)$ average message complexity, where $0 < \epsilon < 1$ is some constant. Moreover, previous routing schemes on (fixed port) dynamic trees support additions and removals of leaves only, and are guaranteed to be correct only at quiet times.

Recently, an efficient compact routing scheme for dynamic trees under the designer port model was constructed in [8]. Our main dynamic scheme bares some similarities with that scheme. For example, both routing schemes use an efficient dynamic ancestry scheme to detect ancestry relations between nodes. Moreover, both dynamic routing schemes are based on adapting the principles of the corresponding static schemes in [5] to the more complex dynamic setting. However, the corresponding static schemes in [5] (the one for the designer port model and the one for the fixed port model) are quite different, and thus require different handling when adapted to the dynamic setting. Specifically, efficient maintenance of a routing scheme with short labels requires the maintenance of an implicit (balanced) decomposition of the tree that strongly depends on the label structure. Thus, the differences in the label structure between the two schemes impose differences in the protocol that maintains the labels, as it must also maintain a different implicit tree decomposition.

2 Preliminaries

The network topology is described by an undirected communication tree $T = \langle V, E \rangle$, where V is a set of nodes, representing processors, and E is a set of edges, representing bidirectional communication links . We consider the standard asynchronous point-to-point message-passing model. Specifically, the communication between nodes is made by exchanging messages over the edges. Each message sent over an edge arrives without errors, at an arbitrary but finite delay. We assume that the computations performed at a node are made instantaneously.

We consider the *fixed port* model, in which, for each node v, an adversary assigns disjoint port numbers pointing at v's incident edges (the assignment is local, and is not necessarily consistent between two neighboring nodes). In the static setting, it is required that each port number is encoded using $O(\log n)$ bits, where n is the number of nodes in the tree.

The ancestry relation in the tree T is defined as the transitive closure of the parenthood relation (in particular, a node is an ancestor of itself). A node v is a *descendant* of node u if u is an ancestor of v. For a node v, let $T(v)$ denote the subtree of T hanging down from v (including v), and let $\omega(v)$, denote the number of nodes in $T(v)$, i.e., $\omega(v) = |T(v)|$. We refer to $\omega(v)$ as the *weight* of v.

Static routing schemes on trees. A static *routing scheme* on trees is composed of the following components.

1) A *marker* algorithm that given a tree T assigns a label $L(v)$ to each node $v \in T$.
2) A *router* algorithm that given the labels $L(w)$ and $L(v)$ of two nodes w and v in T, outputs $\text{Rout}(w, v)$, where $\text{Rout}(w, v)$ is the port number at w leading to the next node on the shortest path connecting w and v.

The most common measure to evaluate a static routing scheme is the *label size*, i.e, the maximum number of bits stored in a label. A routing scheme with asymptotically optimal label size is called *compact*. In our schemes, the labels given to the nodes may contain several fields (we use the symbol ∘ to concatenate such fields). Clearly, one can distinguish between the different fields with the aid of a sequential data structure that does not increase the asymptotic size of a label (see e.g., [7]).

The dynamic models. We assume that we may initialize the labels and data structure of the initial tree, in a *preprocessing stage*, which is completed before the dynamic scenario starts. (Clearly, no scheme can be expected to be correct before the nodes are assigned labels).

We consider the following types of topology changes. **(1)** *Add-leaf:* A new degree one node u is added as a child of an existing node v. **(2)** *Add internal node (between neighbors v and w):* Edge $e = (v, w)$ splits into two edges (v, u) and (u, w) for a new node u. If v was w's parent, then u is a child of v and w is considered a child of u. **(3)** *Remove node of degree at most 2:* A (non-root) node v of degree at most two is deleted. If v was internal node, then its (only) child becomes the child of u's parent.

In the *growing tree* model it is assumed that only the first two types of topology changes may occur, namely, Add-leaf and Add internal node. A *growing tree* consists of an initial tree that may change according to the growing tree model.

When a new leaf u is inserted as a child of an existing node v, the corresponding ports at v and u are assigned (by an adversary) a port-number, under the constraint that at any given moment, the port numbers at each node are distinct. Once an adversary assigns a port number, this number cannot be changed (unless the link is removed). We assume that at any given time t, the port numbers are encoded using $O(\log n)$ bits, where n denotes the maximal tree size until time t. (Note that for a growing tree, this means that the port numbers are encoded using $O(\log n)$ bits, where n is the current tree size.) We would like to point out that this requirement on the size of the port numbers is also used in the static scheme of [5], and is necessary for obtaining short labels, as port numbers must somehow be encoded in labels. Moreover, this requirement seems realistic, as the adversary typically encodes port numbers using $O(\log \Delta)$ bits, where Δ is the maximal degree of the node so far (in some cases, one may run the dynamic routing scheme on a dynamic spanning tree of a dynamic network; in this case the adversary would typically encode the port numbers using $O(\log \Delta)$ bits, where the degree Δ relates to the dynamic graph rather than to the dynamic spanning tree. However, the requirement holds in this case too, as $\Delta < n$).

If a leaf is removed, the corresponding link is removed, and thus the corresponding port number (at the existing parent) is also removed. If an internal node u is removed, then its parent becomes the parent of its child, and the corresponding port numbers (at the parent and child of u) remain the same.

For a routing scheme in a dynamic tree, the definition of a router remains the same, however, the marker algorithm changes to distributed *update protocol*, whose goal is to assign and maintain the labels to fit the requirements of the router.

We consider the *controlled* dynamic model (considered also in [1,8,9,10,13]), in which the topological changes do not occur spontaneously. Instead, when an entity wishes to cause a topological change at some node u, it enters a *request* at u. This request triggers the invocation of the update protocol at u, which must grant a *permit* to the request after a finite time. For this purpose, and for the purpose of updating the labels, the update protocol may send messages over the links of the underlying tree. The requested topology change is performed only after the request is granted a permit from the update protocol. This model can be found useful in various contexts of overlay networks applications, where many of the topology changes are ones that are decided by the designer of the algorithm, and therefore can be delayed, possibly beyond their inherent delay. For more details regarding the applications of the controlled model and the implementations of the topology changes, see [8,9].

For a dynamic routing scheme, we are interested in the following complexity measures.

The *label size* is the maximum number of bits in a label taken over any node v.

The *average message complexity* is the ratio of the number of messages sent during the execution to the number of nodes ever existing in the tree (including deleted nodes).

3   The Compact Routing Scheme for a Growing Tree

In this section we consider the growing tree model and establish our compact routing scheme Dyn-Rout for a growing tree, which incurs $O(\frac{\log^2 n}{\log^2 \log n})$ average message complexity. Let us first recall the compact ancestry scheme on growing trees given in Section 3 in [8].

Theorem 1. *[8] In the designer port model, there exists a dynamic compact ancestry scheme on a growing tree that incurs $O(\log n)$ average message complexity. I.e., using $O(\log n)$ average message complexity, the scheme maintains at each node w in the growing tree an ancestry label $L_{anc}(w)$ of size $O(\log n)$, such that for any two nodes u and v, given the ancestry labels $L_{anc}(u)$ and $L_{anc}(v)$ only, one can detect whether u is an ancestor of v or not.*

Let us denote the ancestry scheme given in Theorem 1 by Protocol Dyn-Anc. As mentioned, Protocol Dyn-Anc operates in the designer port model where the port numbers at each node can be freely assigned (and changed) by the designer of the scheme (as long as the port numbers are disjoint at each node). Note, however, that in contrast to the routing case, the actual enumeration of the ports is irrelevant for the correctness of the ancestry scheme (i.e., the fact weather a node is an ancestor of another node has nothing to do with port numbers). Therefore, the only place where the power of designer port model can be exploited by Protocol Dyn-Anc is to ease the message delivery protocol, and somehow save on messages. However, by maintaining a table at each node which translates port numbers that are assigned by an adversary to ones assigned by the designer of the scheme, one can operate in the fixed port model and simulate the scheme in the designer port model using the same messages and labels. Note, this table may increase the memory stored at each node; however, the table is not part of the label, and therefore does not increase the label size. It follows by the above observations that Theorem 1 also holds for the fixed port model.

Our Protocol Dyn-Rout (that operates in the fixed port model) runs Protocol Dyn-Anc. As promised in Theorem 1, for any node v in the growing tree, given its own ancestry label and the ancestry label of a destination node u, node v can find whether u is its descendant or not. Note that if u is not a descendant of v then the desired port number Rout(v, u) points at v's parent $p(v)$. In addition to other components (that will be described soon), the label $L(v)$ at each node v contains also the ancestry label $L_{anc}(v)$ (given by Protocol Dyn-Anc) and the *parent* label $L_{parent}(v)$, where the port number $port(v, p(v))$ leading from v to its parent $p(v)$ is encoded. If u is not a descendant of v then the router at v simply outputs the port number stored in $L_{parent}(v)$. However, if u is a descendant of v then Rout(v, u) leads to one of v's children, the one which is a ancestor of u. The rest of the section is dedicated to show how short labels can be efficiently maintained so that, in the above case, given the labels of v and u, node v will know the port number leading to its child which is an ancestor of u.

Our general strategy is to adapt the principles of the corresponding (fixed-port) static routing scheme in [5] (the one described in Section 3 in [5]) into the dynamic scenario. In addition to the parent and ancestry labels and other components that will be described later, the label $L(v)$ of a node v contains also the *big* label $L_{big}(v)$ and the *small* label $L_{small}(v)$.

The big label at v, $L_{big}(v)$, is a table containing $O(\log n / \log \log n)$ tuples of the form $\langle Port(v, w), \tilde{L}_{anc}(w) \rangle$, where w is a child of v, and $\tilde{L}_{anc}(w)$ is some label which informally aims to be the ancestry label of w. These 'pointed' children w of v are called *big* and all other children of v (if any) are called *small*.

Let u be a descendant of v. The role of the big label at v is to allow v to know whether one of its big children w is an ancestor of u, and if so, what is the port number at v leading to w. More precisely, given a big child w of v, we would first like to determine whether u is a descendant of w at a given time, simply by looking at $L_{anc}(u)$ and the corresponding tuple $\langle Port(v, w), \tilde{L}_{anc}(w) \rangle \in L_{big}(v)$, at the given time. In the static case, this can easily be done by letting $\tilde{L}_{anc}(w)$ equal $L_{anc}(w)$ and using the decoder of the ancestry scheme. However, in the dynamic setting, maintaining this equality at all times is impossible due to the asynchronous nature of the setting. Still, one can allow v to know (at all times) whether it's descendant u is a descendant of its big child w, using a rather simple handshake procedure, which is invoked between w and v whenever the ancestry label of w is updated, and which updates $\tilde{L}_{anc}(w)$ to be the new ancestry label at w. If v finds that the destination node u is a descendant of its big child w, the router at v simply outputs the port number $Port(v, w)$ (which is encoded in the corresponding tuple in $L_{big}(v)$).

The role of the small labels is to allow v to determine (in case its descendant u is not a descendant of any of v's big children) which of its ports leads to its small child w that is an ancestor of u.

The static scheme of [5] proposed the following. The small label at any big child of v is the same as the small label at v. In contrast, the small label at each small child w of v is the small label at v concatenated with $Port(v, w)$, the port number at v leading to w, i.e., $L_{small}(w) = L_{small}(v) \circ Port(v, w)$. This recursive definition enables v to extract the port number leading to its small child w which is an ancestor of u, simply by comparing the small labels at v and u. We refer to the procedure that compares the small labels and extracts the port number $Port(v, w)$ as Procedure COMPARE&EXTRACT.

In the static case, the $O(\log^2 n / \log\log n)$ bound on the label size follows from the following easy arguments. First, the ancestry label of each node v can be encoded using $O(\log n)$ bits. By the assumption on the size of a port number assigned by the adversary, the parent label of each node is also encoded using $O(\log n)$ bits. Since each big label contains $O(\log n / \log\log n)$ tuples, and since each tuple is encoded using $O(\log n)$ bits, we get that the size of a big label is $O(\log^2 n / \log\log n)$. Since each small label is a concatenation of port numbers, the size of a small label is determined by the sum of the sizes of the concatenated port numbers. The main trick in [5] is to choose the big children to be the $\lambda \sim O(\log n / \log\log n)$ children of v with maximal weight. This choice of the big children, guarantees that the total number of (concatenated) port numbers in a small label is $\log_\lambda n = O(\log n / \log\log n)$. Since each port number is encoded using $O(\log n)$ bits, the $O(\log^2 n / \log\log n)$ bound on the label size follows.

We would have liked to adapt that method to the dynamic setting. However, we could not find an efficient way for maintaining the above trick at all times (or even just at quiet times). In particular, it seems that even just to ensure that the weight of the big child of v is relatively large with respect to the weights of the other children of v, would require the scheme to maintain the approximate weight of the child, and the best known scheme that does that [1,9] already uses $O(\log^2 n)$ average message complexity. Informally, instead of maintaining the above trick at all times for all nodes, we make sure it holds only locally and only occasionally, whenever we invoke Procedure Reset, that is used for balancing and reorganizing certain portions of the tree.

Before dwelling into the description of Procedure Reset, let us first describe the update protocol, whose goal is to schedule and trigger the different invocations of Procedure Reset.

The update protocol: The update protocol operates in *iterations*. A new iteration starts when Procedure Reset is invoked on the whole tree. We assume that for every $j \geq 1$, during the time period between j'th time Procedure Reset is completed on the whole tree until the next time such procedure is initiated, each node knows the value n_j, which is the number of nodes at the beginning of the j'th iteration. (In particular, note that $n_1 = n_0$.) This assumption is implemented by the Reset procedure that is invoked on the whole tree in the beginning of the iteration, as explained later. Let us now describe the operation of the update protocol during the j'th iteration, for $j \geq 1$.

A node may be either *locked* or *unlocked*. Initially, all nodes are unlocked. When a request (for inserting a child) arrives at an unlocked node, it is handled by Protocol Dyn-Anc, that eventually grants it a permit. In contrast, when a request arrives at a locked node v, it is first put in a queue at v. When v becomes unlocked again (which is guaranteed to occur eventually), the requests from its queue are dequeued one by one, according to the First In First Out discipline, and are handled by Protocol Dyn-Anc.

If Protocol Dyn-Anc issues a permit to a request at a locked node v, then v delays the performance of the corresponding topology change until it becomes unlocked again. In contrast, if v is unlocked when the permit arrives, then the following happen.

The ancestry label the inserted w child of v is given by Protocol Dyn-Anc. The port numbers at w are given by the adversary (recall, each port number is encoded using $O(\log n)$ bits). If w is a leaf, then the port $Port(v, w)$ is also assigned by the adversary. In this case, the small label at w is set to be $L_{small}(v) \circ Port(v, w)$ (thus making w a small child of v). However, if w is inserted between v and its child u then the following happen. First, recall that the port leading from v to w remains the same as the port that was leading from v to u. We let the small label of w equal the small of its child u, that is, if u was a small child of v (before w was inserted) then $L_{small}(w) = L_{small}(v) \circ Port(v, w)$, and otherwise, if u was a big child of v then $L_{small}(w) = L_{small}(v)$. If u was a big child of its parent v when w was inserted then w becomes a big child of v (instead of u) and the ancestry label in the corresponding tuple is set to be the new ancestry label of w (this can be implemented instantaneously as the parent v is the one issuing the ancestry label of w, when it inserts it). In addition, the big label at w contains the tuple $\langle Port(w, u), L_{anc}(u) \rangle$, thus making u a big child of w.

Throughout the execution, each node v holds a variable $l(v)$ which informally aims at counting the number of small nodes on the path from v to the root (including v, if v is small). When a node u is inserted to the tree as a child of its parent v, its variable $l(u)$ is set as follows. If u is a leaf then $l(u) = l(v) + 1$ (recall, in this case, u is small). Otherwise, if u is inserted between v and its child w then, $l(u) = l(w)$ (recall, in this case, w is a big child of u, and u is small iff w was small before the insertion of u). Once u is inserted to the tree, its variable $l(u)$ may be updated only by Procedure Reset, in a way to be described soon.

We say that a *triggering event* occurs at some leaf u, if u joins the tree with variable that satisfies $l(u) > 8\lceil \log n_j / \log \log n_j \rceil$. This triggering event will result in an invocation of Procedure Reset$(T(\rho))$, on some subtree whose root $\rho = \rho(u)$ is one of u's ancestors, called a *anchor* node. The specific choice of the anchor ρ guarantees that the chosen subtree $T(\rho)$ is on the one hand unbalanced and on the other hand relatively small (but not too small as that may result in too many invocations of Procedure Reset.) Specifically, the *anchor* node ρ is the closest ancestor of u satisfying the following conditions.

The ANCHOR CONDITIONS: $l(\rho) \leq \frac{4 \log n_j}{\log \log n_j}$ and either one of the following holds.

1. a) ρ is not the root and b) $\omega(\rho) \leq 2n_j$ and c) ρ has a small child w such that $\omega(w) > \frac{2\omega(\rho) \log \log n_j}{\log n_j}$,
2. ρ is the root of the whole tree T.

When a triggering event occurs at a leaf u, Procedure Find_Anchor(u) is invoked at u. The goal of that procedure is to find the anchor $\rho(u)$ and to lock the nodes in the subtree $T(\rho)$ (so that Procedure Reset$(T(\rho))$ can subsequently operate on a static tree). Procedure Find_Anchor(u) can be implemented as follows. First, the leaf u creates an *agent* (see e.g., [9]). This agent then starts walking from u up the tree while locking every node it visits. The agent, coming from a child w to its parent v, informs v of w's weight. When the agent reaches some node v for the first time (coming from its child w), it initiates a broadcast and upcast operation on the subtree $T_v \setminus T_w$. The broadcast locks the nodes in $T_v \setminus T_w$, and the upcast lets each node $z \in T_v \setminus T_w$ know it weight. Subsequently, v checks whether it satisfies one of the anchor conditions. If it does, then the procedure is completed, and otherwise, the agent continues to v's parent. Procedure Find_Anchor(u) incurs $O(|T(\rho)|)$ messages, where $|T(\rho)|$ is calculated when the procedure is completed (it will be guaranteed that each such procedure is eventually completed, as explained later on).

In order to avoid collisions between the invocations of different procedures, we do the following. First, if some procedure S of type Find_Anchor tries to enter a node which initiated a Reset procedure that hasn't been completed yet, then Procedure S first waits for the Reset procedure to be completed and only then enters v and continues its action. Second, regarding collisions between different Find_Anchor procedures, when two (or more) such procedures meet at a node v, only one of them continues from v. To save on messages, the 'winning' procedure will use the outcome of the other procedures instead of redoing their work. The procedure that wins in the 'competition' is the one coming to v from its parent, if indeed one comes from there, and otherwise, it is the one coming from the child of v whose corresponding port number at v is the smallest among all candidates. The formal description of how to implement the above 'traffic rules' is straightforward, and is therefore deferred to the full paper.

Note that the protocol that grants permits to requests is Protocol Dyn-Anc. Therefore, it may happen that while some Procedure Find_Anchor tries to 'catch' a subtree and 'lock' it, nodes are continuing to join the subtree and the procedure is never completed. This undesired phenomena can be avoided as follows. Recall that our update protocol operates in iterations. Similarly, also Protocol Dyn-Anc works in iterations. Without getting into too much details regarding Protocol Dyn-Anc, we just mention the following facts. First, the root decides when an iteration starts. Second, during each iteration the number of nodes in the tree is finite, and third, between iterations, the tree T remains fixed, i.e, no topology occurs in the tree. Therefore, in order to guarantee that each procedure is completed eventually, when an iteration of Protocol Dyn-Anc ends, the next iteration is delayed, and a broadcast and upcast operation is performed on the tree, for making sure that before the next iteration starts, all Find_Anchor procedures are completed. Subsequently, when the upcast is completed, the next iteration of Protocol Dyn-Anc can safely start. We are now ready to describe Procedure Reset.

Procedure Reset: As mentioned, for balancing the tree, Protocol Dyn-Rout occasionally invokes Procedure Reset on different subtrees. (In particular, in the preprocessing stage, before the scenario actually starts, Procedure Reset is invoked on the whole initial tree for initializing the labels.) Procedure Reset, when invoked on a subtree $T(\rho)$ reorganizes it and makes it consistent with the whole tree. In the reorganization, the nodes in $T(\rho)$ are assigned new labels and variables, and may also replace their big children.

It follows from the description of the update protocol that as long as Procedure Reset($T(\rho)$) is operating, all the nodes in $T(\rho)$ are locked. Thus, the subtree $T(\rho)$ remains fixed (i.e., no topology change occurs in $T(\rho)$), and moreover, the ancestry label of each node in $T(\rho)$ remains the same. We assume that when Procedure Reset($T(\rho)$) starts, all the nodes in $T(\rho)$ are already assigned labels (the initial invocation of Procedure Reset(T), that occurs in the preprocessing stage, is assumed to start with empty labels). The assignment of new labels to the nodes in $T(\rho)$ is made carefully, in order to keep the scheme correct at all times. For that, we introduce another two labels at each label (that did not exist in the static scheme of [5]) called the *future* label and the *busy* label. The future label at each node w contains two sublabels, namely, the *future small* sublabel $f\mathrm{L}_{small}(w)$, and the *future big* sublabel $f\mathrm{L}_{big}(w)$. The busy label at each node contains a single bit. Initially, all busy labels are zero.

Procedure $\mathrm{Reset}(T(\rho))$ is initiated at the root ρ of $T(\rho)$. At the first stage, two broadcast and upcast operations are performed on $T(\rho)$, which guarantee that upon their completion, the following holds. The future big sublabel at each node $u \in T(\rho)$ contains the tuple $\langle port(u, w), L_{anc}(w)\rangle$, for each child w of u that satisfies $\omega(w) \geq \omega(u)\log\log n_j/\log n_j$. Each of these children w of u is called *future big*, and all other children of u are called *future small*. The future small sublabel of ρ is simply a copy of the small label at ρ; and the future small sublabel of each $w \in T(\rho) \setminus \{\rho\}$ is the future small label of its parent $p(w)$ concatenated with the port number $Port(p(w), w)$. i.e., $f\mathrm{L}_{small}(w) = f\mathrm{L}_{small}(p(w)) \circ Port(p(w), w)$. These two broadcast and upcast operations can trivially be implemented using $O(|T(\rho)|)$ messages.

Subsequently, after the broadcast and upcast operations are completed, the root ρ of $T(\rho)$ creates an agent that performs a DFS tour in the subtree $T(\rho)$.

Upon returning to $w \in T(\rho)$ after visiting all its children, the agent does:

(1) Replaces the small and big labels of w by the future small and future big labels of w, respectively, (2) Empties the future labels of w, and (3) Sets w's busy label to 1.

When the agent returns to ρ after visiting all the nodes in $T(\rho)$ and implementing the above, it get canceled. Subsequently, ρ initiates a broadcast and upcast operation for making sure that the following hold. (1) The variable $l(v)$ at each node $v \in T(\rho)\setminus\{\rho\}$ is precisely $l(\rho)$ plus the number of small nodes on the path from v to ρ (the path excludes ρ and includes v), (2) The busy label at each node in $T(\rho)$ is zero, and (3) If $T(\rho)$ is the whole tree, then each node knows the value $n_{j+1} = n$ (which is the current tree size).

Finally, when that operation is completed, another broadcast it initiated by ρ for unlocking all the nodes in $T(\rho)$. This completed the description of Procedure $\mathrm{Reset}(T(\rho))$. We are now ready to describe the router of the scheme.

The router: The goal of the router is to find, given the labels of any pair of nodes u and v, the current port number at u leading to the next node on the shortest path connecting u and v, i.e., $\mathrm{Rout}(u, v)$.

Using the ancestry labels and the decoder of Protocol $\mathrm{Dyn\text{-}Anc}$, the router can find whether u is an ancestor of v or not. In the case where v is not a descendant of u, the router outputs the port number stored in its parent label $L_{parent}(u)$. If v is a descendant of one of u's big children w then this is detected using the big label at u and the ancestry label at v. In this case, the router outputs $\mathrm{Rout}(u, v) = Port(u, w)$, which is encoded in the corresponding tuple in the big label of u.

If the future label at u is empty then the router outputs the port number obtained by comparing the small labels of u and v, using $\mathrm{COMPARE\&EXTRACT}$.

Consider now the case that the future label at u is not empty. First, if v is a descendant of one of u's future big children w, then this is detected using the future big sublabel at u and the ancestry label at v. In this case, the router outputs the port number $\mathrm{Rout}(u, v) = Port(u, w)$, which is encoded in the corresponding tuple in the future big sublabel of u.

Now consider the case where v is a descendant of u but not a descendant of neither one of u's big children nor a descendant of one of u's future big children. If the future label at v is not empty then the router outputs the port obtained by comparing the small labels of u and v, using COMPARE&EXTRACT; otherwise (the future label at v is empty), consider two cases. If the busy label at v is 1, then the router outputs the port obtained by comparing the future small label of u with the small label of v, using COMPARE&EXTRACT. Otherwise, if the busy label at v is 0, then the router outputs the port obtained by comparing the small labels of u and v, using COMPARE&EXTRACT.

The proof of the following theorem is deferred to the full version of this paper.

Theorem 2. *Consider the fixed port model. Protocol* Dyn-Rout *implements a routing scheme on a growing tree, which is correct at all times. The label size of the scheme is* $\Theta(\frac{\log^2 n}{\log \log n})$ *and its average message complexity is* $O(\frac{\log^2 n}{\log^2 \log n})$.

The extension of protocol Dyn-Rout for supporting also removals of nodes of degree at most 2 is deferred to the full version of this paper.

References

1. Afek, Y., Awerbuch, B., Plotkin, S.A., Saks, M.: Local management of a global resource in a communication network. J. ACM 43, 1–19 (1996)
2. Abraham, I., Gavoille, C.: Object location using path separators. In: PODC 2006 (2006)
3. Abraham, I., Gavoille, C., Malkhi, D., Nisan, N., Thorup, M.: Compact name-independent routing with minimum stretch. ACM Transactions on Algorithms 4(3) (2008)
4. Afek, Y., Gafni, E., Ricklin, M.: Upper and lower bounds for routing schemes in dynamic networks. In: FOCS 1989, pp. 370–375 (1989)
5. Fraigniaud, P., Gavoille, C.: Routing in trees. In: Orejas, F., Spirakis, P.G., van Leeuwen, J. (eds.) ICALP 2001. LNCS, vol. 2076, pp. 757–772. Springer, Heidelberg (2001)
6. Fraigniaud, P., Gavoille, C.: A Space Lower Bound for Routing in Trees. In: STACS 2002, pp. 65–75 (2002)
7. Korman, A.: General compact labeling schemes for dynamic trees. J. Distributed Computing 20(3), 179–193 (2007)
8. Korman, A.: Improved compact routing schemes for dynamic trees. In: PODC 2008 (2008)
9. Korman, A., Kutten, S.: Controller and estimator for dynamic networks. In: PODC 2007 (2007)
10. Korman, A., Peleg, D.: Compact Separator Decomposition for Dynamic Trees and Applications. J. Distributed Computing (to appear, 2008)
11. Korman, A., Peleg, D., Rodeh, Y.: Labeling schemes for dynamic tree networks. Theory Comput. Syst. 37(1), 49–75 (2004)
12. Korman, A., Peleg, D.: Labeling schemes for weighted dynamic trees. J. Information and Computation 205(12), 1721–1740 (2007)
13. Korman, A., Peleg, D.: Dynamic routing schemes for graphs with low local density. ACM Trans. on Algorithms (to appear); Korman, A., Peleg, D.: Dynamic routing schemes for general graphs. In: Bugliesi, M., Preneel, B., Sassone, V., Wegener, I. (eds.) ICALP 2006. LNCS, vol. 4051, pp. 619–630. Springer, Heidelberg (2006)
14. Santoro, N., Khatib, R.: Labelling and implicit routing in networks. The Computer Journal 28, 5–8 (1985)
15. Thorup, M.: Compact oracles for reachability and approximate distances in planar digraphs. J. of the ACM 51, 993–1024 (2004)
16. Thorup, M., Zwick, U.: Compact routing schemes. In: SPAA 2001, pp. 1–10 (2001)
17. Van Leeuwen, J., Tan, R.B.: Interval routing. The Computer Journal 30, 298–307 (1987)

An Analytical Model of Information Dissemination for a Gossip-Based Protocol

Rena Bakhshi, Daniela Gavidia, Wan Fokkink, and Maarten van Steen

Department of Computer Science, Vrije Universiteit Amsterdam, Netherlands
{rbakhshi,daniela,wanf,steen}@few.vu.nl

Abstract. We develop an analytical model of information dissemination for a gossip protocol. With this model we analyse how fast an item is replicated through a network. We also determine the optimal size of the exchange buffer, to obtain fast replication. Our results are confirmed by large-scale simulation experiments.

1 Introduction

Today, large-scale distributed systems consisting of thousands of nodes are commonplace, due to the wide availability of high-performance and low-cost devices. Such systems are highly dynamic in the sense that nodes are continuously in flux, with new nodes joining and existing nodes leaving.

In practice, large-scale systems are often emulated to discover correlations between design parameters and observed behaviour. Such experimental results provide essential data on system behaviour. However, they usually show only behaviour of a particular implementation, and can be time consuming. Moreover, in general experiments do not give a good understanding of the emergent behaviour of the system, and into how parameter settings influence the extra-functional properties of the system. As a result, it is very difficult to predict what the effects of certain design decisions are, as it is practically infeasible to explore the full range of input data. A challenge is to develop analytical models that capture (part of) the behaviour of a system, and then subsequently optimize design parameters following an analytical rather than an experimental approach.

We aim at developing and validating analytical models for gossip-based systems (cf. [1]), which rely on epidemic techniques for the communication and exchange of information. These communication protocols, while having simple specifications, show complex and often unexpected behaviour when executed on a large scale. Our analytical models of gossip protocols need to be realistic, yet, sufficiently abstract to allow for easy prediction of systems behaviour. By 'realistic' we mean that they can be applied to large-scale networks and can capture functional and extra-functional behaviour such as replication, coverage and other system dynamics (see [2]). Such models are amenable for mathematical analysis, to make precise predictions. Furthermore, we will exploit the fact that as an analytical model presents an abstraction of the original protocol, a simulation

V. Garg, R. Wattenhofer, and K. Kothapalli (Eds.): ICDCN 2009, LNCS 5408, pp. 230–242, 2009.

of the model tends to be much more efficient (in computation time and memory consumption) than a simulation of an implementation of this protocol.

In this paper, we develop an analytical model of a shuffle protocol from [3], which was developed to disseminate data items to a collection of wireless devices, in a decentralized fashion. A decentralized solution considerably decreases the probability of information loss or unavailability that may occur due to a single point of failure, or high latency due to the overload of a node. Nodes executing the protocol periodically contact each other, according to some probability distribution, and exchange data items. Concisely, a node initiates a contact with its random neighbour, pulls a random subset of items from the contacted node, simultaneously pushing its own random subset of items. This push/pull approach has a better performance than a pure push or pull approach [4,5]. Replication ensures the availability of the data items even in the face of dynamic behaviour, which is characteristic of wireless environments. And since nodes relocate data in a random fashion, nodes will eventually see all data items.

The central point of our study is a rigorous probabilistic analysis of information dissemination in a large-scale network using the aforementioned protocol. The behaviour of the protocol is modelled on an abstract level as pairwise node interactions. When two neighbouring nodes interact with each other (gossip), they may undergo a state transition (exchange items) with a certain probability. The transition probabilities depend on the probability that a given item in a node's cache has been replaced by another item after the shuffle. We calculated accurate values for these probabilities. We also determined a close approximation that is expressed by a much simpler formula, as well as a correction factor for this approximation, allowing for precise error estimations. Thus we obtain a better understanding of the emergent behaviour of the protocol, and how parameter settings influence its extra-functional behaviour.

We investigated two properties characterizing the protocol: the number of replicas of a given item in the network at a certain moment in time (replication), and the number of nodes that have 'seen' this item over time (coverage). Using the values of the transition probabilities, we determined the optimal number of items to exchange per gossip, for a fast convergence of coverage and replication. Moreover, we determined formula that captures the dissemination of an item in a fully connected network. All our modelling and analysis results are confirmed by large-scale simulations, in which simulations based on our analytical models are compared with running the actual protocol. To the best of our knowledge, we are the first to develop an accurate, realistic formal model that can be used to optimally design and fine-tune a given gossip protocol. In this sense, our main contribution is demonstrating the feasibility of a model-driven approach to developing real-world gossip protocols.

The paper is structured as follows. Sec. 2 explains the shuffle protocol. In Sec. 3 the analytical model is developed and exploited. Sec. 4 discusses the results of our experimental evaluations. Sec. 5 presents a round-based perspective of replication. Sec. 6 discusses related work. And Sec. 7 contains the conclusions. Several parts of the full version of this paper, available as [6], have been omitted:

notably the calculation of the precise formula for the probability of dropping an item, and a round-based perspective of coverage.

2   A Gossip-Based Protocol for Wireless Networks

This section describes the shuffle protocol introduced in [3]. It is a gossip protocol to disseminate data items to a collection of wireless devices. The protocol relies on replication to ensure the availability of data items in the face of dynamic behaviour, which is characteristic of wireless environments.

The system consists of a collection of wireless nodes, each of which contributes a limited amount of storage space (which we will refer to as the node's cache) to store data items. The nodes periodically swap (shuffle) data items from their cache with a randomly chosen neighbour. In this way, nodes gradually discover new items as they are disseminated through the network.

Items can be published by any user of the system, and are propagated through the network. Several copies of each data item may exist in the network. Replication may occur when a node has available storage space to keep an item it just gossiped to a neighbour.

All nodes have a common agreement on the frequency of gossiping. However, there is no agreement on when to gossip. In terms of storage space, we assume that all nodes have the same cache size c. When shuffling, each node sends a fixed number s of the c items in the cache. The gossip exchange is performed as an atomic procedure, meaning that once a node initiates an exchange with another node, these pair of nodes cannot become involved in another exchange until the current exchange is finished.

In order to execute the protocol, the initiating node needs to contact a gossiping partner. We describe the protocol from the point of view of each participating node. We refer to [3] for a more detailed description.

Node A initiates the shuffle by executing the following steps:

1. picks a neighbouring node B at random;
2. sends s randomly selected items from its local cache to B;
3. receives s items from the local cache of B;
4. checks whether any of the received items are already in its cache; if so, these received items are eliminated;
5. adds the rest of the received items to the local cache; if the total number of items exceeds cache size c, removes items among the ones that were sent by A to B, but not those that were also received by A from B, until the cache contains c items.

In response to being contacted by A, node B consecutively executes steps 3, 2, 4 and 5 above, with all occurrences of A and B interchanged.

According to the protocol, each node agrees to keep the items received from a neighbour. Given the limited storage space available in each node, keeping the items received during an exchange implies discarding some items that the node has in its cache. By picking the items to be discarded from the ones that have been sent to the neighbour, the conservation of data in the network is ensured.

3   An Analytical Model of Information Dissemination

We analyse dissemination of a data item in a network in which the nodes execute the shuffle protocol.

3.1   Probabilities of State Transitions

We present a model of the shuffle protocol that captures the presence or absence of a generic item d after shuffling of two nodes A and B. There are four possible states of the caches of A and B before the shuffle: both hold d, either A's or B's cache holds d, or neither cache holds d.

We use the notation $P(a_2b_2|a_1b_1)$ for the probability that from state a_1b_1 after a shuffle we get to state a_2b_2, with $a_i, b_i \in \{0,1\}$. The indices a_1, a_2 and b_1, b_2 indicate the presence (if equal to 1) or the absence (if equal to 0) of a generic item d in the cache of an initiator A and the contacted node B, respectively. For example, $P(01|10)$ means that node A had d before the shuffle, which then moved to the cache of B, afterwards. Due to the symmetry of information exchange between nodes A and B in the shuffle protocol, $P(a_2b_2|a_1b_1) = P(b_2a_2|b_1a_1)$.

Fig. 1 depicts all possible outcomes for the caches of gossiping nodes as a state transition diagram. If before the exchange A and B do not have d ($a_1b_1 = 00$), then clearly after the exchange A and B do not have d ($a_2b_2 = 00$). Otherwise, if A or B has d ($a_1 = 1 \vee b_1 = 1$), the protocol guarantees that after the exchange A or B has d ($a_2 = 1 \vee b_2 = 1$). Thus, the state $(-, -)$ has a self-transition, and no other outgoing or incoming transitions.

We determine values for all probabilities $P(a_2b_2|a_1b_1)$. They are expressed in terms of probabilities P_{select} and P_{drop}. Here P_{select} expresses the chance of an item to be selected by a node from its local cache when engaged in an exchange. And P_{drop} represents a prob-

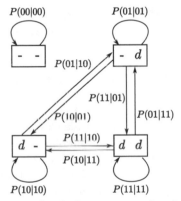

Fig. 1. Symbolic representation for caches of gossiping nodes

ability that an item which can be overwritten (meaning that it is in the exchange buffer of its node, but not of the other node in the shuffle) is indeed overwritten by an item received by its node in the shuffle. Due to the symmetry of the protocol, these probabilities are the same for both initiating and contacted nodes. In Sec. 3.2, we will calculate P_{select} and P_{drop}. We write $P_{\neg select}$ for $1 - P_{select}$ and $P_{\neg drop}$ for $1 - P_{drop}$.

As explained above, $P(00|00) = 1$. We now focus on the case where $a_1b_1 = 01$, meaning that before shuffling, a copy of d is only in the cache of B.

$a_2b_2 = 01$: B did not select (to send) d and, thus, B did not overwrite d; i.e.
$\quad P(01|01) = P_{\neg select}$.
$a_2b_2 = 10$: B selected d and dropped it; i.e. $P(10|01) = P_{select} \cdot P_{drop}$.

$a_2b_2 = 11$: B selected d and kept it; i.e. $P(11|01) = P_{select} \cdot P_{\neg drop}$.
$a_2b_2 = 00$: as said, completely discarding d is impossible; i.e. $P(00|01) = 0$.

Due to the symmetry, the case $a_1b_1 = 10$ is similar. We now deal with the case where $a_1b_1 = 11$, meaning that before shuffling, d is in the caches of A and B.

$a_2b_2 = 01$: A selected d and dropped it, and B did not select d; i.e. $P(01|11) =$
    $P_{select} \cdot P_{drop} \cdot P_{\neg select}$.
$a_2b_2 = 10$: symmetric to the previous one: $P(10|11) = P_{\neg select} \cdot P_{select} \cdot P_{drop}$.
$a_2b_2 = 11$: after the shuffle both A and B have d, because either:
    – A and B did not select d, i.e. $P_{\neg select} \cdot P_{\neg select}$;
    – A and B selected d (thus, both kept it), i.e. $P_{select} \cdot P_{select}$;
    – A selected d and kept it and B did not select d: $P_{select} \cdot P_{\neg drop} \cdot P_{\neg select}$;
    – symmetric case to the previous one: $P_{\neg select} \cdot P_{select} \cdot P_{\neg drop}$.
    Thus, $P(11|11) = P_{\neg select} \cdot P_{\neg select} + P_{select} \cdot P_{select} + 2 \cdot P_{select} \cdot P_{\neg select} \cdot P_{\neg drop}$.
$a_2b_2 = 00$: as before, $P(00|11) = 0$.

3.2 Probabilities of Selecting and Dropping an Item

The following analysis assumes that all node caches are full (that is, the network is already running for a while). Moreover, we assume a uniform distribution of items over the network; this assumption is supported by experiments in [3,4].

Consider nodes A and B engaged in a shuffle, and let B receive the exchange buffer S_A from A. Let k be the number of duplicates, i.e. the items of an intersection of the node cache C_B and the exchange buffer of its gossiping partner S_A (i.e. $S_A \cap C_B$). Recall that C_A and C_B contain the same number of items for all A and B, and likewise for S_A and S_B; we use c and s for these values. The total number of different items in the network is denoted as n.

The probability of selecting an item d in the cache is the probability of a single selection trial (i.e. $\frac{1}{c}$) times the number of selections (i.e. s): $P_{select} = \frac{s}{c}$.

The shuffle protocol demands that all items in S_A are kept in C_B after the shuffle. This implies that: a) all items in $S_A \backslash C_B$ will overwrite items in $S_B \subseteq C_B$, and b) all items in $S_A \cap C_B$ are kept in C_B. Thus, the probability that an item from S_B will be overwritten is determined by the probability that an item from S_A is in C_B, but not in S_B. Namely, the items in $S_B \backslash S_A$ provide a space in the cache for items from $S_A \backslash C_B$. We would like to express the probability P_{drop} of a selected item d in $S_B \backslash S_A$ (or $S_A \backslash S_B$) to be overwritten by another item in C_B (or C_A). Due to symmetry, this probability is the same for A and B; therefore, we only calculated the expected probability that an item in $S_B \backslash S_A$ is dropped from C_B. Let $2s \leq c \leq n - s$. Then

$$E[P_{drop}] = \frac{n-c}{\binom{n}{s}} \sum_{k=0}^{s-1} \left(\frac{(n-c)-1}{(s-k)-1} \right) \sum_{\widehat{s}=0}^{k} \frac{\binom{c-s}{k-\widehat{s}}\binom{s}{\widehat{s}}}{s-\widehat{s}} \tag{1}$$

A detailed explanation of how this formula was calculated can be found [6].

3.3   Simplification of P_{drop}

To gain a clearer insight into the emergent behaviour of the gossiping protocol we make an effort to simplify the formula for the probability P_{drop} of an item in $S_B \backslash S_A$ to be dropped from C_B after a shuffle. Therefore, we re-examine the relationships between the k duplicates received from a neighbour, the $\hat{s}$ items of the overlap $S_A \cap S_B$, and P_{drop}. Suppose that $|S_A \cap C_B| = k$, and let's estimate P_{drop} by considering each item from S_A separately, and calculating the probability that the item is a duplicate (i.e., is also in C_B). The probability of an item from S_A to be a duplicate (also present in C_B) is $\frac{c}{n}$. In view of the uniform distribution of items over the network, the items in a node's cache are a random sample from the universe of n data items; so all items in S_A have the same chance to be a duplicate. Thus, the expected number of items in $S_A \cap C_B$ can be estimated by $E[k] = s \cdot \frac{c}{n}$. And the expected number of items in $S_A \cap S_B$ can be estimated by $E[\hat{s}] = k \cdot \frac{s}{c}$, because only the k items in $S_A \cap C_B$ may end up in $S_A \cap C_B$; $\frac{s}{c}$ captures the probability that an item from C_B is also selected to be in S_B. Thus the probability of an item in $S_B \backslash S_A$ to be dropped from C_B after a shuffle is $E[P_{drop}] = \frac{s-k}{s-\hat{s}} = \frac{s - s \cdot \frac{c}{n}}{s - s \cdot \frac{c}{n} \cdot \frac{s}{c}} = \frac{n-c}{n-s}$. This is valid for $s \le c < n$.

Substituting the expressions for P_{select} and the simplified P_{drop} into the formulas for the transition probabilities in Fig. 1, we obtain:

$$P(01|01) = P(10|10) = \frac{c-s}{c} \qquad\qquad P(01|11) = P(10|11) = \frac{s}{c}\frac{c-s}{c}\frac{n-c}{n-s}$$

$$P(10|01) = P(01|10) = \frac{s}{c}\frac{n-c}{n}\frac{1}{s} \qquad\qquad P(11|11) = 1 - 2\frac{s}{c}\frac{c-s}{c}\frac{n-c}{n-s}$$

$$P(11|01) = P(11|10) = \frac{s}{c}\frac{c-s}{n-s}$$

To verify the accuracy of the proposed simplification for $E[P_{drop}]$, we compare the simplification and formula (1) for different values of n. We plot the difference of the exact P_{drop} and the simplification, for $c = 250$ and $c = 500$ (Fig. 2).

We now examine how closely the simplified formula $E[P_{drop}] = \frac{n-c}{n-s}$ (here referred as $S(n, c, s)$) approximates formula (1) (here referred as $E(n, c, s)$). We compared the difference between these two formulas using an implementation on the basis of common fractions, which provides loss-less calculation. We observe

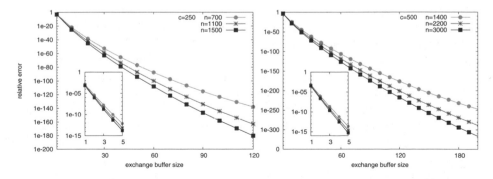

Fig. 2. The difference of the exact P_{drop} and its approximation, for different n and c

that the inverse of the difference of the inverse values of both formulas, i.e. $e_{c,s}(n) = \left(E(n,c,s)^{-1} - S(n,c,s)^{-1} \right)^{-1}$, exhibits a certain pattern for different values of n, c and s. For $s = 1$, $E(n,c,1) = \frac{n-c}{n}$, whereas $S(n,c,1) = \frac{n-c}{n-1}$. We then investigate the correction factor θ in $E(n,c,s) = \frac{n-c}{(n-s)+\theta}$. For $s = 1$, $\theta = 1$; but, for $s > 1$ the situation is more complicated. For $s = 2$, we got $e_{4,2}(7) - e_{4,2}(6) = 3.5$, $e_{4,2}(8) - e_{4,2}(7) = 4$, $e_{4,2}(9) - e_{4,2}(8) = 4.5$, and etc. Thus we calculated the first, the second and other (forward) differences[1] over n. We recognized that the s-th difference of the function $e_{c,s}(n)$ is always $\frac{1}{s}$. Moreover, at the point $n = 0$ the 1st, ..., s-th differences of the function $e_{c,s}$ exhibit a pattern similar to the Pascal triangle [8]; i.e. for $d \geq 1$ the d-th difference is: $(\Delta^d e_{c,s})(0) = \frac{1}{s \cdot \binom{s-1}{d}}$ (assuming $\binom{a}{b} = 0$, whenever $b > a$). The initial difference at $n = 0$ allowed us to use the Newton forward difference equation [7] to derive the following formula for $n > 0$: $E[P_{drop}] = \frac{n-c}{(n-s)+\frac{1}{\gamma}}$, where

$$\gamma = \sum_{d=0}^{s-1} \frac{\binom{n}{d}}{s \cdot \binom{s-1}{d}} = \frac{\binom{n}{s}}{(n-s)+1} \cdot \sum_{d=0}^{s-1} \frac{1}{\binom{n-d}{(s-1)-d}} \tag{2}$$

Extensive experiments with Mathematica and Matlab indicate that $\frac{n-c}{(n-s)+\frac{1}{\gamma}}$ and formula (1) coincide. We can also see in Fig. 2 that the correction factor is small.

3.4   Optimal Size for the Exchange Buffer

We study what is the optimal value for fast convergence of replication and coverage with respect to an item d. Since d is introduced at only one node in the network, one needs to optimize the chance that an item is duplicated. That is, the probabilities $P(11|01)$ and $P(11|10)$ should be optimized (then $P(01|11)$ and $P(10|11)$ are optimized as well, intuitively because for each duplicated item in a shuffle, another item must be dropped). These

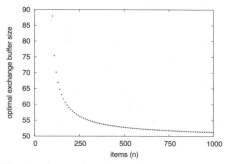

Fig. 3. Optimal value of exchange buffer size, depending on n

probabilities both equal $\frac{s}{c}\frac{c-s}{n-s}$; we compute when the s-derivative of this formula is zero. This yields the equation $s^2 - 2ns + nc = 0$; considering $s \leq n$, the only solution of this equation is $s = n - \sqrt{n(n-c)}$. We conclude that this is the optimal value for s to obtain fast convergence of replication and coverage. This will also be confirmed by the experiments and analyses in the following sections.

---

[1] A forward difference of discrete function $f : \mathbb{Z} \rightarrow \mathbb{Z}$ is a function $\Delta f : \mathbb{Z} \rightarrow \mathbb{Z}$, $\Delta f(n) = f(n+1) - f(n)$ (cf. [7]).

4   Experimental Evaluation

In order to test the validity of the analytical model of information spread under the shuffle protocol presented in the previous section, we followed an experimental approach. We compared properties observed while running the shuffle protocol in a large-scale deployment with simulations of the model under the same conditions. These experiments show that the analytical model indeed captures information spread of the shuffle protocol. We note that a simulation of the analytical model is much more efficient (in computation time and memory consumption) than a simulation of the implementation of the shuffle protocol.

The experiments simulate the case where a new item d is introduced at one node in a network, in which all caches are full and uniformly populated by $n = 500$ items. They were performed on a network of $N = 2500$ nodes, arranged in a square grid topology (50×50), where each node can communicate only with its four immediate neighbours (to the North, South, East and West). This configuration of nodes is arbitrary, we only require a large number of nodes for the observation of emergent behaviour. Our aim is to validate the correctness of our analytical model, not to test the endless possibilities of network configurations. The model and the shuffle protocol do not make any assumptions about the network. The network configuration is provided by the simulation environment and can easily be changed into something different, e.g. other network topology. For this reason, we have chosen this large grid for testing, although other configurations could have been possible. Each node has a cache size of $c = 100$, and sends s items when gossiping. In each round, every node randomly selects one of its neighbours, and updates its state according to the transition probabilities introduced before (Fig. 1). This mimics (the probabilities of) an actual exchange

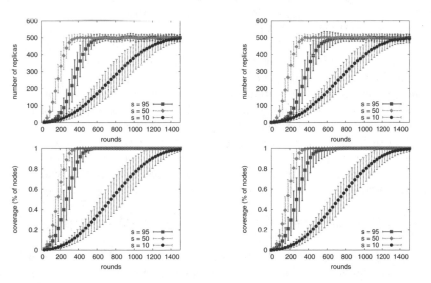

Fig. 4. The shuffle protocol (left) and the model (right), for $N = 2500$, $n = 500$, $c = 100$ and different values of s

of items between a pair of nodes according to the shuffle protocol. In the experiments, after each gossip round, we measured the total number of copies of d in the network (replication), and how many nodes in total have seen d (coverage). To fill the caches of the nodes with a random selection of items, measurements are initiated after 1000 gossip rounds. In other words, 500 different items are inserted at the beginning of the simulation, and shuffled for 1000 rounds. During this time, items are replicated and the replicas fill the caches of all nodes. At round 1000, a copy of the fresh item d is inserted at a random location, and its spread through the network is tracked over the next 2000 rounds.

Fig. 4 shows the behaviour of both the shuffle protocol and the analytical model in terms of replication and coverage of d, for various values of s. Each curve in the graphs represents the average and standard deviation calculated over 100 runs. The experiments with the model calculate P_{drop} using the simplified formula $\frac{n-c}{n-s}$ described in Sec. 3.3. Clearly the results obtained from the model (right) resemble closely the ones from executing the protocol (left). In all cases, the network converges to a situation in which there are 500 copies of d, i.e. replication is $\frac{500}{2500} = 0.2$; this agrees with the fact that $\frac{c}{n} = \frac{100}{500} = 0.2$. Moreover, replication and coverage display the fastest convergence when $s = 50$; this agrees with the fact that $n - \sqrt{n(n-c)} = 500 - \sqrt{500 \cdot 400} \approx 50$ (cf. Sec. 3.4).

5   Round-Based Modelling of Replication

In this section we exploit the analytical model of information dissemination to perform a mathematical analysis of replication with regard to the shuffle protocol. For the particular case of a network with full connectivity, where a node can gossip with any other node in the network, we can find explicit expressions for the dissemination of a generic item d in terms of the probabilities presented in Sec. 3. We construct a differential equation that captures replication of item d from a round-based perspective. Thus we can determine the long-term behaviour of the system as a function of the parameters. In the full version [6], also a differential equation for coverage is determined and exploited.

One node introduces a new item d into the network at time $t = 0$, by placing it into its cache. From that moment on, d is replicated as a consequence of gossiping among nodes. Let $x(t)$ represent the percentage of nodes in the network that have d in their cache at time t, where each gossip round takes one time unit. The variation in x per time unit $\frac{dx}{dt}$ can be derived based on the probability that d will replicate or disappear after an exchange between two nodes, where at least one of the nodes has d in its cache:

$$\frac{dx}{dt} = [P(11|10) + P(11|01)] \cdot (1 - x) \cdot x - [P(10|11) + P(01|11)] \cdot x \cdot x$$

The first term represents duplication of d when a node that has d in its cache initiates the shuffle, and contacts a node that does not have d. The second term represents the opposite situation, when a node that does not have d initiates a shuffle with a node that has d. The third and fourth term in the equation

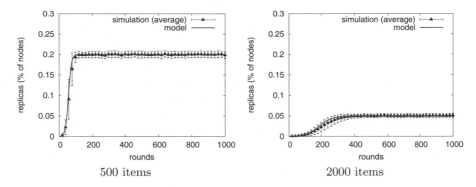

Fig. 5. Percentage of nodes in the network with a replica of item d in their cache, for $N = 2500$, $c = 100$, $s = 50$, and $n = 500$ or $n = 2000$

represent the cases where both nodes have d in their cache, and after the exchange only one copy of d remains. Substituting $P(11|10) = P(11|01) = \frac{s}{c}\frac{c-s}{n-s}$ and $P(10|11) = P(01|11) = \frac{s}{c}\frac{n-c}{n-s}\frac{c-s}{c}$, we obtain

$$\frac{dx}{dt} = 2 \cdot \frac{s}{c} \cdot \frac{c-s}{n-s} \cdot x \cdot \left(1 - \frac{n}{c} \cdot x\right) \tag{3}$$

The solution of this equation, taking into account that $x(0) = \frac{1}{N}$, is

$$x(t) = \frac{e^{\alpha t}}{(N - \frac{n}{c}) + \frac{n}{c}e^{\alpha t}} \tag{4}$$

where α denotes $2\frac{s}{c}\frac{c-s}{n-s}$ and N is the number of nodes in the network. By imposing stationarity, i.e. $\frac{dx}{dt} = 0$, we find the stationary solution $\frac{c}{n}$. This agrees with the fact that the protocol achieves a uniform distribution of items over the network. Namely, since there are Nc cache entries in the network in total, the average number of copies of an individual item in the network converges to $\frac{Nc}{n}$; so replication converges to $\frac{c}{n}$.

We evaluate the accuracy of $x(t)$ as a representation of the fraction of nodes carrying a replica of d, by running a series of experiments where $N = 2500$ nodes execute the shuffle protocol, and their caches are monitored for the presence of d. Unlike the experiments in Sec. 4, we assume full connectivity; that is, for each node, all other nodes are within reach. After 1000 rounds, where items are disseminated and replicated, a new item d is inserted at a random node, at time $t = 0$. We track the number of replicas of d for the next 1000 rounds. The experiment is repeated 100 times and the results are averaged. The simulation results and $x(t)$, presented in Fig. 5, show the same initial increase in replicas after d has been inserted, and in both cases the steady state reaches precisely the expected value $\frac{c}{n}$ predicted from the stationary solution.

We repeat the calculation from Sec. 3.4, but now against $x(t)$, to determine which size of the exchange buffer yields the fastest convergence to the steady-state

for both replication and coverage. That is, we search for the s that maximizes the value of $x(t)$. We first compute the derivative of $x(t)$ with respect to s ($z(t, s)$), and then derive the value of s that maximizes $x(t)$, by taking $z(\cdot, m) = \frac{\partial x}{\partial s}|_m = 0$:
$z(t, s) = \frac{\partial x}{\partial s} = \frac{2e^{kt}(cN-n)(cn+s(-2n+s))t}{(cN+(-1+e^{kt})n)^2(n-s)^2}$, where $k = 2\frac{s}{c}\frac{c-s}{n-s}$. Let $z(t, s) = 0$. For $t > 0$, $cn = s(2n - s)$. Taking into the account that $s \leq n$, the only solution for this equation is $s = n - \sqrt{n(n - c)}$. So this coincides with the optimal exchange buffer size found in Sec. 3.4.

6   Related Work

Two areas of research are relevant to our paper: rigorous analysis of gossip (and related) protocols, and results from mathematical theory of epidemics [9,10]. Results from epidemics are often used in the analysis of gossip protocols [11]. We restrict our overview to relevant papers from the area of gossip protocols.

Allavena et al. [12] proposed a membership protocol, and analysed the evolution of the number of links between two nodes executing the protocol. They calculated the expected time until a network partition occurs. Eugster et al. [13] presented a lightweight probabilistic broadcast algorithm, and analysed the evolution of processes that gossip one message. The states of the Markov chain are the number of processes that propagate one gossip message. From the Markov chain, the distribution of the gossiping nodes is computed. Their analysis shows that the expected number of rounds to propagate the message to the entire system does not depend on the out-degree of nodes. These results are based on the assumption that individual out-degrees are uniform. However, this simplification has shown to be valid only for small systems (cf. [4]). Bonnet [14] studied the evolution of the in-degree distribution of nodes executing the Cyclon protocol [15]. From the Markov chain the distribution to which the protocol converges is determined. Boyd et al. [16] analysed a gossip protocol in which nodes compute the average of their local measurements. The Markov chain is defined by a weighted random walk on the graph. Every time step, a pair of nodes communicates with a certain probability, and sets their values to the average of their current values. The authors considered the optimization of the neighbor selection probabilities for each node, to find the fastest-mixing Markov chain (for fast convergence of the algorithm) on the graph. Deb et al. [17] studied the adaptation of random network coding to gossip protocols. The authors analysed the expected time and message complexity of two gossip protocols for message transmission with pure push and pure pull approaches.

7   Conclusions

We have demonstrated that it is possible to model a gossip protocol through a rigorous probabilistic analysis of the state transitions of a pair of gossiping nodes. We have shown, through an extensive simulation study, that the dissemination of a data item can be faithfully reproduced by the model. Having an accurate model of node interactions, we have been able to carry out the following:

- After finding precise expressions for the probabilities involved in the model, we provide a simplified version of the transition probabilities. These simplified, yet accurate, expressions can be easily computed, allowing us to simulate the dissemination of an item without the complexity of executing the actual shuffle protocol. These simulations use very little state (only some parameters and variables, as opposed to maintaining a cache) and can be executed in a fraction of the time required to run the protocol.
- The model reveals relationships between system parameters. Armed with this knowledge, we successfully optimize one of the parameters (the size of the exchange buffer) to obtain fast convergence of replication.
- Under the assumption of full connectivity, we are able to use the transition probabilities to model replication and coverage. Each property is ultimately expressed as a formula which is shown to display the same behavior as the average behavior of the protocol, verifying the validity of the model.

While gossip protocols are easy to understand, even for a simple push/pull protocol, the interactions between nodes are unexpectedly complex. Understanding these interactions provides insight into the mechanics behind the emergent behavior of gossip protocols. We believe that understanding the mechanics of gossiping is the key to optimizing (and even shaping) the emergent properties that make gossiping appealing as communication paradigm for distributed systems.

References

1. Bakhshi, R., Bonnet, F., Fokkink, W., Haverkort, B.: Formal analysis techniques for gossiping protocols. ACM SIGOPS Oper. Syst. Rev. 41(5), 28–36 (2007)
2. Eugster, P., Guerraoui, R., Kermarrec, A.M., Massoulié, L.: Epidemic Information Dissemination in Distributed Systems. IEEE Computer 37(5), 60–67 (2004)
3. Gavidia, D., Voulgaris, S., van Steen, M.: A gossip-based distributed news service for wireless mesh networks. In: Proc. WONS 2006, pp. 59–67. IEEE, Los Alamitos (2006)
4. Jelasity, M., Voulgaris, S., Guerraoui, R., Kermarrec, A.M., van Steen, M.: Gossip-based peer sampling. ACM TOCS 25(3) (2007)
5. Karp, R., Schindelhauer, C., Shenker, S., Vocking, B.: Randomized rumor spreading. In: Proc. FOCS 2000, pp. 565–574. IEEE, Los Alamitos (2000)
6. Bakhshi, R., Gavidia, D., Fokkink, W., van Steen, M.: An analytical model of information dissemination for a gossip-based protocol (2008), http://arxiv.org/abs/0810.1571
7. Abramowitz, M., Stegun, I.A.: Handbook of Mathematical Functions with Formulas, Graphs, and Mathematical Tables, 9th edn. Dover, New York (1972)
8. Graham, R., Knuth, D., Potashnik, O.: Concrete Mathematics, 2nd edn. Addison-Wesley, Reading (1994)
9. Bailey, N.: Mathematical Theory of Infectious Diseases and Its Applications, 2nd edn. Griffin, London (1975)
10. Daley, D., Gani, J.: Epidemic Modelling: An Introduction. Cambridge University Press, Cambridge (1999)
11. Eugster, P., Guerraoui, R., Kermarrec, A.M., Massoulié, L.: From epidemics to distributed computing. IEEE Computer 37(5), 60–67 (2004)

12. Allavena, A., Demers, A., Hopcroft, J.E.: Correctness of a gossip based membership protocol. In: Proc. PODC 2005, pp. 292–301. ACM, New York (2005)
13. Eugster, P., Guerraoui, R., Handurukande, S., Kermarrec, A.M., Kouznetsov, P.: Lightweight Probabilistic Broadcast. ACM TOCS 21(4), 341–374 (2003)
14. Bonnet, F.: Performance analysis of Cyclon, an inexpensive membership management for unstructured P2P overlays. Master thesis, ENS Cachan Bretagne, University of Rennes, IRISA (2006)
15. Voulgaris, S., Gavidia, D., van Steen, M.: Cyclon: Inexpensive membership management for unstructured P2P overlays. Netw. Syst. Manag. 13(2), 197–217 (2005)
16. Boyd, S., Ghosh, A., Prabhakar, B., Shah, D.: Gossip algorithms: Design, analysis and applications. In: Proc. INFOCOM 2005, vol. 3, pp. 1653–1664. IEEE, Los Alamitos (2005)
17. Deb, S., Médard, M., Choute, C.: Algebraic gossip: a network coding approach to optimal multiple rumor mongering. IEEE/ACM TON 14(SI), 2486–2507 (2006)

A Distributed $O(|E|)$ Algorithm
for Optimal Link-Reversal

Sukhamay Kundu

Computer Sc. Dept, Louisiana State University
Baton Rouge, LA 70803, USA
kundu@csc.lsu.edu

Abstract. We first characterize the minimal link-sets L whose directions must be reversed for reestablishing one or more directed paths from each node x to a fixed destination node d in a network when a link fails. Then, we give a distributed $O(|E|)$ algorithm for determining such a link-set L, where $|E| = \sharp$(links in the network). This improves the previous lower bound $O(n^2)$, where $n = \sharp$(nodes in the network). The minimality of the reversed link-set L has other important consequences.

1 Introduction

We consider a connected network $G = (V, E)$ with a fixed destination node d, where all links E are directed to form an acyclic digraph with one or more directed paths to d from each node x. A message arriving at $x \neq d$ along any of its incoming links is forwarded via one of its outgoing links. Thus, a message originating at any node follows an acyclic path and reaches d. The link-reversal is an important technique to reestablish one or more new xd-paths for each x when a failed link (y, z) destroys all current yd-paths and possibly all xd-paths from some other nodes x as well. Our algorithm differs from other link-reversal algorithms in several ways: (1) we first determine a minimal set of links L whose directions can be reversed to reestablish at least one path to d from each node x, keeping the network acyclic, and then we reverse the direction of the links in L; in particular, we reverse a link at most once. (2) it improves the time complexity to $O(|E|)$ from $O(|V|^2)$ for the previous algorithms [1-4], and (3) each node x knows when its computation terminates so that it can begin to redirect the messages properly towards the destination node d along the new xd-paths.

The importance of minimizing the reversed link-set L can be seen follows. For each link $u \rightarrow v \in L$, the messages currently queued at u for transmission to d have to be redirected now along a new link $u \rightarrow w$. Also, the messages that are queued at v (some of which might have arrived at v via the link $u \rightarrow v$) may be directed now either along $v \rightarrow u$ or $v \rightarrow w'$ for $w' \neq u$ (which might also be in L). Clearly, it would be best if we could choose L that minimizes $|\{v: v$ is one of the end nodes of a link in $L\}|$. Our algorithm does not always achieve this. Some other link-reversal algorithms in the literature are TORA [2, 3] and LMR [4]; they are variations of the original algorithm in [1]. The performance

V. Garg, R. Wattenhofer, and K. Kothapalli (Eds.): ICDCN 2009, LNCS 5408, pp. 243–250, 2009.
© Springer-Verlag Berlin Heidelberg 2009

analysis of a class of link-reversal algorithms is given in [5], [6] gives an overview of link-reversal algorithms, and [7, 8] give some recent surveys.

2   Terminology

We sometimes write $x \to x'$ to emphasize that the undirected link $(x, x') \in E$ is currently directed from x to x'. We say that both x and x' are *incident* with or *belong* to the link $x \to x'$. A path π from x to y (in short, an xy-path) will mean a directed path; we say that a node u is incident with or belongs to π if it belongs to a link in π. We write $N^+(x) = \{x'$: the link (x, x') is directed as $x \to x'\}$; the nodes in $N^+(x)$ are called the *downstream* neighbors of x. Likewise, we write $N^-(x) = \{x'$: the link (x, x') is directed as $x' \to x\}$ and the nodes in $N^-(x)$ are called the *upstream* neighbors of x. The node x is a *source*-node if $N^-(x) = \emptyset$ and is a *sink*-node if $N^+(x) = \emptyset$. Initially, d is the only sink-node.

Let $G(y, z)$ denote the directed network G without the failed link $y \to z$. We assume that the elimination of the link $y \to z$ destroys all yd-paths without disconnecting the network itself, i.e., $G(y, z)$ is still connected as an undirected graph. This means $y \to z$ is the only downstream link from y, and y is the only sink-node other than d in $G(y, z)$. Let $V_b = \{x$: there is no xd-path in $G(y, z)\}$, the set of "bad" nodes; clearly, $y \in V_b$. For $x \in V_b$, all xd-paths in G use the link $y \to z$. Let $V_g = V - V_b$, the set of "good" nodes, i.e., the nodes which still have at least one path to d in $G(y, z)$. See Fig. 1(i). The nodes V_b form an acyclic digraph of G with node y as the only sink-node and the nodes V_g form an acyclic digraph of G with node d as the only sink-node. Also, all links connecting nodes in V_g and nodes in V_b are directed to nodes in V_b, and there is at least one such link. Note that node z can be arbitrarily far away from node d. We write G_b for the subdigraph of G on V_b and G_g for the subdigraph of G on V_g.

We write $V_{bg} = \{x \in V_g$: there is a link $x \to x'$ for some $x' \in V_b\} \subset V_g$. This is the subset of good nodes which have at least one path in $G(y, z)$ to y without using any link in G_g. We define $V_{\overline{bg}} = \{x \in V_g$: there is a path in $G(y, z)$ from x to some node in V_b and hence to $y\} \subset V_g$; this is the subset of good nodes which have at least one path to y using zero or more links in G_g. Clearly, $V_{bg} \subseteq V_{\overline{bg}}$ and the nodes d and z do not belong to $V_{\overline{bg}}$. We write G_{bg} for the subdigraph of G on V_{bg}. We sometimes call a node in V_b simply a b-node, a node in V_{bg} a bg-node, a node in $V_{\overline{bg}} - V_{bg}$ a $\overline{bg}$-node, and finally a node in $V_g - V_{\overline{bg}}$ a g-node. Note that a bg-node is a good-node that has a downstream b-node neighbor, and that not all good nodes are g-nodes. We write type(x) for the $b/g/bg/\overline{bg}$-type of node x. In Fig. 1(i), the sets V_b, V_g, V_{bg}, and $V_{\overline{bg}}$ are unchanged if we remove any one or more of the links in $\{8 \to 7, 8 \to 6, 7 \to 6\}$ except for removing both $8 \to 7$ and $8 \to 6$; in that case, the nodes 8 and 9 become b-nodes.

3   Minimal Link-Sets for Reversal

Definition 1. *A subset of links L in $G(y, z)$ is called a reversal link-set if the reversal of their directions reestablishes at least one xd-path in $G(y, z)$ from*

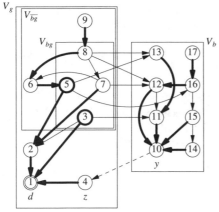

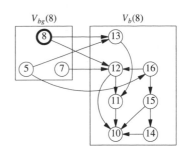

(i) A network G with all links directed to form an acyclic digraph with d as the only sink-node.

(ii) The links $L(8)$, the nodes $V_{bg}(8)$ and $V_b(8)$ belonging to $L(8)$, and the subdgraph $G(8)$ of G.

Fig. 1. Illustration of B_b, V_g, V_{bg}, etc. The bold lines show a spanning-tree T_g on V_g rooted at d and a spanning-tree T_b on V_b rooted at y.

each node x, keeping the digraph acyclic. We write L_{min} for a minimal reversal link-set set L; such a set does not contain any link joining the nodes in V_g.

In Fig. 1(i), the two possible minimal L are $L_{min} = \{3 \to 11,\ 11 \to 10\}$, which corresponds to the links on the paths from node 3 to node 10, and $L_{min} = \{5 \to 16,\ 5 \to 13,\ 16 \to 15,\ 16 \to 12,\ 15 \to 14,\ 15 \to 10,\ 13 \to 11,\ 12 \to 11,\ 12 \to 10,\ 11 \to 10\}$, which corresponds to the links on the paths from node 5 to node 10. There are many non-minimal L's. It is clear that for any reversal link-set L we have L contains at least one link from $L_{bg} = \{x \to x': x \in V_{bg}$ and $x' \in V_b\}$. We now characterize all reversal link-sets L. Let $x \in V_{bg}$ and π_{xy} be an xy-path. If we reverse the directions of all links in π_{xy}, then each node in V_b now has a path to x and hence to d. To see this, let $x_b \in V_b$ which is not on π_{xy} and let π' be a path from x_b to a node x'' in π_{xy}, where x'' may equal y. Let π'' be the initial part of π_{xy} upto the node x''. Clearly, π' together with reversed version of π'' gives an $x_b x$-path and hence we have an $x''d$-path. However, just reversing the links in π_{xy} may create one or more cycles, as is the case in Fig. 1(i) for $x = 8$ and $\pi_{xy} = \langle 8, 12, 11, 10 \rangle$. Some of the cycles formed on reversing the links in the path π_{xy} are $\langle 8, 13, 11, 12, 8 \rangle$ and $\langle 12, 10, 11, 12 \rangle$. Indeed, any cycle formed would involve links of a path π_{uv} joining two nodes u and v on π_{xy} where π_{uv} is disjoint from π_{xy} except for the end nodes u and v. This suggests the following definition. (Note that choosing π_{xy} a shortest or longest xy-path does not resolve this problem, in general.)

Definition 2. *For a node $x \in V_{bg}$, let $L(x) = \{u \to v: u \to v$ is in some xy-path and $v \in V_b\} = \{u \to v: u \to v$ is in some xy-path and not both u and $v \in V_g\}$. Also, let $G(x)$ denote the subdigraph of $G(y, z)$ consisting of the links $L(x)$ and the nodes belonging to those links. See Fig. 1(ii).*

Theorem 1. *For each $x \in V_{bg}$, $L(x)$ is a reversal link-set. Also, each reversal link-set $L = \bigcup \{L(x) : \ x \in V_{bg} \text{ and } x \text{ belongs to a link in } L\}$.* ♡

The proof of Theorem 1 and other proofs are omitted here for want of space. Def. 2 plays a critical role in the proof of Theorem 1.

Definition 3. *A node $x \in V_{bg}$ is called a bg-sink node if there is no path from x in $G(y, z)$ to some other node in V_{bg}. (Although a bg-sink node x is a sink-node in G_{bg}, the converse need not be true; nodes $\{3, 5\}$ are the only bg-sink nodes in Fig. 1(i).) We write $S_{bg} \subseteq V_{bg}$ for the set of bg-sink nodes.*

The following corollary is immediate from Theorem 1 and forms the basis of our algorithms in the next Section.

Corollary 1. *A necessary and sufficient condition for L to be a minimal reversal link-set is $L = L(x)$ for some bg-sink node x.* ♡

4   Minimal Link-Reversal Algorithm

There are several phases in the our algorithm using a minimal reversal link-set $L = L(x)$ for some bg-sink node x. We assume that each node x knows its $N^+(x)$ and $N^-(x)$.

We first identify the node-type (b, g, bg, or $\overline{bg}$) of each node of G by using a standard "flooding" technique on $G(y, z)$. We use four kinds of messages, but only one kind from each node (and only one message on any link). A node x sends the same (b, g, bg, or $\overline{bg}$) message to all its upstream neighbors $N^-(x)$ in the flooding, i.e., backwards along the link to x after it receives the messages from all its downstream neighbors and identifies its type. Thus, a b-node sends only b-messages, a g-node sends only g-messages, etc. In the process, we also determine a directed spanning tree T_b of V_b rooted at y and a directed spanning tree T_g of V_g rooted at d, with all links directed from a children to its parent; see Fig. 1(i). The trees T_b and T_g are used later for choosing a specific bg-sink node x, the associated minimal link-set $L(x)$, etc.

The flooding begins with node d marking itself as a g-node and sending a g-message to all nodes in $N^-(d)$ and similarly with node y marking itself as a b-node and sending a b-message to all nodes in $N^-(y)$. Subsequently, when a node x has received a message from each of its neighbors $N^+(x)$, it determines its node-type and the bg-sink node status according to the criteria (C1)-(C5) below and then forwards the corresponding $b/g/bg/\overline{bg}$-message to each node in $N^-(x)$. Note that a node x can determine its type to be bg before receiving a $b/g/bg/\overline{bg}$-message from each of $N^+(x)$, but we nevertheless wait to send the bg-message out from x till x receives the $b/g/bg/\overline{bg}$-messages from all of $N^+(x)$ for the sake of simplicity.

(C1) If x receives only b-messages, then type$(x) = b$.
(C2) If x receives only g-messages, then type$(x) = g$.
(C3) If x receives at least one b-message and at least one $g/bg/\overline{bg}$-message, then type$(x) = bg$.

(C4) If x receives no b-message and at least one $bg/\overline{bg}$-message (and possibly zero or more g-message), then type$(x) = \overline{bg}$.

(C5) Finally, if type$(x) = bg$ and x has not received any $bg/\overline{bg}$-message, i.e., it has received only b/g-messages, then x is a bg-sink node.

4.1 Algorithm FindSinkNodes S_{bg}

We assume that when the only outgoing link (y, z) from a node y fails, node y initiates the algorithm FindSinkNodes; in addition, it asks node z to inform the destination node d of the link-failure situation (which can be done using at most $O(|E|)$ messages) and then node d on receiving this information initiates the algorithm FindSinkNodes. The other nodes x in $G(y, z)$ start executing the algorithm FindSinkNodes when they receive their first $b/g/bg/\overline{bg}$-message. We also assume that the node failures are sufficiently infrequent that all phases of the link-reversal algorithm terminates before a new link failure occurs. We simply use the conditions (C1)-(C5) as described above to determine the type of each node, including if it is a bg-sink node. For this purpose, each node x maintains a vector of four counts numBmssgRcvd(x), numGmssgRcvd(x), numBGmssgRcvd(x), and num$\overline{BG}$mssgRcvd(x). The termination of FindSinkNodes requires additional work, including identification of the spanning trees T_b and T_g, and is described later.

Theorem 2. *FindSinkNodes uses a total of $O(|E|)$ messages.* ♡

The first column in Fig. 2 shows a possible sequence in which the nodes in Fig. 1(i) can determine their types. Here, we assume that each message takes one unit of time to reach its recipient and zero processing time for the messages. The smallest node x which received all $|N^+(x)|$ messages first is listed first. We indicate type(x) in parentheses next to x in the first column. In the second column, we show the $b/g/bg/\overline{bg}$-message sent by x and the nodes $u \in N^-(x)$ receiving that message; we also show type(u) next to each u provided u can determine its type based on the messages received upto this point. Until all nodes have determined their types, there is always at least one node which is ready to forward its selected $b/g/bg/\overline{bg}$-message. The third column shows the determination of parent-child links in T_b and T_g, which is explained below.

4.2 Terminating Computation of bg-Sink Nodes

We use two other messages for this purpose: a p-message (p for "parent") and an np-message (np for "not parent"). Exactly one of these messages go forward along each link of $G(y, z)$.

We let each node $x \notin \{d, y\}$ maintain a unique parent(x), which is the node from which x receives its first $g/bg/\overline{bg}$-message if type$(x) \in \{g, bg, \overline{bg}\}$ or the node from which x receives its first b-message if type$(x) = b$. Note that x may have to wait till it receives a $b/g/bg/\overline{bg}$-message from each of the neighbors $N^+(x)$ to determine parent(x) simply because x may not know type(x) until

Node x and type(x)	$b/g/bg/\overline{bg}$-message sent to $N^-(x)$	Parent-child link in T_b or T_g
$1(g)$	g: $2(g), 3, 4(g)$	$2{\to}1, 4{\to}1$ in T_g
$10(b)$	b: $11(b), 12, 14(b), 15$	$11{\to}10, 14{\to}10$ in T_b
$2(g)$	g: $3, 5, 7$	
$4(g)$	g: $-$	
$11(b)$	b: $3(bg), 12(b), 13(b)$	$12{\to}10, 13{\to}11$ in T_b and $3{\to}1$ in T_g
$14(b)$	b: $15(b)$	$15{\to}10$ in T_b
$3(bg)$	bg: $-$	
$12(b)$	b: $7(bg), 8, 16$	$7{\to}2$ in T_g
$13(b)$	b: $5(bg), 8$	$5{\to}2$ in T_g
$15(b)$	b: $16(b)$	$16{\to}12$ in T_b
$16(b)$	b: $17(b), 5$	$17{\to}16$ in T_b
$5(bg)$	bg: $6(\overline{bg})$	$6{\to}5$ in T_g
$17(b)$	b: $-$	
$6(\overline{bg})$	$\overline{bg}$: $7, 8(bg)$	$8{\to}6$ in T_g
$7(bg)$	bg: 8	
$8(bg)$	$\overline{bg}$: $9(\overline{bg})$	$9{\to}8$ in T_g
$9(\overline{bg})$	$\overline{bg}$: $-$	

Fig. 2. A possible sequence of the determination of type(x) for nodes x in Fig. 1(i)

that point. This means a node x has to maintain four potential parents, one for each possible value of type(x) and in the order they are found, and then finally select parent(x) to be one of those based on type(x). It is easy to see that the parent-links form two trees, a tree T_b spanning the nodes V_b with the root at y and a tree T_g spanning the nodes V_g with the root at d. The bold links in Fig. 1(i) show these trees assuming that each $b/g/bg$-message takes one unit time to reach its recipient. We have chosen parent(16) to be simply the smaller of $\{12, 15\}$ from which it receives b-message at time 3.

After a node $x \notin \{d, y\}$ has determined type(x) it can safely determine parent(x) and at that point it sends an np-message to each node in $N^+(x)$ other than parent(x). (Sometime, it is actually possible to determine parent(x) even earlier; for example, node 3 in Fig. 1(i) can determine parent$(3) = 1$ after it receives its first message from node 1, which is a g-message.) A node x waits, however, to send the p-message to parent(x) until the number of p/np-messages received by x equals $|N^-(x)|$, and it is at this point that x terminates its computation for determining the bg-sink nodes. This means, in particular, that p-messages are initiated by the source-nodes in $G(y, z)$, which includes node z, and perhaps zero or more other terminal nodes in the trees T_b and T_g. For Fig. 1(i), only the nodes $\{3, 4, 9, 17\}$ initiate p-messages. The terminal node 13 in T_b sends its p-message to node 11 only after receiving np-messages from the nodes 5 and 8; similarly, the terminal node 7 in T_g sends its p-message to node 2 only after receiving np-message from node 8. The special node y (d) terminates its computation last among the nodes in V_b (resp., V_g) and this happens when it receives $|N^-(y)|$ (resp., $|N^-(d)|$) many p/np-messages.

4.3   Selecting One bg-Sink Node

We briefly describes the steps in this task. Only the nodes $V_{bg} \cup V_b$ participates in this step; the only links that participate in this step are L_{bg} and the links in T_b. We use two kinds of s-messages (s for sink-node). (Note that we do not try to choose $x \in S_{bg}$ such that $|L(x)|$ is minimum because this can increase the total number of messages to $O(|V|^3)$.) We use the null s-message, $s()$, to coordinate the starting and ending of computations of the nodes participating in this phase, and use a non-null s-message $s(x)$, where x is a bg-sink node.

We begin by letting each node $x \in S_{bg}$ initiate the message $s(x)$ to the smallest numbered node from which it received a b-message during the execution of FindSinkNodes algorithm and initiate the message $s()$ to all other nodes from which it received b-message. For each node $x' \in V_{bg} - S_{bg}$, we let it initiate the message $s()$ to all nodes from which it received b-message. (This means each terminal node in T_b, which sends b-messages only to nodes in V_{bg}, will receive exactly a total of $|N^-(u)| \geq 0$ many s-messages.) For Fig. 1(i), node 3 initiates the message $s(3)$ to node 11, node 5 initiates the message $s(5)$ to node 13 and $s()$ to node 16, node 7 initiates the message $s()$ to node 12, node 8 initiates the message $s()$ to each of the nodes 12 and 13, and finally node 17 initiates the message $s()$ to node 16.

Each terminal node u in T_b on receiving $|N^-(u)|$ many s-messages does the following: if it does not receive any non-null s-message, then it sends $s()$ to its parent; otherwise, if $s(x)$ is the first non-null s-message received by u, then it sends the entire s-message $s(x)$ to its parent. For a non terminal node u in T_b, exactly the same thing happens except that some of its $|N^-(u)|$ many s-messages come from its children before it sends an appropriate s-message to its parent. When the root node y of T_b receives an s-message from each of its children, it selects the node x in the first non-null s-message it received and terminates its computation for this phase. The other nodes in T_b terminate their computation in this phase on sending their s-message to their parents, and the nodes in V_{bg} terminate their computation on sending their s-messages to the nodes in V_b. Let x_s denote the bg-sink node x selected by y.

The following theorem is immediate from the fact that there will be exactly one s-message along each link of the tree T_b, in addition to at most $\sum |N^+(x)|$, summed over $x \in S_{bg}$, many s-messages originating from the nodes in S_{bg}.

Theorem 3. *The selection of a specific bg-sink node $x_s \in S_{bg}$ by the special node y takes $O(|E|)$ messages.* ♡

4.4   Actual Link-Reversal Phase

This is the final step of our algorithm and has two parts. In the first part, node y informs the bg-sink node x_s that it has been selected, and in the second part each link in the set $L(x_s)$ is reversed, i.e., each node x belonging to the links in $L(x_s)$ updates $N^-(x)$ and $N^-(x)$ to represent the new orientation of G.

For the first part, we assume that during the selection of x_s, each node u in T_b, save $u \neq y$, which forwarded a non-null s-message of the form $s(x)$ remembers both the parameter x in that s-message and the node u' from which it received that s-message. We have u' is either a child of u in T_b or $u' = x$, the gb-sink node where the message $s(x)$ originated. By abuse of notation, we write s-child$(u) = u'$, which is unique. We can follow the trail of nodes backward (from u to u') starting from the root y of T_b corresponding to the s-message $s(x_s)$. We begin by node y sending an f-message (f for find) to s-child(y), which is the child of y that sent the message $s(x_s)$ to y. Then $y' = s$-child(y) sends an f-message to s-child(y'), and so on until we reach the node $x \in V_{bg}$.

The second part begins with the bg-sink node x_s reversing each of the links $x_s \to u$ corresponding to the nodes u from which it received b-message, i.e., adding each such u to $N^-(x_s)$ and deleting u from $N^+(x_s)$, and then sending an r-message (r for reverse) to each of those node u. When a b-node u receives the first r-message, it does exactly the same thing as above, updating its $N^-(u)$ and $N^+(u)$, and then sending an r-message to each node added to $N^-(u)$. The second and subsequent r-messages received by a b-node u, if any, are ignored.

Theorem 4. *The reversal of the links in $L(x_s)$ for the selected bg-sink node x_s takes $O(|E|)$ messages.* $\heartsuit$

5   Conclusion

We have presented a $O(|E|)$ distributed algorithm for the link-reversal problem, where $|E| = \sharp$(links in the network). It first selects a minimal reversal link-set and reverses the direction of those links exactly once.

References

1. Gafni, E.M., Bertsekas, D.P.: Distributed algorithms for generating loop-free routes in networks with frequently changing topology. IEEE Trans. on Communication 29, 11–18 (1981)
2. Park, V.D., Corson, M.S.: A highly adaptive distributed routing algorithm for mobile wireless networks. In: Proc. IEEE Conf. on Computer Communications (INFOCOM 1997) (1997)
3. Park, V.D., Corson, M.S.: A performance comparison of temporally-ordered routing algorithm and ideal link-state routing. In: Proc. IEEE Intern. Symp. on Systems and Communications (June 1998)
4. Corson, M.S., Ephremides, A.: A distributed algorithm for mobile wireless networks. ACM Wireless Networks Journal 1, 61–82 (1995)
5. Busch, C., Surapaneni, S., Tirthapura, S.: Analysis of link-reversal routing algorithms for mobile ad-hoc networks. In: Proc. of 15th ACM Symp. on Parallelism in Algorithms and Architectures (SPAA), San Diego, pp. 210–219 (June 2003)
6. Perkins, C.E.: Ad-hoc Networking. Addison-Wesley, Reading (2000)
7. Rajarama, R.: Topology control and routing in ad-hoc networks: a survey. SIGACT News (June 2002)
8. Samir, R., Robert, C., Jiangtao, Y., Rimli, S.: Comparative performance evaluation of routing protocols for mobile ad-hoc networks. In: Proc. IEEE 7th Intern. Conf. on Computer Communications and Networks (IC3N 1998) (1998)

Two Consensus Algorithms with Atomic Registers and Failure Detector Ω

Carole Delporte-Gallet and Hugues Fauconnier

Laboratoire d'Informatique Algorithmique: Fondements et Applications
Université Paris VII - Denis Diderot
{cd,hf}@liafa.jussieu.fr

Abstract. We present here two consensus algorithms in shared memory asynchronous systems with the eventual leader election failure detector Ω. In both algorithms eventually only the leader given by failure detector Ω will progress, and being eventually alone to make steps the leader will decide. The first algorithm uses an infinite number of multi-writer multi-reader atomic registers and works with an unbounded number of anonymous processes. The second uses only a finite number of single-writer multi-reader registers but assumes a finite number of processes with known unique identities.

1 Introduction

Recall that in the consensus problem each process proposes a value and all processes have to agree on one of these proposed values. As most of the fault-tolerant problems need to solve at least this problem, it is not necessary to insist on the importance of solving the consensus problem in asynchronous systems. From a more theoretical point of view, since the impossibility result of the consensus in asynchronous systems [1,2], several solutions to circumvent this impossibility result have been proposed. One of the solutions consists to assume that processes are equipped with failure detectors [3]. A failure detector is a distributed oracle that gives unreliable information about crashes. Hence Ω is a failure detector that realizes an eventual leader election: eventually one correct process is the unique leader in the system. Failure detectors can be compared by reduction and one of the main results concerning failure detectors proves that Ω is the weakest failure detector for solving the consensus with a majority of correct processes in message passing systems [4,5] or with shared memory or implemented registers [6,7]. Then this means that (1) with help of Ω the consensus problem can be solved (2) if the consensus problem is solved with information about crashes this information can be reduced to Ω. Remark that as a consequence of the impossibility result, Ω cannot be implemented in asynchronous systems. But with some restrictions about the asynchrony, Ω can be efficiently implemented and many implementations have been proposed in partially synchronous systems (e.g. [8,9]).

We present here two consensus algorithms in asynchronous shared memory systems in the crash failure model and using failure detector Ω. For this, we

V. Garg, R. Wattenhofer, and K. Kothapalli (Eds.): ICDCN 2009, LNCS 5408, pp. 251–262, 2009.

first define a general and rather generic consensus algorithm using a specific data structure. Then we consider two cases for which this data structure can be implemented with registers. In this way we get two different algorithms: the first one working with an unbounded number of anonymous processes and the second one is more efficient but working with a known set of processes.

Most of consensus algorithms using failure detectors are designed in message passing asynchronous models. The first consensus algorithm for consensus in shared memory models with failure detector is [5] that uses $\Diamond S$ (a failure detector equivalent to Ω) and the rotating coordinator paradigm.

The way Ω is used here is one of the main interest of the proposed algorithms: only processes that consider themselves as leader make steps. As Ω ensures that eventually only one process is the leader forever, then eventually only this process will be alone to make steps and in this case it is relatively easy to achieve the consensus. We get the a similar approach (but without failure detectors) in the Paxos algorithm [10,11,12,13,14] or in [15]. In this way these algorithms are rather different from other like [16] designed for message passing systems.

These algorithms are also interesting from an another point of view, if instead of assuming Ω, we assume that only one process makes steps, we get an obstruction-free implementation [17]. In the same way, these algorithms are relatively close to randomized consensus algorithms (e.g. [18,19,20,21]). It is not surprising, for algorithms ensuring always the agreement property (i.e. safety), an eventual leader or randomization enable to get the termination (i.e. liveness).

Roadmap: In a first section we define the model and recall most of the classical definitions. In Section 3 we present the general algorithm, for this we first introduce a shared data structure used by this algorithm and give two cases for which this data structure can be implemented. Then in Section 4 and Section 5, we give the two algorithms deriving from the implementation of this data structure.

2   Model

The model we consider here is an asynchronous model with shared atomic registers. Atomic registers are defined by means of two operations *read* and *write* such that the read operation returns the last value written in the register by a write operation. Recall that the atomicity of the registers means that operations on the same register are linearizable [22]: that is there is an order $\prec$ extension of the "precede" relation[1] such that every read or write operations on each register are totally ordered. In particular, we have the following property that will be used later: if process p writes v_1 in register R_1 and then reads register R_2 and process q writes v_2 in register R_2 and then reads register R_1, then p reads v_2 in register R_2 or q reads v_1 in register R_1.

A process can fail by *crashing*. In this case it behaves accordingly to its specification until it (possibly) crashes. A process that does not crash is said *correct*. A *faulty* process is one that is not correct. We do not assume generally that the set of processes is bounded or that processes have unique identities.

---

[1] op_1 precedes op_2 if op_1 completes before op_2 is invoked.

In order to circumvent the impossibility of consensus in asynchronous systems [1], the model is enhanced with the Ω failure detector [4]. Informally a failure detector gives (unreliable) information to processes about crashes. Formal definitions of failure detectors can be found in [3]. Failure detector Ω realized an eventual leader election. More formally, in the classical definition, each process has a local variable, *leader*, containing the identity of a process assumed to be the leader, and failure detector Ω ensures that eventually all these variables for correct processes contain forever the identity of the same correct process. In order to adapt this definition to anonymous processes, we consider a variant of this definition: here each process p has a local boolean variable *is_leader* such that eventually *is_leader* is true for only one correct process.

Recall the specification of the *Consensus Problem*: every process p proposes value v_p and all correct processes have to *decide* on the same value that has to be one of the proposed values. For convenience, we consider here an equivalent specification: a consensus algorithm has to ensure the following properties:

- *Agreement*: if process p decides v and process q decides v' then $v = v'$.
- *Integrity*: the decided value of process p is a value proposed by at least one process.
- *Weak Termination*: at least one correct process eventually decides.

Remark that the specification given here is slightly different from the classical one [23] where the weak termination is replaced by:

- *Strong Termination*: every correct process eventually decides.

The consensus problem with weak termination and the consensus problem with strong termination are equivalent in models we consider here: if a process decides then it writes the decision in a special register and every process that has not yet decided repetitively reads this register (see Figure 1).[2]

```
1  /* Wdecide(m)  is the decide in the weak specification*/
2  /* Sdecide(m)  is the decide in the strong specification*/
3  /* R is a atomic register shared by processes initialized to ⊥ */
4  on Wdecide(m):
5     write(m) in R
6     Sdecide(m)
7  /* each process runs the following task */
8  task:
9     while read R ≠ ⊥ do skip
10    Sdecide(read R)
```

Fig. 1. Broadcast the decision

Recall that in asynchronous systems, the famous result of [1] shows that there is no consensus algorithm if at least one process may crash.

---

[2] With message passing system a reliable broadcast could be used to broadcast the decision.

In the following by consensus we mean consensus with the weak termination property and by strong consensus we mean consensus with the strong termination property.

3 General Algorithm

3.1 Weak Set Data Structure

As a first step describe a shared data structure we will call *weak set*. A *weak set* S is a shared data structure containing a set of values. Initially a weak set is the empty set. Weak set S is defined by two operations: the $get(S)$ operation returns the set of the values contained in the weak set S and the $add(S, v)$ operation that adds v to the weak set S (we say also *get from S* and *add v to S*). Note that we do not consider here operations to remove values from the set. More precisely, after the end of $add(S, v)$ for some value v, v belongs to the set and all $get(S)$ return all the values v such that $add(S, v)$ ended before the beginning of the $get(S)$ operation, but due to the concurrency of accesses to the weak set, values that have been added concurrently to the $get(S)$ may or may not belong to the set returned by this $get(S)$. Notice that weak sets are not necessarily linearizable and then are not atomic objects. For example, if concurrently processes p_1, p_2, make respectively an $add(S, v_1)$ and an $add(S, v_2)$ and p_3, p_4 and p_5 make $get(S)$ operations concurrently with these add_s they could return respectively $\{v_1\}$, $\{v_2\}$ and $\{v_1, v_2\}$ and clearly there is no corresponding linearizable history. Nevertheless we have:

Proposition 1. *Let A and B be two weak sets and let p and q be two processes: Assume that p makes $add(A, v)$ then $get(B)$, and q makes $add(B, w)$ then $get(A)$, then if w does not belong to the set returned by $get(B)$ for p then v belongs to the set returned by $get(A)$ for q.*

In other words, if p does not see the value added by q in weak set B then q sees the value written by p in weak set A.

Proof. To prove the proposition let $t^p_{add(A,v)}$ and $t^q_{add(B,w)}$ be respectively the times at which p and q end their $add(A, v)$ and $add(B, w)$ operations, in the same way define $t^p_{get(B)}$ and $t^q_{get(A)}$ the times corresponding to the beginning of $get(A)$ and $get(B)$ operations. By hypothesis we have: $t^p_{add(A,v)} < t^p_{get(B)}$ and $t^q_{add(B,w)} < t^q_{get(A)}$. By definition, if w is not in the set returned by $get(B)$, then we have: $t^p_{get(B)} \leq t^q_{add(B,w)}$ but then : $t^p_{add(A,v)} < t^p_{get(B)} \leq t^q_{add(B,w)} < t^q_{get(A)}$ proving $t^p_{add(A,v)} < t^q_{get(A)}$ and by definition of weak set, v belongs to the set returned by $get(A)$ operation of q.

The important point is the fact that it is easy to implement weak sets from atomic registers in two cases.

Proposition 2. *If the set of possible values that can be added to weak set S is finite, then weak set S can be implemented with multi-writer multi-reader registers.*

Proof. In the implementation for each possible value v we have a boolean multi-writer multi-reader register $r[v]$. All these registers are initialized by *False*. To implement $add(S, v)$, process p simply writes *True* in $r[v]$. To implement $get(S)$, process p reads all the $r[v]$ registers and returns the set of all v such that $r[v]$ is *True*.

Proposition 3. *If the set of processes using weak set S is bounded and known by all the users of weak set S then weak set S can be implemented with help of single-writer multi-reader atomic registers.*

Proof. In the implementation, for each process p we have a single-writer multi-reader register $r[p]$. To implement $add(S, v)$ process p simply writes v and all the values previously added by p in $r[p]$. To implement $get(S)$, p reads all the registers $r[q]$ and returns all the values read in these registers.

3.2 Consensus with Weak Sets and Ω Failure Detector

It is clear that if only one process makes steps in the decision algorithm the consensus is trivial. With failure detector Ω, eventually only one process is distinguished as leader. Then if, in the consensus algorithm only the leader makes step to decide, eventually only one process will make steps. But this property occurs only eventually and we have to ensure and test the fact that a process is alone to make steps or more generally that all active processes act in a consistent way and make exactly the same steps.

In the algorithm each process works in rounds but a process makes a new round only if it considers itself as the leader. Recall that does not mean that it is a true leader and does not ensure that it will be alone in the round. Each process p maintains an estimate value (Val). Processes share an array of weak sets $T[r]$: $T[r]$ contains the set of estimate values for all processes that have participated to round r. When a process makes a new round r, first it adds its current estimate value to weak set $T[r]$, then it gets the set of estimate values from the current round and from the previous round. The process decides if it sees that the set of estimate values of its current round and of the previous round contains only its own estimate. Intuitively, if it is the case, then the algorithm ensures that the set of estimate values for greater rounds may only contain this value. In this way, no other value may be decided ensuring the safety of the decision.

If a process does not see that the set of estimate values for the current and the previous round contains only its own estimate value, that means that the process is not alone in this round and that other processes do not have a consistent view for the decision. Then the process has to progress and go to a new round. But in fact the process can jump to any round r in which some processes have already added their estimate values in $T[r]$: to do this in a safe way, a process can jump to a round r if it adopts one of the values already in $T[r]$.

Details of the algorithm are in Fig. 2

We have to prove the properties of Integrity, Agreement and Termination.

```
1   ∀r : T[r] is a weak set
2   Val :=value proposed by p
3   Round := 1
4   while true do
5     if is_leader() then
6       if Round = 1 then
7         add(T[1], Val)
8       else
9         add(T[Round], Val)
10        V1 := get(T[Round])
11        V2 := get(T[Round − 1])
12        if V1 = {Val} ∧ V2 = {Val} then
13            decide Val; halt
14      if ∅ = get(T[Round + 1]) then
15          Round := Round + 1
16      else
17          choose v and r > Round such that v ∈ get(T[r])
18          Round := r
19          Val := v
```

Fig. 2. Consensus

Proposition 4. Integrity: if p decides v, v is a value proposed by at least one process.

Proof. By an easy induction on round r, as every process first adds a value on a weak set before it gets value from this weak set, every value added by any process is a value proposed by some process.

Note that in the algorithm process p may change its round in two ways: either by Line 14 (then p do not write Val) or by Line 17 (then p writes Val). In the following, we say that p does not change its estimate value for the first case and that p changes its estimate value for the second case.

Before proving agreement, we give two preliminary lemmas:

Lemma 1. If a process begins add(T[r], v) at some time t for some r then for every weak set T[r'] with $1 \leq r' < r$ at least one process begins an add(T[r'], v) before time t.

Proof. We proceed by induction on rounds r. Let P(r) be the induction property: If a process begins add(T[r], v) at some time t for some r then for every weak sets T[r'] with $1 \leq r' < r$ at least one process begins an add(T[r'], v) before time t.

P(1) is trivial.

Assume the property is true for r. Among the set of processes that begin add(T[r + 1], v), let p be the first to do that and let t be the time at which p begins this add(T[r + 1], v). At time t, p is executing round r + 1.

Consider r' the previous round executed by p. Either p does not change its estimate value in round r' or it does. For the first case, then $r' = r$, when executing round r, p made add(T[r], v). It begins this add strictly before time t and so by induction hypothesis we prove P(r + 1). For the second case, while executing round r', p gets value v from a get(T[r + 1]), this value was added by some process q' contradicting the fact that q was the first process to begin an $add(T[r+1], v)$.

Lemma 2. *If some process p_0 decides v_0 in round r_0 then for any process making an $add(T[r], v)$ for $r \geq r_0$ then $v = v_0$.*

Proof. We prove this lemma by induction. We order the *add* operations by the time at which they begin. Consider the property $P(i)$: if $add(T[r], v)$ is the i-th *add* such that $r \geq r_0$ we have $v = v_0$.

Note that a process p makes an $add(T[r], v)$ only during round r.

We first show $P(1)$. Let p be the process making this first $add(T[r], v)$ for some v and some $r \geq r_0$. By Lemma 1, at the time at which p begins this *add* then for every r' such that $1 \leq r' < r$ at least one process began an $add(T[r'], v)$ before, then necessarily we have $r = r_0$. We have two cases to consider:

– p does not change its estimate value in the previous round.
  Note that the previous round is necessarily $r_0 - 1$. Let z be such that in round $r_0 - 1$ p makes an $add(T[r_0 - 1], z)$. If we consider weak sets $T[r_0]$ and $T[r_0 - 1]$, we have: (1) p_0 before deciding makes an $add(T[r_0], v_0)$ then a $get(T[r_0 - 1])$, (2) p makes an $add(T[r_0 - 1], z)$ then a $get(T[r_0])$, (3) p_0 obtains only $\{v_0\}$ from the $get(T[r_0 - 1])$. By Proposition 1 we deduce that either $z = v_0$ or p obtains a set containing v_0 from its $get(T[r_0])$. In this later case when, in round $r_0 - 1$, p made $get(T[r_0])$, p obtained either $\emptyset$ but in this case we have $z = v_0$ or $\{v_0\}$. And so it goes to round r_0 with its Val equal to v_0 and then makes an $add(T[r_0], v_0)$ proving that $z = v_0$.
– p changes its estimate value in the previous round.
  Let r' be this previous round. At the end of the round r', p has chosen v from $get(T[r_0])$ but by definition p being the first one to make an $add(T[r_0], v)$ it is impossible.

Assume $P(i)$, and let $add(T[r], v)$ be the $i+1$th *add* such that $r \geq r_0$. Assume that this *add* is made by process p. Note that this add occurs when p is in round r. We have to consider the following cases:

– $r = r_0$ and p does not change its estimate value in the previous round.
  The proof is exactly the same as the proof of $P(1)$.
– $r = r_0$ and p changes its estimate value in the previous round.
  Let r' be this previous round. At the end of round r', p made a $get(T[r_0])$ returning a set containing v. By properties of the weak set, some process began an $add(T[r_0], v)$ before. By induction hypothesis this value is v_0 and then $v = v_0$.
– $r > r_0$ and p does not change its estimate value in the previous round.
  Note that this previous round is $r - 1$ and p makes an $add(T[r - 1], v)$. By induction hypothesis this value is v_0 and then $v = v_0$.
– $r > r_0$, and p changes its estimate value the previous round.
  Let r' be this previous round, then at the end of the execution of round r', q makes a $get(T[r])$ returning a value v. By induction hypothesis, this value is v_0 and then $v = v_0$.

In all the cases, when executing round r, q adds v in weak set $T[r]$. This proves $P(i+1)$, and ends the proof of the lemma.

Proposition 5. Agreement: *if p decides v and p' decides v' then $v = v'$.*

Proof. Consider m the first round in which some process decides and let v be the first decided value. By the Lemma 2 no value different of v can be written in round $r \geq m$. And so, no process can decide a value different *of v.*

Note that the properties of Ω are not useful for the integrity and agreement properties. They are used only for the Termination property. Then without failure detector, this algorithm maintains the safety of the consensus (more precisely agreement and integrity are always ensured).

Proposition 6. Termination: *at least one correct process eventually decides.*

Proof. By definition of Ω failure detector, there is a time t_0 after which only one correct process l is leader. Let R be the maximum of the rounds begun at time t_0. Assume that no process decides before round $R+2$. After time t_0 only process l may begin new rounds. And so, except l, no process adds a value in weak set $T[R+1]$ and in weak set $T[R+2]$. Let v_l be the value of variable Val for process l when l begins round $R+1$. When process l executes round $R+1$, it makes an $add(T[R+1], v_l)$. Then, when process l executes round $R+2$, it makes an $add(T[R+2], v_l)$. And then, $get(T[R+1])$ and $get(T[R+2])$ return $\{v_l\}$ ensuring that process l decides v_l.

4   Algorithm with Multi-writer Multi-reader Atomic Registers

Consider here only binary consensus. From Proposition 2 it is then possible to implement weak sets $T[r]$ with help of atomic registers: for this we have two atomic registers $T[r][0]$ and $T[r][1]$ for each $T[r]$.

The proposed algorithm is the adaptation of the general one of Figure 2. For each round r we have two binary registers $T[r][0]$ and $T[r][1]$. All these registers are initialized with $False$. Here the test to get the decision (Line 12 of Algorithm Fig. 2) becomes $T[r][v]$ and $T[r-1][v]$ are equal to $True$ for exactly one v. If the condition is not true (then the process does not decide) it goes to the next round with its own estimate value if no value has been set for the next round or if both estimate values have been set for the next round, else it adopts the unique value set in the next round. It is clear this strategy is a special case of the one of the general algorithm (Line 14 to Line 17 of the general algorithm). Details of the algorithm are in Figure 3.

Remark that (1) it is not necessary for the processes to have an unique identity and (2) the number of processes participating to the algorithm is not necessary bounded, then:

Proposition 7. *Algorithm of Figure 3 realizes a binary consensus with help of multi-writer multi-reader atomic registers and failure detector Ω between an unbounded number of anonymous processes.*

```
1  ∀r ≥ 1 : T[r][0] = T[r][1] = False
2  Val :=binary value proposed by p
3  Round := 1
4  while true do
5    if is_leader() then
6      T[Round][Val] := True
7      if (Round ≥ 2)
8        ∧(T[Round][1 − Val] = False) ∧ (T[Round − 1][1 − Val] = False)
9      then
10         decide Val; halt
11     else
12       if (T[Round + 1][1 − Val] = True) ∧ (T[Round + 1][Val] = False)
13       then Val := 1 − Val;
14     Round := Round + 1
```

Fig. 3. Consensus with an unbounded number of processes

```
1  ∀n : Reg[n] = False
2  /* v is the value proposed by the process */
3  /* StrongBinaryConsensus(v) return the decided value of the Binary Consensus*/
4  write True in Reg[v]
5  for j = 0, · · · , ∞ do
6    if Reg[j] then
7      decision :=StrongBinaryConsensus(1)
8    else
9      decision :=StrongBinaryConsensus(0)
10   if decision = 1 then
11     decide j
12     halt
```

Fig. 4. Multi-valued Consensus

Remarks: Note that this result is very strong and is in some way surprising. But from a more realistic point of view the main difficulty is how to get (an infinite number of) atomic registers shared by an unbounded number of anonymous processes.

In this algorithm processes do not jump rounds. Then when some process becomes the leader forever it could have to make all the rounds made by other processes and then it could have to make an unbounded number of rounds before deciding.

The fact we consider only binary consensus is not really a restriction: Algorithm of Figure 4 realizes a multi-valued consensus from repeated strong binary consensus. Due to the atomicity of the write, the first value written will be read by all processes. This algorithm corresponds to [24] in message passing.

5   Algorithm with One-Writer Multi-reader Registers and a Bounded Number of Processes

Give some explanation on how this algorithm can be derived from the general one.

When the set of processes is known and bounded Proposition 3 proposes an implementation of weak sets $T[r]$ with help of single-writer multi-reader atomic registers: in this implementation each process has its own register and to add a value to the weak set process p simply writes this value to the register. A main drawback of this implementation is the fact that we have for each process an infinite number of atomic registers (one for each round). In fact we are going to see it is not necessary and each process can safely only use one register corresponding to the last round it has made. More precisely each process p maintains an atomic register $Reg[p]$ in which it writes its estimate value and the number of the round.

Consider the condition of consensus of the general algorithm (Line 12 of Algorithm Figure 2); this condition is that (A) in the current and previous round the weak sets of estimate values are reduced to the same singleton equal to the estimate value of the process. It is straightforward to verify that we can assume also that no process has made rounds greater than this one. Then to realize the test for the condition of consensus, a process reads $Reg[q]$ for all q. From this it determines (1) the number of the current maximum round, (2) extracts the set of estimate values for this maximum round, and (3) extracts the set of estimate values for the round preceding this maximum round. Note that clearly (2) gives exactly the weak set of this round, but some value in (3) corresponding to the round preceding the maximum one may be lacking because processes may have already written their value in the maximum round. Nevertheless if some values are lacking, these values have precisely already been written in the maximum round and then are in the set getting from (2). Then if the process is in the maximum round, the condition (A) is equivalent to the fact that the set of values coming from (2) and (3) is reduced to a singleton.

Moreover, here when a process sees that it is not in the maximum current round, it can jump to the round preceding the maximum round and if the set of estimate values of the maximum round is a singleton it adopts it.

```
/* All registers are initialized by (⊥, −1) */
1  Val[p] := v_p value proposed by p
2  Round[p] := 1

3  while true do
4    if is_leader() then
5      write((Val[p], Round[p]) in Reg[p])
6      for i := 1 to n do (Val[i], Round[i]) :=read Reg[i]
7      MaxRound := max{Round[i]|1 ≤ i ≤ n}
8      V1 := {Val[i]|Round[i] = MaxRound}
9      V2 := {Val[i]|Round[i] = MaxRound − 1}
10     if V1 ∪ V2 = {v} ∧ Round[p] = MaxRound ∧ MaxRound > 1
11     then
12        decide v
13        halt
14     else
15        if V1 = {x} then Val[p] := x
16     Round[p] := max(MaxRound − 1, Round[p] + 1)
```

Fig. 5. Consensus with Ω

Proposition 8. *Algorithm of Fig. 5 realizes a consensus between n processes with help of single-writer multiple-reader registers and failure detector Ω.*

Remark that this algorithm is very efficient:

- If n is the number of processes, only n atomic registers are needed. Moreover these registers are single-writer multi-reader registers and such registers are clearly much simpler than multi-writer multi-reader registers.
- When a process becomes leader forever, the convergence of the algorithm is quite fast: in at most three rounds the process decides independently of the history of the system.

6 Conclusion

We have presented a general algorithm to solve the consensus problem in asynchronous shared memory systems with help of failure detectors. From this algorithm we have derived two algorithms. The first one is interesting from a theoretical point of view because it works with an unbounded number of anonymous processes. Then it could be used in very dynamical systems in which processes can be created and destroy infinitely often. The second one assumes only that the set of processes is known (and bounded) but it is very efficient.

Acknowledgments

We are grateful to Michel Raynal for his comments which helped improve the multi-valed consensus algorithm.

References

1. Fischer, M.J., Lynch, N.A., Paterson, M.S.: Impossibility of distributed consensus with one faulty process. Journal of the ACM 32(2), 374–382 (1985)
2. Loui, M., Abu-Amara, H.: Memory requirements for agreement among unreliable asynchronous processes. Advances in Computing Research 4, 163–183 (1987)
3. Chandra, T.D., Toueg, S.: Unreliable failure detectors for reliable distributed systems. Journal of the ACM 43(2), 225–267 (1996)
4. Chandra, T.D., Hadzilacos, V., Toueg, S.: The weakest failure detector for solving consensus. Journal of the ACM 43(4), 685–722 (1996)
5. Lo, W.K., Hadzilacos, V.: Using failure detectors to solve consensus in asynchronous shared memory systems. In: Tel, G., Vitányi, P.M.B. (eds.) WDAG 1994. LNCS, vol. 857, pp. 280–295. Springer, Heidelberg (1994)
6. Delporte-Gallet, C., Fauconnier, H., Guerraoui, R., Hadzilacos, V., Koutnetzov, P., Toueg, S.: The weakest failure detectors to solve certain fundamental problems in distributed computing. In: 23th ACM Symposium on Principles of Distributed Computing (2004)
7. Koutnetzov, P.: Synchronisation using failure detector. Technical report, PhD Thesis, EPFL (2005)
8. Aguilera, M.K., Delporte-Gallet, C., Fauconnier, H., Toueg, S.: On implementing Omega with weak reliability and synchrony assumptions. In: 22th ACM Symposium on Principles of Distributed Computing, pp. 306–314 (2003)

9. Malkhi, D., Oprea, F., Zhou, L.: Omega meets paxos: Leader election and stability without eventual timely links. In: Fraigniaud, P. (ed.) DISC 2005. LNCS, vol. 3724, pp. 199–213. Springer, Heidelberg (2005)

10. Lamport, L.: The Part-Time parliament. ACM Transactions on Computer Systems 16(2), 133–169 (1998)

11. Gafni, E., Lamport, L.: Disk paxos. In: Herlihy, M.P. (ed.) DISC 2000. LNCS, vol. 1914, pp. 330–344. Springer, Heidelberg (2000)

12. Chockler, G., Malkhi, D.: Active disk paxos with infinitely many processes. Distributed Computing 18(1), 73–84 (2005)

13. Boichat, R., Dutta, P., Frolund, S., Guerraoui, R.: Deconstructing paxos. Distributed Computing Column of ACM SIGACT News 34(1) (2003)

14. Boichat, R., Dutta, P., Frolund, S., Guerraoui, R.: Reconstructing paxos. Distributed Computing Column of ACM SIGACT News 34(2) (2003)

15. Guerraoui, R., Raynal, M.: The alpha of indulgent consensus. Comput. J. 50(1), 53–67 (2007)

16. Mostéfaoui, A., Raynal, M.: Leader-based consensus. Parallel Processing Letters 11(1), 95–107 (2001)

17. Herlihy, M., Luchangco, V., Moir, M.: Obstruction-free synchronization: Double-ended queues as an example. In: 23rd International Conference on Distributed Computing Systems (ICDCS), Providence, RI, USA (2003)

18. Chor, B., Israeli, A., Li, M.: On processor coordination using asynchronous hardware. In: Proceedings of the 6th ACM Symposium on Principles of Distributed Computing, pp. 222–231 (1987)

19. Abrahamson, K.: On achieving consensus using a shared memory. In: PODC 1988: Proceedings of the seventh annual ACM Symposium on Principles of distributed computing, pp. 291–302. ACM Press, New York (1988)

20. Aspnes, J., Herlihy, M.: Fast randomized consensus using shared memory. Journal of Algorithms 11(3), 441–461 (1990)

21. Ben-Or, M.: Another advantage of free choice: Completely asynchronous agreement protocols. In: Proceedings of the 2nd ACM Symposium on Principles of Distributed Computing, pp. 27–30 (1983)

22. Herlihy, M., Wing, J.M.: Linearizability: A correctness condition for concurrent objects. ACM Trans. Program. Lang. Syst. 12(3), 463–492 (1990)

23. Lynch, N.A.: Distributed Algorithms. Morgan Kaufmann, San Francisco (1996)

24. Mostéfaoui, A., Raynal, M., Tronel, F.: From binary consensus to multivalued consensus in asynchronous message-passing systems. Inf. Process. Lett. 73(5-6), 207–212 (2000)

Self-similar Functions and Population Protocols: A Characterization and a Comparison

Swapnil Bhatia and Radim Bartoš

Department of Computer Science, Univ. of New Hampshire, Durham, NH
{sbhatia,rbartos}@cs.unh.edu

Abstract. Chandy et al. proposed the methodology of "self-similar algorithms" for distributed computation in dynamic environments. We further characterize the class of functions computable by such algorithms by showing that self-similarity induces an additive relationship among the level-sets of such functions. Angluin et al. introduced the population protocol model for computation in mobile sensor networks and characterized the class of predicates computable in a standard population. We define and characterize the class of self-similar predicates and show when they are computable by a population protocol.

1 Introduction

Mobile wireless sensor networks hold tremendous promise as a technology for sampling a variety of phenomena at unprecedented granularities of time and space. Such networks embody a modern-day "macroscope": an instrument that can potentially revolutionize science by enabling the measurement, understanding—and eventually—control, of a whole new class of physical, biological, and social processes. The source of potential of such networks lies in the following four capabilities endowed to each participating node: the ability to sense environmental data, the ability to compute on such data, the ability to communicate with peers in the network, and the ability to move in its environment. A network of autonomous underwater vehicles (AUVs) deployed to patrol a harbor, to map the locations of underwater mines, to monitor the diffusion of a pollutant in a river, or to build a bathymetric map are some realistic examples of missions that mobile sensor networks are charged with today.

While there has been tremendous interest in building such networks in recent years, most of this work has focused on a proper subset of the four capabilities of mobile sensor nodes described above. Work on mobile ad hoc networks has focused on mobility and communication [1,2,3] and sensor network research has mostly focused on sensing and communication [4,5]. More recently, there has been a growing interest in in-network computation and communication in static sensor networks [6,7]. We believe that all this previous work paves the way for a more comprehensive model that includes all four of the above abilities, particularly computation. Such a model would allow us to frame new questions from the point of view of the *computational mission* of the network and provide us insight into the design tradeoffs of such networks for various classes of missions. This paper represents an intermediate step toward this goal.

In this paper, we focus on two recent papers that deal with distributed computation in dynamic environments—the first by Chandy et al. [8] and the second by Angluin et al.

V. Garg, R. Wattenhofer, and K. Kothapalli (Eds.): ICDCN 2009, LNCS 5408, pp. 263–274, 2009.

[9]—and attempt to characterize the relationship between their work. Both papers are motivated by the need to understand computation in distributed systems that exist in highly dynamic environments similar to those in which mobile sensor networks are deployed. Using approaches that complement each other, these papers attempt to abstract the four capabilities of mobile sensor nodes described above to answer new questions regarding computation in such networks. Chandy et al. propose a methodology for designing algorithms for dynamic distributed systems and identify a class of functions amenable to their method. They outline a method for systematically designing such algorithms which they call "self-similar algorithms." (We call the functions computed by such algorithms self-similar functions.) The approach taken by Angluin et al. complements that of Chandy et al. in that instead of starting with a class of functions, Angluin et al. define a computational model called the population protocol model, which abstracts the four capabilities of mobile sensor nodes described above. Their model comprises a population of anonymous identical nodes, each with a small constant amount of memory, that communicate and compute opportunistically during encounters with each other. In a series of papers [9,10,11], Angluin et al. have characterized the class of predicates computable in a standard population model. The goal of this paper is to further characterize the class of functions defined by Chandy et al. and to understand its relationship to the computational model defined by Angluin et al.

Our contributions are as follows. Restricted to a finite input space (but any number of sensing nodes), we study the structure of self-similar functions and show how their definition imposes an additive relationship on the level-sets of such functions, a property that is similar to the one known to hold for predicates computable by population protocols in a standard population. Using these results and known results about population protocols, we show that although population protocols and self-similar functions are identically motivated, these two concepts do not coincide. For a given convention of representing predicates, we define and characterize the class of self-similar predicates and those computable by a population protocol. While self-similarity more generally captures the properties required of a function to be distributedly computable in a dynamic environment, the constraints that its definition imposes appear to be stronger than those imposed by population protocols. On the other hand, the notion of self-similarity appears to be more general than the notion of opportunistic computation in a population protocol. Our work contrasts these two conceptions of computation in dynamic environments in a mobile sensor network and highlights their particular strengths. We hope that this increased understanding of existing models will usher in better models of mobile sensor networks that incorporate the computational mission of such networks. We also hope that this paper will generate interest in a study of mobile sensor networks that unifies computation, communication, mobility, and sensing.

2   Self-similar Algorithms

Implicit in the paper by Chandy et al. [8] are the following questions: How can we derive distributed algorithms that compute correctly in dynamic environments? Which functions are amenable to distributed computation in dynamic environments? To answer the first question, Chandy et al. begin by enumerating properties that a computation must possess, if it is to execute correctly in a dynamic distributed environment. They restrict their investigation to stable and idempotent functions which can be computed by what they call "self-similar algorithms." By stability, it is meant that once a computation achieves its "final" state, it remains in that state forever, thus providing a stable answer. It follows that a computation in such an environment must be conservative in the sense that it must always transition to only those states that would not result in an incorrect computation; all transitions must conserve the correct final answer. That is, if s_i is the collective state of the computational agents in the system in the ith step and f is the function to be computed, then $f(s_i) = f(s_0)$ for all i. Finally, a self-similar algorithm is one in which any "group behaves like the entire system" [8]. More precisely, suppose f is a function that is to be computed by a collection of agents. Then, a self-similar algorithm A for f is one which can be executed by any (nonempty) subset of identical agents participating in a sequence of arbitrary groupings such that the result of their "local" computation is compatible with and usually contributes to the "global" computation that is to be executed. Chandy et al. show that the above properties—stability, idempotence, conservation, and computability by self-similar algorithms—hold exactly for a class of functions they call *superidempotent*.

Definition 1. *A function f from multisets to multisets is* **superidempotent** *if $f(X \cup Y) = f(f(X) \cup Y)$ [8].*

In this paper, we shall refer to such functions as self-similar functions to emphasize their computability by a self-similar algorithm.

2.1   General Observations

It is easy to see that the class of self-similar functions excludes some familiar functions.

Proposition 1. *Any one-to-one function (except for the identity) is not self-similar, because it is not idempotent.*

On the other hand, self-similar functions include some familiar functions.

Proposition 2. *An idempotent homomorphism is self-similar.*

Proof. If f is an idempotent homomorphism, then the r.h.s. in the definition of superidempotence $f(f(X) \cup Y) = f(f(X)) \cup f(Y)$ (by homomorphism), $= f(X) \cup f(Y)$ (by idempotence) $= f(X \cup Y)$ (by homomorphism), which is the l.h.s. of the definition of superidempotence.   □

Corollary 1. *Let T be a linear transformation such that $T^2 = T$. Then, T is self-similar.*

Proof. By its definition, T is idempotent and linearity implies the homomorphism property.   □

Thus, all projections (i.e., linear transformations T such that $T^2 = T$) are self-similarly computable.

2.2   Finite-Valued Self-similar Functions

While Chandy et al. define self-similar algorithms over infinite input spaces, in order to compare the class of such functions with a realizable model of computation, we study self-similar functions over a finite input space (alphabet) in this paper. Let Q be the finite nonempty set of possible input values for any agent and let $|Q| = q$ be a positive integer. Consider the q-dimensional space $\mathbb{N}^q$ of nonnegative integers.

Lemma 1. *Let $Q^\star$ be the (infinite) set of all finite multisets containing elements from Q. There exists an isomorphism ϕ between the monoids $(Q^\star, \cup)$ and $(\mathbb{N}^q, +)$.* [1]

Thus, the definition of superidempotence can be translated from $(Q^\star, \cup)$ to $(\mathbb{N}^q, +)$ as follows: a function $f : \mathbb{N}^q \to \mathbb{N}^q$ is superidempotent if and only if $f(x + y) = f(f(x) + y)$ for all $x, y \in \mathbb{N}^q$. In this subsection, $f : \mathbb{N}^q \to \mathbb{N}^q$ is a self-similarly computable function. From the definition of superidempotence, we know

Fact 1. *For any $u, v \in \mathbb{N}^q$, $f(u+v) = f(f(u)+v) = f(u+f(v)) = f(f(u)+f(v))$.*

Definition 2. *For any $v \in \mathbb{N}^q$, denote by $\sum v$ the integer $\sum_{i=1}^{q} v_i$, and by H_k^q the hyperplane $\{v \in \mathbb{N}^q | \sum v = k\}$.*

We assume that a computational step is agent conserving in that the number of a agents in a group participating in a computational step does not change during the step. From this we have

Fact 2. *If $f : \mathbb{N}^q \to \mathbb{N}^q$ and $v \in \mathbb{N}^q$, $\sum v = \sum f(v)$.*

That is, any $v \in \mathbb{N}^q$ lives in the $q - 1$-dimensional hyperplane $\{u : \sum u = \sum v\}$ of $\mathbb{N}^q$ and any self-similar f maps v to an $f(v)$ in the same plane. It is useful to know the number of points in each H_k^q. For each $k \in \mathbb{N}$, the number of points in H_k^q is the number of integral solutions of the equation $\sum v = k$ Therefore, $|H_k^q| = \binom{k+q-1}{q-1}$.

Definition 3. *The set of all points (multisets) x such that $f(x) = y$, for some fixed y, is called a **fiber**. A fiber is **trivial** if it contains exactly one point. Any subset of a fiber of f is called a **contour of** f. A contour of f containing u that also contains $f(u)$ is called a **complete contour**. The **value** of a contour is $f(u)$ for any u in the contour.*

Self-similar computations progress along trajectories that must be contained in fibers; if not then f cannot be conservative. Fibers play a central role in self-similar functions. Indeed, self-similarity induces an additive relationship between contours, as we show below.

Theorem 1 (Direct sum of contours). *If U and V are contours, then $U \oplus V = \{u + v | u \in U, v \in V\}$ is also a contour.*

Proof. Since the claim is trivially true if either U or V are empty, we assume that they are both nonempty. For any $w_1, w_2 \in U \oplus V$ let $w_1 = u_1 + v_1$ and $w_2 = u_2 + v_2$ for some $u_1, u_2 \in U$ and $v_1, v_2 \in V$. Now $f(w_1) = f(u_1 + v_1) = f(f(u_1) + f(v_1)) = f(f(u_2) + f(v_2)) = f(u_2 + v_2) = f(w_2)$, where the second and fourth equalities follow from the definition of superidempotence, and the third from the definition of a contour. □

---

[1] We omit this and several other easy proofs below due to lack of space; see [12].

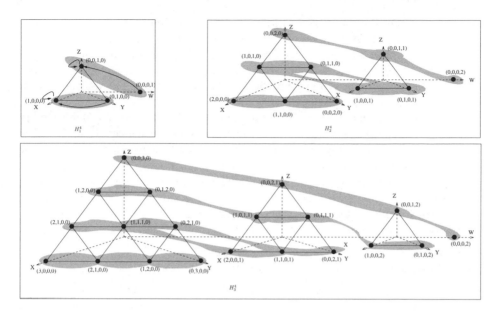

Fig. 1. Relationship between contours of a self-similar function $f : \mathbb{N}^4 \to \mathbb{N}^4$. (The axes in order are X, Y, Z, and W.) Points (black disks) included in the same shaded region form a contour. Notice that H_2^4 contains four copies of H_1^4, and H_3^4 contains four copies of H_2^4. Contours are invariant under translation from H_k^4 to H_{k+1}^4.

Corollary 2 (Translation of a contour). *If U is a contour, then for any $v \in \mathbb{N}^q$, the translation $U + v = \{u + v | u \in U\}$ of U is also a contour.*

Proof. For any $v \in \mathbb{N}^q$, $\{v\}$ is (trivially) a contour. Then by Theorem 1, $U \oplus \{v\}$ is a contour. □

Figure 1 illustrates this relationship between contours of a self-similar function $f : \mathbb{N}^4 \to \mathbb{N}^4$. Over H_1^4, it is defined as follows: $f(0,1,0,0) = f(1,0,0,0) = (1,0,0,0)$ and $f(0,0,0,1) = f(0,0,1,0) = (0,0,1,0)$. Thus, there are two fibers (and contours) in H_1^4: $\{(0,1,0,0),(1,0,0,0)\}$ and $\{(0,0,0,1),(0,0,1,0)\}$. (There are only $\binom{1+4-1}{4-1} = 4$ points in H_1^4 and they are thus partitioned into two fibers.) As per the above results, any translation of these two contours must also be a contour. Thus, $\{(0,0,0,1)+(1,0,0,0),(0,0,1,0)+(1,0,0,0)\} = \{(1,0,0,1),(1,0,1,0)\}$ for example, must be a contour in H_2^4. (There are three more possible translations, one along each of the axes, all of which must also be contours in H_2^4.) Since points in each contour must have the same value, the union of intersecting contours must form a single contour. For example, the intersecting contours $\{(1,0,1,0),(1,0,0,1)\}$, $\{(0,1,1,0),(0,1,0,1)\}$, $\{(1,0,1,0),(0,1,1,0)\}$, and $\{(1,0,0,1),(0,1,0,1)\}$ of H_2^4 together form a single contour, as shown by the overlapping shaded regions of the figure. Similarly, the contours in H_2^4, when translated along any of the four axes must form contours in H_3^4, as shown in the figure.

Viewing contours in translation justifies naming such functions as self-similar: contours in H_k^q are the result of translating contours in H_{k-1}^q in q ways and are thus copies of them; those in H_{k-1}^q are copies of those in H_{k-2}^q; and so on. However, while contours are invariant under translation, the value of a contour in H_k^q, in contrast to the standard notion of self-similarity, need not bear any relationship to the value of a contour in H_{k-1}^q. For example in Figure 1, the value of any point in H_2^4 under f is not determined by its contour membership: the contour only requires that the value of all its points be the same.

The results proved above are fundamental in understanding the structure of self-similar functions. They complement the description given by Chandy et al. that self-similar algorithms are those in which "any group behaves like the entire system" [8]. Our results show that for finite input spaces, such algorithms compute functions in which self-similarity manifests itself in the form of an additive relationship between contours: larger contours are formed by translating smaller contours. This clarifies the notion of self-similarity proposed by Chandy et al. and makes our understanding of it more precise.

We now state two useful results that immediately follow from the above results.

Definition 4. *For any* $u = (u_1, \ldots, u_q) \in \mathbb{N}^q$ *and* $v = (v_1, \ldots, v_q) \in \mathbb{N}^q$, *we define the* **partial order** $\leq$ *as follows:* $u \leq v \iff \forall i \in \{1, \ldots, q\} : u_i \leq v_i$.

Lemma 2. *Let* $\{v^1, \ldots, v^r\}$ *be a contour in* H_k^q *(with k such that $1 \leq r \leq |H_k^q|$) and let* $u \in \mathbb{N}^q$ *such that* $u \leq v^i$ *for* $i = 1, \ldots, r$. *Then the set* $\{u + \sum_{i=1}^{r} m_i(v^i - u) : m_i \in \mathbb{N}, \sum_{i=1}^{r} m_i = m\}$ *is a contour in* $H_{j+m(k-j)}^q$, *where* $j = \sum u$.

Proof. We prove this by induction on r.

Basis. If $r = 1$, then we must show that if $\{v^1\}$ is a contour in H_k^q and $u \leq v^1$, then the set $\{u + m_1(v^1 - u) : m_1 \in \mathbb{N}, m_1 = m\}$ is a contour in $H_{j+m(k-j)}$, where $j = \sum u$. Since $v^1 \in H_k^q$, and $u \in H_j^q$, $u + m(v^1 - u) \in H_{j+m(k-j)}^q$. For any $m_1 = m \in \mathbb{N}$ the set in question contains a single vector and is therefore trivially a contour.

Induction hypothesis. Suppose the statement is true for $r = n$.

Inductive step. For $r = n$, we are given that the set $\{u + \sum_{i=1}^{n} m_i(v^i - u) : m_i \in \mathbb{N}, \sum_{i=1}^{n} m_i = m\}$ is a contour in $H_{j+m(k-j)}^q$. Let $v^{n+1} \in H_k^q$. Let $U_n = \{u : u \leq v^i, i = 1, \ldots, n\}$ and $U_{n+1} = \{u : u \leq v^i, i = 1, \ldots, n+1\}$. Then it must be that $U_{n+1} \subseteq U_n$ because if $u \in U_{n+1}$, then it must necessarily be no larger than $v^1, \ldots, v^n$. Moreover, $(0, \ldots, 0) \in U_{n+1}$ and hence U_{n+1} is nonempty. Thus, the induction hypothesis holds for all $u \in U_{n+1}$, since it holds for U_n. Let $u' \in U_{n+1}$ with $\sum u' = j'$. Therefore, $\{u' + \sum_{i=1}^{n} m_i(v^i - u') : m_i \in \mathbb{N}, \sum_{i=1}^{n} m_i = m\}$ is a contour in $H_{j'+m(k-j')}^q$ as per the induction hypothesis.

Now, the set $\{m_{n+1}(v^{n+1} - u')\}$ is a contour in $H_{m_{n+1}(k-j')}^q$ for any fixed $m_{n+1} \in \mathbb{N}$ because it contains a single point. Therefore, by Theorem 1, $\{u' + \sum_{i=1}^{n} m_i(v^i - u') : m_i \in \mathbb{N}, \sum_{i=1}^{n} m_i = m\} \oplus \{m_{n+1}(v^{n+1} - u')\}$ is a contour in $H_{j'+m'(k-j')}^q$, where $m' = m + m_{n+1}$. But $\{u' + \sum_{i=1}^{n} m_i(v^i - u') : m_i \in \mathbb{N}, \sum_{i=1}^{n} m_i = m\} \oplus \{m_{n+1}(v^{n+1} - u')\} = \{u' + \sum_{i=1}^{n+1} m_i(v^i - u') : m_i \in \mathbb{N}, \sum_{i=1}^{n+1} m_i = m'\}$. Thus, we have shown that this set is a contour in $H_{j'+m'(k-j')}$, where $j' = \sum u'$. □

The union of the contours described in the above result is called a *linear* set. Such sets are closely related to the type of predicates computable in the standard population protocol model.

We now state a useful special case of the above result. We omit the proof, which follows directly from the previous result, due to space restrictions.

Corollary 3. *Let* $u, v^1, v^2, \ldots, v^q \in \mathbb{N}^q$ *be such that* $v^i = u + e_i$ *where* $\{e_1, \ldots, e_q\}$ *is the standard basis for* $\mathbb{N}^q$. *If* $\{v^1, \ldots, v^q\}$ *is a contour, then* f *is constant in each* H_k^q *for all points* $w \geq u$.

Lemma 3. *Any function* $f : \mathbb{N}^q \to \mathbb{N}^q$ *that is constant over each* H_k^q *and maps each* H_k^q *to itself is self-similar.*

Theorem 2. *There exists a function* $f : \mathbb{N}^2 \to \mathbb{N}^2$ *that is not computable but is self-similar.*

Proof. Let $w = w_2, w_3, \ldots$ be an infinite sequence of nonnegative integers such that $0 \leq w_k < |H_k^2|$. Let $f_w : \mathbb{N}^2 \to \mathbb{N}^2$ be a function constant over each H_k^2 such that for any $(i, k - i) \in H_k^2$, $f_w(i, k - i) = (w_k, k - w_k)$: w_k defines the value of the function in H_k^2. If $w \neq w'$ are two sequences as defined above such that $w_k \neq w'_k$, then $f_w(i, k - i) = (w_i, k - w_i) \neq (w'_i, k - w'_i) = f_{w'}(i, k - i)$. Thus, every sequence w defines a distinct function f_w that is constant over each H_k^2. By Lemma 3, each such f_w is self-similar. However, the set $\{f_w | w = w_2, w_3, \ldots; 0 \leq w_k < |H_k^2|\}$ is uncountable, whereas the set of Turing machines is countable. □

3   Population Protocols and Self-similar Functions

In a series of recent papers, Angluin et al. have defined the *population protocol* model of distributed computation and characterized its computational power [9]. A *population* is a collection of n anonymous computational agents with an undirected population graph on n vertices. Each agent is modeled as a deterministic finite automaton, with a finite set of transition rules from pairs of states to pairs of states. In the randomized variant (see [11] for details), an input symbol from an input alphabet is provided to each agent, and a fixed input function maps it to the initial state of the agent. A computation evolves in discrete steps, and at each step, an edge (i, j) of the population graph is chosen uniformly at random by the "environment": this models a pairwise random *encounter* between agents during which they communicate and compute. During such an encounter, agents i and j transition from their current states q_i and q_j to new states according to the population protocol (i.e., $(q_i, q_j) \to (q'_i, q'_j)$). The collective state of all n agents can be completely described by an n-dimensional vector over the states of the protocol, where the ith component is the current state of the ith agent. Thus, an execution is an *infinite* sequence of n-dimensional vectors. At any step, the current output of the computation can be obtained by mapping the current state of any agent to the output alphabet using a given fixed output function. A function f is stably computed by a population protocol iff for any input assignment x, the computation eventually converges to an orbit of n-vectors, all of which map to the unique $f(x)$ under the output function. We recall some definitions below [9].

Definition 5. *A* **population protocol** $\mathcal{A}$ *is a 6-tuple* $\mathcal{A} = (X, Y, Q, I, O, \delta)$ *where:* X *is the* **input alphabet**, Y *is the* **output alphabet**, Q *is a set of* **states**, $I : X \to Q$ *is the*

input function, $O : Q \to Y$ *is the* **output function**, *and* $\delta : Q \times Q \to Q \times Q$ *is the* **transition function**.

Definition 6. *A* **population** $\mathcal{P}$ *is a set* A *of* n *agents with a directed graph over the elements of* A *as vertices and edges* $E \subseteq A \times A$. *The* **standard population** $\mathcal{P}_n$ *is the set of* n *agents* $A_n = \{a_1, \dots, a_n\}$ *with the complete directed graph (without loops) on* A_n.

Definition 7. *A* **semilinear set** *is a subset of* $\mathbb{N}^q$ *that is a finite union of linear sets of the form* $\{u + k_1 v_1 + k_2 v_2 + \dots + k_m v_m\}$ *where* u *is a* q-*dimensional base vector,* $v_1, \dots, v_m$ *are* q-*dimensional basis vectors, and* $k_1, \dots, k_m \in \mathbb{N}$. *A* **semilinear predicate** *is one that is true precisely on a semilinear set.*

The computational power of population protocols was characterized by Angluin et al. [10,11].

Theorem 3 (Theorem 6 in [11]). *A predicate is computable by a population protocol in a standard population if and only if the set of points on which it is true is semilinear.*

3.1 Self-similar Functions Computed by Population Protocols

Theorem 4. *If the population protocol* $\mathcal{A} = (X, X, Q, I, I^{-1}, \delta)$ *stably computes a function* $f : X^\star \to X^\star$ *from multisets to multisets over* X *in the standard population* $\mathcal{P}_n$, *then* f *is self-similar.*

Proof sketch. A population protocol $\mathcal{A}$ that correctly executes in a standard population $\mathcal{P}_n$ must also correctly execute in any population $P \subseteq \mathcal{P}_n$ because it cannot distinguish between the two populations. Partition $\mathcal{P}_n$ into P and P'. Let t be larger than the number of steps required for $\mathcal{A}$ to converge when executed in P and P'. Let $f(P)$ and $f(P')$ denote the output respectively. Now execute $\mathcal{A}$ in $\mathcal{P}_n$ such that for the first t steps no inter-partition encounter is allowed, and after t steps all encounters are allowed. The intermediate output will be $f(P) \cup f(P')$ and the final output will be $f(f(P) \cup f(P')) = f(\mathcal{P}_n)$. $\square$

3.2 Predicates: Semilinear and Self-similar

Definition 8. *A* **predicate** *is a function* $P : \mathbb{N}^q \to \{T, F\}$. *For any predicate* P, *its* **consensus predicate** *form is a function* $f : \mathbb{N}^q \to \mathbb{N}^q$ *such that for any* $v \in \mathbb{N}^q$, $f(v) = (\sum v, 0, 0, \dots, 0)$ *iff* $P(v) = T$ *and* $f(v) = (0, \sum v, 0, \dots, 0)$ *iff* $P(v) = F$. *We call the consensus predicate form* **self-similar** *if* f *is self-similar.*

The consensus predicate defined above follows the "all-agents output convention" as defined by Angluin [9] which requires all agents to agree on the truth-value of the predicate. In the sequel, our results involve only those predicates that are expressible in this convention because this is one of the conventions used by Angluin et al. and we are interested in comparing self-similar predicates to population protocol computable predicates. We postpone the discussion of more robust conventions to future work.

Proposition 3. *Not all semilinear consensus predicates are self-similar consensus predicates.*

Proof. Consider the following consensus predicate: $f(i,j) = (i + j, 0)$ if $j \leq i$ and $f(i,j) = (0, i + j)$ otherwise. It is easy to show that this predicate is semilinear and idempotent but not self-similar. □

If a predicate P is always true or always false, then its consensus form function will be constant over each H_k^q, and by Lemma 3, will be self-similar. We say that a predicate is eventually constant if there is a $k \in \mathbb{N}$ such that the predicate is constant over H_k^q. (Corollary 3 implies that the predicate is then constant for all $k' \in \mathbb{N}$ such that $k' \geq k$.)

Theorem 5. *A predicate $P : \mathbb{N}^q \rightarrow \{T, F\}$ that is not eventually constant has a self-similar consensus form $f : \mathbb{N}^q \rightarrow \mathbb{N}^q$ if f is idempotent and either the set of points on which P is true or that on which P is false has a standard basis.*

Proof. Suppose the set of true points of P has a standard basis T_1^q. Thus, P is true only on points in $\text{span}(T_1^q)$ and hence P is false only on points in $\text{span}(F_1^q \cup (F_1^q \oplus T_1^q))$.

To show that P has a self-similar consensus form f, we must show that $\forall v \in \mathbb{N}^q$: $\forall u \leq v : f(v) = f(f(u) + f(v - u))$. Suppose $P(v) = T$, that is $v \in \text{span}(T_1^q)$. Then $\forall u \leq v : u \in \text{span}(T_1^q)$ because u must have zeroes in at least those coordinates in which v has zeroes. Now since $P(v) = T$, $f(v) = (\sum v, 0, \ldots, 0)$ by definition of the consensus form. On the other hand, $f(f(u) + f(v - u)) = f((\sum u, 0, \ldots, 0) + (\sum(v - u), 0, \ldots, 0)) = f(\sum v, 0, \ldots, 0)$. Since $f(v) = (\sum v, 0, \ldots, 0)$, and since f is idempotent, $f(\sum v, 0, \ldots, 0) = (\sum v, 0, \ldots, 0)$. Thus, we have shown that $\forall v \in \text{span}(T_1^q) : \forall u \leq v : f(v) - f(f(u) + f(v - u))$.

Now suppose $P(v) = F$. Thus $v \notin \text{span}(T_1^q)$, that is $v \in \text{span}(F_1^q \cup (F_1^q \oplus T_1^q)) = \text{span}(F_1^q) \cup \text{span}(F_1^q \oplus T_1^q)$. If $v \in \text{span}(F_1^q)$, then the same argument as above applies because $\forall u \leq v : P(u) = F$.

If $v \in \text{span}(F_1^q \oplus T_1^q)$, then $v = v_F + v_T$ for some $v_F \in \text{span}(F_1^q)$ and some $v_T \in \text{span}(T_1^q)$. Thus $P(v_F) = F$ and $P(v_T) = T$ and therefore $f(v_F) = (0, \sum v_F, 0, \ldots, 0)$ and $f(v_T) = (\sum v_T, 0, \ldots, 0)$. Therefore $f(f(v_F) + f(v_T)) = f(\sum v_T, \sum v_F, 0 \ldots, 0)$. Since P is not eventually constant, $(i, 0, \ldots, 0) \in \text{span}(T_1^q)$ and $(0, j, 0, \ldots, 0) \in \text{span}(F_1^q)$ for all $i, j \in \mathbb{N}$. Hence $(\sum v_T, 0, \ldots, 0) \in \text{span}(T_1^q)$ and $(0, \sum v_F, \ldots, 0) \in \text{span}(F_1^q)$ and therefore $(\sum v_T, \sum v_F, 0 \ldots, 0) \in \text{span}(T_1^q \oplus F_1^q)$. Therefore, $P(\sum v_T, \sum v_F, 0, \ldots, 0) = F$ and hence $f(\sum v_T, \sum v_F, 0 \ldots, 0) = (0, \sum v, 0, \ldots, 0)$. Thus, we have shown that $\forall v \in \text{span}(F_1^q \cup (F_1^q \oplus T_1^q))$ f is self-similar. □

Theorem 6. *If $P : \mathbb{N}^q \rightarrow \{T, F\}$ is a predicate with a self-similar consensus form, then at least one of the following holds: Either the set of points on which P is true or that on which P is false has a standard basis; or P is eventually constant.*

Proof. Consider the q points in H_1^q. If P is true on all q points or false on all q points, then P is eventually constant. So, assume otherwise and let the true fiber $T_1^q \subset H_1^q$ and the false fiber $F_1^q \subset H_1^q$ partition H_1^q (with $e_1 \in T_1^q$ and $e_2 \in F_1^q$ as per the definition of the consensus form convention).

Now consider H_2^q and observe that $H_2^q = (T_1^q \oplus T_1^q) \cup (F_1^q \oplus F_1^q) \cup (T_1^q \oplus F_1^q)$. By Theorem 1, $T_1^q \oplus T_1^q$, $F_1^q \oplus F_1^q$ and $T_1^q \oplus F_1^q$ are all contours and thus P is constant over each of these sets in H_2^q.

For some $v \in T_1^q \oplus F_1^q$, suppose $P(v) = F$. Then, all points in $T_1^q \oplus F_1^q$ must map to $(0, 2, 0, \ldots, 0)$ since P must be false on all these points. Furthermore, $f(0, 2, 0, \ldots, 0) = (0, 2, 0, \ldots, 0)$ since f is self-similar and hence idempotent. But $(0, 2, 0, \ldots, 0) \in F_1^q \oplus F_1^q$ and hence P must be false on all the points in $F_1^q \oplus F_1^q$. Thus, we can write the false fiber $F_2^q \supseteq (F_1^q \oplus F_1^q) \cup (F_1^q \oplus T_1^q) = F_1^q \oplus (F_1^q \cup T_1^q) = F_1^q \oplus H_1^q$. (It is easy to check that $\oplus$ distributes over $\cup$.) The only points remaining in H_2^q are those in the contour $T_1^q \oplus T_1^q$. If P is false on any of these points, then P is constant on H_2^q, and thus P is eventually constant. So assume that P is true on each point in the contour $T_1^q \oplus T_1^q$. Therefore, the set of true points in H_2^q, i.e., the true fiber in H_2^q is $T_2^q = T_1^q \oplus T_1^q$ and the false fiber $F_2^q = F_1^q \oplus H_1^q$. Thus, H_2^q is partitioned into two nonemtpy fibers.

Now $\mathbb{N}^q = \mathrm{span}(H_1^q) = \mathrm{span}(T_1^q) \cup \mathrm{span}(F_1^q) \cup \mathrm{span}(F_1^q \oplus T_1^q) = \mathrm{span}(T_1^q) \cup \mathrm{span}(F_1^q \cup (F_1^q \oplus T_1^q)) = \mathrm{span}(T_1^q) \cup \mathrm{span}((F_1^q \cup F_1^q) \oplus (F_1^q \cup T_1^q)) = \mathrm{span}(T_1^q) \cup \mathrm{span}(F_1^q \oplus H_1^q) = \mathrm{span}(T_1^q) \cup \mathrm{span}(F_2^q)$. Using Corollary 3 and considering F_2^q as the contour we obtain that the $\mathrm{span}(F_2^q) \cap H_k^q$ is a contour in every H_k^q, $k \geq 2$. If the value of this contour in any H_k^q is true, then P is constant over all of that H_k^q and thus is eventually constant. If the value of this contour is false for all H_k^q, and for some k, the value of T_k^q is also false, then P is constant over all of H_k^q and thus is eventually constant. If the value of this contour is false for all H_k^q, and the value of T_k^q is true for all H_k^q, then the set of true points has a standard basis T_1^q.

We assumed that for some $v \in T_1^q \oplus F_1^q$, $P(v) = F$. If we assume that $P(v) = T$, then we can show that the set of false points has a standard basis F_1^q. $\square$

From this, and Angluin et al.'s Theorem 3 immediately follows

Theorem 7. *If predicate $P : \mathbb{N}^q \to \{T, F\}$ is not eventually constant and has a self-similar consensus form, then P is computable by a population protocol.*

Proof. Since P has a self-similar consensus form and is not eventually constant, the set of points on which either P or its negation is true has a standard basis and is therefore a linear set. Population protocols are closed under complement. $\square$

For predicates that are eventually constant, self-similarity imposes no additional constraints within each H_k^q. Thus, for any $k \in \mathbb{N}$, the predicate may be true on all points in H_k^q or false on all points in H_k^q. Therefore, the computability of such predicates by a population protocol is given directly by Theorem 3.

3.3   Self-similar Functions Not Computable by Population Protocols

It is known that all predicates that are computable in the standard population are in the class NL [9], the set of functions computable by a nondeterministic Turing machine with access to memory logarithmic in the size of the input.

Theorem 8. *There exists a self-similar function that is in NL but whose predicate form is not computable by any population protocol.*

Proof. Let $f : \mathbb{N}^2 \to \mathbb{N}^2$ be the constant function such that for any $(i, k - i) \in H_k$, $f(i, k - i) = (k - \lfloor \lg k \rfloor, \lfloor \lg k \rfloor)$. By Lemma 3, f is self-similar. Since f requires

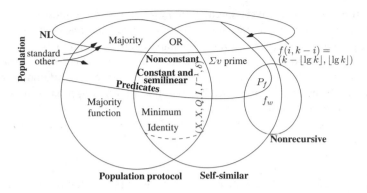

Fig. 2. Relationship between self-similar functions and functions computable by population protocols (Bold names differentiate classes from examples. Not all relationships are known).

an addition, the counting of the number of bits of the result, and a subtraction, it is in L, the set of functions computable with a deterministic Turing machine with access to memory logarithmic in the size of the input. It is known that $L \subseteq NL$ [13] and thus f is in NL. Define the predicate $P_f(v)$ over all points $v \in \mathbb{N}^2$ such that it is true if and only if $v \in H_k^2$ is the image of all $u \in H_k^2$ under f. From Theorem 3 we can deduce that the predicate P_f will be computable by a population protocol if and only if the set of its true points—which are also the fixed points of f—is semilinear. However, the set of fixed points $\{(k - \lfloor \lg k \rfloor, \lfloor \lg k \rfloor)|k = 1, 2, \ldots\}$ of f is not semilinear.   □

4   Conclusions and Future Work

Starting with the class of self-similar algorithms defined by Chandy et al., we studied functions from multisets to multisets computed by such algorithms over a (finite) input alphabet. We showed how the definition of self-similarity of algorithms—a group of any size behaves identically—results in a self-similar additive relationship among the contours of the functions computed by such algorithms. We defined self-similar predicates under the consensus convention used by Angluin et al., and showed that all such predicates that are not eventually constant have a simple structure: the set of points on which they are true or the set of points on which they are false has a standard basis. Using known results about population protocols, we thus showed that nonconstant self-similar predicates are computable by population protocols. We also showed that the notion of self-similarity is more general than, though quite similar to, the notion of opportunistic computability inherent in the population protocol model by showing the existence of a self-similar function not computable by population protocols. Our results, alongwith other examples, are summarized in Figure 2.

Both models discussed in this paper are motivated by distributed computation in dynamic mobile sensor network-like environments. However, neither model attempts to capture in sufficient detail the spatio-temporal nature of the data and its impact on communication and computation. Thus, one cannot frame questions that involve the spatial distribution of data or constraints on communication in the context of these models. If the state space of the population protocol model is endowed with a topology reflecting the space in which the network exists, then such questions may perhaps be framed. The population protocol model is intended to model a large number of frugal sensors. This may not be appropriate for AUV networks where the number of AUVs is small and each AUV is equipped with sufficient resources. While other models may allow us to ask these questions, we believe that a unified approach to studying such networks may be necessary.

Acknowledgments

We thank Prof. Michel Charpentier for reading an early version of this manuscript, the anonymous referees for their comments, and the Office of Naval Research for supporting this work.

References

1. Spyropoulos, T., Psounis, K., Raghavendra, C.: Efficient routing in intermittently connected mobile networks: The single-copy case. IEEE/ACM Trans. on Networking 16(1) (2008)
2. Grossglauser, M., Tse, D.: Mobility increases the capacity of adhoc wireless networks. IEEE/ACM Transactions on Networking 10(4), 477–486 (2002)
3. Chatzigiannakis, I.: Design and Analysis of Distributed Algorithms for Basic Communication in Ad-hoc Mobile Networks. Computer science and engineering, Dept. of Computer Engineering and Informatics, University of Patras (2003)
4. Gnawali, O., Greenstein, B., Jang, K.Y., Joki, A., Paek, J., Vieira, M., Estrin, D., Govindan, R., Kohler, E.: The TENET Architecture for Tiered Sensor Networks. In: ACM Conference on Embedded Networked Sensor Systems (Sensys), Boulder, Colorado (2006)
5. Palchaudhari, S., Wagner, R., Baraniuk, R.G., Johnson, D.B.: COMPASS: An adaptive sensor network architecture for multi-scale communication. IEEE Wireless Communications (submitted, 2008)
6. Giridhar, A., Kumar, P.R.: Computing and communicating functions over sensor networks. IEEE Journal on Selected Areas in Communications 23(4), 755–764 (2005)
7. Giridhar, A., Kumar, P.R.: Towards a theory of in-network computation in wireless sensor networks. IEEE Communications Magazine 44(4), 98–107 (2006)
8. Chandy, K.M., Charpentier, M.: Self-similar algorithms for dynamic distributed systems. In: 27th International Conference on Distributed Computing Systems (ICDCS 2007) (2007)
9. Angluin, D., Aspnes, J., Diamadi, Z., Fischer, M., Peralta, R.: Computation in networks of passively mobile finite-state sensors. Distributed Computing 18(4), 235–253 (2006)
10. Angluin, D., Aspnes, J., Eisenstat, D., Ruppert, E.: The computational power of population protocols. Distributed Computing 20(4), 279–304 (2007)
11. Aspnes, J., Ruppert, E.: An introduction to population protocols. Bulletin of the European Association for Theoretical Computer Science 93, 98–117 (2007)
12. Bhatia, S., Bartoš, R.: Self-similar functions and population protocols: a characterization and a comparison. Technical Report UNH-TR-08-01, University of New Hampshire (2008)
13. Papadimitriou, C.H.: Computational Complexity. Addison-Wesley, Reading (1994)

Byzantine-Resilient Convergence in Oblivious Robot Networks

Zohir Bouzid, Maria Gradinariu Potop-Butucaru, and Sébastien Tixeuil

Université Pierre et Marie Curie - Paris 6, LIP6-CNRS 7606, France

Abstract. Given a set of robots with arbitrary initial location and no agreement on a global coordinate system, *convergence* requires that all robots asymptotically approach the exact same, but unknown beforehand, location. Robots are oblivious— they do not recall the past computations — and are allowed to move in a one-dimensional space. Additionally, robots cannot communicate directly, instead they obtain system related information only *via* visual sensors. We prove ([4]) necessary and sufficient conditions for the convergence of mobile robots despite a subset of them being Byzantine (*i.e.* they can exhibit arbitrary behavior). Additionally, we propose a deterministic convergence algorithm for robot networks and analyze its correctness and complexity in various synchrony settings. The proposed algorithm tolerates f Byzantine robots for $(2f+1)$-sized robot networks in fully synchronous networks, $(3f+1)$-sized in semi-synchronous networks and $(4f+1)$-sized in asynchronous networks. The bounds obtained for the ATOM model are optimal for the class of *cautious* algorithms, which guarantee that correct robots always move inside the range of positions of the correct robots.

1 Introduction

The execution of complex tasks in hostile environments (*e.g.* oceans or planets exploration, decontamination of radioactive areas, human search and rescue operations) makes necessary the use of robots as an alternative to human intervention. So far, robots have been studied mainly through the prism of engineering or artificial intelligence, with success in the case of single powerful robots. However, many of the envisioned new tasks can not or should not (for cost reasons) be achieved by an unique robot, hence low cost swarm of cheap mobile robots executing coordinated tasks in a distributed manner is appealing when considering dangerous environments. In order to capture the difficulty of distributed coordination in robot network two main computational models are proposed in the literature: the ATOM [13] and CORDA models [12]. In both models robots are considered identical and indistinguishable, can see each other via visual sensors and operate in look-compute-move cycles. Robots, when activated, observe the location of the other robots in the system, compute a new location and move accordingly. The main difference between the two models comes from the granularity of the execution of this cycle. In the ATOM model, robots executing concurrently are in phase while in CORDA they are asynchronous (i.e. a robot

V. Garg, R. Wattenhofer, and K. Kothapalli (Eds.): ICDCN 2009, LNCS 5408, pp. 275–280, 2009.
© Springer-Verlag Berlin Heidelberg 2009

can execute the look action for example while another robot performs its move action).

Gathering and convergence are two related fundamental tasks in robot networks. Gathering requires robots to *reach* a single point within finite time regardless of their initial positions while convergence only requires robots to get *close* to a single point. More specifically, $\forall \epsilon > 0$, there is a time t_ϵ such that all robots are at distance at most ϵ from each other. Gathering and convergence can serve as the basis of many other protocols, such as constructing a common coordinate system or arranging themselves in a specific geometrical pattern. The specification of convergence being less stringent than that of gathering, it is worth investigating whether this leads to better fault and Byzantine tolerance. In [3] the authors address convergence with limited visibility in fault-free environments. Convergence with inaccurate sensors and movements is addressed in [7]. Fault-tolerant convergence was first addressed in [5,6], where algorithms based on the convergence to the center of gravity of the system are presented. Those algorithms work in CORDA model and tolerate up to f $(n > f)$ crash faults, where n is the number of robots in the system. To our knowledge, none of the aforementioned works on convergence addresses the case of byzantine faults.

Our contributions. In this paper we focus on the feasibility of deterministic solutions for convergence in robots networks that are prone to byzantine faults. Our contribution is threefold:

1. We draw a connection between the convergence problem in robot networks, and the distributed *approximate agreement* problem (that requires correct processes to decide, for some constant ϵ), values distance ϵ apart and within the range of initial values. In particular, our work uses a similar technique as the one presented in [8] and [1] for the problem of approximate agreement with byzantine failures. They propose approximate agreement algorithms that tolerate up to f byzantine failures and require $n > 3f$, which has been proven optimal for both the synchronous and asynchronous case.
2. We prove necessary and sufficient conditions for the convergence of mobile robots despite a subset of them being Byzantine (*i.e.* that can exhibit arbitrary behavior), when those robots can move in a uni-dimensional space. Due to space limitation, these issues are discussed in [4].
3. We propose a deterministic convergence algorithm for robot networks and analyze its correctness and complexity in various synchrony settings. The proposed algorithm tolerates f Byzantine robots for $(2f + 1)$-sized robot networks in fully synchronous networks, $(3f + 1)$-sized in semi-synchronous networks and $(4f+1)$-sized in asynchronous networks. The bounds obtained for the ATOM model are optimal for the class of *cautious* algorithms, which guarantee that correct robots always move inside the range of positions of other correct robots.

Outline. The remaining of the paper is organized as follows: Section 2 presents our model and robot network assumptions, [4] provides necessary and sufficient conditions for the convergence problem with Byzantine failures, Section 3 describes our protocol and its complexity.

2 Preliminaries

Most of the notions presented in this section are borrowed from [13,11,2]. We consider a network that consists of a finite set of robots arbitrarily deployed in a uni-dimensional space. The robots are devices with sensing, computing and moving capabilities. They can observe (sense) the positions of other robots in the space and based on these observations, they perform some local computations that can drive them to other locations.

In the context of this paper, the robots are *anonymous*, in the sense that they can not be distinguished using their appearance, and they do not have any kind of identifiers that can be used during the computation. In addition, there is no direct mean of communication between them. Hence, the only way for robots to acquire information is by observing each others positions. Robots have *unlimited visibility*, *i.e.* they are able to sense the whole set of robots. Robots are also equipped with a multiplicity sensor.

A robot that exhibits discrete behavior is usually modeled with an I/O automaton [10], while one with continous behavior will be modeled using a hybrid I/O automaton [9]. The actions performed by the automaton that models a robot are as follows:

- *Observation (input type action)*. An observation returns a snapshot of the positions of all robots within the visibility range. In our case, this observation returns a snapshot of the positions of *all* robots denoted with $P(t) = \{P_1(t), ..., P_n(t)\}$. The positions of correct robots are referred as $U(t) = \{U_1(t), ..., U_m(t)\}$. Note that $U(t) \subseteq P(t)$. The observed positions are *relative* to the observing robot, that is, they use the coordinate system of the observing robot.
- *Local computation (internal action)*. The aim of this action is the computation of a destination point (possibly using the relative position of other robots that was previously observed);
- *Motion (output type action)*. This action commands the motion of robots towards the destination location computed in the previous local computation action.

The *local state* of a robot at time t is the state of its input/output variables and the state of its local variables and registers. A *network of robots* is modeled by the parallel composition of the individual automata that model each robot in the network. A *configuration* of the system at time t is the union of the local states of the robots in the system at time t. An *execution* $e = (c_0, \ldots, c_t, \ldots)$ of the system is an infinite sequence of configurations, where c_0 is the initial configuration[1] of the system, and every transition $c_i \rightarrow c_{i+1}$ is associated to the execution of a subset of the previously defined actions.

---

[1] Unless stated otherwise, we make no specific assumption regarding the respective positions of robots in initial configurations.

We now review the main differences between the ATOM [13] and CORDA [11] models. Both models use the notion of a scheduler, that models system asynchrony (or lack of). A *scheduler* can be seen as an entity that is external to the system and selects robots for execution. As more power is given to the scheduler for robot scheduling, more different executions are possible and more difficult it is to design robot algorithms.

In the ATOM model, whenever a robot is activated by the scheduler, it performs a *full* computation cycle. Thus, the execution of the system can be viewed as an infinite sequence of rounds. In a round one or more robots are activated by the scheduler and perform a computation cycle. In the literature, the *fully-synchronous ATOM* model refers to the fact that the scheduler activates all robots in each round, while the *semi-synchronous ATOM* model denotes that the scheduler is allowed to activate only a subset of the robots. In the CORDA model, robots may be interrupted by the scheduler in the middle of a computation cycle. In particular, when a robot goes toward its goal, the move can end anywhere before the destination, yet the robot is guaranteed to move by at least a distance of δ before it can be stopped by the scheduler. Moreover, while a robot performs an action a, where a can be one of the following atomic actions: observation, local computation or motion, another robot may perform a totally different action b. As a result, the set of executions that are possible in the CORDA model are a strict superset of those that are possible in the ATOM model. So, an impossibility result that holds in the ATOM model also holds in the CORDA model, while an algorithm that performs in the CORDA model is also correct in the ATOM model. Note that the converse is not necessarily true.

In the remaining of the paper, we consider that the scheduler is *fair*, that is, in any infinite execution, every robot is activated infinitely often. A scheduler is *k-bounded* if, between any two activations of a particular robot, any other robot can be activated at most k times. The particular case of the fully synchronous ATOM considers a 1-bounded scheduler. Of course, an impossibility result for the most constrained scheduler (bounded) also holds for the least constrained one (fair), and an algorithm for the fair scheduler is also correct in for the k-bounded scheduler. The converse is not necessarily true.

The faults we address in this paper are *Byzantine* faults. A byzantine (or malicious) robot may behave in arbitrary and unforeseeable way. In each cycle, the scheduler determines the course of action of faulty robots and the distance to which each non-faulty robot will move in this cycle. However, a robot is guaranteed to move a distance of at least δ towards its destination before it can be stopped by the scheduler.

Our convergence algorithm performs operations on multisets. A multiset or a bag S is a generalization of a set where an element can have more than one occurence. The number of occurences of an element a is referred as its *multiplicity* and is denoted by $mul(a)$. The total number of elements of a multiset, including their repeated occurences, is referred as the *cardinality* and is denoted by $|S|$. $\min(S)$(resp. $\max(S)$) is the smallest (resp. largest) element of S. If S is nonempty, $range(S)$ denotes the set $[\min(S), \max(S)]$ and $diam(S)$ (diameter of S) denotes $\max(S) - \min(S)$.

2.1   The Byzantine Convergence Problem

In the following we refine the definition of the *point convergence problem* from [2]: given an initial configuration of N autonomous mobile robots, for every $\epsilon > 0$, there is a time t_ϵ from which all correct robots are within distance of at most ϵ of each other.

Definition 1 (Byzantine Convergence). *A system of oblivious robots verify the Byzantine convergence specification if and only if* $\forall \epsilon > 0, \exists t_\epsilon$ *such that* $\forall t > t_\epsilon, \forall\ i,j \leq N, distance(U_i(t), U_j(t)) < \epsilon$, *where* $U_i(t)$ *and* $U_j(t)$ *are the positions of some* correct *robots* i *and* j *at time* t, *and where* $distance(a, b)$ *denote the Euclidian distance between two positions.*

Definition 1 requires the convergence property only from the *correct* robots. Note that it is impossible to obtain the converge of all the robots in the system regardless their behavior since Byzantine robots may exhibit arbitrary behavior and never join the position of correct robots.

3   Deterministic Approximate Convergence

In this section we propose a deterministic convergence algorithm and prove its correctness in both ATOM and CORDA models. Algorithm 1, similarly to the approximate agreement algorithm in [8], uses two functions, $trim_f(P(t))$ and $median(P(t))$. The former removes the f largest and f smallest values from the multiset given in parameter. The latter returns the median point in the input range. Using Algorithm 1, each robot computes the median of the positions of the robots seen in its last LOOK cycle ignoring the f largest and f smallest positions.

Algorithm 1. Byzantine Tolerant Convergence

Functions:

$trim_f$: removes the f largest and f smallest values from the multiset given in parameter.

$median$: returns the points that is in the middle of the range of points given in parameter.

Actions:

move towards $median(trim_f(P(t)))$

Theorem 1. *[4] Algorithm 1 is convergent for* $n > 2f$ *in fully-synchronous ATOM model, for* $n > 3f$ *in semi-syncronous model and for* $n > 4f$ *in CORDA model under a k-bounded scheduler.*

References

1. Abraham, I., Amit, Y., Dolev, D.: Optimal Resilience Asynchronous Approximate Agreement. In: Higashino, T. (ed.) OPODIS 2004. LNCS, vol. 3544, pp. 229–239. Springer, Heidelberg (2005)
2. Agmon, N., Peleg, D.: Fault-tolerant gathering algorithms for autonomous mobile robots. In: Symposium on Discrete Algorithms: Proceedings of the fifteenth annual ACM-SIAM symposium on Discrete algorithms, vol. 11(14), pp. 1070–1078 (2004)
3. Ando, H., Oasa, Y., Suzuki, I., Yamashita, M.: Distributed memoryless point convergence algorithm for mobile robots with limited visibility. IEEE Transactions on Robotics and Automation 15(5), 818–828 (1999)
4. Bouzid, Z., Gradinariu Potop-Butucaru, M., Tixeuil, S.: Byzantine-resilient convergence in oblivious robot networks. Technical Report inria-00329890, INRIA (2008)
5. Cohen, R., Peleg, D.: Robot convergence via center-of-gravity algorithms. In: Proc. of the 11th Int. Colloquium on Structural Information and Communication Complexity, pp. 79–88 (2004)
6. Cohen, R., Peleg, D.: Convergence properties of the gravitational algorithm in asynchronous robot systems. SIAM Journal on Computing 34(6), 1516–1528 (2005)
7. Cohen, R., Peleg, D.: Convergence of autonomous mobile robots with inaccurate sensors and movements. In: Durand, B., Thomas, W. (eds.) STACS 2006. LNCS, vol. 3884, pp. 549–560. Springer, Heidelberg (2006)
8. Dolev, D., Lynch, N.A., Pinter, S.S., Stark, E.W., Weihl, W.E.: Reaching approximate agreement in the presence of faults. Journal of the ACM (JACM) 33(3), 499–516 (1986)
9. Lynch, N., Segala, R., Vaandrager, F.: Hybrid I/O automata. Information and Computation 185(1), 105–157 (2003)
10. Lynch, N.A.: Distributed Algorithms. Morgan Kaufmann, San Francisco (1996)
11. Prencipe, G.: CORDA: Distributed coordination of a set of autonomous mobile robots. In: Proc. 4th European Research Seminar on Advances in Distributed Systems (ERSADS 2001), Bertinoro, Italy, pp. 185–190 (May 2001)
12. Prencipe, G.: On the feasibility of gathering by autonomous mobile robots. In: Pelc, A., Raynal, M. (eds.) SIROCCO 2005. LNCS, vol. 3499, pp. 246–261. Springer, Heidelberg (2005)
13. Suzuki, I., Yamashita, M.: Distributed anonymous mobile robots: Formation of geometric patterns. SIAM Journal of Computing 28(4), 1347–1363 (1999)

Snap-Stabilization in Message-Passing Systems[*]

Sylvie Delaët[1], Stéphane Devismes[2], Mikhail Nesterenko[3],
and Sébastien Tixeuil[4]

[1] LRI UMR 8623, Université de Paris-Sud
sylvie.delaët@lri.fr
[2] VERIMAG UMR 5104, Université Joseph Fourier
stephane.devismes@imag.fr
[3] Computer Science Department, Kent State University
mikhail@cs.kent.edu
[4] LIP6 UMR 7606, Université Pierre et Marie Curie
sebastien.tixeuil@lip6.fr

Abstract. We consider *snap-stabilization* in message-passing systems. Snap-stabilization permits to design protocols that withstand transient faults: Any computation that is started after faults cease *immediately* satisfies the expected specification. Our contribution is twofold, as we demonstrate that in message passing systems *(i)* snap-stabilization is impossible for nontrivial problems if we consider channels with finite yet unbounded capacity, and *(ii)* snap-stabilization becomes possible in the same setting with bounded-capacity channels. The latter contribution is constructive, as we propose two snap-stabilizing protocols.

1 Introduction

Snap-stabilization [2] offers an attractive approach to transient fault tolerance. As soon as such faults end a snap-stabilizing protocol *immediately* operates correctly. Of course, not all safety predicates can be guaranteed when the system is started from an arbitrary global state. Snap-stabilization's notion of safety is *user-centric*: When the user initiates a request, the received response is correct. However, between the request and the response, the system can behave arbitrarily (except from giving an erroneous response to the user).

A related well-studied concept is *self-stabilization* [3]. After the end of the transient faults, a self-stabilizing protocol *eventually* satisfies its specification. Thus, snap-stabilization offers stronger safety guarantee than self-stabilization: It may take an arbitrary long time for a self-stabilizing protocol to start behaving correctly after the faults.

However, nearly every snap-stabilizing protocol presented so far assumes a high level communication model in which any process is able to read the states of every communication neighbor and update its own state in a single atomic step (this model is often referred to as the *state model*). Designing protocols with

---

[*] Due to the lack of space, many technical results have been omitted, see [1] (http://arxiv.org/abs/0802.1123) for more details.

V. Garg, R. Wattenhofer, and K. Kothapalli (Eds.): ICDCN 2009, LNCS 5408, pp. 281–286, 2009.
© Springer-Verlag Berlin Heidelberg 2009

forward recovery properties (such as self-stabilizing and snap-stabilizing ones) in the low level message-passing model is rather challenging. In this model, a process may either send a message to a single neighbor or receive a message from a single neighbor (but not both) together with some local computations; also messages in transit could be lost or duplicated.

Our contribution is twofold:

(1) We show that contrary to the high level state model, snap-stabilization is strictly more difficult to guarantee than self-stabilization in the low level message passing model. In more details, for nontrivial specifications, there exists no snap-stabilizing (even with unbounded memory per process) solution in message-passing systems with unbounded yet finite capacity channels. This is in contrast to the self-stabilizing setting, where solutions with unbounded memory per process [4], unbounded random sequences [5], or operating on a restricted set of specifications [6] do exist.

(2) We prove that snap-stabilization in the low level message passing model is feasible when channels have bounded capacity. Our proof is constructive, as we present snap-stabilizing protocols for *propagation of information with feedback* (PIF) and *mutual exclusion*.

2   Impossibility Results

We introduced the notion of *safety-distributed* specifications and shown that no problem having such a specification admits a snap-stabilizing solution in message-passing systems with finite yet unbounded capacity channels. Intuitively, safety-distributed specification has a safety property that depends on the behavior of more than one process. That is, certain process behaviors may satisfy safety if done sequentially, while violate it if done concurrently. For example, in mutual exclusion, a requesting process eventually executes the critical section but several requesting processes must not execute the critical section concurrently. Since most of classical synchronization and resource allocation problems are safety-distributed, this result prohibits the existence of snap-stabilizing protocols in message-passing systems if no further assumption is made.

This result hinges on the fact that after some transient faults the configuration may contain an unbounded number of arbitrary messages. Note that a safety-distributed specification involves more than one process and thus requires the processes to communicate to ensure that safety is not violated. However, with unbounded channels, each process cannot determine if the incoming message is indeed sent by its neighbor or is the result of faults. Thus, the communication is thwarted and the processes cannot differentiate safe and unsafe behavior.

3   Possibility Results

We shown that snap-stabilization becomes feasible in message-passing systems if the channels are of bounded known capacity. We present solutions to *propagation*

of information with feedback (PIF) and *mutual exclusion.* The protocols assume
fully-connected networks and use finite local memory at each process. The channels are lossy, bounded and FIFO. The program execution is asynchronous. To
ensure nontrivial liveness properties, we make the following fairness assumption:
If a sender process s transmits infinitely many messages to a receiver process r
then, r receives infinitely many of them. The message that is not lost is received
in finite (but unbounded) time. If the channel is full when the message is transmitted, this message is lost. For simplicity, we consider single-message capacity
channels. The extension to an arbitrary but known bounded message capacity
channels is straightforward (see [7]).

3.1 PIF

The PIF scheme can be described as follows: When requested, a process – called
initiator – starts the first phase of the PIF-computation by broadcasting a specific message m into the network (the *broadcast phase*). Then, each non-initiator
acknowledges to the initiator the receipt of m (the *feedback phase*). The PIF-
computation terminates when the initiator receives acknowledgments from every
other process and decides taking account of these acknowledgments. Any process
may need to initiate a PIF-computation. Thus, any process can be the initiator of a PIF-computation and several PIF-computations may run concurrently.
Hence, any PIF protocol has to cope with concurrent PIF-computations.

A basic PIF implementation requires the following input/output variables:

- Req_p. This variable is used to manage the requests for the process p. Req_p
  is set to Wait when p is requested to perform a PIF. Req_p is switched from
  Wait to In at the beginning of each PIF-computation (*n.b.* p starts a PIF-
  computation only upon a request). Finally, Req_p is switched from In to
  Done at the termination of each PIF-computation (this latter switch also
  corresponds to the *decision event*). Since a PIF-computation is started by
  p, we assume that Req_p cannot be set to Wait before the termination of the
  current PIF-computation, *i.e.*, before $\text{Req}_p = $ Done.[1]
- BMes_p. This buffer contains the message to broadcast.
- $\text{FMes}_p[1 \ldots n-1]$. $\text{FMes}_p[q]$ contains the acknowledgment for the broadcast
  message that q sends to p.

Using these variables, a process p is requested to broadcast a message m when
$(\text{BMes}_p, \text{Req}_p)$ is set to (m, Wait). Consequently to this request, a PIF-computation is started, *i.e.*, Req_p is set to In. This computation terminates when Req_p is
set to Done. Between the start and the termination, the protocol has to generate
two types of event at the application level. First, a "**B-receive**$\langle m \rangle$ **from** p"
event at any other process q. When this event occurs, the application at q is
assumed to treat the broadcast message m and then to put an acknowledgment
Ack_m into $\text{FMes}_q[p]$. The protocol then transmits Ack_m to p: This generates a

---

[1] Even if the current computation is due to a fault.

"**F-receive**$\langle Ack_m \rangle$ **from** q" event at p so that the application at p can access to the acknowledgment.

Note that the protocol has to operate correctly despite arbitrary messages in the channels left after the faults. Note also that the messages can be lost. To counter the message loss the protocol repeatedly sends duplicate messages. To deal with the arbitrary initial messages and the duplicates, we mark each message with a flag which takes its value in {0,1,2,3,4}. Two arrays are used to manage the flag marking:

- In $\texttt{State}_p[q]$, process p stores a flag value that it attaches to the messages it sends to its q'th neighbor.
- In $\texttt{NState}_p[q]$, p stores last flag that it receives from its qth neighbor.

Using these two arrays, our protocol proceeds as follows. When p starts a PIF-computation, it sets $\texttt{State}_p[q]$ to 0, for every process q. The computation terminates when $\texttt{State}_p[q] \geq 4$ for every index q.

During the computation, p repeatedly sends $\langle \texttt{PIF}, \texttt{BMes}_p, \texttt{FMes}_p[q], \texttt{State}_p[q], \texttt{NState}_p[q] \rangle$ to every process q such that $\texttt{State}_p[q] < 4$. When some process q receives $\langle \texttt{PIF}, B, F, pState, qState \rangle$ from p, q updates $\texttt{NState}_q[p]$ to $pState$. Then, if $pState < 4$, q sends $\langle \texttt{PIF}, \texttt{BMes}_q, \texttt{FMes}_q[p], \texttt{State}_q[p], \texttt{NState}_q[p] \rangle$ to p. Finally, p increments $\texttt{State}_p[q]$ only when it receives a $\langle \texttt{PIF}, B, F, qState, pState \rangle$ message from q such that $pState = \texttt{State}_p[q]$ and $pState < 4$.

The trick behind the algorithm is the following. Assume that p starts to broadcast the message m. Then, while $\texttt{State}_p[q] < 4$, $\texttt{State}_p[q]$ is incremented only when p received a message $\langle \texttt{PIF}, B, F, qState, pState \rangle$ from q such that $pState = \texttt{State}_p[q]$. So, $\texttt{State}_p[q]$ will be equal to four only after p successively receives $\langle \texttt{PIF}, B, F, qState, pState \rangle$ messages from q with the flag values 0,1,2, and 3. Now, initially there is at most one message in the channel from p to q and at most another one in the channel from q to p. So these messages can only cause at most two incrementations of $\texttt{State}_p[q]$. Finally, the arbitrary initial value of $\texttt{NState}_q[p]$ can cause at most one incrementation of $\texttt{State}_p[q]$. Hence, since $State_p[q] = 3$, we have the guarantee that p will increment $State_p[q]$ to 4 only after it receives a message sent by q after q receives a message sent by p. That is, this message is a correct acknowledgment of m by q.

It remains to see when generating the **B-receive** and **F-receive** events:

- Any process q receives at least four copies of the broadcast message from p. But, q generates a **B-receive** event only once for each broadcast message from p: When q switches $\texttt{NState}_q[p]$ to 3.
- After it starts, p is sure to receive the correct feedback from q since it receives from q a $\langle \texttt{PIF}, B, F, qState, pState \rangle$ message such that $pState = \texttt{State}_p[q] = 3$. As previously, to limit the number of events, p generates a **F-receive** event only when it switches $\texttt{State}_p[q]$ from 3 to 4. The next copies are ignored.

3.2   Mutual Exclusion

A *mutual-exclusion* mechanism ensures that a special section of code, called *critical section* (CS), can be executed by at most one process at any time. We adopt the specification proposed in [8]: Any process that requests CS enters in CS in finite time (*liveness*), and if a requesting process enters in CS, it executes CS alone (*safety*). It is important to note that, starting from any configuration, a snap-stabilizing mutual exclusion protocol cannot prevent several (non-requesting) processes to execute the CS simultaneously. However, it guarantees that every requesting process executes the CS alone.

Our snap-stabilizing mutual exclusion protocol is called $\mathcal{ME}$. As previously, $\mathcal{ME}$ uses the variable Req. A process p sets $\mathcal{ME}.\text{Req}_p$ to Wait when it requests the access to the CS. Process p is then called a *requestor* and assumed to not set $\mathcal{ME}.\text{Req}_p$ to Wait until $\mathcal{ME}.\text{Req}_p = \text{Done}$, *i.e.*, until its current request is done.

The main idea behind the protocol is the following: We assume identities on processes and the process with the smallest identity – called the *leader* – decides using a variable called Val which process can execute the CS. Val takes its value in $\{0 \ldots n-1\}$ and we assume that any process numbers its incoming channel from 1 to $n-1$. A process p is authorized to access the CS, if p is the leader and Val_p is equal to 0, or p is not the leader and the Val-value of the leader designates the link incoming from p to the leader.

When a process learns that it is authorized to access the CS: (1) It first ensures that no other process can execute the CS; (2) It then executes the CS if it wishes to; (3) Finally, it notifies to the leader that it has terminated Step (2) so that the leader (fairly) authorizes another process to access the CS.

To apply this scheme, $\mathcal{ME}$ is executed by phases from Phase 0 to 4 in such way that each process goes through Phase 0 infinitely often. After requesting the CS, a process p can access the CS only after executing Phase 0: p can access to the CS only if $\mathcal{ME}.\text{Req}_p = \text{In}$ and p switches $\mathcal{ME}.\text{Req}_p$ from Wait to In only in Phase 0. Hence, our protocol just ensures that after executing Phase 0, a process always executes the CS alone. We describe the five phases of our protocol below:

Phase 0. When a process p is in Phase 0, it starts a PIF-computation to collect the identities of all processes and to evaluate which one is the leader. It also sets $\mathcal{ME}.\text{Req}_p$ to In if $\mathcal{ME}.\text{Req}_p = \text{Wait}$. Finally switches to Phase 1.

Phase 1. When a process p is in Phase 1, p waits the termination of the previous PIF. Then, p starts a PIF of the message ASK to know if it is authorized to access the CS and switches to Phase 2. Upon receiving a message ASK from the channel p, any process q answers YES if $\text{Val}_q = p$, NO otherwise. Of course, any process will only take account of the answer of the leader.

Phase 2. When a process p is in Phase 2, it waits the termination of the PIF started in Phase 1. After the PIF terminates, p knows if it is authorized to access the CS. If p is authorized to access the CS, p starts a PIF of the message EXIT. The goal of this message is to force all other processes to restart to Phase 0. This ensures no other process executes the CS until p notifies to the leader that it releases the CS. Indeed, due to the arbitrary initial configuration, some process $q \neq p$ may believe that it is authorized to execute the CS: If q never starts Phase 0. On the contrary, after restarting to 0, q cannot receive any authorization from the leader until p notifies to the leader that it releases the CS. Finally, p terminates Phase 2 by switching to Phase 3.

Phase 3. When a process p is in Phase 3, it waits the termination of the last PIF. After the PIF terminates, if p is authorized to execute the CS, then: (1) p executes the CS and switches $\mathcal{ME}$.Req$_p$ from In to Done if $\mathcal{ME}$.Req$_p$ = In, then either (2.a) p is the leader and switches Val$_p$ from 0 to 1 or (2.b) p is not the leader and starts a PIF of the message EXITCS to notify to the leader that it releases the CS. Upon receiving such a message, the leader increments its variable Val modulus $n + 1$ to authorize another process to access the CS. Finally, p terminates Phase 3 by switching to Phase 4.

Phase 4. When a process p is in Phase 4, it waits the termination of the last PIF and then switches to Phase 0.

4 Conclusion

In this paper, we shown that *snap-stabilization* is impossible for a wide class of specifications in message-passing systems where the channel capacity is finite yet unbounded. However, we also show that *snap-stabilization* is possible in message-passing systems if we assume a bound on the channel capacity. The proof is constructive, as we presented two snap-stabilizing protocols for message-passing systems with a bounded channel capacity.

It is worth investigating if these results could be extended to more general networks, *e.g.* with general topologies, and/or where nodes are subject to permanent *aka* crash failures. On the practical side, our results imply the possibility of implementing snap-stabilizing protocols on real networks, and actually implementing them is a future challenge.

References

1. Delaët, S., Devismes, S., Nesterenko, M., Tixeuil, S.: Snap-stabilization in message-passing systems. Research Report 6446, INRIA (2008)
2. Bui, A., Datta, A.K., Petit, F., Villain, V.: Snap-stabilization and pif in tree networks. Distributed Computing 20(1), 3–19 (2007)
3. Dijkstra, E.W.: Self-stabilizing systems in spite of distributed control. Commun. ACM 17(11), 643–644 (1974)
4. Gouda, M.G., Multari, N.J.: Stabilizing communication protocols. IEEE Trans. Computers 40(4), 448–458 (1991)
5. Afek, Y., Brown, G.M.: Self-stabilization over unreliable communication media. Distributed Computing 7(1), 27–34 (1993)
6. Delaët, S., Ducourthial, B., Tixeuil, S.: Self-stabilization with r-operators revisited. Journal of Aerospace Computing, Information, and Communication (2006)
7. Awerbuch, B., Patt-Shamir, B., Varghese, G.: Self-stabilization by local checking and correction (extended abstract). In: FOCS, pp. 268–277. IEEE, Los Alamitos (1991)
8. Cournier, A., Datta, A.K., Petit, F., Villain, V.: Enabling snap-stabilization. In: ICDCS, pp. 12–19. IEEE Computer Society, Los Alamitos (2003)

A Novel Performance Index for Characterizing Stochastic Faulty Patterns in Mesh-Based Networks*

Farshad Safaei[1,2] and Mohammad Mahdi Gilak[3]

[1] IPM, School of Computer Science
[2] Dept. of ECE, Shahid Beheshti Univ., Tehran, Iran
[3] Faculty of Mathematical Sciences, Shahid Beheshti Univ., Tehran, Iran
safaei@ipm.ir, mo.gilak@mail.sbu.ac.ir

Abstract. In this paper, we propose a new performance index of network reliability namely, probability of message facing the faulty patterns, to assess the performance-related reliability of adaptive routing schemes in mesh-based interconnect networks with a variety of common cause faulty patterns. These patterns comprise of both convex and concave regions which are being widely used in the literature. Experimental examples are also presented in which the results of the suggested modeling approach are confirmed through simulation results.

1 Introduction

Almost all of the performance evaluation studies for functionality of complex hardware-software systems, however, have made use solely of simulation experiments [1-4]. The limitations of simulation-based studies are that they are highly time-consuming and expensive. This paper presents the mathematical model for analyzing the performance and reliability of a mesh-based interconnect network in the presence of the common cause failures caused by the occurrence of stochastic faulty patterns in a given communication network.

This paper is organized as follows. Section 2 presents relevant preliminary information. Section 3 describes the mathematical approach for determining the probability of facing the faulty patterns. In Section 4, experimental examples are presented, in which the values obtained by the mathematical expressions are compared with our simulated results. Finally, Section 5 concludes the paper.

2 Preliminaries

2.1 Fault Models and Fault Patterns

The failure does not only reduce the computational power, but also deforms the structure of interconnect network, which may consequently lead to a *disconnected* network.

---

* This research was in part supported by a grant from IPM. (No. CS1387-4-07).

V. Garg, R. Wattenhofer, and K. Kothapalli (Eds.): ICDCN 2009, LNCS 5408, pp. 287–293, 2009.

Definition 1 [2, 4]. *A network is disconnected if there exist two nodes without any fault-free path to route messages between them.*

Adjacent faulty nodes are coalesced into *faulty regions*, which may lead to different patterns of failed components. These regions, which have been introduced in [4] may have different patterns and are classified as convex or concave regions.

Definition 2 [4]. *A convex region is defined as a region* $\mathcal{R}$ *in which a line segment connecting any two points in* $\mathcal{R}$ *lies entirely within* $\mathcal{R}$. *If we change the "line segment" in the standard convex region definition to "horizontal or vertical line segment", the resulted region is called rectilinear convex segments. Any region that is not convex is a concave region.*

Examples of convex regions are I-shape, ⊡-shape and that of concave regions are L-shape, U-shape, T-shape, H-shape, +-shape.

3 Mathematical Model Formulation

3.1 Assumptions

  a. Messages are uniformly destined to other network nodes.
  b. Messages are routed adaptively through the network. Moreover, a message is assumed to always follow one of the available shortest paths in the fault-free segments of the network.
  c. Fault patterns are static [2, 4] and do not disconnect the network.
  d. Nodes are more complex than links and thus have higher failure rates [2]. Thus, we assume only node failures.

3.2 Calculating the Probability of Message Facing Faulty Patterns

Consider an $R \times C$ mesh network in which there exist some faulty nodes that have formed a I-shaped, II-shaped, +-shaped, H-shaped, T-shaped, U-shaped, L-shaped, or ⊡-shaped faulty pattern, such that the faulty nodes do not disconnect the network. We refer to such a network as a connected $R \times C$ mesh with the $X - shape$ faulty pattern.

Definition 3 (The minimum path from point $a = (x_a, y_a)$ **to point** $b = (x_b, y_b)$ **).**
We denote by S *the set of all sequences containing forward, backward, upward and downward directions, so that all* S *elements start from* $a = (x_a, y_a)$ *and terminate at* $b = (x_b, y_b)$. *We let* s_0 *be the length of the shortest sequences of* S. *Therefore, one path from* a *to* b *is an element of the set* S *with the length of* s_0.

Definition 4. *The set of* $R \times C$ *mesh network vertices, denoted by* $v(M_{R \times C})$, *is defined formally as*

$$v(M_{R \times C}) = \{(x, y) : 1 \le x \le R, 1 \le y \le C\} \tag{1}$$

Let a and b be two non-faulty points in an $R \times C$ mesh network, then the number of paths (minimal) between two points $a, b \in v(M_{R \times C})$ is given by

$$\binom{|x_b - x_a| + |y_b - y_a|}{|x_b - x_a|} \tag{2}$$

In this section, our goal is to calculate the probability of a message facing the existing faulty pattern in the connected $R \times C$ mesh in the presence of the $X - shape$ faulty pattern. A path facing the faulty pattern means that there exist one or more points from the set of points residing on the given path. In order to calculate the probability of facing faulty pattern, we should enumerate the number of all existing paths facing the $X - shape$ faulty pattern and divide them by the number of all existing paths in the connected $R \times C$ mesh network. This quantity is expressed formally as

$$P_{hit} \triangleq \frac{The\ number\ of\ all\ minimal\ paths\ crossing\ the\ fault\ region}{The\ number\ of\ minimal\ paths\ existing\ in\ the\ network} \tag{3}$$

In the mesh network, the position of the faulty patterns is important. Therefore, to calculate the parameter P_{hit} in the presence of the $X - shape$ faulty pattern, we should know the coordinates of all the faulty points. We denote the set of these characteristics in the $X - shape$ faulty pattern by $F(X)$.

Theorem 1. *In a connected $R \times C$ mesh network with the $X - shape$ faulty region, the number of all existing paths between any pair of non-faulty nodes is given by*

$$\sum_{a,b \in v(M_{R \times C}) \backslash F(X)} \binom{|x_b - x_a| + |y_b - y_a|}{|x_b - x_a|} \tag{4}$$

where the symbol "\" signifies the difference between two sets.

Proof. Consider two non-faulty points a and b in a connected $R \times C$ mesh network in the presence of the $X - shape$ faulty pattern. The number of paths crossing from a to b is denoted by

$$\binom{|x_b - x_a| + |y_b - y_a|}{|x_b - x_a|}$$

Thus, the total number of paths in the above mentioned network can be calculated as the aggregate of the total number of paths between any two of non-faulty points in the network. That is

$$\sum_{a,b \in v(M_{R \times C}) \backslash F(X)} \binom{|x_b - x_a| + |y_b - y_a|}{|x_b - x_a|}$$

which completes the proof.   ∎

Table 1. Description of the direction to be used for adaptive routing messages in the mesh network

Condition satisfied	Message direction
$x_b - x_a \geq 0$	The message is routed from $a = (x_a, y_a)$ to $b = (x_b, y_b)$ in X^+
$x_b - x_a < 0$	The message is routed from $a = (x_a, y_a)$ to $b = (x_b, y_b)$ in X^-
$y_b - y_a \geq 0$	The message is routed from $a = (x_a, y_a)$ to $b = (x_b, y_b)$ in Y^+
$y_b - y_a < 0$	The message is routed from $a = (x_a, y_a)$ to $b = (x_b, y_b)$ in Y^-

To continue the work, it is required to determine the direction of each path in the network with respect to the coordinate axes. Consider two points $a = (x_a, y_a)$ and $b = (x_b, y_b)$ in the $R \times C$ mesh. Table 1 gives the information for the direction of a message utilizing the X and Y dimensions. The symbols $-$ and $+$ reveal the orientation in the negative or positive side of the coordinate axes, respectively.

Now, if we consider an arbitrary path from a to b and multiply the set of the first components of the existing nodes of that by the set of the second components of the existing nodes in a Cartesian way, we will obtain a mesh subnetwork, $|x_b - x_a| \times |y_b - y_a|$, from the $R \times C$ mesh in which node a is placed in one corner of that and node b is placed in the corner opposite a in the mesh subnetwork. This subnetwork from the $R \times C$ mesh network is denoted by $M(a,b)$. It is straightforward to show that all the existing paths from a to b are in $M(a,b)$.

Before we proceed to calculate (3), we pause to give a few definitions; then we present and prove a theorem.

Definition 5. *The function* $\mathcal{F} : \mathcal{P}(M_{R \times C}) \rightarrow v(M_{R \times C})$ *is called the restriction function of* $M_{R \times C}$ *network in which* $\mathcal{P}(M_{R \times C})$ *is the set of all mesh subnetworks of* $M_{R \times C}$, *and it's criterion is expressed as*

$$\mathcal{F}(M(a,b)) = M(a,b) \cap F(X) \tag{5}$$

Definition 6. *Let* a *and* b *be two non-faulty points of* $v(M_{R \times C})$. *For any two arbitrary points* $C_i, C_j \in \mathcal{F}(M(a,b))$, *the number of possible paths from* C_j *to* C_i *is indicated by* $LM_{a,b}(C_j, C_i)$ *so that the direction of each path in dimension* X *(or* Y) *is collinear with the direction of a path from* a *to* b *in dimension* X *(or* Y). *The parameter* $LM_{a,b}(C_j, C_i)$ *is defined as follows*

$$\begin{pmatrix} \Delta_x^{a,b}(C_j, C_i) + \Delta_y^{a,b}(C_j, C_i) \\ \Delta_x^{a,b}(C_j, C_i) \end{pmatrix} \tag{6}$$

where $\Delta_x^{a,b}(C_j, C_i)$ is a function denoting the number of orientations along a path from C_j to C_i in dimension X which are collinear with the orientations along a path from a to b and it's criterion is expressed as

$$\Delta_x^{a,b}(C_j,C_i) = \begin{cases} \left| |x_{C_i} - x_{C_j}| \right| & \left(x_b - x_a \geq 0 \ \ and \ \ x_{C_i} - x_{C_j} \geq 0\right) \ or \\ & \left(x_b - x_a < 0 \ \ and \ \ x_{C_i} - x_{C_j} \geq 0\right) \\ \\ -\left| x_{C_i} - x_{C_j} \right| & otherwise \end{cases} \qquad (7)$$

Similarly, we can obtain the criterion of function $\Delta_y^{a,b}(C_j,C_i)$ by interchanging the roles of X and Y as

$$\Delta_y^{a,b}(C_j,C_i) = \begin{cases} \left| |y_{C_i} - y_{C_j}| \right| & \left(y_b - y_a \geq 0 \ \ and \ \ y_{C_i} - y_{C_j} \geq 0\right) \ or \\ & \left(y_b - y_a < 0 \ \ and \ \ y_{C_i} - y_{C_j} \geq 0\right) \\ \\ -\left| y_{C_i} - y_{C_j} \right| & otherwise \end{cases} \qquad (8)$$

Theorem 2. *Given that a and b are two non-faulty points of a mesh network and $\mathcal{F}(M(a,b)) = \{C_1,C_2,...,C_k\}$, the number of paths from a to b that do not traverse the points $C_1,C_2,...,C_k$ is given by*

$$\det_{0 \leq i,j \leq k} d_{ij}(a,b) \qquad (9)$$

in which

$$\begin{aligned} d_{0j}(a,b) &= LM_{a,b}(C_j,b) & j &= 0,1,...,k \\ d_{ij}(a,b) &= LM_{a,b}(C_j,C_i) & i &= 1,2,...,k \quad j = 0,1,...,k \\ C_0 &= a \end{aligned} \qquad (10)$$

Proof. The proof is quite involved and we omit it due to lack of space. The interested reader is referred to [5] for the proof. ∎

Theorem 3. *Let $M_{R \times C}$ be a connected $R \times C$ mesh network in the presence of $X - shape$ faulty region with faulty points $F(X)$. The number of paths not facing the $X - shape$ is calculated as*

$$\sum_{a,b \in v(M_{R \times C}) \setminus F(X)} \det_{0 \leq i,j \leq C_{a,b}} d_{ij}(a,b) \qquad (11)$$

where $C_{a,b}$ is the number of elements of $\mathcal{F}(M(a,b))$; that is

$$\| \mathcal{F}(M(a,b)) \| = C_{a,b}$$

Proof. Consider two arbitrary points a and b from the set $v(M_{R \times C}) \setminus F(X)$. According to Theorem 2, the number of minimal paths from a to b, not crossing the points $\mathcal{F}(M(a,b))$, is equal to $\det_{0 \leq i,j \leq C_{a,b}} d_{ij}(a,b)$. Thus, the number of minimal paths from a to b not crossing the $F(X)$ points, will be equal to $\det_{0 \leq i,j \leq C_{a,b}} d_{ij}(a,b)$.

Therefore, the number of all existing paths in $M_{R \times C}$ not traversing the $F(X)$ points is equal to the aggregate of the total number of paths between any two non-faulty points in $M_{R \times C}$ not crossing the points of $F(X)$. That is,

$$\sum_{a,b \in v(M_{R \times C}) \backslash F(X)} \det_{0 \leq i,j \leq C_{a,b}} d_{ij}(a,b) . \qquad \blacksquare$$

It follows from Theorems 2 and 3, the probability that a path in $M_{R \times C}$ not facing the fault pattern, P_{miss}, can be calculated as

$$P_{miss} = \sum_{a,b \in v(M_{R \times C}) \backslash F(X)} \frac{\det_{0 \leq i,j \leq C_{a,b}} d_{ij}(a,b)}{\left(\begin{array}{c} |x_b - x_a| + |y_b - y_a| \\ |x_b - x_a| \end{array} \right)} \qquad (12)$$

Thus, it is trivial that the probability of message facing the faulty pattern, P_{hit}, is given by

$$P_{hit} = 1 - P_{miss} \qquad (13)$$

4 Experimental Results

An experimental approach is necessary to validate the analytical evaluation to which mathematical analysis led. A program for calculating the probability of message facing the faulty patterns was written in C and executed to simulate the failure of nodes and the subsequent constructing of the corresponding faulty patterns. Table 2 gives the results obtained from simulation experiments and the mathematical models.

Table 2. Experimental results of the probability of message facing faulty patterns

Faulty pattern	Mesh network ($M_{R \times C}$)				
	5×6	7×6	9×11	10×10	13×9
‖-shape $F(\|) = \{(1,2),(2,2),(3,2),(2,3),(3,3),(4,3)\}$	0.751	0.612	0.325	0.322	0.274
T-shaped $F(T) = \{(2,2),(2,3),(2,4),(1,4),(3,4),(4,4)\}$	0.733	0.765	0.391	0.421	0.416
□-shape $F(\Box) = \{(1,1),(1,2),(2,1),(2,2),(3,2),(3,1)\}$	0.227	0.134	0.011	0.01	0.005
+-shape $F(+) = \{(1,3),(2,3),(3,3),(4,3),(2,4),(2,2)\}$	0.818	0.66	0.393	0.379	0.307

5 Conclusions

This paper introduces probability of message facing faulty patterns as a novel performance index of network reliability, and presents the mathematical approach for its evaluation for arbitrary shapes in a given network with mesh architecture. It is shown that for a variety number of faulty patterns, mathematical expressions of this probability are in good agreement with those obtained through simulation experiments.

References

1. Levitina, G., Xieb, M., Zhang, T.: Reliability of fault-tolerant systems with parallel task processing. European Journal of Operational Research 177(1), 420–430 (2007)
2. Gómez, M.E., et al.: A Routing Methodology for Achieving Fault Tolerance in Direct Networks. IEEE Transactions on Computers 55(4), 400–415 (2006)
3. Suh, Y.J., et al.: Software-based rerouting for fault-tolerant pipelined communication. IEEE Trans. on Parallel and Distributed Systems 11(3), 193–211 (2000)
4. Wu, J., Jiang, Z.: On Constructing the Minimum Orthogonal Convex Polygon in 2-D Faulty Meshes, IPDPS (2004)
5. Safaei, F., Fathy, M., Khonsari, A., Gilak, M., Ould-Khaoua, M.: A New Performance Measure for Characterizing Fault-Rings in Interconnection Networks. Journal of Information Sciences (submitted, 2007)

Optimizing Multi-hop Queries in ZigBee Based Multi-sink Sensor Networks

Bing Han[1,2,3] and Gwendal Simon[1]

[1] Institut TELECOM - TELECOM Bretagne, Brest, France
[2] Institut TELECOM - TELECOM ParisTech, Paris, France
[3] State Key Laboratory of Networking and Switching Technology,
Beijing University of Posts and Telecommunications, Beijing, China
{bing.han,gwendal.simon}@telecom-bretagne.eu

Abstract. Wireless sensor networks with multiple users collecting data directly from the sensors have many potential applications. An important problem is to allocate for each user a query range to achieve certain global optimality while avoid congesting the sensors in the meanwhile. We study this problem for a ZigBee cluster tree by formulating it into a multi-dimensional multi-choice knapsack problem. Maximum overall query range and max-min fair query range objectives are investigated. Distributed algorithms are proposed which exploit the ZigBee cluster tree structure to keep the computation local. Extensive simulations show that the proposed methods achieve good approximation to the optimal solution with little overhead and improve the network performance.

1 Introduction

Wireless Sensor Networks (WSNs) with multiple mobile sinks can be very useful in emergency applications. A typical example is a monitoring system with some device-equipped firemen gathering data from the fire site in order to determine a safe perimeter, while others operating on the hearth are under real-time alert about risks of nearby explosions. The firemen send requests to and collect data from the sensors within a specific area in multi-hop fashion. Since the firemen are generally interested in what happens nearby, it is beneficial to interact *directly* with the sensors around them instead of via an infrastructure. Under this case, firemen are reasonably considered as *sinks*. Fig. 1 illustrates WSNs with and without an infrastructure. Users in Fig. 1(b) are considered as sinks.

Due to the queries imposed by the sinks, a sensor spends a certain amount of bandwidth for either sending its own data or forwarding data from other sensors. Obviously, if a sensor is impacted by many sinks, it may experience congestion. Packets dropped due to congestion not only waste energy but also degrade query coverage of all related sinks. Thus, it is a natural requirement that each sink sets a proper impact range to avoid congestion and to achieve a global optimality at the same time. Congestion control in WSN has been studied in recent years and proposed solutions have focused on the transport layer [1]. Furthermore, all existing studies have emphasized on providing fairness for sources (sensors)

V. Garg, R. Wattenhofer, and K. Kothapalli (Eds.): ICDCN 2009, LNCS 5408, pp. 294–305, 2009.

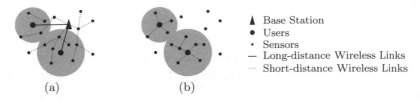

(a)   (b)

Fig. 1. Multi-sink WSN structures. (a) With infrastructure, data retrieved from base station. (b) Infrastructure-less, data retrieved directly from sensors.

i.e. allocating for each sensor a fair amount of bandwidth. In contrast, we investigate both maximality and fairness objectives *in favor of sinks*, *i.e.* allocating for each sink a proper query impact range to achieve global optimality while not congesting the sensors. We emphasize that doing so has practical significance. When sinks are independent users of the WSN, we usually would like to give each of them a fair chance to access the network thus prevent certain users from being starved. When the users act towards the same goal, one may want to maximize the sum of their impact range. We also argue that whole-network query coverage on the sensors, as a usually studied problem, is less important under the aforementioned application scenario. Instead, data from sensors within a reasonable query range should be reported with high reliability. Thus, sensors far away from all sinks may have no query on them, as shown in Fig. 1(b).

We investigate this *impact range allocation problem* and confine our study with the following assumptions: (i) Each fireman tends to set its impact range as large as possible in order to maximize individual security. The impact range is measured by hop numbers such that a k hop impact range will cover all k hop neighbors of the sink. (ii) ZigBee network will be employed since it is especially suitable for low power, low rate wireless sensor networks and supported by many off-the-shelf WSN products. Because energy supply is usually scarce in WSN, cluster tree mode of the ZigBee will be considered. (iii) No in-network data aggregation or compression. (iv) We will investigate two global optimization objectives: maximizing the overall impact range and allocating max-min fair impact range for the sinks although other objectives may be applied.

The contributions of this study are three-fold. Firstly, the impact range allocation problem is formulated and studied as a Multi-dimensional Multiple choice Knapsack Problem (MMKP) with two optimization objectives. Secondly, distributed heuristic is proposed based on solving a local optimization problem on congested sensors. Finally, simulation results show that the proposed algorithm obtains a good approximation to the optimal solution and is able to alleviate congestion therefore improve network performance. The rest of the paper is organized as follows: Related works are briefly surveyed in Section 2. ZigBee standard is briefly introduced and a multi-sink WSN architecture is proposed in Section 3. In Section 4, we formally describe the proposed problems. Distributed algorithms are discussed in Section 5 and evaluated by simulations in Section 6. Some perspectives of these first results may deserve further investigation. We discuss them and conclude the paper in Section 7.

2   Related Works

We will formulate the impact range allocation problem as an MMKP in Section 4. For detailed descriptions of MMKP, please refer to [2]. In general, MMKP can be solved with branch and bound strategy and there are several off-the-shelf Mixed Integer Programming (MIP) solvers available, e.g. the GLPK package[3]. Besides, various algorithms have been proposed to solve the MMKP either exactly or approximately. Due to the NP-completeness of the problem, only approximate algorithms are suitable for large or/and online problems [4,5,6]. In particular, an MMKP with a single constraint degrades to a Multiple Choice Knapsack Problem (MCKP). The lexicographic Max-Min Fairness (MMF) is a generalization of the traditional max-min fairness defined in [7]. They are equivalent on convex solution sets but MMF solution exists on general sets as well. We will employ the former because the problem has discrete parameter values. MMF has been used in formulating various resource allocation problems in the networking area and general MMF concepts and formal problem formulations, algorithms as well as example design problems can be found in [8].

Similar query allocation problem has been studied based on queries with continuous radius in our previous work [9]. We investigate hop-based query in the current paper. Under this discrete setting, the problem becomes combinatoric which is harder and deserves methods other than those employed in [9].

Concluding the discussions above, our MMKP formulation of the maximum overall impact range problem is exactly the same MMKP problem mentioned above and can be solved by those algorithms. So we emphasize on formulating the MMKP problem with MMF as an objective which is novel. Furthermore, we will consider solving both problems in a distributed way in contrast to the centralized algorithms already proposed.

Note also that our work is based on the ZigBee cluster tree operating mode which necessitates a beacon enabled 802.15.4 network. Beacon scheduling, beacon period and superframe length have great impact on the performance of the network, as investigated in [10,11,12]. In our study, we will focus on solving a distributed optimization problem, thus we schedule the beacons only between parents and children and fix beacon period and superframe length.

3   ZigBee Based Wireless Sensor Networks

The ZigBee specification [13] defines addressing, network maintenance and routing for unicast, multicast or broadcast packets at network layer for LR-WPANs. It specifies IEEE 802.15.4 [14] as its MAC layer, which provides sleep mode feature based on superframes bounded by the beacons. This feature is available only in the synchronized tree network. A ZigBee network is initiated and controlled by a single ZigBee coordinator, while other devices act as either a router, if they participate in routing, or end devices otherwise. The routing mechanism employed by ZigBee combines the flat routing known as AODV [15] and the hierarchical routing based on the cluster tree. When the network operates in ad hoc mode, the data is generally delivered by AODV and only when AODV routing fails, the cluster tree routing is used. The network can also operate in pure cluster tree mode where only tree routing is used. Under this case, a router only need to decide to forward a packet to either its parent or one of its children based on its own address, destination address of the packet, the maximum children number (Cm), maximum router number (Rm) and maximum network depth (Lm). The last three parameters are pre-configured for a given ZigBee network and are known to every device. Cluster tree routing does not employ any route discovery message thus is more appealing for energy constrained networks such as WSNs. Besides, a sink (user) in a ZigBee-based WSN may act as either end devices or routers. If mobility is considered, the movement of a sink router may result in reconstruction of the subtree rooted at itself. Thus we consider only the case that sinks are end devices in this paper.

In order to collect data from the sensors, a sink sends a query to all sensors within a certain number of hops around it. All queried sensors send data back at the required rate until modified by another query. The queries are sent via hop-bounded flooding on the tree and data is sent back via unicast cluster tree routing, both supported by the ZigBee specification. Especially for the latter, we assume sensors send a copy of the same data to each querying sink rather than using multicast. Fig. 2 illustrates an example multi-sink WSN with two sinks and a query at radius of 3 hops.

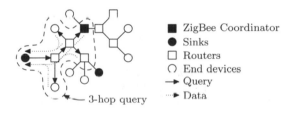

Fig. 2. Multi-sink WSN based on ZigBee tree structure

4   Model and Problem Formulation

We consider a set $\mathcal{V}$ of n sensors and a set $\mathcal{M}$ of m sinks. The communication tree employed by ZigBee is defined as $T = (\mathcal{V} \cup \mathcal{M}, E)$ with $\mathcal{V} \cup \mathcal{M}$ the node set and E the link set. There is a link between two nodes of $\mathcal{V} \cup \mathcal{M}$ if they have a parent-child relationship between them. The available bandwidth r_i of a sensor is assumed to be the shared bandwidth seen by the application and we assume all r_is take the same value. A **query** of sink p is disseminated to all sensors within $u(p)$ hops on the tree from p. $u(p)$ is also referred to as the impact range of query p. Sensors under query will generate data at a certain constant rate in response. Because the data are routed back to the sink along the communication tree, the amount of bandwidth a sensor i has to spend, as a result of the impact of p, is equal to or larger than its upstream sensors along the route. This holds as long as we assume there is no compression or aggregation on the data. A **configuration** is a set of impact range chosen by all sinks, noted as $C = \{u(p) : \forall p \in \mathcal{M}\}$. We say that a configuration is *feasible* when the bandwidth required to handle the queries on each sensor is less than its available bandwidth. The set of feasible configurations will be referred to as C.

The impact range allocation problem is to find a subset of C which achieves certain optimization objectives. We formulate it into a generalized MMKP. Let each possible impact range of sink p correspond to an item to be selected and the value of the items is the hop-distances in T, then we have $u(p) \in [1, d_T]$ where d_T is the diameter of T. Since each sink sets its impact range to a particular value at a certain time, the items can be seen as grouped into m classes each corresponding to a certain sink. A binary variable x_{pu} is then associated with sink p where $x_{pu} = 1$ indicates that $u(p) = u$ and $x_{pu} = 0$ otherwise, with $u \in [1, d_T]$. The bandwidth provided by a sensor i to a sink p when p takes impact range level u is denoted as r_{ipu} and is mapped to the ith dimension of weight of item u in class p. Each sensor forms a constraint dimension with its available bandwidth r_i. The general MMKP is formulated as follows:

Achieve: General Objective

$$\text{Subject to:} \sum_{p \in \mathcal{M}} \sum_{u=1}^{d_T} r_{ipu} x_{pu} \leq r_i, \ i \in \mathcal{V} \tag{1}$$

$$\sum_{u=1}^{d_T} x_{pu} = 1, \ p \in \mathcal{M} \tag{2}$$

$$x_{pu} \in \{0, 1\}, \ p \in \mathcal{M}, \ u \in [1, d_T] \tag{3}$$

We propose two explicit objectives in place of the general one: (i) to maximize the sum of impact range of all sinks *i.e.* $\sum_{p \in \mathcal{M}} u(p)$, noted as **Maximum Impact Range** (**MMKP-MIR**) problem, and (ii) to find **Max-Min Fair** impact range allocations (**MMKP-MMF**). Searching for MMF solutions in discrete solution space has been proven to be NP-hard [16]. Similarly, we can also prove MMKP-MIR is NP-hard but this is considered as technical thus omitted.

5   Distributed Algorithms

The basic idea of the distributed algorithm is to solve a smaller local problem at the congested sensor based on its estimation of the potential traffic. Algorithms for MMKP-MMF and MMKP-MIR are similar thus are put under a uniform algorithmic framework.

5.1   Uniform Algorithmic Framework

At the sink side, the algorithm starts with a *slow start* phase. As shown in Algorithm 1, function `initLevel` increase the query level with exponential growth to quickly discover a potentially congested sensor. On the sensors, the `congested` function detects a potential congestion state. We propose using the collision intensity information obtained from MAC layer as a simple congestion identification mechanism. Accurate congestion detection methods can be applied but they are out of scope of this paper. On congestion, function solveMCKP calculates an impact range allocation for the related sinks. We exploit GLPK for MMKP-MIR or a heuristic we will propose for MMKP-MMF in the simulation implementation. Note that GLPK is obviously infeasible for an implementation on real sensor devices, we use it the simulations only for simplicity. Then the congested sensor sends an adjust-level message to the related sinks with the local solution. On receiving an adjust-level message, the sink sets its impact range to the suggested level if the suggested level is smaller than the current value. Then the increaseLevel function increases the impact level linearly because the suggested impact range is already near the optimal.

In the following, we first present the traffic estimation mechanism, then we propose a heuristic for the MMF version of the local problem, finally, we explain why linear increment in increaseLevel of the impact level is necessary.

Algorithm 1. Distributed Heuristic

```
Sink Part   : Run at sink p
send < level, p, 1 >
while no < adjust-level > message do
    level ← initLevel()
    send < level, p, level >
level ← adjustLevel()
while true do
    while no < adjust-level > message do
        level ← increaseLevel()
        send < modify-level, p, level >
    level ← adjustLevel()
    send < modify level, p, level >

Sensor Part: Run at sensor i
while true do
    if congested() then
        C ← solveMCKP()
        for ∀p · l_p ∈ C do
            send < adjust-level, l_p > to p;
```

Algorithm 2. Local MCKP-MMF

```
input  : S ⊆ M, U, h, h_p, d, r_i
output : MCKP-MMF configuration C

for p ∈ S do
    C ← {S_p = (level_p ← 0, state_p ← active)}
for u_m ∈ U, m ← 1 to |U| do
    A ← {S_p : state_p = active}
    if A = ∅ then break
    equclass ← (d − h + h_p)/2
    sort(A, Δ_T(equclass, h_p, u_m))
    for a_j ∈ A, j ← 1 to |A| do
        C' ← C, level'_{a_j} ← u_{m+1}
        if feasible (C') then level_{a_j} ← u_{m+1}
        else
            for a_k ∈ A, k ← j to |A| do
                state_{u_k} ← stop
            break
return C
```

5.2 Traffic Estimation

The aim of traffic estimation is to provide information about the additional traffic load offered on a certain router if the impact range of a query becomes one hop larger. We propose a local estimation profiting the ZigBee cluster tree structure, instead of measuring the real traffic.

Consider the ZigBee tree T rooted at the ZigBee coordinator, as shown in Fig. 3(a). For the querying sink s, the whole network can be seen as a tree T_s rooted at itself as in Fig. 3(b). Thus for a router (the ZigBee Coordinator is considered also as a router), the additional traffic passing through it comes from the to-be-covered devices that are his descendent on T_s. We assign a label (h, h_s) to each device in the network, where h and h_s denote the depth of the device on T and T_s, respectively. Note that every device knows h on joining the network and h_s is actually its hop distance to s which could be obtained from the query messages. Then we classify the routers whose label satisfies $h - h_s = d - 2i$ into equivalent classes EQ_i, and the router with $h_s = i$ is referred to as the

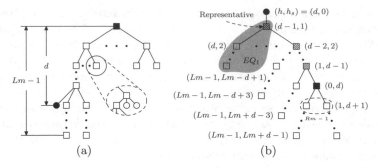

Fig. 3. Different views of a ZigBee routing tree. (a) Tree T, rooted at the ZigBee coordinator. (b) Tree T_s, rooted at the sink, labels assigned to devices.

representative router of the equivalent class. As shown in Fig. 3(b), the routers belong to EQ_1 are grouped into a shadowed area.

Now consider a router in $r \in EQ_i$ with label (h, h_s), let $\Delta_R(i, h_s, k)$ be the number of additional routers and $\Delta_E(i, h_s, k)$ the number of additional end devices that will be handled by r when the impact range of the query increases from k to $k + 1$. If every device sends data at constant rate B, the additional traffic load $\Delta_T(i, h_s, k)$ on router r should be:

$$\Delta_T(i, h_s, k) = B \left(\Delta_R(i, h_s, k) + \Delta_E(i, h_s, k) \right). \tag{4}$$

We first derive $\Delta_R(i, h_s, k)$, then $\Delta_E(i, h_s, k)$ can be obtained as:

$$\Delta_E(i, h_s, k) = \Delta_R(i, h_s - 1, k - 1)(Cm - Rm). \tag{5}$$

Let Δ_R^n and Δ_R^r be the Δ_R functions of non-representative and representative routers respectively. Then we have:

$$\Delta_R^n(i, h_s, k) = \begin{cases} Rm^{k-h_s+1}, & \text{if } h_s - 1 \le k \le Lm - d + 2i - 2 \\ 0, & \text{otherwise} \end{cases} \tag{6}$$

where $1 \le i \le d$ and $i + 1 \le h_s \le Lm - d + 2i - 1$, and for a representative router, which implies $h_s = i$, we have:

$$\Delta_R^r(1, 1, k) = \begin{cases} Rm\Delta_R^n(1, 2, k) + \Delta_R^r(2, 2, k), & \text{if } 0 < k \le Lm + d - 2 \\ 1, & \text{if } k = 0 \\ 0, & \text{otherwise} \end{cases} \tag{7}$$

$$\Delta_R^r(i, i, k) = \begin{cases} (Rm - 1)\Delta_R^n(i, i + 1, k) \\ \quad + \Delta_R^r(i + 1, i + 1, k), & \text{if } i - 1 < k \le Lm - d + 2i - 2 \\ 1, & \text{if } k = i - 1 \\ 0, & \text{otherwise} \end{cases} \tag{8}$$

where $2 \le i \le d$.

Remark: the estimation above is an upper bound of the traffic and it is accurate only when the network address is fully used by the devices, which is hardly true in practice. Therefore, we propose to apply a scaling parameter on the estimation to take address utilization into account, *e.g.* the number of children devices.

5.3   Local MCKP Solution

Various existing algorithms can be applied to solve an MCKP with maximum impact range objective (MCKP-MIR). We will solve it with GLPK and for a more practical implementation, a light weight heuristic algorithm could be applied. We propose a heuristic for the MMF local problem (MCKP-MMF) here.

MCKP-MMF heuristic starts at a trivial configuration $C = (0, \ldots, 0)$ with all sinks marked as 'active', then discovers a partial feasible solution by greedily increasing the impact range of the sink that generates the least extra traffic, round by round. At each round, the active sinks are sorted by their extra traffic load estimated by Δ_T at the corresponding impact level in ascending order. Then the algorithm increases their impact levels by one, one sink after another, from the least costly sink to the most costly one. Similar idea based on the *savings* has been used in [4]. If the constraint is violated at a certain round, the first sink that violates the constraint and all sinks after it are marked as 'stopped'. The algorithm terminates once all sinks are marked as 'stopped'.

Algorithm 2 describes this heuristic. The input S of the algorithm is a subset of the sinks which have query on sensor i, as each sensor records each query it is handling, S is known to i. Parameter h and h_p are the depth of sensor i on tree T and tree T_p, respectively. The sort function in the algorithm sorts the active sinks in A in ascending order with Δ_T as keys.

5.4   Dynamic Impact Range Adaption

A sink may receive multiple notifications from multiple congested sensors. In order to satisfy the most stringent constraint, it needs to adjust its impact range only when the new range is lower than its current one. The side effect of this policy is the impact range tends to decrease in the long run and a sink may not be able to know its optimal impact range. To help the sinks to jump out of a potential local optimal assigned by Algorithm 2, each sink tries to increase its impact level periodically. Thus, increaseLevel is employed after the sink adjusts its impact range. Similar effects have been observed and the same countermeasure has been employed in [9].

6   Evaluation

We implemented the algorithms and the basic functionalities of ZigBee network layer on top of IEEE 802.15.4 implementation [17] in ns2 [18]. The algorithm is evaluated with the metrics defined in Table 1. The simulation parameters are summarized in Table 2. The size of the network is chosen to include a small

Table 1. Evaluation metrics

$$\gamma = \frac{\text{Query data receiving rate at sinks (bps)}}{\text{Query data sending rate (bps)}}$$

$$T_{app} = \text{Query data receiving rate at sinks (bps)}$$

$$O_{mac} = \frac{\text{MAC control message sending rate (bps)}}{\text{Query data receiving rate (bps)}}$$

$$O_{app} = \frac{\text{Application control message sending rate (bps)}}{\text{Query data receiving rate (bps)}}$$

$$I = \frac{\text{sum of impact level of sinks}}{\text{number of sinks}},$$

at a certain simulation time.

$$I^* \quad \text{same as } I, \text{ obtained by an exact algorithm.}$$

$$FI = \frac{\left(\sum_{i=1}^{m} x_i\right)^2}{m \sum_{i=1}^{m} x_i^2}, \ m: \text{number of queries}$$
$$x_i: \text{impact range of query } i$$

Table 2. Simulation parameters

Node distribution	Uniform
Topology	50 nodes at 100m × 100m
	100 nodes at 140m × 140m
Number of sinks	4% number of the nodes,
	randomly chosen
MAC layer	IEEE 802.15.4, $BO = SO = 6$,
	$Lm = 10$, $Cm = 3$, $Rm = 3$
NWK layer	ZigBee cluster tree routing
Wireless Tx/Rx	15m, two ray ground model,
	omniscient antenna
Bandwidth	250kbps at 2.4GHz band
Query data rate	Light load: 100bps,
	Heavy load: 800bps
Simulation time	Query starts: 70s,
	query stops 300s,
	simulation stops: 350s

and a large network. We also select two representative values of the required data rate to simulate a light load network and a heavy load network. During the simulation, ZigBee network formation takes about 60 seconds so we start the queries at 70 seconds.

6.1   Data Arrival Ratio and Throughput

The effectiveness of the two algorithms in controlling the congestion is shown by comparing the query data arrival ratio against a network without impact range allocation algorithms, where the sinks take the maximum allowed impact range. From Fig. 4, we observe that the uncontrolled network delivers the data at a relatively lower ratio than the controlled network. For a heavy load network, less of congestion control is generally detrimental: arrival ratios can be as low as about 0.37, which is unacceptable. In Fig. 5, we present the aggregated throughput of the query data. Under congestion, the throughput could be even lower, as observe in the heavy load cases in Fig. 5.

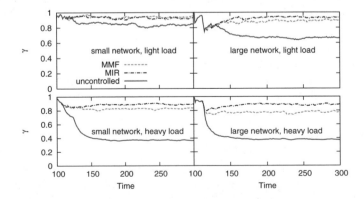

Fig. 4. Data arrival ratio

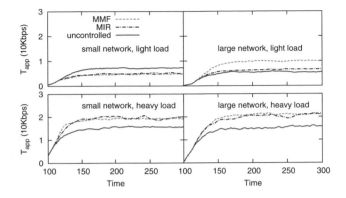

Fig. 5. Aggregated data throughput

6.2 Control Message Overhead

We are also interested in how much it costs to achieve query control with the
distributed algorithm. Both the MAC layer and the application layer overhead
are investigated. At MAC layer, the overhead comes from the beacon, acknowledgment and ARP requirement/response messages, while at application layer,
it comes from the query message and the adjust-level message as described in
Algorithm 1. Note that there is no routing overhead in the network layer and the
network formation overhead is negligible since it is done only at the beginning
of the network operation period and we do not consider network re-formation.
Fig. 6 shows these results. The values shall be interpreted as how many bits of
control message is needed to successfully deliver one bit of query data. At MAC
layer, advantages of impact range control are obvious under high load case as
the overhead is comparable or even lower than that of uncontrolled network. At
application layer, the uncontrolled networks always have negligible overhead. In
contrast, the control overhead goes abruptly for networks with either MIR or

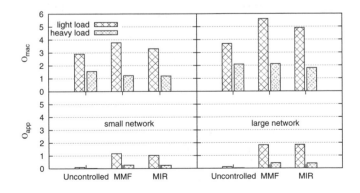

Fig. 6. Control message overhead

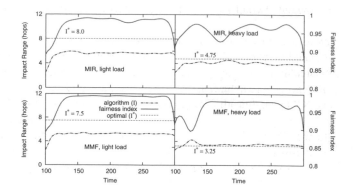

Fig. 7. Impact range and fairness index

MMF when the query load is light. However, the overhead keeps at a very low level under heavy load cases.

6.3   Impact Range and Fairness Index

The average impact range of the 4 sinks in the large network, obtained by both the distributed algorithms and an external problem solver is plotted in Fig. 7. The external problem solver obtains an *optimal* solution for both MIR and MMF with the traffic information traced from the uncontrolled network. We see that for MMF case, the approximation is quite near to the optimal. While for MIR in a light load network, the optimal is further above what the distributed algorithm can achieve. This is because the 'select the minimum' strategy used in Algorithm 1 gives a sink more chances to follow a smaller impact range. The problem becomes less obvious when the local solution gives sinks similar impact ranges. We observe also that the heuristic over-performs the optimal under heavy loaded MMF case. This is because when the local solution suggested by the congested sensor is already very near the optimal, the linear increment procedure of the sink may generate transient congestion state in the network. We leave these problems for future works. Concerning the fairness index, MMF performs slightly better, as can be expected.

7   Conclusion

We have proposed and solved the impact range allocation problem for a WSN based on ZigBee tree. Optimizing such networks in favor of the sinks (users) has practical significance. MMF and MIR, two commonly used optimization objectives have been studied in the paper and they conform with the MMKP formulation. Distributed algorithms have been proposed to solve the problems through cooperation between sinks and sensors. By exploiting the ZigBee cluster tree structure, the computation was done fully locally. Simulation results have shown that the proposed algorithms perform well in congestion control with little overhead. They especially efficient in large networks with heavy queries.

As future works, it will be interesting to cope with dynamic networks, mobility of sinks is a challenge on the way to a realistic network. On the other hand, although only bandwidth is considered in this study, the problem formulation and the algorithms may be adapted to cope with other types of resources, for example, energy, storage, computation power, *etc.*

References

1. Wang, C., Sohraby, K., Li, B., Daneshmand, M., Hu, Y.: A survey of transport protocols for wireless sensor networks. IEEE Network 20(3), 34–40 (2006)
2. Martello, S., Toth, P.: Knapsack problems: algorithms and computer implementations. John Wiley & Sons, Inc., New York (1990)
3. http://www.gnu.org/software/glpk/
4. Khan, S., Li, K.F., Manning, E.G., Akbar, M.M.: Solving the knapsack problem for adaptive multimedia systems. Stud. Inform. Univ. 2(1), 157–178 (2002)
5. Hifi, M., Michrafy, M., Sbihi, A.: Heuristic algorithms for the multiple-choice multi-dimensional knapsack problem. Journal of the Operational Research Society 55(12), 1323–1332 (2004)
6. Hifi, M., Michrafy, M., Sbihi, A.: A reactive local search-based algorithm for the multiple-choice multi-dimensional knapsack problem. Computational Optimization and Applications 33(2-3), 271–285 (2006)
7. Radunovic, B., Boudec, J.Y.L.: A Unified Framework for Max-Min and Min-Max Fairness with Applications. ACM/IEEE Trans. on Networking 15(5), 1073–1083 (2006)
8. Ogryczak, W., Pioro, M., Tomaszewski, A.: Telecommunications network design and max-min optimization problem. Journal of Telecom. and Information Tech. 3, 43–56 (2005)
9. Han, B., Simon, G.: Fair capacity sharing among multiple sinks in wireless sensor networks. In: Proc. of the IEEE MASS Conf., pp. 1–9 (October 2007)
10. Yeh, L.W., Pan, M.S., Tseng, Y.C.: Two-way beacon scheduling in zigbee tree-based wireless sensor networks. In: The IEEE Int. Conf. on Sensor Networks, Ubiquitous and Trustworthy Computing (SUTC 2008) (2008)
11. Pan, M.S., Tseng, Y.C.: Quick convergecast in zigbee beacon-enabled tree-based wireless sensor networks. Comput. Commun. 31(5), 999–1011 (2008)
12. Kohvakka, M., Kuorilehto, M., Hännikäinen, M., Hämäläinen, T.D.: Performance analysis of ieee 802.15.4 and zigbee for large-scale wireless sensor network applications. In: PE-WASUN 2006: Proc. of the 3rd ACM Int. workshop on Performance evaluation of wireless ad hoc, sensor and ubiquitous networks, pp. 48–57 (2006)
13. ZigBee Specification, Document 053474r17 (2008)
14. IEEE 802.15.4 Standard (2006)
15. Perkins, C., Royer, E.: Ad-hoc on-demand distance vector routing. In: Proc. of the Second IEEE Workshop on Mobile Computing Systems and Applications (WMCSA 1999), pp. 90–100 (1999)
16. Sarkar, S., Tassiulas, L.: Fair allocation of discrete bandwidth layers in multicast networks. In: Proc. of the IEEE INFOCOM Conf. (March 2000)
17. Zheng, J., Lee, J.M.: Low rate wireless personal area networks - ns2 simulation platform, http://www-ee.ccny.cuny.edu/zheng/pub/
18. http://www.isi.edu/nsnam/ns/

QDMAC: An Energy Efficient Low Latency MAC Protocol for Query Based Wireless Sensor Networks

Abhishek Anand, Shikhar Sachan, Kalpesh Kapoor, and Sukumar Nandi

Indian Institute of Technology Guwahati, India
{a.abhishek,s.sachan,kalpesh,sukumar}@iitg.ernet.in

Abstract. Design of a MAC protocol for a wireless sensor network requires ensuring efficient utilization of energy and minimization of interference and latency. We present QDMAC, a MAC protocol designed to excel on these parameters for query based wireless sensor networks. The paper includes various phases of the proposed protocol viz. allotment of mote-ids, formation of convergecast tree topology, allocation of collision free schedules to the motes and the technique for maintaining the time synchronization in the network. The protocol has been implemented and tested on a test-bed of twenty micaz motes. The implementation of the protocol is found to be satisfactory.

Keywords: Wireless Sensor Networks, MAC Protocols, Latency, Time Synchronization.

1 Introduction

Wireless Sensor Networks (WSN) consist of a large number of sensor nodes deployed in an adhoc manner over a sensing area to gather information. Deployments of WSN pose a number of technical challenges. They differ significantly from traditional networks as motes have very limited energy resource, computational power and data storage capabilities [1]. Also, WSN are often deployed in ad-hoc manner and are prone to failures.

There are mainly two kinds of data gathering mechanisms for WSN. First, event based data gathering in which the motes on detection of an event attempt to transfer the information to the sink in the minimum possible time. Second, query based data gathering in which the sink first disseminates a query to all the motes and then expects a response from them. Example of the same being a habitat monitoring application [2].

In this paper we present QDMAC, a protocol that uses the concept of data gathering trees and staggered schedule, and show its ability to efficiently support query based monitoring systems. The rest of the paper is organized as follows. Section 2 gives an overview of related work and proposed protocols for query based WSNs. In Section 3, we introduce our protocol design and explain its working in detail. In Section 4, a mathematical analysis of our protocol in terms of energy consumptions and latency is given. In Section 5, we present the observations for our implementation of the protocol on a testbed of micaz motes. Finally, conclusions are presented in Section 6.

V. Garg, R. Wattenhofer, and K. Kothapalli (Eds.): ICDCN 2009, LNCS 5408, pp. 306–317, 2009.
© Springer-Verlag Berlin Heidelberg 2009

2   Related Work

Several query based approaches have been proposed earlier, see for example Cougar [1] and Acquire [3]. Cougar addressed issues of MAC layer fairness and energy efficiency by using wave scheduling mechanism [4]. This eliminates interference between nodes but at the cost of latency as the edges are activated independently of the location of view-nodes (sinks). In case of **ACQUIRE** it is evident that at MAC layer protocol with duty cycle similar to S-MAC and T-MAC can be used but not DMAC. Therefore, there could be high sleep latency [5]. Moreover, in some situations it might not be useful to send stale data from the cache. **QMAC**[6] has a bidirectional staggered schedule. However, there is a high possibility of collision due to hidden terminal problem in one of the cases where the sink knows the destination (see Figure 1). The phase in which there is a high possibility of collision is marked by a blue circle in the figure. In this case, the query packet sent by node B and the reply packet sent by node D can collide often at C due to the hidden terminal problem. Especially if B, C, D are in a straight line with C in middle, B will sense the channel to be free even though D might be communicating with C. This situation has been taken care in our protocol by not concurrently propagating the query and replies.

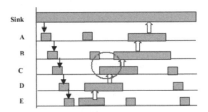

Fig. 1. Figure from [6] showing the schedules for a case where the sink knows the destination. The blue circle denotes the possibility of collision due to hidden terminal problem.

Some other MAC protocols for WSNs, such as SMAC [7] and TMAC [8] adapt duty cycling in order to be energy efficient. However they suffer from high sleep latency because an intermediate node may have to wait until the receiver wakes up before it can forward the packet. DMAC [5] protocol solved the packet delivery latency issue efficiently by having staggered schedule for the various nodes at different level in the data gathering tree. However, interference among the nodes that are at the same level in a data gathering tree could be an issue. This problem is most severe for the first-level nodes since the replies of all their descendants flow through them. For DMAC, it is important to have an efficient mechanism to maintain time synchronization among the nodes and to form the initial data gathering tree. The currently available time synchronization protocols are not optimized for DMAC type MAC protocols where nodes follow a staggered schedule. In [9], a technique for initial tree formation for event driven networks is presented.

3 QDMAC: The Proposed MAC Protocol

As mentioned in Section 2, one of the main issues in DMAC is the interference among the nodes that are at the first level. Since the data of all descendants of first-level nodes pass through them, they will be active most of the time. As a result, contention among them will be very high to cause significant increase in latency. Also for the level one nodes on the opposite side of the sink, collision due to hidden terminal problem could arise if they try to send packets at the same time to the sink. For this reason, we divide the whole tree into *branches* which are lead by *branch-heads*. A node which can listen to the sink is a branch-head and all its descendants are members of the branch. An example of such a tree with five branches is shown in Figure 2. The formation of this tree is explained in the next section. We use the terms branch and group interchangeably. In addition, *branch-heads* are also called *group-leaders*. The novelty of our protocol lies in reduction of interference without sacrificing latency by allotting different but overlapping schedules to different branches. Moreover, we have also implemented regular-time synchronization after the nodes enter the sleep-wake up cycle.

The working of our protocol is divided into two phases; the *Initiation Phase* and the *Data Transmission Phase*. We further subdivide the Initiation Phase into *Topology Learning Phase* and *Scheduling Phase*. We assume that the deployed motes are in radio on state during the Initiation Phase. Each node has a *nodeID* which is randomly generated and a *groupID* which is equal to the *nodeID* of its level one ancestor. It is set after the *Topology Learning Phase* and helps to identify the node's group.

Topology Learning Phase: In this phase the sink constructs the data gathering tree and each node comes to know of its level and its group. We follow a ripple based approach to construct the tree whereby control packets flow from level to level. We use the *Topology Learning Packet* (TLP) to form the data gathering tree. A TLP has the following three fields: group ID of the sender, level of sender of this TLP and expected maximum level of the network. The tree formation is similar to the breadth first search. Whenever a node receives a TLP, it waits for a better TLP (one with lower level or better RSSI [10] in case levels are equal). Then it sets its level to one more than the best TLP received and group id same as of that TLP. The nodes which receive TLP directly from the sink however set group id as their node-id since they are branch-heads. Then they

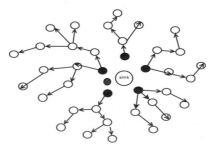

Fig. 2. A sample data collection tree indicating the branch-heads (black). A red singleton branch is also indicated.

broadcast a TLP containing their own level and group id. The sink starts the process by transmitting a TLP with level set to zero (group id is not used by sink). The transmission power is set such that only the nodes close to the sink are able to hear it. These TLPs propagate down level by level to the leaves. In this process, all the nodes come to know about their level and group id.

All the nodes after broadcasting their TLP remain in the listening mode and try to listen to the broadcast from the nodes in the next higher level. If they hear a TLP with level value higher than their level values, they understand that they are not the leaf nodes and wait indefinitely for a *Return Packet* (RP). If a node does not listen to any TLP or RP for sufficient time (Section 5.2 reports the optimal choice of this wait duration), it assumes that it is a leaf. It then broadcasts the RP and sets its `isLeaf` flag to true for future use. An RP has the following fields: group id, maximum level of the branch and the level of the sender which is used to ensure that these packets only propagate towards sink.

The leaf nodes set the highest level field of the RP as their level. The nodes that receive this RP forward this packet (after setting the `senderLevel` field) only if their group id matches the group id in the packet and their level value is lower than the `senderLevel` field of the packet. They use the CSMA scheme with random back off before transmission. This process of forwarding the packets continues until the RPs reach the sink. The sink waits for sufficient time to receive all the RPs.

Scheduling Phase: First we introduce some terms which we will use in describing the schedules mathematically

- μ : This is similar to the μ of DMAC [5]. This is the basic unit of transmission interval of the network. In this duration, a node can send a single small packet to another node after a random initial back off. It should be a little more than the sum of the max initial back off time and transmission time for a packet of max length supported by the network. Moreover, that maximum length of a packet should be kept less to reduce re-transmission penalty in case interference occurs while transmission.
- `TimePeriod` : This is the time duration after which all the schedules start repeating. During this time, all the nodes of the network are allocated exactly 1μ time for each of the following:
  - Listen for query - this time instant within a TimePeriod is denoted by `QRx`
  - Forward query - this time instant within a TimePeriod is denoted by `QTx`
  - Listen to response of children- this time instant within a TimePeriod is denoted by `RRx`
  - Broadcast child's or own response - this time instant within a TimePeriod is denoted by `RTx`

  Figure 3 shows a complete *data-cycle* of length *TimePeriod*.
- `glQRx of a group` - the time instant within a TimePeriod when the group leader(branch-head) is scheduled to receive the query from the sink
- `glRTX of a group` - the time instant within a TimePeriod when the group leader(branch-head) is scheduled to send a reply to the sink

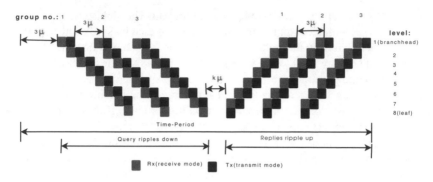

Fig. 3. The sleep-wake up schedules of the nodes in a network having 3 branches

As shown in the figure 3, first the query propagates from the sink to the leaves and then the reply ripples up. The gap of 3μ between schedules of branches ensures that when a node is transmitting, no other node in the higher three levels is transmitting in any of the branches. This eliminates the possibility of collision due to the hidden terminal problem. The same time difference is maintained even when the replies ripple up. Also, the order in which the sink disseminates the query to the group leaders is same as the order in which the response is received from the branch heads. This ensures that all the leaves have sufficient and almost equal time to prepare the response. If all the branches have exactly the same number of motes, all the leaves get exactly same time to prepare the response.

At the end of the Topology Learning Phase, the sink knows about the total number of branches and the maximum level in each branch. Now it prepares special schedules for them. In the Mathematical section, we show that if a node knows the Timeperiod, μ, g1QRx and g1RTx time instants, it can calculate its schedules. So the scheduling packets contain only the following fields: group id, TimePeriod, μ, g1QRx and g1RTx.

The Scheduling Phase starts with time synchronization as the motes are switched on at different times. The system time of the motes (in TinyOS) is the time since boot. Every mote has a `time_zero_error` which they use to calculate the network time. The time synchronization begins with the sink transmitting its own timestamp in a *sync packet* (SP). These sync packets contain the level of sender and this helps to ensure that the sync packets only travel from the sink to the leaves. Extreme care must be taken in implementation of this synchronization scheme. Because the random back off of the CSMA later will make the timestamp wrong by the time the packet is actually transmitted. We removed the random back off at MAC layer and introduced a random back off before the packet contents are filled. This ensures that the timestamp is correct. After this, the sink sends one scheduling packet for each group.

Data Transmission Phase: On receiving a scheduling packet, a node enters the data transmission phase. The sleep-wake up cycle begins. Each node maintains a queue for storing replies. We implemented a FIFO queue but one may wish to maintain a priority queue to reduce the latency for high-priority replies. Our query packet contains the following fields: query id, query type, group id, start target level, end target level, query parameter and timestamp of the query. Our reply packet contains the following fields: query id, group id, sender id and timestamp of the sensed values and number of reply packets yet to be transmitted.

A node accepts a query only if it has same group id and its level is less than that *end target level*. If its level is also more than *start target level* then it initiates the sensors for the response. The sensors sample the value independently of the data transmission schedules and when the sensor is ready with the queried value, it is encapsulated in a reply packet and added to the queue which stores the replies which are yet to be sent. Otherwise it just forwards the query in its QTx slot. In some situations, the sensors can be sampled continuously and if values detected are above thresholds (eg. extremely high temperature), they can be encapsulated in a reply packet with dummy query id and added to the queue. Thus, this protocol also supports events. Just before transmitting a reply packet, it adds to the moreNum field of the packet (the number of elements in its reply queue -1). When the sensor values are ready, a mote sets this parameter to 0 before adding it to the reply-packet queue. So when the reply reaches the sink, it contains the total number of reply packets yet to be transmitted for all the nodes that lie in the path between the replier and the sink. This helps the sink to ensure that it does not send too many queries which might result in overflow of reply-queue on the motes.

Another important optimization implemented is programming of the motes to reject any reply-packet whose sender id and query id match the corresponding values of a reply packet which was recently received. After implementing this, we almost always got only one reply per sender. The exceptions to this were because the sink over-heard transmissions of second level nodes also.

Interference Minimization within the Same Group: Since all the nodes in the same group and same level have exactly the same RTx schedules, interference minimization is very important. For this, we used a random back off scheme. At the start of a RTx slot, a node backs off for a random amount of time. After that, it senses the channel and transmits the response only if the channel is clear. If not, it attempts again only in the next RTx slot. So it goes to sleep until the next QRx slot. This scheme is not followed in case of query transmission. If a query could not be sent in a QTx slot, it will be simply dropped. This worked fine in dense deployments as almost all the nodes get the query packet from some or parent or the other.

Time Synchronization: In the absence of regular time synchronization among the nodes, clock drift will render all the protocols based on staggered schedules useless. An accurate time synchronization will allow smaller μ value and hence reduce latency and energy consumption. In our earlier experiments with the micaz motes we observed that despite initial time synchronization, the staggeredness of the schedules went haywire within an hour and query could not propagate down. So we made provisions for regular time synchronization during the data transmission phase.

But time synchronization in the data transmission phase proved to be non-trivial because during this phase, the nodes are already in sleep-wake up cycle and they wake up for a very short period. We cannot use the MAC layer random back off that we used for the query packets because that will introduce a random error in the timestamp. To solve this problem, we programmed every mote to transmit the sync packet in a QTx slot without any random back off but after leaving a random number (say r) of TimePeriods since the receipt of the sync packet. Had they sent the sync packet in the very next QTx slot after the QRx slot in which they received the sync packet(as they do for queries), all the sync packets would have collided at all levels since we have removed the random back off. During this wait for r TimePeriods, all other operations such as receiving and forwarding queries and responses will occur normally in their respective slots. If after r TimePeriods, the node finds that it already has a query to forward in the QTx slot, it will reschedule the transmission of the sync packet after a very small random number(say r') of TimePeriods. A node accepts a sync packet only from a lower level node. This ensures that the sync packets only travel from the sink to the leaves. The sink regularly broadcasts its timestamp in a sync packet during the g1QRx slots of each branch.

4   Mathematical Evaluation of the Protocol

Calculation of Schedules: If a node of level l knows the QRx instant and RTx instant of it's group leader, it can calculate its schedules as follows:

$$QRx = glQRx + (l - 1) * \mu \tag{1}$$
$$QTx = glQRx + (l) * \mu \tag{2}$$
$$RRx = glRTx - (l) * \mu \tag{3}$$
$$RTx = glRTx - (l - 1) * \mu \tag{4}$$

(note that in real implementation, the time taken to start the radio should be subtracted from QRx and RRx)

The sink calculates TimePeriod, g1QRx and g1RTx times for each branch as follows. From figure 3, the derivation of these formulae is trivial. l_{max} denotes the maximum of maximum levels of each branch.

If there are n branches, then for the i^{th}(one based indexing) branch,

$$TimePeriod = (2 * (l_{max}) + 8 * (n - 1) + 3 + k) * \mu, \text{where} k > 0 \tag{5}$$
$$glQRx = (4 * i - 1) * \mu \tag{6}$$
$$glRTx = TimePeriod - \mu * (4 * n - 4 * i + 1) \tag{7}$$

The parameter k helps us to achieve lower duty cycles(but at the cost of a higher latency of response).

Energy Consumption: The TimePeriod of a network with n branches and maximum level as l_{max} is defined as equation (5). During this period, a node is awake for only 4μ time and sleeps for the rest time. So the duty cycle, η, is:

$$\eta = \frac{4}{2 * (l_{max}) + 8 * (n - 1) + 3 + k} \tag{8}$$
$$= \frac{4}{2 * l_{max} + 8 * n - 5 + k} \tag{9}$$

So the maximum achievable duty cycle is:

$$\eta_{max} = \frac{4}{2 * l_{max} + 8 * n - 5} \tag{10}$$

If we wish to achieve a smaller duty cycle $\eta <= \eta_{max}$, we can choose a positive k. Please note that it is a simplified analysis as we have ignored the spikes in power consumption when the radio is switched on. Also, this is only the upper bound on the power consumption of the nodes of the network. This is because a node will not use it's RTx if it has no pending replies. Also, if there is no query, the QTx slots will remain unused. The nodes near the sink will use their RTx slots more frequently than nodes near the leaves. So the batteries of the nodes near the sink will exhaust earlier.

Latency: We define latency as the time difference between the instant at which the sink disseminates the query and the instant when it gets back the response. Calculation of latency for out protocol is also trivial. It is equal to difference between the g1QRx and g1RTx instants for a given group. Thus latency, L, is:

$$L = glRTx - glQRx \tag{11}$$
$$= TimePeriod - \mu * (4 * n - 4 * i + 1) - (4 * i - 1) * \mu \tag{12}$$
$$= TimePeriod - 4 * n * \mu \tag{13}$$
$$= (2 * l_{max} + 8 * n - 5 + k) * \mu - 4 * n * \mu \tag{14}$$
$$= (2 * l_{max} + 4 * n - 5 + k) * \mu \tag{15}$$

Throughput: We can receive n replies (1 from each branch) in a TimePeriod which is $(2 * l_{max} + 8 * n - 5 + k) * \mu$. In these equations, l_{max} and n depend upon the deployment. k can be safely assigned any non-negative value. We will discuss about the choice of μ in Section 5.4.

5   Experimental Study

We tested our protocol extensively using a testbed of twenty micaz motes. We already discussed about the practical problems faced (and their solutions) in the previous sections. Here we will discuss in brief about the implementation of our protocol and mention some experimental observations.

5.1   Implementation

Programming of motes was done using TinyOS 2.x-nesC environment. A regular micaz mote connected to the PCs usb port (via a mib520 programming board) acted as the sink. Our implementation consisted of three modules:

Base-Station (Mote): This program runs on the sink mote. It has the responsibility of receiving the packets from the PC and transmitting them through the radio at appropriate time only. Also it forwards the radio packets it hears to the PC as soon they are received. It snoops the scheduling messages sent by the PC before for-warding them to know μ, the g1QRx and g1RTx times and the TimePeriod. So when PC sends the queries, it broadcasts them at the appropriate time(g1QRx time of that group) and timestamps them properly. It is also responsible for sending its timestamp in a sync packet regularly at g1QRx times of each group without random back off during the data transmission phase.

Base-Station (PC): This program is written in Java and uses the SerialForwarder utility provided in the TinyOS 2.x distribution to communicate with the base-station (mote). It allows a user to control the network by sending initialization/re-initialization packets. After all the RPs are received, it prepares the scheduling packets and sends them to the base-station mote transmission. It also sends the queries based on user-input and displays the responses.

Node (Mote): A copy of this program runs on every mote of the network except the sink. This program is the main implementation of our protocol and consists of two finite-state machines controlling the initiation state and the data transmission state respectively.

For determining optimum values of μ, random back off before transmitting various control packets, r and r', we arranged our 20 motes according to the topology of figure 4(a).

5.2   Optimal Wait Durations

After broadcasting its own TLP in the initiation phase, a node waits for TLPs or RPs from higher levels before assuming that it is a leaf. We had initially set this wait duration for all the nodes to be constant. However, we observed that many fake leaves were created near the sink. This was because the wait duration starts earlier for nodes near the sink and hence ends earlier. If such a node fails to hear any TLP of its children, it will transmit RP before the actual leaves transmit. So we made this wait duration proportional to expected (max level - node's level). The expected max level is a field of TLP which is set by the user via the UI of the base-station (PC) program. In the experimental setup described above, we set this delay as 1000 * (expected level - own level) ms.

The wait duration for better TLP after receiving the first TLP was set to 400 ms. The nodes which receive the TLP from the sink are branch-heads and they do not wait for a better TLP. These nodes just wait for a random time between 0 and 400 ms to reduce inter-branch collision of TLPs at all lower levels. RPs were forwarded without any extra delay (except for the CSMA random back off which was between 0.3 ms to 1 ms).

5.3   Singleton Branches

The data gathering tree for a deployment was formed as shown in figure 4(a). The red node indicates a *singleton branch*. Singleton branch is a level one node with no children. By trying various other deployments, we observed that a singleton branch is a node which is near to sink but is not well connected to its children. The nodes in its vicinity are better connected to other nodes. It turned out that we can safely exclude the

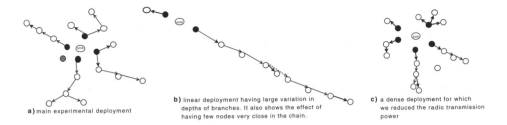

b) linear deployment having large variation in depths of branches. It also shows the effect of having few nodes very close in the chain.

a) main experimental deployment

c) a dense deployment for which we reduced the radio transmission power

Fig. 4. Experimental deployments

singleton branches from the network without affecting the connectivity of other nodes. The RP of that singleton was automatically discarded by the base-station (PC) software and hence no scheduling packet would be created for it.

5.4   Choice of μ

The choice of μ is very critical in our protocol. If we choose a small μ, time synchronization has to be done very often during the data transmission phase. It can be recalled that μ is a little more than the sum of the max initial back off time and transmission time for a packet of max length supported by the network. So to achieve a very small μ, we need to reduce the random back off. But reduction of random back off increased the number of packet losses due to collisions. At best, we could reduce μ to 5 ms. The CC2420 radio transceiver has a transmission rate of 250 Kbps. The reply packet(along with header and preamble) required a little less than 2 ms to transmit. The max random back off was of 3 ms. With this μ and k as 1,

$$TimePeriod = (2 * (4) + 8 * (4 - 1) + 3 + 1) * 5ms \quad \text{from eqn.(5)} \qquad (16)$$
$$= 180ms \qquad (17)$$

$$Latency = (2 * 4 + 4 * 4 - 5 + 1) * 5ms \quad \text{from eqn.(15)} \qquad (18)$$
$$= 100ms \qquad (19)$$

5.5   Choice of r, r′ and Time Synchronization Frequency

These choices depend upon the clock-drift rates and the value of TimePeriod which in turn depends on the choice of μ and deployment. Without regular time synchronization, we found that in a network with five nodes arranged in a straight line and the value of μ as 5ms, we stopped getting replies after 20 minutes since initialization. In the deployment as shown in Figure 4(a) and μ=5ms, we chose r to be a random number between 1 to 100 and r′ to be a random number between 1 to 10. The sink broadcasts a sync packet every 3 min in the respective g1QRx slots. With this choice, the time synchronization remained perfect throughout the test period (8hrs) and we got the responses from all levels in the same manner as we got at the beginning of the experiment.

In the data transmission phase, we queried for the photo-sensor values and got correct replies almost always (except some packet losses). If the target was a single node, the reply packet was received almost always in the same data cycle (i.e after a delay of approximately 100ms since the transmission of query by the base-station mote). So the latency of response was as described in the mathematical section. In some rare cases, the reply was received in the next data cycle (after approximately 100ms+180ms=280ms since the transmission of query by the base-station mote). We also tried bulk queries where more than one nodes of the network were queried. Within the next few data cycles, almost all the reply packets rippled up to the sink.

Other worth mentioning deployments are shown in figures 4(b) and 4(c). 4(c) had a dense deployment. To reduce the number of collisions, we had to reduce the transmission power. But reduction of transmission power to a large extent created some isolated nodes. For our protocol to work properly, it is important to find an optimal transmission power so that the transmission range is slightly more than one-hop distance. Moreover, latency can be further improved for deployments like 4(b) where the depths of branches vary to a large extent by having the schedules of a branch going only upto the depth of that branch. We can sort the branches in descending order of their depth and allocate schedules in that order i.e the `g1QRx` slot of the branch with max depth starts earliest and its `g1RTx` slot ends at the last.

6   Conclusion and Future Work

We proposed QDMAC, a MAC protocol for query based wireless sensor networks. We developed mathematical expressions for latency, duty cycle and verified those expressions experimentally. We experimentally found out a suitable value of μ. To the best of our knowledge, this is the first experimental evaluation of these parameters for DMAC type staggered schedule MAC protocol. The proposers of DMAC [5] simulated with μ=10ms. With $\mu = 5ms$, k=0, n branches and max depth of tree as l_{max}, TimePeriod of the network was observed to be $(10 * l_{max} + 40 * n - 25)ms$ and latency as $(10 * l_{max} + 20 * n - 25)ms$. In this TimePeriod, we can receive a reply from each of the branches. Moreover, a high priority event can be delivered to the sink within one TimePeriod. This is considerably better than QMAC whose simulation results show that latency increases at a rate of 1 second per unit increase in hop-length (comparable to l_{max}).

In terms of energy consumption, it is considerably better than Acquire which is not suitable for low duty cycle MAC protocols. The duty cycle of our MAC protocol is

$$\frac{4}{2 * l_{max} + 8 * n - 5 + k}$$

Another attractive feature of our protocol is a unique regular time synchronization technique tailor-made for this MAC protocol. This time synchronization protocol was successfully tested experimentally.

There were some packet losses because of seldom collisions between transmissions of nodes of same level and same group (if the random back off periods are too close). In our protocol, all the packets are broadcasted. Packet losses can be eliminated by implementing packet-acknowledgments as suggested in DMAC. But for that we need to unicast the packets to specific receiver-ids. So the random numbers we use for the purpose of id allocation should be such that all the nodes which are in each other's transmission range have different ids. Also in the initiation phase, a node needs to store the ids of their parents for unicasting the packets later.

As mentioned in Section 4, the batteries of nodes near the sink will exhaust earlier than those near the leaves. A recent work [11] suggests the use of mobile sinks to minimize this problem. However in case of QDMAC, it would be easier to replace the batteries (or add new nodes) when the batteries start exhausting and then re-initialize the network. Our implementation of QDMAC has provision for on-the-fly re-initialization of the network from the base station. Also the nodes having less remaining battery life indicate this on their LED's on reinit command. Although some aggregate queries such as getting average light sensor's value can be easily implemented in our protocol, further research is required to implement all type of aggregate queries.

References

1. Yao, Y., Gehrke, J.: The Cougar Approach to In-network Query Processing in Sensor Networks. ACM SIGMOD Record Archive 31, 9–18 (2002)
2. Mainwaring, A., Culler, D., Polastre, J., Szewczyk, R., Anderson, J.: Wireless Sensor Networks for Habitat Monitoring. In: First ACM International Workshop on Wireless Sensor Networks and Applications, pp. 88–97 (2002)
3. Sadagopalan, N., Krishnamachai, B., Helmy, A.: Active Query forwarding in sensor Networks. In: IEEE Internatioanl Workshop on Sensor Network Protocols and Applications, pp. 149–155 (May 2003)
4. Cornell-University: The Cougar Project: A Work in Progress Report (2003)
5. Lu, G., Krishnamachari, B., Raghavendra, C.S.: An Adaptive Energy-Efficient and Low-Latency MAC for Data Gathering in Wireless Sensor Networks. In: 18th International Parallel and Distributed Processing Symposium, p. 224 (April 2004)
6. Vasanthi, N.A., Annadurai, S.: An Energy Efficient Sleep Schedule for Achieving Minimum Latency in Query based Sensor Networks. In: IEEE International Conference on Sensor Networks, Ubiquitous, and Trustworthy Computing (SUTC 2006), vol. 2, pp. 214–219 (2006)
7. Ye, W., Heidemann, J., Estrin, D.: Medium Access Control with Coordinated, Adaptive Sleeping for Wireless Sensor Networks. IEEE/ACM Transactions on Networking 12, 493–506 (2004)
8. Dam, T.V., Langendoen, K.: An Adaptive Energy-Efficient MAC Protocol for Wireless Sensor Networks. ACM Sensys., 171–180 (November 2003)
9. Parmar, S.N., Nandi, S., Chowdhury, A.R.: Power Efficient and Low Latency MAC for Wireless Sensor Networks. In: IEEE Sensor and Ad Hoc Communications and Networks (SECON) Conference, vol. 3, pp. 940–944. IEEE Communications Society, Los Alamitos (2006)
10. Berkely-University: The Datasheet of the CC2420 Radio Tranceiver Present in Micaz Motes (2008),
    http://inst.eecs.berkeley.edu/~cs150/Documents/CC2420.pdf
11. Friedmann, L., Boukhatem, L.: Efficient Multi-sink Relocation in Wireless Sensor Network. In: Third International Conference on Networking and Services, p. 90 (June 2007)

Field Sensing and Target Tracking Using Mobile Sensors*

Parchand Amit Madhukar and R.K. Ghosh

Indian Institute of Technology, Kanpur

Abstract. We investigate the problem of gathering of sensory data from a non-convex area (without a hole) using mobile sensors when certain regions of the area are under attacks from intruders. The theory of sensing and tracking targets is based on the idea of a potential field wherein the sensors move towards the areas of intrusion due to the existence of mutually attractive forces between intruders and sensors, and move away from each other due the existence of mutually repulsive forces between themselves. A set of algorithms have been proposed on the basis of the fore-mentioned potential field theory which accomplishes the twin objectives of field sensing and target tracking efficiently.

1 Introduction

Wireless sensor network consists of a large number of spatially distributed autonomous micro-sensors cooperating together to gather sensory data. Sensors are battery powered and usually injected into sensing space by air droppings. Sometimes sensors are mounted on robots, moving vehicles or tagged to live animals which provide mobility, and allow them to cover larger, possibly important areas of the region of sensing. Mobility also helps in tracking the intruders through some intuitive knowledge about the nature and likely direction of their movements. The key to effective monitoring is ensure that no part of the environment is left without surveillance for an extended period of time [1]. The approach presented here, takes the environment to be sensed as input and schedules the mobility of sensors in a way that meets the above conditions. Scheduling of the movement of sensors so as to balance both gathering of environmental data, and tracking intruders is quite challenging due to limited energy of sensors.

Hui et al. [2] proposed a sentry based approach for power management to sense and track intruders; wherein sensors are divided into two types depending on their tasks, namely sensing and tracking. A challenging problem which arises while considering target tracking is to avoid *sinkhole attack* due to many-to-one communication. Nagai et al. [3] have proposed certain ways for scheduling of sensors which allows sensors to avoid such situations, and track intruders effectively. The aim of this paper is to handle both the issues of sensor scheduling, and tracking intruders in a uniform manner through a novel potential field based approach.

---

* This research was sponsored by Research I Foundation.

V. Garg, R. Wattenhofer, and K. Kothapalli (Eds.): ICDCN 2009, LNCS 5408, pp. 318–324, 2009.

2   Overview of Our Approach

The preferred area of coverage is first partitioned into unit areas (hexagons) of sensing [4]. The benefit of hexagonalizing is that on placing the sensors at the centers of the hexagons, the boundaries of the sensed areas will overlap, and it helps in eliminating the possible spatial errors by matching the boundaries. After hexagonalizing the sensing area, a graph is constructed by replacing each regular hexagon by one vertex and introducing an edge between a pair of vertices if and only if they represent two adjacent hexagons. Then the trajectory of each sensor is planned so that it always traverses along a selected simple path of this graph. Our approach is to determine a connected path cover for sensing the given area [5]. The traversals of sensors is scheduled by assigning paths of similar lengths to them. When the sensors traverse along their respective assigned paths the whole region is covered. As the sensing task is evenly distributed, no sensor is expected experience early energy drain out. This works most efficiently for the environments without intruders.

An intruder is defined as an entity which enters a region where it is not supposed to be; and affects that region (in some disastrous way). The aim is to track an intruder (target) by intuitive knowledge about its nature and direction of movements. We propose a *potential field* approach which tracks the targets effectively in bounded time, while providing the sensing coverage at the same time. The potential fields methods are well established in robotics for robot motion path planning [6, 7]. We use similar approach to plan sensor scheduling.

3   Clustering or Path Allocation

Consider the region as a non-convex, non-hollow polygon. Hexagonalize the polygon as in [4], and construct a graph G as explained in the previous section.

To form the paths to be allocated to a sensor, we proceed as follows. At each instance of time, one sensor is placed at some initial position and then allowed to traverse the path along the edges of the graph till it covers a fixed length. The length of the path a sensor is supposed to cover is estimated as the total number of nodes in G divided by the number of sensors available. However, if there is no neighboring unvisited node, the path is clipped and other sensors are made to compensate for the traversal of shorter paths by some sensors. While traversing over the edges, we use the following heuristics:

– Node having lesser number of unvisited neighboring nodes should be preferred.
– If there is a tie on the first condition, then the node having more number of visited neighbors should be preferred next.

The algorithm for path-allocation to the sensors is presented next. Before actual allocation of paths, some initializations are needed. The objective of these initializations are to cluster nodes of G forming a path that can be traversed by one mobile sensor. A data structure is maintained to store all the nodes (and their connectivity) with each node linked to all its neighbors. A queue Q is used to store the nodes with connectivity 1. The first sensor at start will be at xth node in Q. A node $temp$ with highest preference is determined (as in conditions (a) and (b) in Traversal algorithm). Let T be the maximum time in which all sensors should at least traverse the path once. We also define

Algorithm 1. Traversal

1 Take a node x where the sensor is supposed to be.
2 Traverse along the valid nodes which are adjacent to the node x. In case there are more than one choice for valid nodes, choose a node according to the following preferences:
   (a) Node having lesser number of neighboring nodes that are not traversed should be preferred.
   (b) Node having more number of neighboring traversed nodes hould be preferred next (i.e. if from the above condition (a) we get two or more such nodes to be traversed then prefer as stated in this step here).
3 Every time a node is traversed, modify the connectivity of every node in its adjacency list.
4 Update the *temp* node with preference order as in preference (a) and (b). Update the queue Q with untraversed nodes having connectivity 1.
5. Perform steps 1, 2, and 3 repeatedly till a path of expected length k is found.
6 Remove node x from Q. Move the pointer ahead in Q.
7 Perform steps 1, 2, 3, 4, and 5 for each node in Q. In case Q is empty and not every node from the list is traversed yet, choose a node x as the *temp* node.
8 Repeat steps 2, 3 and update Q.
9 Repeat the above procedure till every node is traversed.
10 In case, the path length of k is not achieved update the path lengths of the remaining paths accordingly for further traversals.
11 In case the length of k is greater than `max.length` add an extra sensor and increase the number of available sensor by 1. Update the path lengths accordingly.

`max.length` $= T *$ (speed of the sensor). Additional sensors have to be provided in the cases, where algorithm demands for extra sensors. The complexity of the algorithm is quadratic with the number of the hexagons; and, therefore, quadratic with the size of the region under consideration. Thus, the algorithm gives a very economic way to cluster the nodes in order to allocate the paths to the sensors.

4 Scheduling

The base station take the responsibility of scheduling each sensor every time it requests for the next node to be traversed. The sensor visits the node and takes sensing measurements in the corresponding local area. After measurements are taken, sensor requests for the next node to be traversed. The above two tasks are performed repeatedly until the sensor has spent out its battery. At each request, the scheduler uses the available information about the environment and directs the sensor. It also updtes its database storing the information about the sensed area, every time it receives information from a sensor. Thus, at each step the latest information from the database is made available to sensor. While performing this action, one of the major requirements is to ensure that base station is able satisfy each sensor's request in constant time after it it receives the request. It is needed to ensures efficient and fast sensing. So, the main aim is to process the information available with the base station in bounded time and direct the sensor accordingly.

Let us first examine the proposed *potential field* [6, 7] method to direct sensors in areas invaded by intruders. It becomes an optimization issue. Two conflicting objectives need to be balanced:

- Traversing the paths in minimum time.
- Tracking the intruders in minimum time.

The specific requirements for optimization depends on the particular scenario. The ratio of the preference for traversing the paths versus the preference for tracking the intruders is called the *preference ratio*. We provide a general approach for optimization, given the preference ratio between the two conflicting objectives.

We propose a potential field for a sensor in the whole environment using the information stored at the base station provided by the sensors in the following way:

1. A unit positive charge is assigned to each target/intruder. The potential is inversely proportional to the distance between the sensor s and the target t.
2. A sensor s is assigned a unit negative charge (or proportional to the range of the sensor if different sensors have different sensing range). The potential is inversely proportional to the distance between the sensor s and the other sensors in the coverage area.
3. The next node n that sensor s is supposed to traverse according to the path allocation produces a field directly proportional to the distance between n and the present location of s. This field is attractive and proportional to the preference ratio.

The direction of the produced field specifies the node that the sensor should traverse next.

Calculating the force requires O(# of sensors + # of targets). Thus, the sensor waits after making a request to the base station. The average computation time can be reduced to a constant by storing the information about the sensors and the targets in an appropriate way. For each sensor, the information of the sensors and targets that are local to it are stored in a database. The database is incrementally updated recording the movement of each entity (i.e. sensor or target). As the net force will be affected mostly by local entities, we consider only these to calculate the net force. Assuming the localization area to be of bounded by constant area, the total time to find net force for a sensor will be proportional to entities inside the area. Assume that there can be only one entity at any hexagonal node. In a local area there are constant number of hexagons. Thus maximum number of entities is a constant. Consequently, for all the sensors, the total time to find the net forces will be constant.

4.1 Scheduling Algorithm

In the scheduling algorithm described below, let w_{NN} [sensor$_{num}$] represent the factor of importance of the node (hexagonal cell) to be traversed next by the sensor (sensor$_{num}$) according to the path allocation scheme. It is initialized to 1.

5 Results

Clustering or assigning paths. The algorithm for clustering or assignment of paths to sensor nodes was also executed over a number of test cases. Figure 1(a) shows one

Algorithm 2. Scheduling

On request from the sensor x:

1. Find the entities that are in the local area of x from the database.
2. Calculate the net force on the sensor due to these entities: $Fnet = F + k * V * w_{NN}[sensor_{num}]$, where F is the force due to sensor-target fields by the sensors and targets in that area. V is the force due to the next node of the path allocated. k is the preference ratio.
3. Update the information in the database with the information sent by the sensor.
4. **if** the next node to be traversed is not the next node in the path **then**
   $w_{NN}[sensor_{num}] = h * w_{NN}[sensor_{num}]$, where h is a constant (affinity to next node in the path) greater than one and is fixed according to preference ratio. Preferably h = preference ratio.
   else $w_{NN}[path] = 1$;

example depicting paths to be traced by two sensors (indicated by filled circles) after hexagonalization of the area has been obtained.

Scheduling. For scheduling, the preference ratio will be very high, i.e., the nodes on the assigned path are given minimal importance. In this case, the time required for the sensors to track a target (assumed to have a speed lower than the sensor's speed) is bounded; and given by $time = 2 * extent$ of the region/speed of the sensor. On the other hand, if the target tracking is accorded a reduced importance, then the sensing of the environment is efficiently done in bounded time.

During the scheduling based on the problem, the preference ratio should be modified according to the relative importances of the target tracking versus the field sensing. A plot indicating the relative importances of tracking over sensing with varying the preference ratios is shown in figure 1(b). It shows that preference ratio as a parameter to be determined for a given scenario.

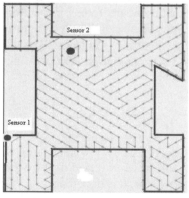

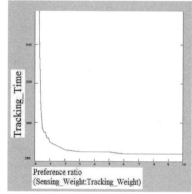

(a) Path allocations to two sensor.   (b) Sensing : tracking time with preference ratio.

Fig. 1. Path allocation, and relative importance of preference ratio

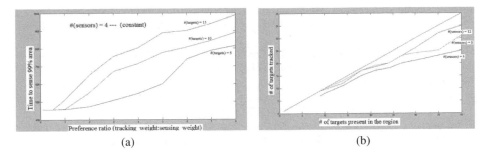

Fig. 2. Tracking targets with sensors

Figure 2(a) shows the variation of time taken to sense 99% of the area against the preference ratio with the presence of varying number of targets. The graph being non-linear tends to rise after a particular preference ratio P_0. P_0 increases with the decrease in the number of targets, which can be justified in the following way. With small number of targets, the affinity of the sensors to track targets must be high enough to make the sensors to reduce their responsibilities for sensing and concentrate on tracking. Hence, the preference ratio must be high to balance the anomaly.

Figure 2(b) shows the number of targets that are tracked versus the total number of targets present with varying number of sensors. Ideally, all the targets should be tracked, which is actually the case if small number of targets are present and considerable time is spent on tracking these. But, as the number of targets increases, the small number of sensors are not enough to track all the targets. Hence, the graphs deviates quickly with decrease in the number of available sensors.

6   Conclusion

In this paper we proposed algorithms and techniques to cover a non-convex, non-hollow sensing area, and to track intruders with the help of a few mobile sensors having low processing ability. Our techniques provides a practical mechanism to strike a reasonable balance between the conflicting goals of sensing and tracking targets within a time bound with help of mobile sensors if some parts of a sensing area were left unattended due to a sparse deployment of sensors.

References

1. Huang, T., Tseng, Y.: Coverage problems in wireless sensor networks. ACM Mobile Networks and Applications (MONET), special issue on Wireless Sensor Networks 10(4), 519–528 (2003)
2. Hui, J., Ren, Z., Krogh, B.H.: Sentry based power management in wireless sensor networks. In: Zhao, F., Guibas, L.J. (eds.) IPSN 2003. LNCS, vol. 2634, pp. 459–472. Springer, Heidelberg (2003)
3. Ngai, E.C.H., Liu, J., Lyu1, M.R.: On the intruder detection for sinkhole attack in wireless sensor networks. In: IEEE International Conference on Communication (ICC), vol. 8, pp. 3383–3389 (2006)

4. Yu, Z., Guan, Y.: A robust group-based key management scheme for woreless sensor networks. In: Wireless Communications and Networking Conference, vol. 4, pp. 1915–1920. IEEE, Los Alamitos (2005)
5. Gupta, H., Zhou, Z., Das, S.R., Gu, Q.: Connected sensor cover: self-organization of sensor networks for efficient query execution. IEEE/ACM Transactions on Network 14(1), 55–67 (2006)
6. Ge, S.S., Cui, Y.J.: New potential functions for mobile robot path planning. IEEE Transaction on Robotics and Automation 16(5), 615–620 (2000)
7. Barraquand, J., Langlois, B., Latombe, J.C.: Numerical potential field techniques for robot path planning. IEEE Transactions on Systems, Man and Cybernetics 22(2), 224–241 (1992)

Q-Coverage Problem in Wireless Sensor Networks

Manju Chaudhary[1] and Arun K. Pujari[1,2]

[1] LNM Institute of Information Technology, Jaipur
Rupa Ki Nangal, Kanota, Jaipur, 303012, India
manju_nunia@gmail.com
[2] Artificial Intelligence Lab
University of Hyderabad, Hyderabad, 500 046, India
akpcs@uohyd.ernet.in

Abstract. The target coverage problem in wireless sensor networks is concerned with maximizing the lifetime of the network while continuously monitoring a set of targets. We add a QoS requirement to the target coverage such that the targets are covered by more than one sensor at any time. Given an integer vector Q, where q_i is the minimum number of sensors to simultaneously cover targets i, the problem becomes Q-coverage problem. In this paper, we study the target Q-coverage problem. The objective is to maximize sensor network lifetime satisfying Q-coverage requirement. The problem is shown to be NP-complete and there is no known practical algorithm. We propose a heuristic and show that the proposed algorithm yields solution very near to the optimal solution. Our algorithm has two important features. It uses a greedy heuristic to generate Q-covers by prioritizing sensors in terms of the residual battery life and the algorithm assigns a small constant of lifetime to Q-covers so generated. In this process, it allows the sensors to participate in many Q-covers. We observe that the smaller the constant, the closer is the solution to optimal solution. Through experiments on randomly generated problem instances, we show that the proposed algorithm yields near-optimal solution.

Keywords: Target Q-coverage problem, Wireless sensor networks, energy efficiency, network lifetime, QoS requirement.

1 Introduction

One major application of sensor networks is to monitor a set of targets by an overly deployed set of sensors. A target is said to be covered if it falls within the sensing range of at least one sensor. The sensors have limited battery life. Given a vector Q = $\{q_1, q_2, ..., q_m\}$ for m targets, the Q-coverage problem is concerned with maximizing the lifetime of the network when at least q_j number of sensors cover the jth target at any given time. The Q-coverage problem is NP complete and we propose a heuristic to solve the problem. In this paper, we address the Q-coverage problem and propose a heuristic that prioritizes the sensors in terms of the residual battery life and then greedily selects sensors to generate a Q-cover. We assign a small constant lifetime (instead of full battery life) to each generated Q-covers so that sensors can participate in many Q-covers to provide near optimal solution.

V. Garg, R. Wattenhofer, and K. Kothapalli (Eds.): ICDCN 2009, LNCS 5408, pp. 325–330, 2009.

The paper defines the Q-coverage problem and show that it is NP-complete in section 2. In section 3, we propose the heuristic to solve Q-coverage problem. Experimental results are shown in section 4 and section 5 discusses the future directions of research.

2   Q-Coverage Problem

Let s_1, s_2, ..., and s_n be randomly deployed n sensor nodes and t_1, t_2, ..., and t_m be m targets. Every sensor s_i has available battery life, b_i. Let $Q = \{q_1, q_2, \ldots, q_m\}$ be a coverage vector such that at any given instance, target t_j should be covered by at least q_j $(q_j \geq 1)$ active sensor nodes. A Q-cover S is a set of sensors that jointly cover all the targets satisfying the coverage vector specification. Formally, $S = \{s_i \mid$ for each t_j, there are at least q_j number of $s_i \in S$ covering $t_j\}$. The objective is to find a set of Q-covers and assign lifetime to each Q-cover so that the aggregated lifetime of all Q-covers is maximum subject to the constraint that no individual sensor can be used longer than its initial battery life.

The Q-coverage problem is introduced by Gu et al [4] and in [5], the domatic partition problem is discussed where every target must constantly be covered by at least k number of sensors. This problem is the special case of Q-coverage problem where $q_j = k$ for all j. The Q-coverage problem can be formulated as linear programming problem. Let us define a matrix C as follows.

$$C_{ij} = \begin{cases} 1, & \text{if sensor } s_i \text{ is in } Q-\text{cover } S_j \\ 0, & \text{otherwise} \end{cases}$$

The columns of C correspond to all Q-covers and the rows correspond to all sensors. The linear programming formulation of the energy efficient Q-coverage problem can be formulated as follows.

$$\text{Maximize} \sum_p x_p$$

$$\text{subject to} \sum_p C_{ip} x_p \leq b_i \text{ for allsensors } s_i$$

$$x_p \geq 0, \text{ for all } Q-\text{covers } S_p.$$

The constraint matrix C is explicitly known if the set of all Q-covers is known in advance. This is not practical. So the other approach is to generate covers (columns of C) as and when necessary (the typical column generation method of linear programming) .

Let us define n×m sensor-target coverage matrix M as follows.

$$M_{ij} = \begin{cases} 1, & \text{if sensor } s_i \text{ covers target } t_j \\ 0, & \text{otherwise} \end{cases}$$

Given M, a Q-cover S is a set of rows of M (equivalently, set of sensors) such that for every column j, there are at least q_j rows i_1, i_1, ..., i_{qj} in S such that $M_{ij} = 1$.

A Q-cover S is a *minimal cover* if for any Q-cover S', $S' \subseteq S$ if and only if $S' = S$.

The maximum allowable lifetime of a Q-cover S is the smallest available lifetime of its sensors. Thus

$$\text{max\_lifetime}(S) = Min_{s_i \in S} \, b_i$$

Let us define a quantity u as follows. [p] is the integer part of p.

$$u = Min_j \left[\frac{\sum_i M_{ij} * b_i}{q_j} \right]$$

Lemma 1: The optimal solution of Q-coverage problem is bounded above by u.

The problem of selecting the minimum number of sensor such that each target is covered by at least one sensor (Cardei et al [2]) is NP-complete and is indeed an instance of Q-coverage problem. So, it is straight forward to conclude that Q-coverage problem is NP-complete. Hence we have the following theorem.

Theorem 1: Target Q-coverage problem is NP–complete.

3 Heuristic with High Energy and Small Lifetime (HESL)

In this section, we develop a new heuristic to solve the Q-coverage problem. There are three generic steps involved in the proposed heuristic.

Step 1: Initially some sorts of priorities based on available battery life are assigned to each sensor. The heuristic generates Q-cover by iteratively selecting sensors with highest residual battery life till all the targets are covered according to the coverage vector Q. The obtained Q-cover is not minimal, so we minimalize it by removing one sensor at a time from it and then checking whether it is a Q-cover or not.

Step 2: For a Q-cover S generated in the previous step, we assign lifetime x(S). Instead of assigning maximum allowable lifetime, the algorithm assigns small constant w units of lifetime. By this process, we do not consume the total energy of sensors and make these sensors available for other Q-covers.

Step 3: In order to avoid the repeated generation of the same Q-cover in consecutive iterations, the priority of a sensor reduces once it is used in a Q- cover and as a result the greedy construction of Q- cover in the next iteration tries to avoid such a sensor. The pseudocode of the proposed algorithm is given below. We term the algorithm as HESL (High-energy & small-lifetime) algorithm.

INPUT M, Q, w
We assume initial value of b_i is 1, for each sensor i.
repeat while for each target $\sum_i M_{ij} \, b_i \geq q_j$
    1. generate a Q- cover
        $S = \varnothing$
        for all targets t
          uncover_label(t) $= q_i$
        do while *uncover_label*(t) $\neq 0$ for some t
          select a sensor s with highest $b_i > 0$ that covers at least
            one target with *uncover_label*(t) > 0.
        $S \leftarrow S \cup \{s\}$

for all targets t covered by s,
   $uncover\_label(t) = uncover\_label(t)-1$
  end do
 minimalize S
2. *assigning lifetime to Q- cover S*
  compute $max\_lifetime(S)$
  $w' = \text{Min}\ (w, max\_lifetime(S))$
  $lifetime(S) \leftarrow lifetime(S) + w'$
3. update priorities
  for each $s \in S$
  $b_s \leftarrow b_s - w'$

Algorithm. HESL

4 Experimental Results

We assume a sensing area of 800×800m inside the monitored area of 1000×1000m. We also assume that sensors have the same energy equal to 1 unit and sensing range equals 70m. For our experiments, we vary the number of sensors in interval [20, 150] and the number of targets in [20, 90] with an increment of 10.

In our experiment, we study the quality of the solution of the proposed heuristic. We experimented for various values of w and vector Q. For each set of parameters, 10 random problem instances are solved and the average of the solution and the upper bounds are taken to examine the closeness of the solution to the upper bound.

In Figure 1, the graphs depicts the quality of solution against the upper bound for different values of w and for fixed $q_m = 2$ for all m targets. Fig. 1a shows results for different m and Fig 1b shows results different n. Figure 2 reports the same experiment when $q_m = 3$ for all m targets.

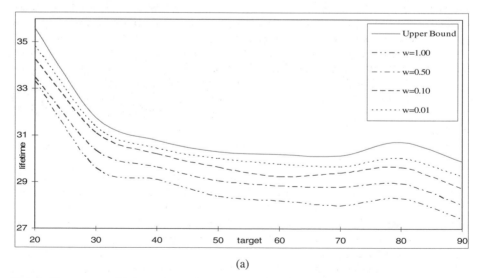

(a)

Fig. 1. The average lifetime obtained by HESL for $q_m = 2$ and different m (Fig.1a) and for different n (Fig.1b)

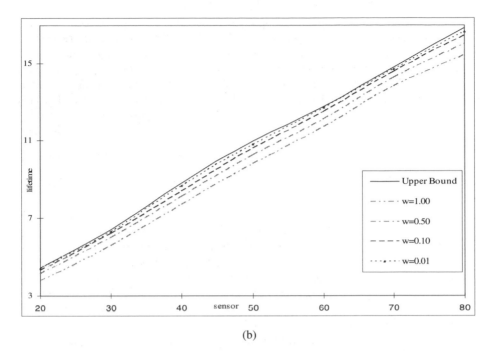

(b)

Fig. 1. (*continued*)

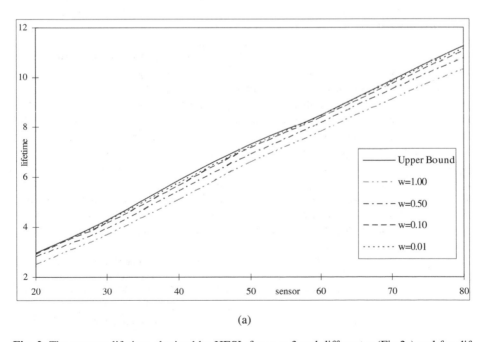

(a)

Fig. 2. The average lifetime obtained by HESL for $q_m = 3$ and different n (Fig.2a) and for different m (Fig.2b)

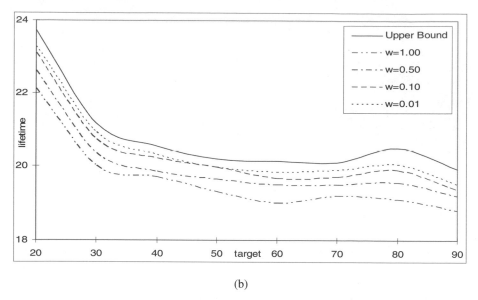

(b)

Fig. 2. (*continued*)

We observe from above graphs that HESL yields solutions very close to the optimal solution and for smaller values of w and q_m, the solution is closer to the optimal value.

5 Conclusion

In this paper, we propose a centralized algorithm for coverage problem with QoS requirement. We show that the problem is NP-complete. HESL is based on greedy approach, and selects that sensor with highest residual energy. Our exhaustive experiments reveal that the proposed method yields solution very close to the actual optimal solution. One can have many variations of the problem with additional constraints of coverage and connectivity or directional sensing [1, 3, 6] etc.

References

[1] Ai, J., Abouzeid, A.A.: Coverage by directional sensors in randomly deployed wireless sensor networks. J. Comb. Optim. 11, 21–41 (2006)
[2] Cardei, M., Wu, J.: Energy efficient coverage problems in wireless ad hoc sensor networks. Computer Communications 29(4), 413–420 (2006)
[3] Funke, S., Kesselman, A., Kuhn, F., Lotker, Z., Segal, M.: Improved approximation algorithms for connected sensor cover. Wireless Networks 13, 153–164 (2007)
[4] Gu, Y., Liu, H., Zhao, B.: Target Coverage with QoS Requirements in Wireless Sensor Networks. In: IPC 2007, pp. 35–38 (2007)
[5] Moscibroda, T., Wattenhofer, R.: Maximizing the Lifetime of Dominating Sets, IPDPS 19, p. 8 (2005)
[6] Wang, L., Xiao, Y.: A survey of energy-efficient scheduling mechanisms in sensor networks. Mobile Networks and Applications 11, 723–740 (2006)

On Providing Reliability and Maximizing Network Lifetime in Multi-Sink Wireless Sensor Networks

Saamaja Vupputuri, Kiran Rachuri, A. Antony Franklin, and C. Siva Ram Murthy

Department of Computer Science and Engineering
Indian Institute of Technology Madras
Chennai-600036, India
{saamaja,kiranr,antony}@cse.iitm.ac.in, murthy@iitm.ac.in

Abstract. In this paper, we focus on maximizing network lifetime of Multi-Sink Wireless Sensor Networks without compromising on reliability requirements. We propose Multi-Sink Multi-Path (MSMP) protocol which achieves the desired reliability by selecting the sink nodes based on their Total Reaching Probabilities (TRPs) and using multiple paths for forwarding to each selected sink. MSMP maximizes the network lifetime by reducing the load on the one hop neighbors of the source node. In addition, MSMP shuffles among all the sink nodes, to distribute the load on all the nodes in the network. This shuffling is based on the energy levels of the nodes in the paths to the sink nodes. We compare MSMP with the existing approaches via simulations and show that MSMP achieves the maximum network lifetime compared to that of other approaches without compromising on the reliability requirements.

1 Introduction

Wireless Sensor Networks (WSNs) [1] consists of tiny sensor nodes which have limited communication, computation, sensing and occasionally controlling capabilities. Typically, these sensor nodes are driven by a finite battery source. In addition to sensor nodes, WSNs consists of multiple sink nodes [2] that are powered and act as destination points for the event data sensed by the sensor nodes. Providing Quality of Service (QoS) in terms of reliability is one of the important requirements of WSNs. In this paper, reliability of an event data packet is defined as the probability with which the packet reaches at least one of the sink nodes. Another important consideration in WSNs is to maximize the lifetime [3] of network. We define the network lifetime as the time at which all the one hop neighbors of a source node are dead. In this paper, we focus on maximizing the network lifetime of WSNs with multiple sink nodes without compromising on the QoS requirements in terms of reliability metric.

The rest of the paper is organized as follows: In Section 2, we discuss about the related work. In Section 3, the details of the proposed protocol are presented. This is followed by a discussion on simulation results in Section 4. Finally, we conclude the paper in Section 5.

V. Garg, R. Wattenhofer, and K. Kothapalli (Eds.): ICDCN 2009, LNCS 5408, pp. 331–336, 2009.

2 Related Work

In [4], the authors introduce the concept of service differentiation in terms of reliability for WSNs. They presented an adaptive multi-path multi-packet forwarding scheme for achieving the desired level of service using probabilistic flooding. The main problem with this approach is that it requires flooding of forwarding parameters to adapt to the dynamics of the network. In [5,6], the authors present a multi-path forwarding protocol to achieve the requested reliability for a data packet by sending it to a single sink node. They use path redundancy to increase the data delivery probability. Both these protocols do not consider the energy levels of the forwarding nodes.

In [7], the authors propose Multi-Constrained Multi-Path (MCMP) routing mechanism which uniformly maps the end-to-end QoS requirements into hop by hop requirements among all downstream hops. One of the main drawbacks of this proposal is that it does not consider energy levels of sensor nodes. In [8], the authors propose a new aggregate routing model and a localized algorithm (DARA) which sends the sensed event data to all the sink nodes simultaneously. They consider energy levels of the sensor nodes, but sending event data to all the sink nodes will increase the load on the one hop neighbors of the source node leading to adverse effect on the network lifetime.

3 Protocol Details

Problem Statement: Given a reliability requirement (R), the source node which sensed the event should send the event packet to a set of sink nodes such that it should achieve R while maximizing the lifetime of the network. The basic principle of MSMP is to send the packet with a fraction r_i of the total desired reliability R to each sink selected.

The basic idea is that when a node has to send a data packet with reliability R, it first selects a set of sink nodes based on their Total Reaching Probabilities (TRPs) that can together satisfy R. Then, the node sends the data packet to each of the selected sink nodes via multi-path forwarding [6]. The nodes in each of these paths, achieve a fraction of the total reliability assigned to it by the previous hop node. This way, the total reliability requested is achieved. In case an intermediate node is not able to achieve the assigned reliability, it sends an *UPDATE* packet back to the source node.

We consider a WSN consisting of N sensor nodes and M sink nodes which are static and distributed uniformly in a rectangular terrain. Each node periodically broadcasts *HELLO* packet by embedding its location coordinates and residual energy level (E_i). The *UPDATE* packet mentioned above contains the following fields: average μ_i and standard deviation σ_i of the residual energies of its neighbors, number of neighbors n_i, and TRP_{s_i} which is defined as the TRP it can achieve by sending the packet to the destined sink s_i using all its neighbors. The TRP_{s_i} field in the *UPDATE* packet gets updated at each node in the reverse path to the source node, with the new TRP_{s_i} from that node.

When a node has to send a sensed event data packet, it first calculates the energy threshold E_{th}, which is the average of the $E_{th_{s_i}}$ of each sink s_i. $E_{th_{s_i}}$ is the energy threshold value for each sink s_i. Initially, when the node does not have any update information, $E_{th_{s_i}}$ for each sink is calculated based on neighborhood μ_i and σ_i values. Once, the node starts receiving *UPDATE* packets from the network then the $E_{th_{s_i}}$ values are updated based on the μ_i and σ_i values in the updates received from the intermediate nodes respectively. Therefore, $E_{th_{s_i}}$ is based on the combined μ and σ which are calculated from the μ_i and σ_i values from the updates received for that sink s_i and the neighborhood μ_i and σ_i values $i.e$, $E_{th_{s_i}} = (\mu) - n \times (\sigma)$, where n is a positive integer.

Based on $E_{th_{s_i}}$ to each sink, the TRP_{s_i} for each sink is calculated as follows:

$$TRP_{s_i} = 1 - \prod_{E_i > E_{th_{s_i}}} (1 - RP_{ij}^d) \tag{1}$$

where RP_{ij}^d is the reaching probability as defined in [6]. Neighbors whose residual energy E_i is more than $E_{th_{s_i}}$ are used as next hop forwarding nodes towards the sink node s_i.Based on the reliability requested R, the sink nodes are selected in the increasing order of their TRP_{s_i}, until the condition $(1 - R) >= \prod_{s_i}(1 - TRP_{s_i})$ is satisfied.

The fraction r_i of total desired reliability R with which the data packet is to be sent to the sink node s_i is allocated based on this condition. Thus, the r_i and E_{th} values are embedded in the *DATA* packet copies to be sent to the sink nodes selected. These values are used for selecting the forwarding nodes in the network. Also, at the source node, on receiving the *UPDATE* packet, the corresponding sink node TRP_{s_i} value is updated. However, the E_{th} value at the source node is updated only when a new set of sinks are selected for the next data packet. This means, for a E_{th} value, the set of sinks selected do not change, till they can satisfy R. This results in spreading the load across the nodes towards different sink nodes. In addition to this, the task of sending the multiple copies of the data packets across multiple paths from the selected one hop neighbors of the source node is delegated to the nodes which are K hops away from the source node in the direction of destined sink node to increase the network lifetime.

4   Simulation Results

We simulated MSMP and some of the existing approaches in the ns-2, a discrete event network simulator. We compare MSMP with single-sink approach and all-sinks approach. The single-sink approach is based on [6] with some modifications. Essentially, in a single-sink approach the desired reliability R is achieved by sending the packet via multiple paths to one of the nearest sink nodes that satisfy the condition $TRP_{s_i} > R$. All-sinks approach is based on [6,8] and for achieving the desired reliability, the packet is sent to all the sinks each with $r_i = 1 - (1 - R)^{1/M}$. The following are the performance metrics used in our simulations. a)*Network lifetime*: The time at which all the one hop neighbors of a source node are dead $i.e$, the time at which a source node gets disconnected from the network. b) *Standard deviation of residual energy*: The standard deviation of remaining energy levels of all the sensor nodes at the end of network lifetime. c) *Percentage of reliability requests satisfied*: Percentage of total reliability requests satisfied till the network lifetime. d) *Average latency of a data packet*:The average of latencies of all the data packets in the network.

4.1   Simulation Setup and Results

We consider a rectangular terrain of area $200m \times 200m$ where, the sensor nodes and sink nodes are static and deployed uniformly. The transmission range of sensor nodes is

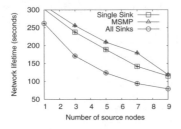

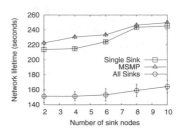

Fig. 1. Network lifetime Vs number of sources   **Fig. 2.** Network lifetime Vs number of sinks

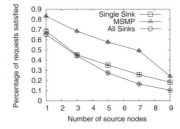

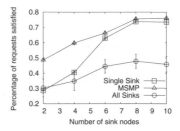

Fig. 3. Percentage of requests satisfied Vs number of sources

Fig. 4. Percentage of requests satisfied Vs number of sinks

fixed to $30m$. Packet loss probability e is assumed to be uniform in the network and is set to 0.1 [6]. The packet generation rate at each source node is fixed to $1\ packet/sec$. In the MSMP approach, for the calculation of E_{th}, the value of n is fixed to 4. We have fixed the reliability request R value for a data packet to 0.9. The value of K is randomly selected from $[3, 5]$. Source nodes are picked randomly, ensuring that the sink nodes are not in their direct transmission range $i.e$, not in their 1-hop range. Also, the sink nodes are placed uniformly across the boundaries of the rectangular terrain. The MAC protocol used is IEEE 802.11. The following are the two scenarios considered in the simulations. a) Source node variation. b) Sink node variation.

Figure 1 shows the effect of varying the number of source nodes on the network lifetime. It can be observed that MSMP performs better than the other two approaches. This is because, in MSMP the load on one-hop neighbors is reduced thereby increasing the network lifetime. On the other hand in the all-sinks approach, the load on the one-hop neighbors per packet is more, as it has to send to all the sinks for each packet leading to early neighbor deaths. Figure 2 shows the effect of varying the number of sink nodes on the network lifetime. It can be inferred that more sinks imply high probability of availability of sink nodes nearer to source nodes leading to reduced load on one hop neighbors inturn increasing the network lifetime. Also, we can observe that all-sinks approach has a lower network lifetime when compared to other approaches because of more load on the one hop neighbors per packet.

Figure 3 shows the effect of varying the number of source nodes on the percentage of requests satisfaction. It can be observed that, in cases where sending to single sink node can not achieve R, MSMP can select more than one sink node for achieving the

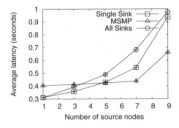

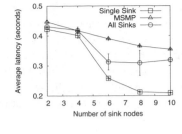

Fig. 5. Average latency of data packet Vs number of sources

Fig. 6. Average latency of data packet Vs number of sinks

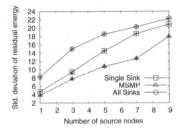

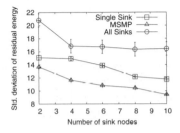

Fig. 7. Standard deviation of residual energy Vs number of sources

Fig. 8. Standard deviation of residual energy Vs number of sinks

same R thereby leading to higher percentage of successful requests. On the other hand, in all-sinks approach though it sends the data packet to all the sink nodes, the number of unsatisfied requests is very high, because of early neighbor deaths. Figure 4 shows that more the number of sinks, more requests can be satisfied before the end of network lifetime. Also, the difference between single-sink and MSMP narrows down because the probability of finding a single sink which can satisfy the request R increases with increase in the number of sinks.

Figure 5 shows the effect of the number of source nodes on the average latency of a data packet. It can be observed that, with increase in the number of source nodes MSMP fares better than the other two approaches. This is because the probability that the number of source nodes using a particular sink node increases with an increase in the number of source nodes. Due to which, in the single-sink approach the nodes in the shortest paths to the sink nodes get drained earlier, necessitating the use of longer paths. This causes increase in the average delay of a packet. From Figure 6, as the number of sink nodes increases the average latency of a packet decreases due to high probability of availability of sink nodes nearer to source nodes. However, in MSMP, due to the selection of sink nodes based on the E_{th} and TRP values, the sink nodes farther from the source node are also selected. This causes a higher average latency than the other two approaches.

Figure 7 shows the effect of varying the number of source nodes on the standard deviation of energy levels. The concept of E_{th} for selecting the forwarding nodes used in MSMP ensures that the load is distributed uniformly among the sensor nodes towards each sink node leading to uniform residual energy levels in the network. In all-sinks approach, though it sends data packet copies uniformly to all the sink nodes, the high standard deviation value is due to early neighbor deaths of the sources in the network leaving the other nodes in the network with comparatively high energy levels thereby resulting in non uniform residual energy levels in the network. In Figure 8, the probability of each source node using a different sink node increases with an increase in the number of sink nodes, therefore the nodes are used uniformly across the network leading to decrease in standard deviation of energy levels.

5   Conclusions

In this paper, we have presented MSMP protocol to maximize the network lifetime of WSNs and at the same time respect the reliability requirements. The basic principle of MSMP is that, the packet is sent with a fraction r_i of the total desired reliability R to each of the sink node s_i selected. Also, it maximizes the network lifetime by delegating the task of diverging into multiple paths to the nodes K hops away from the source node instead of 1-hop neighbors. We showed that MSMP performs better in terms of percentage of reliability requests honored and at the same time achieves higher network lifetime compared to the other approaches via simulations.

References

1. Akyildiz, I., Su, W., Sankarasubramaniam, Y., Cayirci, E.: A survey on sensor networks. IEEE Communications Magazine 40(8), 102–114 (2002)
2. Oyman, E., Ersoy, C.: Multiple sink network design problem in large scale wireless sensor networks. In: ICC 2004: Proceedings of the 17th IEEE International Conference on Communications, pp. 3663–3667 (2004)
3. Chang, J.H., Tassiulas, L.: Maximum lifetime routing in wireless sensor networks. IEEE/ACM Transactions on Networking 12(4), 609–619 (2004)
4. Bhatnagar, S., Deb, B., Nath, B.: Service differentiation in sensor networks. In: WPMC 2001: Proceedings of the 4th International Symposium on Wireless Personal Multimedia Communications (2001)
5. Deb, B., Bhatnagar, S., Nath, B.: ReInForM: Reliable information forwarding using multiple paths in sensor networks. In: LCN 2003: Proceedings of the 28th Annual IEEE Conference on Local Computer Networks, p. 406 (2003)
6. Felemban, E., Lee, C.G., Ekici, E.: MMSPEED: Multipath multi-SPEED protocol for QoS guarantee of reliability and timeliness in wireless sensor networks. IEEE Transactions on Mobile Computing 5(6), 738–754 (2006)
7. Huang, X., Fang, Y.: Multiconstrained QoS multipath routing in wireless sensor networks. Wireless Networks 14(4), 465–478 (2008)
8. Razzaque, A., Alam, M.M., Or-Rashid, M.M., Hong, C.S.: Multi-constrained QoS geographic routing for heterogeneous traffic in sensor networks. In: CCNC 2008: Proceedings of the 5th Annual IEEE Consumer Communications and Networking Conference, pp. 157–162 (2008)

Fault-Tolerant Implementations of Regular Registers by Safe Registers with Applications to Networks

Colette Johnen[1,*] and Lisa Higham[2]

[1] LRI, Univ. Paris-Sud, CNRS, F-91405 Orsay, France
colette@lri.fr, johnen@labri.fr
[2] Computer Science Department, University of Calgary, Canada
higham@ugalgary.ca

Abstract. We present the first wait-free and self-stabilizing implementation of a single-writer/single-reader regular register by single-writer/single-reader safe registers. The construction is in two steps: one implements a regular register using 1-regular registers, and the other implements a 1-regular register using safe registers. In both steps, if the initial register is bounded then the implementation uses only bounded registers.

1 Introduction

Lamport [10] defined three models of single-writer/multi-reader registers, differentiated by the possible outcome of read operations that overlap concurrent write operations. These three register types, in order of increasing power, are called safe, regular, and atomic. Program design is easier assuming atomic registers rather than regular registers but the hardware implementation of an atomic register is costlier than the implementation of a regular register. Safe registers, which capture the notion of directly sensing the hardware, are cheaper still. This motivated Lamport and other researchers to find wait-free constructions for assembling atomic registers from regular ones and regular registers from safe ones. One natural extension to this research arises from asking whether these implementations of strong registers from weaker ones can be made self-stabilizing.

This paper addresses this question. The core contribution is an implementation of a single-writer/single-reader regular register using single-writer/single-reader safe registers. The implementation is both self-stabilizing and wait-free. To implement a single-writer/single-reader regular register of M bits, our construction uses 9 single-writer/single-reader safe registers of M bits and 12 single-writer/single-reader safe registers of 2 bits. Thus, if a program uses only bounded regular registers then it can be implemented using bounded safe registers.

Related research. A body of research [2,5,11,3], initiated by Lamport [10], gave constructions of strong registers types from weaker ones. By combining these results, even the strongest register being considered (a multi-writer/multi-reader atomic register) has a wait-free construction from a collection of the weakest (single-writer/single-reader

---

* Colette Johnen has moved to Labri, Univ. Bordeaux 1, CNRS, F-33405 Talence, France.

V. Garg, R. Wattenhofer, and K. Kothapalli (Eds.): ICDCN 2009, LNCS 5408, pp. 337–348, 2009.
© Springer-Verlag Berlin Heidelberg 2009

338   C. Johnen and L. Higham

safe bits). The fault-tolerance sought in all these constructions was wait-freedom; none of these original constructions addressed self-stabilization. More recently, Abraham *et al.* [1] introduced 1-regular registers, which lie between safe and regular registers, and presented a wait-free implementation of a regular register by 1-regular registers. This construction is also not self-stabilizing and relies on timestamps to distinguish the latest value, thus requiring 1-regular registers of unbounded size.

Hoepman, Papatriantafiou and Tsigas [8] presented self-stabilizing versions of some of these well-known constructions. For instance, they present a wait-free and self-stabilizing implementation of a multi-writer/multi-reader atomic register using single-writer/single-reader regular registers of unbounded size. Dolev and Herman [4] designed a variant of Dijkstra's self-stabilizing token circulation on unidirectional rings that uses only regular registers. In contrast to the wait-free case, however, no self-stabilizing construction of strong registers starting from only safe ones was known.

Algorithm 1. A binary regular register from a binary safe register

Shared registers:
The single-writer/single-reader binary register, R, is replaced by a single-writer/single-reader binary safe register, Rs.

Code for writer:
τ (REGULAR-WRITE(R, new_bit))   # *old_bit* is a local binary variable #
    if (*old_bit* $\neq$ new_bit) then SAFE-WRITE(Rs, new_bit); *old_bit* $\longleftarrow$ new_bit.

Code for reader:
τ (REGULAR-READ(R)):: return SAFE-READ(Rs).

Lamport's wait-free implementation of a single-writer/single-reader regular binary register from only one single-writer/single-reader safe binary register (Algorithm 1) is straightforward – the safe register is over-written only if the new value is different from what was most recently written. This simple idea does not work in the self-stabilizing setting, because the value of *old_bit* could be corrupted and thus not equal to the value of the safe register. In fact, as established by Hoepman *et al.* [8], there is no wait-free and self-stabilizing implementation of a single-writer/single-reader regular binary register with only one single-writer/single-reader safe binary register.

Outline of paper. The description of our implementation is separated into two pieces. Section 3 presents an implementation of a single-writer/single-reader 1-regular register by single-writer/single-reader safe registers. Section 4 implements a single-writer/single-reader regular register by single-writer/single-reader 1-regular registers. Both of these implementations are wait-free and self-stabilizing; hence, so is their composition. We only sketch the proofs, trying to provide the essential insights for correctness. A lot of detail is omitted, most notably, that needed to completely establish the correctness of the second piece, which is the most intricate of the two. Our technical report [9] has the complete proofs. Section 5 overviews how this work applies to network models of distributed computation, and how it relates to research on fault-tolerant compilers between different variants of network models.

2 Definitions and Preliminaries

2.1 Model

Shared registers.   Let R be a single-writer/multi-reader register that can contain any value in domain T. R supports only the operations READ and WRITE. Each READ and WRITE operation, o, has a time interval corresponding to the time between the invocation of o, denoted inv(o), and the response of o, denoted resp(o). An operation o *happens-before* operation o' if resp(o) < inv(o'). If neither o happens-before o' nor o' happens-before o, then o and o' *overlap*. Because there is only one writer, WRITE operations to R happen sequentially, so the happens-before relation is a total order on all the WRITE operations. READ operations, however, may overlap each other and may overlap a WRITE. Lamport [10] defined three kinds of such registers depending on the semantics when READ and WRITE operations overlap. Register R is *safe* if each READ that does not overlap any WRITE returns the value of the latest WRITE that happens-before it, and otherwise returns any value in T. Register R is *regular* if it is safe and any READ that overlaps a WRITE returns the value of either the latest WRITE that happens-before it, or the value of some overlapping WRITE. Register R is *atomic* if it is regular, and if any READ, r, overlaps a WRITE, w, and returns the value written by w, then any READ, r', that happens-after r must not return the value of any WRITE that happens-before w. We also use another register type, which was defined by Abraham *et al.* [1]. Register R is *1-regular* if it is safe and any READ with *at most one* overlapping WRITE returns the value of either the latest WRITE that happens-before it, or the value of the overlapping WRITE.

Systems, configurations and executions.   Each of the two technical results of this paper is an implementation of a single-writer/single-reader register (called the *specified register*) using weaker single-writer/single-reader registers (called the *target registers*). As discussed further in Section 5, the implementations extend to any system of such shared registers, because the individual implementations are independent. Thus, the specified system consists of just two processors, a writer p and a reader q, sharing a single specified register. This system is implemented using several registers of the target register type. Since our target registers are also single-writer/single-reader, they can be partitioned into two sets. One contains the registers written by p and read by q; the other contains the registers read by p and written by q.

   A *configuration* of the system is an assignment of values to each of the the shared target registers and the internal variables, including the program counter, of the writer and reader implementations. In a *computation step*, a processor executes the next action of its program. Each action is an invocation or a response of an READ or a WRITE on a shared target register, or a read or a write of an internal variable.

2.2 Fault-Tolerance

Wait-freedom.   An operation on a shared object is *wait-free* if every invocation of the operation completes in a finite number of steps of the invoking processor regardless of the number of steps taken by any other processor. Wait-freedom provides robustness; it implies that a stopping failure (or very slow execution) of any subset of processors cannot prevent another processor from correctly completing its operation.

Self-stabilization. Let PS be a predicate defined on computations. A distributed system is *self-stabilizing to PS* if and only if there is a predicate, L, on configurations such that:

- **L is attractor:** Starting from any configuration, any computation reaches a configuration satisfying L. For any configuration C satisfying L, the successor configuration reached by any computation step applied to C also satisfies L.
- **correctness from L:** Any computation starting from a configuration satisfying L satisfies PS.

L is called the *legitimacy predicate*. Informally, an algorithm is self-stabilizing to a behaviour specified by PS if, after a burst of transient errors of some components of a distributed system (which leaves the system in an arbitrary configuration), the system recovers and eventually returns to the specified behaviour.

2.3 Proof Obligation of Register Implementations

The possible operations on a register are READ and WRITE.

Therefore, to implement a strong register, R, using only weaker registers requires defining two programs $\tau\,(\text{READ}(R))$ and $\tau\,(\text{WRITE}(R, \cdot))$ each accessing only registers of the weaker type. Consider an execution E of the implementation. It consists of a sequence $r_1, r_2, \ldots$ of successive computation steps of $\tau\,(\text{READ}(R))$ by the reader, and a sequence $w_1, w_2, \ldots$ of successive steps of $\tau\,(\text{WRITE}(R, \cdot))$ by the writer. Furthermore, r_1 (respectively, w_1) could begin part way through $\tau\,(\text{READ}(R))$ (respectively, $\tau\,(\text{WRITE}(R, \cdot))$); there could be arbitrary initial values in registers; and the two sequences of computation steps could overlap arbitrarily.

The proof that an algorithm is a correct wait-free and self-stabilizing implementation of a strong register is decomposed into four components:

Termination: Normally, establishing wait-freedom would require showing that any execution of $\tau\,(\text{READ}(R))$ or of $\tau\,(\text{WRITE}(R, \cdot))$ terminates in a finite number of steps. Since our algorithms must simultaneously be self-stabilizing, we need to show the stronger requirement that any execution of any suffix of $\tau\,(\text{READ}(R))$ or of $\tau\,(\text{WRITE}(R, \cdot))$, with any values in the registers, terminates.

Legitimate configurations: We define a predicate $\tilde{L}$ on the values of the target registers and on values of the internal variables used by $\tau\,(\text{WRITE}(R, \cdot))$ and $\tau\,(\text{READ}(R))$.

Attractor: We show that $\tilde{L}$ is an attractor.

Correctness: We show that every every execution of $\tau\,(\text{READ}(R))$ that begins from any configuration that verifies the predicate $\tilde{L}$, returns only values that are consistent with the semantics of the stronger register, R.

3 Implementing 1-Regular Registers from Safe Registers

Theorem 1. *Algorithm 2 is a wait-free and self-stabilizing implementation of 1-regular register, R, using safe registers, provided* 1-REGULAR-WRITE($R, \cdot$) *is executed at least once after any transient fault.*

Algorithm 2. A 1-regular register constructed from safe registers

---

Shared registers:
Each single-writer/single-reader 1-regular register, R, is replaced by 3 single-writer/single-reader safe registers, $R1$, $R2$, $R3$.

Code for writer:
τ (1-REGULAR-WRITE(R, new_state))
   # line 1: # SAFE-WRITE($R1$, new_state);
   # line 2: # SAFE-WRITE($R2$, new_state);
   # line 3: # SAFE-WRITE($R3$, new_state).

Code for reader:
τ (1-REGULAR-READ(R))
   # $v1$, $v2$, and $v3$ are local variables of the function. #
   $v3 \longleftarrow$ SAFE-READ($R3$); $v2 \longleftarrow$ SAFE-READ($R2$); $v1 \longleftarrow$ SAFE-READ($R1$);
   if ($v3 = v2$) then return $v2$ else return $v1$.

Termination: It is immediate from the code that any execution of any suffix of either τ (1-REGULAR-WRITE) or τ (1-REGULAR-READ) will terminate since each consists of three read or write operations on safe registers.

Legitimate configurations: We define a predicate $\widetilde{Leg}1$ on configurations that (informally) captures the property that there is substantial agreement between the value of the three shared safe registers $R1$, $R2$ and $R3$. This agreement is related to the value of the writer's program counter (denoted PC).

$L1_s \equiv [\ R3 = R2 \wedge \text{PC is in line 1 of } \tau \, (1\text{-REGULAR-WRITE}(R, \cdot))\ ]$
$L2_s \equiv [\ R1 = \nu \wedge \text{PC is in line 2 of } \tau \, (1\text{-REGULAR-WRITE}(R, \nu))\ ]$
$L3_s \equiv [\ R1 = R2 = \nu \wedge \text{PC is in line 3 of } \tau \, (1\text{-REGULAR-WRITE}(R, \nu))\ ]$
$L0_s \equiv [\ R1 = R2 = R3 \wedge \text{PC is not in } \tau \, (1\text{-REGULAR-WRITE}(R, \cdot))\ ]$
$\widetilde{Leg}1 \equiv L1_s \vee L2_s \vee L3_s \vee L0_s.$

Attractor: Once verified, $L0_s$ remains verified as long as the writer is not executing τ (1-REGULAR-WRITE(R, ν)), since registers $R1$, $R2$, and $R3$ are only written inside τ (1-REGULAR-WRITE(R, ν)). If $L0_s$ is verified and the PC enters line 1, then $L1_s$ becomes verified because only the value of $R1$ is modified in line 1. When the PC moves to line 2, $R1 = \nu$. Thus, $L2_s$ becomes verified and remains so while PC stays in line 2, because the value of $R1$ is not modified in line 2. When the PC enters line 3, $R1 = R2 = \nu$. Thus $L3_s$ becomes verified and remains so while PC stays in line 3, because only the value of $R3$ is modified. When the PC exits line 3, $R1 = R2 = R3 = \nu$. Thus $L0_s$ is verified. We conclude that $\widetilde{Leg}1$ is closed.

  At the end of a complete execution of τ (1-REGULAR-WRITE(R, $\cdot$)), $L0_s$ is verified; so $\widetilde{Leg}1$ is verified after one complete execution of τ (1-REGULAR-WRITE(R, $\cdot$)).

Correctness: Any execution of the transformed system consists of an arbitrary overlapping of two sequences: a sequence of executions of τ (1-REGULAR-WRITE(R, $\cdot$)) by the writer and a sequence of executions of τ (1-REGULAR-READ(R)) by the reader. Let $E1$ be any such execution that starts from a configuration $c1$ satisfying $\widetilde{Leg}1$. Define $ghost(R)$ to be the value of $R3$ in configuration $c1$.

Let Rd be an execution of τ (1-REGULAR-READ(R)) by the reader in $E1$. We need to show that Rd returns a value that could have been returned by the corresponding operation 1-REGULAR-READ(R) on the original 1-regular register.

If Rd has two or more overlapping executions of τ (1-REGULAR-WRITE($R, \cdot$)) by the writer, then, by the definition of 1-regular registers, any value in the domain of the register can be returned.

Suppose that Rd has at most one overlapping execution of τ(1-REGULAR-WRITE($R, \cdot$)), say W.

Case 1: W was preceded by W-prev, an execution of τ (1-REGULAR-WRITE($R, \cdot$)). Since the three safe registers are accessed in the opposite order by Rd and W, at most one of the safe registers in $\{R1, R2, R3\}$ could be being read by Rd while there is an overlapping write to the same register by W. If the SAFE-READ of $R1$ is overlapped then $v3 = v2$, and the value written by W-prev is returned. If the read of $R3$ is overlapped then $v1 = v2$, and the value written by W is returned. If the read of $R2$ is overlapped then Rd returns either $v2 = v3$ (the value written by W-prev), or $v1$ (the value written by W).

Case 2: W is the first execution of τ (1-REGULAR-WRITE($R, \cdot$)). This is similar to Case 1, except that Rd returns either the value written by W or the value $ghost(R)$.

Suppose that Rd has no overlapping execution of τ (1-REGULAR-WRITE($R, \cdot$)). Then L_0 holds throughout the duration of Rd. So $v3$ is returned; and $v3$ is either the value written by the most recent preceding execution of τ (1-REGULAR-WRITE($R, \cdot$)) or $v3 = ghost(R)$.

4   Implementing Regular Registers from 1-Regular Registers

4.1   Overview of Algorithm 3

If we could ensure that no more than one write could overlap a read operation, a 1-regular register would suffice in place of a regular register. For a single-writer/single-reader model, this observation suggests that we try to avoid overlap by having more than one 1-regular register available for the writer and arranging communication from the reader to direct the writer which one to use. To implement this idea, the regular register R is implemented with three 1-regular copies. There is also a color with value in $\{0, 1, 2\}$ associated with R. The color value is written by the reader and read by the writer (also using a 1-regular register). The writer implements a REGULAR-WRITE to R by writing to the copy $R[i]$ if it believes the current color is i. Three additional 1-regular registers are needed, $Flag[i]$ where $i \in \{0, 1, 2\}$, which are used to help the reader determine which of the three copies has the latest value.

Consider a regular register with writer p and reader q. In a τ (REGULAR-WRITE($R, \cdot$)) execution, p first reads RC to get a color $i \in \{0, 1, 2\}$. It then writes its new state to $R[i]$, and set both registers $Flag[i \oplus 2]$ and $Flag[i \oplus 1]$ to i thus making them "point to" the register just written.

In an execution of τ (REGULAR-READ(R)), the reader q executes a loop three times. In iteration $i \in \{0, 1, 2\}$ of the loop, the reader q first writes i to RC, and then reads $Flag[i]$ to get a pointer value. Depending on the value returned, q reads either $R[i \oplus 1]$

Algorithm 3. A regular register constructed from 1-regular registers

Shared registers:

The single-writer/single-reader regular register, R is replaced by 7 single-writer/single-reader 1-regular registers: $R[c]$ and $Flag[c]$ $\forall c \in [0..2]$ each written by the writer and read by the reader, and RC written by the reader and read by the writer.

$\oplus$ denotes addition modulo 3.

Code for writer:

τ (REGULAR-WRITE(R, new_state))   # color is a local variable of the procedure. #

      # line 1: # $color \longleftarrow$ 1-REGULAR-READ(RC);
            1-REGULAR-WRITE($R[color]$, new_state);
      # line 2: #   if ($color \neq 2$) then 1-REGULAR-WRITE($Flag[2]$, $color$);
      # line 3: #   if ($color \neq 1$) then 1-REGULAR-WRITE($Flag[1]$, $color$);
      # line 4: #   if ($color \neq 0$) then 1-REGULAR-WRITE($Flag[0]$, $color$).

Code for reader:

τ (REGULAR-READ(R))   # $f[0..2]$, $v[0..2]$, and c are local variables. #

      for $c \longleftarrow$ 0 to 2 do
            1-REGULAR-WRITE(RC, c);
            $f[c] \longleftarrow$ 1-REGULAR-READ($Flag[c]$);
            if $f[c] \neq c \oplus 1$ then $f[c] \longleftarrow c \oplus 2$;
            $v[c] \longleftarrow$ 1-REGULAR-READ($R[f[c]]$);
      if ($f[0] = f[1] = 2$) then return($v[1]$) else return($v[2]$).

---

or $R[i \oplus 2]$. Thus the reader q gets a pair of values $f[i]$, $v[i]$ in iteration i. Reader q returns either $v[1]$ or $v[2]$ depending on the flag values read during iterations 0 and 1.

4.2   Sketch of Algorithm 3 Correctness

Theorem 2. *Algorithm 3 is a wait-free and self-stabilizing implementation of regular register, R, using 1-regular registers, provided* REGULAR WRITE(R, $\cdot$) *is executed at least once after any transient fault.*

Termination: It is immediate from the code that any execution of any suffix of either τ (REGULAR-WRITE(R, $\cdot$)) or τ (REGULAR-READ(R)) will terminate since each consists of nine or fewer read or write operations on 1-regular registers.

Legitimate Configurations: Observe that the local variables are overwritten with values that do not depend on their previous values. This leads to the intuition that, after each is overwritten, the configuration is the same as one that could arise from a complete fault-free execution. Define a legitimacy predicate $\widetilde{Leg2}$ on the configurations as follows.

$L1_r \equiv$ [PC is in line 1 or is not in any line of τ (REGULAR-WRITE(R, $\cdot$))
          $\wedge \exists\, c \in \{0,1,2\}$ satisfying $Flag[c \oplus 2] = Flag[c \oplus 1] = c$]
$L2_r \equiv$ [PC is in line 2 of τ (REGULAR-WRITE(R, ν)) $\wedge$ $R[color] = \nu$]
$L3_r \equiv$ [PC is in line 3 of τ (REGULAR-WRITE(R, ν)) $\wedge$ $R[color] = \nu$ $\wedge$
          $((Flag[2] = color) \vee (2 = color))$]
$L4_r \equiv$ [PC is in line 4 of τ (REGULAR-WRITE(R, ν)) $\wedge$ $R[color] = \nu$ $\wedge$
          $[(Flag[2] = color = 0 = Flag[1]) \vee (Flag[2] = color = 1) \vee$

$$(Flag[1] = color = 2)]\ ]$$
$$\widetilde{Leg2} \equiv L1_r \vee L2_r \vee L3_r \vee L4_r$$

Attractor: It is easily confirmed from the code that $\widetilde{Leg2}$ is verified after one complete execution of τ (REGULAR-WRITE($R, \cdot$)) and that once it is verified it remains verified. So $\widetilde{Leg2}$ is an attractor.

Correctness: We start with some notation to facilitate the correctness argument. Let Rd denote an execution by the reader of τ (REGULAR-READ(R)) starting from a legitimate configuration. Denote by Rd-loop(i) the interval within the execution of Rd when the reader is executing iteration i of its loop, for $i \in \{0, 1, 2\}$. Let W denote an execution of τ (REGULAR-WRITE($R, \cdot$)). Say that W *writes with color j* if the operation 1-REGULAR-READ(RC) done during the execution of W returns j.

Consider a computation $E2$ starting from a configuration $c2$ satisfying $\widetilde{Leg2}$. Rather than treat the starting point $c2$ separately, we define a *ghost* W that writes with a color and value defined by the values of the 1-regular registers in $c2$. Specifically, if in configuration $c2$, there is $c \in \{0, 1, 2\}$ satisfying $Flag[c \oplus 2]= Flag[c \oplus 1] = c$ then define initialize_value $= R[c]$ and define initialize_color $= c$. Otherwise define initialize_value $= R[c']$ where $c' = Flag[2]$, and define initialize_color $= c'$. The *ghost* W writes the value initialize_value with color initialize_color.

Define $Set.i = \{ Flag[i], R[i \oplus 1], R[i \oplus 2] \}$. Say that W *interferes* with Rd-loop(i) only if it both overlaps with Rd-loop(i) and it writes to at least one 1-regular register that is read by the reader during Rd-loop(i).

We have to prove that a τ (REGULAR-READ(R)) satisfies the requirement of a regular register. The proof has three main steps.

Step 1.   At most one W can interfere with a given Rd-loop(i). As a consequence, by the definition of 1-regular registers, 1-regular registers in $Set.i$ for any i, satisfy the stronger semantics of regular registers.

Step 2.   The pair of values $(f[i], v[i])$ returned by Rd-loop(i) is the same as the pair of values that would have been computed had Rd-loop(i) been executed instantaneously either (1) at the end of the most recent preceding W, or (2) at the end of the interfering W.

Step 3.   The final value returned by Rd is either the value of an overlapping or the most recent preceding W.

Step 1:   Observe from the code that Rd-loop(i) reads only from registers in $Set.i$, and if the writer writes with color i, it does not access any registers in $Set.i$. Thus, to interfere with Rd-loop(i), W must write with color $j \neq i$, implying it must begin 1-REGULAR-READ(RC) before Rd-loop(i) completes 1-REGULAR-WRITE(RC, i).

Also, it must overlap at least the first read, 1-REGULAR-READ($Flag[i]$), by Rd-loop(i). Because there is only one writer, there can be is at most one such W that spans this interval. In the Fig. 1, W (writing with the color 2) interferes with Rd-loop(0).

Step 2:   If no W interferes with Rd-loop(i), then by the definition of 1-regular registers, the pair $(f[i], v[i])$ computed in Rd-loop(i), will be the same as would be computed had Rd-loop(i) been executed any time after the registers it accesses were last written, which is no later than at the end of the most recent preceding W. Suppose, that some W

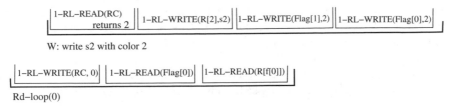

Fig. 1. Illustration of step 1

interferes with Rd-loop(i) and let W-prev denote the τ (REGULAR-WRITE($R, \cdot$)) that most recently precedes W. Notice that W first writes to the R 1-regular register and then to the $Flag$ 1-regular registers, whereas Rd-loop(i) first reads a $Flag$ 1-register and then an R 1-register. Suppose W writes with color k ($k \neq i$). The value $f[i]$ is either the value, say j, in $Flag[i]$ at the end of W-prev, or the value k written by W to $Flag[i]$. Figure 2 illustrates this, for the case where $j = 2$ and $k = 1$. If $f[i] = j$ and $j \neq k$ then the read of $R[j]$ in Rd-loop(i) returns the value of $R[j]$ at the end of W-prev because W does not write to $R[j]$. If $f[i] = k$ and $j \neq k$, then the read of $R[k]$ in Rd-loop(i) will return the value just written by W. If $f[i] = j = k$, then the read of $R[k]$ in Rd-loop(i) will return either the value written by W or by W-prev. In all cases, the pair of values $(f[i], v[i])$ is the pair of values from either the end of W-prev or the end of W.

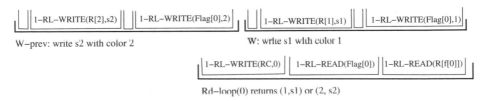

Fig. 2. Illustration of step 2

Step 3: Consider Rd-loop(c) of Rd, for some $c \in \{0, 1, 2\}$. The value, $v[c]$, computed by Rd-loop(c) is the value written by a real or ghost τ (REGULAR-WRITE($R, \cdot$)) execution named W_stale or it is the initial value of $R[f[c]]$. We denoted by $t0$ the ending time of W_stale if W_stale exists otherwise $t0$ denoted the time $t - 1$ - assuming that the ghost τ (REGULAR-WRITE(R, initialize_$value$)) execution ends at time t. Let W_previous denote the latest execution of τ (REGULAR-WRITE($R, \cdot$)) preceding Rd, and $t1$ be its ending time. We will show that Rd will not return $v[c]$ as its final value if $t0 < t1$. It will therefore follow that the final value returned by Rd is either the value of an overlapping or the most recent preceding τ (REGULAR-WRITE($R, \cdot$)) execution.

Let $I(c)$ denote the interval from $t0$ to the beginning of Rd-loop(c).

$R[f[c]]$ has not been overwritten during interval $I(c)$. Any write with color $f[c]$ writes to $R[f[c]]$. Thus, all writes during $I(c)$ do not have color $f[c]$. According to Rd-loop(c) property, the flag value returned by Rd-loop(c) is the the value of $f[c]$ at $t1$ or at $t2$ (where $t2$ is the end of the interfering W with Rd-loop(c)). Observe that if a write with color j such that $c \neq j \neq f[c]$ is done during $I(c)$ then $f[c]$ would be equal to j at $t1$ and at $t2$. Thus, all writes during $I(c)$ have color c.

Observe from the code, that the final value returned by Rd is either $v[1]$ (if $f[0] = f[1] = 2$) or $v[2]$ (otherwise). Assume that $c > 0$; let k be an integer such that $0 \leq k < c$. Notice that the time interval $I(k)$ is a prefix of $I(c)$. If $t0 < t1$ then a write with color c (ghost or real) occurs during $I(k)$.

Rd-loop(k) property implies that Rd-loop(k) computes $f[k] = c$. If $c = 2$ then Rd returns $v[1]$ ($f[0] = f[1] = 2$) otherwise Rd returns $v[2]$ ($f[0] = 1$).

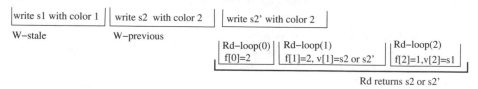

Fig. 3. Illustration of step 3

We conclude that the final value returned by Rd is either the value of an overlapping or the most recent preceding τ (REGULAR-WRITE($R, \cdot$)) execution.

In Figure 4, a sequence of three τ (REGULAR-WRITE($R, \cdot$)) executions is concurrent with a τ (REGULAR-READ(R)).

The possible values returned by the τ (REGULAR-READ(R)) execution are indicated.

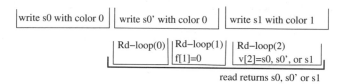

Fig. 4. Example of an execution

Combining the implementations. The composition of Algorithms 2 and 3 is a self-stabilizing implementation of a single-writer/single-reader regular register using only single-writer/single-reader safe registers. Also observe that both implementations are clearly wait-free — each transformation is straight-line code of at most 10 operations on shared registers. Hence, their composition is also wait-free. The size of each shared safe register used by the composition is $9M + 24$ bits where M is the size of the regular register being implemented. Thus, any self-stabilizing algorithm that uses only bounded single-writer/single-reader regular registers, can be implemented with bounded single-writer/single-reader safe registers.

5   Application to Network Simulations

A network that uses shared registers can be modelled as a graph where nodes represent processors and there is an edge between two nodes if and only if the corresponding processors communicate directly by reading or writing registers shared between them.

Two variants are defined by specifying whether the registers are single-writer/multi-reader and located at the nodes (*state* models) or single-writer/ single-reader and located on the edges (*link* models). By specifying either state or link communication, via shared registers that are either safe, regular, or atomic, we arrive at six different register-based network models. For a graph G, strength-location(G) denotes the network with topology G and network model strength-location, where strength $\in$ {safe, regular, atomic} and where location $\in$ {link, state}. For example, the regular-link model has single-writer/single-reader regular registers located on the links of the network.

In a network model, two processors can share a register only if they share a edge in G. In contrast, in the stronger globally shared memory model, even when the globally shared memory contains only single-writer/single-reader registers, *any* pair of processors can share registers.

The research cited earlier (Lamport and others) on wait-free implementations of strong register types using weaker ones exploited globally shared memory for some of the implementations of multi-reader (respectively, multi-writer) registers using only single-reader (respectively, single-writer) registers. A natural generalization of this research is to determine which of these implementations remain possible in the register-based network model.

Our research seeks to answer this question as well as to generalize by adding self-stabilization to the fault-tolerance requirement. Specifically, we ask whether it is possible to transform wait-free (respectively, self-stabilizing) algorithms for one of the stronger network models into a wait-free (respectively, self-stabilizing) algorithms for a weaker network model.

The implementations in this paper immediately answer one part of this question: there is a wait-free and self-stabilizing implementation of algorithms designed for regular-link(G) on safe-link(G), for any topology G.

By combining our previous work with either existing results or straightforward extensions of known results, we can also answer all parts of the question concerning conversions from atomic to regular strength. Specifically, 1) Previous research [7] presents a self-stabilizing implementation of atomic-state(G) on regular-state(G), and proves that no such wait-free implementation exists [6]. 2) Lamport (construction 5 of [10]) gave a wait-free implementation of an atomic single-writer/single-reader register by regular single-writer/single-reader registers. It is easily confirmed that this implementation is also self-stabilizing, and constitutes a wait-free and self-stabilizing implementation of atomic-link(G) on regular-link(G). 3) A natural way to transform an algorithm from a state model into an algorithm for a link model is to implement a WRITE by sequentially writing to each adjacent link. While this algorithm fails to preserve atomicity, it suffices for regular (or safe) registers. It is straightforward to confirm that this naive idea provides a wait-free and self-stabilizing implementation of regular-state(G) on regular-link(G).

Given these previously known results and the contributions of this paper, the only remaining open piece of the general question is whether or not there is a wait-free and/or self-stabilizing implementation of regular-state(G) on safe-state(G) for any graph G.

References

1. Abraham, I., Chockler, G., Keidar, I., Malkhi, D.: Wait-free regular storage from byzantine components. Information Processing Letters 101(2), 60–65 (2007)
2. Abraham, U.: On interprocess communication and the implementation of multi-writer atomic registers. Theoretical Computer Science 149(2), 257–298 (1995)
3. Attiya, H., Welch, J.L.: Distributed computing: fundamentals, simulations and advanced topics. McGraw-Hill, Inc., New York (1998)
4. Dolev, S., Herman, T.: Dijkstra's self-stabilizing algorithm in unsupportive environments. In: Datta, A.K., Herman, T. (eds.) WSS 2001. LNCS, vol. 2194, pp. 67–81. Springer, Heidelberg (2001)
5. Haldar, S., Vidyasankar, K.: Constructing 1-writer multireader multivalued atomic variables from regular variables. Journal of the Association of the Computing Machinery 42(1), 186–203 (1995)
6. Higham, L., Johnen, C.: Relationships between communication models in networks using atomic registers. In: IPDPS 2006, the 20th IEEE International Parallel & Distributed Processing Symposium (2006)
7. Higham, L., Johnen, C.: Self-stabilizing implementation of atomic register by regular register in networks framework. Technical Report 1449, L.R.I. (2006)
8. Hoepman, J.H., Papatriantafilou, M., Tsigas, P.: Self-stabilization of wait-free shared memory objects. Journal of Parallel and Distributed Computing 62(5), 818–842 (2002)
9. Johnen, C., Higham, L.: Self-stabilizing implementation of regular register by safe registers in link model. Technical Report 1486, L.R.I. (2008)
10. Lamport, L.: On interprocess communication. Distributed Computing 1(2), 77–101 (1986)
11. Li, M., Tromp, J., Vitanyi, P.M.B.: How to share concurrent wait-free variables. Journal of the Association of the Computing Machinery 43(4), 723–746 (1996)

A General Approach to Analyzing Quorum-Based Heterogeneous Dynamic Data Replication Schemes*

Christian Storm and Oliver Theel

Department of Computer Science
Carl von Ossietzky University of Oldenburg
D-26111 Oldenburg, Germany
{christian.storm,oliver.theel}@informatik.uni-oldenburg.de

Abstract. Choosing a strict quorum-based data replication scheme for a particular application scenario in the decision space spawned by static and dynamic, unstructured and structured, homogeneous and heterogeneous data replication schemes is a crucial decision w.r.t. the resulting quality properties of the distributed system and therefore needs a careful evaluation. To date, the analysis of data replication schemes is limited to only a very specific subclass, namely to homogeneous unstructured schemes: Existing approaches are specifically tailored towards a particular instance of a homogeneous unstructured data replication scheme. In this paper, we present a novel approach to the analytical evaluation of strict quorum-based data replication schemes by means of a compositional GSPN system model. This model allows to evaluate structured and moreover heterogeneous (as well as unstructured and homogeneous) dynamic data replication schemes and also applies for static schemes. Because of being compositional, different data replication schemes can be easily evaluated with the same general system model.

1 Introduction

Data replication employing strict quorum systems is a well-established means for improving the availability of critical data objects in distributed systems [1,2,3,4,5] that are a composite of several interconnected processes, each managing a copy of the data object. A strict data replication scheme manages the multiple replicas and guarantees sequential consistency by employing a strict quorum system that consists of two sets of subsets of the set of processes, namely a read and a write quorum set. It is constructed such that every write quorum intersects with every other write quorum and with every read quorum in at least one process, whereas two read quorums need not to intersect. Prior to performing a read (write) operation, the unanimous agreement of all processes of a read (write) quorum for this operation is needed. Due to the strict intersection property, conflicting, i.e., consistency violating operations cannot be performed concurrently.

---

* This work was supported by the German Research Foundation (DFG) under grant GRK 1076/1 "TrustSoft" (http://www.trustsoft.org).

V. Garg, R. Wattenhofer, and K. Kothapalli (Eds.): ICDCN 2009, LNCS 5408, pp. 349–361, 2009.

Choosing a quorum system implies choosing a particular trade-off between different qualities such as load, capacity, availability [6], scalability, and operation costs [7]. Because of this quorum system-specific trade-off and highly varying application scenario quality demands, there is no single data replication scheme that is best-suited for every application scenario. Hence, a plethora of quorum-based data replication schemes classifiable into unstructured and structured data replication schemes has been proposed. *Unstructured* data replication schemes such as, e.g., Majority Consensus Voting [3], use combinatorics and minimal quorum cardinalities to create the quorum system. Unfortunately, unstructured schemes suffer from bad scalability because of linearly increasing quorum cardinalities in the number of processes. In contrast, *structured* data replication schemes such as, e.g., the Grid Protocol [2], impose a logical structure on the set of processes and use structural properties to specify the quorum system, resulting in sub-linear operation costs but also in high operation availability. The aforementioned unstructured and structured data replication schemes are *static* meaning they use an immutable and *a priori* defined quorum system. Such schemes have an upper bound on the operation availability [8] as they cannot react to process failures beyond a scheme-specific threshold. In contrast, *dynamic* data replication schemes [4,5] can consistently adapt their quorum system at runtime, e.g., via the concept of epochs [5], and thereby generally provide highly increased operation availabilities for slightly higher costs. Traditional dynamic data replication schemes are *homogeneous* in the sense that a single scheme-inherent rule is used for deriving the adapted quorum systems: For example, in Dynamic Voting – the dynamic counterpart of the static Majority Consensus Voting – each quorum system is built in a Majority Consensus manner for "every stage" n' of the dynamics, $1 \leq n' \leq n$, with n being the total number of processes in the system. In the same sense as there is no single data replication scheme superior for every application scenario, there is also none superior for every stage of the dynamics as both, unstructured and structured schemes have their specific pros and cons. *Heterogeneous* dynamic data replication schemes overcome this restriction by enabling the usage of a particular quorum system construction rule per stage of the dynamics and thereby provide advanced means to trade-off different quality measures like operation availability and costs.

The choice of a data replication scheme and thus a particular quality measure trade-off needs to be carefully evaluated as it is crucial w.r.t. the quality properties of the distributed system. Evaluation methods using simulation are not a good choice because of their massive time complexity and their simulation-inherent inaccuracy of results. Contrarily, methods based on stochastic analysis are fast and accurate but demand for a higher level of abstraction since an analytical model as detailed as a simulation model is in general not solvable due to exponential time- and space requirements. The analytical model must be as precise as possible and as abstract as necessary to provide meaningful results. While static data replication schemes are easily analyzable by solving combinatorial equations, analyzing *dynamic* data replication schemes is a difficult task and needs careful modeling of the system as the dynamics greatly increases the complexity of the system model such that it is no longer easily solvable – if solvable at all. There have been approaches to analytically evaluate dynamic data replication schemes [9, 10, 11, 4, 12, 13, 14]. All these approaches are restricted to *homogeneous* and *unstructured* dynamic data replication schemes which drastically limits their application to only this very specific subclass. Besides, they are specifically tailored to evaluate a single particular data replication scheme and are therefore unsuitable for the evaluation of other schemes.

In this paper, we present a novel approach to the analytical evaluation of strict quorum-based data replication schemes by means of a compositional system model based on generalized stochastic petri nets (GSPN). We believe our model to be holistic in the sense that it allows to evaluate structured and moreover heterogeneous (as well as unstructured and homogeneous) dynamic data replication schemes and also applies for static schemes being a particularly simple case. Moreover, different data replication schemes can easily be evaluated without altering the general model simply by exchanging the quorum system specification whereby a different data replication scheme is described.

The remainder of the paper is structured as follows. The next section relates previous work to our approach. Section 3 presents the proposed system model in detail. An exemplary evaluation of data replication schemes is given in section 4. Finally, section 5 concludes the paper.

2   Related Work

Various approaches to analytically evaluate dynamic data replication schemes have been proposed. Initially, continuous-time Markov chains (CTMC) were used [4, 9, 10]. Conceptually, they explicitly enumerate the state space and define a predicate on each state that evaluates to true if an operation is available and to false otherwise. As it is a very complex task to manually construct CTMCs for large systems, GSPNs – which can be seen as a high-level representation of CTMCs as the reachability graph of a GSPN is isomorphic to a CTMC – were used instead, for example, in [11]. In these models, links are assumed to be perfect while processes are subject to failures (or also vice versa as in [4]). Process failures and recoveries are assumed to be independent with identical failure and recovery rates, thus the single processes are identical w.r.t. their availability. Assuming perfect links and neglecting network partitioning seems contradictory to using quorum systems as they are actually designed to tolerate network partitions. Nonetheless, in order to give generally comparable results this assumption may be well justified given the very large number of possible network topologies. Contrarily, for evaluating a data replication scheme for a specific application scenario, link failures cannot be disregarded. The GSPN system model presented in [12, 13, 14] allows both, processes and links to fail and to recover. Links are modeled as bidirectional point-to-point connections between processes. Process (link) failures and recoveries are also assumed to be independent but with potentially different failure resp. recovery rates [13, 14]. In [12] only failures are assumed to be independent (with potentially different failure rates) whereas recoveries are dependent on a single shared repairman resource.

All aforementioned approaches are restricted to unstructured and homogeneous dynamic data replication schemes, hence (1) only one type of data replication scheme that is used for every stage of the dynamics must be modeled and (2) logical structures are simply not used and thus process identities can be neglected as all processes are considered equal. These facts help to keep the system models small and easily tractable but also drastically limit their application to only this very specific subclass of data replication schemes. Moreover, the system model of each approach discussed is specifically tailored towards a particular data replication scheme thereby rendering the respective model unsuited for the evaluation of other schemes. In contrast, our system model allows the evaluation of structured, unstructured, homogeneous, and heterogeneous dynamic data replication schemes as well as static data replication schemes, the latter being a simple special case. Additionally, different data replication schemes can easily be evaluated simply by exchanging the quorum system specification whereby a different data replication scheme is described. In this paper, we *exclusively* focus on the aspect of *modeling* and *analyzing* (heterogeneous) dynamic data replication schemes. For a more concise presentation we do not consider link failures albeit our model actually does support link *and* process failures. In favor of a simpler presentation, we furthermore assume operations to be triggered by process failure and recovery events. Note that under this assumption the derived operation availabilities represent upper bounds. The next section describes our GSPN system model and the modeling of data replication schemes in detail.

3   System Model

The GSPN system model consists of three major conceptional components, namely the process template subnet, the quorum system representation subnets, and the operation execution control subnet. These subnets are instantiated and composed to form a system model for the analysis of a specific configuration of data replication schemes and processes.

The modeling of structured data replication schemes requires the encoding of logical structures in the system model and therefore requires the processes to have unique identities in order to differentiate them in the logical structures. Consequently, the process template subnet described next is instantiated n times for a scenario comprising n processes. Note that – besides being required for modeling structured data replication schemes – having different instances of the process subnet allows to model non-uniform process availabilities.

Process Template Subnet. The process template subnet (cf. Fig. 1) models the behavior of a process. A process p_i, $1 \leq i \leq n$, is either correct or (transiently) failed corresponding to its state place p_i having i token or zero token. Modeling processes as either correct or failed and disregarding the state of their respective replicas is justified as follows: because of the strict quorum intersection property at least one process in every quorum participated in the last write operation and has a current version of the replica. During the course of a read operation execution we assume processes having an outdated replica to update themselves from processes having a current replica. In case of a write operation, the replica of each process in the write quorum will be assigned the new value anyway making an update unnecessary. We furthermore assume both, read and write operations to be executed instantaneously, i.e., no process fails while an operation is being executed. In effect, these assumptions abstract from network and processing time delay due to replica updates and operation execution. Thereby, the need for tracking the individual replica states of the processes – which account for a state space of size 4^n – is avoided and only 2^n states are needed for the processes. The failure resp. recovery of a process p_i is modeled by two timed transitions T_{fail_i} which draws i token from place p_i and $T_{recover_i}$ which puts i token back on p_i given that p_i has zero token, i.e., the process p_i is actually failed. A failure resp. recovery of a process triggers the execution of an operation by putting a token on the shared place $ctrl_{op}$. An operation execution involves (1) probing a quorum consisting of correct processes and (2) afterwards, if possible, consistently adapting the quorum system using the concept of epochs [5]. The next section presents the encoding of quorum systems in the system model.

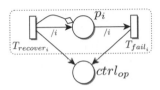

Fig. 1. Process Template Subnet

Quorum System Representation Subnets. An explicit encoding of quorum systems in the system model, i.e., encoding the enumeration of all possible quorums, is not viable as it leads to a system model that scales exponentially in the number of processes and becomes intractable: for any combination of correct processes a subnet specifying the quorum system must be encoded resulting in $2^n - 1$ quorum system subnets for a system of n processes. For example, the model for Dynamic Voting with $n = 3$ processes requires $2^3 - 1$ quorum system subnets: $\{p_1, p_2, p_3\}$, $\{p_1, p_2\}$, $\{p_1, p_3\}$, $\{p_2, p_3\}$, and $\{p_1\}$, $\{p_2\}$, $\{p_3\}$ for one, two, and three processes being failed. Therefore, an implicit representation by means of a quorum system construction subnet that is able to dynamically derive quorums for unstructured and structured data replication schemes is mandatory. Moreover, modeling heterogeneous data replication schemes requires the encoding of n potentially different construction subnets in the system model for every stage of the dynamics.

For this purpose the concept of *tree-shaped voting structures* (tVS) is used and applied to petri nets: tVSs specify quorum systems via tree graphs and are interpreted by a universal algorithm that is able to derive an operation-specific quorum at run-time. By simply redefining the specification, another data replication scheme is easily modeled. Conceptually, a tVS is a voting structure [15] transformed from a directed acyclic graph into a tree graph. Therefore, the universality of voting structures for specifying (static) data replication schemes is also given for tVSs. In a tVS (cf. Fig. 2) the leaf nodes represent real processes (with replicas) while the inner nodes serve grouping purposes. For the unique labeling of (leaf) nodes, multiple leaf nodes referring to the same process are suffixed with primes. Each node is equipped with a vote (upper right index) being a natural number and a pair of minimal votes to collect among its subsequent nodes in order to form a read or write quorum (lower left resp. right index). Each node's minimal votes to collect per operation must be equal to or less than the sum of the votes of its subsequent nodes. Some data replication schemes such as, e.g., the Tree Quorum Protocol [1] define a partial order on the list of quorums specifying the ordering in which they must be probed. The edges are annotated with priorities reflecting this ordering where 1 represents the highest and ∞ the lowest priority. A default edge priority of ∞ is assumed for edges without an explicitly stated priority. The tVS in Fig. 2 specifies the quorum system of the optimized version [16] of the structured Grid Protocol [2] with four processes. The (optimized) Grid Protocol arranges the $n = 4$ processes in a logical $k \times j$ grid with $n = k \cdot j$ where k is the number of

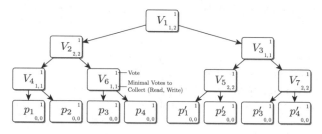

Fig. 2. Tree-shaped Voting Structure of the optimized 2×2 Grid Protocol

columns and j is the number of rows in the logical grid. A read quorum consists of all processes from a complete column (CC-Cover) or one process from each column (C-Cover), while a write quorum requires both, a C-Cover and additionally a CC-Cover to meet the intersection property for ensuring sequential consistency. The recursive algorithm for interpreting tVSs in order to derive a quorum is as follows: starting with the root node, each node queries as many of its subsequent nodes for their votes as needed to meet its minimal vote requirement for the read (write) operation while obeying the query ordering specified via edge priorities. A queried non-leaf node casts its vote if sufficiently many queried subsequent nodes also cast their votes and the sum of their votes meets the minimal vote requirement. A queried leaf node casts its vote if it is not failed and has not currently casted its vote for a concurrent conflicting operation. If a queried node refuses to positively vote then one of its adjacent nodes is queried for its vote alternatively, respecting the query ordering specified via edge priorities. Eventually, the root node will either receive sufficiently many votes and grants permission to execute the read (write) operation or must refuse to do so. In the latter case the operation is not available. For example, the exhaustive interpretation of the tVS in Fig. 2 yields the read quorums $\langle \{p_1, p_3\}, \{p_1, p_4\}, \{p_2, p_3\}, \{p_2, p_4\}, \{p_1, p_2\}, \{p_3, p_4\} \rangle$ which can be used in any order.

A tVS as shown in Fig. 2 is transformed into its petri net counterpart called *tree-shaped voting structure petri graph* (tVSPG) – which is a petri net without an initial assignment of token – as shown in Fig. 3 by (1) substituting the tree nodes by places, (2) substituting the tree edges by immediate transitions and marking dependent outgoing edge cardinalities, (3) augmenting the transitions with priorities and guards, and (4) stating guards for a successful or failed quorum derivation. Incoming transition edges always have a cardinality of one while outgoing transition edge cardinalities – with the exception of transitions connecting to leaf places – are marking dependent on whether a read or a write quorum is to be formed: it corresponds to the respective minimal number of votes to collect from the subsequent node of the replaced edge's destination node in the tVS. For example, the transition $t_{V_1-V_2}$ has an incoming edge cardinality of one, i.e., draws one token from place V_1 and an outgoing edge cardinality of two, i.e., if fired it will put two token on place V_2 (in this case regardless of the operation). The outgoing edge cardinality of transitions connecting to leaf places matches the number of token corresponding to the process identity. For example, the outgoing transition cardinality of the transi-

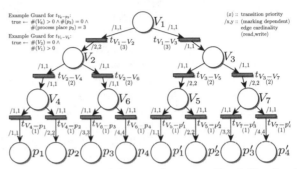

Fig. 3. Tree-shaped Voting Structure Petri Graph of the optimized 2×2 Grid Protocol (Conceptual)

tion $t_{V_7-p'_4}$ connecting the places V_7 and p'_4 is four. The transformed tVS is initially unmarked in order to enable the derivation of read and write quorums from a single tVSPG by putting an operation-specific number of token on the root place that matches the minimal number of votes to collect of the original tVS's root node. For example, if a read quorum should be formed then one token is put on the place V_1, while for forming a write quorum two token are placed on V_1. Due to the non-deterministic firing behavior of petri nets, a firing sequence resulting in a quorum not expressed in the original tVS is possible such that the quorum intersection property and thereby sequential consistency is violated. For example, while forming a write quorum only the transitions in the C-Cover (left subgraph of V_1) may fire thereby consuming all token and thus preventing a CC-Cover (right subgraph of V_1) from being formed. Therefore, the firing sequences of tVSPGs (1) must be sequentialized in a vertical order on the levels of the tVSPG (which increase with farther distance from the root node) and (2) must follow the logic expressed in the tVS via votes resp. votes to collect among subsequent nodes. The vertical ordering of firing sequences is established via assigning higher priorities to transitions on lower levels of the tVSPG such that all potentially enabled transitions on a level k fire before any transition at level $k+1$ is enabled. The horizontal ordering among the edges in each level of a tVS defined by edge priorities is adopted to petri nets by accordingly prioritizing the transitions on each level of the tVSPG. For example, if for the read operation the C-Cover should be prioritized over the CC-Cover then the transition $t_{V_1-V_2}$ gets assigned a higher priority than $t_{V_1-V_3}$. Besides the vertical (and horizontal) ordering of firing sequences, they must also follow the logic expressed in the tVS. For example, in order to form a correct write quorum complying to the Grid Protocol, the transitions $t_{V_1-V_2}$ and $t_{V_1-V_3}$ must fire exactly once such that the quorum building is triggered for both, the C-Cover and the CC-Cover. Such logic constraints are realized by attaching guards to transitions: for example, the transition $t_{V_1-V_2}$ ($t_{V_1-V_3}$) is only enabled if V_2 (V_3) has zero token and V_1 has at least one token. For deciding whether a quorum of non-failed processes can be built, the state of processes referenced in the tVSPG must be considered. Therefore, a guard is attached to each transition connecting to a leaf place that is only enabled if the leaf place has zero token and its corresponding process has not failed. For example, the transition $t_{V_6-p_3}$ is only enabled if (1) the place V_6 has at least one token, (2) the leaf place p_3 has zero token, and (3) the process place p_3 has three token meaning that the process p_3 has not failed. A quorum is successfully built if all potentially enabled transitions have fired. The quorum then consists of the processes corresponding to the leaf places having non-zero token. Otherwise, some process has failed and the quorum building process is restarted by putting the operation-specific number of token on the root place. Because the transition guards hinder firing a transition if its destination place has non-zero token, the token pile up until eventually the root place has non-zero token while restarting the quorum building. In this case no quorum can be formed. Finally, all the net's places are emptied. These three cases are monitored and acted upon by a guarded success-, retry-, and failure-transition.

Via both, attaching guards to transitions and vertical (and horizontal) ordering of firing sequences, tVSPGs resemble the semantics of their respective tVSs. Because of the simple and deterministically applicable transformation steps, tVSs can be automatically transformed into their petri graph counterparts. The next section describes how tVSPGs are embedded in the overall system model and how operations are performed.

Operation Execution Control Subnet. A tVSPG represents the (unstructured or structured) quorum system for a *particular subset* of the set of processes resulting in the need for $2^n - 1$ tVSPGs in the system model and thereby in an exponential scaling of the model size. This problem is accounted for by decoupling the process subnets from the tVSPGs by means of sorted lists such that tVSPGs and process subnets are both connected to the sorted lists rather than directly to each other whereby only n as opposed to $2^n - 1$ tVSPGs are needed. The epoch list (cf. Fig. 4) consisting of the places $q_{e_1}, \ldots, q_{e_n}$ holds the processes that are in the current epoch ordered by process identities in ascending order such that q_{e_i} has k token and q_{e_i+1} has j token with $k < j$. The place *stage* represents the number of processes in the epoch list. Initially, the place *stage* is assigned n token and the epoch list contains the process identities of all processes in ascending order. The process list $q_{p_1}, \ldots, q_{p_n}$ represents the non-failed processes and is initially empty. The quorum list $q_{q_1}, \ldots, q_{q_n}$ contains the processes of a quorum after it has been successfully built and is initially empty. Conceptually, the quorum list places are the common leaf places for all tVSPGs and further reduce the place count of the model. Putting a token on the place $ctrl_{op}$ – which initially has one token – triggers an operation execution and fires the transition

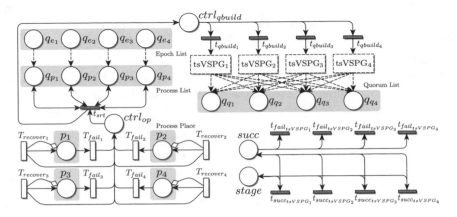

Fig. 4. Schematic Control Flow of the System Model with Four Processes

t_{srt} which empties the n process list places. Then, the process list places are filled with non-failed process identities: if the epoch list place q_{e_i} and its corresponding process place p_j are not empty then the process list place q_{p_i} gets assigned j token. Finally, a token is put on the place $ctrl_{qbuild}$. Depending on the token count k of the place *stage* the transition t_{qbuild_k} fires and triggers the quorum building with the tVSPG for the current stage k (that models the quorum system for k processes). For decoupling the processes and tVSPGs, the leaf places of each tVSPG are identified with their respective quorum list places and the guards are adapted accordingly. For example, the outgoing edge of the transition $t_{V_6-p_3}$ in Fig. 3 is connected to the quorum list place q_{q_3} instead of a dedicated tVSPG-local process place p_3 and its outgoing cardinality resembles the token count of the process list place q_{p_3} instead of the process place p_3; the transition is only enabled if (1) the place V_6 has at least one token, (2) the quorum list place q_{q_3} has zero token, and (3) the process list place q_{p_3} has non-zero token, i.e., the process it corresponds to has not failed. By this means, each tVSPG represents the quorum system for a specific *number* of processes rather than a specific subset of the set of processes. A successful formation of a write quorum implies a successful formation of a read quorum: if the write operation is available, so is the read operation. If a write quorum cannot be formed (the write operation is not available) then the tVSPG is activated again to form a read quorum. If this fails then the read operation is also not available. If a read (write) quorum can be formed then the success transition of the tVSPG puts one (two) token on the place *succ*; if both operations are available then three token are put on the place *succ*. Otherwise, the place *succ* is emptied by the failure transition of the tVSPG. Finally, the quorum list places are emptied. Subsequently, if a write quorum was successfully formed then the epoch change is performed by emptying the *stage* place and the epoch list places and afterwards filling the epoch list places in ascending order with non-failed processes from the process list: the epoch list place q_{e_i} gets assigned the token count of the first process list place q_{p_j} having non-zero token, thereby emptying the process list place q_{p_j}

and putting a token on the place *stage*. Eventually, the process list places are emptied, the epoch list places reflect the currently non-failed processes, and the place *stage* contains the number of currently non-failed processes.

Evaluating Quality-of-Service Measures. The evaluation of a composed system model is facilitated via assigning rewards to the states of the system. For example, for finding the steady state read operation availability, a reward of one is assigned to each state in which *succ* has non-zero token, and a reward of zero otherwise. In the same way other information as, e.g., the relative times spent in each stage of the dynamics is evaluated. The time distribution is used to derive quality-of-service measures of the overall dynamic data replication scheme from already known ones of the static data replication schemes used in the single stages. An exemplary evaluation of operation availability and message complexity – as a measure for operation costs in terms of the number of processes in a quorum and thus messages needed to effectuate a quorum – is presented in the next section.

4   Example Evaluation of Data Replication Schemes

Data replication schemes should provide both, high operation availability and low operation costs. Majority Consensus Voting, for example, has a good resilience to process failures because of its unstructured nature but only a linear message complexity. In contrast, the Grid Protocol has a message complexity in the order of $O(\sqrt{n})$ for read and $O(2 \cdot \sqrt{n})$ for write operations but because of being a structured scheme it is vulnerable to structure-specific process failure patterns and is in general not as resilient to process failures as Majority Consensus Voting. While traditional homogeneous data replication schemes force to favor operation availability over message complexity or vice versa, a heterogeneous data replication scheme allows for a more flexible trade-off. Figure 5(a) and 5(c) relate the "number of nines" (behind the decimal point) of the read and write operation availability to process availability for Dynamic Voting, the Grid Protocol, and the heterogeneous protocol, each with nine processes. The heterogeneous protocol uses the Grid Protocol for the stages 4, 6, 8, 9, and Majority Consensus Voting for the other stages of the dynamics. The *mean time to repair* for each process was set to 1.201 days [17] and the processes in this example have a uniform availability. The heterogeneous protocol clearly outperforms the Dynamic Grid Protocol in terms of read and also write operation availability; it even has the same operation availability as the highly resilient Dynamic Voting. Figure 5(d) and 5(b) relate process availability to message complexity which calculates to the sum of the relative time span spent in each stage of the dynamics multiplied by the message complexity of the static data replication scheme used in that stage. If a static scheme has quorums of different cardinalities to choose from then the average quorum cardinality is chosen for message complexity due to fairness of comparison. For the write operation, the heterogeneous protocol has a comparable message complexity to both, the Dynamic Grid Protocol and Dynamic Voting, while for the read operation it resembles the message

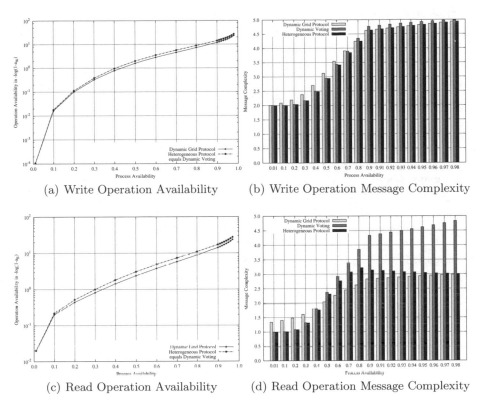

(a) Write Operation Availability   (b) Write Operation Message Complexity

(c) Read Operation Availability   (d) Read Operation Message Complexity

Fig. 5. Operation Availability of the Dynamic Grid and the Heterogeneous Protocol/Dynamic Voting (left), and Message Complexity of the Dynamic Voting, the Dynamic Grid, and the Heterogeneous Protocol (right)

complexity of the Dynamic Grid Protocol and has clearly less message complexity than Dynamic Voting.

The composed system model of the above example was analyzed with SPNP [18] on a dedicated core of a Core2 Duo processor fixated at 1.2 GHz as SPNP is not able to benefit from multi-cores. The analysis involves reachability graph construction and calculating the stationary probability distribution of the resulting CTMC. For nine processes, the markings of the 20 state space-constituting places $stage$, $succ$, $p_1, \ldots, p_9$, $q_{e_1}, \ldots, q_{e_9}$ must be encoded in the CTMC resulting in an unoptimized state space of $2^{20} = 1,048,576$ states. The optimized CTMC due to SPNP for the Dynamic Grid Protocol has $40,821$ states and $367,389$ transitions which took 179s to analyze while the optimized CTMCs for the heterogeneous protocol and for Dynamic Voting both have $14,326$ states and $128,934$ transitions and took 68s resp. 44s to analyze. The difference in the analysis times stems from (1) different state space sizes which correlate with operation availability, (2) from manually optimized tVSPGs for Majority Consensus Voting, and (3) from higher complexity and therefore longer run-times of the Grid Protocol tVSPGs.

Of course, a system model that explicitly models the processes scales exponentially in the number of processes: in our approach, for example, the model of Dynamic Voting with 10 (11) processes has $35,573$ $(86,516)$ states and $355,730$ $(951,676)$ transitions and takes 133s (405s) to analyze.

5   Conclusion and Future Work

We presented a novel approach to the analytical evaluation of strict quorum-based data replication schemes by means of a compositional GSPN system model. In contrast to previous approaches, our model allows the analytical evaluation of homogeneous and heterogeneous as well as structured and unstructured dynamic data replication schemes and also applies for static schemes. Moreover, different data replication schemes can easily be evaluated without altering the general model. Additionally, the model allows to evaluate other quality-of-service measures besides operation availability such as, e.g., message complexity. In future work we will investigate more optimizations regarding the system model size and reachability graph construction by using, for example, state space partitioning.

References

1. Agrawal, D., Abbadi, A.E.: The tree quorum protocol: An efficient approach for managing replicated data. In: Proceedings of the 16th Very Large Data Bases Conference, pp. 243–254. Morgan Kaufmann, San Francisco (1990)
2. Cheung, S.Y., Ahamad, M., Ammar, M.H.: The grid protocol: A high performance scheme for maintaining replicated data. In: Proceedings of the 6th International Conference on Data Engineering, pp. 438–445. IEEE, Los Alamitos (1990)
3. Thomas, R.H.: A majority consensus approach to concurrency control for multiple copy databases. ACM Transactions on Database Systems 4(2), 180–207 (1979)
4. Jajodia, S., Mutchler, D.: Dynamic voting algorithms for maintaining the consistency of a replicated database. ACM Transactions on Database Systems 15(2), 230–280 (1990)
5. Rabinovich, M., Lazowska, E.: Improving fault tolerance and supporting partial writes in structured coterie protocols. In: Proceedings of the ACM SIGMOD, pp. 226–235 (1992)
6. Naor, M., Wool, A.: The load, capacity, and availability of quorum systems. SIAM Journal on Computing 27(2), 423–447 (1998)
7. Jiménez-Peris, R., Patiño-Martínez, M., Alonso, G., Kemme, B.: Are quorums an alternative for data replication? ACM Transactions on Database Systems 28(3), 257–294 (2003)
8. Theel, O., Pagnia, H.: Optimal replica control protocols exhibit symmetric operation availabilities. In: Proceedings of the 28th International Symposium on Fault-Tolerant Computing, pp. 252–261. IEEE, Los Alamitos (1998)
9. Pâris, J.F.: Voting with a variable number of copies. In: Proceedings of the 16th International Symposium on Fault-tolerant Computing, pp. 50–55. IEEE, Los Alamitos (1986)
10. Pâris, J.F.: Voting with witnesses: A consistency scheme for replicated files. In: Proceedings of the 6th International Conference on Distributed Computing Systems, pp. 606–621. IEEE, Los Alamitos (1986)

11. Dugan, J.B., Ciardo, G.: Stochastic petri net analysis of a replicated file system. IEEE Transactions on Software Engineering 15(4), 394–401 (1989)
12. Chen, I.R., Wang, D.C.: Analysis of replicated data with repair dependency. The Computer Journal 39(9), 767–779 (1996)
13. Chen, I.R., Wang, D.C.: Analyzing dynamic voting using petri nets. In: Proceedings of the 15th Symposium on Reliable Distributed Systems, pp. 44–53. IEEE, Los Alamitos (1996)
14. Chen, I.R., Wang, D.C., Chu, C.P.: Analyzing user-perceived dependability and performance characteristics of voting algorithms for managing replicated data. Distributed and Parallel Databases 14(3), 199–219 (2004)
15. Theel, O.: General structured voting: A flexible framework for modelling cooperations. In: Proceedings of the 13th International Conference on Distributed Computing Systems, pp. 227–236. IEEE, Los Alamitos (1993)
16. Theel, O., Pagnia-Koch, H.H.: General design of grid-based data replication schemes using graphs and a few rules. In: Proceedings of the 15th International Conference on Distributed Computing Systems, pp. 395–403. IEEE, Los Alamitos (1995)
17. Long, D.D.E., Muir, A., Golding, R.A.: A longitudinal survey of Internet host reliability. TR UCSC-CRL-95-16, Department of Computer Science, University of California Santa Cruz(1995)
18. Ciardo, G., Muppala, J.K., Trivedi, K.S.: SPNP: Stochastic petri net package. In: Proceedings of the 3rd International Workshop on Petri Nets and Performance Models, pp. 142–151. IEEE, Los Alamitos (1989)

Tree-Based Dynamic Primary Copy Algorithms for Replicated Databases

Pradhan Bagur Umesh, A.R. Bharath Kumar, and V.S. Ananthanarayana

Department of Information Technology
National Institute of Technology Karnataka, Surathkal, Mangalore, India
pradhan@ieee.org, a.r.bharathkumar@gmail.com, anvs@nitk.ac.in

Abstract. With increasing demand for performance, availability and fault toler-ance in databases, data replication is gaining more and more importance. Re-solving or serializing conflicting update requests is the main challenge in large scale deployment of replicated databases. In this paper, we propose the first to-ken based dynamic primary copy algorithms for resolving conflicting requests among different sites of replicated databases. The contribution being reduction in the number of messages required per update request.

1 Introduction

Data replication refers to storage of same data at multiple devices or sites. Availability, high throughput and fault tolerance are the driving factors for replication. Maintaining consistency and resolving conflicting requests are the crucial needs of replicated data-bases. Conflicting requests arises when there exists multiple requests on a single data item and at least one of them is write or update request. Replicated databases may re-ceive a large number of conflicting requests and hence it is necessary to handle these efficiently such that maximum of one site is updating the data at any point in time and, that site should have obtained the latest data before it starts updating.

Replication strategies can be classified as Lazy and Eager replication [1], [2], [3], [4]. Traditionally, for updating, these use primary copy approach, where any update request is directed to the site holding the primary copy and updates are later propa-gated to other sites. In dynamic primary copy approach [5], [6], [7] notion of primary copy is dynamic in nature where the update is done at the same site where the request is submitted.

The dynamic primary copy approach in [5] uses lesser number of messages per up-date with increase in number of conflicting requests. Further performance improve-ment was proposed in [6] and [7]. In [6] the number of messages per update is of order $\sqrt{N}$. Here, we propose the *first token based dynamic primary copy algorithms* which would be referred as tree-based Lazy Dynamic Primary Copy Algorithm (t-LDPC) and tree-based Eager Dynamic Primary Copy Algorithm (t-EDPC). The t-LDPC algorithm uses number of messages of order log(N) and t-EDPC algorithm uses 'N' messages more than t-LDPC but converts the replication strategy Eager. The proposed algorithm has the flavor of Kerry Raymond's mutual exclusion algorithm [8], but the context of

V. Garg, R. Wattenhofer, and K. Kothapalli (Eds.): ICDCN 2009, LNCS 5408, pp. 362–367, 2009.
© Springer-Verlag Berlin Heidelberg 2009

the algorithms is different. In [8], the aim was to address the problem of distributed mutual exclusion, whereas here we address the problem of resolving conflicting requests in replicated databases.

The rest of the paper is organized as follows: In section 2, we briefly describe the existing conflict resolution algorithms. We then propose our algorithms in section 3 including the system model and definitions. Analysis of the proposed algorithms is presented in section 4 and we compare our algorithm with the existing algorithms in section 5. Finally we conclude in section 6.

2 Replication Strategies

A distributed database system (DDBS) is a system consisting of data items stored in a set of sites S_1, S_2, S_3,..., S_N and communicate by message passing via underlying communication network. Replicated data in such systems (e.g. Replicated Databases) poses the challenge of maintaining consistency of all the data items and resolution of conflicting update requests. Here, we outline the existing replication strategies

In Primary copy method, data is updated only at the site which hosts the primary copy for that data. The replicas just apply the changes propagated by the primary copy site and all coordination and ordering happens only at primary site. This method has both lazy and eager implementations. CDDR [10] uses this method to update the replicas of data.

Dynamic Primary copy with Piggy-Backing (DPCP) method uses a blend of Lazy and Eager replication. The idea of primary copy is dynamic in nature. The database is divided into pages. When a site wants to update, an update request for a particular page is broadcasted. Upon receipt of permission from all the sites, it updates the page locally.

In Lazy Dynamic Primary Copy (LDCP) and Eager Dynamic Primary Copy (EDPC) methods, the sites are grouped and the communication for each site is restricted to the nodes of its group. EDPC broadcasts each update to all the nodes in the network. LDPC uses Lazy strategy where the updates are multicast to only the nodes of same group.

3 Proposed Algorithm

3.1 System Model

The system has 'N' sites (S_1, S_2, S_3, ..., S_N). The underlying communication channel is assumed to be error free and reliable, and message passing between nodes to be asynchronous. Without loss of generality, database is assumed to be fully replicated at all the sites and that each site executes a maximum of one database accessing process.

We assume a non-rooted tree structure of arrangement of nodes in the system which means there exists a unique path any two nodes. Each node can have the knowledge about its neighbors only.

3.2 Definitions

Timestamp (TS): Timestamp at any site S_i (where $1 \le i \le N$), TS_i is an ordered pair (L_i, S_i), containing the Lamport's logical clock [9] value L_i and the site id S_i and $TS_i < TS_j$ iff ($L_i < L_j$) or ($L_i = L_j$ and $S_i < S_j$). Here the Lamport's logical clock represents the number of updates that have been carried out to obtain the data at that site.

Request_List: Each site maintains a request list in which it stores the request it receives and the list is always sorted in timestamp order.

HOLDER: It is a variable which identifies the neighboring node that is in the path of the token-holder and the node.

3.3 Algorithm

We divide the algorithm for resolution of conflicting update requests into five phases.

1. Request phase: The request submitted by the client must be propagated to the respective node holding the token which would currently be the root of the tree. When a REQUEST message is received by a node which does not posses the token, it sends a REQUEST message to its Parent node if it has not yet requested for the token or the timestamp of the current request has lesser timestamp than one for which it has requested and updates the request in its Request_List based on timestamps.

2. Server Co-ordination: When a site which posses the token receives the request message, it sends the token to the node from which it received the request. It also makes a request (after deleting the corresponding entry from its Request_List if its request queue is not empty). Then it updates its HOLDER variable to the node to which it sent the token.

Whenever a site receives a token, and its request is not at the head of its Request_List it sends the token to the site whose request is at the head of the list, deletes the respective entry, and updates its HOLDER variable to the node to which it sent the token.

If Request_List is non-empty at this point, a request (with the time-stamp of the request at the head of its Request_List) is sent to the node pointed by HOLDER variable.

3. Execution Phase: Whenever a site receives the token and its request message is the head of its Request_List, it changes the HOLDER variable to point to itself, then updates the data item based on the latest data received, and deletes its entry from its Request_List. It then updates its timestamp which is sent along with the updated data item.

4. Agreement Co-ordination Phase: Here, we two variations, one of them uses lazy strategy which we call as tree-based Lazy Dynamic Primary Copy Algorithm (t-LDPC) and the other uses eager strategy which we call as tree-based Eager Dynamic Primary Copy Algorithm (t-EDPC).

t-LDPC: After the execution phase, if its Request_List is non-empty, the token, the update and a request (with the time-stamp of the request at the head of its Request_List) are sent to the node in the head of its Request_List as a single message, and the corresponding entry from the Request_List is deleted. Else the token is retained.

t-EDPC: After the execution phase, the *update is broadcasted* to all the nodes in the system. Now, if its Request_List is non-empty, the token and a request (with the time-stamp of the request at the head of its Request_List) are sent to the node it the top entry in the head of its Request_List as a single message, and the corresponding entry from the Request_List is deleted. Else the token is retained.

5. Response Phase: The client is intimated of the change.

The read requests are satisfied as follows: In t-EDPC, the read request is satisfied locally i.e. the sites need not obtain read permission form any other sites. In t-LDPC, the procedure to obtain read permission is same as that for update/write permission. The only difference being the node holding token can send any number of read-grants unlike in the case of update requests. Timestamp is not incremented for read requests.

Since there is only one token in the system for any data and since only the node with token can update the data, the maximum number of sites updating the data at any point in time. And, since the token carries the latest data with timestamp, it is assured the node has received latest data before satisfying its read or update requests.

The algorithms can be combined with distributed two-phase locking to preserve one-copy serializability similar to [10]. The proposed algorithms are free from deadlock and starvation. As the nodes in the system maintain tree structure for message passing there would be no deadlocks due to the acyclic nature of trees and as we use time stamp ordering, starvation is prevented. It can be noted that since time-stamping is done only to prevent starvation and increase fairness, any time-stamping method which gives priority to the starving request can be used with these algorithms. The t-LDPC algorithm gives preference to the nodes which have not participated for a longer time while the eager algorithm tries to maintain uniform timestamp knowledge all over the system. The memory requirements at each node is also lesser compared to other algorithms as each node is supposed to be aware of its tree-neighbors only. The length of the request list is also bounded. The algorithms are also robust against link failures as failure of any link can be substituted by creating an alternative connected tree-structure in the network excluding the failed link if the network is strongly connected. For more details on handling failures see [11].

4 Analysis

t-LDPC: For each update request, in the best case two messages are required (one for request and one to send the token) which happens when token is transferred to the child node. In the worst case, $4\log(N)$ messages are required ($2\log(N)$ messages for propagation of request to the node holding token and $2\log(N)$ messages for propagation of token to the requesting node) which is the case when the token is transferred to the farthest leaf node of the tree. So, the number of messages exchanged per update request ranges from 2 to $4\log(N)$. In t-LDPC as satisfaction of read requests follows same logic as that of update request, the number of messages exchanged per read request ranges from 2 to $4\log(N)$.

t-EDPC: Here, handling of update request is same as in t-LDPC, but in addition we broadcast the update to all the nodes in the system. So here in the best case '$2+N$' messages are required and in the worst case '$4\log(N)+N$' number of messages are required. t-EDPC requires zero messages for satisfaction of read request. The base to the logarithms here is the number of children for each node in the system.

5 Comparison

In this section we compare the number of message required in case of Eager Middleware Replication, $DPCP_M$, $DPCP_P$ and LDPC with that of the proposed algorithms. Here, we compare the best case of these algorithms with worst case of the proposed algorithms.

Let r be the read/write ratio, q be number of simultaneous requests to be handled and N is the number of nodes.

Table 1. Comparison of the proposed algorithm with the other algorithms

Algorithm	Given equation with q conflicting requests	Number of messages per Read	Number of messages per update (with proportional reads r) (best case)
EMR	$(3Nq - 3q)$	0	$3 (N - 1)$
$DPCP_M$	$(6Nq-q^2-q)/2$	0	$2.5 N - 0.5$
$DPCP_P$	$(4Nq-q^2+3q + 2N - 4)/2$	2	$1.5N + 2.5 + 2r$
LDPC	$3\sqrt{N}$ to $5\sqrt{N}$	$2\sqrt{N}$	$3\sqrt{N} + r2\sqrt{N}$
EDPC	$(2\sqrt{N} + N)$ to $(4\sqrt{N} + N)$	0	$2\sqrt{N} + N$
t-LDPC	2 to $4\log(N)$	2 to $4\log(N)$	$4\log(N)+r4\log(N)$ (worst case)
t-EDPC	$(2+N)$ to $(4\log(N)+N)$	0	$(4\log(N)+N)$ (worst case)

Here, as we can observe from the equation, t-LDPC algorithm runs in $O(\log(N))$ which is clearly better than all other methods. We can also observe that LDPC is better than t-EDPC, but in LDPC (as well as t-LDPC) all the sites do not have latest copy of the data items as they employ lazy strategy where as in t-EDPC, as the respective updated data item is broadcasted to all the nodes in the system after each update, it avoids dirty reads except in certain rare situations where a remote site may read the data while the update is propagating in the network. System knowledge for t-EDPC (as well as EDPC) comes at a cost of N messages per update.

6 Conclusion

In this paper we have presented two efficient token based algorithms for handling the conflicts in replicated databases. These are the first token based strategies proposed to handle the conflicting requests. The performance of t-LDPC algorithm is better than all other algorithms, performing better as N increases. We have reduced the number of messages required and thus the network traffic, by many folds using tree arrangement of nodes which can be simulated easily in any connected network. The algorithm can be further optimized by increasing the degree of each node which also reduces the network delay. Unlike t-EDPC, the only drawback of the t-LDPC algorithm is the absence of the global knowledge. Further work can be done to reduce the latency in these algorithms.

As the processing power of the processors and number of data sources in the system increases drastically, the network traffic becomes the bottleneck of a distributed database implementation. Thus the algorithm which reduces the network traffic would the need of the hour. Here we have proposed algorithms which not only reduce the network traffic satisfying all the requirements of conflict resolution but also requiring very little knowledge about the network (only information about the neighbors) which is a critical factor as the networks are becoming bigger everyday.

References

[1] Sun, C., Lin, Y., Kemme, B.: Comparison of UDDI Registry Replication Strategies. In: ICWS 2004, pp. 218–225 (2004)

[2] Wolski, A.: Applying Replication to Data recharging in Mobile Systems. Solid Information Technology 7(2) (2001)

[3] Breitbart, Y., Komondoor, R., Rastogi, R., Seshadri, S.: Update Protocols for Replicated Database. In: ICDE, pp. 469–476 (1996)

[4] Anderson, T.A., Breibart, Y., Korth, H.F., Wool, A.: Replication, Consistancy and Pratcality: Are these Mutually Exclusive? In: ACM SIGMOD 1998, pp. 485–495 (1998)

[5] Ananthanarayana, V.S., Vidyasankar, K.: Dynamic Primary Copy with Piggy-Backing Mechanism for Replicated UDDI Registry. In: Madria, S.K., Claypool, K.T., Kannan, R., Uppuluri, P., Gore, M.M. (eds.) ICDCIT 2006. LNCS, vol. 4317, pp. 389–402. Springer, Heidelberg (2006)

[6] Bharath Kumar, A.R., Pradhan, B.U., Ananthanarayana, V.S.: An Efficient Lazy Dynamic Primary Copy Algorithm for Replicated UDDI Registry. In: ICIP 2008, pp. 564–571 (2008)

[7] Pradhan, B.U., Bharath Kumar, A.R., Ananthanarayana, V.S.: An Efficient Eager Dynamic Primary Copy Algorithm for Replicated UDDI Registry. In: ICCNS 2008, pp. 161–166 (2008)

[8] Raymond, K.: A tree-based algorithm for distributed Mutual Exclusion. ACM Transactions on Computer Systems 7(1), 61–77 (1989)

[9] Lamport, L.: Time, Clocks and the ordering of Events in a Distributed System. Communications of the ACM, 558–565 (1978)

[10] Huang, Y., Wolfson, O.: A Competitive Dynamic Data Replication Algorithm. In: Proceedings of the Ninth International Conference on Data Engineering, April 1993, pp. 310–317 (1993)

[11] Revannaswamy, V., Bhatt, P.C.P.: A Fault Tolerant Protocol as an Extension to a Distributed Mutual Exclusion Algorithm. In: ICPADS 1997, p. 730 (1997)

FTRepMI: Fault-Tolerant, Sequentially-Consistent Object Replication for Grid Applications

Ana-Maria Oprescu, Thilo Kielmann, and Wan Fokkink

Department of Computer Science, Vrije Universiteit Amsterdam, The Netherlands
{amo,kielmann,wanf}@cs.vu.nl

Abstract. We introduce FTRepMI, a simple fault-tolerant protocol for providing sequential consistency amongst replicated objects in a grid, without using any centralized components. FTRepMI supports dynamic joins and graceful leaves of processes holding a replica, as well as fail-stop crashes. Performance evaluation shows that FTRepMI behaves efficiently, both on a single cluster and on a distributed cluster environment.

1 Introduction

Object replication is a well-known technique to improve the performance of parallel object-based applications [13]. Java's remote method invocation (RMI) enables methods of remote Java objects to be invoked from other Java virtual machines, possibly on different hosts. Maassen introduced Replicated Method Invocation (RepMI) [11], which was implemented in Manta [12]. He obtained a significant performance improvement by combining object replication and RMI. His mechanism, however, uses a centralized *sequencer node* for serializing write operations on object replicas, which makes it vulnerable to crashes.

We present FTRepMI, an efficient and robust, decentralized protocol for RepMI in which processes progress in successive rounds. To increase efficiency, local writes at different processes are combined in one round. Inspired by virtual synchrony [18], FTRepMI provides object replication [7], while offering flexible membership rules governing the process group (called *world*) that is dedicated to an object. A process interested in an object can obtain a replica by joining its world; when it is no longer interested in the object, it can leave the world. Each member of a world can perform read/write operations on the replica. In case of a write, the replicated object needs to be updated on all processes in its world. A failure detector is used to detect crashed processes, and an iterative mechanism to achieve agreement when a crash occurs. In case of such a process failure, the other processes continue after a phase in which processes query each other whether they received a write operation from the crashed process.

FTRepMI provides sequential consistency for the replicated object, meaning that all involved processes execute the same write operations, in the same order. We slightly digress from Lamport's definition [9] in that we provide the means to

V. Garg, R. Wattenhofer, and K. Kothapalli (Eds.): ICDCN 2009, LNCS 5408, pp. 368–376, 2009.

ensure sequential consistency (by executing all write operations on all processes in the same order), but we do not enforce it ourselves for read operations on the replicated object (the programmer still has to use Java's *synchronized* methods for both read and write). We sketch a correctness proof, and moreover we analyzed FTRepMI by means of model checking, on the Distributed ASCI Supercomputer, DAS-3 (`www.cs.vu.nl/das3/`).

The strength of FTRepMI, compared to other decentralized fault-tolerant protocols for sequential consistency, is its simplicity. This makes it relatively straightforward to implement. Simplicity of protocols, and decentralized control, is of particular importance in the dynamic setting of grid applications, where one has to take into account extra-functional requirements like performance, security, and quality of service. A prototype of FTRepMI has been implemented on top of the Ibis system [16], a Java-based platform for grid computing. Results obtained from testing the prototype on DAS-3 show that FTRepMI behaves efficiently both on a single cluster and on a distributed cluster environment.

Related work. Orca [1] introduced conceptually shared, replicated objects, extended in [4] with a primary/backup strategy, and partial replication with sequential consistency. *Isis* [2], on which *GARF* [5] relies for communication management, proposes a framework for replicated objects with various consistency requirements. *Isis* presents a per-request chosen-coordinator/cohorts design approach, providing for fault tolerance and automatic restart. Chain replication [17] is a particular case of a primary/backup technique improved by load-balancing query requests. It is latency-bound as a result of "chaining" latencies between servers, leading to performance problems in multi-cluster grids. As support for fault tolerance it uses a central master. *Eternal* [15] addresses *CORBA* applications, providing fault tolerance through a centralized component. It delegates communication and ordering of operations to *TOTEM* [14], a reliable, totally ordered multicast system based on *extended virtual synchrony* as derived from the virtual synchrony model of *Isis*. General quorum consensus, used in [8], is another replication technique, allowing for network partitions and process failure. RAMBO [10] takes the same approach to address atomic memory operations. It supports multiple objects, each shared by a group of processes; groups may overlap. It is considerably more sophisticated, but induces a cost on crash-free operations of eight times the maximum point-to-point network delay.

2 FTRepMI

In our model, a parallel program consists of multiple processes, each holding some threads. A process is uniquely identified by a rank r, which prescribes a total order on processes. All processes can send messages to each other; we assume non-blocking, reliable and stream-based communication. Processes can crash, but their communication channels are reliable. There is no assumption on how the delivery of messages from a broadcast is scheduled.

During crash-free runs, FTRepMI uses a simple communication pattern to dissipate a write operation in the world. The protocol proceeds in successive rounds, in which the processes progress in lockstep, based on binary-valued logical clocks. If a process receives a local write while idle (this includes reading the replica), it broadcasts the write; we use function shipping [11]. Then it waits for all processes to reply, either with a write operation or a *nop*, meaning that the process does not have a write operation to perform during this round. If a process receives a remote write while idle, it broadcasts a *nop* and waits for messages from all other processes (except the one which triggered this *nop*). Processes apply write operations in some (*world*-wide) pre-defined order (e.g. ascending, descending), based on the ranks attached to these write operations.

FTRepMI can in principle support multiple replicated objects. To simplify our presentation, however, we assume there is only one shared object. The *world* consists of the processes holding a replica of the object, at a given moment in time. The world projection at each process is a set of ranks. Processes can join or leave the world, so at a given moment, this set of ranks may contain gaps.

2.1   The Protocol – Crash-Free Runs

As previously explained, a process interested in accessing a replicated object has to first join the world of that object. If there is no world for that object, the process will start one. (This could be done using an external directory, e.g. a file on stable storage, but the exact details are outside the scope of this paper.) When trying to access the replica, a thread invokes the FTRepMI protocol. If it is a read request, the thread can simply read the local copy. In case of a write access, the thread must grab the local lock to contact the Local Round Manager (LRM) at this process. The LRM is at the heart of FTRepMI: it keeps track of the local and remote writes the process received, is in charge of controlling which local writes pertain to which round, and executes writes on the local replica.

Dealing with world changes. Processes are allowed to join or leave the world. This is achieved by two special operations, called *join* and *leave*. In our implementation of FTRepMI, for a smooth integration of these operations into the protocol, they are processed as if they were write operations.

Handling a join request. When a new process N, with rank n, wants to join the world, it contacts an external directory (e.g. stable storage) for the contact address of another process O which already hosts a replica. Upon receiving N's request, O constructs a special local operation $join(n)$, which contains information about the joining process. This operation is handled by the protocol as a local write operation. Its special semantics is noticed upon its execution: all processes add n to their R set. The contact process O sends N the initialization information (the current state of the replicated object, the current sequence number, its world projection), and N joins the world in the round in which $join(n)$ is performed. In case O no longer accepts join requests because it is leaving, process N stops and retries to join via another contact process.

If a process gets many *join* requests within a short time, its local writes (or the *join*s) may be delayed for multiple rounds. To avoid this, one can alternatively piggyback *join*s onto other messages. A process would then have to maintain four queues of *join* requests: local requests which need to be acknowledged, remote requests, and local and remote requests pertaining to the next round.

Handling a leave request. When a process O, with rank o, wants to leave the world, it performs a special operation $leave(o)$ that results in the removal of rank o from R on all other processes. It is handled as a local write operation.

Dealing with write operations. Local and remote write operations on the replica are handled differently. A local write needs to be communicated to the other processes, while the arrival of a remote write may get a process into action, if this write operation is for the current round and the process is idle (i.e. did not receive remote writes or generate a local write for the current round yet). In the latter case, the process generates as a local write for the current round a special *nop* operation. An alternative would be to generate *nop*s at regular time intervals. However, finding suitable intervals is not easy, and this would lead to unnecessary message flooding during periods in which the entire system is idle.

Handling a local write. A thread wanting to perform a write operation op on the local replica, must first grab the local write lock. Then it asks the LRM at this process to start a new round. If the process is idle, op is placed in the queue $\mathcal{WO}$ at this process, which contains write operations waiting to be executed on the local replica in the current round in the correct order; each write operation is paired with the rank of the process where it originates from. Then the next round is started, and the thread that performs op broadcasts op to all other processes. If there is an ongoing round, op is postponed until the next round, by placing it in the queue $\mathcal{NWO}$, which stores write operations for the next round.

Handling a remote write. A round can also be started by the arrival of a remote write operation, which means this process has so far been idle during the corresponding round, while another process generated a write operation for this round and broadcast it to all other processes. When this remote operation arrives, the LRM is invoked. If the process is idle, it starts a new round and broadcasts a *nop* to all other processes. During its current round, a process also buffers operations pertaining to the next round ($\mathcal{NWO}$).

Starting a new round. When the current round at a process has been completed, the time stamp is inverted, $\mathcal{NWO}$ is cast to $\mathcal{WO}$, and $\mathcal{NWO}$ is emptied. If the new $\mathcal{WO}$ contains a local write, then the process initiates the next round, in which this write is broadcast to the other processes. If $\mathcal{WO}$ does not contain a local write, but does contain one or more remote writes, then the process also initiates the next round, in which it broadcasts *nop* to the other processes. If $\mathcal{WO}$ is empty, then the process remains idle.

2.2   Fault Tolerance

For the fault-tolerant version of FTRepMI, we require known bounds on communication delay, so that one can implement a perfectly accurate failure detector.

Fault tolerant consistency is provided by ensuring that operations issued by a failing process are executed either by all alive processes or by none. When a process n has gathered information from/about each process in the current round, either by a remote write or by a crash report from the local failure detector, it checks if recovery is needed. If for some crashed process there is no operation in the $\mathcal{WO}$ of n, then n starts the recovery procedure by broadcasting a SOS-message. To answer such messages, each process preserves the queue $\mathcal{CWO}$, i.e. $\mathcal{WO}$ of the previous round, in case the requester is lagging one round behind. Recovery procedure at process n terminates when either it obtains all missing ops or it has received replies from all asked processes. If more processes crashed while n was in recovery procedure and n is still missing ops, then n continues the recovery procedure; namely, a newly crashed process may have communicated missing ops to some processes but not to n. After the recovery procedure ends, all crashed processes for which n still does not hold a remote write in $\mathcal{WO}$ are deleted from n's world, while crashed processes whose missing operations were recovered are taken to the next round. A process q in crash recovery broadcasts a message $S(q, sn_q)$, to ask the other processes for their list of write operations in q's current round sn_q. A process p that receives this message sends either $\mathcal{WO}$ or $\mathcal{CWO}$ to q; if $sn_p = sn_q$, then p sends $\mathcal{WO}$, and if $sn_p = 1 - sn_q$, then p sends $\mathcal{CWO}$. Note that, since q's crash recovery is performed at the end of q's current round, q cannot be a round further than p, due to the fact that p did not send a write in that round yet. Therefore, in the latter case, sn_q must refer to the round before p's current round.

This recovery mechanism assumes that the time-out for detecting crashed processes ensures that at the time of such a detection no messages of the crashed process remain in the system. This is the case for our current implementation of FTRepMI. If this assumption is not valid, a request from a crash recovery must be answered by a process only when it has received either a write or a crash detection for each process in the corresponding round. That is, a process can always dissipate $\mathcal{CWO}$, while it can dissipate $\mathcal{WO}$ only after collecting information on all processes in its world projection.

As a process n is joining the world, the contact process may crash before sending the join accept to n, but after it sent $join(n)$ to some other processes. Now these processes consider n as part of the world, but n is unaware of this and may try to find another contact process. To avoid such confusion, when n retries to join the world, either it must use a different rank, or it must wait for a sufficient time. Then, the alive processes detect that n is no longer in the world, and in the ensuing recovery it is decided that n did not perform a write.

As a process n is joining the world, the contact process o may crash after sending the join accept to n, but before it has sent a $join(n)$ to the other active processes. Then n could join the world while no process is aware of this. The solution is that o gives permission to n to join the world in the round $1 - sn$ after the round sn in which o broadcast $join(n)$, and only after o received in this round $1 - sn$ a remote write or crash detection for each process that took part in previous round sn (i.e. o becomes certain that all active processes that took part in the previous round have received $join(n)$). o's join accept contains not only o's world projection but also the number of detected crashes in the current round. To ensure that n will not wait indefinitely for round $1 - sn$ to start, o will start it with a *nop*, if o's $\mathcal{NWO}$ is empty (i.e. no process is in round $1 - sn$).

3   Validation

Model checking analysis. We specified the fault-tolerant version of FTRepMI in the process algebraic language μCRL [3]. We performed a model checking analysis for three types of properties, on a network of three processes, with respect to several configurations of threads. We used a distributed version of the μCRL toolset on 32 CPUs of DAS-3. First, we verified that the order in which processes execute their writes complies to the order in which they occur in the programs on the threads. Second, we verified that two processes will never execute different writes in the same round. Third, we verified that FTRepMI is deadlock-free, that is, if one process executes writes, and another process does not crash, then the other process will eventually execute the same writes.

Correctness proof. We will now argue the correctness of FTRepMI. We focus on sequential consistency, deadlock-freeness and joins. Note that given two active processes, either they are in the same round, or one process is one round ahead of the other. (That is why two round numbers are enough.)

Sequential consistency. Suppose that processes p and q have completed the same round, and have not crashed. We will now argue that they performed the same writes at the end of this round. That is, if p performs a write operation WO, then q also performs WO. The operation WO must be a local write at some process r in this round. If r does not crash, it will communicate WO to q, and we are done. So let's consider what happens if r crashes in this round, before communicating WO to q. Then q will detect, either in the previous or in the current round, that r crashed. In the first case, q is guaranteed to receive (e.g. from p) in a crash recovery at the end of the previous round, r's local write in that round, after which q shifts r's crash to the current round. Since p obtains WO, r has managed to communicated WO to some processes $s_1, \ldots, s_k$ in the current round. If at least one of these processes does not crash, WO is communicated to q in the crash recovery procedure that q performs at the end of the current round, and we are done. So let's consider what happens if $s_1, \ldots, s_k$ all crash without replying to q's SOS-message. Since q detects these crashes, and did not receive a write operation for r in the current round yet, q will start a crash recovery for the current round once again. This iterative crash recovery mechanism guarantees that ultimately q will receive WO.

Deadlock-freeness. Suppose that process p does not crash, and is not idle, and that all active processes are in p's current or next round. We will now argue that eventually p will progress to the next round. Each active process is guaranteed to become active in p's current round, either by the local write (possibly *nop*) at p in this round, or by a write from some other process. If none of the processes active in this round crash, then p is guaranteed to receive a write from each of these processes, and complete this round. So suppose that one or more processes crash before sending a write to p in this round. The failure detector of p will report these crashes, meaning that at the end of the round p starts the crash recovery procedure, and asks all processes it thinks to be active in this round for their $\mathcal{WO}$ (if they are in p's current round) or $\mathcal{CWO}$ (if they are in the next round). Active processes that have not crashed will eventually answer with an *SOSReply*-message. And those that crash before sending an *SOSReply* to p will be reported by p's failure detector, possibly leading to an iteration of p's crash recovery procedure. Since only a limited number of processes can join a round, eventually p will complete its crash recovery procedure, and thus the round.

Joins. Suppose a process N is allowed by its contact process O to join the world. Then all alive processes participating in the round that N joins are informed of this fact. Namely, in the previous round, O has broadcast $join(n)$ to all processes that participated in that round. In the current round, O only gives permission to N to join the world after having received a remote write or crash detection for all processes that participated in the previous round. These processes can only have progressed to the current round after having received $join(n)$. And they will pass on this information to other processes that join in the current round.

4   Performance Evaluation

We tested the performance of the FTRepMI Ibis-empowered prototype on a testbed of two DAS-3 clusters, both having 2.4 GHz AMD Opteron dual-core nodes interconnected by Myri-10G; the clusters are connected by a StarPlane-based [6] wide-area network, with 1ms round-trip latencies and dedicated 10Gbps lightpaths. As a first test, a process generates 1000 write operations on the replica; the rest of the processes only read the replica. Up to 16 CPUs performance is dependent only on the network delay; for 32 CPUs, bandwidth becomes a bottleneck. Second, we analyze the performance of two processes each generating 1000 write operations on the replica. To validate the advantage of combining in the same execution round write operations issued by different processes, each process computes the time per operation as if there were only 1000. There is no significant performance overhead when more writers are present in the system. Third, to analyze FTRepMI in terms of network delay and bandwidth, we repeat the same tests for an equal distribution of CPUs over two clusters. We also look at how distributing the "writing" processes over the clusters affects the performance. We found that FTRepMI performs efficiently also on a wide-area distributed system. The performance penalty incurred is maximum 10%.

We then analyzed the performance of crash-recovery for the simple scenarios of one process generating 1000 write operations on the replica in worlds of up to 32 processes, equally distributed on two clusters. Half-way through the computation (i.e., after 500 write operations are executed), all processes in one cluster (not containing the writer) crash. The remaining processes spend between 2 to 200 ms before resuming normal operation. Note that recovery time is not performance critical. FTRepMI caters for applications which require more than FTRepMI's recovery time to recompute a lost result (if at all possible).

Future work. Scalability can be improved by decreasing the size of exchanged messages. Tests on a wide-area network with higher latency (e.g., using clusters from Grid5000) would add more insight on the performance of FTRepMI. We also plan to develop a version of FTRepMI that does not require the presence of perfectly accurate failure detectors.

Acknowledgments. We thank Niels Drost and Rena Bakhshi for their helpful comments, and Stefan Blom for his help with the μCRL model checking exercise.

References

1. Bal, H., Kaashoek, F., Tanenbaum, A.: Orca: A language for parallel programming of distributed systems. IEEE TSE 18(3), 190–205 (1992)
2. Birman, K.: Replication and fault-tolerance in the Isis system. In: SOSP 1985, pp. 79–86. ACM, New York (1985)
3. Blom, S., Fokkink, W., Groote, J.F., van Langevelde, I., Lisser, B., van de Pol, J.: μCRL: A toolset for analysing algebraic specifications. In: Berry, G., Comon, H., Finkel, A. (eds.) CAV 2001. LNCS, vol. 2102, pp. 250–254. Springer, Heidelberg (2001)
4. Fekete, A., Kaashoek, M.F., Lynch, N.: Implementing sequentially consistent shared objects using broadcast and point-to-point communication. J. ACM 45(1), 35–69 (1998)
5. Garbinato, B., Guerraoui, R., Mazouni, K.R.: Implementation of the GARF replicated objects platform. Distributed Systems Engineering 2(1), 14–27 (1995)
6. Grosso, P., Xu, L., Velders, J.-P., de Laat, C.: Starplane: A national dynamic photonic network controlled by grid applications. Emerald Journal on Internet Research 17(5), 546–553 (2007)
7. Guerraoui, R., Schiper, A.: Fault-tolerance by replication in distributed systems. In: Strohmeier, A. (ed.) Ada-Europe 1996. LNCS, vol. 1088, pp. 38–57. Springer, Heidelberg (1996)
8. Herlihy, M.: A quorum-consensus replication method for abstract data types. ACM TOCS 4(1), 32–53 (1986)
9. Lamport, L.: How to make a multiprocessor computer that correctly executes multiprocess programs. IEEE TOC 28(9), 690–691 (1979)
10. Lynch, N.A., Shvartsman, A.A.: RAMBO: A reconfigurable atomic memory service for dynamic networks. In: Malkhi, D. (ed.) DISC 2002. LNCS, vol. 2508, pp. 173–190. Springer, Heidelberg (2002)
11. Maassen, J.: Method Invocation Based Programming Models for Parallel Programming in Java. PhD thesis, Vrije Universiteit Amsterdam (2003)
12. Maassen, J., van Nieuwpoort, R., Veldema, R., Bal, H., Kielmann, T., Jacobs, C., Hofman, R.: Efficient Java RMI for parallel programming. ACM TOPLAS 23(6), 747–775 (2001)
13. Maassen, J., Kielmann, T., Bal, H.: Parallel application experience with replicated method invocation. Concurrency and Computation: Practice and Experience 13(8-9), 681–712 (2001)
14. Moser, L., Melliar-Smith, P., Agarwal, D., Budhia, R., Lingley-Papadopoulos, C.: Totem: A fault-tolerant multicast group communication system. Commun. ACM 39(4), 54–63 (1996)

15. Narasimhan, P., Moser, L., Melliar-Smith, P.: Strongly consistent replication and recovery of fault-tolerant Corba applications. Computer System Science and Engineering 17(2), 103–114 (2002)
16. van Nieuwpoort, R., Maassen, J., Wrzesinska, G., Hofman, R., Jacobs, C., Kielmann, T., Bal, H.: Ibis: A flexible and efficient Java-based grid programming environment. Concurrency and Computation: Practice and Experience 17(7-8), 1079–1107 (2005)
17. van Renesse, R., Schneider, F.: Chain replication for supporting high throughput and availability. In: OSDI 2004, pp. 91–104. USENIX Association (2004)
18. Schiper, A.: Practical impact of group communication theory. In: Schiper, A., Shvartsman, M.M.A.A., Weatherspoon, H., Zhao, B.Y. (eds.) Future Directions in Distributed Computing. LNCS, vol. 2584, pp. 1–10. Springer, Heidelberg (2003)

Effective Layer-3 Protocols for Integrating Mobile Ad Hoc Network and the Internet

Khaleel Ur Rahman Khan[1], Rafi U. Zaman[1],
A. Venugopal Reddy[2], and Mohammed Asrar Ahmed[1]

[1] CSE Department, M. J. College of Engineering and Technology, Hyderabad, India
[2] CSE Department, Univ. College of Engg. Osmania University, Hyderabad, India
{khaleelrkhan,rafi.u.zaman,asrar.mohammed}@gmail.com,
avgreddy@osmania.ac.in

Abstract. The next generation mobile communication systems will be based on infrastructure wired/ wireless LAN technologies and ad hoc networks. Such hybrid networks benefit the extension of infrastructure network coverage using ad hoc connectivity apart from offering the ad hoc nodes access to the resources of the wired/infrastructure networks. In most of the integration strategies Mobile IP is integrated with the ad hoc network routing protocol to provide Internet access and in few of the strategies the routing protocol has been enhanced to provide the connectivity without using Mobile IP. Few strategies use fixed gateways, others use mobile gateways. In this paper, we proposed two different approaches of integrating ad hoc network and the wired network using two different protocols. In the first part of this paper, an extended DSDV protocol, named as Efficient DSDV (Eff-DSDV) protocol is used to provide bi-directional connectivity between exclusive ad hoc hosts and the hosts on the Internet (wired network). The proposed framework uses one of the ad hoc hosts known as Mobile Gateway Node (MGN) to act as a bridge between ad hoc network and the Internet. The performance comparison is made between the proposed approach and one of the leading strategies based on packet delivery ratio, end-end delay, and control overhead. The experimental results indicate that the performance of the proposed strategy is better than the existing strategies.

Later in the paper, we propose a framework for integrating mobile ad hoc network and the Internet using both fixed and mobile gateways. The ad hoc hosts can access the Internet using either fixed or mobile gateway, based on criteria of distance, load on the gateway. An extended version of AODV routing protocol is used in the framework. The objective behind using both fixed and mobile gateways is to increase the reliability of the Internet access, scalability, providing transparent Internet access to the ad hoc hosts and in general improve the performance of the integrated framework. The proposed framework is a hybrid architecture involving two-layer and three-layer approaches of integration. The performance comparison of the two proposed strategies has been done under common metrics.

Keywords: Mobile Ad Hoc Network (MANET), Integration Strategy, Mobile Gateway Node (MGN), Routing Protocol, Eff-DSDV, Fixed Gateways, Mobile Gateways.

V. Garg, R. Wattenhofer, and K. Kothapalli (Eds.): ICDCN 2009, LNCS 5408, pp. 377–388, 2009.
© Springer-Verlag Berlin Heidelberg 2009

1 Introduction

Mobile Ad Hoc Network (MANET) is a wireless network which is created dynamically without the use of any existing network infrastructure or centralized administra-
tion [1]. The MANET nodes communication is limited to the ad hoc network only.
Several applications may require a connection to an external network such as Internet
or LAN to facilitate the users with the resources present in the external network.

In this paper, the MANET and the wired network (Internet) are integrated into a
hybrid network. The major issues for providing Internet connectivity for ad hoc networks includes reducing the Mobile IP overhead, routing protocol overhead, improved gateway connectivity ratio and providing bi-directional connectivity.

The main focus of the first strategy is to provide bi-directional connectivity between
the ad hoc hosts and the wired hosts with optimal control overhead. In this strategy,
one of the ad hoc hosts is used as Mobile Gateway Node (MGN) acting as a bridge
between the MANET and the wired network. The MGN runs the Eff –DSDV [2] protocol and takes care of the addressing mechanisms to ensure the transfer of packets
between the hybrid networks. In this framework, it is assumed that the connectivity is
provided to exclusive ad hoc hosts only. We are ignoring the case of visiting mobile
nodes of the Internet or wireless infrastructure network, for Internet access.

The objective of the second strategy is to design a hybrid framework wherein both
fixed and mobile gateways are used to achieve the benefits of both the fixed and mobile
gateway based strategies. The mobile gateway based strategy uses three tier architecture
providing access transparency, location transparency and migration transparency [3]. It
is scalable and adaptable to the growth of MANET. This hybrid approach is also expected to improve the gateway discovery faster than the other approaches. The framework uses extensions of AODV [4] and mobile IP [5] protocols. The Mobile Gateway
(MG) is configured with AODV and Mobile IP, whereas the Fixed Gateway (FG) uses
AODV and IP. The Foreign Agent is the Mobile IP Foreign Agent (FA).

The rest of the paper is organized as follows. Section 2 discusses the previous work
done in this area. Section 3 describes the basic model of the framework of the first
strategy. Section 4 gives the design of the strategy by highlighting the Eff–DSDV
protocol. Section 5 describes the experimental configuration and also discusses the
experimental results. Section 6 gives the design of the hybrid architecture using fixed
and mobile gateways, along with a discussion on experimental results of the second
strategy. Section 7 makes a comparison between the two strategies. Section 8 concludes the paper.

2 Previous Work

The existing approaches for integrating MANET and the Internet are classified into
two categories based on two criteria. The outer most criterion is related to the type of
architecture of the hybrid network. This classification leads to *two-tier* and *three-tier*
strategies. Further, the gateway discovery process and their selection are considered
as other criteria to produce a finer classification of the existing approaches [6]. Few of
the two-tier strategies are given in [7-13]. A couple of three-tier strategies can be
found in [3 and 14-15].

3   Model of the Connectivity Framework

The objective of this framework is to integrate the ad hoc network and the infrastructure (wired) network by means of the mobile hosts, which are located under the radio range of Mobile Gateway Node (MGN), which acts as the bridge between the hybrid networks. The MGN is configured with the Eff-DSDV routing protocol with the necessary addressing mechanisms so as to forward the data packets destined to the wired host via the switch as shown in Figure 1. There are two ways for the mobile host to obtain the global connectivity. In the first scenario, the mobile host may be directly under the coverage of the MGN i.e. one hop away from MGN, can send its data directly to the MGN. In the second case, the ad hoc hosts which are outside the range of the MGN communicate with the MGN using multi-hop communication links.

When a mobile host outside the range of the MGN wishes to send packets to the wired host, first sends it to the MGN via multi-hop links using Eff-DSDV protocol. MGN then forwards the packets via the switch to the wired host using the normal IP routing mechanisms. On the other hand if the wired host wishes to send data to the ad hoc host, first send it to the switch. The switch then forwards the packets to the MGN via the access point. MGN after making the necessary changes to the data packets forward them to the ad hoc host using the Eff-DSDV protocol. As stated earlier, one of the limitations of this framework is that it allows global connectivity between the exclusive ad hoc hosts and the wired hosts.

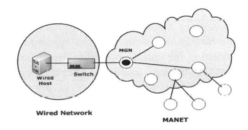

Fig. 1. Basic Model of the Connectivity Framework

4   Design of the Connectivity Framework

4.1   Efficient DSDV Protocol (Eff-DSDV)

In DSDV [16] protocol, each mobile host maintains a routing table that stores the number of hops, and the sequence number for all the destinations. The routing table updates may be time-driven or event-driven. The interval between the two updates is known as the periodic route update interval. In DSDV the low packet delivery is due to the fact that, it uses stale routes in case of broken links. In DSDV the existence of stale route does not imply that there is no valid route to the destination. The packets can be forwarded thru other neighbors who may have routes to the destination. The details of the Eff-DSDV protocol can be found in [2].

4.2 Full Duplex Connectivity between MANET and Internet

In the proposed Eff-DSDV protocol, ad hoc hosts and the MGN know each others presence via routing update of the Eff-DSDV protocol. Whenever the ad hoc host "A" loses the link and comes up again , it broadcasts DSDV advertisements to its neighbors with sequence number of '0'. Each host takes a note of it and makes an entry about host "A" in their routing tables. Later they broadcast with increased sequence number to their neighbors. This broadcasting process continues until the advertisements reach all the destinations i.e. the diameter of the network. The MGN also comes to know about the host "A" and makes an entry in its routing table. The host "A" also gets routing updates from its neighbors and thereby creates its routing table, including the route to MGN. Thus all the nodes know routes to every other node in the network including the MGN. The ad hoc node uses the protocol stack that is similar to the wired nodes except that it uses Eff-DSDV protocol to route packets. To commission two protocol stacks, MGN uses two wireless interfaces. The first one is configured for the infrastructure mode and has the protocol stack of normal wired nodes. With this interface the MGN is able to connect to the access point. The access point is the connection between wireless and wired communication. It converts from wired to wireless and the other way round. The other interface of the MGN is configured for the ad hoc mode and has the Eff-DSDV ad hoc routing protocol.

Communication Scenarios in the Proposed Framework
The proposed framework provides the following three modes of communication in order to provide full duplex communication:

- *Communication within the MANET (Intra-MANET routing):* This form of communication is the conventional communication within the ad hoc network by means of Eff-DSDV routing protocol. To send data to another host, the ad hoc host checks its routing table. If the destination is within the ad hoc network, then there will be an entry in the routing table leading to the destination. Accordingly the packets will be routed to the next-hop and continues till it reaches the destination.
- *Communication from ad hoc host to Internet host:* This type of communication happens between an ad hoc host and a wired host in the infrastructure network. The ad hoc host checks its routing table for the wired host address. If no entry for such host is found, then it searches for the route to the MGN. If the route is found to MGN then the packets are forwarded to the MGN thru intermediate ad hoc nodes (if required) using Eff-DSDV routing protocol. Then the MGN noticing that, this packet's destination lies outside the network, processes the packet in a similar way as is done in [8]. Then it forwards it to the switch thru the access point. If the routing entry to the MGN is not found, then the packet is discarded.
- *Communication from correspondent wired host to an ad hoc host:* This type of communication is initiated by the wired host. The wired host, when wishing to send packets to the ad hoc host, first sends them to the switch using IP routing. The switch then forwards the packet thru the access point to the MGN. The MGN in consultation with its routing table forwards the packet to the ad hoc host using the Eff-DSDV routing protocol.

5   Simulation Results Analysis

5.1   Simulation Setup

The effectiveness of the proposed framework is evaluated by carrying out the simulation experiments, in which the ad hoc hosts and the MGN runs the Eff-DSDV routing protocol. The simulation experiments were conducted using NCTUns 3.0, network simulator [17]. The parameters that are common to all the simulations are as follows. The topology size is 800x800m. Number of ad hoc hosts are 20. One MGN and one wired host are taken. Three traffic sources were taken. The transmission range of the hosts is 250m. The traffic type is CBR. The packet size is 512bytes. Standard host speed is 20 m/s. MGN speed 2m/s. The random waypoint model is used. The pause time is 5 sec. The total simulation time is 600 sec. Wireless channel bandwidth is 2 Mbps. Wired link bandwidth 10 Mbps. Eff-DSDV periodic route update interval 3-5 sec. No. of times the Eff-DSDV ROUTE REQUEST may be resent 2. Time duration before sending a new route-request is 1. The performance of the proposed framework is analyzed with respect to packet delivery ratio, end-end delay and the routing protocol overhead.

5.2   Simulation Results Discussion

The metrics have been obtained as a function of ad hoc node speed and as a function of the traffic load. Figures 2-4 shows the performance comparison of the proposed approach and the Ratanchandani [11] strategy. Each data point in the graph is an average of three simulation runs. Figure 2 shows the impact of the ad hoc host speed on the packet delivery fraction. As is seen the packet delivery ratio goes down as the node speed increases. It can be seen that the performance of our strategy is superior to that of Ratanchandani [11], The better performance of our strategy is due to the Eff-DSDV.

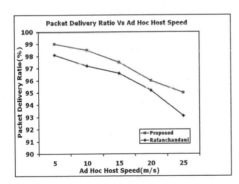   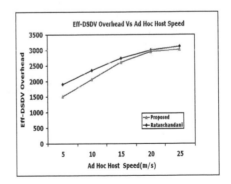

Fig. 2. Packet delivery ratio as a function of ad hoc host speed

Fig. 3. Routing protocol overhead as a function of ad hoc host speed

Figure 3 shows the relationship between routing protocol overhead and the node speed. The increase in routing protocol overhead is relatively lesser than in comparison with [11]. It is even lesser than other strategies like [3 and 12]. This is due to the fact that the AODV protocol used in other strategies requires substantial latency for the routes to be established due to node mobility.

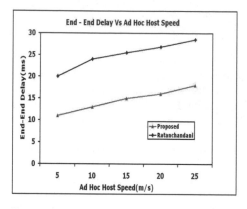

Fig. 4. End-End packet delay as a function of ad hoc host speed

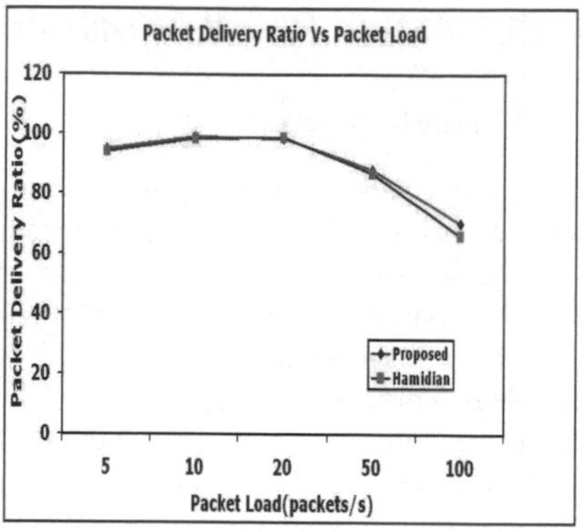

Fig. 5. Packet delivery ratio as function of packet load

Figure 4 shows the relationship between packet delivery latency i.e. end-end delay and node speed. The figure shows that the packet delivery delay increases with the increase in the speed. But the increase in the proposed framework is lesser than in comparison with the approach of [11]. The advantage of proactive protocol is that it has global view and hence achieves lesser packet delays due to non involvement of route discovery as is required every time in AODV protocol.

In the second part of our simulation, we have compared the performance of the proposed strategy with Hamidian approach [18]. Hamidian approach uses fixed gateways without mobile IP and is based on the AODV protocol. The performance comparison between them has been made as a function of packet load.

Figures 5 and 6 show the relationship of the packet delivery ratio and end-end delay with respect to packet load. The packet load is the number of packets transmitted per second per source. The Figure 5 shows that the packet delivery ratio is slightly higher for low packet load but it decreases with increase in the traffic load. It may be

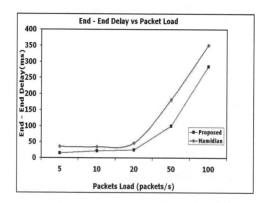

Fig. 6. End-End delay as a function of Packet load

observed that the packet delivery ratio of both the strategies is almost the same. Figure 6 shows the comparison between the two approaches with regard to end-end delay. It may be observed that the delay of the proposed approach is better than the Hamidian approach. The increase in the delay is due to more collisions, retransmissions and routing dumps.

6   Hybrid Framework Using Fixed and Mobile Gateways

As stated earlier, the strategies for integrating MANET and the Internet use either fixed or mobile gateways. In this strategy, we propose to use both the types of gateways for providing Internet access to the ad hoc hosts in a uniform and transparent manner. The architecture of proposed framework is shown in Figure 7. It consists of both the fixed and mobile gateways. The fixed gateways running the extended AODV protocol are connected to the router directly. The router using normal IP routing mechanisms can send and receive IP packets to the wired nodes and the FG. The FG on the ad hoc domain side uses extended AODV protocol to communicate with the Ad hoc hosts. Whereas it uses on the router link the usual IP routing as is used in [13]. The other part of the strategy uses three-tier architecture, using mobile gateways providing Internet access to the ad hoc nodes, similar to [3]. As shown in the Figure 7, the inner layer contains the wired backbone consisting of Routers and Mobile IP Foreign Agents (FA). The middle layer contains the mobile gateways and mobile Internet nodes which are just one hop away from the FA. The outer layer contains MANET nodes and visiting mobile Internet nodes. The mobile gateways should be registered with some FA at any time. Likewise the MANET nodes should be registered with the MG to get the Internet access.

One of the interesting aspects of our framework is that, the MG and FG use the same control message formats, so that the MANET nodes cannot distinguish whether the control message is from the FG or MG.

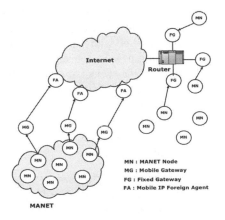

Fig. 7. Architecture of Hybrid Framework

6.1 Mobile Gateway Functionality

The mobile gateways are assumed to be registered with some FA. Similarly the MANET nodes are assumed to be registered with the MG in order to access the Internet. In our simulation experiments, we use distance first and if it is same, then we select the least loaded gateway for registration of ad hoc hosts.

Mobile gateways can register with only one FA at any time using proactive, reactive or hybrid approach. In the proactive approach, the FAs on the Internet willing to serve broadcast agent advertisements which will be received by mobile gateways. The other nodes ignore this. In the case of reactive approach, the MG and the interested MANET nodes will send the agent solicitations respectively to the FA and MG for registration with the FA and the MG, respectively. In our implementation, we use proactive approach for MG registration with FA and reactive approach for registration of MANET nodes with the gateways.

6.2 Combined Approach to Provide Internet Connectivity to the MANET Nodes

As stated earlier, in order to provide a transparent Internet connectivity to the MANET nodes, the FG and MG uses the same *Gateway Solicitation (GSol), Gateway Advertisements (GAdv), Gateway Registration Request (GRReq), Gateway Registration Reply (GRRep)*.

MANET host H, wishing to access an Internet host known as correspondent node D, first registers with a gateway which may be FG or MG. Host H starts by sending a GSol message which is broadcasted in the network. The GSol message traverse thru other MANET nodes perhaps until it reaches a FG or MG. Any gateway willing to serve H will send back a Mobile GAdv message. Note that a MG can send GAdv only if it is registered with the FA. The responding gateway will mention in the GAdv packet some important attributes of the gateway like its address, GAdv lifetime, number of registered nodes with the gateway (load) and a sequence number of the GAdv. Once the host H receives the GAdv packets, it will select the appropriate gateway based on the distance and the load metric. After which the host will send GRReq packet and wait for the GRRep from the gateway. A GRRep packet includes the registration lifetime, gateway IP address and the load. Now the host is registered with the gateway and all its communication will be with this gateway only. On expiration of the registration lifetime, the host has to renew its registration with the gateway. The host may renew with the same gateway or may select an alternate gateway. Once the registration process is completed the host H sends data packets. Data packets from the H to D will have to reach the registered gateway using the AODV protocol. For addressing, the node uses the routing table structure using the default route concept as in [13, 18].

6.3 Simulation Setup and Results Discussion

The parameters that are common to all the simulations are as follows. The topology size is 800x700m. Number of ad hoc hosts are 20. Two fixed gateways and four mobile gateways are used. Five traffic sources were taken. One Foreign Agent is used. Two wired hosts were placed. The transmission range of the hosts is 250m. The traffic type is CBR. The packet size is 512bytes with a packet sending rate of 5 packets/sec. Standard

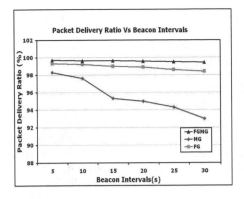

Fig. 8. Packet delivery Ratio as a function of Beacon Intervals

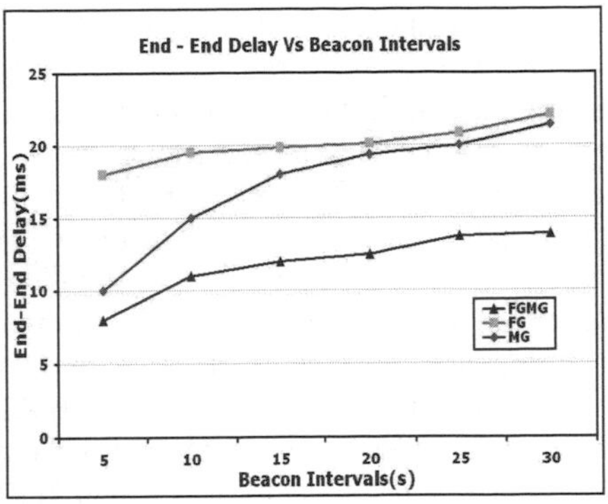

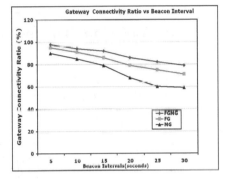

Fig. 9. End-End Delay as a function of Beacon Intervals

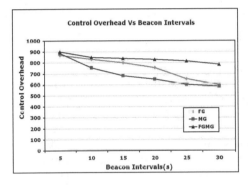

Fig. 10. Control Overhead as a function of Beacon Intervals

Fig. 11. Gateway Connectivity ratio as function of Beacon Intervals

host speed is 20 m/s. The pause time is 5 sec. The total simulation time is 600 sec. Beacon time of FA 5 sec. Beacon time of gateways 10 sec (Standard). Agent advertisement lifetime of FA is 15 sec. Agent advertisement lifetime of gateways is 20 sec. MANET node registration lifetime is 15 sec. Mobile gateway registration lifetime is 20 sec. Time interval between two agent solicitations of FA is 3 sec.

The performance of the proposed framework is analyzed with respect to performance metrics, packet delivery ratio, end-end delay, control overhead in terms of AODV and MIP messages and node-gateway connectivity ratio. The performance is first evaluated by varying FG and MG beacon time (from 5 to 30 seconds of the simulation time). Figures 8 to 11 shows the performance with respect to the metrics of packet delivery ratio, end-end delay and control overhead, gateway connectivity ratio respectively. Each data point in the graph is an average of three simulation runs. The performance of the proposed architecture has been compared with the strategies using fixed gateways and mobile gateways independently. In the graphs, the fixed gateways based strategy is marked as FG and mobile gateways based is marked as MG. The proposed hybrid architecture is marked as FGMG (Fixed and Mobile Gateway).

Figure 8 shows that the packet delivery ratio decreases slightly as the beacon interval increases. When the interval increases, route updates for the gateways are performed less frequently. When the beacon interval is short, the gateway advertisements play a role in keeping the routes fresh. When the interval increases, these messages have much less effect on the route updates. It can be seen that the performance of the proposed strategy is superior to that of FG or MG independently. Figure 9 shows the impact of beacon interval on the end-end delay. The delay increases with the beacon intervals. The increase in the beacon interval reduces the benefit of the proactive route maintenance that occurs at nodes close to the gateway. The delay using FGMG approach is lesser than the other two approaches. Figure 10 shows the control overhead in terms of AODV and Mobile IP messages. The overhead reduces due to less frequent traffic. Therefore as stated earlier, the overhead is higher for the proposed approach than in comparison with FG or MG. Figure 11 shows the percentage of time the MANET nodes are connected to the gateways. As is clear from the graph, the connectivity ratio for the Fixed and Mobile Gateway (FGMG) of our approach is higher than FG or MG alone.

7   Comparison of the Two Strategies

The performance of the both the proposed strategies is analyzed with respect to performance metrics, packet delivery ratio, end-end delay, by varying the ad hoc host speed under similar simulation environment and conditions. The first strategy is using the Eff-DSDV protocol and the second strategy is the hybrid architecture using the extended AODV protocol.

As is seen in Figure 12, the packet delivery ratio of the first strategy is superior to the second strategy due to the fact that under mobility conditions the performance of the Eff-DSDV protocol is better than the AODV protocol. Figure 13 indicates that the end-end delay of the first strategy is better due to the fact that the Eff-DSDV is a proactive protocol and provides a global view to all the hosts and hence the latency of route discovery is not required, which is otherwise required in the on demand protocols. However the second strategy has the advantage of being scalable and more reliable and

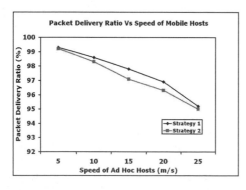

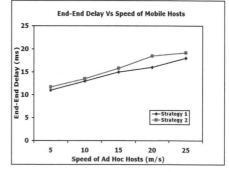

Fig. 12. Comparison of Packet Delivery Ratio   **Fig. 13.** Comparison of End-End Delay

provides better connectivity ratio than in comparison with the first strategy. The main drawback of the first strategy is the reliability. If the MGN fails then the communication gets affected.

8 Conclusion

In this paper we have presented a solution for integrating mobile ad hoc network using two different approaches using an extended DSDV and AODV routing protocols. In the first strategy using Eff-DSDV routing protocol, it uses one of the ad hoc hosts as the Mobile Gateway Node (MGN) to interconnect the two networks. The framework provides full duplex connectivity for ad hoc network nodes. Another advantage of this strategy is that it does not require the flooding of the gateway advertisements for registration of ad hoc hosts with the MGN. The simulation results indicate that the performance of the proposed strategy is superior to the strategy of Ratanchandani. In order to provide the Internet access for visiting mobile nodes, Eff-DSDV has to be integrated with Mobile IP, which could be the future work. In the second strategy, extended AODV protocol is used in the implementation of a hybrid architecture using fixed and mobile gateways providing a transparent Internet access to the ad hoc hosts. This strategy is more reliable and scalable than the first one. This strategy is a novel hybrid approach which can be used in a situation where both the types of gateways are available. The performance comparison between the two strategies indicates that the performance of the first strategy is slightly better to the second one in terms of packet delivery ratio and end-end delay. The only drawback of the first strategy is vulnerability of MGN.

References

1. Royer, E.M., Toh, C.-K.: A Review of Current Routing Protocols for Ad Hoc Mobile wireless networks. IEEE Personal Communications Magazine, 46–55 (April 1999)
2. Khan, K.U.R., Zaman, R.U., Venugopal Reddy, A., et al.: An Efficient DSDV routing protocol for MANET and its usefulness for providing Internet access to ad hoc hosts. In: IEEE Tencon International Conference, University of Hyderabad. IEEE Press, Los Alamitos (2008)
3. Ammari, H., El-Rewini, H.: Integration of Mobile Ad Hoc Networks and the Internet Using Mobile Gateways. In: Proceedings of the 18th International Parallel and Distributed Processing Symposium (IPDPS 2004) Workshop 12, p. 218b (2004)
4. Perkins, C.E., Royer, E.M.: Ad-Hoc on - Demand Distance Vector Routing. In: Proc. workshop Mobile Computing Systems and Applications (WMCSA 1999), pp. 90–100 (February 1999)
5. Perkins, C.E.: Mobile IP. IEEE Communications Magazine 3(5), 84–99 (1997)
6. Khan, K.U.R., Zaman, R.U., Venugopal Reddy, A.: Integrating Mobile Ad Hoc Networks and the Internet: challenges and a review of strategies. In: 3rd International Conference on Communication Systems Software and Middleware and Workshops, COMSWARE 2008, January 6-10 (IEEE CNF), pp. 536–543 (2008)
7. Lei, H., Perkins, C.E.: Ad Hoc Networking with Mobile IP. In: Proceedings of the 2nd European Personal Mobile Communications Conference, Bonn, Germany, pp. 197–202 (1997)

8. Broch, J., Maltz, D.A., Johnson, D.B.: Supporting Hierarchy and Heterogeneous Interfaces in Multi-Hop Wireless Ad Hoc Networks. In: Proceedings of the Workshop on Mobile Co7 Computing, Perth, Australia (June 1999)
9. Jonsson, U., Alriksson, F., Larsson, T., Johansson, P., Maguire Jr., G.Q.: MIPMANET – Mobile IP for Mobile Ad Hoc Networks. In: The First IEEE/ACM Annual Workshop on Mobile Ad Hoc Networking and Computing (MobiHOC), Boston, Massachusetts, USA, August 11, 2000, pp. 75–85 (2000)
10. Sun, Y., Belding-Royer, E.M., Perkins, C.E.: Internet Connectivity for Ad Hoc Mobile Networks. International Journal of Wireless Information Networks, Special Issue on Mobile Ad Hoc Networks (MANETs): Standards, Research, Applications, 75–88 (April 2002)
11. Ratanchandani, P., Kravets, R.: A Hybrid approach to Internet connectivity for Mobile Ad Hoc Networks. In: Proceedings of IEEE Wireless Communications and Networking Conference (WCNC), New Orleans, Louisiana, USA, March 16-20, pp. 1522–1527 (2003)
12. Tseng, Y., Shen, C., Chen, W.: Mobile IP and Ad Hoc Networks: An Integration and Implementation Experience. IEEE Computer 36(5), 48–55 (2003)
13. Kumar, R., Misra, M., Sarje, A.K.: An Efficient Gateway Discovery in Ad Hoc Networks for Internet Connectivity. In: Proc. of the International Conference on Computational Intelligence and Multimedia Applications 2007, pp. 275–281 (2007)
14. Michalak, M., Braun, T.: Common Gateway Architecture for Mobile Ad-Hoc Networks. In: Proc. of the Second Annual Conference on Wireless On -Demand Network Systems and Services (WONS 2005), vol. 00, pp. 70–75 (2005)
15. Denko, M.K., Wei, C.: An architecture for integrating mobile ad hoc networks with the Internet using multiple mobile gateways. In: Proc. of the Canadian Conference on Electrical and Computer Engineering, pp. 1097–1102 (2005)
16. Perkins, C.E., Bhagwat, P.: Highly Dynamic Destination Sequence- Vector Routing (DSDV) for Mobile Computers. Computer Communication Review 24(4), 234–244 (1994)
17. Wang, S.Y., Chou, C.L., Huang, C.H., Hwang, C.C., Yang, Z.M., Chiou, C.C., Lin, C.C.: The Design and Implementation of the NCTUns 1.0 Network Simulator. Computer Networks 42(2), 175–197 (2003)
18. Hamidian, A., Körner, U., Nilsson, A.: Performance of internet access solutions in mobile ad hoc networks. In: Kotsis, G., Spaniol, O. (eds.) Euro-NGI 2004. LNCS, vol. 3427, pp. 189–201. Springer, Heidelberg (2005)

Performance Analysis of a UMTS Cell with Underlying Tunnel-WLANs

Sibaram Khara[1], Iti Saha Misra[2], and Debashis Saha[3]

[1] Dept of ECE & EIE College of Engineering and Management Kolaghat, India
sianba@rediffmail.com
[2] Dept of ETCE, Jadavpur University, India
itisahamisra@yahoo.co.in
[3] CS & MIS Group, IIM Calcutta, India
ds@iimcal.ac.in

Abstract. Users' preference of WLAN-access has potential effect on the performance of a UMTS cell with underlying WLANs. In the models with complementary-WLANs, the hybrid users (i.e., UMTS users having WLAN privileges) are permitted to access WLAN only in the event of blocking of their data-requests in UMTS. So, a user sometimes misses the high speed data services of WLAN because he/she does not access WLAN as long as UMTS bandwidth is available. Though, this model decreases the dropping probability of a UMTS request (i.e., call), the complementary benefit, at high traffic load, decreases. We develop an analytical model with tunnel-WLANs in which a hybrid user always accesses the WLAN as soon as he/she enters a WLAN hotspot. The numerical results show that the dropping probabilities of requests in the models with complementary-WLANs and with tunnel-WLANs are almost same at low traffic environment. But, at higher traffic load, the dropping probability of a request in a model with tunnel-WLANs is better than that in a model with complementary-WLANs.

Keywords: Complementary-WLAN, handoff, request, tunnel-WLAN.

1 Introduction

Request handling scheme in a hybrid cell (a UMTS cell with embedded WLANs) decides the users' preference of WLAN-access. In some proposals [1], a hybrid user is permitted to access WLANs only when his/her request is blocked in UMTS, i.e., a hybrid user is not permitted to access WLANs if UMTS bandwidth is available. Such WLANs are called complementary-WLANs (C-WLANs). An analytical model of a hybrid cell with embedded C-WLANs is called C-WLAN model. In this model, a user sometimes misses the high speed data services of WLANs while residing in a hotspot itself. Moreover, C-WLAN model restricts vertical handoff of a new WLAN data session to UMTS. But, vertical handoff from WLAN to UMTS is essential to continue some data sessions when a user moves out of WLAN [2]. This model requires a separate air interface for user equipment (UE) on reserved WLAN bandwidth. Thus, a C-WLAN model incurs difficulties to implement UMTS-WLAN integration using conventional WLANs.

V. Garg, R. Wattenhofer, and K. Kothapalli (Eds.): ICDCN 2009, LNCS 5408, pp. 389–394, 2009.
© Springer-Verlag Berlin Heidelberg 2009

On the other hand, a data session may always be handed over to WLAN as soon as a user enters a hotspot. Such WLANs are called tunnel-WLANs (T-WLANs) [3]. The analytical model of a hybrid cell with embedded T-WLANs is called T-WLAN model. In this study, we develop a T-WLAN model and compare its performance with C-WLAN models. Results show that a T-WLAN model provides better performance in high traffic environment.

2 Overview of a T-WLAN Model

We consider a loose coupling architecture of a UMTS-WLAN integrated network [4]. The coverage of all WLAN hotspots in a hybrid cell is called equivalent WLAN (Fig. 1). Unless specified, WLAN means equivalent WLAN in this article.

2.1 User Classes

A *UMTS-only* user has subscriptions for only UMTS services and he/she cannot access the WLAN. A *back-up* user is a hybrid user currently residing in the UMTS-only coverage and he/she can initiate vertical handoff from UMTS to WLAN. A *hotspot user* is a hybrid user currently residing in a WLAN hotspot and he/she can initiate VHR from WLAN to UMTS. A *WLAN user* can access only WLAN.

2.2 Coverage Probability

The hybrid user's density (users per unit area) in a WLAN hotspot d times the subscriber's density in the UMTS-only coverage. Coverage probability g is defined as the ratio of *hotspot* users to total hybrid users in a hybrid cell. Say, A is the ratio of WLAN coverage to the coverage of a UMTS cell.

$$g \approx \left[(Ad)^{-1} + 1 \right]^{-1}, \quad \text{where } A^{-1} \gg 1$$

2.3 Request Handling Scheme

We specify following call handling scheme for a hybrid cell with M UMTS data channels out of which m channels are used to handle handoff requests and there are K data channels in WLAN.

In the UMTS system:

- Both horizontal handoff requests (HHRs) and vertical handoff requests (VHRs) are handled with same priority.
- A new request (NR) is blocked if m data sessions are already going on.
- A HHR or VHR is blocked if there are $(M - m)$ ongoing handed over data sessions or total M ongoing data sessions.

In the WLAN system:

- All data-requests are handled with same priority in a WLAN cell.
- A NR or VHR is blocked if there are K ongoing data sessions.

2.4 States of Requests

Request-life is defined as the duration of time elapsed between the instant a request is initiated and the instant it is dropped or completed. A request may undergo at most seven states during its *request-life; arrival, blocked, dropped, successful, completion, VHR arrival, HHR arrival* (Figure 1(a)). A *request (NR or, HHR* or VHR) attains *arrival* state as soon as it is initiated by a user. In the *blocked* state, *a request is denied* and in the dropped state, a request is rejected. In the successful state, a data session is established and in the *Completion state,* a user's data session is completed. When a request in successful state, initiates an HHR, it reaches to *HHR arrival* state and when it initiates a VHR, it reaches to *VHR arrival* state.

2.5 Session-Mobility Scenarios

- A new or handed over data session of a *UMTS-only user* may be completed in the same cell or it may initiate HHR in a neighbor UMTS cell (Fig. 1(b)).
- A new or handed over data session of a *back-up user* may be complemented in the UMTS-only coverage of the same cell or it may initiate HHR in the UMTS-only coverage of neighbor cell or it may initiate VHR in WLAN.
- A new or handed over data session of *hotspot user* may be completed in WLAN itself or it may initiate VHR in the UMTS-only coverage.
- A new data session (NDS) of a *WLAN user* is completed in the WLAN itself.

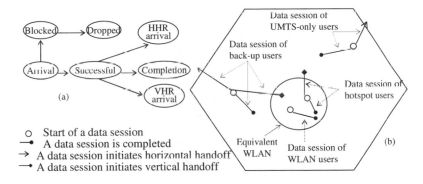

Fig. 1. (a) States of requests and (b) Handoff scenarios

3 Handoff Calculation

Assume $p, b_1, b_2, b_3,$ b , $P_1, P_2,$ $P_3, P_4,$ $P_5,$ $R^G,$ $H^G,$ $R^W, H^W, R_r^G,$ $H_r^G,$ R_r^W, H_r^W are percentage faction of UMTS-only users, blocking probability (in UMTS) of an NR, of an HHR, of a VHR, blocking probability of a request in WLAN, handoff probability (of UMTS requests) of an NR, of an HHR, of a VHR, handoff probability (of WLAN requests) of an NR, of a VHR, cell residence time (CRT) in

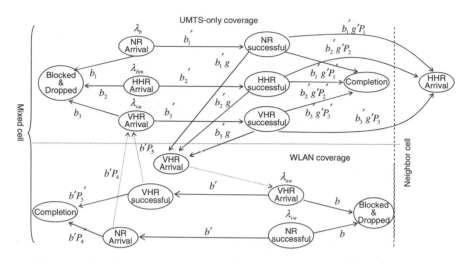

Fig. 2. Handoff scenarios with state transition probabilities

UMTS, session holding time (SHT) in UMTS, CRT in WLAN, SHT in WLAN, residual CRT in UMTS, residual SHT in UMTS, residual CRT in WLAN and residual SHT in WLAN, respectively. We also assume, for any value x, $x' = (1-x)$.

Figure 2 shows the handoff scenarios using the states of requests. λ_b, λ_{hm} and λ_{vu} are NR, HHR and VHR arrival rates in UMTS and λ_{nw} and λ_{vw} are NR and VHR arrival rates in WLAN. Using flow balance equation across UMTS cell [5], i.e., *flow in = flow out*, we can write the following. From figure 2(a) we can write the following.

$$\lambda_{hm} = \lambda_b b_1' g' P_1 + \lambda_{hm} b_2' g' P_2 + \lambda_{vu} b_2' g' P_3$$

$$\lambda_{hm} = K_1 \lambda_b + K_2 \lambda_{vu}$$

$$K_1 = \frac{P_1 b_1' (1-g)}{1 - P_2 b_2' (1-g)} \quad \text{and} \quad K_2 = \frac{P_3 b_3' (1-g)}{1 - P_2 b_2' (1-g)}$$

$$\frac{dK_1}{dg} = \frac{-b_1' P_1}{\left\{1 - P_2 b_2' (1-g)\right\}^2} \quad \text{and} \quad \frac{dK_2}{dg} = \frac{-b_2' P_2}{\left\{1 - P_2 b_2' (1-g)\right\}^2}$$

Both K_1 and K_2 decrease with increasing g i.e., with increasing WLAN coverage and density ratio.

$$\lambda_{vw} = \lambda_b b_1' g + \lambda_{hm} b_2' g + \lambda_{vu} b_3' g$$

From figure 2 we can write the following.

$$\lambda_{vu} = b' P_4 \lambda_{nw} + b' P_5 \lambda_{vw}$$

The distribution of channel holding time (CHT) in a cell is the minimum of the distributions of CRT and SHT. So, CHT of NDS, horizontally handed over data session (HHDS) and vertically handed over data session (VHDS) in UMTS are given by $\min(H^G, R_r^G)$, $\min(H_r^G, R^G)$ and $\min(H^G, R^G)$, respectively. CHT of NDS and VHDS in WLAN are given by $\min(H^W, R_r^W)$ and $\min(H^W, R^W)$, respectively. Using Laplace transform approach, from [6], we can calculate the mean CHT of each data session. Each cell can be modeled as M/M/m queuing system in which the data channels assigned to a base station (i.e., Node B in UMTS) are the servers, while any data-request forms the arrival process, and then the CHT is equivalent to the service time. We consider the hiper-Erlang distribution of CRT because of its universal approximation of all distributions [6]. P_1, P_2, P_3, P_4 and P_5 can be estimated from [1].

4 Numerical Results

Then we estimate dropping probabilities of an NR and handoff request (HHR or VHR) in a C-WLAN and T-WLAN models with $M = 30, m = 25$ and $K = 50$. We

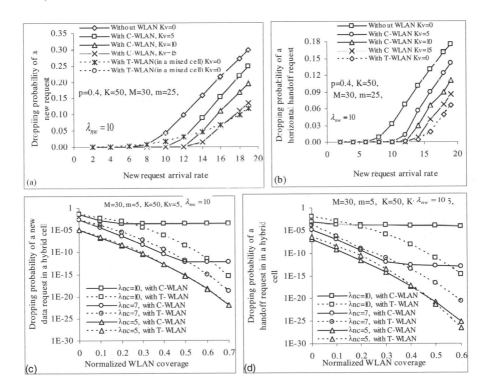

Fig. 3. Dropping probabilities of a (a) new request (b) handoff request, with increasing new arrival rate. Dropping probabilities of a (a) new request and (b) handoff request, with increasing normalized WLAN coverage.

use $R^G = 3.31$min, $H^G = 2.25$min, $R^W = 2.73$min and $H^W = 2.5$min. The solid lines of the graphs of figures 3(a) and 3(b) show that the dropping probabilities of an NR and handoff request improve with increasing reserved WLAN channels in C-WLANs. These results honestly agree with those in [1]. At $\lambda_{nc} = 5$ per minute (Fig. 3(a)), the performance of the both models are almost similar. But, at high traffic condition, the dropping probability of an NR in T-WLAN model improves over C-WLAN model.

Figure 3(c) shows that the dropping probabilities of C-WLAN and T-WLAN models are comparable at low NR arrival rate (at $\lambda_{nc} = 5$). But, the dropping probabilities of an NR (Fig. 3(c)) and handoff request (Fig. 3(d)) in a T-WLAN model is superior if the WLAN coverage is more than 22% and 18% ($\lambda_{nc} = 10$, $K_v = 5$), respectively.

5   Conclusion

In a high traffic environment, a T-WLAN model shows better performance over C-WLAN model with increasing WLAN coverage. The model is useful to estimate the requisite WLAN to maintain a threshold blocking probability in a UMTS cell.

References

1. Tang, S., Li, W.: Performance Analysis of the 3G Network with Complementary WLANs. In: Proceeding of IEEE Globecom 2005, pp. 2637–2641 (2005)
2. Liu, H., Bhaskaran, H., Raychaudhuri, D., Verma, S.: Capacity Analysis of a Cellular Data System with UMTS/WLAN Interworking. In: Proceeding of IEEE VTC 2003, vol. 3, pp. 1817–1821 (2003)
3. Steven-Navarro, E., Wong, V.W.S.: Resource Sharing in an Integrated Wireless Cellular/WLAN System. In: Canadian Conference on Electrical and Computer Engineering (CCECE 2007), Vancouver, Canada, pp. 631–634 (April 2007)
4. Khara, S., Misra, I.S., Saha, D.: A One-pass Method of MIP Registration by WLAN Host through GPRS Networks. In: Chaudhuri, S., Das, S.R., Paul, H.S., Tirthapura, S. (eds.) ICDCN 2006. LNCS, vol. 4308, pp. 570–581. Springer, Heidelberg (2006)
5. Tang, S., Li, W.: Modeling and Analysis of Hierarchical Cellular Networks with Birectional Overflow and Takeback Strategies under Generally Cell Residence Time. Intl. journal of Telecommunication Systems 32(1), 71–91 (2006)
6. Fang, Y.: Hyper-Erlang Distribution Model and its Application in Wireless Mobile Networks. Intl. Journal of Wireless Networks: Special issue: Design and modeling in mobile and wireless systsems 7(3), 211–219 (2001)

Performance Comparison of Orthogonal Gold and Walsh Hadamard Codes for Quasi-Synchronous CDMA Communication

Sujit Jos[1], Preetam Kumar[2], and Saswat Chakrabarti[2]

[1] Dept. of Electronics and Electrical Communication Engineering
[2] G. S. Sanyal School of Telecommunications
Indian Institute of Technology Kharagpur
sujit@gssst.iitkgp.ernet.in, preetam@gssst.iitkgp.ernet.in,
saswat@ece.iitkgp.ernet.in

Abstract. Orthogonal codes are integral part of DS-CDMA based communication systems. Walsh Hadamard orthogonal codes are extensively employed in present day CDMA systems. In this paper, Orthogonal Gold codes are presented as a possible option for spreading sequences in Quasi-Synchronous CDMA (QS-CDMA). These codes are compared with Walsh Hadamard codes in terms of individual user performances and average BER performance. It is observed that codewords from Orthogonal Gold set perform more uniformly compared to individual codewords of Walsh Hadamard set and also give comparable average BER performance.

1 Introduction

Orthogonal codes are widely used for uplink and downlink transmissions of cellular DS-CDMA systems like cdma2000 and WCDMA/UMTS. Perfect synchronization is necessary to maintain the orthogonality between different users. In presence of synchronization error, multi access interference is present due to the timing mismatch between different user spreading codewords. Also, received signal power of desired user degrades due to the reduced value of autocorrelation function [1]. When the synchronization error present in the system is less than a chip period, the DS-CDMA system is referred to as Quasi-Synchronous CDMA system (QS-CDMA)[2]. Walsh Hadamard codes are the most popular orthogonal codes employed in present day DS-CDMA systems. The performance of Walsh Hadamard codes in presence of timing error has been well addressed in [3]-[4].

In this work, Orthogonal Gold codes are compared with Walsh Hadamard codes for quasi-synchronous CDMA applications. The comparison is accomplished in terms of individual user performances as well as average BER performance. It has been shown that Orthogonal Gold codes may be a better option than Walsh Hadamard codes in presence of timing synchronization error.

To carry out the comparison of the two orthogonal codes, we begin by describing the system model of QS-CDMA with BPSK modulation. Numerical and simulation results are presented in section 3. Finally we conclude the paper.

V. Garg, R. Wattenhofer, and K. Kothapalli (Eds.): ICDCN 2009, LNCS 5408, pp. 395–399, 2009.
© Springer-Verlag Berlin Heidelberg 2009

2 System Model for QS-CDMA with BPSK

The system model of QS-CDMA is referred from [4]. In a system employing BPSK signalling, the BER expression of user i could be written as

$$BER_i = Q\left(\sqrt{\frac{A_i^2 \varphi_{ii}^2(\tau_i)}{\frac{N_0}{2} + \sum_{k=0,k\neq i}^{K-1} A_k^2 \varphi_{ik}^2(\tau_k)}}\right) \qquad (1)$$

Here, A_k is the amplitude of user k, N_0 is the one-sided power spectral density of the AWGN noise process in the channel. K is the number of different users simultaneously signalling over the common transmission channel and $\varphi_{ik}(\tau_k)$ is the correlation between the user spreading codewords $s_i(t)$ and $s_k(t)$ at delay τ_k. $\varphi_{ik}(\tau_k)$ is defined as

$$\varphi_{ik}(\tau_k) = \frac{1}{NT_c} \int_0^{NT_c} s_i(t)s_k(t-\tau_k)dt \qquad (2)$$

where, $s_k(t)$ is the spreading codeword for user k.

The system is synchronous when $\tau_k = 0$ for all k. When $\tau_k \neq 0$, individual codewords within the codeset give different performances due to different values of autocorrelation and crosscorrelation with other codewords in the codeset. From (1), it is evident that codewords with higher value of autocorrelation and lower values of MAI gives better BER performance in quasi-synchronous environment. Hence, a simple figure merit for individual users from BER perspective maybe a ratio μ such that

$$\mu = \frac{\varphi_{ii}^2(\tau_i)}{\sum_{k=0,k\neq i}^{K-1} \varphi_{ik}^2(\tau_k)} \qquad (3)$$

Codewords with higher value of μ give better BER performances and codewords with similar value of μ give similar BER performances. It is desired that all codewords have similar values of μ so that every user enjoys similar quality of signal. Codewords with all 1's or all -1's are excluded from the discussion since their autocorrelation remains unity and MAI remains zero for all possible delays in a quasi-synchronous environment leading to a performance near theoretical BPSK curve at perfect synchronization. Moreover, they give no spreading of the user data symbols. With the above exception, the number of different levels of BER will be equal to the number of different values of μ in the codeset. Hence, codeset with a row of all 1's or -1's have a total of $\mu + 1$ different BER levels.

3   Numerical and Simulation Results

Based on the previous discussion, we compare Orthogonal Gold codes with Walsh Hadamard codes. The values of μ for individual codewords from the two orthogonal sets have been computed for spreading gain of 8. As mentioned earlier, codewords with all 1's or all -1's have been excluded. Table 1 shows the number of different values of μ for Walsh Hadamard and Orthogonal Gold sets of order 8. Table 2 shows similar results for order 64. The codesets are expected to have the same number of different BER levels as the different values of μ. Monte-Carlo simulation has been carried out to verify these implications.

Table 1. Number of different values of μ and the expected number of BER levels for orthogonal codeset of order 8

Orthogonal codeset of order 8	Number of different μ's	Expected number of BER levels
Walsh Hadamard	4	5
Orthogonal Gold	3	3

Table 2. Number of different values of μ and the expected number of BER levels for orthogonal codeset of order 64

Orthogonal codeset of order 64	Number of different μ's	Expected number of BER levels
Walsh Hadamard	32	33
Orthogonal Gold	8	8

Fig. 1 shows the BER performances of individual codewords from Walsh Hadamard set of order 8 at a synchronization error of 0.3Tc. By synchronization error of 0.3Tc, we mean that all codewords are at a constant synchronization error of 0.3Tc. Theoretical BPSK curve at perfect synchronization is also shown for reference. As observed from the figure, we have five different levels of BER corresponding to four different values of μ and a row of all 1's in the Walsh Hadamard matrix of order 8. The BER curve for the first codeword overlaps with the theoretical BPSK curve because of the unity autocorrelation and zero crosscorrelation at all values of time delay. The simulation results are in agreement with the numerical results given in table 1. Fig. 2 shows the BER performances of individual codewords from Orthogonal Gold set of order 8. Orthogonal Gold set has three levels of BER corresponding to three different values of μ given in the numerical results. As with Walsh Hadamard set, the results are in agreement with the numerical results. Fig. 3 shows the average BER performance of the two codes at synchronization error of 0.3Tc. It is observed from the figure that the two orthogonal sets give more or less the same average performance.

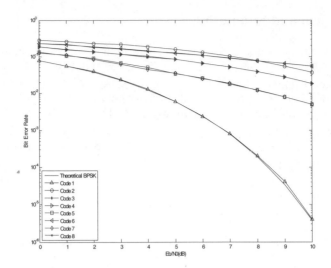

Fig. 1. BER performances of individual codewords from Walsh Hadamard set of order 8 at synchronization error of 0.3Tc, when K=N=8

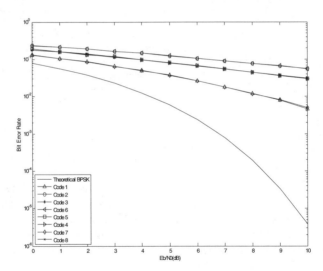

Fig. 2. BER performances of individual codewords from Orthogonal Gold set of order 8 at synchronization error of 0.3Tc, when K=N=8

From the figures, we can observe that individual codewords of Orthogonal Gold codes perform more uniformly compared to corresponding codewords from Walsh Hadamard set. This trend is expected to continue in higher order codesets as indicated by table 2. Hence, Orthogonal Gold codes perform better than Walsh Hadamard codes since all the users enjoy more or less the same performance. Codewords from Walsh Hadamard set behave diversely resulting in a larger number of BER levels thereby putting some users at disadvantage. The performance of Walsh Hadamard codes in terms average BER performance is similar to Orthogonal Gold codes with no extra advantage.

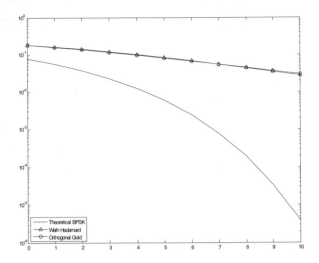

Fig. 3. Average BER performance of the two orthogonal sets of order 8 at synchronization error of 0.3Tc, when K=N=8

Hence, we can conclude from the above discussions that Orthogonal Gold codes may be a better option than Walsh Hadamard codes in practical scenarios where perfect orthogonality cannot be maintained.

4 Conclusion

Orthogonal Gold codes were presented as possible options for spreading sequences in QS-CDMA. These codes were compared with Walsh Hadamard codes in terms of individual user performances and average BER performance. It is observed that individual codewords of Orthogonal Gold set perform more uniformly compared to codewords from Walsh Hadamard set and also give an average BER performance comparable to Walsh Hadamard set.

References

1. Jos, S., Kumar, P., Chakrabarti, S.: A Code Selection Criterion Based on Autocorrelation Properties for Quasi-Synchronous CDMA Communication System. In: Proceedings of ISSSTA 2008, pp. 156–160 (2008)
2. Lin, X.D., Kyung, H.C.: Optimal PN sequence design for quasi-synchronous CDMA communication systems. IEEE Trans. Commn. 45, 221–226 (1997)
3. Dasilva, V.M., Sousa, E.S.V.: Multicarrier Orthogonal CDMA signals for quasi-synchronous communication systems. IEEE JSAC 12, 842–852 (1994)
4. Houtum, W.J.V.: Quasi-synchronous codeword-division multiple access with high-order modulation. IEEE Trans. Commn. 49, 1240–1249 (2001)

Analysis of Optimum Interleaver for Receivers in IDMA Systems

Manoj Shukla[1], V.K. Srivastava[2], and S. Tiwari[2]

[1] Department of Electronics Engineering, Harcourt Butler Technological Institute,
Kanpur, India
manojkrshukla@rediffmail.com
[2] Department of Electronics & Comm. Engineering,
Motilal Nehru National Indtitute of Technology, Allahabad, India

Abstract. In this paper, we are analyzing a new Tree Based Interleaver (TBI) to generate user specific chip-level interleaving sequences for different users in an IDMA system, which reduces computational complexity with optimum memory requirement. This method of generation also solves the memory cost problem and reduces the amount of information exchange between mobile stations and base stations required to specify the interleaver. Simulation results are presented to show that the proposed interleavers perform well as compared to Random Interleavers in an IDMA system.

Keywords: Interleave Division Multiple Access, Random Interleaver, Tree Based Interleaver, Master random Interleaver Iterative Receivers.

1 Introduction

Interleave division multiple access (IDMA) is a technique which is based on interleaving as only means for user separation in comparison to Code Division Multiple Access (CDMA) where the signature sequences are responsible for user separation. IDMA not only inherits many advantages from conventional CDMA, such as robustness against fading and mitigation of cross-cell interference, but also allows very simple chip-by-chip (CBC), iterative multiuser detection (MUD) strategy while achieving impressive performance. In [1] [3] [5], an IDMA system that uses randomly and independently generated interleavers is presented. The IDMA system with random interleaver [1] performs better than a comparable CDMA system.

If the user specific interleavers are generated independently and randomly, the base station (BS) has to use a considerable amount of memory to store these interleavers as they are required at transmitter and receiver for interleaving and deinterleaving purpose, which may cause serious concern, when the numbers of users is large.

In [4], the method for generation of peg interleaver is merely using an algorithm to generate the sequence of random interleavers, orthogonal in nature, instead of random selection of respective interleavers [1]. So, the problem of memory requirement is still present for high number of users.

V. Garg, R. Wattenhofer, and K. Kothapalli (Eds.): ICDCN 2009, LNCS 5408, pp. 400–407, 2009.

If the user specific interleavers are generated by master random interleaver method [2], then problem of high memory requirement is reduced considerably, but the computational complexity required to generate the interleaving sequence is increased extensively, especially when the number of users is large. It is also an important point to mention that at the receiver, in the turbo processor frequent interleaving and deinterleaving is required during the process of iterative decoding. Therefore, lots of calculations are required for in turbo processing and hence, the computational complexity is further increased when   number of users is high.

In this paper, we examine the Tree Based Interleaver (TBI) generation to alleviate this concern. With this method, not only the interleaver assignment scheme is simplified and memory cost is greatly reduced, but also the computational complexity required to generate the interleaving matrix is greatly reduced without sacrificing performance.

Section 2 contains an introduction of the IDMA communication system. In section 3, we have a brief look over power interleaving method discussed in [2], and explain the computational complexity and memory requirement factors of the interleaver generation methods. In section 4, we present a Tree Based Interleaver that reduces both the computational complexity and memory requirement factors of the interleavers. Section 5 presents computer simulations of IDMA systems with the Tree Based Interleaver (TBI). Section 6 concludes the paper.

2   IDMA Scheme

We consider an IDMA system [1] shown in Figure 1, with K simultaneous users using a single path channel. At the transmitter, a N-length input data sequence $d_k = [d_k(1),$ ...., $d_k(i)$, ... $d_k(N)$]^T of user k is encoded into $c_k = [c_k(1),$ ...., $c_k(j)$, ... $c_k(J)$]^T based on low rate code C, where J is the Chip length.

The code C is constructed by serially concatenating a forward error correction code and repletion code of length-sl. The forward error correction code used here is Memory-2 Rate-1/2 Convolutional coder. We may call the elements in c_k 'chips'.

Then c_k is interleaved by a chip level interleaver 'Π_k', producing a transmitted chip sequence $x_k = [x_k(1),$ ...., $x_k(j)$, ... $x_k(J)$]^T . After transmitting through the channel the bits are seen at the receiver side as $r = [r_k(1),$ ...., $r_k(j)$, ... $r_k(J)$]^T . The Channel opted for simulation purpose is additive white Gaussian noise (AWGN) channel.

After chip matched filtering the received signal form the K users can be written as

$$r(j) = \sum_{k=1}^{K} h_k x_k(j) + n(j), j = 1, 2, ...J.$$ (1)

where h_k is the channel coefficient for k^{th} user and $\{ n(j) \}$ are the samples of an additive white Gaussian noise (AWGN) process with mean as zero and variance σ^2 =$N_0/2$. An assumption is made that $\{h_k\}$ are known priori at the receiver.

The receiver consists of a signal estimator block (SEB) and a bank of K single user a *posteriori* probability (APP) decoders (DECs), operating in an iterative manner. The modulation technique used is binary phase shift keying (BPSK) signaling. The outputs of the SEB and DECs are extrinsic log-likelihood ratios (LLRs) about $\{x_k\}$ defined as

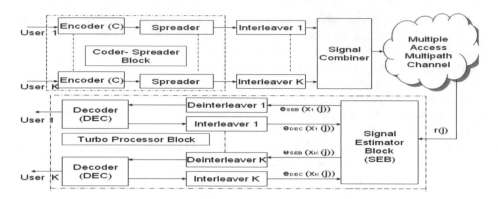

Fig. 1. Transmitter and Receiver structures of IDMA scheme with K simultaneous users

$$e(x_k(j)) = \log\left(\frac{p(y/x_k(j)=+1)}{p(y/x_k(j)=-1)}\right), \forall k, j. \tag{2}$$

These LLRs are further distinguished by the subscripts i.e., $e_{SEB}(x_k(j))$ and $e_{DEC}(x_k(j))$, depending upon whether they are generated by SEB or DECs.

Due to the use random interleavers $\{\Pi_k\}$, the SEB operation can be carried out in a chip-by-chip manner, with only one sample r(j) used at a time. Rewrite (2) as

$$r(j) = h_k x_k(j) + \zeta_k(j) \tag{3}$$

where

$$\zeta_k(j) = r(j) - h_k x_k(j) = \sum_{k' \neq k} h_{k'} x_{k'}(j) + n(j) \tag{4}$$

is the distortion in $r(j)$ with respect to user-k.

Now the data based on log likelihood ratio (LLR) is generated as shown below.

$$e_{SEB}(x_k(j)) = 2h_k \cdot \frac{r(j) - E(r(j)) + h_k E(x_k(j))}{Var(r_j) - |h_k|^2 Var(x_k(j))}$$

Further the data is duly updated in the receiver.

$$e_{DEC}(x_k(\pi(j))) = \sum_{j=1}^{S} e_{SEB}(x_k(\pi(j)))$$

$$j = 1, \ldots, S$$

Now, the steps are repeated depending on no. of iterations and users.

3   Master Random Interleaver Generation Method

In an IDMA system, each user has a user specific interleaver $\{\Pi_k\}$ having length equal to chiplength 'J'. A considerable amount of memory will be required to store the indexes for these interleavers.

To minimize this memory cost problem, a master random interleaver method is proposed in [2]. In this paper, it is stated that a master interleaver Φ is taken, and the subsequent k-interleavers are generated using $\Pi_k = \Phi^k$.

where $\Phi^k(c)$ is defined as $\Phi^1(c) = \Phi(c)$.
$$\Phi^2(c) = \Phi\,(\Phi(c)).$$

where Φ is an ideal random permutation.

This method not only reduces the amount of information exchange between Base Station (BS) and Mobile Stations (MSs), but also greatly reduces the memory cost.

In generation of interleaver, if the intermediate variables like Φ^2, $(\Phi^2)^2$, are not stored, then for generating the interleaving sequence for the kth user needs (k-1) cycles. Even if the intermediate values of the stored as stated in the paper with reference [2], it is mentioned that a maximum of (n-1) cycles are needed for generating, if $k = 2^n$.

If the no. of users is too large, let us say for the 96th user, we have to wait for 95 cycles for the interleaving sequence, which is very time consuming.

In this paper, we examine a Tree Based Interleaver (TBI) to alleviate this concern.

4 Tree Based Interleaver

The Tree Based Interleaver is basically aimed to minimize the computational complexity and memory requirement that occurs in power interleaver and random interleavers respectively.

In a Tree Based Interleaver generation, two randomly generated interleavers are chosen, let Π_1 and Π_2 is the two randomly selected interleavers. These interleavers are tested to have zero cross correlation between them. The combinations of these two interleavers in a particular fashion as shown in the figure 2 are used as interleaving masks for the users.

The allocations of the interleaving masks follow the tree format. The interleaving masking diagram is shown upon fourteen users for simplicity. It is clearly shown through the figure that, for obtaining the interleaving sequence of the 14th user, it needs only 2 cycles of clock, as compared to thirteen cycles needed in case of master random interleaver method.

$$\Pi_{14} = \Pi_2\,(\,\Pi_2\,(\Pi_2)).$$

The memory required by the Tree Based Interleaver generation method is only slightly more than that required for master random interleaver generation method [2].

In Tree Based Interleaver tree, initially two master interleavers are selected randomly with zero cross correlation. The data related to first and second user is interleaved according to these master interleavers. The subsequent interleavers are decided based on tree which is based on tree algorithm. In the tree algorithm, the even users are allotted the space on downside while odd users are placed upside on the tree respectively. If the tree algorithm is known at the receiver, the interleaver for any particular user can be calculated immediately and its data can be retrieved easily.

Table 1. Type Sizes for Paper Comparison of the computation complexity in terms of no. of cycles required to obtain the interleaving mask

User Number	Tree Based Interleaver Generation	Master Random Interleaver Generation
2	0	1
6	1	5
14	2	13
30	3	29
62	4	61
126	5	125

For Tree Based Interleaver:
$$=ceil\ (log2\ (i))$$
Ceil(x) rounds the elements of x towards infinity.

For Master Random Interleaver:
$$= i$$
where i is user number.

The TBI scheme reduces the computational complexity that occurs in the power interleaving scheme. It is shown by the help of a table below. The results in the table I am shown if the intermediate variables are not stored.

The mechanism involved in generation of user specific interleavers is shown in figure 2. The two randomly selected interleavers are solely responsible for generation of other interleavers related to other users.

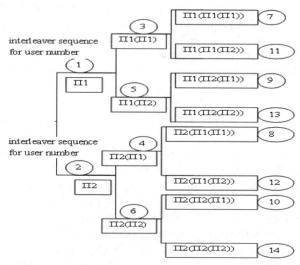

Fig. 2. Interleaving Figure mask allocation for the proposed Tree Based Interleaving scheme

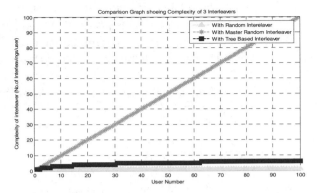

Fig. 3. Graph Showing Computational Complexity between Random Interleaver, Power Interleaver, and Tree Based Interleaver

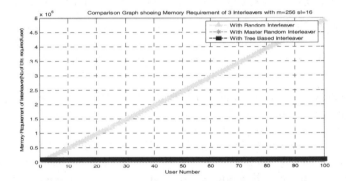

Fig. 4. Graph Showing Memory Requirement between Random Interleaver, Power Interleaver, and Tree Based Interleaver

The Tree Based Interleaving scheme is extremely efficient for reduction of computational complexity as compared to that in Master Random Interleaving scheme [2] as shown in figure3.

The Memory requirement of Tree Based Interleaver is extremely low as compared to that of the Random Interleaver, while is slightly high if compared with master random interleaver [2], as shown in figure 4. The memory requirement is for all the interleavers are shown below,

Memory required for Random Interleaver = $n*cl*log2\ (cl)$.
Memory required for Master Random Interleaver = $cl*log2\ (cl)$.
Memory required for Tree Based Interleaver = $2*\ cl*log2\ (cl)$.
where cl is chip lengh.

5   Simulation Results

For simplicity, assume IDMA system with BPSK signaling in single path AWGN channels and $h_k=1$, $\forall$ k. Without loss of generality, a uniform C_{REP} {+1, -1, +1, -1, --------}

is used with spread length sl =16, for all users and 20 iterations. In figure 5, uncoded IDMA cases are considered, i.e., without any forward error correction (C_{FEC}) coding. The data length is 256 bits is used, for an uncoded system. In figure 6, Memory-2 Rate-1/2 Convolutional code is used. The data length used in the coded system is 64.

From these two figures, the performances of IDMA scheme is similar for random and tree based interleavers, while on the front of computational complexity, the tree based interleaver is outperforming the master random interleaver while having very small hike when compared with random interleaver.

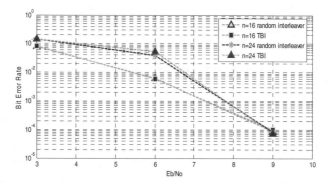

Fig. 5. Comparison of uncoded IDMA systems in single path AWGN channels, using both random and TBI with different no. of users

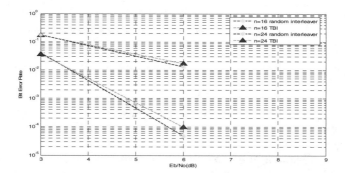

Fig. 6. Comparison of coded IDMA systems in single path AWGN channels, using both random and TBI with different no. of users

In case of memory requirement, tree based interleaver which means that the proposed Tree Based Interleaver is far better than random interleaver while having slight increment when compared with master random interleaver. So, we may conclude that Tree Bases Interleaver may replace the random interleaver and master random interleaver.

6   Conclusion

The proposed 'Tree Based Interleavers' are easy to generate and they are better than the random interleavers in terms of memory cost problems. The TBI will be better than master random interleaver in terms of computational complexity. The proposed interleavers can take the place of the random and master random interleaver techniques without performance loss.

References

1. Ping, L., Liu, L., Wu, K., Leung, W.K.: Interleave-Division Multiple-Access. IEEE Trans. Wireless Commun. 5, 938–947 (2006)
2. Wu, H., Ping, L., Perotti, A.: User-specific chip-level interleaver design for IDMA systems. IEEE Elec. Lett. 42(4) (February 2006)
3. Ping, L., Liu, L.: Analysis and design of IDMA systems based on SNR evolution and power allocation. In: Proc. VTC 2004, Fall, Los Angles, CA (September 2004)
4. Bie, Z., Wu, W.: PEG Algorithm Based Interleavers Design for IDMA System. In: Proceedings of IEEE 41st Annual Conference, pp. 480–483 (March 2007)
5. Liu, L., Leung, W.K., Ping, L.: Simple chip-by-chip multi-user detection for CDMA systems. In: Proc. IEEE VTC, Spring, Korea, pp. 2157–2161 (April 2003)

Enhancement of QoS in 802.11e for Different Traffics

P. Hemanth, D. Shankar, and P. Jayakrishanan

School of Electrical Sciences, VIT University, Vellore 632 014, India
hemanth_guna@yahoo.com, itzdshankar@yahoo.com,
pajayak@gmail.com

Abstract. This paper presents how Enhanced Quality of Service (QoS) in IEEE802.11e is achieved by providing different traffic types with different priorities to access the radio channel. Treating all traffics (voice, video and data) equally without considering the individual characteristics such as delay, jitter and datadrop of each application is not appropriate. The access method in IEEE 802.11e is called Hybrid Coordination Function and combines functions from both the DCF and the PCF. The EDCF parameter set defines the priorities in medium access by setting individual interframe spaces , contention windows (CW), Arbitrary IFS and many other parameters per AC. Wireless LAN with QoS stations (QSATs) for different traffic types under different network traffic loads has been designed and simulated using OPNET. Performance metrics of QoS, like delay, throughput, datadrop, and retransmission attempt is evaluated.

1 Introduction

The demand for Wireless LAN (WLAN) applications is increasing in public areas like offices and airports because of easy deployment, high mobility and high transmission speeds. For example, a conference call or other real-time services require less delay than a file downloading application. The various user applications with delay and packet loss tolerance are given in Figure 1 [7]. Extensive research is being carried out to increase data rates and for providing QoS of wireless networks to values comparable with wired networks. The emerging technologies for WLANs are defined by the IEEE802.11 standards [2], which started by 802.11b with physical layer (PHY) data rates of up to 11 Mbps and were enhanced in 802.11a/g [3] to provide up to 54 Mbps by using Orthogonal Frequency Division Multiplexing (OFDM).

The fundamental access method of the IEEE802.11 MAC is a DCF known as carrier sense multiple accesses with collision avoidance in the contention period. There is no priority for the real time traffics in this access method. All stations compete for the channel with the same priority so we go for PCF. The IEEE802.11 MAC may also incorporate an optional access method called a PCF, which is only usable on infrastructure network configurations in contention free period.

To solve this problem, the IEEE802.11e draft [1] defines MAC enhancements to support LAN applications with different QoS requirements. The access method in 802.11e is called the Hybrid Coordination Function and the HCF uses a contention based channel access method called the Enhanced DCF (EDCF), concurrently with a polled channel access mechanism based on PCF.

V. Garg, R. Wattenhofer, and K. Kothapalli (Eds.): ICDCN 2009, LNCS 5408, pp. 408–413, 2009.
© Springer-Verlag Berlin Heidelberg 2009

Fig. 1. G.1010- Mapping of user-centric QoS requirements

This paper will briefly review the main features and functions of the IEEE802.11 standard in section 2. Traffic Differentiation and EDCF mechanism is described in 3. Simulation environment is described in 4 and performance comparison between DCF, EDCF, n-EDCF is given in section 5. The conclusion is stated in section 6.

2   Over View of IEEE802.11 MAC

DCF defines a basic access mechanism and an optional RTS/CTS MAC mechanism. A station with a frame to transmit monitors the channel activities until an idle period equal to a Distributed Inter-Frame Space (DIFS) is detected. After that the backoff time counter is decremented in terms of slot time as long as the channel is sensed as idle. The counter is suspended when a transmission is detected on the channel, and resumed with the old remaining backoff counter when the channel is sensed as idle again for more than a DIFS. The station transmits its frame when the backoff timer reaches zero. For each new transmission attempt, the backoff interval is uniformly chosen from the range [0; CW-1] in terms of time slots, where CW is the current backoff contention window size, and is clearly described in reference [4].

Time bounded multimedia applications (e.g., voice over IP, video conferencing) require certain bandwidth, delay, and jitter guarantees. The DCF will treat all Traffic with same priority. There is no differentiation mechanism to provide better service for real time multimedia traffic than for best effort traffic applications.

3   Mechanism of IEEE802.11e

Interpretation of User Priority and Backoff Procedure:
Outgoing MSDUs with UP values 0 through 7 are handled by MAC entities at STAs in accordance with the UP and are identical to the IEEE802.1D priority tags. At the MAC layer there are four queues that specify four access categories (ACs) which has different EDCAF parameter values for access to the medium. The mapping of User Priority to access categories is given in Table 1.

Table 1. UP-to-AC mappings

User Priority (802.1D)	Access Category	Traffic Type
1, 2	AC-BK	Background
0, 3	AC-BE	Best Effort
4, 5	AC-VI	Video
6, 7	AC-VO	Voice

The HCF uses both a contention-based channel access method, called the *enhanced distributed channel access* (EDCA) mechanism for contention-based transfer and a controlled channel access, referred to as the *HCF controlled channel access* (HCCA) mechanism, for contention free transfer. The EDCA mechanism provides differentiated, distributed access to the WM for STAs using eight different UPs. The EDCA mechanism defines four access categories (ACs) that provide support for the delivery of traffic with UPs at the STAs. TXOPs using a set of EDCA parameters from the EDCA Parameter Set element like AIFS[AC], $CW_{min}[AC]$ and $CW_{max}[AC]$ which is different for each AC.

The duration AIFS[AC] is a duration derived from the value AIFSN[AC] by the relation. AIFS[AC] = AIFSN[AC] × aSlotTime + aSIFSTime.

Where AIFSN[AC], aSlotTime and aSIFSTime are physical channel dependent. On specific slot boundaries, each EDCAF initiate the transmission of a frame exchange sequence, or decrement the backoff timer, or invoke the backoff procedure due to an internal collision, or do nothing for that access function.

EDCAF shall initiate a transmission sequence if there is a frame available for transmission, and the backoff timer for that EDCAF has a value of zero, and initiation of a transmission sequence is not allowed to commence at this time for an EDCAF of higher UP. EDCAF shall decrement the backoff timer if the backoff timer for that EDCAF has a nonzero value.

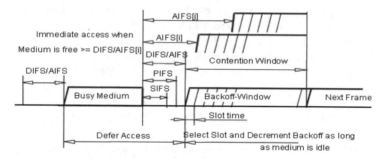

Fig. 2. AIFS and Backoff Time Contend for Channel Access in EDCF

EDCAF shall invoke the backoff procedure due to an internal collision if there is a frame available for transmission, and the backoff timer for that EDCAF has a value of zero, and initiation of a transmission sequence is allowed to commence at this time for an EDCAF of higher UP. EDCAF shall do nothing if none of the above actions is taken. Each EDCAF shall maintain a variable CW[AC], which shall be initialized to the value of the parameter $CW_{min}[AC]$.

CW[AC] = AIFS[AC] + Backoff Time[AC]. The Contention Window (CW) is used to determine the number of slot times in the backoff period. Like the AIFS, CW is AC specific. Backoff Time[AC] = Random[AC] × aSlotTime The Random[AC] is a pseudorandom integer drawn from a uniform distribution over the interval [0, CW[AC]], where $CW_{min}[AC]$ <= CW[AC] <= $CW_{max}[AC]$ [5]. The initial value of CW[AC], or the reset of CW[AC] after a successful transmission attempt, is $CW_{min}[AC]$.EDCA mechanism timing relationships is shown in Figure 2 [1].

4 Simulation of IEEE 802.11e for QSTAs Using OPNET

The network consists of eight Adhoc QSTAs which generates four equal traffics of voice, video, besteffort and background. The OPNET Modeler standard node model wlan_station_adv is used to develop IEEE802.11e model. The MAC process model is developed based on the OPNET standard process model *wlan_mac_hcf* which will describe the functionality of enhanced MAC for QoS.

Simulations are carried out using the OPNET standard model with and without QoS. The Network Traffic load is set as 8QSTA* 3Mbps=24Mbps (6Mbps per AC). The network model is shown in Figure 3. Simulations are run over each of the eight PHY modes of 802.11a, 6, 9, 12, 18, 24, 36, 48 and 54Mbps. The simulation is also carried for different loads 12, 24, and 36 Mbps by changing the number of nodes 4, 8 and 12 respectively. The length of each packet is 1500 bytes and the interarrival time has a 4ms exponential distribution. So the data rate for each node is 3Mbps. The table 2 will give EDCA parameters values that are set in OPNET while simulation.

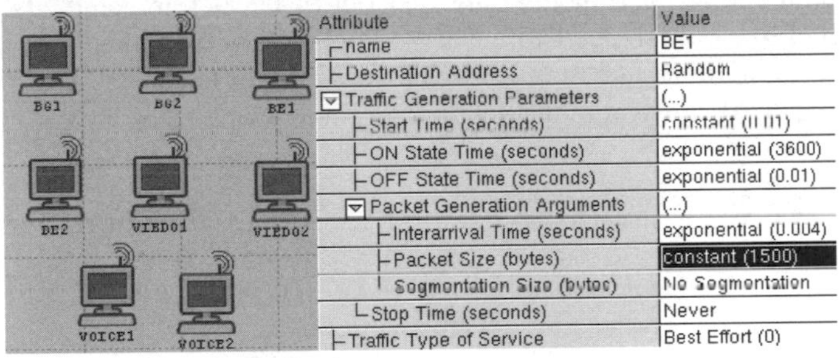

Fig. 3. Network Model and Packet Generation Arguments

Table 2. EDCA Parameter values

AC	AIFSN	CWmin	CWmax
AC_VO	2	3: (aCWmin+1)/4-1	7: (aCWmin+1)/2-1
AC_VI	2	7: (aCWmin+1)/2-1	15: aCWmin
AC_BE	3	15: aCWmin	1023: aCWmax
AC_BK	7	15: aCWmin	1023: aCWmax

5 Performance Evaluation

A. Delay and Datadrop Performance
The major performance metrics of QoS will include Delay and Datadrop. Since traffic generation rate is much greater than the physical channel speed large number of packets will be discarded. Figure 4 illustrate the delay and datadrop of each AC in the Adhoc network with eight QSTAs over eight PHY speeds. When the network operates less than 24Mbps PHY speeds i.e., in overloaded scenarios, AC_VO and AC_VI delay is less than the DCF. The data dropped is less for voice and video than besteffort and background and decreased to zero when PHY speed increases.

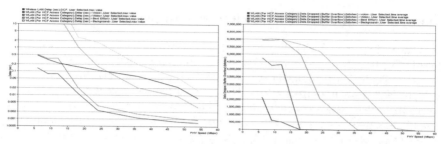

Fig. 4. Delay and Datadrop over 8 PHY modes

Figure 5 gives Queue Size for each AC and Retransmission Attempts in EDCF and DCF mode over 8 PHY speeds. The retransmission attempts mean the number of retries a QSTA makes to successfully transmit a packet, or if a packet is dropped because of reaching the retry limit. In the busy network, among 10 packets to be transmitted in EDCF mode, there are 6 packets on average that need one retransmission attempt. While in DCF mode, only four out of ten is retransmitted. The highest priority traffic, like conference calls, which is delay sensitive, always enjoys a better service; data applications like the file downloading might not work at all with a heavy loading of higher AC present in the network.

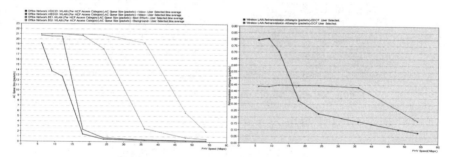

Fig. 5. ACs Queue Size and Retransmission Attempt over 8 PHY modes

When a TXOP is obtained to QSTA we can transmit more than one frame which will give better performance of delay when compared to single packet transmission. EDCA mechanism will transmit single frame, n-EDCA means the TXOP limit is set as more than one frame. As shown in Figure 6 the n-EDCA has less delay over EDCA in both voice and video.

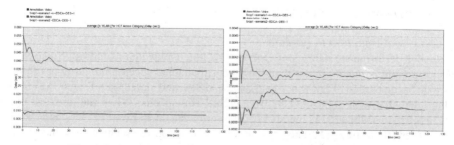

Fig. 6. Delay of video and voice with n-EDCA and EDCA TXOPs

B. Simulation Results with Different loads

In this three simulation scenarios the PHY speed is set as constant (6Mbps), and traffic load generated is 12, 24, and 36Mbps for 4, 8, and 12 QSTAs respectively. Since all are overload conditions the datadrop is much higher. Even then the delay and throughput performance of voice and video is very good when compared to the besteffort and background traffics as shown in Figure 7 with scenarios on x-axis.

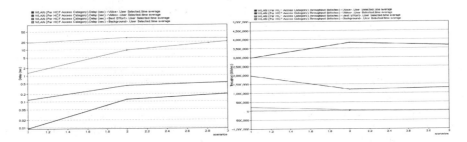

Fig. 7. Delays and Throughputs of voice, video, BE and BG

From simulation results it is clear that highest priority traffic, like conference calls, which is delay sensitive, always enjoys a better QoS. It also shows the improved performance over the mechanisms that is proposed in [4],[5]and[6] and more realistic.

6   Conclusions

In this paper, the enhanced MAC for QoS in IEEE 802.11e model developed using the OPNET Modeler was presented. Our two simulations models (i.e., different PHY speeds and diff QSTA) showed that this is an effective improvement on the ability to support low delay services as compared to the Legacy MAC and more realistic. The access to radio channel by the higher priority traffic is much more aggressive than lower priority. Higher priority traffic benefited, while lower priority traffic suffered.

References

1. IEEE 802.11e/D6.0, Draft Amendment to IEEE Std 802.11, 1999 Edition: Medium Access Control (MAC) Quality of Service (QoS) Enhancements (November 2005)
2. IEEE Std. 802.11-1999, Part 11: Wireless LAN MAC and Physical Layer (PHY) Specifications, Reference number ISO/IEC 8802-11:1999(E), edition 1999 (1999)
3. IEEE Std. 802-11a, IEEE Standard for Wireless LAN MAC and Physical Layer (PHY) Specifications: High-Speed Physical Layer in the 5 GHz Band (September 1999)
4. Gu, D., Zhang, J.: Mitsubishi Electric Research Laboratories, QoS Enhancement in IEEE802.11 Wireless Local Area Networks. IEEE Communications Magazine (June 2003)
5. Choi, S., Prado, J., Shankar, S.: IEEE 802.11e Contention-Based Channel Access (EDCF) Performance Evaluation. In: Proc. IEEE ICC 2003, Anchorage, Alaska, USA (May 2003)
6. Mangold, S., Choi, S.: Analysis of IEEE 802.11e for QoS Support in Wireless LANs. IEEE Wireless Communications (December 2003)
7. ITU-T G.1010. End-user multimedia QoS categories (2001)

Flooding-Assisted Threshold Assignment for Aggregate Monitoring in Sensor Networks*

Ali Abbasi[1], Ahmad Khonsari[1,2], and Mohammad Sadegh Talebi[2]

[1] ECE Department, University of Tehran, Iran
[2] School of Computer Science, IPM, Iran
a.abbasi@ece.ut.ac.ir, {ak,mstalebi}@ipm.ir

Abstract. The research community has witnessed a large interest in monitoring large scale distributed systems. In these applications typically we wish to monitor a global system condition which is defined as a function of local network elements parameters. In this paper, we address *Aggregate Threshold Queries* in sensor networks, which are used to detect when an aggregate value of all sensor measurements crosses a predetermined threshold. The major constraint in designing monitoring applications is reducing the amount of communication burden which is the dominant factor of energy drain in wireless sensor networks. In this study, we address the aggregate threshold monitoring problem by proposing a distributed algorithm to set local thresholds on each sensor node so as to minimize the probability of global polling. We adopt the FPTAS optimization formulation of the problem [2] and propose a distributed algorithm as the solution to the problem. Simulation results demonstrate the validity of the proposed distributed algorithm in attaining very close performance as the centralized schema.

1 Introduction

In recent years, with the abundance of emerging large scale distributed systems such as sensor networks, and peer to peer networks, monitoring scenarios is progressively more considered vital to track these systems. In monitoring either we are interested in supervising the network itself (e.g. traffic engineering, routing optimization, anomaly detection in data networks), or environment that network deployed in it (e.g. wildlife behavior, moving objects in sensor networks). Network monitoring includes measuring system parameters to react to different network conditions. There are two ways of getting knowledge from the network; the first is to send requests into the network to poll all relevant information. Another option is that all network elements push all possibly important readings to the management station. The nature of network monitoring applications imposes specific requirements on design of monitoring algorithm: 1- the algorithm should provide real time detection of noteworthy events 2- The algorithm must be scalable to large number of nodes. 3- The detection process should incur minimum communication in the network. This is a very critical requirement in

---

* This work is partially supported by Iran Telecommunication research Center (ITRC).

V. Garg, R. Wattenhofer, and K. Kothapalli (Eds.): ICDCN 2009, LNCS 5408, pp. 414–424, 2009.
© Springer-Verlag Berlin Heidelberg 2009

sensor networks, because communication is the primary source of energy consumption in these networks. Sensors are powered by batteries and replacing these if not impossible is usually cumbersome. It is also important in wired networks. In these Networks, the monitoring application should not hamper the normal operation of the network. Thereby, a challenge in monitoring applications is to devise plans to reduce communication while fulfilling application requirements. A common method is to install local constraints or filters at remote sources to filter out unnecessary updates. Local constraints should have the property such that preserving all of them ensures that there was not any anomalous event. Each new measurement is compared to the filter and in case it violates (exits) the corresponding range of the filter an update is sent to the base station. Apparently efficient decomposition of global system constraint into local constraint has a great impact on reducing communication. Filter setting is dependent on a number of parameters including the associated cost with sending an update from each node to the management station and the changing patterns of measurements. Often the monitoring task is the need to detect when a function of individual network element readings crosses a given threshold. Typically, monitored functions are aggregate functions like SUM, or AVG which gives global insights concerning the state of the network. These functions are specially important in sensor networks where individual sensor readings are inherently unreliable and don't convey much information. Consider the following queries:

- Report when the number of enemy troops detected in a region of the network crosses 20.
- Report when variance of temperature in a building crosses 3.

Aggregate functions like SUM, AVG are linear functions of individual sensor readings, thus the global property of $\sum_i A_i T_i \leq T$ can be decomposed to a set of $X_i \leq T_i$ constraints which checked locally at each node. In this work, we concentrate on the problem of determining optimal values fo T_i's. Previous works [2] [18] assume that the monitoring station computes the optimal thresholds based on individual nodes probability distribution functions and assigns thresholds for nodes. Thus each node should update its histogram constructed over recent measurements either periodically or based on a change detection algorithm to the base station. But there is limitation on the applicability of such an approach for sensor networks. The structure of such networks has necessitated the design of asynchronous, distributed and fault-tolerant computation and information exchange algorithms [5].

This is mainly because of sensor networks operational constraints: (i) the network topology may not be completely known to the nodes of the network, (ii) nodes may join or leave the network (even expire), so that the network topology itself may change. These issues specially occurs in mobile sensor networks. In this work, we propose a distributed algorithm for optimal threshold assignment so as to minimize the probability of global system polling.

The remainder of the paper is organized as follows: Section 2 reviews related works. Section 3 defines the system model and problem definition. Section 4 provides the optimal solution for the threshold assignment problem. Section 5 presents a distributed threshold assignment algorithm based on the problem's optimal solution. Section 6 validates experimental evaluation of the proposed method. Finally section 7 concludes the study.

2   Related Works

In recent years, continuous query processing for monitoring distributed data streams has attracted much research. Different query types have been mentioned in this environment includes top-k[3], quantiles[7], joins[6]. Monitoring aggregate threshold queries in networks initially mentioned by the pioneering work of Raz et al. [12]. They introduced installing local mathematical constraints at remote sites and present a simple approach for threshold assignment assuming uniform data distributions of system variables. Olston et al. [18] suggested an adaptive filter based approach for tracking error bounded values of aggregate functions. According to the precision specified in continuous query filters are assigned for local values of data objects. Keralpera et al.[16] presented several algorithm for static and adaptive threshold setting for monitoring thresholded counts queries and analyzed the communication complexity of each algorithm. Sharfman et al[20] introduced a geometric approach for monitoring arbitrary threshold functions. Recent work of kashyap et al.[14] considers the problem of non-zero slack threshold assignment which adaptively dedicate fraction of total threshold to monitoring node to absorb small local threshold crossing that eliminate the need to global system polling. All the above works assume centralized threshold computation and assignment but in this paper we propose a distributed algorithm for optimal threshold setting.

3   System Model and Problem Formulation

We assume that there is a base station being responsible for monitoring the network. The base station disseminates queries to sensors and responds to user queries. Each sensor node i continuously reads the requested local phenomenon x_i which is in the range $[0, M_i]$ at a fixed sampling rate. Amongst the local phenomenon are temperature, humidity, light, etc. The measured values of all sensors can be represented in a vector of values $\mathbf{x} = (x_i, i = 1..n)$.

The goal is to detect when the aggregate value of all the measurements $\sum_{i=1}^{n} A_i x_i$ crosses a predetermined threshold T. A common method to reduce communication is to install local constraints or filters (in the form of an interval $I_i = [0, T_i]$) at remote sources. Local constraints setting should maintain the property that preserving all of them, ensures that the aggregate value has not exceeded the threshold (covering property). Each sensor i after measuring the new value of x_i, checks condition $L_i \equiv (x_i \in [0, T_i])$, and the condition upon being violated, an update is sent to the base station to initiate global aggregate computation. Using such a method, vast amount of updates are filtered out at the source and are not transmitted to the base station. The efficiency of this approach is largely dependent on filter setting method. But what values should we choose for T_i's? Selection of values must satisfy the global property

$\sum_{i=1}^{n} A_i T_i \leq T$ to conform covering property. However, this equation leads to great flexibility in choosing T_i's. In this respect, we face to another question: what is the best selection?

We aim at maximizing the communication cost via minimizing the probability of global polling. Every local filter violation leads to global computation, thus we should maximize the probability of preserving all local constraints $\max F(x_1 \leq T_1, \ldots, x_n \leq T_n)$, where F is the joint cumulative frequency distribution over all the sensors. Computing the multi-dimensional histograms is somewhat cumbersome in terms of communication burden, and hence we consider more communication convenient assumption of independence between sensor's data distributions. With this simplifying assumption, we come up to the optimization problem

$$\max_{\mathbf{T}} \prod_{i=1}^{n} F_i(T_i) \tag{1}$$

subject to:

$$\sum_{i=1}^{n} A_i T_i \leq T \tag{2}$$

where $\mathbf{T} = (T_i, i - 1..n)$ is the vector of local thresholds. It has been proven that local threshold selection problem is *NP-hard* [2] wherein the authors have introduced a centralized scheme, referred to as FPTAS. This centralized scheme was used to solve the problem within ϵ relative error for arbitrarily small ϵ. The solution was based on the assumption that all the values of $F_i(T_i)$ are integral powers of a constant α, which is assumed to be slightly greater than 1. Thus, each $F_i(T_i)$ will correspond to some α^{r_i} and maximizing $\prod_{i=1}^{n} F_i(T_i)$ will be equivalent to maximizing $\alpha^{\sum r_i}$. If $T_i(r)$ denotes the local threshold value such that

$$\alpha^{r_i} \leq F_i(T_i(r_i)) < \alpha^{r_i+1} \tag{3}$$

the problem becomes

$$\max_{\mathbf{r}} \sum_{i-1}^{n} r_i \tag{4}$$

subject to:

$$\sum_{i=1}^{n} A_i T_i(r_i) \leq T \tag{5}$$

where $\mathbf{r} = (r_i, i = 1..n)$ is the vector representation of powers.

This problem is a variant of *knapsack problem* that can be solved using dynamic programming.

In order for (4) to admit a unique maximizer, F_i must satisfy the following assumptions:

A1: F_i is positive, strictly increasing and twice-continuously differentiable.
A2: F_i is log-concave, i.e. $\log F_i$ is a concave function.

Indeed, we assume that optimization variable, $\mathbf{r}$, belongs to a domain in which F_i satisfies the abovementioned assumptions.

4   Optimal Solution

In this section, we solve problem (4). Problem (4) is a constrained problem, whose constraint (5) is coupled across the network. Such a constrained optimization problem can be efficiently solved using Interior Point Method [5], which necessitates the coordination among possibly all nodes of the networks, which is undesirable or infeasible. However, in the context of wireless ad-hoc and sensor networks, we are interested in distributive algorithms to solve (4).

Towards this end, we aim at solving the problem (4) through its dual. In the sequel, we proceed to derive the dual problem of (4) and then present a distributively iterative algorithm as the solution to the dual problem.

We start by writing the Lagrangian of problem (4), as follows

$$L(\mathbf{r}, \mu) = \sum_{i=1}^{n} r_i - \mu \left(\sum_{i=1}^{n} A_i T_i(r_i) - T \right) \tag{6}$$

where $\mu > 0$ is the Lagrange multiplier associated with constraint (5). Using Karush-Kuhn-Tucker (KKT) conditions for convex optimization, to find optimal powers $\mathbf{r}^*$, we should find the stationary points of the Lagrangian and satisfy complementary slackness conditions. The complementary slackness conditions for optimal primal variable $\mathbf{r}^*$ and dual variable μ^*, are

$$\mu^* \geq 0; \tag{7}$$

$$\sum_{i=1}^{n} A_i T_i(r_i^*) \leq T; \tag{8}$$

$$\mu^* \left(\sum_{i=1}^{n} A_i T_i(r_i^*) - T \right) = 0 \tag{9}$$

In order to find the stationary points of the Lagrangian, we solve

$$\nabla L(\mathbf{r}^*, \mu^*) = \mathbf{0} \tag{10}$$

where $\mathbf{0}$ is a vector with all zero. For the ith element of (10) we have

$$\frac{\partial L}{\partial r_i} = 1 - \mu A_i \frac{dT_i(r_i)}{dr_i} \tag{11}$$

From (3), recall that $T_i(r_i)$ is selected so that $\alpha^{r_i} \leq F_i(T_i(r_i)) < \alpha^{r_i+1}$, also, recall that α is a constant slightly greater than 1. Therefore, the lower and upper bounds of $F_i(T_i(r_i))$ are sufficiently close to each other, leading us to approximate $F_i(T_i(r_i))$, using the concept of geometric mean as following:

$$F_i(T_i(r_i)) \approx \sqrt{\alpha^{r_i} \alpha^{r_i+1}}$$
$$\approx \sqrt{\alpha} \alpha^{r_i} \tag{12}$$

Such an approximation would also be done through the concept of average mean, which for $\alpha = 1 + \delta$, $\delta \to 0$ gives the same results, as in (12).

Recalling the monotonicity assumption of F_i, it admits a unique inverse, which yields the explicit expression for T_i as

$$T_i(r_i) = F_i^{-1}(\alpha^{r_i}\sqrt{\alpha}) \tag{13}$$

Substituting (13) in (11), yields

$$\frac{\partial L}{\partial r_i} = 1 - \mu A_i \frac{dF_i^{-1}}{dr_i}(\alpha^{r_i}\sqrt{\alpha}) \tag{14}$$

$$= 1 - \mu A_i \frac{d}{dr_i}(\alpha^{r_i}\sqrt{\alpha})\left.\frac{dF_i^{-1}}{dr_i}\right|_{\alpha^{r_i}\sqrt{\alpha}}$$

$$= 1 - \mu A_i \alpha^{r_i}\sqrt{\alpha}\ln\alpha\left.\frac{dF_i^{-1}}{dr_i}\right|_{\alpha^{r_i}\sqrt{\alpha}} \tag{15}$$

Setting (15) to zero and doing some algebraic manipulation, gives an explicit expression for the optimal exponent $\mathbf{r}^*$, in terms of optimal Lagrange multiplier μ^* and other network parameters. For the sake of presentation, we define

$$G_i(z) = \left.\frac{dF_i^{-1}}{dr_i}\right|_z \tag{16}$$

Substituting $G_i(.)$ in (15), we come up to the following implicit equation to obtain $\mathbf{r}^*$

$$\alpha^{r_i^*} G_i(\alpha^{r_i^*}\sqrt{\alpha}) = \frac{1}{\mu^* A_i \ln\alpha\sqrt{\alpha}} \tag{17}$$

In order to solve problem (4) through its dual, we need to obtain the Lagrange dual function, or simply dual function. The Lagrange dual function $D(\mu)$ is defined as the maximum of the Lagrangian $L(\mathbf{r},\mu)$ over the primal variable $\mathbf{r}$, for a given μ. Thus, $D(\mu)$ can be expressed as

$$D(\mu) = \max_{\mathbf{r}} L(\mathbf{r},\mu) \tag{18}$$

Based on the results of the KKT condition mentioned above, maximization in (18) is already solved with $\mathbf{r}^*$ given by (17), which results in

$$D(\mu) = L(\mathbf{r}^*,\mu) \tag{19}$$

The dual problem is formulated as

$$\min_{\mu} D(\mu) \equiv \min_{\mu} L(\mathbf{r}^*,\mu) \tag{20}$$

$$\text{subject to:}$$

$$\mu \geq 0 \tag{21}$$

Dual problem defined above can be solved using iterative methods. In order to obtain a distributed algorithm, we solve the dual problem (20) using Gradient Projection Method. To solve the dual problem, Gradient Projection Method adjusts μ in opposite direction to the Gradient of dual function, i.e. $\nabla D(\mu)$. Precisely speaking, in the kth iteration step, $\mu^{(k)}$ is updated as follows

$$\mu^{(k+1)} = \left[\mu^{(k)} - \gamma \frac{dD(\mu^{(k)})}{d\mu} \right]^+ \tag{22}$$

where $[z]^+ = \max\{z, 0\}$ and γ is a sufficiently small constant step size. Using the Danskin's Theorem [4], the derivative of $D(\mu)$ is given by

$$\frac{dD(\mu)}{d\mu} = T - \sum_{i=1}^{n} A_i T_i(r_i) \tag{23}$$

Substituting (23) in (22), yields

$$\mu^{(k+1)} = \left[\mu^{(k)} + \gamma \left(\sum_{i=1}^{n} A_i T_i(r_i^{(k)}) - T \right) \right]^+ \tag{24}$$

where $r_i^{(k)}$ is the solution to (17) for a given $\mu^{(k)}$. In this equation, γ is chosen sufficiently small so as to guarantee the convergence.

In the economics literature, Lagrange multiplier or dual variable, μ is called *shadow price* [15] and accordingly, (24) is called shadow price update. This stems from the interpretation of its role in solving the primal problem via its dual. From (17) it's apparent that $\mathbf{r}^*$ is a decreasing function of μ; therefore μ can be construed as the price which must be paid by node i to achieve the threshold $T_{(r_i)}$. As the nature of such a price is hidden to the sources from the primal problem perspective, it is called *shadow price*.

(17) and (24) can be utilized as an iterative solution to problem (20) and thereby (4). At each iteration step k, dual variable μ will be updated based on the history of itself and the primal variables $\mathbf{r}$. Then, it would be utilized by to update primal variable $\mathbf{r}$, accordingly. Therefore, after spending enough iteration steps, primal and dual variables tends to primal-optimal $\mathbf{r}^*$ and dual-optimal μ^*, respectively.

Based on the above iterative solution, we propose a distributed algorithm as a solution to threshold selection problem. We deffer the algorithm until the Section 5.

5   Distributed Threshold Assignment Algorithm

In this section, we propose a distributed algorithm based on the iterative solutions obtained in Section 4. Considering (24) and (17), it is clear that the iterative solution to problem (4) can be regarded as a distributed algorithm.

The algorithm is devised by directly utilizing the update equation (17) and (17), over the network. Clearly, for μ to be updated using (24), the knowledge about the evolution of all nodes in the network is required. Although the nature of solution is distributive, this is a global information of the network and can be elaborated using well-known algorithms such as Flooding, etc.

In particular, each sensor i in the iteration step k benefits from all other nodes' current power $\mathbf{r}_{-i}$'s, thanks to Flooding-like algorithms, to update the current shadow price $\mu^{(k)}$. Since all other nodes have access to such information too, they will obtain the same value for $\mu^{(k+1)}$ and therefore, we don't introduce additional notation to distinguish between the realized update process.

Upon updating $\mu^{(k)}$, each sensor i calculates its power r_i, accordingly. The above rule will proceed until reaching some predefined notions of convergence.

We will refer to this algorithm as DTA. The DTA Algorithm is stated below.

DTA Distributed Threshold Assignment Algorithm

Initialization
Initialize A_is and T $\forall i = 1..n$.

Main Loop
Do until $\max_i |r_i^{(k+1)} - r_i^{(k)}| < \epsilon$

1. t each sensor node, update the shadow price as following:

$$\mu^{(k+1)} = \left[\mu^{(k)} + \gamma \left(\sum_{i=1}^{n} A_i T_i(r_i^{(k)}) - T \right) \right]^+$$

2. Update r_i according to the following equation:

$$\alpha^{r_i^{(k)}} G_i(\alpha^{r_i^{(k)}} \sqrt{\alpha}) - \frac{1}{\mu_i^{(k+1)} A_i \ln \alpha \sqrt{\alpha}}$$

DTA. Distributed Threshold Assignment Algorithm

6 Experimental Evaluation

We have conducted simulation experiments to evaluate the performance of our proposed algorithm. We verify that the algorithm, locally executed on each node, may indeed achieve the desired global optimal threshold assignment.

In our simulation scenario, we consider a sensor network consisting of 100 sensor nodes which randomly scattered over an area.

We assume that each node i incessantly takes measurements of a physical phenomenon, whose CDF obeys an exponential distribution with the exponent parameter λ_i. Although such a distribution may sound to be of limited interest, it is worth mentioning that many significant real world applications might fall within such a framework. Amongst such applications are monitoring the dwell time of a traffic flow which pursue a Poisson distribution. The corresponding coefficient A_i is assumed to be randomly drawn from a uniform distribution over $[0, 5]$. Step size is chosen to be $\gamma = 1.2$ and the total threshold T is set to 10.

The most significant issues of interest are the evolutions of primal and dual (shadow price) variables. Evolution of assigned thresholds T_is and shadow price

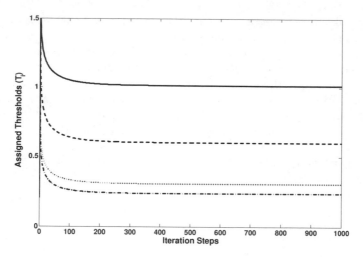

Fig. 1. Evolution of The Assigned Thresholds $T_i(r_i)$ for Some Nodes Using DTA Algorithm

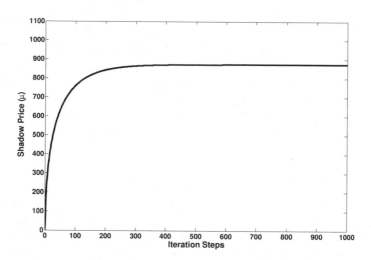

Fig. 2. Evolution of The Shadow Price μ Using DTA Algorithm

μ for DTA Algorithm are depicted in Fig. 1 and 2, respectively. It is apparent from these figures that by spending less than 300 iteration steps, convergence was achieved and thereafter, μ and T_is had intangible variations.

7   Conclusion

There have been many studies exploring various applications of WSNs such as monitoring. In the context of WSNs, we are interested in the design of asynchronous, distributed algorithms for exchanging the information among the sensor nodes. In this paper, we focused on the problem of distributed threshold selection for aggregate threshold monitoring in WSNs. Towards this end, we formulated threshold selection as an optimization problem that considers the cumulative distribution function of distinct monitoring variables. The fundamental objective of the optimization problem was to minimize the probability of global polling. The original problem was non-convex, thus we adopted the so called FPTAS reformulation which was convex and has been solved using a centralized approach. We elaborated their method and solved the problem via its dual so as to achieve a distributed solution. Our distributed solution leads to a distributed algorithm; called DTA Algorithm which acts based on the global evolution of the network information. Such information is gathered by a flooding-like algorithm. The results extracted from the experimental evaluation was promising and demonstrated the achieved performance of the suggested algorithm are quite comparable to the results of the centralized approach.

References

1. Akyildiz, I.F., Su, W., Sankarasubramaniam, Y., Cayirci, E.: A Survey on Sensor Networks. IEEE Communications Magazine 40(8), 102–114 (2002)
2. Aggrawal, S., Deb, S., Naidu, K.V.M., Rastogi, R.: Efficient Detection of Distributed Constraint Violations. In: Proc. of IEEE ICDE, pp. 1320–1324 (2007)
3. Babcock, B., Olston, C.: Distributed Top-k Monitoring. In: Proc. of ACM SIGMOD, pp. 28–39 (2003)
4. Bertsekas, D.: Nonlinear Programming. Athena Scientific (1999)
5. Boyd, S., Ghosh, A., Prabhakar, B., Shah, D.: Gossip Algorithms: Design, Analysis, and Applications. In: Proc. IEEE INFOCOM, pp. 1653–1664 (2005)
6. Cormode, G., Garofalakis, M.: Sketching streams through the net: Distributed approximate query tracking. In: Proc. VLDB, pp. 13–24 (2005)
7. Cormode, G., Garofalakis, M., Muthukrishnan, S., Rastogi., R.: Holistic aggregates in a networked world: Distributed tracking of approximate quantiles. In: Proc. ACM SIGMOD, pp. 25–36 (2005)
8. Cormode, G., Muthurikshnan, S., Yi, K.: Algorithms for Distributed Functional Monitoring. In: Proc. ACM SODA, pp. 1076–1085 (2008)
9. Das, A., Ganguly, S., Garofalakis, M., Rastogi, R.: Distributed set-expression cardinality estimation. In: Proc. VLDB, pp. 312–323 (2004)
10. Deshpande, A., Guestrin, C., Madden, S., Hellerstein, J.M., Hong, W.: Model-Driven Data Acquisition in Sensor Networks. In: Proc. VLDB, pp. 588–599 (2004)
11. Deshpande, A., Guestrin, C., Madden, S.: Using Probabilistic Models for Data Management in Acquisitional Environments. In: Proc. CIDR, pp. 317–328 (2005)
12. Dilman, M., Raz, D.: Efficient Reactive Monitoring. In: Proc. IEEE INFOCOM, pp. 1012–1019 (2001)
13. Jadbabaie, A., Lin, J., Stephen Morse, A.: Coordination of Groups of Mobile Autonomous Agents Using Nearest Neighbor Rules. IEEE Transactions on Automatic Control 48(6), 988–1001 (2003)
14. Kashyap, S., Ramamirtham, J., Rastogi, R., Shukla, P.: Efficient Constraint Monitoring Using Adaptive Thresholds. In: Proc. IEEE ICDE, pp. 526–535 (2006)
15. Kelly, F.P., Maulloo, A., Tan, D.K.H.: Rate Control for Communication Networks: Shadow Prices, Proportional Fairness, and Stability. Operational Research Society 49(3), 237–252 (1998)

16. Keralapura, R., Cormode, G., Ramamirtham, J.: Communication-Efficient Distributed Monitoring of Thresholded Counts. In: Proc. ACM SIGMOD, pp. 289–300 (2006)
17. Kifer, D., Shai, B., Gehrke, J.: Detecting Change in Data Streams. In: Proc. VLDB, pp. 180–191 (2004)
18. Olston, C., Jiang, J., Widom, J.: Adaptive filters for continuous queries over distributed data streams. In: Proc. ACM SIGMOD, pp. 563–574 (2003)
19. Poosala, V., Ioannidis, Y.: Selectivity Estimation Without The Attribute Value Independence Assumption. In: Proc. VLDB, pp. 486–495 (1997)
20. Sharfman, I., Schuster, A., Keren, D.: A Geometric Approach to Monitoring Threshold Functions over Distributed Data Streams. In: Proc. ACM SIGMOD, pp. 301–312 (2006)

A Mechanism to Structure Mission-Aware Interaction in Mobile Sensor Networks

Michel Charpentier, Radim Bartoš, and Swapnil Bhatia

Department of Computer Science,
University of New Hampshire,
Durham, NH, USA
{charpov,rbartos,sbhatia}@cs.unh.edu

Abstract. One of the main appeals of mobile sensors is the variety of environments in which they can operate as an autonomous network. Different environments, however, present different challenges, especially in terms of inter-sensor communication. In sparse environments, it may not be possible to maintain full connectivity at all times, setting off the need for agents to communicate opportunistically when they are close to each other. This, in turn, suggests that communication needs be taken into account in the design of agents' trajectories. In this paper, we introduce a notion of *tour* and *meeting point* as an abstraction of trajectories designed for both sensing and communication, and we study the tradeoffs involved between motion to sense and sample and motion to communicate and interact.

1 Introduction and Motivation

1.1 Motivation

Mobile sensor networks hold tremendous promise as a technology. Thanks to controlled mobility, the network can now be made autonomous and thus, more adaptable to the phenomenon it is deployed to study, making it possible to build and deploy networks that can sense and act in the physical world in programmable ways. Network designers, however, need to consider *sensing*, *motion*, *communication*, and *computation* issues simultaneously, which is a true challenge to mission preparation and deployment. In our broader effort, we are investigating methods that would provide mobile sensor network operators with means to deal with all these features in a unified way.

In this paper, we focus on networks in which mobile agents (or nodes) cooperate towards a common mission and the geographical region in which they operate is vast relative to the number of agents and their communication range. In such networks, inter-agent communication changes from a commodity, used by the system when cooperation is needed, to a limited resource that impacts the network's mission-solving strategy—very much like energy, computational power and the ability to move.

This shift in perspective leads us to reexamine the overall network communication architecture. For instance, mobility makes it difficult to maintain the

V. Garg, R. Wattenhofer, and K. Kothapalli (Eds.): ICDCN 2009, LNCS 5408, pp. 425–436, 2009.
© Springer-Verlag Berlin Heidelberg 2009

structure necessary to the realization of standard communication protocols, while at the same time knowledge of the network's mission can result in a better exploitation of available communication opportunities. As a result, it may not be as beneficial as it was before to maintain a clear separation between communication and computation. We believe that the time has come to look for communication strategies that are better adapted to the new challenges of mobile computing. This paper presents some of our exploratory steps towards such novel communication architectures.

1.2   Contributions

Consider agents with limited communication capabilities, charged with a mission that requires them to interact with each other while sampling vast areas. We assume that when agents move towards each other, they can rely on a local, efficient form of communication. In this context, agent trajectories cannot be designed in terms of sensing duties alone but must take into account communication needs as well. Agent trajectories are thus constrained by their individual tasks (what parts of the space they must explore) as well as their collaborative behavior (what other agents they need to communicate with and when).

As a possible structure to help design such trajectories, this paper defines and studies the notion of a *tour*. Tours involve a combination of motion and communication and can be used to model requirements and tradeoffs between the individual sensing tasks of mobile agents and their collaboration with respect to the mission. Tours are a simple model that can be used to investigate mission-solving strategies in order to assess their compliance with desired performance and overall network behavior.

2   Background

This paper is motivated in part by our past and current efforts in the field of autonomous underwater vehicles (AUVs) [1]. The underwater environment poses numerous challenges. Submerged AUVs typically utilize acoustic links with limited range and bit rates, high error rates, and propagation latencies many orders of magnitude larger than those of radio frequency links. At the same time, AUVs are typically used for sensing missions that span areas that are vast when compared to the communication range. Since nodes must be relatively close for the acoustic data transmission to be successful, mobility of AUVs is the key enabler of communication in such a sparse environment. The cost of AUVs and the cost of deployment prohibits the use of a large number of vehicles. On the other hand, mobility in the underwater environment is free of some of the constraints typical in the ground and air-based mobile sensor networks. Furthermore, modern AUVs are typically equipped with navigational aids that provide them with their absolute location and with precise clocks that facilitate maintaining synchronicity during a mission. As a result, networks of cooperating AUVs provide an important case for the study presented in this paper.

Much of the work in the area of networks operating in a challenging environment has been done under the umbrella of *Disruption/Delay Tolerant Networks* (DTNs). Fall [2] proposes a non-interactive messaging based overlay architecture for DTNs. Ho et al. extends the DTN architecture to sensor networks [3]. There has been significant work in the area of routing protocols for such networks. Zhao et al. [4,5] and Burns et al. [6,7] propose routing protocols that can influence and exploit mobility patterns to improve routing in DTNs. Subramanian et al. propose a utility-driven routing protocol that can optimize a given metric such as delay and deadline violations [8]. The DTN architecture provides a simple message delivery primitive appropriate for intermittent bandwidth-constrained transmission opportunities. Using clever and sophisticated replication heuristics, DTN routing protocols strive to minimize packet delays. However, by design, the DTN architecture is oblivious to the purpose of the network, which is a defining feature of mission-centric networks. We believe that a mission-aware communication subsystem will be able to better utilize the scarce communication opportunities in a mission-centric network.

Underwater communication, an area that has received significant attention in recent years [9,10,11,12], represents a compelling example of networking in a challenging environment. Underwater networking problems are studied at many different levels starting from acoustic communication links all the way to multihop routing in connected underwater networks. The results of our field experiments [13] have shown the importance of proper handling of intermittent connectivity during a mission due to the challenging environment. We have already taken the first steps toward addressing this issue at the vehicle code level [14]. This paper presents some of our initial steps to address the difficulty of designing AUV missions in challenging environments at a more fundamental level.

3   Tours and Meeting Points

3.1   Motion, Sensing, Communication and Computation

We consider networks of mobile sensing agents deployed to perform a mission that involves periodic data acquisition and distributed computation. Agents are charged with the task to monitor (sense, scan, collect data) an area of interest in a periodic way and to compute relevant information from this sensed data in a distributed fashion. We assume that the area is vast compared to the communication capabilities of agents and agents will need to move towards each other in order to communicate efficiently. When they are close enough, agents can rely on local communication mechanisms to form groups, exchange information and compute their new states according to some predetermined algorithm.

When solving these missions, in which effective communication involves movement, the motion of agents must be programmed so they all visit their share of the area of interest *and* they form groups often enough to carry out a distributed computation from the acquired data. We propose to design this combination of motion, sensing, computation and local communication in terms of *tours*.

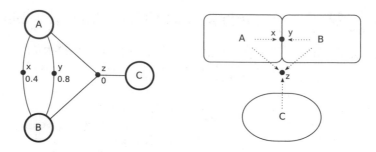

Fig. 1. Tour graph and possible corresponding tour areas and meeting points

A tour is defined by an *area* (to be repeatedly sampled) and a collection of *meeting points* (to be visited by groups of agents). The overall space to be covered by the network is partitioned into several tours and each tour is the responsibility of a single agent. This agent's task is, for each period of the cyclical computation, to sense and sample its tour area while maintaining a schedule of visits to its meeting points in order to exchange information and perform joint computational steps with agents from other tours.

A tour is thus implemented by a trajectory that covers the entire area to sample and returns to the meeting points at regular intervals to interact with other agents. The frequency with which a trajectory visits each meeting point is one of the key parameters of a tour implementation. We denote by t the amount of time between consecutive visits to a given meeting point. Low values of t correspond to trajectories that visit their meeting points many times while scanning the tour area. High values of t correspond to trajectories that complete large amounts of sensing between meetings.

3.2 Tours as Network Building Blocks

Tours can be connected through their meeting points and assembled into a network that implements the desired mission. Formally, such a network of tours is a graph in which the vertices are tours and the edges are meeting points. This graph is both a multigraph (the same tours can be connected through several meeting points) and a hypergraph (meeting points can connect more than two tours). Fig. 1 represents a network that consists of three tours (A, B and C) and three meeting points (x, y and z). The figure also shows a possible physical realization of this network. In this realization, agents[1] A and B monitor adjacent rectangular areas and rely on two meeting points x and y that share the same location in the middle of the side common to the two rectangles. Agent C monitors a circular area and interacts with agents A and B through meeting point z. This point is located outside the tour areas and all three agents will need to leave their assigned area to attend meetings at this point. A given tour graph can have several different physical realizations.

---

[1] Here, "agent A" is used as a shortcut to mean "the agent in charge of tour A".

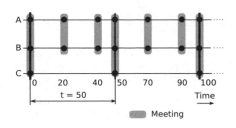

Fig. 2. Schedule of meetings

In a tour connecting graph, each meeting point is labeled with a number between 0 and 1 that specifies when, during the tours, this meeting point must be visited (the labels 0 and 1 are equivalent and both denote the edge of a cycle). This graph is associated with a time-between-visits t that is common to all tours (considerations involved in choosing t are discussed later in the paper). This time-between-visits and the labels together define the schedules that the tour trajectories must implement in order to guarantee that groups of agents will form at meeting points.

For instance, suppose the desired time-between-visits t of the network of Fig. 1 is 50 minutes. This means that all tour trajectories are based on a repetition of a 50 minute cycle of visits. Each 50 minute time slot includes sensing (of some given part of the tour area) as well as visits to the meeting points as specified by the labels. The label 0.4 associated with meeting point x means that this point will be visited by agents A and B at times $0.4 \times 50 = 20$, $(1 + 0.4) \times 50 = 70$, $(2 + 0.4) \times 50 = 120$, etc. Fig. 2 shows what groups of agents are formed at what times during the first 100 minutes in this network.

3.3 Implementing Tours

In our vision, networks are built by assembling tours in accordance with the mission to solve and the strategy and algorithms chosen to solve it. The task of programming the movement of agents so they achieve the desired sensing and interaction is pushed into the tour implementation. Although the details of tour implementation are not the focus of this paper, this section aims to define the implementation problem precisely and present some of the difficulties and tradeoffs that such implementations involve.

A tour-based design of a network results in a desired time-between-visits t and a meeting schedule (in the form of numbers associated with each meeting point). Together with the geometrical definition of the area to be sensed during the tour, these represent the constraints to be satisfied by a tour implementation. The output of a tour implementation process consists of a trajectory that satisfies the following requirements:

- It visits all the meeting points at their specified times. If a meeting point x is labeled with $v_x \in [0, 1]$ and the desired time-between-visits is t, the trajectory must visit this point at times $v_x \times t$, $(1 + v_x) \times t$, $(2 + v_x) \times t$, etc.
- It covers (for sensing and data gathering) the entire tour area as quickly as possible. In other words, the area A of the tour should be visited entirely every $R \times t$, where R is as small as possible.

This trajectory design problem can be thought of as an optimization problem, in which the goal is to minimize R given the other parameters. A tour implementation should attempt to cover as much of the area as possible between meetings because it will allow agents to use more recent samples when they interact with other agents in the course of the distributed computation performed by the network. If, given the best possible R, the duration $R \times t$ between samples is still too high for the given mission, the network will have to use smaller tours and hence more agents, as expected.

3.4   Tradeoff between Agent Interaction and Individual Activities

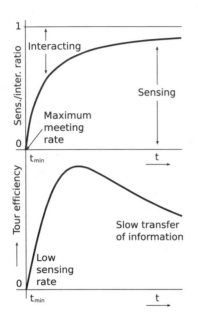

Fig. 3. Sensing / meeting tradeoff

The tradeoff between desired sensing rates, the overall area to monitor and the number of agents is unavoidable and has little to do with tours. Tours, however, involve another, more interesting tradeoff due to the fact that agents have to share their time between sensing and traveling to meeting points. Low values of t, the time-between-visits, means more interaction with other agents, which benefits distributed algorithms in general. However, this also implies that agents need to interrupt their sensing task more often to attend meetings, and this results in a smaller proportion of agent time dedicated to sampling and sensing activities, thus in a lower overall sensing rate and the need for agent to rely on inaccurate (out-of-date) data during meetings. For most missions and associated algorithms, we expect that there will be an optimal time-between-meetings t_{opt}. If known, this optimum can be fed to the tour implementation optimization problem in order to minimize the time to sample the entire tour area.

Fig. 3 illustrates the tradeoff that is involved when deciding on a suitable time-between-visits. As this parameter decreases, agents have to spend more time traveling to meeting points and hence have less time for sensing. There is a minimum time-between-visits t_{min} for which agents spend all their time attending meetings and no sensing takes place. As t increases, agents can fit more sensing in each tour period and as a result will bring data that is more up-to-date when they attend meetings. Transfer of information, however, becomes slower as agents attend fewer meetings, which is certain to have a negative impact on most distributed algorithms. In many situations, there will be an optimal time-between-visits t_{opt} that results in maximum efficiency. Efficiency will decrease when $t > t_{opt}$ because of lack of interaction among agents; efficiency will also decrease when $t < t_{opt}$ because of agents using stale data from lack of sensing.

4 Application

4.1 Tour-Based AUV Missions

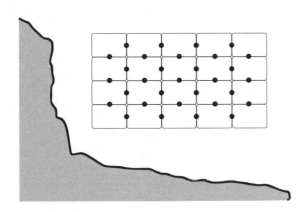

Fig. 4. Typical environmental monitoring mission: cooperating AUVS continuously sample an area of interest looking for an event of interest

Many of the typical missions are amenable to the concept of tours. A broad category of AUV deployments aim at providing continuous environmental sensing of an area. In the cases of larger areas or higher required temporal resolution, the total sampled area is subdivided and assigned to vehicles as shown in Fig. 4. Sub-areas are typically sensed by a single AUV performing some variation of the "lawn mower" pattern. A recent field experiment performed at an AUV event in Monterrey Bay, where AUVs were tasked to detect transient "thin layers" of biological activity [13], is an example of such a mission. Persistent barrier patrol (fig. 5) is an example of a security or law-enforcement AUV mission where a line of AUVs monitor a passageway for unusual activity [15]. Another example of a mission is inspired by the RiverNet project [16] where AUVs are used to monitor pollutants in the Hudson River. Fig. 6 shows several groups of AUVs performing vertical profiling of the river and facilitating cooperative adaptive sampling by intra- and inter-group communication.

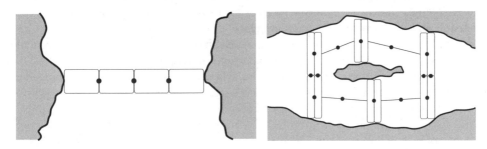

Fig. 5. Surveillance mission: a narrow waterway is monitored for unusual activity

Fig. 6. An example of a pollutant monitoring mission in a river channel

4.2   Event-Detection Mission on a Regular 3D Pattern

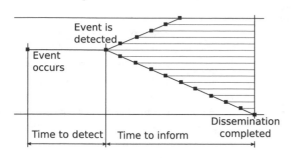

Fig. 7. Time to detect and time to inform

Consider an event-detection mission in which agents are assigned different areas, which they repeatedly sample to decide if the event of interest has occurred. In accordance with the tour pattern, agents also meet regularly to inform other agents (or be informed by them) whether the event has happened in their own individual areas. We assume that the event of interest is such that it can be observed by a single agent independently, and that the goal of the agents as a group (the mission) is that they all know that the event has happened as quickly as possible after any occurrence of the event. Accordingly, performance is measured in terms of the amount of time between an occurrence of the event and the moment awareness of this occurrence reaches the last agent.

Fig. 7 describes the two stages involved in solving such a mission: event detection *per se*, by some agent, followed by a propagation of information. This example illustrates the tradeoff between individual work and collaboration. With more interaction, agents spend less time monitoring their area and the time to detect increases. However, once the event is detected, the propagation of information benefits from this high-level of interaction and the time needed for this information to reach all agents decreases. Conversely, agents can detect the event more quickly if they spend less time attending meetings, but the propagation stage will then take longer. We are interested in finding the optimum amount of interaction that results in the best overall performance.

Case Study: Underwater Event Detection in Straight Lines. In order to keep this illustrative example simple, we use the following model of costs for sensing and interaction. N agents navigate in circles, looking for the event of interest along the line of their circle (Fig. 8). Each circle has length (circumference) L and we assume that agents sense and travel horizontally with speed λ.

Each circle is explored by a single agent as a tour (the "area" monitored in each tour is the circle itself). Tours are connected via meeting points in a linear graph (inner tours have two meeting points and the top and bottom tours only have one). The distance between two adjacent circles is $2d$ and agents meet at distance d from their circle, which means that agents travel a roundtrip vertical distance of $2d$ for each meeting they attend. We assume that agents travel vertically with speed μ.

Let t be the time-between-visits as before. Each agent will attend two meetings per t period (1 up and 1 down), except for the top and bottom agents, which only do one meeting (and could either sense more slowly or wait at meeting points to stay in sync with the rest of the group, depending on other considerations like

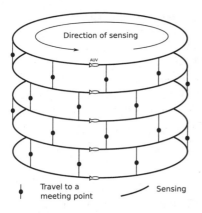

Fig. 8. Event detection example

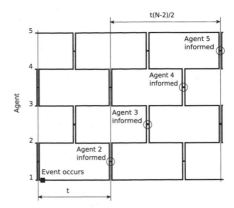

Fig. 9. Information propagation (worst case scenario)

energy consumption). We are interested in finding the optimal time-between-visits t that will result in the fastest completion time for the mission.

In this section, we analyze the network via a worst-case calculation of how much time elapses between one occurrence of the event and the earliest moment all agents are aware that the event has occurred. We carry out this calculation in terms of the parameters t, L, d, λ and μ. It is straightforward to see that the worst case scenario is one where there is a single occurrence of the event and the following conditions hold:

- the event happens on the top or bottom line, which causes the information to travel from one end of the network to the other;
- it is located right after a meeting point, which means with the longest possible time before the next opportunity to communicate with other agents;
- it happens when the agent has just traveled past this point, forcing the agent to travel one full circle back to this point before the event is detected.

During each period t, agents on the inner lines attend two meetings and need to travel a vertical distance of $2d$ at speed μ for each one of these meetings. Overall, agents spend $2 \times \frac{2d}{\mu}$ in each period t traveling to meeting points. There must be enough time in each period for agents to travel to their meeting points, which defines t_{min}, the smallest possible t:

$$t_{\mathsf{min}} = \frac{4d}{\mu}$$

We assume $t > t_{\mathsf{min}}$, which leaves $t - \frac{4d}{\mu}$ out of each period t for agents to sense while they cover a horizontal distance of $\lambda(t - \frac{4d}{\mu})$. Therefore, it takes $\frac{Lt}{\lambda(t-\frac{4d}{\mu})}$ for an agent to complete one full circle. As discussed before, this is also the time for event detection in the worst case:

$$\text{Time to detect} = \frac{L}{\lambda}\frac{1}{1 - \frac{4d}{\mu t}}$$

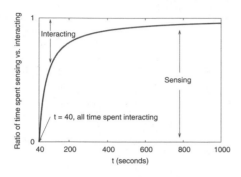
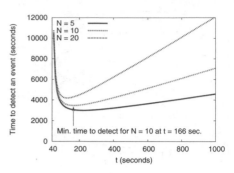

Fig. 10. Proportion of the total tour time spent sensing and interacting (L=10 km, d=10 m, λ=5 m/s, μ=1 m/s)

Fig. 11. Worst case time to detect an event (L=10 km, d=10 m, λ=5 m/s, μ=1 m/s) for varying number of nodes

Fig. 9 shows the propagation of information after the event is detected. It takes t units of time for the top (or bottom) agent to reach its meeting point and inform another agent. It then takes $\frac{t}{2}$ for this agent to inform the next one, and so on. Overall, it takes $t + (N - 2)\frac{t}{2} = \frac{Nt}{2}$ for the information to reach all N agents:

$$\text{Time to inform} = \frac{Nt}{2t}$$

The overall duration between event occurrence and the end of information dissemination is the sum (Time to detect + Time to inform), minimized when:

$$t_{\text{opt}} = \frac{4d}{\mu} + \sqrt{\frac{8Ld}{\lambda \mu N}}$$

Note that $\frac{4d}{\mu}$ is t_{min}, the time spent traveling to (and back from) meeting points, which leaves $\sqrt{\frac{8Ld}{\lambda \mu N}}$ for scanning and sensing.

Illustration. As an illustration, consider a situation where L=10km, d=10m, λ=5m/s, μ=1m/s and N=10. In this case, the optimum t_{opt}=166 seconds, of which 40 seconds are spent traveling to meeting points and 126 seconds are spent scanning. Fig. 10 shows the proportion of time spent sensing versus traveling to meeting points as a function of t. With an amount of interaction set to t_{opt}, it takes 44 minutes for an agent to complete a full circle (instead of about 33 minutes if agents didn't need to attend meetings to communicate) and the overall time to mission completion is 58 minutes. As a comparison, reducing agent interaction by half (t=333 seconds) allows agents to cover the tour in 38 minutes but increases the time to completion to 66 minutes; doubling agent interaction t=83 seconds) results in a tour time of 64 minutes and a time to completion of 71 minutes. At one extreme (t=40 seconds), all the agents' time is spent interacting and no sensing takes place; at the other extreme, the smallest (meaningful) amount of communication to complete the mission (the circle is entirely sampled before each meeting) corresponds to $t=4040$ seconds, in which case agents need only 33.7 minutes to sample the circle but leads to a time to completion of 6 hours and 10 minutes. Fig. 11 shows the time to mission completion as a function of t and for different values of N. Fig. 10 and 11 illustrate, for this case study, the general tradeoff discussion of sect. 3.4 (Fig. 3).

5   Current and Future Work

Mobile sensor networks, and other applications in which mobile agents carry out distributed computations in a challenging environment, present the networking task with new difficulties. In many situations, standard networking techniques can be modified, extended and adapted to address these new challenges. We feel, however, that there is also an opportunity for a fresh look at some of the assumptions that underlie the networks in use today.

In our broader effort, we are seeking primitives that combine communication with other tasks central to the new networks, like sensing, moving and comput-ing. By moving away from communication as an address-based, always-on service more or less independent (in its interface, not necessarily its implementation) from other agent activities, we hope to explore novel designs and architectures better adapted to the inherent needs of mobile networks.

The notion of tours presented in this paper is an example of a mechanism that combines motion and communication so they can be jointly optimized based on other network parameters, such as sensing range, energy consumption and the definition of the mission to be implemented. We are currently exploring other mechanisms, and we plan to continue to study tours based networks. In particular, we would like to have the steps of the distributed computation play a more explicit role in the model. For instance, the event detection mission used as an illustration in the paper relies on extremely simple agent states (boolean) and computational steps at meetings (logical OR). More involved functions and/or states can have a substantial impact on the design and optimization of tours. We have started to explore classes of functions that will give network designers more freedom in the way they can arrange tours [17] and we are also looking at tradeoffs between the size of agents' states and the amount of interaction needed to solve a mission with the desired performance. We have also completed preliminary work on techniques that can be used to design tour-implementing trajectories in such a way that the cost of high meeting rates is minimized.

As presented in this paper, the notion of tours does not deal with agent failures, such as missed meetings because of delays or temporary failures. These are important in the context of mobile sensor networks and we have started to investigate techniques that will let agents use meetings to adjust at runtime their tour trajectories and future meeting schedules.

References

1. Bartoš, R., Chappell, S.G., Komerska, R.J., Haag, M.M., Mupparapu, S., Agu, E., Katz, I.: Development of routing protocols for the solar-powered autonomous underwater vehicle (SAUV) platform. Wireless Communications and Mobile Computing 8(8), 1075–1088 (2008)
2. Fall, K.: A delay tolerant networking architecture for challenged internets. In: SIG-COMM 2003 (2003)
3. Ho, M., Fall, K.: Poster: Delay tolerant networking for sensor networks. In: First IEEE Conference on Sensor and Ad Hoc Communications and Networks (SECON 2004), Santa Clara, CA (2004)
4. Zhao, W., Ammar, M., Zegura, E.: A message ferrying approach for data delivery in sparse mobile ad hoc networks. In: ACM MobiHoc. (2004)
5. Zhao, W., Ammar, M., Zegura, E.: Controlling the mobility of multiple data transport ferries in a delay-tolerant network. In: IEEE INFOCOM (2005)
6. Burns, B., Brock, O., Levine, B.N.: MV routing and capacity building in disruption tolerant networks. In: IEEE INFOCOM (2005)
7. Burns, B., Brock, O., Levine, B.N.: MORA routing and capacity building in disruption-tolerant networks. Ad Hoc Netw. 6(4), 600–620 (2008)
8. Balasubramanian, A., Levine, B.N., Venkataramani, A.: DTN routing as a resource allocation problem. In: Proc. ACM SIGCOMM (2007)
9. Sozer, E.M., Stojanovic, M., Proakis, J.G.: Underwater acoustic networks. IEEE Journal of Oceanic Engineering 25(1), 72–83 (2000)
10. Akyildiz, I.F., Pompili, D., Melodia, T.: Underwater acoustic sensor networks: research challenges. Ad Hoc Networks 3(3), 257–279 (2005)
11. Cui, J.H., Kong, J., Gerla, M., Zhou, S.: The challenges of building mobile underwater wireless networks for aquatic applications. IEEE Network 20(3), 12–18 (2006)
12. Partan, J., Kurose, J., Levine, B.N.: A survey of practical issues in underwater networks. In: WUWNet 2006: Proceedings of the 1st ACM international workshop on Underwater networks, Los Angeles, CA, pp. 17–24. ACM Press, New York (2006)
13. Chappell, S.G., Komerska, R.J., Blidberg, D.R., Duarte, C.N., Martel, G.R., Crimmins, D.M., Beliard, M.A., Nitzel, R., Jalbert, J.C., Bartoš, R.: Recent field experience with multiple cooperating solar-powered AUVs. In: 15th Intl. Symposium on Unmanned Untethered Submersible Technology (UUST 2007), Durham, NH (2007)
14. Haag, M.M., Agu, E., Komerska, R., Chappell, S.G., Bartoš, R.: Status packet deprecation and store-forward routing in AUSNET. In: First ACM International Workshop on UnderWater Networks (WUWNet), Los Angeles, CA (2006)
15. U.S. Department of the Navy: The Navy Unmanned Undersea Vehicle (UUV) Master Plan (2000), http://www.npt.nuwc.navy.mil/UUV/UUVMP.pdf
16. Popa, D., Sanderson, A., Komerska, R., Mupparapu, S., Blidberg, D., Chappel, S.: Adaptive sampling algorithms for multiple autonomous underwater vehicles. In: Proc. of IEEE/OES AUV 2004: A Workshop on Multiple Autonomous Underwater Vehicle Operations, Sebasco Estates, ME (2004)
17. Chandy, K.M., Charpentier, M.: Self-similar algorithms for dynamic distributed systems. In: 27th International Conference on Distributed Computing Systems (ICDCS 2007) (2007)

Balancing Energy Dissipation in Data Gathering Wireless Sensor Networks Using Ant Colony Optimization

Ayan Acharya, Anand Seetharam, Abhishek Bhattacharyya,
and Mrinal Kanti Naskar

Department of Electronics and Telecommunication Engineering, Jadavpur University,
Kolkata: 700032, India
masterayan@gmail.com, anandsthrm@yahoo.co.in,
abhishek.bhattacharyyya@gmail.com, mrinalnaskar@yahoo.co.in

Abstract. Formulation of energy efficient protocols is of utmost importance for wireless sensor networks because of energy constraints of sensor nodes. When a number of nodes is deployed in a field located away from the base station, the nodes undergo unequal energy dissipation while transmitting information to the base station primarily due to two reasons: i) the difference in the distances of nodes from the base station and ii) the variation in inter-nodal distances. The schemes presented here better network lifetime by taking into account these two issues and try to equalize the energy dissipation by the nodes. While constructing the chain we also use Ant Colony Optimization algorithm instead of greedy approach used in PEGASIS. Application of ACO ensures that the chain formed is of shortest possible length and thus further helps enhance network performances by reducing the inter-nodal transmission distances as much as possible. Extensive simulations performed corroborates that the proposed schemes outperform PEGASIS by a significant margin.

Keywords: Wireless sensor network, data gathering round, Ant Colony Optimization, network lifetime.

1 Introduction

Wireless sensor networks (WSN) can be considered as a collection of mobile or static nodes capable of collecting data more cost-effectively as well as autonomously without any fixed infrastructure. The sensor networks are required to transmit gathered data to the base station (BS) or sink. Network lifetime thus becomes an important parameter for sensor network design as replenishing battery power of sensor nodes is an impractical proposition. The definition of network lifetime in case of sensor networks may be regarded to be application specific [3]. For most situations it can be said a network is useless if a major portion of the nodes die. Moreover it is accepted universally that balancing the energy dissipation by the nodes of the network is a key factor for prolonging the lifetime [3].

Here we consider a WSN where the base station is fixed and located far off from the sensed area. Furthermore it is assumed that all the nodes are static, homogenous, energy constrained and capable of communicating with the BS. The network being homogenous no high energy nodes are available hence communication between the

V. Garg, R. Wattenhofer, and K. Kothapalli (Eds.): ICDCN 2009, LNCS 5408, pp. 437–443, 2009.

nodes and the base station is expensive affair. Moreover all nodes have information about their respective distances from the BS in the static environment as stated in [2]. Individual nodes thus take rounds in transmitting to the base station which also distributes the dissipated energy more or less uniformly amongst the nodes.

The LEACH [1] and PEGASIS [2] propose elegant solutions to the problem. In this paper we try to provide a far more competent solution than the existing ones to the energy utilization problem. In our scheme a chain is formed in a way similar to PEGASIS but instead of using greedy algorithm we use Ant Colony Optimization (ACO) for chain formation. Though ACO is a widely accepted optimization tool its use in wireless sensor networks so far has been limited. Only a few applications of ACO in sensor networks [4-5] are available. Unlike [4-5], in our schemes we have tried to analytically remove the factors resulting in uneven energy dissipations and have only used ACO as a tool to enhance the performance.

In our paper here, instead of making all nodes transmit to the base station the same number of times, the network lifetime and performance has been increased by allowing the individual nodes to transmit unequal number of times to the base station depending on their distances from it.

2 Energy Dissipation Model

We consider the first order radio model as discussed in [1,2] with identical parameter values. The energy spent in transmission of single bit is given by

$$etx(d) = e_{t1} + e_{d1}d^n \qquad (1)$$

where e_{t1} is the energy dissipated per bit in the transmitter circuitry and $e_{d1}*dn$ is the energy dissipated for transmission of a single bit over a distance d, n being the path loss exponent (usually $2.0 \leq n \leq 4.0$). For simulation purposes we have considered a first order model where we assume n=2. Thus the total energy dissipated for transmitting a K-bit packet is

$$Etx(K,d) = (e_{t1} + e_{d1}d^2)K = e_t + e_d d^2 \qquad (2)$$

where $e_t = e_{t1}*K$ and $e_d = e_{d1}*K$. If e_{r1} be the energy required per bit for successful reception then energy dissipated for receiving a K-bit packet is

$$Erx(K) = e_{r1}K = e_r \qquad (3)$$

Where, $e_r = e_{r1}*K$. In our simulations we take $e_{t1} = 50$ nJ/bit, $e_{d1} = 100$ pJ/bit/m2 and $e_{r1} = e_{t1}$ as mentioned in [2] with K = 2000 bits. It is assumed that the channel is symmetric so that the energy spent in transmitting from node i to j is the same as that of transmitting from node j to i for any given SNR.

3 Balancing Energy Dissipation in Data Gathering WSNs

In our schemes we aim at building a system that would ensure that total energy dissipation is divided equally among all the nodes of the network. Let us assume that there are 'N' nodes in the network. The nodes are at first distributed randomly in the play field. The central idea in our schemes is similar to PEGASIS in which a chain is formed among all the nodes. One node is elected as leader. Each node receives a data packet from it neighbor, fuses it with its own data packet and then transmits it to its other neighbor in the chain. The data packet thus reaches the leader which is entrusted with the duty of transmitting the data packet the sink. Hence so far the work is just an illustration of PEGASIS.

But here we take this opportunity to bring into focus some of the drawbacks of PEGASIS. Although [2] tries to distribute the load evenly among all the nodes in the network this goal has not been fully achieved. Firstly, because the chain is formed using the greedy approach the inter-nodal distances tend to become larger towards the end of the chain resulting in greater energy dissipation. This is one of the primary reasons why we have considered ACO for chain formation. Another aspect which has been ignored in [2] is the variable distances of the nodes from the base station. A greater balancing in energy dissipation may be achieved if one burdens the nodes to transmit to the base station depending on their distances from it. An important point needs to be emphasized here. A network may last for a considerable amount of time with the nodes in the network gradually dying as time elapses. But it needs to be noted that the network may not serve its purpose at all after a certain percentage of node deaths. Hence the objective must be to ensure that all nodes remain completely functional for a larger length of time.

4 Chain Formation Using Ant Colony Optimization (ACO)

In this section we discuss the Ant Colony optimization algorithm used for chain construction. ACO makes sure that none of the inter-nodal distances becomes extremely large during chain construction ie. they never exceed a threshold value. Ant Colony Optimization is inspired by the behavior of real ants searching for food. The main objective of ACO is to utilize both local information (visibility) as well as information about good solutions obtained in the past (pheromone), when constructing new solutions.

To apply ant algorithm in our problem, we place ants arbitrarily on the nodes. Each ant is a simple agent with certain memory attributed. According to a probability, an ant chooses the next node into which it has to move into. This probability is a function of inter-nodal distance and pheromone deposited upon the link. Every ant has a taboo table recording nodes which the ant has already accessed. The Taboo table forbids the ant to move into previously visited nodes. At the end of travelling an ant deposits pheromone on the paths it has travelled through. Based on the information collected an ant determines an ant's choice of anode from its neighborhood. The mathematical formulations are omitted here due to the lack of space. In this way the entire chain is constructed. The chain is reconstructed using ACO when a node dies, but by bypassing it and by following all the above mentioned facts.

5 Energy Efficient Protocols

In this section we propose certain energy efficient protocols and assess how these perform when compared with PEGASIS.

Scheme A: In this scheme we construct the chain using ACO instead of the greedy algorithm as proposed by PEGASIS. The basic approach of the network functioning is similar to that in PEGASIS and as described in Section 3. However the use of ACO helps to form chains with uniform intermodal distances. This fact is demonstrated in Section 6. This strategy no doubt indicates an enhancement in the network performance but this improvement gradually weans away and we get similar performance as compared to PEGASIS for larger percentage of node deaths. Therefore we see that there is surely further scope of amelioration.

Scheme B: In **Scheme A** we tried to nullify the differences occurring in energy dissipation of the nodes due to varying inter- nodal distances by constructing the chain using ACO. However the varying distances from the base station still need to be taken into account. To address this issue and to prevent a degradation of network performance Scheme B allows the individual nodes to become leader variable number of times depending on their distances from the base station. This is achieved in the following way. Let d_{Bi} denote the distance of the ith node from the base station. Thus making use of (2), the energy dissipated (E_{Bi}) by the ith node when it transmits a data packet to the base station is given by

$$E_{Bi} = (e_t + e_d d_{Bi}^2).$$ (4)

Now among the 'N' nodes constituting the network we choose the node which is farthest away from the base station as reference, because it has to dissipate the maximum amount of energy during its turn of transmitting to the base station as compared to the other nodes. This node is denoted as the reference node. Let x_i be the number of times the ith node is elected as the leader. The above discussion leads to the following relation,

$$x_i = (d_{Bref}^2/d_{Bi}^2) \, x_{ref}.$$ (5)

To determine the precise value of x_i for various values of i we choose $x_{ref} = 10$. The reason for not choosing $x_{ref}=1$ and using its scaled version $x_{ref} = 10$ for determining the different x_is is to minimize the error obtained by rounding of the value of x_i to its nearest integer.

Scheme C: A further enhancement in network performance may be achieved if somehow the nodes are made to dissipate equal amount of energy in a round. We assume that 'C' data gathering rounds constitute a cycle and that the ith node is selected as the leader x_i number of times in one data gathering cycle. Now let d_i be the inter-nodal distance corresponding to i^{th} node where d_i is the average of distances of the ith node from its two neighbors. Let d_{Bi} denote the distance of the ith node from the base station. Thus we have, the energy dissipated (Esi) by the ith node in each round as,

$$Esi = A_i C + B_i x_i$$ (6)

with $A_i=(e_t+e_r+e_d d_i^2)$ and $B_i=e_d(d_{Bi}^2-d_i^2)$. Since it is desired that every node should spend an equal amount of energy in each round we assume Esi=Ess for all i. Therefore, from equation (6), we have

$$x_i = (Ess - A_i C)/B_i; \therefore C = \sum_i x_i = Ess \sum_i \frac{1}{B_i} - C \sum_i \frac{A_i}{B_i}; \Rightarrow x_i = \left(\frac{C}{B_i}\right)[(1+\sum_i \frac{A_i}{B_i})/(\sum_i \frac{1}{B_i}) - A_i]$$

Now for the system to be realizable, we should have, $C > x_i \geq 0$. Now, $x_i \geq 0$ is only possible if

$$[(1+\sum_i A_i / B_i)/(\sum_i 1/B_i) - A_i] \geq 0 \Rightarrow (1+\sum_i A_i / B_i) \geq A_i \sum_i 1/B_i$$

As $B_i=e_d(d_{Bi}^2 - d_i^2)+e_r$ is positive for all i as $d_{Bi}> d_i$ in all cases. Further under most circumstances, the relation $d_{Bi} >> d_i$ is also valid. This discussion helps us to write the above inequality as,

$$A_i \leq (1+\sum_i A_i / B_i)/(\sum_i 1/B_i) \tag{7}$$

Therefore, A_i can be approximated as (e_t+e_r) and B_i as $e_d d_{Bi}^2$ .However in order to ensure that $x_i \geq 0$ is valid for all values of i, we need to estimate an upper limit on the inter-nodal distance from the above inequality expressed in (7). The inequality in (7) takes the form

$$(e_t +e_r +e_d d_i^2) \ (A_i \text{ corresponding to maximum possible } d_i) \leq e_d / \sum_i \frac{1}{d_{Bi}^2}+(e_t +e_r)$$

$$\therefore d_i^2 \leq (d_{Brms}^2 / N) \tag{8}$$

with d $_{Brms}$ as the root mean square of distances from the base station of the nodes. The other condition $x_i < C$ with identical approximations also gives the same inequality as found in (8). Therefore our system will be always viable if condition (8) is ensured. This is not very difficult to ensure as we also consider that the base station is placed away from the play field. The chain formation in this case too was done with ACO as before now but with the constraint that the inter-nodal distance satisfied (8). This distance satisfying (8) was taken as the threshold while simulating PEGASIS.

6 Simulation Results

In this section we demonstrate how our schemes outperform PEGASIS which in turn means that our schemes would perform far better than LEACH.

Results for Scheme A

We now demonstrate how ACO based chain construction approach performs better than the greedy chain. All simulations were done on a 50m*50m area and nodes were randomly distributed in this region. As mentioned in Section 5 in majority of the cases chain formation with the greedy approach results in chains with large inter-nodal distances towards the chain end. Table 1 demonstrates the fact that the greedy algorithm forms inferior chains with large inter-nodal distances.

Table 1. Number of rounds passed when 1% of nodes die for a node distribution in which the greedy algorithm forms a chain with large inter-nodal distances

Base Station Location	Energy/node(J)	Greedy chain	ACO chain	Percentage Improvement
(25,175)	0.75	1940	2703	39.33
(25,200)	0.25	697	841	20.67
(25,150)	1.00	3256	3890	19.47
(25,250)	0.75	1890	2218	17.35

Figures 2 and 3 portray the chains formed by greedy and ant algorithm for the same node distribution. It depicts clearly how the inter-nodal distances increase towards the end of the chain when the greedy algorithm is used. The lines in black indicate the inter-nodal distances which are larger than the threshold.

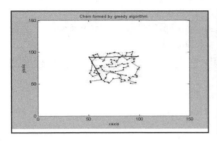
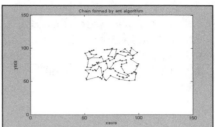

Fig. 2. Chain formed by Greedy Algorithm   **Fig. 3.** Chain formed by ACO

Results for Schemes B and C

Our motive in this paper has been to make the network survive without degradation in performance for larger time durations. Schemes B and C take us a step further in this regard. The following table provides a comparative study between PEGASIS, Scheme B and Scheme C.

Table 2. Number of rounds passed when 1%, 10%, 20%, 30%, 40% and 50% nodes die with base station location at **(25,225)**

Energy (J/node)	Protocol	Percentage of node death					
		1	10	20	30	40	50
0. 5	PEGASIS	1490	1659	1680	1702	1726	1751
	Scheme B	1627	1693	1725	1738	1748	1758
	Scheme C	1692	1711	1725	1735	1745	1756
0.75	PEGASIS	2245	2460	2504	2542	2571	2622
	Scheme B	2469	2549	2577	2590	2608	2636
	Scheme C	2551	2563	2582	2597	2608	2628
1.00	PEGASIS	3042	3283	3355	3424	3459	3508
	Scheme B	3287	3416	3457	3484	3502	3521
	Scheme C	3400	3433	3454	3473	3497	3505

A close examination of the above table helps us appreciate the fact that both Schemes B and C perform better than PEGASIS till more than 50% of the nodes die. In many of the cases depicted, improvement can be seen even when more than 60% of the nodes. After the death of a major percentage of the nodes, the network may be regarded as nonfunctional because the service provided by it would be so inferior in quality that it would be hardly of any use. Thus we have succeeded in our goal that the degradation in network performance is delayed. Furthermore although PEGASIS shows an improvement over our schemes after the death of more than 50% of the nodes, this enhancement is minimal and the remaining nodes die within a very short span of time.

7 Conclusion

The protocols considered in this paper ensures that a near energy utilization occurs thereby increasing network lifetime. The ACO scheme also helps to enhance the performance of our scheme. The simulation results also help to understand and appreciate the facts stated in the paper. In future we would also like to use other optimization tools for chain construction and observe how they perform as compared to ACO and the greedy algorithm.

References

1. Heinzelman, W., Chandrakasan, A., Balakrishna, H.: Energy-Efficient Communication Protocol for Wireless MicrosensorNetworks. In: Proceedings of 33rd Hawaii International Conference on System Sciences, pp. 1–10 (January 2000)
2. Lindsey, S., Raghavendra, C.S.: PEGASIS: Power Efficient Gathering in Sensor Information Systems. In: Proceedings of IEEE ICC 2001, pp. 1125–1130 (June 2001)
3. Chen, Y., Zhao, Q.: On the Lifetime of Wireless Sensor Networks. IEEE Communications Letters 9(11) (November 2005)
4. Ding, N., Xiaoping Liu, P.: Data Gathering Communication in Wireless Sensor Networks Using Ant Colony Optimization. In: Proceedings of the IEEE Conference on Robotics and Biomimetics, Shenyang, August 22-26, 2004, pp. 822–827 (2004)
5. Ye, N., Shao, J., Wang, R., Wang, Z.: Colony Algorithm for Wireless Sensor Networks Adaptive Data Aggregation Routing Schema. In: Li, K., Fei, M., Irwin, G.W., Ma, S. (eds.) LSMS 2007. LNCS, vol. 4688, pp. 248–257. Springer, Heidelberg (2007)

Rate Adaptive Channel MAC

Manzur Ashraf and Aruna Jayasuriya

Institute for Telecommunications Research
University of South Australia
Mawson Lakes Bvd, Mawson Lakes, SA 5072, Australia
Manzur.Ashraf@postgrads.unisa.edu.au

Abstract. A novel 'Rate adaptive Channel MAC paradigm' has been proposed considering perfect channel prediction and optimal rate adaptation. Simulation results reveal a significant performance gap between the theoretical rate adaptive Channel MAC and existing rate adaptive protocols- such as 'Opportunistic Auto Rate' (OAR).

1 Introduction

Rate adaptive transmission schemes use bandwidth efficient coded modulation techniques to increase throughput over the channels with variable Signal-to-Interference and Noise (SINR) ratio due to fading and interference from other transmissions [1]. At each SINR point, the coded modulation scheme which gives the highest throughput with minimal bit error rate (i.e. below a certain bit error rate threshold) is selected. Following this principal, standards such as IEEE 802.11 medium access protocols have introduced the physical layer multi-rate capability. As the multi-rate schemes exists in the physical layer, adaptive MAC mechanisms are required to exploit this capability. Sender based rate adaptation schemes (e.g. [2]) and receiver based adaptation schemes (e.g. [3], [4]) enables multi-rate features into MAC. Generally receiver based rate adaptive MAC performs better than the sender-based rate adaptive MACs [3]. In receiver-based rate adaptive MACs, the channel quality measurement is done at the receiver during the RTS/CTS exchange. Hence, the channel estimates in these MACs are close to the channel condition during the actual data transmission time opposed to the sender-based approaches. Receiver Based Auto Rate (RBAR) [3] and Opportunistic Auto Rate (OAR) [4] are two prominent examples of receiver-based MACs. In RBAR, every RTS-CTS-DATA-ACK handshaking mechanism (we define it as a cycle) is rate adaptive. In other words, all data packets within a cycle is transmitted with the optimal data rate selected by the receiver based on the received RTS power within that cycle. In OAR, on the other hand, a number of packets is transmitted within a cycle (i.e. after a single RTS-CTS exchange) based on the channel coherence interval and the feasible data rate selected in the same way of RBAR protocol. However, it is possible that the channel condition will significantly change during the multi-packet transmission sequences of OAR. If the transmission at the original rate is maintained (selected by RTS-CTS exchange), error rates may become large if the channel quality worsens leading to

V. Garg, R. Wattenhofer, and K. Kothapalli (Eds.): ICDCN 2009, LNCS 5408, pp. 444–449, 2009.

packet losses. Conversely, the rate selection becomes sub-optimal if the channel quality is further improved during the multiple data transmissions.

In OAR, throughput improvement is possible (i.e. decrease the packet loss or improve the sub-optimal to optimal rate selection) if the sender and receiver adapt the data rate during a cycle. Moreover, considering perfect channel prediction and time-share fairness constraint, each transmitter-receiver pair can fully utilise its non-fade duration using a rate-adaptive transmission, if a common probability of good channel[1] persists in the network. The scope of this paper is thus to combine both (a) scheduling and (b) rate adaptive transmission based on the channel state information at the receiver, to design a rate adaptive opportunistic MAC. The channel utilisation of single-rate 'Channel MAC' described in [5] only considers the scheduling policy. The channel of a user, which goes up the threshold first, is given access to the medium provided that no one else is transmitting. The single-rate 'Channel MAC' (which calculates the channel utilisation only) is extended in this paper including the rate adaptation features similar to [1]. We assume a perfect data rate adaptation based on the channel condition during multiple data packet transmissions during the non-fade duration. The aim is to identify the theoretical maximum throughput limit of the Channel MAC paradigm considering data rate adaptation. We name this technique "Rate adaptive Channel MAC".

2   System Model

Let us define a neighborhood of $2n$ nodes, where $N_T \in (1, 2, \ldots, n)$ are the transmitters and $N_R \in (1, 2, \ldots, n)$ are the receivers. For symmetry let us assume that each transmitter $i \in N_T$ is communicating with receiver $i \in N_R$. We assume a constant transmission power for the system. Each transmitter is sending DATA packets to its receiver without any intermittent delay. No control frame is used.

2.1   Channel Model

We consider a two-state channel model. It has either a non-fade state "ON" state with gain $g[t] > 0$ or a fade state "OFF" with $g[t] = 0$. we assume that the non-fade duration, termed Average Non-Fade Duration (ANFD), l, is constant, after which the channel goes into a fade with an arbitrary distributed fade duration with the mean Θ. Hence probability of good channel, p, is calculated as follows:

$$p = \frac{l}{l + \Theta} \qquad (1)$$

We assume each ANFD consists of a number of block. The block-length depends on the the data-rate given a fixed length packet. Suppose data-rate is selected based on the instantaneous channel states. Then the packet transmission time, l_i, for a constant $\bar{P}$ sized packet at data-rate R_i is $l_i = \bar{P}/R_i$. We assume $g[t]$ is constant over the block-length l_i where the channel is optimally suitable to support the data-rate R_i.

---

[1] Which is equivalent to a common average non-fade duration in all channels.

3   Rate Adaptive Channel MAC Throughput

3.1   Rate Selection Probability in Rayleigh Fading Channel

Number of threshold-based techniques for rate selection have been used in literature [1],[3],[4]. In a threshold based scheme, the rate is chosen by comparing the received SNR against an array of thresholds representing performance limits of the available modulation techniques. The modulation technique with the highest data rate and the bit error rate less than a constraint value for the estimated SNR is chosen. The selected modulation technique results in the feasible data rate to be used in subsequent transmissions. Let $r_1, r_2, r_3, ..., r_{m-1}$ are power threshold for different suitable rate limits. For example, r_1 dB indicates that if the received power level is below r_1 dB, rate R_1 is feasible. In case the received power level is above r_1 but below r_2, rate R_2 is feasible and so on. A region surrounded by two subsequent power threshold, which is suitable for a particular rate is called a "rate-region". For example, R_2 rate-region is surrounded by r_1 and r_2 power thresholds.

Case 1. $l_k \rightarrow 0$ (l_k is the packet transmission time of $\bar{P}$ sized packet with the data-rate R_k): First, we identify the rate region where the cutoff threshold, P_c is located. Assume P_c is located in R_k rate-region ($k < m$). That is $P_c \in R_k$. According to [6], the probability that DATA packet is transmitted with R_k feasible rate is $(R_k) = p - e^{-r_k/P_{av}}$. Here p is the probability of good channel condition beyond the selected threshold P_c. The second part denotes the probability of received power is above the cutoff r_k. P_{av} is the average received power. Similarly

$$P(R_z) = e^{-r_{z-1}/P_{av}} - e^{-r_z/P_{av}} \text{(when } k < z < m) \tag{2}$$

$$P(R_m) = e^{-r_{m-1}/P_{av}} \tag{3}$$

Hence, the mean data rate for such a transmission is:

$$\bar{R} = \frac{1}{\sum_{i=k}^{m} P(R_i)} \sum_{i=k}^{m} [P(R_i) \times R_i] \tag{4}$$

As the packets are assumed to be infinitesimally small in this case, the channel conditions should remain the same during each packet transmission. Hence this case corresponds to the optimum rate achieved with the proposed scheme.

Case 2. $l_k > 0$: We identify total number of $l_i | (k \le i \le m)$ fitted within an ANFD duration with corresponding feasible data rates. The total transmission time at R_i data rate within an ANFD is

$$T_{R_i} = l \frac{P(R_i)}{\sum_i P(R_i)} \tag{5}$$

Hence the number of transmitted packet x_i at R_i data rate is $x_i = \lfloor T_{R_i}/l_i \rfloor$. Therefore mean data rate is

$$\bar{T} = \frac{\sum_{i=k}^{m} x_i l_i}{l} \frac{1}{\sum_{i=k}^{m} P(R_i)} \sum_{i=k}^{m} [P(R_i) \times R_i] \qquad (6)$$

3.2   Channel Utilisation in Channel MAC Considering Collision

We define Normalised propagation delay w.r.t ANFD as $\bar{a} = \frac{a}{l}$. Total arrival rate by n node pairs is $O = nr$ where r is the level crossing arte by a single channel.

Following [7], we derive

$$U = \frac{\frac{1}{O}e^{-\bar{a}O}}{O(1 + 2\bar{a}) + e^{-\bar{a}O}} \qquad (7)$$

3.3   Rate Adaptive Channel MAC

We define the throughput of Channel MAC as the product of utilisation and the average rate during a transmission period.

(i) $l_k \to 0$: Combining Equation 7 and 4, we get the throughput for rate adaptive Channel MAC as follows:

$$S_{rate-adaptive1} = \bar{R} \times U \qquad (8)$$

(ii) $l_k > 0$: Combining Equation 7 and 6, we get the throughput for rate adaptive Channel MAC as follows:

$$S_{rate-adaptive2} = T \times U \qquad (9)$$

4   Simulation Study

The simulation in this paper is conducted using MATLAB. However, the OAR simulation is done using NS2. The available rates for both protocols are assumed to be 2, 5.5 and 11 Mbps.

We consider Rayleigh fading as a small scale fading incorporated with the channel. The packet level simulator described in [8] is used to model the time-scale fading with parameters 10 kmph node velocity and 2 GHz carrier frequency.

4.1   Single-Hop Environment

We consider a single-hop scenario. Transmit power, P_t is set to 0.2818W. The transmission range is set to 250 m. Thus receiver sensitivity at 250m is -71.4dBm. Rate threshold for 5.5Mbps and 11Mbps are selected as -67.4 and -55.41 dBm as in [4]. The maximum Doppler frequency is set to 20 Hz^2.

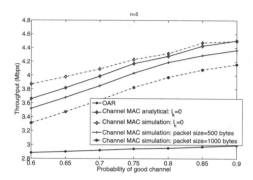

Fig. 1. Throughput performance of rate adaptive Channel MAC and OAR

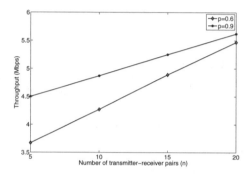

Fig. 2. Throughput performance of analytical Channel MAC ($l_k = 0$) at different n and p values

Figure 1 shows throughput performance of rate adaptive Channel MAC for l_k 0 and $l_k > 0$ (packet size= 500 and 1000 bytes) for $n = 5$. Corresponding OAR throughput results (packet size=1000 bytes) are also included in this figure for comparison. The discrepancy between the analytical and simulation results for the rate adaptive Channel MAC is due to the assumption that arrivals are poisson distributed in the analytical calculations, while the simulation uses actual rayleigh channel fading models, as explained in [9]. Figure 1 shows that throughput decreases with the increasing packet sizes. This is due to the fact with increasing packet sizes, the probability of changes in fading conditions during a packet transmission increases, leading to sub-optimum rate selections or packet losses. Both of these conditions leads to overall throughput degradation. However, at $p = 0.9$, the rate adaptive Channel MAC throughput is 40% higher than the OAR throughput considering 1000 byte packet size. In rate adaptive Channel MAC, the good channel conditions are fully utilised, resulting in relatively linear throughput increases with p, which is in contrast to the under-utilisation of the channel in OAR.

---

[2] If carrier frequency, f_c is 2000 MHz and velocity of node is 10 Kmph, the maximum Doppler frequency, $f_m = f_d = \frac{v}{c} f_c cos(0)$, results in 18.5 Hz.

In figure 2,the throughput results of the analytical Channel MAC ($l_k = 0$) at different p and n values are given. It can be observed that rate adaptive Channel MAC achieves higher throughput at lower p values with increasing n, improving the potential operating range. Due to the multiuser diversity effect in the Channel MAC, the probability of finding at least one good channel at a given time increases with higher number of nodes, which improves the transmission opportunities.

5   Conclusion

In this paper we propose a mechanism to provide rate adaptation to the Channel MAC protocol. The objective of the rate adaptation scheme is to find the transmission rates for each transmission interval to maximise the throughput. We analytically evaluate the rate adaptive MAC based on perfect channel state information. We then demonstrate the effectiveness of the protocol using the analytical equations and a separate simulation study. The simulation results reveal up to 75% throughput improvement can be achieved with Channel MAC as compared to OAR in a single hop network.

References

1. Balachandran, K., Kadaba, S.R., Nanda, S.: Channel quality estimation and rate adaptation for cellular mobile radio. IEEE JSAC 17(7), 1244–1256 (1999)
2. Kamerman, A., Monteban, L.: WaveLAN-II: a high-performance wireless LAN for the unlicensed band. Bell Labs Technical Journal, 118–133 (1997)
3. Holland, G., Vaidya, N., Bahl, P.: A rate-adaptive MAC protocol for multi-hop wireless networks. In: MobiCom., pp. 236–251 (2001)
4. Sadeghi, B., Kanodia, V., Sabharwal, A., Knightly, E.: Opportunistic media access for multirate ad hoc networks. In: MobiCom., pp. 24–35 (2002)
5. Ashraf, M., Jayasuriya, A., Perreau, S., Rasmussen, L.: Channel MAC: A novel medium access control paradigm for wireless ad hoc networks. In: Australian Telecommunication Networks and Applications Conference, pp. 404–408 (2006)
6. Wang, H.S., Moayeri, N.: Finite-state markov channel- a useful model for radio communication channels. IEEE Transactions on Vehicular Technology 44(1), 163–171 (1995)
7. Kleinrock, L., Tobagi, F.: Packet switching in radio channels: Part 1- carrier sense multiple access modes and their throughput-delay characteristics. IEEE Transactions of Communications 23(12), 1400–1416 (1975)
8. Punnoose, R.J., Nikitin, P.V., Stancil, D.D.: Efficient simulation of ricean fading within a packet simulator. In: Proc. of IEEE VTC, pp. 764–767 (2000)
9. Ashraf, M., Jayasuriya, A., Perreau, S.: Analytical throughput for the channel MAC paradigm. In: Zhang, H., Olariu, S., Cao, J., Johnson, D.B. (eds.) MSN 2007. LNCS, vol. 4864, pp. 375–386. Springer, Heidelberg (2007)

Efficient Load Balancing on a Cluster for Large Scale Online Video Surveillance

Koushik Sinha, Atish Datta Chowdhury, Subhas Kumar Ghosh, and Satyajit Banerjee

Honeywell Technology Solutions,
151/1, Doraisanipalya, Bannerghatta Road, Bangalore 560076, India
{koushik.sinha,atish.chowdhury,subhas.kumar,
satyajit.banerjee}@honeywell.com

Abstract. In this paper we present a new load distribution strategy tailored to real-time, *large scale* surveillance systems with the objective of providing best effort timeliness of on-line automated video analysis on a cluster of compute nodes. We propose a novel approach to fine grained load balancing, modeled as a *makespan minimization* problem to reactively minimize the tardiness of processing individual camera feeds. The proposed approach is also robust in the sense that it is not dependent on either the estimates of future loads or the worst case execution requirements of the video processing load. Simulation results with real-life video surveillance data establish that for a desired timeliness in processing the data, our approach reduces the number of compute nodes by a factor of two, compared to systems without the load migration heuristics.

1 Introduction

With the advancements in video processing technologies, high bandwidth network communications and computational capabilities of commodity computers, *automated real time video analysis* is becoming increasingly important [1]. Timeliness of generating alerts is naturally the most important issue for such video based surveillance systems. While a hard real time solution may be a necessity for extremely critical applications, it can prove to be too costly in general. For wide spread deployment of automated surveillance solutions, it would therefore be more economical to have a smaller cluster of nodes and use dynamic load balancing and scheduling techniques to handle temporal surges in computational loads of individual cameras so as to provide an overall low response time, while ensuring efficient utilization of system resources.

Current video surveillance systems tend to focus on the issues of efficient storage and retrieval, remote monitoring, data streaming, forensics, ease of configurability and real-time analysis - but not explicitly on the timeliness issues of large scale online analysis vis-a-vis resource utilization [1,10]. Timeliness, in this context, can be quantified in terms of the delay between the time of availability of image frames from cameras and completion of their processing.

If efficient resource utilization were not a key issue, one could design a computation cluster by pre-allocating the compute-capability (i.e., number of nodes) required for the worst-case (i.e., most computation intensive) scenarios across all cameras for the above soft real-time requirement. As an example, theoretically, a sufficient condition for

V. Garg, R. Wattenhofer, and K. Kothapalli (Eds.): ICDCN 2009, LNCS 5408, pp. 450–455, 2009.

bounded tardiness under *earliest pseudo-deadline first Pfair* (EPDF Pfair) scheduling [6] can be used with worst case processing requirements for each of the tasks. While this approach would provide the best timeliness guarantee, more often than not, it would lead to gross over-engineering, as the computational loads that the individual cameras bring in generally tend to exhibit sporadic behavior with time.

Alternatively, best-effort resource utilization may be achieved by a systemic load balancing mechanism. For a load balancing algorithm, a load index is a key design parameter, i.e. in order to fare well, it must correlate well with the task response times [2,3]. A systemic load balancing mechanism like LSF, Condor, OpenMosix, Fractiling, Hectiling, etc. [4,3,5] aim at reducing the overall average response times of the submitted tasks based on application agnostic load indices comprised of CPU queue length, CPU usage, load average etc. Although an application aware load balancing scheme based on future video processing loads would be ideal, a reasonably accurate estimation of the computational load associated with a camera stream is a difficult task. It is not only dependent on the actual physical phenomenon but also on the placements of the individual cameras with respect to the zones they are trying to cover. Thus the use of an estimation based load balancing strategy would not only be difficult to model, but also would make it difficult to deploy a surveillance system quickly and at the same time maintain a high degree of reconfigurability in terms of camera deployments.

In the context of automated online video surveillance, it is also important that all the cameras be processed equally fast, such that the value provided by real time intelligent analysis is not undermined, e.g., by an adversary which gets monitored only by the cameras with delayed processing, thereby taking more time to be detected. The timeliness objective addressed in this paper therefore is to reduce the *collective response times* of frame-processing across all the cameras.

1.1 Our Contribution

In the absence of mechanisms of accurate load estimation and suitable dynamic load balancing algorithms for our objective, in this work we propose and show the viability of a simple load balancing heuristic that addresses the objective of collectively reducing the processing latencies of all the camera feeds. Towards this end, we define the notion of lag for individual camera feeds at the level of a polling interval and propose a fine grained load balancing approach modeled as a *makespan minimization* problem to reactively minimize the processing of the lags. The usefulness of our approach lies in its suitability in the absence of estimates of future loads and also on its lack of dependency on the worst case execution requirements of video frame processing.

Simulation results show that our approach provides a reduction in the requirement of compute nodes by nearly a factor of two for achieving desired timeliness.

2 Preliminaries

We consider a computation cluster (as depicted in Figure-1) with the nodes sharing a data and a control bus (LAN). The *data bus* is used to stream compressed or uncompressed digital video surveillance data from n number of cameras while the *control*

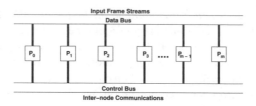

Fig. 1. Network of compute nodes

bus is dedicated to transmission of information required by our load balancing scheme. There are m compute or *slave* nodes and a *master* node. Multiple master nodes may also be considered, in order to provide the necessary fail-over capabilities. The master node coordinates the load distribution between the compute nodes over the control bus by explicitly scheduling the load transfers. Compute nodes are denoted by p_i, $1 \le i \le m$, and the master as p_0. The scheduling of communication over the control network assumes a reasonable degree of time synchronization amongst the nodes.

The generic video analytic engine that we have considered in this paper consists of two distinct computational stages or modules, namely: i) Video Motion Detection (VMD) and ii) Video Motion Tracking (VMT). Extensive profiling over a large number of video streams leads to the following observation.

Observation 1. *Though the analysis of the basic VMD algorithm has negligible computational complexity compared to that required by the detailed video analysis (VMT), it correlates well with the latter. Thus, it is possible to derive a reasonably good estimation of the total computational load in a frame utilizing only basic VMD.*

3   Problem Formulation

For a given real-time video processing system, we assume that the camera streams have the same periodicity τ and arrive synchronously. Our approach is based on *periodically* ensuring that there are no leftover frames to be analyzed across all the cameras. The precise choice of the *period* would depend upon a specific implementation. In the rest of the paper, we refer to this *period* as the *polling interval* or *slab* and denote its duration by τ_{poll}.

Let T_j^i be the completion time of the ith frame of jth camera relative to its arrival. Hence the tardiness of the ith frame of the jth camera is given by $d_j^i = \max((T_j^i - \tau), 0)$. We define tardiness associated with the kth polling interval of the jth camera as the tardiness associated with its last frame in the kth polling interval as denoted by D_j^k. Assuming $\tau_{poll} = q \cdot \tau$ for some integer $q > 0$, we have $D_j^k = d_j^l$ where $l = k \cdot q$. Maximum tardiness at a given polling interval k is given by $D_k = \max_j D_j^k$. Our objective is to *minimize* $\max_k(D_k)$ subject to:

- Frames of a camera can only be processed sequentially by at most one machine at any point in time.
- Frame processing of a given camera cannot be migrated across machines within a polling interval.
- No frame is ever dropped.

After each polling interval, we collect the set of frames that are yet to be analyzed (excess frames) and try to minimize their completion times (using Observation-1), subject to the restrictions stated above. This results in a schedule (camera-node association) which is followed during the next polling period for processing the frames, where we first process the excesses, thereby reactively minimizing the makespan of the lags generated in the previous slab.

4 Algorithm Description

We now present our centralized load balancing algorithm that is based on makespan reduction of accumulated excesses from individual cameras after every τ_{poll}. For ease of representation, henceforth we shall refer to this algorithm as the *Excess Makespan Reduction* algorithm or the *EMR* algorithm and use the following notations. Let $\mathcal{M}$ be the set of all machines. In the kth polling period, let $J(p_i, k)$ denote the set of cameras associated with machine p_i. Excess of each camera j at the end of polling period is defined as $e(j)$. Let $\mathcal{E}(p_i, k) = \{e(j) : j \in J(p_i, k)\}$, denotes the set of excesses at machine p_i at the end of kth polling period. By $\mathcal{A}_{\max}(\mathcal{E}(k), \mathcal{M})$ we shall denote the makespan minimization algorithm that, after each polling period k, takes the set of all excesses $\mathcal{E}(k) = \bigcup_{p_i \in \mathcal{M}} \mathcal{E}(p_i, k)$ and the set of machines $\mathcal{M}$ as input and produces a packing as to which task should be executed on which machine in order to minimize $C_{\max}$, where $C_{\max}$ denotes the makespan of the processing times of the set of excesses.

Algorithm 1. Algorithm *EMR*

1: **procedure** *EMR*(At the end of kth polling period)
2:     Each compute node p_i determines $\mathcal{E}(p_i, k)$ ▷ vide Observation-1
3:     Master node p_0 receives all the $\mathcal{E}(p_i, k)$ and computes $\mathcal{E}(k)$
4:     Master p_0 executes $\mathcal{A}_{\max}(\mathcal{E}(k), \mathcal{M})$
5:     Let $J(p_i, k+1) \leftarrow \mathcal{A}_{\max}(\mathcal{E}(k), \mathcal{M})$
6:     Master broadcasts all $J(p_i, k+1)$ to all compute nodes   ▷ on the control bus
7:     Execute according to new camera-node associations.
8: **end procedure**

Depending on the machine environment model (identical, related or unrelated), we use different *makespan minimization* approximation algorithms $\mathcal{A}_{\max}(\mathcal{E}, \mathcal{M})$ to obtain a solution for C_{max}. Using the standard scheduling notations, we note that for makespan minimization problem following algorithms can be considered depending on the objective function:

- $Pm||C_{max}$: Graham's $(4/3 - 1/m)$–approximation algorithm, known as *longest processing time first* or the LPT algorithm [7].
- $Qm||C_{max}$: 3/2-approximation algorithm of Gonzales et. al [8].
- $Rm||C_{max}$: Shchepin and Vakhania's algorithm having approximation ratio 2 [9].

4.1 Complexity of Algorithm EMR

We measure the time complexity of the algorithm *EMR* as observed by the master node. Step-2 takes $O(n)$ time to compute for each camera. The sending of the values of the excesses in Step-3 is done in a single round, using one message per node and in $O(m)$ time slots using a round-robin scheme. Assuming identical machines [7], in Step-4 $\mathcal{A}_{\max}(\mathcal{E}(k), \mathcal{M})$ requires $O(n(\log n + \log m))$ time as we maintain two heaps - one for the set of excesses, with the largest excess on top of the heap and one for the processors, with the least loaded processor on top. In Step-6, the master node p_0 broadcasts the computed schedule using a single message. Since our system model assumes a single-hop network (Figure-1), Step-6 takes $O(1)$ time slots. Thus, the worst case time complexity of algorithm *EMR* is $O(n(\log n + \log m))$.

5 Results

We compare the performance of our proposed *EMR* algorithm (referred as cluster scenario) against a strategy where the mapping of cameras to nodes is done one time initially and not changed for the entire duration of a simulation run (referred as static scenario). For the purpose of simulation, we assume the *identical machines environment model* with no preemption, i.e., $Pm||C_{max}$ and use Graham's 2-approximation LPT algorithm [7] for makespan reduction in the *EMR* algorithm. The simulation was repeated 10 times, for number of cameras $n = 8, 16, 24, 32, 40$ and 48. For initial camera to node assignment, the cameras are evenly distributed among the nodes using a random association. For every simulation run, both the static and the cluster scenario start with the same camera to node mapping. The computational load for each frame from all the cameras is determined by simulating the processing of individual video streams on an Intel Xeon 5150, 2.66 GHz dual core HT enabled machine, with 2GB RAM.

⌐ A set of compute nodes processing a set of camera streams is said to be in *stable state* if there is no monotonic increase in the excesses across slabs owing to the inadequacy of

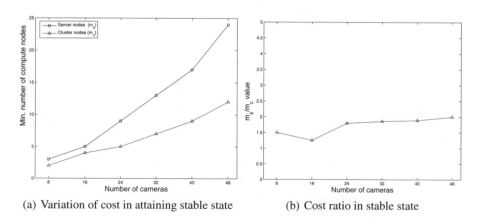

(a) Variation of cost in attaining stable state   (b) Cost ratio in stable state

Fig. 2. Cost comparison between server and cluster scenario

computational resources. For each run, we denote by m_c (resp. m_s) the *minimum* number of compute nodes required to attain stable state for the cluster (resp. static) scenario. Figure-2 demonstrates that as the number of cameras is increased, m_s/m_c gradually increases and becomes 2 for $n = 48$. We also experimented with different τ_{poll} values and observed that for small τ_{poll} our proposed fine granularity load balancing performs significantly better than the static scenario.

6 Conclusion

We have proposed a new centralized load distribution algorithm for real-time, large scale surveillance systems with the aim of providing best effort timeliness of on-line video frame processing on a cluster of compute nodes. While simulation results are encouraging, in the future, we plan to formally analyze the performance of our algorithm.

References

1. Brown, L., Hampapur, A., et al.: IBM smart surveillance system (S3): an open and extensible architecture for smart video surveillance. Intl. Conf. on Comp. Vision (2005)
2. Shivaratri, N.G., Krueger, P., Singhal, M.: Load distributing for locally distributed systems. Computer 25(12), 33–44 (1992)
3. Szelag, M., Terry, D., Waite, J.: Integrating Distributed Inter- Process Communication with PANTS on a Bewoulf cluster. Major Qualifying Project CS-DXF-0021 (March 2001)
4. Lee, G.-H., Woo, W.-D., Yoon, B.-N.: An Adaptive Load Balancing Algorithm Using Simple Prediction Mechanism. In: Quirchmayr, G., Bench-Capon, T.J.M., Schweighofer, E. (eds.) DEXA 1998. LNCS, vol. 1460, pp. 496–501. Springer, Heidelberg (1998)
5. OpenMosix, an open source linux cluster project (2008),
   http://openmosix.sourceforge.net/documentation.html
6. Devi, U.C., Anderson, J.H.: Improved conditions for bounded tardiness under EPDF fair multiprocessor scheduling. J. IPDPS, IEEE Comp. Soc. 3 (2004)
7. Graham, R.L.: Bounds on multiprocessing timing anomalies. SIAM Journal on Applied Mathematics 17, 416–429 (1969)
8. Gonzalez, T., Sahni, S.: Preemptive scheduling of uniform processor systems. Journal of the ACM 25, 92–101 (1978)
9. Shchepin, E.V., Vakhania, N.: An optimal rounding gives a better approximation for scheduling unrelated machines. Oper. Res. Lett. 33(2), 127–133 (2005)
10. Haynes, S.D., Cheung, P.Y.K., Luk, W., Stone, J.: SONIC - a plug-in architecture for video processing. In: Seventh Annual IEEE Symposium on Field-Programmable Custom Computing Machines (1999)

Cluster Performance Forecasting Using Predictive Modeling for Virtual Beowulf Clusters

Abhijit Rao, Rajat Upadhyay, Nirav Shah, Sagar Arlekar,
Jayanth Raghothamma, and Shrisha Rao

International Institute of Information Technology, Bangalore,
India

Abstract. In this paper we discuss our implementation of a virtual Beowulf cluster, and the results of experiments using which we have built a predictive model. Estimating a cluster's performance is difficult, and investing in a real cluster without any idea of the performance that will be delivered is not recommended. We aim to suggest a way to address this problem by using a virtual Beowulf cluster. A virtual Beowulf cluster is a virtualized setup to simulate and understand the working of a real Beowulf cluster, but without extensive investments in hardware. This virtual setup is used to build a predictive model.

Keywords: Beowulf cluster, virtualization, predictive modeling, regression analysis.

1 Introduction

There are significant challenges in creating a cluster, such as the time required to design and create a cluster that is easily configurable and scalable. A cluster requires constant maintenance and dedicated personnel to maintain, and the time required to bring a failed cluster up or the time required in recreating a setup to rerun any problem is high.

The most important problem in creating a cluster is to estimate the hardware needed to deliver the performance required to solve a particular problem. We try to predict the performance of real clusters by simulating the cluster behavior using a virtual setup. Our virtual cluster is composed of virtual machines that act as the nodes in the cluster. The entire cluster has one master and several slaves nodes. The master is the only machine through which the user can interface with the cluster, giving the user the illusion that it is just a single machine. The cluster is networked using a gigabit ethernet network.

The cluster was built for the following experimental purposes. First, estimate variation of cluster performance with changes in task sizes. Second, to get a rough estimate of cluster size (number of machines) for a particular problem. Third, to make an estimate of the time taken to run a particular problem. These results can be used to estimate the hardware required to create a real cluster.

V. Garg, R. Wattenhofer, and K. Kothapalli (Eds.): ICDCN 2009, LNCS 5408, pp. 456–461, 2009.

The results of the experiments conducted on the cluster have been used to build a predictive model using regression analysis, which enables us to understand the behavior of the system and predict the performance of the real cluster. This model offers insights regarding the optimum cluster size required for any given task, the most suitable parallelization thread count for the same task. These insights could help system designers decide on the trade-off point between cost and performance leading to better investment decisions.

In short, this research supplements the existing research by enabling performance forecasting using a predictive model (derived using a virtual cluster), rather than serving as a mere comparison tool between virtual and physical environments of clusters [5] as is the state of the art at present.

There has been considerable work done in building and implementing virtual Beowulf clusters [6]. Software such as cluster simulators have been the topics of major discussion. The most active area of work in this field is the implementation of virtual clusters with minimal investment in hardware. This is to create a simulator, or to create an environment for testing and experimenting with an economy of time. Predictive modeling techniques have been widely used for creating predictive models in the field of cluster computing, data mining, and have been influenced by statistics and machine learning [1,2]. Performance management systems in distributed computing have been used to develop a framework for solving performance management problems using approximation theory [4]. The virtual machine concept for implementation, management of computational grids has been discussed in [3], and extensive work has been done to create efficient algorithms to predict the performance of check pointing systems in a cluster [5].

The rest of the paper is as follows. In Section 2 we describe the model and process of calibration for our cluster results and evaluation of the result. Section 3 describes the conclusion of the paper.

2   Our Model of a Virtual Beowulf Cluster

Our Model is an assembly using virtual machines where each virtual node runs an instance of a Linux based OS, supported by virtualization software. We have used Intel Core-2 Duo, 1.6 GHz processors to support the virtual nodes.

2.1   Calibrating the Cluster with Goldbach

The Goldbach conjecture is one of the best-known unsolved problems in number theory and in all of mathematics. It states that every even integer greater than 2 can be written as the sum of two primes. We chose a program to verify the Goldbach conjecture, implemented using OpenMPI constructs, to test our cluster. The master allocates a number n, the number for which the conjecture is to be verified and the range of prime numbers to use for the test to the slave. The slaves perform the actual verification of the conjecture and return pairs of numbers ,each pair being of the form a, b such that $n = a + b$ to the master as and when they are found.

2.2   Experimental Results and Inferences

The observations from the Goldbach program execution on the virtual cluster are as follows. The chosen problem size are: Range of Numbers: 32 million numbers. Number of Primes considered: 2 million.

Figure 1 depicts the performance of our cluster for the Goldbach problem.

1. The general trend is that as the number of VMs increase the time taken decreases.
2. The decrease of time stagnates as the number of VMs exceed the number of processes.
3. There is an optimal point for the number of VMs to be used. The optimal point is when the number of VMs equals the number of processes.
4. As the number of VMs is increased, the number of nodes available for computation increases, due to which the time taken decreases. If the number of VMs exceeds the number of processes, some of the VMs remain unutilized, hence there is no effective decrease in the time taken.

From Figure 2, for each curve we observe the following:

1. The time decreases as the ratio P/V (number of processes/number of VMs) approaches 1. The optimal point is when the number of VMs equals the number of processes.
2. As long as the number of processes is less than the number of VMs, the increase in number of processes will utilize more VMs for computation resulting in decrease in time taken. After number of processes exceeds the number of VMs, as the available computation power is constant, the increase in parallelism results in more communication overhead. Hence the increase in processing time

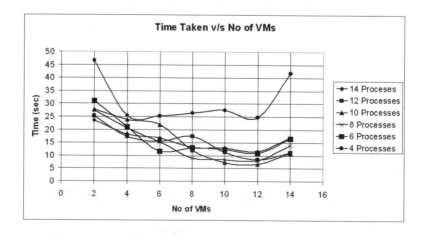

Fig. 1. Time Taken vs. Number of VMs

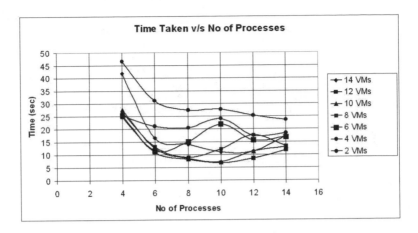

Fig. 2. Time Taken vs. Number of Processes

2.3   Building a Predictive Model for a Real Cluster Using Virtual Cluster as a Test Bed

We have chosen regression analysis as the method for extrapolating the data obtained from the experiments. Polynomial extrapolation was used to arrive at the equation for predictive values of computation times of the cluster while it scales. For the regression approach we have selected, we assume the chosen problems computation time dominates the network latency time of the cluster. Based on the observations made in section 2.2, it was noted that the cluster performance reaches the optimum level when the number of process threads is equivalent to the number of VMs (virtual nodes) in the cluster as in Figure 3. Thus considering this as a indicative factor, we extrapolate the computation time for greater number of cluster nodes, i.e., with the cluster scale up, to determine the best possible count for the number of VMs required.

The table describes the experimental results for the combination, i.e., number of VMs − number of processes.

The polynomial equation for the regression plot turns out to be:

$$y = 0.5528x^2 - 10.76x + 58.633,$$

which is of the form $y = \alpha x^2 + \beta x + \varepsilon$, resembling the standard regression equation $I = \alpha + \beta E + \varepsilon$, where α, β and ε are constants, y is the time taken to complete the task and x is the number of virtual machines or virtual nodes. The R2 value in purview of regression model indicates the goodness of fit for the line through the given points. An R2 value of 1 would indicate a perfect fit, meaning that all points lie exactly on the line. We have obtained an R2 value of 0.9587 which indicates a near-perfect fit. In order to verify if the equation arrived for the given problem is correct, we extrapolate for 4, 6, 8, 10, 12 VMs to match the results with the experimental results. The results are shown in the table below. The table shows a maximum deviation of 2.39 seconds as shown in

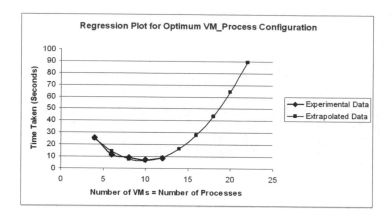

Fig. 3. Regression Plot for Predictive Modeling of Cluster Performance

Table 1. Experimental Values vs. Exrapolated Values

No of Process	No of VM's	Experimental (Time in secs)	Extrapolated (Time in secs)	Deviation (Time in secs)	Deviation (Percentage)
14	14	17.02	16.34	0.68	4.17
12	12	8.46	9.12	0.66	7.25
10	10	7.29	6.31	0.97	15.43
8	8	8.99	7.93	1.06	13.40
6	6	11.59	13.97	2.39	17.09
4	4	25.46	24.44	1.02	4.16

table below which can be explained owing to the fact goodness of fit value being 0.9587. Thus the equation is near correct with experimental and theoretically extrapolated values almost in sync.

2.4   Translating the Results to Real Clusters

The problem dealt and the program run on the real cluster would be the same as run in the virtual cluster thus achieving a similar test conditions. Thus for the problem considered a 10 node cluster with task parallelized into 10 processes would prove to be optimum. The same regression analysis can be applied to various problems to arrive at the optimal cluster size.

3   Conclusion

In this study of cluster performance forecasting using predictive modeling for virtual Beowulf clusters, we have described how a virtual cluster's results can be extrapolated to understand the performance patterns of a real cluster with scaling up of its size. The virtual clusters performance is of course not identical to that of a real Beowulf cluster, but even so, it can prove a valuable tool for testing and experimenting in a virtual environment with economy of time. The nuances of a cluster can be understood with the help of standard programs run on our cluster and estimations can be made when investing in a real Beowulf cluster. While our work gives useful insights into cluster performance, we realize that more work will have to be done in simulating real cluster environments and examining machine learning techniques of predictive modeling to arrive at a very precise estimation that would offer deeper insights, sufficient to enable detailed and precise advice for cluster investments.

Acknowledgments

We would like to thank Abhilash L.L., Deependu Saxena, and Sukanta Samanta for their helpful suggestions.

References

1. Alpaydin, E.: Introduction to Machine Learning. MIT Press, Cambridge (2004)
2. Hong, S.J., Hong, S.J., Weiss, S.M., Weiss, S.M.: Advances in predictive model generation for data mining. In: Perner, P., Petrou, M. (eds.) MLDM 1999. LNCS, vol. 1715. Springer, Heidelberg (1999)
3. Keahey, K., Foster, I., Freeman, T., Zhang, X.: Virtual workspaces in the grid. In: Cunha, J.C., Medeiros, P.D. (eds.) Euro-Par 2005. LNCS, vol. 3648, pp. 421–431. Springer, Heidelberg (2005)
4. Kusic, D., Nagarajan, K., Jiang, G.: Approximation modeling for the online performance management of distributed computing systems. Technical report (2007).
5. Plank, J.S., Thomason, M.G.: Processor allocation and checkpoint interval selection in cluster computing systems. Journal of Parallel and Distributed Computing 61, 1590 (2001)
6. Spigarolo, M., Davoli, R.: Berserkr: A virtual beowulf cluster for fast prototyping and teaching. In: CF 2004: Proceedings of the 1st conference on Computing frontiers, pp. 294–301. ACM, New York (2004)

A Hierarchical Approach to Handle Group Mutual Exclusion Problem in Distributed Systems

Abhishek Swaroop[1] and Awadhesh Kumar Singh[2]

[1] Department of Computer Science and Engineering, G.P.M. College of Engineering,
G.T. Karnal Road, Delhi, India 110036
abhi_pu1@yahoo.co.in
[2] Department of Computer Engineering, National Institute of Technology,
Kurukshetra, Haryana, India 136119
aksinreck@rediffmail.com

Abstract. A hierarchical algorithm to solve the group mutual exclusion problem has been proposed. We consider a hierarchical arrangement where the nodes are divided in to clusters. The algorithm uses a token-based protocol to handle inter-cluster requests and a centralized protocol for intra-cluster requests. The algorithm also uses a two-level priority scheme in order to assign relative weights to fairness and concurrency. Unlike other algorithms, the message complexity of our algorithm is proportional to the number of clusters rather than the number of nodes. Also, a new metric has been proposed to measure the level of coherence. The proposed algorithm is the first hierarchical solution to the group mutual exclusion problem.

Keywords: Cluster, Concurrency, Fairness, Group mutual exclusion.

1 Introduction

Joung proposed the group mutual exclusion (GME) [3] as generalization of the classical mutual exclusion (ME) problem. In GME problem, the nodes requesting the same resource (also termed as group) are allowed to be in their critical section (CS) simultaneously. However, the nodes requesting different resources, must execute their CS in mutually exclusive way.

We assume a distributed environment in which the nodes are arranged in hierarchical clusters. Further, the nodes inside a cluster may behave in a coherent manner because in practical scenario, usually, the nodes within a single cluster would have alike requests. We consider the example of a CD juke box storing e-books shared by various departments in a technical institution. It is highly likely that large number of nodes from a particular department, e.g. mechanical engineering, would make an access request for an e-book related to the mechanical engineering curriculum rather than the nodes from any other department. Such distributed systems perform better, when a hierarchical approach is used to solve their synchronization problem.

V. Garg, R. Wattenhofer, and K. Kothapalli (Eds.): ICDCN 2009, LNCS 5408, pp. 462–467, 2009.

The GME problem, since its inception [3], has been handled by a number of researchers. The hierarchical approach has been used to handle ordinary mutual exclusion [1], [4]. However, the hierarchical solution to GME is being proposed first time here.

We assume a message passing asynchronous distributed system consisting n nodes, divided in to p clusters. Each cluster i contains n_i nodes such that $\sum_{i=1}^{p} n_i = n$. Each node can be identified by a cluster *id* and a node *id*. Node $P_{i,1}$ is designated as coordinator in cluster i. Further, each coordinator is connected with all other coordinators. We use a centralized algorithm at the intra-cluster level and a token-based algorithm, adapted from Chang-Singhal-Liu [2], at the inter-cluster level. In [2], token-based approach, using dynamic request sets, has been used to solve the mutual exclusion problem. Later on, Swaroop-Singh [5], [6] used the concept of dynamic request sets to solve the GME problem; however, the algorithms presented in [5], [6] are non-hierarchical in nature.

The proposed algorithm uses a two-level priority scheme to select the next group, in which the relative weight of the concurrency and the fairness can be varied depending upon the application. Further, we propose a new metric to measure the coherence, shown by the nodes, of a cluster during a particular time period. The worst case message complexity is independent of the total number of nodes in the system; however, it depends upon the number of clusters.

2   The Working of Algorithm

In this section we present the high level description of our hierarchical group mutual exclusion algorithm (called HGME henceforth) to solve the GME problem. The pseudo code of the algorithm is given in appendix.

A process $P_{i,j}$ requesting a group g, sends its request to its coordinator $P_{i,1}$, enters in its CS upon receiving permission and informs the coordinator on exiting from CS. Upon receiving a request for a group g from some node in its cluster, if a coordinator possesses the idle primary token, that is, currently no session is open, it sends permission to the requesting node, and adds the requesting node in the list of allowed nodes. If the coordinator possesses the non-idle primary token and the group g is currently being used then if there are no pending requests then the coordinator sends the permission to the requesting node and adds the requesting process in the list of allowed nodes. Otherwise, the request is added in the local queue. If the coordinator does not posses token, it sends a request for token to all the coordinators in its request set, if it is not already waiting for token.

When a coordinator $P_{i,1}$ holding the idle primary token, receives a request from some other coordinator $P_{j,1}$, it immediately sends the primary token to the $P_{j,1}$ and adds $P_{j,1}$ in its request set. However, if the $P_{i,1}$ is holding non-idle primary token, it sends a secondary token to $P_{j,1}$ only if the group requested by $P_{j,1}$ is the currently open group and there are no pending requests at $P_{i,1}$. Otherwise, the request of $P_{j,1}$ is added in the cumulative queue. On the other hand, if $P_{i,1}$ does not possess the primary token , it adds $P_{j,1}$ in its request set, if it is not already there.

Upon receiving secondary token, the coordinator $P_{j,1}$, sends permission to all local nodes requesting for the currently open group g, remove these nodes from its local queue, and waits for their exit from CS. However, in order to avoid starvation, if $P_{j,1}$ receives a request for group g from some node in its cluster, while it is waiting for the allowed nodes to exit from their CS, $P_{j,1}$ does not send permission and add the request in its local queue. Once all local nodes have exited from CS, $P_{j,1}$ returns the secondary token to the primary token holder. Along with the secondary token, it piggybacks a vector containing the local priority of those groups having pending requests in its local queue. The priorities are calculated as per the scheme suggested in section 3.

When a coordinator returns a secondary token to $P_{i,1}$, $P_{i,1}$ removes it from the list of coordinators to which it has sent the secondary tokens. If $P_{i,1}$ has received back all the secondary tokens and all local nodes of cluster i have exited from their CS, it announces the termination of the session and selects the next group g and the next primary token holder using the priority scheme suggested in section 3. $P_{i,1}$ sends permission to all local nodes requesting the group g and removes these requests from cumulative queue and from its local queue. $P_{i,1}$ sends secondary tokens to all other coordinators (except the newly selected primary token holder) requesting the group g and remove their requests from the cumulative queue. $P_{i,1}$ adds all the coordinators having pending requests in cumulative queue, in its request set and sends primary token (along with the list of coordinators to which the secondary tokens have been issued) to the newly selected primary token holder. When the newly selected primary token holder receives the primary token, it empties its request set, sets its current group as g, and sends permission to all local nodes requesting group g.

3   The Priority Scheme

The priority scheme calculates priorities at two levels. The priorities calculated at the local level are forwarded to the primary token holder, where these are used for the calculation of global priorities. The method of calculation of priorities is explained below:

(i) *Local Priority:* Let L is the total number of requests that is the number of nodes in the local queue of the coordinator $P_{i,1}$. Let $P_{i,x1}$, $P_{i,x2}...P_{i,xq}$ be the nodes requesting group g_k. The request of $P_{i,x1}$ is the first request for g_k in local queue at position y_1. α and β are constant parameters. The local priority of group g_k in cluster i (local_$prio_{i,k}$) can be calculated as follows: $local\_prio_{i,k} = \alpha \times \dfrac{L - y_1 + 1}{L} + \beta \times \dfrac{q}{n_i}$.

(ii) *Global Priority*: Let $P_{i1,1}$, $P_{i2,1}$, ... $P_{iq,1}$ are the coordinators requesting g_k and r is the total number of coordinators in the cumulative queue. The cum_prio_k for a group g_k can be calculated as follows:

$$cum\_prio_k = \frac{local\_prio_{i1,k} + local\_prio_{i2,k} + ... + local\_prio_{iq,k}}{p}$$. Here $p \geq q$

is the total number of clusters in the system. Assume that the first request for group g_k in cumulative queue is at position z_1. The global priority of group g_k (global_$prio_k$)

can be calculated as follows: $global\_prio_k = \gamma \times \dfrac{r - z_l + 1}{r} + \delta \times cum\_prio_k$ .While calculating the global priority of a group g_k ($global\_prio_k$), the first term represents the fairness and the second term represents both the local priority and concurrency. We can select the values of constant parameters α, β, γ, and δ depending upon the nature of the application. The group having the highest global priority is selected as the next group and the coordinator having the oldest request for that group in the cumulative queue is selected as the next primary token holder.

4   The Performance Analysis

We analyze the performance of our algorithms using following performance metrics: synchronization delay, waiting time, message complexity, message size, and maximum concurrency. We propose a new metric to measure the level of coherence shown by the nodes of a cluster.

If p is the number of clusters then in the worst case $p+4$ messages/CS request will be required, however, in the best case three messages per CS will be required. As far as, the message complexity is concerned HGME lies in between a centralized algorithm and a non-hierarchical distributed algorithm. In contrast to the centralized algorithm, the load in HGME will be divided among all the coordinators. Further, a cluster will remain stable together; therefore it is better to have one coordinator for each cluster instead of having a single coordinator for the entire system. The waiting time of the algorithm under light load condition is $4T$ in the worst case and $2T$ in the best case, where T is the maximum message propagation delay. Further, the synchronization delay under heavy load condition will be $4T$ in the worst case and $2T$ in the best case. All messages used in our algorithm except RET_SEC ($O(m)$) and P_TOKEN ($O(p*m)$) are of constant size. The maximum concurrency of our algorithm is n.

4.1   Level of Coherence

We propose a metrics ($L\_coherence_i$) to measure the level of coherence shown by the nodes of the cluster i during a particular time period. Let r_1 is the number of groups requested and r_2 is the total number of requests in a clusters i during the time period under consideration. Now, $L\_coherence_i$ can be calculated as follows: $L\_coherence_i = \dfrac{r_2}{r_1}$. The higher is the value of $L\_coherence_i$, the higher is the coherence among the nodes of the cluster i. The performance of the HGME will improve with higher level of coherence.

5   Conclusion

The HGME is first hierarchical algorithm to solve the GME problem. The approach used has resulted in very significant improvement in the message complexity.

Moreover, the two-tier priority scheme provides an efficient trade off mechanism between fairness and concurrency. The newly proposed metric, that is, level of coherence, can serve as objectively verifiable performance indicator for hierarchical GME algorithms.

References

1. Bertier, M., Arantes, L., Sens, P.: Distributed Mutual Exclusion Algorithms for Grid Applications: A Hierarchical Approach. J. of Parallel and Distributed Computing 66(3), 128–144 (2006)
2. Chang, Y.I., Singhal, M., Liu, M.T.: A Dynamic Token Based Distributed Mutual Exclusion Algorithm. In: 10th annual International Phoneix Conference on Computers and Communications, pp. 240–246 (1991)
3. Joung, Y.J.: Asynchronous Group Mutual Exclusion (extended abstract). In: 17th annual ACM Symposium on Principles of Distributed Computing, pp. 51–60 (1998)
4. Madhuram, S., Kumar, A.: A Hybrid Approach for Mutual Exclusion in Distributed Computing Systems. In: 6th IEEE Symposium on Parallel and Distributed Processing, pp. 18–25 (1994)
5. Swaroop, A., Singh, A.K.: A Token-Based Fair Algorithm for Group Mutual Exclusion in Distributed systems. J. of Computer Science 3(10), 829–835 (2007)
6. Swaroop, A., Singh, A.K.: A Fault Tolerant Token-Based Algorithm for Group Mutual Exclusion in Distributed systems. J. of Electronics, Circuits, and Systems 2(1), 194–200 (2008)

Appendix: Pseudo Code of the Algorithm

Each node may remain in any one of the flowing three states

```
R: requesting, N: not requesting, CS: executing in CS.
```

Each coordinator maintains following data structure:

```
state_c_{i,1}: W(waiting for token), NW(not waiting), HPT(holding primary
token),HST(holding secondary token),HIPT(holding idle primary token).
local_q _{i,1}: A queue which is used to store local requests.
allow_l _{i,1}: Set of processes to which coordinator has sent permission.
allow_r _{i,1}: The coordinators to which secondary tokens have been sent.
mygroup_{i,1} : The current group being accessed by nodes of cluster i.
session_no_{i,1} : It stores the latest session number known to P_{i,1}.
myprimary_{i,1} : Stores the id of the primary token holder node to which
                 secondary token has to be returned
RS_{i,1}: Set of node id's to which the global request has to be sent.
```

The primary token contains following arrays:

```
cum_q: It stores all the global requests.
session_pt: An array of size p, it stores the session number of each
coordinator known to primary token.
allow_sec: set of coordinators to which secondary tokens have been sent.
```

Initialization:
For $i=1$ to p
  $RS_{i,1}$=id's of other coordinators
  $local\_q_{i,1}$=$\emptyset$; $cum\_q_{i,1}$=$\emptyset$;
  $state\_c_{i,1}$=NW; $allow\_r_{i,1}$= $\emptyset$
  $myprimary_{i,1}$=NULL; $allow\_l_{i,1}$=$\emptyset$;
  $sesion\_no_{i,1}$=0; $session\_pt[i]$=0;
  $mygroup_{i,1}$=NULL
  For j = 1 to n_i $state\_m_{i,j}$=NR
  $state\_c_{i,1}$=HIPT; $RS_{i,1}$= $\emptyset$;
  $allow\_sec$= $\emptyset$; cum_q= $\emptyset$
$P_{i,j}$ **Requesting for group** g:
Send REQUEST ($P_{i,j}$, g) to $P_{i,1}$
$state\_m_{i,j}$=R
$P_{i,j}$ **receives ALLOW** (g) **from** $P_{i,1}$:
Enter CS; $state\_m_{i,j}$=CS
...executing in CS.....
Exit CS; $state\_m_{i,j}$=N
Send COMPLETE ($P_{i,j}$) to $P_{i,1}$
$P_{i,1}$ **receives REQUEST** ($P_{i,j}$, g)
Switch ($state\_c_{i,1}$)
  Case NW: Add req. in $local\_q_{i,1}$
    $state\_c_{i,1}$=W
    Send G_REQUEST ($P_{i,1}$, g, sesion
    $\_no_{i,1}$) to coordinators in $RS_{i,1}$
  Case HIPT :Send ALLOW (g) to $P_{i,j}$
    $session\_no_{i,1}$++; $mygroup_{i,1}$=g
    $session\_pt[i]$++; $state\_c_{i,1}$=HPT;
    $allow\_l_{i,1}$=$P_{i,j}$
  Case   HPT: if(($myqroup_{i,1}$=q)
    && ($local\_q_{i,1}$=$\emptyset$) && (cum_q=$\emptyset$))
    Send ALLOW (g) to $P_{i,j}$
    $allow\_l_{i,1}$=$allow\_l_{i,1} \cup P_{i,j}$
  Else
    Add REQUEST($P_{i,j}$,g) in $local\_q_{i,1}$
  Default: Add REQUEST($P_{i,j}$,g) in
    $local\_q_{i,1}$
$P_{i,1}$ **receives COMPLETE** ($P_{i,j}$):
Remove $P_{i,j}$ from $allow\_l_{i,1}$
If ($state\_c_{i,1}$=HPT)
  If($allow\_l_{i,1}$=$\emptyset$)&&($allow\_r_{i,1}$=$\emptyset$)
  Call sel_next_coord ( )
Else
  If ($allow\_l_{i,1}$=$\emptyset$)
    $mygroup_{i,1}$=NULL;
    $myprimary_{i,1}$=NULL
    If ($local\_q_{i,1} \neq \emptyset$)
      $state\_c_{i,1}$=W;store priority
      of all groups in $vect$
    Else
      $state\_c_{i,1}$=NW; $vect$= $\emptyset$
    Send RET_SEC ($P_{i,1}$, $vect$) to
    $myprimary_{i,1}$
$P_{i,1}$ **receives P_TOKEN (**g, **al-
low_sec, session_pt, cum_q):**
$state\_c_{i,1}$=HPT;$RS_{i,1}$=$\emptyset$;$mygroup_{i,1}$=g
$allow\_r_{i,1}$=$allow\_sec$;
$session\_no_{i,1}$=$session\_pt[i]$
Send ALLOW (g) to local nodes
requesting   for g
Remove these from $local\_q_{i,1}$
$allow\_l_{i,1}$=id's of nodes to which
ALLOW has been sent
$P_{i,1}$ **receives   S_TOKEN   (**$P_{j,1}$,
g,**session):**
$session\_no_{i,1}$=$session$;$mygroup_{i,1}$=g
$state\_c_{i,1}$=HST; $myprimary_{i,1}$=$P_{j,1}$

Send ALLOW (g) to nodes request-
ing for g add these in $allow\_l_{i,1}$
Remove the nodes from $local\_q_{i,1}$
$P_{i,1}$**receives RET_SEC(**$P_{j,1}$, $vect$**)** :
Remove $P_{j,1}$ from $allow\_r_{i,1}$
Add requests in $vect$ in cum_q
If ($allow\_r_{i,1}$=$\emptyset$)&& ($allow\_l_{i,1}$=$\emptyset$)
  $mygroup_{i,1}$=NULL;$myprimary_{i,1}$=NULL
  Call sel_next_cord ( )
$P_{i,1}$**receives   G_REQUEST(**$P_{j,1}$,g,
session)
If ($state\_c_{i,1}$=HIPT)
  If ($session$=$session\_pt[j]$)
    $RS_{i,1}$=$P_{j,1}$; $session\_pt[j]$++;
    $allow\_sec$= $\emptyset$;cum_q= $\emptyset$;
    Send P_TOKEN (g, $allow\_sec$,
    $session\_pt$, cum_q)to $P_{j,1}$
Else if ($state_{i,1}$=HPT)
  If ($session$=$session\_pt[j]$)
    If($mygroup_{i,1}$==g)&&(cum_q=$\emptyset$)
      $allow\_r_{i,1}$=$allow\_r_{i,1} \cup P_{j,1}$;
      $session\_pt[j]$++
    Send S_TOKEN   ($P_{i,1}$, g
    ,$session\_pt[j]$)   to $P_{j,1}$
  Else
    Add request of $P_{j,1}$ in cum_q
Else
  If ($P_j \notin RS_{i,1}$)
    $RS_{i,1}$=$RS_{i,1} \cup P_{j,1}$
    If ($state\_c_{i,1}$=W)
      Send G_REQUEST ($P_{i,1}$,
      g') to $P_{j,1}$
Proc Sel_next_coord ( )
Add local priority of groups for
current token holder in cum_q
If ($cum\_q \neq \emptyset$)
  Calculate priority of groups,
  find next group 'g' and next
  primary token holder(P_j).Send
  "ALLOW" to local nodes requesting for 'g' and S TOKEN to coordinators, add these coordinators in allow_sec,send P_TOKEN
  to $P_{j,1}$, and remove the requests
  from cum_q. Add $P_{j,1}$ and other
  coordinators in cum_q in $RS_{i,1}$
Else $state\_c_{i,1}$=HIPT

Virtual Time Fair Queuing Algorithm for a Computational Grid

Daphne Lopez[1] and S.V. Kasmir Raja[2]

[1] School of Computing Sciences, VIT UNIVERSITY, Vellore - 632 014, India
daphne.lopez@gmail.com
[2] Department of Computer Science and Engineering, SRM University, Chennai, India
svkr@yahoo.com

Abstract. Grid scheduling is the process of making scheduling decisions involving resources over multiple domains. This process can include searching multiple administrative domains to use a single machine or scheduling a single job to use multiple resources at a single site or multiple sites. In an increasing number of scientific disciplines the enormous potential of the grid can be realized with the fundamental development of potential new scheduling techniques. Conventional scheduling techniques are queue based and provide only one level of service. In this paper we propose an algorithm for effective scheduling of jobs by the local scheduler considering the virtual time and proportional fairness to have a high rate of accuracy and low overhead. We describe the various scheduling algorithms that are in use and next, we explain the virtual time fair queuing algorithm with its implementation and the results.

Keywords: Grid computing, Schedulers, Proportional share algorithms, Shares, Virtual Time.

1 Introduction

Grid computing is the effective utilization of computer resources across networks. This technology assists organizations in gaining immense computing power by utilizing the resources more efficiently [1]. With the increase of jobs in all businesses and the need to have these jobs run more quickly, applications are turning towards grid to enhance computation speed and data storage. One of the most important functions of a grid is the scheduling of jobs. The Grid scheduler must make decisions in an environment where the resources are distributed and dynamic in nature. The grid scheduling architecture has three phases as resource discovery, system selection and job execution [2]. Resource discovery involves the collection of information about all the resources available. System selection uses the information to dynamically choose a system for the user's application. Job execution is to use the dynamic information gathered and to complete the job [2]. The schedulers and the various scheduling algorithms play a major role in the execution of jobs. Existing Grid schedulers can be classified according to three factors, namely their organization (that may be centralized, hierarchical, or distributed), their scheduling policy (that may optimize either

V. Garg, R. Wattenhofer, and K. Kothapalli (Eds.): ICDCN 2009, LNCS 5408, pp. 468–474, 2009.
© Springer-Verlag Berlin Heidelberg 2009

system or application performance), and the state estimation technique they use to construct predictive models of application performance. Scheduling policy is an important feature of a grid scheduler. The policy could be system oriented – aimed at optimizing system performance, or application oriented – maximize user performance, possibly disregarding the overall system performance. [3] Given the large amount of resources available on the grid, it is more appropriate to give preference to user performance enhancing the quality of service given to the users. The scheduling policies used in the grid do not address this need. The grid scheduling policy currently in use makes sure that jobs do not starve but not much attention is given to user performance.

1.1 Review of Algorithms Used in a Grid

The algorithms used for a local scheduler in the grid are FCFS, Round Robin and the like. These algorithms do not pay heed to proportional fairness. The term proportional fairness can be defined as an ideal state in which each client has received service exactly proportional to its share. Assuming three jobs $j1, j2, j3$ in the run queue with lengths 100, 2 and 1 respectively (in millions of instructions) having arrived in the order $j1, j2, j3$. Applying round robin policy in one cycle let each of them be assigned one share (that is the processor executes one million instructions of each job in one cycle). So at the end of a cycle, the remaining shares of the jobs $j1, j2, j3$ will be 99, 1, and 0 respectively. We see that though $j1$ arrived earliest, it didn't get the amount of shares it deserved. Also it is not wise to complete $j1$ and then switch over to $j2$ or $j3$ as it will result in starvation. Hence we have to make sure that all the jobs are fairly executed and also that there is no (or minimal) starvation.

1.2 Shares

A processor's processing capacity can be expressed in terms of Millions of Instructions Per Second (MIPS). In a single scheduling cycle, the processor will process the jobs in the run queue. Say job j is processed for s seconds. And the processor's MIPS rating is m. so the processor processes ($m*s$) million instructions of job j in this cycle. Hence this $m*s$ is the share of the job j. Similarly all jobs in the queue will have their own shares. Shares can be assigned depending on various factors, for example weights / priorities of the jobs. In our experiment, the share is assigned based on the arrival time of the job. The job which comes first is given a better share than that which arrived later.

1.3 Proportional Share Algorithms

Proportional share resource management is based on the concept that each client has a weight associated with it and resources are allocated to the client in proportion to its weight. It provides a flexible and useful abstraction for multiplexing scarce resources among users and applications.. The Scheduler orders the clients in a queue and runs the first client in the queue for its time quantum. Proportional fairness is achieved either by adjusting the position of the job in the queue or by changing the time quantum Because of its usefulness, many proportional-share scheduling mechanisms have been developed, [3],[4],[5],[10].

Different users will have different priorities that determine the amount of Grid resources allocated to their applications [5]. This may determine the weight to be assigned to the jobs submitted by the client.

1.3.1 Fair Share (FS)

Fair Share [8] implements proportional sharing among users. by setting priorities to the clients to the clients based on the submitters group priority.. In order to have a proportional sharing the priorities are adjusted as it executes. The overhead is in the changing of the priorities which required $O(N)$ time, where N is the number of clients.

1.3.2 Weighted Round Robin (WRR)

Weighted round-robin (WRR) provides proportional sharing by running all clients with the same frequency but adjusting the size of theisr time quanta. WRR is simple to implement and schedules clients in $O(1)$ time. However, it has a relatively weak proportional fairness as the execution purely depends on the weight assigned and the size of the job.

When the assigned weights are large the error range also varies widely where certain clients get the service all at once and certain others do not get it all resulting in weak proportional fairness [7].

1.3.3 Weighted Fair Queuing (WFQ)

Weighted Fair Queuing (WFQ) [5] introduced the idea of a virtual finishing time (VFT) to do proportional sharing scheduling. To explain what a VFT is, we first explain the notion of virtual time [7]. The virtual time of a client is a measure of the degree to which a client has received its proportional allocation relative to other clients. When a client executes, its virtual time advances at a rate inversely proportional to the client's share.   Given a client's virtual time, the client's virtual finishing time (VFT) is defined, as the virtual time the client would have after executing for one time quantum. WFQ then schedules clients by selecting the client with the smallest VFT. Fair queuing provides stronger proportional fairness guarantees than round robin or fair-share scheduling. Unfortunately, fair queuing is more difficult to implement, and the time it takes to select a client to execute is $O(N)$ time for most implementations, where N is the number of clients. With more complex data structures, it is possible to implement fair queuing such that selection of a client requires $O(\log N)$ time.

1.3.4 Virtual Time Round Robin (VTRR)

VTRR is an accurate, low-overhead proportional share scheduler for multiplexing time-shared resources among a set of clients [7]. VTRR combines the benefit of low overhead round robin scheduling with the high accuracy mechanisms of virtual time and virtual finishing time used in fair queuing algorithms.

At a high-level, the VTRR scheduling algorithm can be briefly described in three steps:

1. Order the clients in the run queue from largest to smallest share. Unlike fair queuing, a client's position on the run queue only changes when its share changes, an infrequent event, not on each scheduling decision.

2. Starting from the beginning of the run queue, run each client for one time quantum in a round-robin manner. VTRR uses the fixed ordering property of round robin in order to choose in constant time which client to run. Unlike round robin, the time quantum is the same size for all clients.

3. In step 2, if a client has received more than its proportional allocation, then skip the remaining clients in the run queue and start running clients from the beginning of the run queue again. Since the clients with larger share values are placed first in the queue, this allows them to get more service than the lower-share clients at the end of the queue [3].

1.3.5 Service Time Error Based

Perfect fairness is a state when there is a zero service time error for all jobs at all times. But perfect fairness cannot be achieved practically. Instead of perfect fairness, the aim of the proportional share algorithms is to be as near perfect fairness as possible. The service time error $E_A(t1; t2)$ for client A over interval $(t1; t2)$, is the difference between the amount time allocated to the client during interval $(t1; t2)$ under the given algorithm, and the amount of time that would have been allocated under an ideal scheme that maintains perfect fairness for all clients over all intervals [3].

Service time error is computed as:

$$E_A (t1; t2) = W_A (t1; t2) - (t2 - t1) * S_A / \sum_i S \qquad (1)$$

Where,

E_A _ is the service time error for client A

W_A - is the amount of time allocated to A

S_A - is the count of the shares of A

$\sum_i S_i$ - is the sum of all the shares of the clients in run queue.

A positive service time error indicates that a client has received more than its ideal share over an interval; a negative error indicates that a client has received less. To be precise, the error E_A measures how much time client A has received beyond its ideal allocation. The goal of a proportional share scheduler should be to minimize the allocation error between clients [12].

2 Virtual Time Fair Queuing Algorithm-Basic Algorithm

This algorithm combines the basic ideas of VTRR and WFQ and is hence more advantageous. The service time error is low. It maintains high accuracy (low error), reduced cost, and low overhead ($O(1)$).

The aim of the algorithm is to avoid hogging. It maintains a run queue where the clients to be run are inserted. All the clients are arranged in decreasing order of shares. Initially, the first client on the queue is assigned the next time quantum since it is most deserving.

The terms used in the algorithm below are:

j – The job that has been assigned the current time quantum

E_C - The service time error value of the current job if it is assigned the next time quantum

E_F - The service time error value of the first job if it is assigned the next time quantum

Initially, all error values are zero since none of the clients have got their services. Now, once the initial time quantum has been assigned, the currently executing job is examined. The time interval between the job's arrival to the current instant is considered for measuring E_C and E_F. The service time error E_C is calculated for this client assuming it will be given the next time quantum. If E_C is greater than the service time error of the first job in the queue E_F, this shows that the job has already received the deserved execution time so far and should not be assigned the next time quantum. At this point, the next job to be run is the first one at the head of the queue. Only one decision is to be made in one pass and hence the overhead is O(1). The algorithm is as follows:

```
1. Insert the jobs into the run queue according to
   decreasing order of shares
2. j = 1
3. While there are jobs remaining in the run queue,
     perform the steps 4 to 5
4. Assign the next time quantum to job j and increment j
5. If Ec > EF (If the job j, does not deserve the next
   time quantum)
          j=First job in queue
6. If there are no more jobs to be run, perform other
   tasks
```

Whenever a job completes, go to the head of the queue, which is assign first job in the queue as *j*. The overhead incurred is hence minimal since it only involves the calculation of error at the end of every time quantum and the decision to run the job at the head of the queue.

2.1 Virtual Time Fair Queuing Algorithm — Dynamic Considerations

Let a new job be inserted into the run queue at a time *t*. Now, it has to be placed in the queue at a right place and also given its fair share. If the job has more number of shares than the others in the queue, it must not receive more attention than those other processes already in the queue as they arrived earlier. It is also unfair to execute all other jobs and then come to the new one. It is hence appropriate to assume that this job has got its proportional share until its arrival. The error is calculated as shown in equation 1. (*t2 – t1*) clearly indicates that the period from the jobs arrival to the current instant is always considered. The case of arrival of a new job is automatically handled in this algorithm. The new job is placed in the queue, such that the decreasing order of shares in preserved.

2.2 Comparison of Algorithms with Examples

Two examples are presented here to compare the results of WFQ, VTRR and virtual time fair queuing algorithms. The simulated results are shown as sample1, sample 2, sample 3 and sample 4. Simulation was performed using GridSim Toolkit 4 which is supposed to be the best tool for simulating scheduling [10]. Consider an example with three clients A,B,C each with shares 3,2,1 respectively. The sequence of executions with the algorithms is as below

WFQ : A, B, A, A, B, C
VTRR : A, B, C, A, B, A
VTFQ : A, B, A, A, B, C

And if the shares had been 3, 3, 1 respectively, then the sequence would be

WFQ   : A, B, A, B, A, B, C
VTRR : A, B, C, A, B, A, B
VTFQ : A, B, A, B, A, B, C

In both the cases, the disadvantages of the other algorithms are:

1. VTRR executes client C much earlier than it deserves to be.
2. WFQ has the ideal allocation sequence but takes O (N) time for the same.

Table 1. Simulated Results with shares 3, 2, 1   **Table 2.** Simulated Results with shares 6, 3, 1

Algorithm	Average Cost
VTRR	200064.4
WFQ	218058.4
VTFQ	150463.2

Algorithm	Average Cost
VTRR	236232.0
WFQ	220345.2
VTFQ	186256.2

But in case of virtual time fair queuing algorithm, the clients are prevented from hogging; thereby maintaining a sequence that is as accurate as WFQ's sequence and at the same time the time complexity is low like in the case of VTRR. Table 3 Compares the performance of the other algorithms with Virtual Time Fair Queuing in terms of cost proportional sharing accuracy and the overhead incurred in the scheduling of jobs.

Table 3. Comparative study of WRR, WFQ, VTRR, Error Based and VTFQ

Algorithm	Cost	Proportional sharing accuracy	Scheduling overhead
WRR	Very High	Unpredictable (Usu. Not accurate)	Very low
WFQ	Moderate	Very accurate	High
VTRR	Moderate	Accurate	Moderate
Error Based	Moderate (Usu. Less than VTRR)	Accurate	Moderate
VTFQ	Low	Accurate	Low

3 Conclusion

We have proposed in this an approach to fairness based scheduling. It is designed, implemented and has proved to have less overhead, less cost and good proportional sharing accuracy. It combines the benefits of the accuracy of WFQ and the less overhead of VTRR. Also, as in VTRR, the scheduling overhead is constant irrespective of the number of clients. Virtual Time Fair Queuing algorithm is been tested with a wide range of data values and has given better results than the other algorithms we have considered.

References

1. IBM Redbook : Introduction to grid computing with Globus : IBM Corporation (2003)
2. Schopf, J.M.: A general architecture for scheduling on the grid. Argonne National Laboratory (2002)
3. National Institute of Advanced Industrial Science and Technology: Grid technology research center (2002), http://www.aist.go.jp/
4. Bennett, J., Zhang, H.: WF2Q: Worst-case Fair Weighted Fair Queuing. In: Proceedings of INFOCOM 1996, San Francisco, CA (March 1996)
5. Demers, A., Keshav, S., Shenker, S.: Analysis and Simulation of a Fair Queuing Algorithm. In: Proceedings of ACMSIG - OMM 1989, Austin, TX, pp. 1–12 (September 1989)
6. Donno, F., Gaido, L., Ghiselli, A., Prelz, F., Sgaravatto, M.: Data Grid Prototype 1, EU-Data Grid Collaboration (2002)
7. Nieh, J., Vaill, C., Zhong, H.: Virtual-Time Round-Robin: An O(1) Proportional Share Scheduler. In: Proceedings of the USENIX Technical Conference (2001)
8. Kleban, S.D., Scott, H.: Clearwater: Fair Share on high Performance Computing System: what does Fair Really Mean? In: Proceedings of the 3rd IEEE/ACM International Symposium on Cluster Computing and the Grid (2003)
9. Ranganathan, K., Foster, I.: Decoupling Computation and Data Scheduling in Distributed Data- Intensive Applications (2002)
10. Murshed, M., Buyya, R.: Using the Grid Sim Toolkit for Enabling Grid Computing Education (2002)
11. Essick, R.: An Event –Based FairShare Scheduler. In: Proceedings of the Winter 1990 USENIX Conference. USENIX, Berkeley (1990)
12. Lopez, D., Rasika, M.: A Service Time Error Based Scheduling Algorithm for a computational Grid. In: Proceedings of the IEEE-ICSCN (February 2007)

Author Index

Printing: Mercedes-Druck, Berlin
Binding: Stein+Lehmann, Berlin